WILLIAM J. CHAMBLISS, University of California, Santa Barbara

ROBERT B. SEIDMAN, University of Wisconsin

LAW, ORDER, AND POWER

ADDISON-WESLEY PUBLISHING COMPANY
Reading, Massachusetts · Menlo Park, California · London · Don Mills, Ontario

0

C

This book is for our wives and children:
Lou, Lauren, Jeffrey, and Kenton Chambliss
Ann, Jonathan, Judy, Katha, Gay, and Lynn Seidman

THE AUTHORS

William J. Chambliss teaches sociology at the University of California, Santa Barbara. He received the B.A. degree from the University of California at Los Angeles and the M.A. and Ph.D. degrees from Indiana University. The author formerly taught at the University of Washington and was Visiting Lecturer and Russell Sage Resident in Law and Sociology at the University of Wisconsin, Madison. From 1969 to 1970, he was a Visiting Professor at the University of Ibadan, Nigeria, where he also did research on Nigerian criminal law. A specialist in the sociology of law, deviance, crime, and delinquency, Dr. Chambliss has written many articles on these subjects. He is the author of the highly successful book *Crime and the Legal Process* and coeditor with Robert B. Seidman of *A Research Bibliography on the Sociology of Law*. The author is a member of the American Sociological Association, Law and Society Association, and the Society for the Study of Social Problems.

Robert B. Seidman is Professor of Law at the University of Wisconsin Law School and Director of the African Law Association in America. He was awarded the B.A. degree by Harvard College and the L.L.B. degree by Columbia University. Dr. Seidman has taught and done extensive research on African law at the University of Ghana; the University of Lagos, Nigeria; and University College, Dar Es Salaam, Tanzania. A member of Phi Beta Kappa and Fellow of the African Studies Association, he is the author of *A Sourcebook of the Criminal Law in Africa* and coeditor with William J. Chambliss of *A Research Bibliography on the Sociology of Law*. He has also published numerous articles in professional journals.

Preface

This work grew out of an association developed when the senior author was Russell Sage Resident in Law and Sociology at the University of Wisconsin. For that we are both grateful to the Russell Sage Foundation.

Many persons have contributed to the making of this book. Alfred R. Lindesmith, Tom Russell, and Jerome Skolnick read the entire manuscript and made many excellent suggestions. Professor Lindesmith read it at two different stages and gave us invaluable help with the work from the beginning. The cogent suggestions of Leon Mayhew, Antoinette Hetzler, and Jim Driscoll, who read the manuscript in its final form, contributed greatly to its improvement. Jim Driscoll also handled the mailing of materials to us while we were in Africa—a chore that was much more demanding than anyone but he would appreciate. Michael Weiden and Ronald Tropp helped immeasurably by doing much of the spadework of research, and James W. Behrens helped us put the manuscript through the press. Mary Beth Shiels and Pamela Virene did most of the typing of the manuscript, and we thank them for their unfailing good humor in times of trial.

Of course, despite all the help that all these good people have given us, any errors that remain are ours.

February 1971   W. J. C.
                                                                        R. B. S.

v

Contents

Part I

Perspective

1

Introduction: a perspective on the systematic study of the legal order

No other phenomenon can claim to be the subject of such a plethora of knowledge and ignorance as the law. Even those who are most intimately involved with it—judges, law professors, attorneys, prosecutors, and law enforcement agents—are frequently proficient in one or another of its many facets without having any general understanding of the broad expanse of the legal order. It is the primary aim of this work to introduce the readers to systematic study of the legal order.

The book represents a contribution to the trend begun by the American legal realists, who insisted that we must study the *law in action* as well as the *law in the books*. The vacuum in general knowledge about the law which characterized legal thinking for many years was in large measure a result of the failure to take seriously this dictum of the realists. Significantly, the realists' case has nominally been won; legal scholars in America at least have by and large accepted the proposition that we must investigate systematically the law in action before we can fully understand the law in all its complexities.

Nevertheless, despite islands of concerted effort to implement the dictum of the realists, the prevailing mode of research by legal scholars and social scientists alike remains aloof from the day-to-day practices of the law. When the day-to-day practices are heeded, there has been a tendency to look at the findings of a particular study in isolation from other studies and especially to fail to see the general implications of the particular study. It is only when the studies are grasped *in toto* that their full implications become apparent. It is our intention to spell out these implications.

We do this by seeking explanations for the shape and character of the law in action in contemporary social theory. In attempting to make sense of the law in action, we have found it necessary to move back and forth from general theoretical perspectives to "theories of the middle range." It is our hope that we have succeeded in presenting a perspective *and* a set of middle-range propositions which together constitute a theory of the law in action.

Most courses in law schools, and virtually every course in high school that touches on the law, continue to assume that the prescriptions of the American Constitution, the common law, and the statutes are descriptions of the real world. How many courses taught in law schools utilize carefully done empirical studies of the social dynamics of legal controls? How many undergraduate courses in law taught in political science departments rely to any significant degree on empirical studies of the law in action? In high school, the Pollyanna perspective is even worse: the "ought" defined by law is blindly taught as the "is." As a result, the teaching of the law is usually the perpetuation of a myth.

The central myth about the legal order in the United States is that the normative structures of the written law represent the actual operation of the legal order. This is a myth that is based on the assumption that in the main, except for legislators, officials lack discretion to create law; in applying it, they merely carry out its dictates. "Ours is a government of laws, not of men."

A corollary to this myth is the notion, less well articulated but nevertheless widely prevalent, that despite the existence of sharp conflicts between interest groups in the society, the State itself, as represented by the courts and the police, as well as by other elements, provides a value-neutral framework within which struggle can take place. The legislature, of course, is not itself value-neutral, but the framework of elections is thought to be so. The legislature is therefore conceived of as an arena within which groups reflecting the power configurations of society itself can peacefully resolve their conflicts. The police are seen as carrying out the laws which the legislature enacts, the courts as deciding which side of a dispute is telling the truth and then fairly and impartially applying the law and meting out the sanction required by the law itself.

This myth of the operation of the law is given the lie daily. We all know today that the blacks and the poor are not treated fairly or equitably by the police. We know that judges have discretion and in fact make policy (as the Supreme Court did in the school desegregation cases). We know that electoral laws have been loaded in the past in favor of rural elements, that the electoral process is loaded in favor of the rich, that the average Presidential candidate is not a poor man, that one-fifth of the Senators of the United States are millionaires. Yet the myth persists. These aberrations are thought to be merely temporary biases. The framework is nevertheless "on the whole" impartial and neutral. Predetermined rules are believed to ordain decisions of government, not the value-loaded discretion of police, judges, or bureaucrats.

It is our contention that, far from being primarily a value-neutral framework within which conflict can be peacefully resolved, the power of the State is itself the principal prize in the perpetual conflict that is society. The legal order—the rules which the various law-making institutions in the bureaucracy that is the State lay down for the governance of officials and citizens, the tribunals, official and unofficial, formal and informal, which determine whether the rules have been breached, and the bureaucratic agencies which enforce the law—is in fact a self-serving system to maintain power and privilege. In a society sharply divided into haves and have-nots, poor and rich, blacks and whites, powerful and weak, shot with a myriad of special interest groups, not only is the myth false because of imperfections in the normative system: It is *inevitable* that it be so.

We propose to test our contention by following the methodology anticipated long ago by O. W. Holmes, who in 1881 stated a whole philosophy of law in a sentence when he asserted that the life of the law has not been logic, but experience. The way in which the rules actually operate to influence behavior can be understood only by considering the total social milieu of the persons whose behavior is supposed to conform to the rules and thus achieve the higher goals implicit in the rules.

This is a contention by no means new or eye-opening. It has been made for generations. If our only purpose were to add another book to the long bibliography of the judicial process or the penal system, the book would not be particularly worth the writing.

What we do hope to do is to add to the growing literature which looks at the law as a special sort of science, behavioral on the one hand, policy-making on the other. One cannot consider the universe of norms without considering whether the activity they prescribe is what ought to be the case. One cannot consider what is the case in the light of the norms without considering how what is the case can be aligned with what ought to be the case. With regard to the law, we must answer the question posed so long ago by Robert S. Lynd: Knowledge for what?

In venturing into such an enterprise, one must make countless decisions as to perspectives and methods. The social sciences are alas! not sufficiently close to consensus that one can easily adopt "the social science stance" and be assured that even a reasonable portion of the members of the enterprise will concur that the stance chosen is a wise one. The stance we have adopted, however, is one we think well suited to the study of the legal order. We have adopted a flexible and eclectic view of methodology. While the results of a particular study may be questioned, we have not eliminated or included studies simply because they represent a particular research methodology. We have ranged widely for ideas, perspectives, propositions, and data which would help us to understand the law in action.

2

A model of law and society

In the nature of things, one cannot describe all the empirical data involved in an area of investigation. One must pick and choose the data that are to be described. The principle of choice is a function of one's "perspective"; and that "perspective" is a function of what the observer proposes to do with his information—a function, in short, of the observer's values or goals. At the outset, therefore, it is appropriate that we identify our interest in the sociology of law. Before we can state that interest, however, it is necessary to chop our way through some terminological thickets.

2.1 THE PROBLEM OF TERMINOLOGY

One tack that has frequently been taken in the effort to define the word "law" is to identify phenomena in various societies which are sufficiently similar to warrant comparative study. To try to do this by the use of a definition, however, raises the danger that substantive judgment of what is most worthy of study will be smuggled under a linguistic cover. For example, a widely used definition of law is that adopted by William B. Harvey: law is a "technique of social ordering deriving its essential characteristics from its ultimate reliance on the reserved monopoly of systematically threatened or applied force in politically organized society."[1] It seems, then, plainly a misnomer to use the same word "law" for systems of social control in primitive societies, which lack any centralized monopoly of force, and which do not have a bureaucratic structure to determine when a rule of law has been breached, or to apply a sanction for its breach.[2] In an effort to find institutions common to both simple and complex societies susceptible of comparative study, therefore, the American anthropologist E. A. Hoebel stipulated a rather broader definition of "law."[3] He saw as the "fundamental *sine qua non*" of law in any society, primitive or civilized, "the legitimate use of physical coercion by a socially organized agent."[4] He then defined law as follows: "A social norm is legal if its neglect or infraction is regularly met, in threat or in fact, by the application of physical force by an individual or group possessing the socially recognized privilege of so acting."[5]

Hoebel has obviously made a preselection among the many potential attributes of what one might call "law" in a modern centralized society—the aspect of forceful sanctions—and masked his choice under a definitional guise. He does this by quietly asserting what is not at all clear, that force is the *sine qua non* of law. Force can be the *sine qua non* of law only if the concept of law exists as an essence in some unreal world of absolute, Platonic Ideas or if there is general agreement in advance about the phenomenon to which the word "law" refers, neither of which is the case. In sum, what Hoebel says by his definition is that he is interested in studying the use of socially approved force to sanction norms of conduct. This is a perfectly valid area of study, but hardly the "*sine qua non*" or "essence" of law. There are many other aspects of the institutions of social control manipulated by the bureaucracy of a centralized state which can serve as the focus of study, withoug necessarily constituting the "essence" of such institutions—the dispute-settling mechanism, the adjudicative mechanism, the systems of decision-making in the legal order, the fact-finding mechanism, the content of the norms, the interrelationship of the norms, and a host of others.

A schema that seems to us more fruitful for identifying the phenomena in society which we propose to study is to relate them to the basic concepts of modern sociology.

2.2 THE NORMATIVE SYSTEM AND THE LAW[6]

Ever since Auguste Comte (1798–1857), sociologists have been intrigued by the observable fact of the continuity of society. If any particular person is removed from society, society as a functioning system nevertheless continues. It is not too extreme a statement to say that the entire corpus of modern social science consists of the study of the implications of this truth.

Modern sociology conceives of a social system as consisting of the interrelated acts of people. Its structure arises out of the regularity or recurrence of these acts. One of the most important inquiries that one can make about any particular aspect of a social system is to seek the nature of, and the reasons for, the observed regularities.

The members comprising a social system are differentiated according to the positions they occupy in it. The observed regularities of the position, i.e., its content, arise because the person or persons who occupy the position fulfill a complex of obligations, and exercise a complex of rights, associated with the position. These "rights" and "obligations" are, of course, not necessarily the same sort of rights and obligations that lawyers customarily associate with the terms "right" and "duty," for most of them are not ordained or sanctioned by the State. One may have an "obligation" to surrender his seat in a train to a pregnant woman, but the State will not punish him if he does not. Hence most lawyers would deny that this "obligation" is a *legal* duty. The complex of obligations that define a social position are collectively called its *role*, and the equivalent complex of rights its *status*.

These obligations and rights are defined in prescriptive rules called *norms*. They may be more or less well articulated. The norms defining the role of father are, in large part, not articulated, although children may let their father know unmistakably when he acts in a way that to them seems to violate his role. ("Do act your age, Daddy!") Other norms, such as those embodied in statutes, are very explicitly stated.

Both human and animal colonies exhibit a high degree of regularity of behavior. The human condition, however, is distinguished from that of the lower orders by the normative system.

By contrast, the intricate interactions of an ant colony or a beehive, like those of a prairie dog village, are governed mainly by the instinctive reactions of natural and social stimuli . . . Obviously then, if the structure of human societies is to be understood, if human behavior is to be adequately explained, the normative aspect must be dealt with.[7]

A very wide range of questions may be asked about the norms, the role, and the way in which the occupant fulfills his role. What is the content of the norms, and how relevant are they to the task which the role-occupant is required to perform? To what extent are they institutionalized—i.e., to what extent do the persons in the system accept the norms, treat them seriously, and expect the role-occupant to be guided by it under appropriate circumstances? How are the norms sanctioned by society? To what extent are they articulated? How closely does the role performance of the occupant match the role expectation of those concerned? To what extent are the consequences of compliance with the norm those anticipated by the persons affected or by the role-occupant, and to what extent are the consequences unanticipated?

It can be seen that the normative system is the societal device by which consciousness is manifested in action. Norms reflect the subjective, internal conception that human beings hold, describing how people occupying certain positions ought to act. They state the *role expectation* for the position. *Role performance* refers to how people in fact act, either in pursuit of the norms defining the position or, deviantly, in defiance of the norms. The problem of the normative system therefore, is the sociological analogue to what in philosophy is called the mind-body problem. Role expectation is the internal, subjective conscious understanding of how the individual believes role-occupants ought to act. Role performance is the external, objective description of how role-occupants behave.

The rules of law are a particular order of norms. Like all norms, they define how people or collectivities ought to act. Some, like the laws against murder, are directed to everyone. Some, like the traffic laws, are addressed only to a particular category of persons (automobile drivers). Others are pertinent to very specific positions (such as the laws which define the role of the President of the United States). Still others are addressed to collectivities (corporation law). But they are all norms as we have defined that word.

The most obvious characteristic of the rules which laymen speak of as "law"—statutes, case law, administrative regulations—is that they are norms. In a centralized State, they are norms which are created or stated by State agencies; such as legislatures, courts, administrative agencies, and officials. One of the "law jobs" for any society is to create rules of law; and part of the study of law is to study how the norms are created and to determine their content.

But the creation of the norms and determination of their content, do not exhaust what one must consider if he is to comprehend a normative system. He must also understand how the norms are enforced—their accompaning sanctions. Most (but, as we shall see, not necessarily all) rules of law in a centralized State are enforced by sanctions imposed by State authority. If one violates a criminal law, the State sanction is usually imposed on the initiative of a State official (the policeman or the prosecutor), and the punishment is inflicted directly by other State officials (the jailer). If one violates other sorts of law—for example, one forbidding negligent automobile driving—he may become liable in damages at the behest of the injured party, who can enlist State power to enforce the judgment.

Thirdly, disputes arise concerning a variety of issues in connection with the normative system. There may be a dispute concerning the content of the norms; there may be a factual dispute as to whether the person in question actually did violate the norm. There must be, therefore, a dispute-settling mechanism to resolve these conflicts in society.

All these various "law jobs" constitute a set of processes: the processes of law-creation, of authoritatively defining the content of the norms, and those involved in settling disputes, in sanctioning the breach of the norms. The touchstone by which we, the authors of this book, distinguish the normative system in a centralized State and its associated processes, which we comprehend under the term "law," from other norms and processes is that what we call "laws" are

A MODEL OF LAW AND SOCIETY

those in which the State has a finger, whether as creator of the norms, adjudicator of conflict, or sanctioning agent.

Thus viewed, the law in a centralized State is not merely a body of rules. Rather, it is a dynamic process involving every aspect of State action, for State action will involve at some point either creation of a norm, adjudication about its content, adjudication that it has been violated, or a sanctioning process. It is this set of processes, then, which make up "the law."

2.3 THE SOCIAL-ENGINEERING FUNCTION OF LAW

As we have suggested, the normative system is the link between consciousness and social action. Conscious control over the normative system provides a tool by which man's intelligence and consciousness can control social processes to achieve the good society.

The development of organizations explicity devoted to the creation and sanctioning of norms creates the potential for the rational control over social process. Norms structure society. By the conscious manipulation of the normative system in which the State has a finger—the law—society today possesses the power to change itself by the rational and conscious effort. Roscoe Pound called this control through law the process of "social engineering."

Society is not, however, infinitely plastic. Social engineering, like any sort of engineering, must take careful account of the constraints imposed by the material with which one is dealing. At any given time and place, the relative difficulty of bringing about change in deeply engrained habits, the limited resources available to invest in a given program, the imperviousness of related institutions, the prevalent system of ideas, resistance of entrenched interests to planned social change, and a host of other factors, limit the range of choice. We conceive that it is an important task of the sociology of law to examine these constraints, thus to pose to the policy-makers the actual range of choice with which they are confronted. Such an empirical examination of the situation is the indispensable first step toward planned social engineering.

What is required is a guide to that investigation, an heuristic model to instruct the investigator where to look for relevant information.

2.4 THE LEGAL SYSTEM

Just as the word "law" cannot be defined except stipulatively, so the term "legal system" lacks any objectively ascertainable content. Like every subsystem of the total society, it performs a myriad of functions, both manifest and latent; to resolve disputes, to create official norms, to educate the people in certain value-sets, to provide employment for a professional class, etc. In studying a system so complex as to comprise such a variety of functions, all connected with the normative system sustained by State power, much depends upon the ingenuity and prespicacity of the observer.

Which of these functions is the "essence" of the legal system? It is no more possible to answer this question then it is to determine the "essence" of law. We are forced, therefore, also to define the "legal system" stipulatively.

Our definition starts from the observable fact that people make certain demands upon the bureaucratic organization that constitutes the State. They demand that disputes be settled, that certain services be performed, that resources be redistributed, and that certain kinds of decisions be made. These demands lead either to the creation of new norms or to a change in the application of existing rules.

Every norm, whether legal or nonlegal, is directed at the activity of a role-occupant. With most norms, the sanction takes place through direct interaction between the person aggrieved by the breach of the norm in question and the role-occupant. If my children disobey me, my parental role authorizes me directly to punish them; if my secretary displeases me, I can rebuke her or (in the absence of a union) discharge her.

There is a relatively small group of norms, rather formal in character, for which separate institutions are entrusted with the sanctioning process. Law is the outstanding example. There are also other, law-like norms for which there are separate, although non-State, sanctioning bodies.[8]

Practically every norm of law addressed to a role-occupant is simultaneously addressed to a sanctioning body, as Hans Kelsen has pointed out. The rule that commands the citizen not to murder, simultaneously commands the judge to apply a sanction if the prosecutor proves to him that someone committed murder. Thus the same demand by people that a rule-creating institution formulate a new norm of conduct for the citizen, simultaneously demands a new norm for the rule-sanctioning agencies, instructing them to impose a sanction if the norm directed at the citizen is breached.

We can, therefore, very tentatively and very abstractly diagram the flow of demands into the legal system, their conversion by rule-making and rule-sanctioning institutions into norms, addressed both to role occupants and to the rule-sanctioning agencies, and into sanctioning activity. (See Fig. 2.1.)

Every normative system induces or coerces activity. The normative system we have defined as "law" uses State power to this end. Our model, therefore, suggests that demands are made by various segments of the population that State power be exercised through law to induce or coerce certain desired behavior by some set of role-occupants. In the nature of things, demands of this sort are made in the interest of those making the demands. They call for the exercise of State power to *induce* or *coerce* the desired activity because the role-occupants do not necessarily want so to act. The legal system, thus defined, is a system by which one part of the population uses State power to coerce another segment. It is a system for the exercise of State power.

A MODEL OF LAW AND SOCIETY

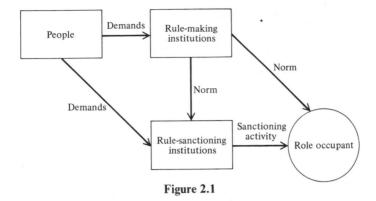

Figure 2.1

This model is, however, entirely normative in character. It traces the flow of demands: demands put to the State by segments of the population, demands made by the rule-making institutions upon role-occupants and upon rule-sanctioning institutions. The only activity it refers to is sanctioning activity. It tells us nothing about how in fact rule-sanctioning institutions act, or how role-occupants respond to the various pressures upon them, nor does it suggest the operation of feedback flows.

The use of the law as an instrument of social engineering requires that the policy-maker be able to predict that the rule he is proposing will bring about the sort of activity desired. If we are to understand how the legal system affects the behavior of the role-occupant, which is the ultimate question for the social engineer, we must go further. We must examine, not only the system of role expectations—the law in the books—but the actual role performance, that is, the law in action.

2.5 ROLE-PERFORMANCE AND ROLE-EXPECTATION

How a role-occupant acts is the resultant of all the forces, personal, and societal, acting on him. So much is a truism, which might be asserted of every role in society, whether defined by law or otherwise. Where the role is defined by law, however, a significant societal force operating on the role-occupant is the activity of officials. Officials create the rules to which the role-occupant is expected to conform, and officials occupy positions where they determine whether a sanction is appropriate and, when it is, assess and enforce it.

One might diagram the problem thus presented as shown in Fig. 2.2. The critical factors in determining how a role-occupant will act appear to be the norm to which he is expected to conform, the societal and personal forces operating upon him, and the activity of the law-sanctioning agencies. But the law-making and the law-sanctioning agencies do not operate *in vacuo*. They, too, are subject to

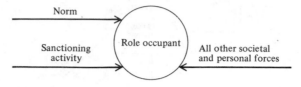

Figure 2.2

norms defining their positions, and to societal and personal forces and influences. In order properly to understand the pressures upon the role-occupant, one must also examine the positions of the law-makers and the law-sanctioning agencies. More completely, the system can be diagrammed as in Fig. 2.3.

The use of law as a tool of social engineering implies the use of rules articulated by law-makers to affect the role-performance of citizens and officials. The role-occupant, however, acts within a "field" of forces, much as a particle in nuclear physics operates within a field—except, of course, that a human being's field includes consciousness. In order to understand the actual range of choice available to the law-makers, i.e., the range within which social engineering by law is feasible, the first task is to examine the existing rules defining a *particular* role and also the role performance. The effort must be to determine whether the role-occupant is achieving the goals set for the position. If he is not, then the forces which are preventing him from so doing must be analyzed, so that we can deter-

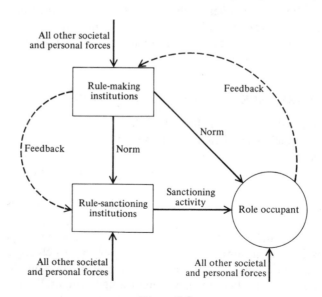

Figure 2.3

A MODEL OF LAW AND SOCIETY

mine the reasons for the failure and the range of possible remedial measures open to the rule-makers. Only then is one in a position to determine what policy ought to be followed and what program might be devised to implement it. This is what the American realists implied by their call for the study of the law in action, as opposed to the traditional study of the law in the books.

The common factors which affect every effort to utilize the law as a tool of social engineering are the activity of the law-makers and the activity of the law-sanctioning officials. The behavior of these officials becomes the keystone to any attempt at an effective change in society through the use of law. For each of these officials there are goals set for their position and norms defining how they are supposed to act. The preliminary but essential task of the sociology of law is the investigation of official behavior. Unless appellate judges, legislatures, and administrators create law wisely, unless policemen, sheriffs, and a host of minor officials enforce the law in a way consonant with its goals, every effort at social engineering must fail. That is why in this book we have concentrated our attention on the positions of the law-making and law-enforcing authorities.

2.6 THE ORGANIZATION OF THIS BOOK

These, then, are the basic issues which we take up in this book. We want to *describe* and to *explain* the characteristics and the shape of the legal order. We propose to do this by inquiring into some of the roles that comprise the legal system, the rules that circumscribe those roles, and the behavior of the role-occupants in those positions. We shall constantly seek to bring to bear sociological, political, and legal theory to explain *why* the legal order is constituted as the empirical data show it to be.

From a slightly different perspective, what we are about to do can be seen as viewing the law as a conscious tool of social engineering. Social engineering requires as its basis empirical information about the existing norms defining the positions at issue, and about the role performance of the role-occupants. Most important of all, it requires control over the machinery of the State itself—the roles which create law, and the roles which adjudicate and enforce it. We shall direct our attention principally to some of these roles in an effort to discover whether they achieve the goals set for them and, if not, the source of the deviancy.

NOTES

1. W. B. Harvey, *Law and Social Change in Ghana*, Princeton University Press, 1966, p. 343.
2. The problem of terminology has exercised anthropologists who have considered the issue. Compare Paul Bohannan, *Justice and Judgment Among the Tiv*, Oxford University Press, 1957, p. 69, with Max Gluckman, *Politics, Law, and Ritual in Tribal Society*, Blackwell, Oxford, 1965, p. 209.

3. E. Adamson Hoebel, *The Law of Primitive Man*, Harvard University Press, Cambridge, Mass., 1964, p. 26.

4. *Ibid.*, p. 28. Reprinted by permission.

5. *Ibid.*, Reprinted by permission.

6. Since this book is written for persons in law as well as those in the social sciences, it will sometimes be necessary to present what will appear as elementary points to members of one or the other group. However, we would rather err on the side of being too explicit than on the side of being too obscure. What follows is very simple sociology indeed, and those with some preliminary experience in the field might well skip this section.

7. Judith Blake and Kingsley Davis, "Norms, values and sanctions," in Robert E. L. Farris (ed.), *Handbook of Modern Sociology*, © 1964 by Rand McNally and Company, Chicago, p. 457. Reprinted by permission.

8. See, e.g., S. Macauley, *Law and the Balance of Power: The Automobile Manufacturers and their Dealers*, Russell Sage Foundation, New York, 1966.

Part II

The creation of formal rules of law

3

The creation of rules and value-choice

Our model suggests that the formulation of new rules of law by law-makers responds to demands made by some part of the population. These demands are invariably in the form such that a new rule requires some other part of the population to act in a new and different way. A demand by blacks for federal intervention to guarantee their right to vote is a demand that white registrars cease discriminatory application of voter registration rights. A demand by a newspaper for a harsher law to punish student protestors is a demand that the students moderate their protests. A demand by a business group that taxes be eased for them is a demand that the tax collectors permit them to retain more of their earnings than they would otherwise be allowed to keep, and that others bear proportionately more of the total tax burden.

That demands put to law-makers are demands that other people act in a different way results from the fact that every rule of law is normative. It is an "ought" statement. It describes how people are officially expected to act (and, incidentally, how the State's sanctioning agents—courts, administrators, police, sheriffs, and many others—are expected to act when a violator is brought before them).

Every law, therefore, expresses a valuation. It embodies somebody's ideas about what ought to be the case. Even a law that commands us to drive on the right-hand side of the street expresses the value-choices of order over chaos, of right-handedness over left-handedness, retaining historical custom over innovation.[1]

A society is composed of individuals occupying positions that are defined by the normative structure. Every demand for a change in the rules of law, therefore, is a demand that the society be changed to that extent. Every demand for a change in the law reflects the sort of society envisaged by those who demand it; that is, it reflects their values and goals.

The problem is to determine whose values are, and whose values ought to be, embodied in the law and whose conception of what society ought to be like determines the legal structure of the State.

On the highest level of generalization two answers to this question are offered by jurisprudents and social scientists. One group suggests that the State is a value-neutral framework within which conflict takes place. The other suggests that the State itself is an integral part of the unending social struggle between the antagonistic interests and classes which comprise society. The one assumes that at the bottom there is a fundamental value-consensus in society which is reflected in the law-making, law-applying, and adjudicating machinery of the State. The other proposes that control of the State and its awesome machinery of compulsion is itself the prize for which antagonistic interests struggle.

3.1 TWO MODELS OF SOCIETY

Two very general models of society purport to answer the question whether society is based on a value-consensus or a value-antagonism. This question is crucial to our discussion. If society represents a value-consensus, then the whole problem raised earlier disappears. The State of course must represent that value-consensus. The only legal problem, then, is to ensure that individual role-occupants do not substitute their own deviant motivations for the values of the polity. If, on the other hand, society is not based on value-consensus at every point, then the issue which we have raised is sharply poised.

Thus, it is argued on the one hand that, even if society is racked by conflict, the State is itself value-neutral. No matter how antagonistic toward one another the several groups and strata in the society may be, on this much they must agree: the peaceful settlement of conflict is better than violence and open warfare. The State, in this view, represents the entire population, but only to a limited degree. Every specific law or activity of the State is value-loaded, but the machinery by which the State comes to the decision to create and enforce any particular law is itself value-neutral, permitting conflict to work itself out peaceably.

On the other hand, conflict theorists argue that even so limited a conception of the value-free character of the State is false. State power is the most important weapon in the unceasing struggle that takes place beneath the more or less smooth and peaceful façade masking social reality. Whoever is in control of the State uses it in his own interest. Since his own interest requires the exclusion of his antagonists from participation in decision-making, even the processes by which the struggle for State power is carried on are warped in favor of one contending group or another.

The first question that must be answered, therefore, is whether society is in fact based on a value-consensus or a value-antagonism. In many discussions of the problem, the answer is assumed. Roscoe Pound, for example, whose writings on jurisprudence did an enormous service in advancing the whole concept of social engineering through law, urged that in a democratic society, the values of the law ought to respond to the values of those to whom it applied. He therefore urged that the claims and demands made upon the legal system be catalogued, the values subsuming them synthesized and then used to determine the serial order in which these claims and demands should be paid. It is a system which is based on the assumption that there is in every society a basic consensus of values reflected in the totality of social demands.

Exactly that claim has been made by Talcott Parsons and the entire school of sociology of which he is the outstanding exponent. Parsons bases his model on four principal assertions:

1   Every society is a relatively persisting configuration of elements.
2   Every society is a well-integrated configuration of elements.
3   Every element in a society contributes to its functioning.
4   Every society rests upon the consensus of its members.[2]

Given such a consensus, the only problem for the legislator is to determine what in fact the values of the society are just as Pound urged.

In opposition to this model, Ralf Dahrendorf and others have urged a conflict model. This model takes a diametrically opposed position on every point:

1   Every society is at every moment subject to change; social change is ubiquitous.
2   Every society experiences at every moment social conflict; social conflict is ubiquitous.
3   Every element in a society contributes to its change.
4   Every society rests on constraint of some of its members by others.[3]

Dahrendorf asserts that it is impossible empirically to choose between these two sets of assumptions. "Stability and change, integration and conflict, function and 'dysfunction,' consensus and constraint are, it would seem, two equally valid aspects of every imaginable society."[4] Like the dual theories of light, each model may be useful to explain specific aspects of social process.

When applied to the study of the legal order, Dahrendorf's claim that one cannot choose between the value-consensus and conflict models is not very persuasive. Indeed, the empirical studies of the law reported in this book make it quite clear that the value-consensus model is not only incapable of accounting for the shape and character of the legal system, but it even fails to raise the most fundamental and sociologically relevant questions about the law. The conflict model, by contrast, while having many shortcomings and not providing a complete answer to the questions raised by the study of the law, is nonetheless much more useful as a heuristic model for analyzing legal systems.

Why this is so will become clear in the analysis of the rule-making and rule-enforcing institutions which follows. In one sense, it is the purpose of this book to evaluate the relative explanatory utility of these competing theories of social order insofar as they pertain to the legal order. We begin this assessment by looking first at the law of "primitive" or "simple" societies in order to see how closely the expectations derived from these competing perspectives fit with the reality of law and social order in those societies.

3.2 THE CREATION OF NORMS IN SIMPLE SOCIETIES

Social scientists once generalized from a kind of naïve Darwinism that societies as well as species developed linearly from simple to complex. While a modified version of this notion can still be found in many social theories, in the form of an assumption that progress is inevitable in societies, for the most part social scientists have discarded the idea of inevitable progress as both naïve and empirically false.[5] Observation of societies by anthropologists and the social scientists have made it abundantly clear that (a) some societies, for example that of the Australian aborigines, have remained relatively unchanged for thousands of years, and (b) although one can see a semblance of "progress" in some particular fields, such as medicine, the progress of society or man generally is unmeasurable. Technology undoubtedly progresses. Whether societies in gross do is more questionable. To paraphrase Milton Mayer, one can scarcely argue very persuasively that a society where friends' heads are cut off with two-toned convertibles and enemies' heads are removed with flame-throwers has really shown any progress over a society where friends' and enemies' heads are removed with a machete. The point, of course, is that the idea that one society has progressed over another assumes that we can discover measures to determine that one society viewed in gross is better or superior to the other. By their nature, such measures must be culture-bound. They can only reflect *my* values. We are forced to conclude that the idea of "progress" has no merit as a scientifically useful construct.

Many of the earlier anthropologists, confronting variations in the several primitive legal systems, tried to explain their differences by placing them on a continuum from the most simple to the most complex. They postulated that their continuum represented a historical process through which every legal system must pass.[6] There is an insufficiency of historical materials to attempt any verification of such a thesis. What evidence there is seems ambiguous.

The real utility of the study of the law of primitive societies is not different from the advantages to be derived from the study of any comparative system of law. By contrasting and comparing legal systems, one may be able to generate meaningful propositions relating the different sorts of variables which seem to control the kind of legal system that obtains. We consider in this chapter, then, the emergence of law-like norms in primitive (i.e., technologically undeveloped) societies.

The Significance of Technology

Every society exists in a specific historical and geographical environment. This environment exercises significant constraints upon the society, and therefore, the understanding of any society must begin with an understanding of its physical parameters. The most significant of these parameters is not the geographical but, rather, the technological environment. The geography of a society of course restricts its choices in the modes of existence to those possible in the environment. But the obvious fact that societies of very different levels of complexity and culture have existed at various times in precisely the same environment, or even, as today, coexist in physical environments which are substantially the same, suggests that the geographical environment cannot be the dominant force which shapes society. The fact that many of the most primitive societies exist in tropical countries is a function, not of the temperature and humidity, but of the historical development of technologies.

Primitive societies have primitive technologies; that is precisely what makes them "primitive." Technologies are primitive when they are simple: the tools are not complicated, and the various tasks to be performed not readily susceptible to division into easily learned, repetitive bits. In a technologically complex society, on the other hand, the nature of the unbelievably complex tools which have been developed requires that the various tasks be capable of division into small, easily learned, and repetitive actions. In a modern automobile manufacturing plant, for example, fantastically complex machines are used to create almost equally complex automobiles by men each of whom does a relatively simple job.

Two consequences important to the development of law flow from the consequences of simple technologies. In the first place, the simpler the technology, the smaller is the number of differentiated jobs in the economy. Now, this is not to say that everyone in the society will do exactly the same thing. Even in a Bushman band, living on as low a level of technology as exists in the world, the women do different sorts of jobs than the men. But it is nevertheless true that the *variety* of jobs is much smaller, and the jobs are infinitely less differentiated from each other, than in highly complex societies.

A second consequence of primitive technology is the simple fact of privation. In most instances, simple technologies do not produce even the minimum required

tions and justifications for what is. William Graham Sumner said long ago, "The folkways are the 'right' ways."[16] Religious ideologies, economic theory, mythological explanations, philosophy, moral and secular literature, all tend to provide rationalizations and indeed imperative reasons for the selections made.

Any choice that is made must therefore be made within the constraints of time and place, and must, in the nature of things, be made in light of the existing conceptual patterns. Hoebel, following Pound, called these conceptual patterns "jural postulates." As Hoebel put it, quoting Julius Stone,

"The jural postulates . . . are generalized statements of the tendencies actually operating, of the presuppositions on which a particular civilization is based . . . They are ideals presupposed by the whole social complex, which can thus be used to bring the law into harmony with it, so that the law 'promotes rather than hampers and oppresses it.' They are, as it were, directives issuing from the particular civilized society to those who are wielding social control through law within it."[17] . . . As for Stone's formulation of the matter, he need not have limited the existence of jural postulates to civilized society, for every society, primitive or civilized, that has a law system has its jural postulates.[18]

Hoebel was dealing with relatively simple societies. In such societies, what choices are made are rarely made explicitly and consciously by the community. Rather, the choices arise as the individuals comprising the society each make their choices, and then, in the course of common living, come to reach a consensus. Simple societies lack marked specialization of function and require cohesion for common protection against a harsh environment. These constraints exert continuing pressures toward a value-consensus, reflecting the common experience of practically every member of the community. Under such circumstances, the community makes choices without consciously realizing that choices have been made.

3.3 SUMMARY

The form or content of a society's culture is largely determined by the choices it has earlier made. But as features of the social structure change, the normative system will adapt to these changes. A change, for example, in the economic conditions of a society will necessarily bring about a change in at least segments of the normative system. The adaptation which is made takes the form of new rationalizations or justifications which "make sense" of doing apparently wise things under the prevailing circumstances. This adjustment of norms to fit prevailing conditions is, it seems likely, the source of norms and normative change in primitive societies. Characteristically, in primitive societies we find a much higher degree of consensus on norms, and a higher degree of internalization of those norms, than is the case in complex societies. That this is true is not surprising, since the range of experiences of the members of the primitive group are much more similar than in complex societies, since communication among the members is more intimate, and since changes in the set of life conditions are more gradual and therefore less likely to lead to rapidly changing normative systems.

Given such a value-consensus, the absence of specialized institutions to develop new norms, and to sanction the breach of agreed norms, seems easy enough to understand. How, then, did specialized law-making and law-sanctioning institutions emerge?

NOTES

1. F. S. Cohen, *Ethical Systems and Legal Ideals*, Falcon Press, New York, 1933, pp. 15–19.

2. Ralf Dahrendorf, "Toward a theory of social conflict," *Journal of Conflict Resolution*, **2**. 1958, pp. 170–183. Reprinted by permission.

3. *Ibid.*, p. 174. Reprinted by permission.

4. *Ibid.*, pp. 174–175. Reprinted by permission.

5. J. B. Bury, *The Idea of Progress*, Macmillan, New York, 1932.

6. An interesting modern extension of the notion of continuum by the use of scalogram analysis has been attempted; it suggests a kind of historical evolution, but the result is hardly conclusive. See Robert L. Cameiro and Stephan F. Tobias, "The application of scale analysis to the study of cultural evolution," *Trans. New York Acad. Sci.*, Series II, **26**, December 1963, pp. 196–207; and cf. Melvin Ember, "The relationship between economic and political development in nonindustrialized societies," *Ethnology*, **2**, 1963, pp. 228–248.

7. Thomas Hobbes, *Leviathan*, Blackwell, Oxford, 1946, Chapter 13.

8. William Seagle, *The Quest for Law*, Knopf, New York, 1941, p. 33. Reprinted by permission.

9. Friedrich Karl von Savigny, *Ueber den Beruf unserer Zeit zur Gesetzgebung und zur Rechtswissenschaft*, 1814; tr. A. Howard, London, 1832, pp. 24, 27, 30; quoted in Wolfgang Friedmann, *Legal Theory*, Columbia University Press, New York, 1967, pp. 159–160.

10. Bronislaw Malinowski, *Crime and Custom in Savage Society*, Humanities Press, Inc., Routledge and Kegan Paul Ltd., London, 1926, pp. 58–59. Reprinted by permission.

11. E. E. Evans-Pritchard, *Social Anthropology and Other Essays*, Free Press of Glencoe, New York, 1962, P. 76; see also Seagle, *op, cit.*, p. 31.

12. Max Gluckman, *Politics, Law, and Ritual in Tribal Society*, Blackwell, Oxford, 1965, pp. 205–206.

13. Robert Redfield, "Primitive law," *U. Cinn. Law Rev.*, **33**, 1964, p. 1; reprinted in Paul Bohannan (ed.), *Law and Warfare: Studies in the Anthropology of Conflict*, Natural History Press, Garden City, N. Y., 1967, pp. 3–4.

14. Malinowski, *op. cit.*, p. 26. Reprinted by permission.

15. R. F. Benedict, *Patterns of Culture*, New American Library, New York, 1934, p. 237; quoted in E. A. Hoebel, *The Law of Primitive Man*, Harvard University Press, Cambridge, Mass., 1964, p. 10.

16. W. G. Sumner, *Folkways*, Dover, New York, 1959, p. 28.

17. Julius Stone, *The Province and Function of Law*, Harvard University Press, Cambridge, Mass., 1950, p. 337. Reprinted by permission.

18. E. A. Hoebel, *The Law of Primitive Man,* Harvard University Press, Cambridge, Mass., 1964, p. 16. Reprinted by permission.

4

From stateless societies to the state

It is a striking fact that all of society's dispute-settling mechanisms can be divided into two ideal types. With one, the decision is in terms of compromise—what Laura Nader calls "give a little, get a little." With the other, the decision is that one party is right and the other wrong, so that the decision is of the sort that she calls "winner takes all." Typically, in simple societies the system of dispute-settlement is based on compromise, while in a complex, stratified society like our own the official role of the courts is based on winner taking all. In this chapter we shall first offer a hypothesis as to why there is this difference; then we shall examine the consequences of these two different conceptions of the role of dispute-solving agencies on the law-making activity of the dispute-solving agency.

4.1 COMPROMISE V. NORM-ENFORCEMENT

Disputes invariably arise because one party does not act in the way the other party to the dispute expects or wants him to act. Since norms express the role-expectation held by others, disputes necessarily arise over the claim that one party violated the norm that the party claiming to be aggrieved holds for the former's position. When the matter comes to be decided by a third party, obviously the principal argument to be made in order to persuade the third party to decide the case in favor of one side or the other is to appeal to commonly held norms to justify the action taken by the defendant or the claim of the plaintiff. Hence, whether the nominal objective of the tribunal is to settle the dispute in terms of compromise or with a one-sided winner, the argument before the tribunal will be in terms of the rules alleged to have been broken.

Common human experience teaches us that the consequences, on the future relationship of the parties to conflict depend, to a degree, on their sense of equitable treatment in the conflict. Where parties want or must have continuing interactions of a nonantagonistic nature after the dispute, both must leave the dispute-settlement procedures without too great a sense of grievance. If, however, the parties need not live together thereafter, then it is irrelevant whether either of the parties continues to be antagonistic to the other after the proceedings.

As a result, whether the principal objective of dispute-settling is continued relationships or not determines whether the tribunal will base itself on "give a little, get a little," or "winner takes all." In the one case, a bargaining relationship is established during the dispute-settling process. The aim of the bargain is not to determine that one side or the other breached the norm at issue so much as it is to discover a compromise solution which will leave neither party so strongly aggrieved as to make future relationships impossible. If, on the other hand, the tribunal is indifferent whether the parties will live together after the dispute-settlement, then there is no reason why it should not determine unequivocally whether the defendant in fact violated the norm, and then award a decision based on the principle of "winner taking all."

"Give a little, get a little" is the appropriate principle of decision-making in our society in cases where a continued relationship between the disputants is anticipated. Stewart Macauley has demonstrated that businessmen do not bring law suits against customers whose trade they want to keep after the particular dispute has been settled.[1] Married couples who want to preserve their marriage do not take their disputes to courts; they take them to marriage counselors, who usually try to help find compromise solutions. Arbitration is a familiar form of dispute-settlement between trade unions and employers, who must after the dispute continue their relationship.

"Winner takes all," on the other hand, is the typical principle of dispute-settlement when there is no desire to continue the relationship. When a person is injured in an automobile accident, usually he had no prior relationship with the other party and anticipates no future relationship. In such cases, the parties typically expect, in the end, to settle their dispute in court on a "winner takes all" basis. So also in criminal matters: either the accused is guilty or he is not guilty.

In every "winner-takes-all" situation, of course bargaining may take place, and often the actual disposition will be on the basis of compromise. But the objective of such a compromise is markedly different from the objective of compromise in a true "give-a-little, get-a-little" situation. Bargaining over a negligence claim has really only the objective of saving the parties the time and expense of an actual trial. They bargain, not in an effort to make possible a future relationship, but in light of their estimates of the probabilities of a favorable outcome of the potential "winner-takes-all" litigation. Guilty plea bargaining in criminal cases is likewise based on the convenience in avoiding the possibilities of a "winner-takes-all" result of the potential trial. (This case is complicated by the fact that although the parties themselves, the criminal and the prosecutor, of course have no anticipation of a continuing relationship, the defense counsel and the prosecutor may well anticipate a continuing relationship and hence may bargain in an attempt to preserve that relationship.)

A one-sided decision has the consequence of sanctioning the breach of a norm. A compromise solution does not necessarily have that consequence. The man who has committed a first-degree murder, but is permitted to plead guilty to manslaughter (with a considerably lighter penalty), has not been sanctioned to the degree consistent with the norm relating to murder. The man who breaches a contract, but ultimately compromises the claim at much less than it should have been, has not been fully sanctioned for his breach.

We can therefore regard the difference between "give a little, get a little" and "winner takes all" as the difference between the objectives of dispute-settlement *simpliciter*, and of norm enforcement. One can hypothesize that the difference between the objectives of dispute-settlement processes in simple and in complex societies is a function of the different imperatives imposed by their different social structures.

Viewing the various types of societies roughly, it is apparent that there are two marked characteristics which exercise significant constraints on every social institution. One of these is the relative differentiation of roles in the various societies; the other is the relative degree of their stratification.

Max Gluckman has said that

When we contrast tribal society with modern society we are . . . working with a distinction the implications of which have been elaborated by many sociologists and anthropologists: the difference between Durkheim's mechanical and organic solidarity, Tonnies' *gemeinschaft* and *gesellschaft*, von Wiese's sacred and secular societies, Weber's traditional and bureaucratic societies, Stalin's patriarchal and industrial societies, Redfield's folk society and urban civilization.[2]

These two ideal types of society differ in many different ways; the very names attached to them by the several authors mentioned by Gluckman suggest that each of the authors saw in the two types different points of emphasis. Viewed in the light in which Durkheim saw them, however, the central difference lies in the relative differentiation of roles. In a society marked by what Durkheim called "mechanical solidarity," each individual does many different sorts of tasks. Economically the level of technology is low, and the whole macroeconomy is usually character-ized as a subsistence economy. There is little interchange of goods. In a stratified subsistence economy, even the chief or leader will live no more elegantly than a lesser member of the clan or tribe, and his actual day-to-day activities may not be significantly different from those of the ordinary member.

The advent of more advanced technologies led to the marked differentiation of roles which characterizes any modern, advanced society. Economically people do very specialized jobs for the most part. There is a high interchange of goods and services, required by the very specialization of roles which characterize the society. This sort of society Durkheim characterized as one of "organic soli-darity."

It should be stressed, of course, that these categories constitute ideal types. In fact, there is not now nor has there been in the past a pure society of mechanical solidarity, any more than there is or has been one of organic solidarity. On the contrary, one could place societies on a continuum from the less complex to the more complex, from societies with relatively little differentiation of roles to the society with a relatively high degree of role differentiation.

The first variable in our theoretical model is the relative complexity of the society. It is a corollary from this proposition that societies may be ranked in order of their relative differentiation of roles, that the more highly differentiated the roles in a society—the greater the number of different roles there are—the greater the number of the norms there must be operative in the society if it is to function.

It is a further corollary that the greater the differentiation of roles, the more complicated and sophisticated the roles necessarily become, and the more highly detailed and sophisticated the norms become. This is so because the more differentiated the roles are in a society, the more the norms defining them must differ from each other in details, and hence the more complex and sophisticated, they must be.

Perhaps the most striking character of the societies marked by mechanical solidarity is, as we said, the low level of technology. As a result, their standards of living are very low; hence derives the apt characterization of their economies as "subsistence" economies. Faced by so low a level of technology in a harsh environment, a community necessarily becomes more dependent on social solidarity. Social relationships are based on the extended family. Difficult com-munications force people to remain close to their birthplace for most of their lives. Every man is dependent in times of crisis on his family and neighbors, a relationship that cannot readily be dissolved if life is to continue. Relatively simple norms of behavior are learned through elementary socialization, and are enforced through sanctions in which the community at large participates— sanctions in the forms of scorn, disapproval, anger, or sometimes even group excommunication. Formal institutions to sanction the breach of the norms are not required; institutions to maintain social solidarity are.

In a complex society, on the other hand, the opposite is true. While economic existence is dependent on a fantastically complex interchange of goods and services, it is the goods and services which are important, not the identities of the individuals performing those services. The relatively high level of technology reduces the threat of starvation and death, and hence lowers the requirement for mutual support in the future as between any particular individuals. Easy communication at once raises the level of interdependence upon the system as a whole, but reduces the interdependence of specific individuals on each other. To use a fashionable term, alienation increases. The institutionalization and enforcement of complex norms and roles in conditions of alienation require more formal processes. In such conditions, whether or not litigants "live together" after the dispute is unimportant.

As a result of these different characteristics, the dispute-settlement processes of the two kinds of societies will be markedly different. We may formulate, therefore, the following proposition: The lower the level of complexity of a society, the more emphasis will be placed in the dispute-settling process upon reconciliation; the more complex the society, the more emphasis will be placed on rule-enforcement.

Durkheim infers precisely the opposite conclusion in originally postulating the differences between mechanical and organic solidarity. He separates juridical rules into "two great classes, according as they have organized repressive sanction or only restitutive sanctions."[3] He reaches his conclusion by first asserting that "the only common characteristic of all crimes is they consist . . . in acts universally disapproved of by members of each society."[4] He finds the source of this disapproval in the "collective" or "common conscience" of the society, which he defines as "the totality of beliefs and sentiments common to average citizens of the same society," and which "forms a determinate system which has its own life."[5] The same collective conscience is the source of repressive punishments: "because they are found in all consciences, the infraction committed arouses in those who have evidence of it or who learn of its existence the same indignation. Everybody is attacked; consequently, everybody opposes the attack."[6] Hence the relative strength of this reaction will be a function of the solidarity of the collective conscience.

Durkheim then reasons that in societies in which there is little differentiation of roles, i.e. in which all the members of the group resemble one another the common conscience is reinforced by that very fact.[7] Hence he concludes:

. . . there exists a social solidarity which comes from a certain number of states of conscience which are common to all the members of the same society. This is what repressive law materially represents . . . The part that it plays in the general integration of society evidently depends upon the greater or lesser extent of the social life that the common conscience embraces and regulates. The greater the diversity of relations wherein the latter makes its action felt, the more also it creates links which attach the individual to the group; the more, consequently, social cohesion derives completely from this source and bears its mark.[8]

Restitutive law—i.e., law in which the sanction is "not expiatory, but consists of a simple *return in state*"[9]—is an index, says Durkheim, of a society with relatively highly differentiated roles. The infraction of rules which apply only to a specialized segment of the community does not strike at the common conscience, and hence does not elicit the retributive passions occasioned when a delict violates the beliefs that aminate the entire body politic.[10] Hence the more differentiated the roles of a society, the more its law will be restitutive.

Our disagreement with Durkheim at this point arises because we believe that Durkheim fails sufficiently to take into account the very real community of interests of the members of simple societies, largely arising out of the difficult and indeed dangerous environment of practically all societies based on a subsistence economy with a low technological level.[11] Whether the basis of law in societies of mechanical solidarity is repressive and punitive or whether it is directed toward the objective of reconciliation is an empirical question that we shall examine later.

The most important corollary to our proposition would seem to be that the sorts of institutions society creates in order to deal with disputes will vary depending on their purposes. Where the purpose of an institution is to reconcile the parties so that they can live together after the breach has been resolved amicably and cooperatively, one would expect to find the institution to reflect a greater emphasis on mediation and compromise. If the purpose of the institution is rule-enforcement, then a bureaucracy would likely to be developed whose primary objective is the determination of the precise content of the norms and of whether it has in fact been broken, together with devices for assessing and enforcing the sanction.

A second important variable is the extent of stratification in the society. The earliest societies are notable for the lack of economic distinction between the various members. As societies grow more complex technologically, then for a wide variety of reasons—greater aggressiveness or competence of individuals, territorial conquests, accidental control of significant resources, and no doubt others—significant economic differences between members tend to arise. Just as in the case of the relative complexity of societies, one could place societies in rank order with respect to their relative stratification. Again, as with respect to the relative complexity of societies, it is important to emphasize that without much more evidence than is now available, it is not possible to assert that this ranking reflects more than a classificatory device; it does not necessarily represent the route of a historical progress.

The more economically stratified a society becomes, the more it becomes necessary for the dominant groups in the society to enforce through coercion the norms of conduct which guarantee their supremacy. It would seem probable that the more the social structure creates and enforces inequality, the more the life experiences of various groups differ and consequently the norms internalized by people in different strata can be expected to vary as well. Under such circumstances, the central thrust of the dispute-settling process shifts from accomplishing an accommodation between the disputants, and thus their reconciliation, to the enforcement of the rule by imposition of a sanction.

Thus we can formulate a second proposition: The less stratified the society, the more emphasis will be placed in the dispute-settling process on reconciliation; the more stratified the society, the more emphasis will be placed on rule-enforcement.

We can combine these two propositions in a simple four-cell table:

	Less complex societies	More complex societies
Less stratified societies	reconciliation reconciliation	rule-enforcement reconciliation
More stratified societies	reconciliation rule-enforcement	rule-enforcemen rule-enforcement

What this table tells us is that in less stratified, less complex societies, we would expect a maximum emphasis to be placed on reconciliation of parties alienated by reason of a claimed breach of a norm. We would also expect that in a more highly complex, more stratified society, emphasis would be placed almost entirely on rule-enforcement. In less complex but more highly stratified societies, we would expect the dispute-settling process to seek simultaneously to achieve both objectives, as also in a less stratified but more complex society.

4.2. DISPUTE-SETTLEMENT AND THE CREATION OF NEW NORMS

Where disputes are settled by compromise, it is indifferent to the tribunal what the precise content of the norm is, because this content is not so important as the search for an appropriate middle position between the parties that will reestablish their original relationship. Norms are appealed to in the argument before the tribunal, but the decision of compromise negates the importance of precise ascertainment of the applicable, authoritative norm.

As societies become more complex and stratified, and hence tend to emphasize rule-enforcement as the objective in settling disputes, a different set of institutions is required for the maintenance of order. Instead of institutions directed toward the achievement of compromise and the maintenance of solidarity, institutions designed to sanction the breach of norms are required.

In the common-law system, this sanctioning function developed out of the dispute-settling function. Courts became institutions by which the breach of norms was sanctioned, and no longer a device by which reconciliation and compromise were accomplished. In addition, there slowly developed institutions devoted to the enforcement of specific sets of norms, too complex or too important to be left to private adversary litigation. Police forces appeared, ultimately to take over the enforcement of criminal laws which earlier had been relegated to private criminal litigation. Administrative agencies enforced the rules of the Welfare State.

As courts become norm-enforcing institutions instead of dispute-settling mechanisms aimed mainly at compromise, however, a new function is forced upon them: they become norm-creating institutions. As soon as disputes must be settled on a winner-takes-all basis—i.e., on the basis that if a rule has been breached, the guilty party must suffer a sanction, in the form of either recompensing the aggrieved party or submitting to punishment—the forum for settling disputes must also determine the correct content of the norm. To determine the correct or authoritative content of the norm, in cases where the norm is unclear, the agency is required to create a new authoritative norm to resolve the problem. In such cases, the agency is permitted, under the guise of determining what is the authoritative norm, to create a new one. The process of dispute-settling thus merges into the process of norm-creation.

The strange fact, however, is that during the long evolution of the common-law tradition in England, the courts continued to deny their rule-creating role even as they were creating new rules; and they continue to deny it to this day. We turn now to examine that paradoxical development.

NOTES

1. S. Macauley, "Non-contractual relations in business: preliminary study," *Am. Soc. Rev.* **28**, 1963, p. 55.

2. Max Gluckman, *Politics, Law, and Ritual in Tribal Society*, Blackwell, Oxford, 1965, p. 213. Reprinted by permission of New American Library, publishers.

3. Emile Durkheim, *The Division of Labor in Society*, George Simpson (tr.), Free Press, New York, reprinted 1964, p. 69.

4. *Ibid.*, p. 73.

5. *Ibid.*, p. 79.

6. *Ibid.*, p. 102.

7. *Ibid.*, p. 105.

8. *Ibid.*, p. 109.

9. *Ibid.*, p. 110.

10. See Talcott Parsons, *The Structure of Social Action*, Free Press of Glencoe, New York, 1937, p. 318.

11. See R. K. Merton, "Durkheim's division of labor in society," *Am. J. Soc.*, **40**, 1934, pp. 319–328; reprinted in R. A. Nisbet, *Emile Durkheim*, Prentice-Hall, Englewood Cliffs, N.J., 1965, p. 109.

5

The creation of law in modern societies, rule-creation and the enforcement of custom

Although it is impossible to trace any clear path of evolution of societies, it is nevertheless clear that societies have evolved in parallel with the development of simple technologies into complex technologies, from mechanical solidarity to organic solidarity; and there has been an evolution from relatively unstratified societies into relatively stratified ones. If our hypothesis is at all valid, therefore, courts must have developed in the Western world at least from institutions with the primary purpose of settling disputes into institutions with the corollary purpose of enforcing norms.

We recall that norms in very simple societies evolve through the repetitive activities of the population at large. In the simplest societies there are no legislatures, no appellate courts, or other specific rule-making bodies. The norms which structure such a society, if we are to follow Hoebel's model, are the resultant of the choices made by the various members of the community through time.

Dispute-settling institutions in such communities tend to have the objective of compromise, though the arguments put before them generally urge the propriety of following the norms. Whatever it ultimately does, the dispute-settling mechanism does not primarily sanction the breach of norms. The ascertainment of the precise content of a norm is relatively unimportant in the dispute-settling process.

The common law courts in England developed out of the continuing struggle between the Crown and the great feudatories for supremacy. Under feudal constitutional law, a feudatory, to all intents and purposes, had his own government and particularly his own courts. One of the early efforts of the Crown to eat away that jurisdiction came when the King's judges were sent to the countryside to try cases. English society at the time was, of course, already highly stratified. The common-law courts from the beginning seem to have tried cases on a winner-takes-all basis.

The substantive law appealed to was purported to be, not the King's law, but local custom. For example, while primogeniture was the prevalent rule for the distribution of a decedent's estate, in those parts of England which had the custom of gavelkind, a dead man's property was distributed equally among his children. The common-law courts originally enforced both types of customs. The judges supposedly applied, not laws which they invented, but laws which represented the customs of the people involved, thus legitimatizing their decisions by appeal to local values. As a body of decisions accumulated, the authoritative declaration of "custom" came to be, not what the people involved said it was, but what other judges in precedent cases had declared the "custom" to be.

As we have seen, however, to decide which norm applies to a case, the court may have to decide what the law actually is. It may, therefore, be necessary for a court to create the law. Thus the common-law courts came to be a primary source of new rules of law, despite the fiction that they only followed the prevailing custom. They were for centuries in England, the most important law-making institutions. They remain a most important source of law to this day throughout the common-law world.

Even legislation was at first conceived of primarily as a device to declare and fix the custom of the realm. The importance of this belief can be seen in an interesting aspect of English constitutional law concerning the settlement of Englishmen overseas in a new colony.

It was the rule that Englishmen colonizing overseas carried their law with them as their birthright. That law, however, did not include *all* the law of England, but only part of it.

The common law of England is the common law of the plantations, and all statutes *in affirmance of the common law* passed in England, antecedent to the settlement of a colony, are in force in that colony, unless there is some private Act to the contrary ...[1]

The reason for the constitutional rule is plain enough. It seemed only fair and just to judge the disputes of Englishmen overseas by the rules to which they were accustomed: the common law of the realm and those statutes which affirmed that custom. Statutes which departed from the common law were not included because it was felt that the colonial settlers might not have internalized those norms, and therefore, it would be unjust to judge their disputes by them.

The development of law-creating institutions out of dispute-settling institutions based on "enforcing custom" required courts to deny that they create law, which is also to deny that they make a value-choice. Instead, any change in law can be attributed to the slow transformation of social values and standards. A custom, to be a custom, must be a custom of all of us. Just as any custom in a simple society is the resultant of multiple choices made by the members of the community, so custom, and law, in common-law theory is conceived of as the resultant of community determination. This is a theory which necessarily assumes that a society *does* have a common set of values as manifested in the common choice of norms. Law is then conceived of, not as a molder of society or a creator of institutions, but only as the institutionalized form of preexisting norms, developed in the course of the imperceptible, glacial movement of societies.

5.1 NORM-CREATION AND THE DEVELOPMENT OF COMMODITY EXCHANGE

The notion that courts do not create norms but merely enforce the customs of the community conforms nicely with the development of contract as the principal form of economic cooperation. In feudal England, economic cooperation was based on customary institutions, upheld by State power against deviation. The serf had certain obligations to the owner of the manor; the vassal had obligations to his lord. These obligations ensured that what economic cooperation was required would be achieved. They ensured that the serfs would perform the labor upon which the entire superstructure of feudal society rested.

As commodity exchange supplanted the subsistence economy of feudal England, agreements relating to the sale and exchange of land and goods and services slowly replaced feudal customs as determining the dominant form of economic cooperation. The employers hired employees on contract; importers sold to wholesalers, wholesalers to retailers, and retailers to consumers. Entrepreneurs entered into large commercial undertakings with one another, based on their agreement to cooperate in certain specified ways. At every point in the economy, private contracts more and more replaced feudal law as the glue for the economy.

In a contract, the parties agree on the sort of conduct that each expects of the other. For purposes of the transaction at hand, they lay down the role-expectations each holds of the other. It is easy for a court to believe that in settling a dispute involving a contract, it is merely ascertaining what the parties intended, that it is not itself creating a new norm of conduct. A court can easily believe that in general it is merely enforcing the custom to comply with contractual obligations and, therefore, that it is not creating any new law by requiring the parties to comply with the rules which the parties themselves have created in the contract. The slow development from a feudal economy to an economy based on the exchange of goods and services fits nicely with the notion that courts do not create law, but merely enforce custom.

5.2 MODELS DENYING VALUE-CHOICE BY LAWMAKERS

A whole collection of theories, both jurisprudential and in the social sciences, have been proposed which generalize from the reasoning in the last section into full-blown philosophies of law. Since the reasoning is focused on dispute-settlement and is based on a denial of the rule-creating role of the courts, these theories have in general assumed that the courts (and sometimes the entire State structure) stand above and apart from society, comprising a neutral framework within which social struggle and conflict takes place. Since they are thought to be neutral, it is assumed there is at least a minimum consensus upon the existence of the State as arbiter of conflict. We shall discuss very briefly certain natural-law theories: the schema put forward by Von Savigny; Sir Henry Maine's famous notion of the movement from status to contract; and certain modern theories, especially those of Paul Bohannan, Jerome Skolnick, and Lon Fuller.

Natural Law

For two millennia and more mankind has sought a standard of absolute justice against which to measure the law as it is. Obviously such a search can have two opposite and contradictory results. On the one hand, the derived absolute standard can become a revolutionary credo with which to attack the existing structure, as it did in the case of the American Revolution. Perhaps more frequently, however, it can become a strong support for the existing law. If the law represents what is thought to be absolutely just, then it must partake of divinity.

The standards of absolute justice have varied. In the earliest forms, the criterion of rightness is thought to derive from divine guidance through authoritative texts such as the Bible (or, in Moslem law to this day, the Koran), through direct intuition of divine will, or through direct intuition guided by "right reason." In more modern forms, the standard tends to be derived from the conception of what is necessary for man to be able to live in society. Since such criteria are incapable of empirical proof or disproof, they tend to find their wellspring in the intuition of the good life held by a particular philosopher or writer.

The natural-law conception played an enormous part in the formation of the common law. That all the problems posed to judges could not be solved in terms of custom was inevitable. Some statutes from the very beginning bore little relationship to customs, whatever the nominal tradition may have been. The Statute of Wills (1540), for example, for the first time permitted a man to direct the distribution of his property after his death in defiance of the customary modes of distribution of property. Which kinds of promises should be enforced, and which not, was not a matter that in the nature of things could be determined by reference to custom alone. (Why should a promise to make a gift ordinarily not be enforceable by law, but a promise to pay for goods sold and received be enforceable? Why should a promise made under seal to make a gift be enforceable, but one not under seal unenforceable?) The judges frequently answered these questions by reference to the natural law. The common law, said Sir Edward Coke, a great seventeenth-century English judge, resides in the breasts of the judges.

The conception of natural law of whatever mold presupposes that the choice of the values embodied in the law derives from a source equally authoritative for all mankind. It assumes, therefore, that that set of authoritative values is appropriate for determining what the law ought to be—i.e., the serial order in which claims ought to be paid. It has the effect of denying that there can be any significant value-antagonism between different interest groups.

The form of conservative natural law which identifies the law that is with the law that ought to be, necessarily tends to be a prop for the existing State structure. If law generally is divinely ordained or otherwise justified by an authoritative standard, then it is likely that laws creating the existing State are likewise justified. The State becomes divinely inspired or at least justified by reference to an authoritative standard.

Von Savigny

The historical school of which Friedrich Karl von Savigny (1779–1869) was the leader stood in stark opposition to theories based on natural law, but ultimately reached much the same conclusion.

Von Savigny's notion that law is a function of the *Volksgeist*, just as is language, nicely fits the myth on which English common law is based. Customs evolved out of the people; the judges merely enforce the customs. The guiding force is the common consciousness of the people, a unitary, mystical force that, like Parson's common set of value-orientations, is supposed to tie together the entire community. Like the schools of thought based on conceptions of the natural law, the historical school ends in a conception of the State as the will of the entire people.

Maine

Sir Henry Maine (1822–1888), an English jurist and legal historian in the Victorian tradition, sought a grand evolutionary scheme in legal history. He first postulated two types of legal system: "static" and "progressive." In the former case, the development of the law is frozen at some point in history; in the latter case there is constant movement and change. He then postulated his most famous proposition: "The movement of progressive societies has hitherto been a movement from Status to Contract."[2]

What did Maine mean by this proposition? In the laws of earlier societies, both in the customary laws of simple societies and generally in the laws of societies based on mechanical solidarity, right was related to status. In primitive law, one's membership in a corporate group—the family, tribe, or village—determined his rights to land, choice in marriage, and obligations in the support of others. In feudal law, too, one's status at birth determined everything. On the other hand, in the nineteenth-century world of which Maine was a part—the world of commodity exchange and separation of labor, the world of organic solidarity—social mobility was at least the ideal, if not the rule. Social mobility was legally based on contract. Contract provided a device by which individuals could create their own norms through agreement. Their rights were determined by the contract, not by status. Maine's statement that the movement of "progressive" societies had hitherto been from status to contract was an accurate description of what had occurred "hitherto."

While Maine was careful to limit his statement to what had "hitherto" occurred, his contemporaries were not. Professor Wolfgang Friedmann writes:

Maine's theory . . . commended itself to a society which had witnessed the American Civil War. That war resulted in the triumph of the industrial, commercial and progress-minded North over the agricultural, feudal, and status-minded South. This meant, in terms of legal development, the victory of "free contract," indispensable to an industrialized and capitalist society, which wanted—at the same time—mobility of labour and capital. It meant the eclipse of status conceptions which tie the worker to an estate by an unchangeable slave status.[3]

Maine, rather more clearly than most of his contemporaries, perceived what was in fact taking place. But he believed that societies could have a "movement" as a whole. Implicit in his proposition is the notion that there is a general sense of the community, i.e. a consensus on values, which is an idea easy enough succumbed to if one fails to perceive the crucial innovating roles of the courts. If judges are genuinely believed merely to be following preexisting laws and preexisting customs, then it is inevitable that one would believe that society, acting through its value-consensus, will first generate the custom, and then the courts will apply it in specific cases.

Bohannan

Paul Bohannan has perhaps gone farthest of contemporary writers in urging that law properly consists only of rules drawn from custom and reinstitutionalized as law. He writes:

...a fairly simple distinction can be drawn between law and custom. Customs are norms or rules...about the ways in which people must behave if social institutions are to perform their tasks and society is to endure. All institutions (including legal institutions) develop customs. Some customs, in some societies, are *re*institutionalized at another level: they are restated for the more precise purposes of legal institutions. When this happens, therefore, law may be regarded as a custom that has been restated in order to make it amenable to the activities of legal institutions . . .[4]

This is a thesis which assumes that for each society there is one, and only one, "legal culture." By "legal culture" Bohannan means "...that which is subscribed to (whether they know anything about it or not, and whether they act within it or 'agree' with it or not) by the people of a society. The secondary institutionalization forms a more or less consistent cultural unit."[5] In the typical municipal system of law, Bohannan says, there is only one "legal culture." In the colonial situation, on the other hand, where the metropolitan power imposes its municipal law in large part on the dependency but permits certain forms of customary law to survive, there are two (or more) legal cultures.

Bohannan conceives of law, therefore, much as did the common-law judges. Custom arises first; then the legal institutions adopt and, to a degree, transform the custom in the process of adoption. Since the legal institutions and the secondary institutionalization of law form "a more or less consistent cultural unit" the entire system rests upon a consensus within the society. Again, the implication of Bohannan's thesis is that law and the legal system, and the State of which it is a most important part, are value-neutral, an expression of the common values of all of us.

Fuller and His Followers

Lon Fuller has initiated an entire school of jurisprudence and sociological thought by his seminal book, *The Morality of Law*.[6] We shall briefly glance at the book's central thesis so far as it applies to this discussion, and then the position of its principal sociologist exponent, Jerome H. Skolnick.

Fuller is at pains to discover what he calls "the inner morality of law." He views law as "the (purposive) enterprise of subjecting human conduct to the governance of rules." He then proposes to discover the necessary and sufficient conditions of a government of rules. He identifies eight ways in which a purported system of law may fail to achieve legality:

The first and most obvious of these lies in a failure to achieve rules at all, so that every issue must be decided on an *ad hoc* basis. The other routes are: (2) a failure to publicize, or at least to make available to the affected party, the rules he is expected to observe; (3) the abuse of retroactive legislation, which not only guides action, but undercuts the integrity of rules prospective in effect, since it puts them under the threat of retrospective change; (4) a failure to make rules understandable; (5) the enactment of contradictory rules or (6) rules that require conduct beyond the powers of the affected party; (7) introducing such frequent changes in the rules that the subject cannot orient his action by them; and, finally, (8) a failure of congruence between the rules as announced and their actual administration.[7]

Jerome Skolnick builds upon this scheme to make some preliminary assertions about the relationship between law and social organization. "First, not all rules are lawful rules, even though these had been created by a 'legitimate' polity . . . A rule of law . . . not only suggests controls upon the arbitrary use of authority, but also implies the construction of institutions prizing and supporting man's ability to use reason to rise above subjective desire."[8] Skolnick explicitly uses the Fuller criteria to determine whether or not a rule of a "legitimate" polity is nevertheless not a "lawful" rule.[9]

Like the natural lawyers, Fuller and Skolnick invoke an authoritative standard to determine whether or not what purports to be "law" in fact is "law." It is a standard which assumes that man can, by the use of reason alone, determine what is necessary for a system of law to meet the demands of all of us. That system of law is based, in Fuller's scheme, on the assumption that the central human demand is for certainty and predictability, and thus assumes that these are the highest values to be obtained from a legal order. He insists that the internal morality of law is neutral toward its substantive aims,[10] although he denies that it is possible to conceive of a system at once faithful to the imperatives of legality and indifferent to justice and human welfare.[11]

Fuller's philosophy of law, like that of the natural lawyers, assumes a common morality. His eight criteria of legality presuppose that the central concern of the law ought to be its predictability. No doubt man wants predictability; but one would think that, for the impoverished, the prediction that the next meal would be forthcoming would be more significant than the formal prediction that the coercive machinery of the State would act in a certain way toward him. The *Declaration of New Delhi*, in its definition of the Rules of Law, said:

[T]he Rule of Law is a dynamic concept . . . which should be employed not only to safeguard and advance the civil and political rights of the individual in a free society, but also to establish social, economic, educational and cultural conditions under which his legitimate aspirations and dignity may be realized . . .[12]

To assume that the primary value to be realized by law, the basis of its "inner morality," is predictability of the action of the State organs is to assume a common set of values for all mankind.

Moreover, it probably is not the case that Fuller's eight criteria of legality are indifferent to the substantive content of the law. For example, when a government decides to expropriate the property of private entrepreneurs, Fuller's criteria would demand that its act be in accordance with the expectations of the owners of the property. No doubt that expectation might be met by paying the owners the fair value of the property expropriated. Yet there are many people in the world who believe that private ownership of productive property is itself immoral, and that the only morality is to "expropriate the expropriators." By insisting on the criterion of predictability as the central value, Fuller has made a choice between value-sets. That choice, in Fuller's argument, however, is in fact obscured by the appeal to an authoritative standard of legality.

Summary

All these several jurisprudential and sociological notions of the nature of law have two factors in common. On the one hand, they appeal to an authoritative standard by which to measure law. In some cases (von Savigny, Bohannan, Maine), they appeal to the notion that law must follow custom. State procedures must follow folkways. Others, like the traditional theories of natural law or its modern garb in the writings of Fuller and Skolnick, find the authoritative standard in intuitive apprehensions of verity. Such intuitive apprehensions of truth invariably reflect the subjective values of the author. By identifying those subjective values with eternal truth, whether drawn from immediate apprehension of the deity, from the nature of man living in society, or the inner morality of a government of rules, they all end by assuming that a single set of values is appropriate and necessary for the society.

By the same token, the necessary inference from all these models is that the legal order and the State are neutral, value-free frameworks within which conflict may be adjudicated. If conflict can be resolved by appeal to a single authoritative standard, the arbiter need not make a value-choice. His is a mere mechanical task, for by consultation with the standard described as authoritative he can determine the appropriate specific value to be embodied in his decision. He need not choose between conflicting rules; indeed, the authoritative standard forbids him to do so.

5.3 MODELS ASSERTING VALUE-CHOICE BY LAWMAKERS

The literature on the conflict models of law and society is far smaller than the literature which assumes that the State exercises power in the impartial interest of the entire population. The reason for this relative paucity appears easy enough to discover. Jurisprudential theory has always been more than a disinterested search for truth. It is a legitimizing weapon of the highest order. The class of jurisprudents as a whole has not been noticeably overloaded with revolutionaries.

Indeed, the very fact that the literature defining conflict models is so sparse should give pause. Jurisprudential models denying value-choice by the State have been proposed in every era, and they all try to justify the *existing* State.

Natural-law theories justified feudalism as divinely ordained and therefore in the interests of all of us; Hobbes justified the Stuart monarchy, von Savigny the German State, Austin the Victorian State. Few people, looking backward, would assert that any of those states were in fact value-neutral. Theories claiming that the existing twentieth-century liberal democratic state is uniquely value-neutral require careful analysis, lest they, too, be merely ideologies for legitimizing the existing law and State. What legitimacy, after all, could better protect the State than that grounded on the common belief that the State equitably represents the interests of all—white and black, rich and poor, draftee and civilian—by providing a neutral framework that protects us all from authoritarianism and anarchy alike?

The first step in the development of a conflict model of law and society was the separation of notions of morality from the notion of law. This was accomplished by the *positivists*.

The Positivists

The development of the modern state was accompanied by a variety of theories that rationalized this development. At first, as in the work of Hugo Grotius (1583–1645), the rationalization was cast in the language and metaphor of natural law. Grotius viewed natural law as based on the nature of man and his instinctual need to live in society.[13] Hobbes (1588–1679) stood this theory on its head, and thus became the first legal positivist. Where Grotius had emphasized that man had an instinctive drive to live in society, Hobbes believed that man in a state of nature lived in a state of war with his fellows, and that his life was "solitary, poor, nasty, brutish and short."[14] Hobbes lived in the period of the Civil War in England, and the tensions, distress, and dislocations of that period plainly affected his view of man. He believed, therefore, that for self-preservation man must escape the misery of anarchy. The solution lay in the securing of order through the imposition of a superior power, the sovereign.

The only effective device for securing order out of the anarchy of the state of nature, Hobbes believed, was by the imposition of a super-will who could command obedience from all. Thus he postulated the sovereign as the only source of law, who was himself above the law and who alone had the power to change it.[15]

Hobbes' aim was to justify absolutism, which he thought was necessary for the peace and good order of society. His theory was in perfect accord with the imposition of the aristocratic government in England in 1688 and served as an ideological justification for it. But his theory was more than a mere justification for sovereignty. To the extent that there *was* a strong State structure, which in fact seemed to lay down laws for the citizenry to follow, Hobbes' theory was empirically verifiable.

In fact, norms officially sanctioned do emanate from legislatures, from bureaucrats, from judges, kings, and emperors—in short, from the sovereign however constituted. Hobbes' theory directs our attention to the State structure as the source of law, and ultimately to the particular persons who play significant roles in that structure.

Hobbes' theory is two-sided. On the one hand, as we have already discussed, it emphasizes that law derives its authority from politically organized society. On the other hand, it is basically a natural-law theory which justifies absolutism on the ground that man's primitive nature is savage and warlike. The first portion of this theory has remained and been accepted as an accurate perception of the source of law; the latter portion has all but disappeared from modern legal theory.

Jeremy Bentham (1748–1832) seized upon the first element of Hobbes' theory and again turned it on its head. Bentham was the bourgeois man par excellence, the representative of the new commercial and industrial classes which had already taken over the economy of England and were pounding on the locked doors that barred their entry into the corridors of power. Bentham believed that the great engine of prosperity was individual initiative and freedom of action.[16] But he was faced by a society in which ancient inequities and remnants of feudalism strengthened the aristocrats' stranglehold on British government through rotten boroughs, institutionalized corruption, and a narrow electoral base. At the same time, the increasing militancy of the working classes also represented a threat to the freedom of action of the entrepreneurs and their ability to maximize profits.

Bentham devised a psychological theory to explain what the law ought to be, and seized upon Hobbes' notion of the State as Leviathan to buttress his assertion that the state should change the law. This psychological theory is known as Utilitarianism.

Nature has placed man under the empire of pleasure and pain. We owe to them all our ideas, we refer to them all our judgments, and all the determination of our life. He who pretends to withdraw himself from this subjection knows not what he says. His only object is to seek pleasure and to shun pain . . .[17]

In fact, Bentham's psychological theory is itself as much a kind of natural-law theory as Hobbes', although his notions of the nature of man differ sharply from that of the latter. Marx was later to remark of Bentham:

To know what is useful for a dog, one must study dog nature. This nature itself is not to be deduced from the principle of utility. Applying this to man, he who would criticize all human acts, movements, relations, etc., by the principle of utility must first deal with human nature in general, and then with human nature as modified in each historical epoch. Bentham makes short work of it. With the driest naïvete he takes the modern shopkeeper, especially the English shopkeeper, as the normal man. What is useful to this queer normal man and to his world is absolutely useful. This yard-measure, then, he applies to past, present and future.[18]

Bentham then elevates this psychological theory into a theory of legislation. The State and law ought to provide subsistence, to aim at abundance, to encourage equality, and to maintain security, for only in this framework can the individual exercise his individual, laissez-faire initiative and thus achieve the goals of his natural drive toward pleasure and away from pain.

Just as many do in much of the developing world today, Bentham perceived in the State the only instrument which might readily carry out the reforms he advocated. Since he advocated conscious law-making, he emphasized the necessity of legal change through legislation rather than through interstitial and frequently uncoordinated judicial law-making. The source of law, for Bentham, was therefore not divine inspiration, but the State acting through specific institutions: the legislature and the judges. A theory of sovereignty, which for Hobbes had been the ground for sanctifying the aristocratic government, was now invoked to sanction legislation, whose purpose was ultimately to destroy aristocratic control of government.

John Austin (1790–1859) seized upon the concept of sovereignty which Bentham had espoused, and again turned the earlier theory upon its head. He defined law as "a rule laid down for the guidance of an intelligent being by an intelligent being having power over him."[19] Law is thus conceived, not as a matter of morality, but as a matter of power. The rules of law are norms of human conduct, laid down by the sovereign and sanctioned by the sovereign. The central task of the lawyer is to determine what rules have in fact been laid down by the political superior, not to speculate on what the law ought to be. By thus divorcing Bentham's theory of sovereignty from his theory of justice, Austin converted what in Bentham's formulation had been a revolutionary theory into a theory which directed the attention of lawyers and judges to maintaining the status quo. The center of attention became the activity of judges, not of legislators. The thrust of Austin's work was therefore to remove the law from tampering by social reformers and radical revolutionaries alike.

Austin's theory remains to this day probably the dominant jurisprudential theory in the common-law world outside the United States. Even in this country, however, the notion that law finds its source in the State and constitutes the central expression of State power, remains the principal theme in the writings of modern jurisprudents. It is the principal theme because empirically it is undoubtedly verifiable that there are norms of conduct which are sanctioned by the exercise of State power, and that lawyers and judges are primarily concerned with this particular normative system.

Austin's crude model of law has been refined by the modern positivist school, of whom Hans Kelsen and H. L. A. Hart are the leading exponents. They have, however, retained its essential, positivistic characteristic. Law is conceived of as having the quality of "law," not because it fits some abstract standard relating to the values which it expresses, but because of its formal utterance by a body of a certain sort, i.e. an organ of the State.

The Realist Movement

Where the natural-law and the historical schools direct the attention of the law-makers to an authoritative standard, the Austinian model denies that a judge ever creates law—his only job is to discover the will of the law-maker. What law ought to be is a question to which Austinians do not significantly direct their attention. The result of Austinianism in the nineteenth century was that judicial decision-making in cases involving issues of law tended to be a highly conceptual process of determining the exegesis and harmonization of the texts of precedent cases and statutes, and in this practice the policy-making function of the court was explicitly denied. In this way, the whole problem of choice was, as it were, swept under the bed.

Oliver Wendell Holmes, then a practicing lawyer in Boston, shattered the elegant world of Austinianism in the first of a series of lectures that he gave at Harvard in 1881, published as *The Common Law*. Cardozo later said that he had packed a whole philosophy of legal method into a fragment of a paragraph, the opening sentences of *The Common Law*:

The life of the law has not been logic; it has been experience. The felt necessities of the time, the prevalent moral and political theories, institutions of public policy, avowed or unconscious, even the prejudices which judges share with their fellowmen have had a good deal more to do than the syllogism in determining the rules by which men should be governed.[20]

To assert that law has been influenced by the felt necessities of the time is to assert the possibility of choice. To assert the possibility of choice in the rule of law requires that the criteria for choice can be determined. While denying choice, the Austinians had in fact made choices. Because they denied that they were making choices, in fact the only value which their choices consciously enhanced were most frequently elegance and consistency in law. Holmes' philosophy would have the law-maker look not to the antecedents of the rule, or its interconnections with the rest of the normative system, but to its consequences in the social order. Holmes again charted the course:

I think that judges themselves have failed adequately to recognize their duty of weighing considerations of social advantage. The duty is inevitable, and the result of the often proclaimed judicial aversion to deal with such considerations is simply to leave the very ground and foundation of judgments inarticulate, and often unconscious . . .[21]

The study of the problem of choice in law in terms of its social consequences must start with a study of how past or existing rules have in fact affected the way people act. Karl Llewellyn wrote:

Ferment is abroad in the law. The sphere of interest widens; men become interested again in the life that swirls around things legal. Before rules, were facts; in the beginning was not a Word, but a Doing. Behind decisions stand judges; judges are men; as men they have human backgrounds. Beyond rules, again, lie effects: beyond decisions stand people whom rules and decisions directly or indirectly touch... *Beyond rules lie effects*—but do they? Are some rules mere paper? And if effects, what effects? Hearsay, unbuttressed guess, assumption or assertion unchecked by test—can such be trusted in this matter of what law is *doing*?[22]

Although, so far as one can see, the legal realists were largely unsullied by intellectual contact with modern sociology, and their reasoning followed a rather different route from that of the sociologists, they also came to consider the difference between norm and action, between role-expectation and role-performance, or, as Llewellyn repeatedly called it, the "law in the books" and the "law in action."

The debt to the positivists, however, was explicit. Llewellyn, in the same article quoted above, insisted on "the *temporary* divorce of Is and Ought for purposes of study."[23] One cannot study squarely and honestly the role-expectation and the role-performance if at the stage of the investigation one permits one's spectacles to be fogged by one's notion of what ought to be the case. Only after the present position has been carefully assessed can one move forward to ask what ought to be the case. The recognition of a potential difference between the law in the books and the law in action necessarily implies a recognition that the rule might be changed in order to bring about the sort of activity that is desired. To speak of the possibility of changing the rule is to open wide the range of choice. It is to regard the function of law as primarily an instrument of social control.

Pound, perceiving this function of law, spoke of law as a form of social engineering. Law, he said, was a tool to meet the demands of men in society. He emphasized the importance of empirical research, just as did Llewellyn and the Realists (among whose ranks Pound himself denied that he had a place, although it is sometimes difficult to see why he did so). He urged that the values to be embodied in the rules of law be adjusted to change with the changing tides of public sentiment.

The Concept of Conflict

The positivists divorce "law as it is" from an authoritative standard which purports to prescribe what the law ought to be. The Realists divorce the "law as it is" in the books from the role-performance of the role-occupants toward whom the norm is directed. To the extent that a role-occupant fails to achieve the goal set for that position or to abide by the norm embodied in the rule of law, two questions arise: What sort of activity do we want of the role-occupant? What sort of rule will bring about that activity?

The question "What sort of activity do we want of the role-occupant?"

is deceptive. In practice, the question is not the activity that *we* want of the role-occupant, but rather, the activity that the policy-makers in the State want of him. Their decision will be the decision of all of us only (a) insofar as there is in fact a common set of values for all of us, and (b) insofar as the policy-makers do not reject this value-consensus for personal and idiosyncratic reasons.

As we have seen, Pound apparently believed that there was only a single set of values—he called them "jural postulates"—in society. He believed that the role of the policy-maker demanded that he canvas the claims and demands made upon the legal order by the population; that he distill from these the overriding value-sets that subsumed "practically all" the demands; and then adjudicate between conflicting demands in terms of the jural postulates then derived. The adjudication between conflicting demands was mainly a matter of assigning serial numbers to them to determine the order of pay-out. The jural postulates, it was assumed, would tell the policy-maker what the serial order ought to be.

But what if the claims and demands made upon the legal system are not so readily subsumed within a single set of jural postulates? Suppose the values of the society are not unitary, but plural? Whose values are then to be used to determine the serial order in which claims and demands are to be met?

Pound's student, Julius Stone, perceived that the problem was a real one at least in the underdeveloped world, where the conflict between the jural postulates of the various orders within post-Colonial plural societies was too apparent to fob off. He suggested that in such cases, Pound's jurisprudential system might not be appropriate.

Yet there are those who argue that in every society, and not only in those of the underdeveloped world, there are value-conflicts as deep and far-reaching as those of Africa and India, although perhaps, they are better hidden under a veneer of common dress, language, and fashion. If there is no value-consensus, how are the law-makers to determine the jural postulates which ought to control their rule-making?

Values and the State

Two contradictory answers are given in contemporary political theory, as we have seen. One view is that the political framework is itself value-neutral, even if the society is not. The other is that the State itself is a weapon of the dominant classes or interest groups in the society.

It is a popular viewpoint of present-day political theory in the United States, that while society no doubt is made up of interest groups with divergent goals and values, it is in everybody's interest to maintain a political framework which permits these conflicts to be resolved through peaceful bargaining, always reserving the right of the minority group to change the law through peaceful persuasion and dissent. In this view, the State is a vast neutral framework within which struggle and debate and negotiation can take place; Robert A. Dahl and Charles E. Lindblom call these activities the processes of polyarchy.[24] It is held that, while no doubt specific substantive laws reflect the interests of specific groups, the constitutional framework is value-free and represents the interests of the polity.

The problem with this viewpoint is that the State itself simply *cannot* be value-free. In the first place, the activities of the government are not confined merely to the application of fixed rules to facts, but in large part consist in the exercise of discretion in creating (or not creating) rules (*institutions*). Such rules are normative; they describe how people ought to act. Every normative statement, as we have seen, is value-laden.

Secondly, the processes by which bargaining is done to a substantial degree control the result. Congress, ideally, may be a place where political bargaining and trading can take place. The success of the various parties to that bargaining, however, depends in very large part on the rules of the game within Congress. If the rules of seniority, for example, place conservative Southern legislators in seats of power, the legislative framework cannot be "neutral." The Constitution itself cannot be value-free. If it prescribes, as it does, a government based on checks and balances, then that very prescription becomes a weapon in the hands of those who would oppose extensive governmental intervention in the economy.

Thirdly, the very nature of the governmental framework requires that there be certain costs involved in contesting issues of law. No matter how neutral the court may be, it costs money and time to invoke its processes. No matter how fair the election procedures are, it is expensive to be a candidate. Those better able to afford the invocation of governmental processes will inevitably be advantaged by that fact. Since it is in their interest to maintain that advantage, the relative costliness of governmental processes is itself a value-loaded issue.

Finally, every system of government is *de facto* or *de jure* inclusive of some people and exclusive of others as to political participation. Provisions determining the qualifications for election necessarily favor some and disadvantage others. Even citizenship provisions may be more or less restrictive. In the South in the United States, and in our great cities, the system has for many generations *de facto* excluded the blacks from any effective participation in the political process—a situation which is today only slowly beginning to change, and this change primarily as the result of pressure from outside the local system. Whatever may be the relative neutrality of the State structure with respect to those included within the system, the structure is not neutral with respect to those excluded from the system.

If the society does not rest on a value-consensus but is itself rent by value-conflicts between the various special interest groups of the community, and if the State is not a value-free framework to moderate and contain the struggle, then what model of the State and law is left? It is a model which conceives of society as constantly in strife, in which the State and its vast machinery for creating myth and symbol, for inspiring support even from those whose interests are most injured by its activity, and, in the final analysis, its monopoly of the means of violence and coercion, is itself at once the principal weapon and the main prize of the struggle.

In this view, the State can rule by coercion, "power," alone if it has the resources to do so. Usually it does not. It therefore must rule with at least the acquiescence, if not the active support, of the governed. That acquiescence can be elicited only if the governed believe the State to be acting in pursuit of their value-sets. In Weber's language, the State must be thought legitimate by those who are so ruled.

The processes of the State, its costs, its system of inclusions and exclusions, its success in legitimizing the rulers—all these are factors which are frequently crucial in determining which particular interest group will control the State itself. The State is not, therefore, in this view, value-neutral; it is itself a weapon in the hands of those who control it.

This view was given powerful stimulus by the work of Karl Marx. In the Marxist view (as expounded mainly by Engels and Lenin), the State consists of the institutions of coercion: the police, the army, prison officials. These are the principal weapons in the hands of the ruling classes. Law, which rests finally upon the State's self-perpetuating monopoly of violence or instruments of coercion, therefore represents the will of the ruling classes; in more modern terms, we would say that it embodies the values of the ruling class. This is a view which conceives of society in terms of sharp conflict between different classes, each with its own set of values, and the State as a weapon in the hands of the class in control of it.

5.4 SUMMARY

Two models of the State, the law, and their relationship to the problems of values have been presented. These models may be contrasted in their respective views either of the existence of value-consensus in society, or of the neutrality of the State structure, or both. If society rests on a value-consensus either because it accepts an authoritative standard to determine the law or because its customs are deemed to be common to all, then the State structure will be equally value-neutral in nature. If, however, society is racked by value-antagonisms, then, it is claimed, the State might still be value-neutral in the sense that it is a framtwork within which the antagonisms of classes and interests can be negotiated without destroying the society completely. Finally, there are those who assert that society is structured on conflict, and that the State is itself a weapon in the hands of the dominant class.

Of these two models, there can be no doubt that the value-neutral version is the one embodied in the myths that give legitimacy to the State. Historically, the development of dispute-settlement processes from compromise to "winner takes all," from dispute-settlement to norm-enforcement and, as part of norm-enforcement, norm-creation, masked the fact that courts had become, not merely impartial judges of disputes in accordance with fixed rules, but the source of new norms. At the same time, the notion of the State as a value-neutral framework representing all of us is obviously the most powerful legitimizing myth that could be imagined. If in fact the State is a coercive weapon in the hands of the minority of the rich and powerful, and if it were so perceived by the masses of the population, then the costs of maintaining the authority of the State would become enormous, if indeed this authority could be successfully maintained. The realists, by directing our attention to behavior as well as to the normative structure, pointed the way to understanding. We turn, therefore, to a brief examination of how laws are in fact enacted by legislatures, and then to a more detailed examination of appellate court law-making.

NOTES

1. Opinion of West, Counsel of the Board of Trade (later Lord Chancellor of Ireland, 1720); quoted in Forsyth, *Cases and Opinions on Constitutional Law and Various Points of English Jurisprudence*, Stevens and Haynes, London, 1869. Italics are ours.

2. Sir Henry Maine, *Ancient Law*, J. Murray, London, 1905, p. 174.

3. Wolfgang Friedmann, *Legal Theory*, Stevens, London, 1967, p. 217.

4. Paul Bohannan, "The differing realms of law." Reprinted by permission of the American Anthropological Association from *American Anthropologist*, Vol. 67, No. 6, 1965, pp. 33–42.

5. *Ibid.*, p. 51.

6. Lon Fuller, *The Morality of Law*, Yale University Press, New Haven, 1964.

7. *Ibid.*, p. 39. Reprinted by permission.

8. Jerome Skolnick, "The sociology of law in America: overview and trends," in *Law and Society*, Supplement to Summer 1965 issue of *Social Problems*, 1965, pp. 5, 37.

9. Jerome Skolnick, "Social research on legality: a reply to Auerbach," *Law and Society Rev.*, **1**, 1966, pp. 105, 108.

10. Lon Fuller, *op. cit.*, p. 153.

11. *Ibid.*, p. 154.

12. International Commission of Jurists, *The Rule of Law in a Free Society: A Report on the International Congress of Jurists*, 1959, p. 3.

13. Hugo Crotius, *De Iure Belli ac Pacis*, Book 1, Chapter i.10.1.

14. Thomas Hobbes, *Leviathan*, Blackwell, Oxford, 1946.

15. *Ibid.*, Chapter 17.

16. See Friedmann, *op. cit.*, p. 270.

17. J. Bentham, *The Works of Jeremy Bentham*, Vol 1, Bowring (ed.), Simpkin, Marshall, London, 1843, pp. 396, 402.

18. Karl Marx, *Das Kapital*, Kerr (ed.) C. H. Kerr, Chicago, p. 688.

19. John Austin, *Lectures on Jurisprudence*, J. Murray, London, 1890.

20. O. W. Holmes, *The Common Law*, Little, Brown, Boston, 1881, p. 1.

21. O. W. Holmes, "The path of the law," *Harvard Law Rev.*, **10**, 1897, p. 457.

22. Karl Llewellyn, "Some realism about realism—responding to Dean Pound," *Harvard Law Rev.*, 1931, p. 1222. Reprinted by permission.

23. *Ibid.*, p. 1236.

24. Robert A. Dahl and Charles E. Lindblom, *Politics, Economics, and Welfare: Planning and Politico-economic Systems Resolved into Basic Social Processes*, Harper, New York, 1953.

6

The institutions of law-making:
the legislature

How are we to judge between these models of law and society described in Chapter 5? We recall that Dahrendorf asserted that one could not demonstrate empirically that the conflict rather than the structural-functionalist model of society accurately represented society. The two models that we traced out in the preceding chapter are, of course, precisely the structural-functionalist and conflict models of society as applied to a specific system, the legal order. Is it significant to determine which model is "correct"? Is it *possible* to determine which model is correct?

6.1 CAN THE LEGAL ORDER BE VALUE-NEUTRAL?

The substantive content of the legal system inevitably reflects some value-systems to the exclusion of others. What is one man's pleasure is another's vice. If the man who sees the act as a vice is in a position to define what is right and wrong and the other man is defenseless to keep that definition from being imposed on him, then in a complex society, partaking of that pleasure may have to be weighed against the possibility of state imposed sanctions.

Even the structural-functionalists, therefore, tend to limit the scope of the claimed value-consensus, to the maintenance of the society as a going concern instead of letting it fall apart into anarchy and disorder and similar seemingly "basic" or "fundamental" propositions. Auerbach, Garrison, Hurst, and Mermin attempted a listing of minimal elements of "the public interest."

a) It is in the "public interest" that our nation be free from outside dictation in determining its destiny; that it have the power of self-determination . . .

b) It is in the public interest to preserve the legitimated institutions through which conflicts in our society are adjusted and peaceful change effected, no matter how distasteful particular decisions reached by these institutions may be to particular groups in our society. In other words, the preservation of democracy—government with the freely given consent of the governed—is in the public interest.

c) It is in the public interest that no group in our society should become so powerful that it can submerge the claims of all other groups.

d) It is in the public interest that all claims made by individuals and groups in our society should at least be heard and considered by the law-making authorities. This proposition, which calls for recognition of the freedom to speak and to associate with others in pursuit of group interests, is a fundamental assumption of the democratic order.

e) It is in the public interest that every individual enjoy a minimum decent life and that the degree of inequality in the opportunities open to individuals be lessened.[1]

A variety of arguments suggest that this statement of a national value-consensus is invalid. Even assuming that there was a value-consensus on these propositions, the range of questions that come before law-making agencies and the State is largely outside their scope. If the structural-functional perception of the consensus is as narrow as this, it cannot be a very useful or interesting guide to the study of law-making, for very few questions coming before law-makers actually touch on any of these generalized objectives. Rather, they tend to be much narrower: How much should the minimum exemption from income tax be? Should the State automatically suspend a driver's license for thirty days on every conviction for speeding? Should automobile manufacturers be required to provide safety belts for all automobiles? Should students engaged in disruption in State universities automatically be expelled upon conviction? The usual questions coming before law-making authorities only rarely touch on the large questions suggested by any list of supposed "public interests."

Second, even if one were to accept these statements of "the public interest," the actual questions coming before law-makers that even touch on these questions are never very simple. Whether or not the United States ought to simply turn itself over to a foreign power, for example, is a question that has never come and doubtless never will come before any legislature. Rather, the question is always partial and problematical: Is joining the United Nations, and the surrender of sovereignty *pro tanto*, for example, too serious an invasion of the "public interest" in independence? If "freedom to speak" is "a fundamental assumption of the democratic order," then it can be argued that no private individual or corporation ought to control newspapers, television, or other institutions of the mass media, which instead should be equally available to all without regard to their financial resources. That would require government control of the mass media, which might well be regarded as the negation of free speech. While no doubt it is in the public interest that every individual should enjoy the minimum essentials of a decent life, exactly how much is a "minimum"? Is it in the public interest to reduce the size of "big business" in order to keep that group from attaining too much power, even if it can be shown that large economic units are more efficient than smaller ones? And if one decides to reduce the size of "big business," what is to be the standard of acceptable maximum size?

Thirdly, is it true that even this list of "the minimal elements of the public interest" would be unanimously accepted? It is notable for omitting any reference to minimum protection for property. Many members of the propertied classes, at least in the American society, would insist that such a guarantee is an essential component of "the public interest." The list omits any statement that equality of treatment before the law regardless of race or color is a necessary ingredient of "the public interest"; yet white racists would hardly complain of this omission.

Fourthly, what a majority conceives of as "the public interest" at any period in history is not a constant. Not so long ago a majority of the law-makers believed that it was in the public interest to prevent any citizen from buying alcoholic beverages. Not very long before that, in the long view of history, no doubt a majority believed that it was in the public interest to burn wretched old women at the stake as witches. How can one be sure that today's perception of "the public interest" is not merely an evanescent reflection of the value-sets of the majority?

Finally, consider the second of the propositions put forward, the broadest and most overarching of all: "It is in the public interest to preserve the legitimated institutions through which conflicts in society are adjusted and peaceful change effected . . ." So long as real poverty exists, it seems clear that the fifth assertion of "the public interest," i.e. "that every individual enjoy a minimum decent life," is sharply in conflict with the second. Which of these interests is to be overriding? The repeated phenomenon of urban rioting in the ghettos of America suggests that there is no value-consensus on the relative weight to be given to any of these propositions which purport to define "the public interest."

The reason why this or any other set of claimed "public interest," a commonly held *summum bonum*, can never adequately describe the actual state of affairs can be explained philosophically as well as empirically. John Dewey has argued that a distinction must be made between *that which is prized* and the *process of valuation*. No doubt we all have general, culturally acquired objectives, i.e. things which are prized. In any specific instance, however, how we define these generalized goals depends on a complex process of considering objective constraints, relative costs and benefits, and the valuation of alternative means. In this process of valuation, our generalized objectives are necessarily modified and changed as they become concrete and definite—i.e. in Dewey's language, as they become ends-in-view. Whatever the relative cultural agreement on general, broadly phrased prizings, there is never any complete agreement on any specific end in view.[2]

The particular norms prescribed by law always are specific. They always command the role-occupant to act in specific ways. It is always a statement, not of generalized prizings, but of a specific end-in-view. It is the result of a process of valuation. On that valuation there is never complete agreement, for there is no complete agreement on the relative weightings to be given the various prizings held in different strata of the society, nor on the relative valuation to be given to different means.

In short, every assertion that a specific law should have a certain content must necessarily reflect the process of valuation of its proponents, and by the same token, it will be opposed to the processes of valuation of its opponents. The nature of law as a normative system, commanding what ought to be done, necessitates that it will favor one group as against another. The proof, whatever academic model-builders may say, lies in the fact that there is some opposition to *every* proposed new rule; whether or not the law-makers themselves are unanimous. Even a declaration of war in the face of armed attack is never supported by the *entire* population.

That the law necessarily advances the values of some groups in society and opposes others reflects the fact that in any complex, modern society there is no value-consensus that is relevant to the law. That is so because of the very nature of the different "webs of life" that exist. It is a function of society itself.

6.2 VALUES AND THE WEB OF LIFE

Regardless of how homogeneous a society may at first glance appear, behind the cloud of consensus and unanimity there always lurks the fact of widespread disagreement on what constitutes the "right and proper" thing to do. This is inevitably the case because *what people do* is a major determinant of *what they see as right*. In general, man has the unique and unfailing capacity to endow whatever he does with the loftiest ideological underpinnings. What people do, their behavior, in turn are a direct reflection of what the ecologists call man's "web of life"— that is, his experiences with life as he moves from Monday to Tuesday, from New Year's to Easter, from bureaucracy to family. In stratified, technologically developed societies, there are wide differences in the experiences of groups of people. The "working man's" world has little in common with the world of the farmer, and even less in common with the world of the upper-class aristocrat. In America, one finds the differences in life experiences in striking contrast and inevitably conflicting. Compare, to cite on an extreme case, the web of life surrounding the Puerto Rican immigrant in an urban setting with the experiences of the American Navajo Indian on a reservation in New Mexico,[3] or compare the experiences of the

Vanderbilts, the Rockefellers, or the Fords with those of the Negro share-cropper in the Mississippi Delta. The point is nicely illustrated by contrasting the web of life implicitly and explicitly brought out in the following passage describing life in the Cumberland Plateau in the 1960's with the life experiences of most urbanized Americans:

In community after community one can visit a dozen houses in a row without finding a single man who is employed. Most are retired miners and their wives who live on social security and union pension checks. Hundreds of other houses are occupied by aged widows, some of whom have taken in a grandchild or other youngster for "company" in their old age.

One row of camp houses has twenty-one residences. Seven are occupied by widows, the youngest of whom is fifty-two years of age and four of whom are more than seventy. Five are the homes of aged couples. Four shelter unemployed miners in their early fifties—men "too old to get a job and too young to retire." Three families draw state aid because the men are disabled from mining accidents. Only two houses are supported by men who still have jobs in a nearby mine.

One may walk the streets of camps and wander along winding creek roads for days and rarely find a young man or woman. For years the young and the employable have turned their backs on the plateau. Each spring when warm weather begins to enliven the land the more energetic and ambitious of the young men and women develop a yen for a more hopeful region. One by one they slip away. A year after high school diplomas are distributed, it is hard to find more than 4 or 5% of the graduates in their home counties. In the autumn of 1960 one high-school principal assured me that not a single graduate of his school in 1958, 1959, or 1960 was living in the county. A couple of dozen are in military or naval service, but 70% had found jobs (or at least lodgment) in Ohio, Indiana and Michigan. The others were scattered over New York, Illinois and California.[4]

Lest one be deluded by the foregoing into thinking that urban America is a homogeneous package which contrasts only with rural America, note the following description of life in a black ghetto as presented by an anthropologist and contrast this picture with life in a white suburb of urban north.

. . . since, at the moment, [the men] are neither working nor sleeping, and since they hate the depressing room or apartment they live in, or because there is nothing to do there, or because they want to get away from their wives or anyone else living there, they are out on the street, indistinguishable from those who do not have jobs or do not want them. Some, like Boley, a member of a trash-collection crew in a suburban housing development, work Saturdays and are off on this weekday. Some, like Sweets, work nights cleaning up middle-class trash, dirt, dishes and garbage, and mopping the floors of the office buildings, hotels, restaurants, toilets and other public places dirtied during the day. Some men work for retail businesses such as liquor stores which do not begin the day until ten o'clock. Some laborers, like Tally, have already come back from the job because the ground was too wet for pick and shovel or because the weather was too cold for pouring concrete. Other employed men stayed off the job today for personal reasons: Clarence to go to a funeral at eleven this morning and Sea Cat to answer a subpoena as a witness in a criminal proceeding.

Also on the street, unwitting contributors to the impression taken away by the truck driver, are the halt and the lame. The man on the cast-iron steps strokes one gnarled arthritic hand with the other and says he doesn't know whether or not he'll live long enough to be eligible for Social Security. He pauses, then adds matter-of-factly, "Most times, I don't care whether I do or don't." Stoopy's left leg was polio-withered in child-hood. Raymond, who looks as if he could tear out a fire hydrant, coughs up blood if he bends or moves suddenly. The quiet man who hangs out in front of the Saratoga apart-ments has a steel hook strapped onto his left elbow. And had the man in the truck been able to look into the wineclouded eyes of the man in the green cap, he would have realized that the man did not even understand he was being offered a day's work.

Others, having had jobs and been laid off, are drawing unemployment compensation (up to $44 per week) and have nothing to gain by accepting work which pays little more than this and frequently less.

Still others, like Bumdoodle the numbers man, are working hard at illegal ways of making money, hustlers who are on the street to turn a dollar anyway they can; buying and selling sex, liquor, narcotics, stolen goods, or anything else that turns up.

Only a handful remains unaccounted for. There is Tonk, who cannot bring himself to take a job away from the corner, because, according to the other men, he suspects his wife will be unfaithful if given the opportunity. There is Stanton, who has not reported to work for four days now, not since Bernice disappeared. He bought a brand new knife against her return. She had done this twice before, he said, but not for so long and not without warning, and he had forgiven her. But this time, "I ain't got it in me to forgive her again." His rage and shame are there for all to see as he paces the Carryout and the corner, day and night, hoping to catch a glimpse of her.

And finally, there are those like Arthur, able-bodied men who have no visible means of support, legal or illegal, who neither have jobs nor want them. The truck driver, among others, believes the Arthurs to be representative of all the men he sees idling on the street during his own working hours. They are not, but they cannot be dismissed simply because they are a small minority. It is not enough to explain them away as being lazy or irresponsible or both because an able-bodied man with responsibilities who refuses work is, by the truck driver's definition, lazy and irresponsible. Such an answer begs the question. It is descriptive of the facts; it does not explain them.

Moreover, despite their small numbers, the don't-work-and-don't-want-to-work minority is especially significant because they represent the strongest and clearest ex-pression of those values and attitudes associated with making a living which, to varying degrees, are found throughout the streetcorner world. These men differ from the others in degree rather than in kind, the principal difference being that they are carrying out the implications of their values and experiences to their logical, inevitable conclusions. In this sense, the others have yet to come to terms with themselves and the world they live in.

Putting aside, for the moment, what the men say and feel, and looking at what they actually do and the choices they make, getting a job, keeping a job, and doing well at it is clearly of low priority. Arthur will not take a job at all. Leroy is supposed to be on his job at 4:00 p.m. but it is already 4:10 and he still cannot bring himself to leave the free games he has accumulated on the pinball machine in the Carry-out. Tonk started a construction job on Wednesday, worked Thursday and Friday, then didn't go back again. On the same kind of job, Sea Cat quit in the second week. Sweets had been working three months as a busboy in a restaurant, then quit without notice, nor sure himself why he did so. A real estate agent, saying he was more interested in getting the job done than in the cost, asked Richard to give him an estimate on repairing and painting the inside of a house, but Richard, after looking over the job, somehow never got around to submitting an estimate. During one period, Tonk would not leave the corner to take a job because his wife might prove unfaithful; Stanton would not take a job because his woman had been unfaithful.

Thus, the man—job relationship is a tenuous one. At any given moment, a job may occupy a relatively low position on the streetcorner scale of real values. Getting a job may be subordinated to relations with women or to other non-job considerations; the commitment to a job one already has is frequently shallow and tentative.

The reasons are many. Some are objective and reside principally in the job; some are subjective and reside principally in the man. The line between them, however, is not a clear one. Behind the man's refusal to take a job or his decision to quit one is not a simple impulse or value choice but a complex combination of assessments of objective reality on the one hand, and values, attitudes and beliefs drawn from different levels of his experience on the other.

Objective economic considerations are frequently a controlling factor in a man's refusal to take a job. How much the job pays is a crucial question but seldom asked. He knows how much it pays. Working as a stock clerk, a delivery boy, or even behind the counter of liquor stores, drug stores and other retail businesses pays one dollar an hour. So, too, do most busboy, car-wash, janitorial and other jobs available to him. Some jobs, such as dishwasher, may dip as low as eighty cents an hour and others, such as elevator operator or work in a junk yard, may offer $1.15 or $1.25. Take-home pay for jobs such as these ranges from $25 to $50 a week, but a take-home pay of over $45 for a five-day week is the exception rather than the rule.

One of the principal advantages of these kinds of jobs is that they offer fairly regular work. Most of them involve essential services and are therefore somewhat less responsive to business conditions than are some higher paying, less menial jobs. Most of them are also inside jobs not dependent on the weather, as are construction jobs and other higher-paying outside work.[5]

Each of these people and literally hundreds of other groups in complex societies cope with different problems, find different pleasures, and discover different ways of solving their problems and picking the fruits of joy from their environment. Not surprisingly, each group also develops its own unique and characteristic normative system. In a word, complex societies are pluralistic societies.

That society does not represent a value-consensus on every level of course by no means answers the question which we posed concerning the value-neutrality of the State. Both the conception of the State as a value-neutral framework for conflict and the view that it is itself a weapon in social conflict can (and, in the more sophisticated versions do) presuppose that society is pluralistic.

In accordance with our general model, we can try to analyze the problem

INSTITUTIONS OF LAW-MAKING: THE LEGISLATURE

posed by examining the role of the law-maker. That model directs us, first, to examine the norms and goals describing society's role-expectations for the role-occupant. Second, it directs us to examine his actual behavior, in the light of the other societal and personal forces creating the "field" within which he moves, and of the activities of the various sanctioning agencies.

6.3 LEGISLATION AND INTEREST GROUPS

Both the model of a value-free law-making structure and that of a law-making structure which responds to pressures of interest groups have been urged. Edmund Burke wrote of the Parliamentary ideal:

Parliament is not a congress of ambassadors from different and hostile interests; whose interests each must maintain, as an agent and advocate, against other agents and advocates; but parliament is a deliberative assembly of one nation, with one interest, that of the whole, where, not local purposes, nor local prejudices, ought to guide, but the general good, resulting from the general reason of the whole.[6]

Arthur F. Bentley, on the other hand, describes legislative behavior as follows:

Logrolling is . . . the most characteristic legislative process. When one condemns it "in principle," it is only by contrasting it with some assumed pure public spirit which is supposed to guide legislators, or which ought to guide them, and which enables them to pass judgment in Jovian calm on that which is best "for the whole people." Since there is nothing which is best literally for the whole people, group arrays being what they are, the test is useless, even if one could actually find legislative judgments which are not reducible to interest-group activities. And when we have reduced the legislative process to the play of group interests, then logrolling, or give and take, appears as the very nature of the process. It is compromise, not in the abstract moral form, which philosophers can sagely discuss, but in the practical form with which every legislator who gets results through government is acquainted. It is trading. It is the adjustment of interests. . . There never was a time in the history of the American Congress when legislation was conducted in any other way.[7]

Whatever may have been Burke's normative ideal, it seems plain enough that legislation has invariably been the result of interest-group activity. That is the result of the structure of complex society itself. Divergent interest-groups will seek to obtain laws that reflect their interests as opposed to the interests of other groups. Moreover, it is a corollary of the fact that every governmental system is itself the resultant of power relationships, that the system of representation in the corridors of power will operate to the benefit of some interest groups and to the disadvantage of others. Most states in the United States had electoral systems heavily biased in favor of rural populations until the Supreme Court, in *Baker v. Carr*,[8] decided that the Constitution commanded that the votes of all citizens must be weighted as equally as possible. The decision necessarily had the consequence of advantaging urban populations as against the rural. The effect on legislative apportionment and the consequent work product of State legislatures is incalculable.

It is a mistake to assume from this perspective, however, that laws always reflect the imposition of one value system or another. While this is usually the case, it is not always so. Often an act may be defined as "against the law," not because the act itself is viewed as particularly heinous, but rather because outlawing certain kinds of behaviour serves other purposes. Anglo-American vagrancy laws provide an excellent illustration of how this happens.[9]

Once the idea and the structure of what has come down as the Anglo-American criminal law was established in England between the eleventh and thirteenth centuries,[10] the particular activities which were included as crimes varied from time to time. In the Middle Ages in England, it was commonplace for beggars to wander from town to town stopping for food and shelter at alms houses run by the church. Although these activities did not confer very high status on the persons engaged in them, during the twelfth and thirteenth centuries it was not considered a matter of any concern to the State. However, the growing number of beggars and "wanderers" was of concern to the church, and as a consequence, the first vagrancy statute was passed specifically for the purpose of relieving the financial burden on the church caused by the maintenance of alms houses which had suddenly increased dramatically as a result of the hardships caused by the plague epidemic, the Black Death, in 1348. The wording of the first vagrancy statute in 1349 makes this reason for passing the law abundantly clear:

Because that abbies and houses of religion have been overcharged and sore grieved, by the resort of great men and other, so that their goods have not been sufficient for themselves, whereby they have been greatly hindered and impoverished, that they cannot maintain themselves, nor such charity as they have been accustomed to do; it is provided, that none shall come to eat or lodge in any house of religion, or any other's foundation than of his own, at the costs of the house, unless he be required by the governor of the house before his coming hither.[11]

There have of course been many changes in the focus of vagrancy statutes since the first one.[12] The *specific* reasons for changing their focus have varied. In every case, however, the *acts* which came to be defined as criminal behavior were so defined because their continuation was a threat to the economic interests of groups in positions of power. Initially it was the economic interests of the church which brought about the legislation; later (in the fifteenth and sixteenth centuries) it was the economic interest of the landowners which brought about a broadening and strengthening of the vagrancy statutes in an effort to keep serfs from leaving the farms for better employment in the cities.[13]

Not all laws so clearly reflect the attempt by groups in power to protect their economic interests. But in one way or another, the laws which are passed, implemented, and incorporated into the legal system reflect the interests of those groups capable of having their views incorporated into the official (that is legal) views of the society.

Societies vary, of course, with respect to the specific groups who possess the ability to influence legislation and the implementation of laws. Societies vary also with regard to the total number of such groups. In some societies, a feudal society for example, the governmental structures are such that a relatively small number of people occupy positions with the capacity to affect the laws. These people for the most part represent one group: the party in power. Some states such as Switzerland among the western nations have governmental structures which provide for a large number of conflicting and divergent interest groups to affect the content of the legal structure.

In all societies, regardless of how the interest groups vary in number, those which are most likely to be effective are the ones that control the economic or political institutions of the society. The most influential groups will of course be those which control both. As a consequence, legislation typically favors the wealthier, the more politically active groups in the society. Not surprisingly, in America this means that the managers and owners of the large corporations and mammoth business complexes will enjoy more success in getting laws passed which benefit them than will the "average citizen" or, in a more extreme contrast, the unemployed resident of a slum.

It seems to be the case that two things characterize laws passed which superficially seem inimical to the best interests of the powerful. First, some laws are passed primarily as a token gesture to assuage some group that has the capacity to disrupt the ongoing processes of society. Secondly, laws which are passed under these conditions are rarely if ever enforced with the same vigor as characterizes the enforcement of those laws which are in the best interests of persons in positions of power.[14]

The anti-trust laws illustrate nicely how laws may energe which appear to conflict with the interests of those in power without actually doing so. The expressed purpose of the Sherman Antitrust Act was to restrict the freedom of large corporations in manipulating the economic life of the country. One of the more controversial sections of these laws prohibits collusion between companies. It made into a criminal offence any agreement between sellers fixing the price of a commodity.

Since the managers and owners of the large companies and corporations most affected by this legislation were also persons who had vast economic and political power, the passage of these laws would appear to contradict the general proposition that laws are enacted in the interests of the powerful. An understanding of the climate of opinion at the time of the passage of these laws makes it clear, however, that even these laws are no exception to the general principle.

The nation had been shocked by a series of scandals disclosing widespread irresponsibility and callousness on the part of the "captains of industry." Their persistent disregard for the interest of consumers widely agitated the public. Under these circumstances, a show of concern that went beyond mere verbal assurances was seen by those in power as absolutely necessary if a total disruption of the generally advantageous system was to be avoided. In this context, then, passing laws to control business activities was indeed an act quite consistent with the best interests of those in power. Without some affirmative gesture which would allay public hostility there appeared to be the very real possibility that the entire free-enterprise system as practiced by the owners and managers of industry might well have been destroyed. The anti-trust laws, then, were tantamount to giving up a room in the basement to the servants in order to save the castle.

This interpretation of the emergence of the anti-trust laws is, in fact, clearly supported by the expressed sentiments of legislators at the time these laws were passed. It was commonly agreed that these laws should never be *enforced* (God forbid!) but should only be enacted to cool down the temper of the "radicals."

Occasionally the heavy hand of interest groups emerges into full daylight. Surprisingly, even this rarely deters legislators from acting in the interests of their clients. Daniel Dykstra has documented a legislative power struggle over a bill permitting certain lumber interests to build a dam on a Wisconsin river. What made this event particularly unusual was not that economic interests were involved but, rather, that each of two competing interests engaged in strenuous lobbying efforts to sway the legislature to do its will. In the ensuing melee over the bill it came to light that legislators had been bribed, and that the merits of the bill were not really at issue. Furthermore, as Dykstra stresses, the more general issues of conservation of public waterways and a long-range consideration of the implications of the dam were never even raised as side issues much less were they, as they should have been, considered as central to the question. The only matter of concern to the legislators, as to the interest groups concerned about the bill, was how the building or not building of the dam would affect the economy of the community.

As Dykstra also points out, corruption in the legislature is not an historical anachronism. It is as pervasive today as in the past. For example, the Natural Gas Bill of 1956 was vetoed by President Eisenhower because in the course of considering the bill it had come to light that some legislators had received money from "friends" of companies representing the natural gas interests.

While there are mechanisms built into the legislative process for investigating such misuse of the legislative power, they are so seldom employed with any real intention of altering the legislative process that for all practical purposes they may as well not exist. One can scarcely count the scandals that have racked the federal legislature in the United States over the past ten years. Not one of these instances—Bernard Goldfine, Bobby Baker, Senator Case, Senator Dodd, Congressman Powell—has prompted the legislature to take the steps at its disposal to minimize the likelihood that such things will recur. One can only conclude that bribes and corruption are institutionalized in the legislative process of America. To interfere with the ongoing practices is viewed with alarm by at least a majority, if not all, of the legislators. Under these circumstances it is possible for small groups to bring to bear considerable legislative pressure to pass bills and laws favorable to their interests, providing they have sufficient wealth to bribe the necessary legislators.

Bribery is not, however, usually necessary to protect the interests of the dominant social classes. The majority of federal Congressmen and Senators, for example, earn far more than their salaries of $30,000, which is already sufficient to place them in the upper one percent of salary earners in the country.[15] Congress has consistently refused to require its members to make public all their holdings and interests, although they have grudgingly gone a step or two along the long mile. Even that brief step is revealing. For example, a majority of members of the House Committee on Money and Banking in 1969 held financial or managerial interests in banks. One fifth of the members of the Senate are said to be millionaires. It can hardly be doubted that the central tendency among so wealthy a segment of the population is automatically to view the world in ways that make legislation favorable to the ruling elites merely a matter of "common sense."

The laws that define deviancy or illegality, therefore, are the result of political activity. Deviancy is not a moral question; it is a political question. No act, nor any set of acts, can be defined as inherently "beyond the pale" of "community tolerance." Rather, there are in effect an infinite number and variety of acts occurring in any society which may or may not be defined and treated as criminal. Which acts are so designated depends on the interests of the persons with sufficient political power and influence to manage to have their views prevail. Once it has been established that certain acts are to be designated as deviant, then how the laws are implemented will likewise reflect the political power of the various affected groups.

Even acts about which there is an apparent societal consensus at one time are in all likelihood acts about which consensus was once lacking. Interest groups were invariably active in promoting the laws in question before their creation. Jerome Hall's analysis of the emergence of the laws of theft illustrate this. In the early history (between the Twelfth and Fourteenth centuries) of English criminal law it was not considered a crime (although it was a civil wrong) for one man transporting the goods of another man to convert those goods to his own use. It was only with the rise of commerce and increased demands by merchants for protection of their goods that such acts came to be defined as criminal. One interesting feature of this change is that the courts effectively created the change without any corresponding change in the statutes. The interests of persons with considerable economic and political power were sufficiently tied in with the interests of the judiciary so that new laws emerged to protect these interests without the organization of particular efforts. Sociologically, however, the process remains essentially the same; that is, it is for the protection of the interests of groups in power that laws emerge.

As societies grow more highly differentiated into groups with special interests, the characteristics of the relevant interest groups undergo considerable transformation. This is illustrated by the particular groups in America which currently hold great influence over the content of the criminal laws. Psychiatrists, for example, have come to play a significant role in determining the particular types of offense that will be considered criminal. (Sutherland's analysis of the emergence and promulgation of sexual psychopath laws shows quite clearly how this transformation of relevant interest groups takes place.) Psychiatrists have also come to play an important role in determining the circumstances under which a person should be considered insane. Consequently, the psychiatric profession has been instrumental in shaping the criteria by which an act shall be judged to be criminal or not, since an act committed by someone who is legally insane is not a crime.

In complex societies the law-enforcement agencies themselves emerge as vested interest groups with considerable influence over legal norms. Their influence flows largely from the ignorance of society and legislators generally about the relevant facts and explanations for criminality. Law-enforcement personnel are assumed to be experts in this area. It is often possible, therefore, for law enforcement agencies to define what constitutes the "best" rules for them to enforce. Not surprisingly, these people rarely advocate the passage of laws which are likely to create problems of enforcement. On the whole, they can be expected to seek the enactment of laws prohibiting acts which they feel are deserving of state sanctions, and which will permit enforcement with a minimum of organizational strain.[16]

The emergence of anti-drug laws in the United States illustrates the important role of law-enforcement agencies in shaping legal norms. The first anti-drug law in the United States was the Harrison Act of 1914. The legislative intent was ostensibly to pass a law which would make it possible to better collect tax revenues on drugs brought into the country.[17] Negatively, the intention was *not* to punish drug users, nor to restrict the physicians' freedom in administering drugs to drug addicts. Subsequently, however, as a consequence of the efforts of Federal enforcement authorities, the law-enforcement agency reponsible for enforcing the drug laws, the courts broadened the interpretation of the Harrison Act to preclude the administering of drugs to addicts by physicians and the possession and taking of drugs by addicts. In addition, the Federal Narcotics Bureau has waged an intensive propaganda and lobbying campaign in state as well as federal governmental agencies. Consequently most states now have anti-drug laws which make it a crime to possess, distribute, or give drugs to addicts.

It is significant that court decisions have not always coincided with the intention of the Federal Narcotics Bureau. There exists today substantial legal precedent for permitting physicians under certain circumstances to administer drugs to addicts. The Bureau, however, is in a position to select for prosecution only those cases which are not likely to be overturned by higher courts (including the practice of not prosecuting cases where appeals to higher courts are likely to occur). Some of the earlier decisions have, therefore, never been reinforced in later cases. As a consequence, there is widespread ignorance on the part of physicians as to the freedom they could in fact enjoy in the treatment of drug addicts. The end result, of course, is that the general practice in the medical profession with respect to drug addiction is a function not of medical wisdom, but of the pressures generated by the Federal Narcotics Bureau, partly on legislatures and partly through the threat of prosecution.

More recently the efforts of the Federal Narcotics Bureau and local police agencies have been largely responsible for the expansion of the anti-drug laws to include marijuana and LSD.[18] For years the enforcement of drug laws was concentrated in the lower classes. Marijuana was originally a "problem" among the Mexican-American population; other drugs were most prevalent in the ghettos. "Respectable" members of the community were generally able to maintain their drug habits with the help of their physicians or other sources of drugs (including at times enforcement agents themselves) that ran little risk of arrest. The activities of the law-enforcement agencies in expanding these laws, because they anticipated that this was in their own bureaucratic interests, did not at the time appear to commit them to a program that would involve arresting persons who could cause them "trouble."

The situation has not turned out to be exactly as anticipated. Marijuana and a host of other so-called drugs have been adopted as part of the way of life of students in colleges and high schools. As a consequence, the police have frequently been exposed for using time-tested techniques of entrapment and general harassment of "drug users" in law-enforcement efforts. Since these techniques have been used against the children of the middle and upper classes, considerable criticism has been leveled at the police which they would normally have avoided.

There is currently underway a strong movement to eliminate marijuana and some other drugs from the list of harmful drugs prohibited by law. This movement, although originally opposed by the law-enforcers, is gaining favor with them precisely because the enforcement of these laws against middle and upper class youths has not brought forth praise and rewards for the enforcement agencies. On the contrary, it has exposed them to a great deal of criticism. In the last analysis it is likely that this fact, and not scientific evidence demonstrating that marijuana is less harmful to users than alcohol, will bring about changes in the laws in question. The harmful effects of an action are largely irrelevant to whether or not it is defined as criminal.

Significantly, law-enforcement agencies rarely lobby or propagandize to obtain laws which might require them to arrest persons of high social standing. Concerns, for example, with illegitimate business practices are virtually never touched by law-enforcement agencies. To insist on stringent enforcement of such laws would only make life difficult for the agencies. Laws against disorderly conduct, drug use, prostitution, and the like, by contrast, provide law-enforcers with readily available grist for the legal machinery, with no particular risk of creating countermovements to interfere with their activities.

Most laws, then, emerge as a consequence of the activities of the relatively small minority of the population who hold positions of political and economic power. The remaining small proportion of the legislation can be accounted for by more amorphous interest groups. On occasion, a particular social class can effectively influence legislation through the expression of "public" sentiment— that is to say, by generating significant expressions of opinion from their own class.

In the most highly industrialized and technologically developed societies there has burgeoned a large middle class. On occasion, this class has displayed its influence in the legislative process. Middle-class pressure is frequently evoked by the activities of members of other classes in the society which threaten the economic or personal well-being of members of the middle class and by some event which brings to their awareness this potential threat.

In the process of making the middle class aware of potential threats to its well-being, the mass media play a critical role. The history of the Pure Food and Drug laws brings out this fact. Essentially what brought these laws into existence was Upton Sinclair's book, *The Jungle*, which graphically portrayed the then prevailing practices of the meat-packing industry. This book received widespread publicity through other media, primarily the newspapers, and was widely read. As a consequence, an aroused middle class placed pressure on legislators to pass laws restricting the behavior of manufacturers. A bureau was formed to investigate possible illegal activities on the part of manufacturers and the bureau expanded to include law-enforcement.

In recent years television and newspapers have brought to the attention of the middle classes the violence that periodically erupts in the slums of major cities. The responses of legislators have been diverse. A few measures have been taken which are aimed at relieving the conditions presumed to lead to the riots in the first place. More have been aimed at increasing the penalties for rioting. New laws have been created imposing severe sanctions against persons who attempt to provoke violence.

Many people, while conceding that most legislation proceeds from interest-group pressures on the legislature, argue that nevertheless some of the criminal laws, at least, express a consensus in the community. Surely, it is argued, rape, murder, theft, aggravated assault—the whole array of conventional crime—represent a value-consensus of the whole community.

Doubtless it is true that on a verbal level nobody will say that he believes people should be free to rape and murder. These categories, however, have no unanimously definite content even within a single society. Does a man have a right to defend himself against an attack with a murderous weapon when he can avoid the attack by fleeing? (There is a disagreement even in judicial opinions among the States on this point.) Is it murder for a policeman to kill a spectator at a "student riot" with buckshot presumably aimed at breaking up the riot in which the spectator is not participating? Is it rape if a man has forcible intercourse with a girl who picked him up at a bar, encouraged him to think that she was available, went out with him in his car to a lonely spot, but said "No" at the last moment?

It is a truism that every person arrested for crime perceives himself as innocent, for there are always circumstances which to him seem to place his action outside the appropriate definition of the crime. This is not simply to make the trivial point that accused persons are capable of rationalization to excuse themselves. Rather, it is to emphasize that moral dictates (prescriptions and proscriptions), like other values, are at best broad, culturally defined objectives. They have meaning, however, only in special circumstances. Everyone will agree that murder is immoral and ought to be punished. The penal law itself provides innumerable qualifications. It is not a crime to kill an enemy in wartime, for the public hangman to execute a man, to kill in self-defence if reasonably necessary (and what a vague qualification *that* is!), to kill in a blind rage induced by "reasonable" provocation, to kill in effecting an arrest (there is no agreement among the States whether the right to kill can be sustained only in arrests for felony or for any crime). These are all exceptions where there is no value-consensus. Moreover, there are many who would assert that it ought not be considered murder to kill a person suffering severe and incurable pain (euthanasia), or to kill a "no-good bum" who "deserved to die" because he was so "stupid" as to be wandering the streets at night flashing large sums of money or who had raped the killer's sister. Others may assert that stealing is not immoral if done to alleviate starvation of oneself or one's family. (The great Macauley, the author of the Indian Penal Codes and one of England's most illustrious writers on crime, believed this.)

Conceptions of what ought to be criminal vary even more dramatically from society to society. We detail a number of cases below in connection with a brief study of a problem frequently raised in Africa: a defendant in a murder trial defends himself on the ground that he had to kill to protect himself against witchcraft. Other cases abound.

In English law the only property which a man may kill to defend is his own home, reflecting the traditional axiom that an Englishman's home is his castle. It is manslaughter (at least) to kill in defense of other personal property. A Masai in Tanganyika killed in defense of cattle. The Masai is a nomadic, pastoral tribe, and each of its members considers himself bound in symbiotic relationship with his cattle; indeed, there is only one word in the Masai language for the Masai and their cattle. Under English law, the Masai was found guilty of manslaughter.

A tribe in Nigeria believes that the fish in the adjoining river embody the souls of their ancestors. Is it murder if they kill a stranger fishing in the river? Members of the Nuer tribe in the Sudan are trained from babyhood to support their close kin in a fight, under pain of extreme social sanctions if they do not. Is a Nuer who comes upon his kinsmen fighting, and joins in, guilty of conspiracy to commit murder if one of the enemies dies? Among the Kikuyu of Kenya, it is the pleasant custom that a young man has the right to lie all night with any girl in his age set, engaging in love-play but not intercourse. Is it kidnapping if a young man holds a girl all night in accordance with the custom but against her will?

Different societies tolerate different kinds of actions that to others appear criminal. It is said that incest is the only act which is uniformly held to be a crime in every society, but there is no agreement about the degrees of consanguinity required to constitute the offence. The particular acts that are prohibited are, as Holmes said long ago, a matter of "expediency," not of universal morality. Sociologically, what constitutes right and wrong behavior can be discovered only by examining, not some presumed society-wide moral code, but the decision-making processes in the society which determine what activity is to be made criminal.

That fact is masked, however, by the culturally induced consensus which exists on broad categories of proscription: "murder," "rape," and so forth. So long as one concentrates merely on the words used in the titles of criminal statutes, a significant amount of apparent value-consensus no doubt can be demonstrated. Only when the actual details of the establishment of legal norms are examined—only when specific, detailed study is made of the process of valuation, rather than superficial examination of generalized objectives on the order of Mother, Virtue, and the Flag—does the reality of value-discord emerge.

In sum, the enforcement of any law necessarily involves certain benefits and costs. The particular laws which comprise any given legal system will be those which certain groups, ranging from small professional associations to the amorphous "middle class," see as primarily benefiting themselves. Whatever the interest groups may strive to achieve, of course the stance taken will invariably be to defend the legislation in terms of its intrinsic beneficent consequences for "all" of society. But "all" of society never really includes everyone but necessarily excludes that group whose behavior the law is intended to control. Much of the confusion over the inherent "naturalness" of the law has stemmed from a failure to realize this very basic fact about legislation. It is significant that it has been the interplay of empirical research and general theoretical perspectives which has led to a realization of the relative importance of interest groups as contrasted with the previously accepted "natural law" interpretations.

Legislation arises to further the interests of one group or another, against other interest groups and, sometimes, the entire society. In order to understand how the legislature becomes a weapon in the inter-group and class struggles of a society, one must also examine specifically the norms controlling the processes of the legislature and of the elections through which legislators are recruited. The norms governing these processes themselves make the influence of legislation by one interest group or another easier or more difficult. The interests represented by Southern congressmen in the Federal Congress have been immeasurably strengthened by the seniority rules that determine the committee chairmanships.

The election system is controlled not so much by the elections themselves as by the internal workings of the two major parties and their nominating procedures, which tend to put power in the hands of the wealthiest minority in the country. The rules of procedure in the two houses of Congress, for example the filibuster rule, have enormous importance in determining which groups can, and which cannot, influence legislation. The importance of procedure as a determinant of decision can be seen even more sharply in the instances of rule-making by appellate courts than in examples of legislative activity. We shall discuss in some detail the workings of the appellate courts in the following three chapters.

6.4 SUMMARY

Legal literature has for centuries given prominent attention to the question of how laws emerge in complex societies. A central feature of disagreement has been the degree to which the laws that emerge express the necessary arrangements for smooth and stable social relationships. One group of legal scholars has placed the emphasis on "natural law" or the demands of human social organizations. Specific legal innovations have been seen as necessary to solutions of social problems.[19]

Systematic research of legal norms has failed to turn up evidence consistent with such an interpretation. On the contrary, every detailed study of the emergence of legal norms has consistently shown the immense importance of interest-group activity, *not "the public interest,"* as the critical variable in determining the content of legislation. To hold to the notion of natural laws emerging from the needs of society requires that we accept the highly questionable assumption that somehow interest groups operate in the best interests of society. It may be true that "what's good for General Motors is good for the society," if all the members of the society benefit from the triumph of special interests. Rarely does this happen. Laws inevitably improve things for some people and make things worse for others.

The legislature is, therefore, not a mere neutral forum where pluralistic interest groups can bargain out a compromise solution representing their respective power positions. The output of the legislature means rags or riches, servility or power, weakness or strength, to every interest group in the country.[20] The institution which produces such extraordinary benefits or detriments cannot in its very nature be a merely impartial framework for struggle. Like every bureaucratic organization, it responds to the pressure of the powerful and the privileged. It is a weapon in the struggle.

NOTES

1. C. Auerbach, L. K. Garrison, W. Hurst, and S. Mermin, *The Legal Process: An Introduction to Decision-Making by Judicial, Legislative, Executive and Administrative Agencies*, Chandler, San Francisco, 1961, p. 661. Reprinted by permission.

2. John Dewey, *Theory of Valuation*, University of Chicago Press, Chicago, 1939.

3. A few recent works that illustrate those contrasts are: Oscar Lewis, *La Vida*, Random House, New York, 1965; Charles Keil, *Urban Blues*, Indiana University Press, Bloomington, 1965; John T. Liell, "Levittown," unpublished Ph.D. dissertation, Yale University, 1958.

4. From *Night Comes to the Cumberlands* by Harry M. Caudill, by permission of Atlantic-Little, Brown and Co. Copyright © 1962, 1963 by Harry M. Caudill.

5. Elliot Liebow, *Tally's Corner*, Little, Brown, Boston, 1967. Reprinted by permission.

6. Edmund Burke, *Works*, H. J. Bohn, London, 1893, p. 447.

7. Arthur Bentley in *The Process of Government*, Peter H. Odegard (ed.), The Belknap Press of Harvard University Press, Cambridge, Mass., 1949, pp. 370–371. Reprinted by permission.

8. 369 U.S. 186 (1962).

9. See William J. Chambliss, "A sociological analysis of the law of vagrancy," *Social Problems*, **12**, 1964, pp. 67–77; see also Caleb Foote, "Vagrancy type law and its administration," *U. Pa. Law Rev.*, **104**, 1956, pp. 603–650. Both articles reprinted in William J. Chambliss (ed.), *Crime and the Legal Process*, McGraw-Hill, New York, 1969.

10. See Clarence Ray Jeffrey, "The development of crime in early English society," *J. Criminal Law, Criminology, and Police Science*, **47**, 1956, pp. 647–666. Also in Chambliss (ed.) *Crime and the Legal Process*.

11. Quoted in William J. Chambliss, "A sociological analysis of the law of vagrancy," p. 68.

12. *Ibid.*, p. 69.

13. Jerome Hall's analysis of theft makes the same point for another type of behavior.

14. Gabriel Kolko, *The Triumph of Conservatism*, Free Press of Glencoe, New York, 1963.

15. C. Wright Mills, *The Power Elite*, Oxford University Press, New York, 1959, pp. 248–259. The annual salary of Congressmen is now (1970) $42,500.

16. The question of the importance of organizational considerations for law-enforcement agencies is taken up in Chapter 14.

17. See Alfred Lindesmith, "Federal law and drug addiction," *Social Problems*, **7**, 1959, pp. 48–57.

18. Alfred R. Lindesmith, *The Addict and the Law*, Indiana University Press, Bloomington, 1965.

19. See Jerome Hall, *Theft, Law, and Society*, Bobbs-Merrill, Indianapolis, 1952.

20. Gabriel Kolko, *Wealth and Power in America*, Praeger, New York, 1962.

7

The appellate courts: inputs

Many people can accept the idea that legislatures as law-making institutions necessarily reflect the values of the groups with the largest influence over the law-makers. It seems more difficult, however, to accept the conflict model of the State with respect to appellate courts. After all, appellate courts are the institution *par excellence* for which society most carefully cherishes the ideal of value-neutrality. In this and the succeeding chapters we shall examine in some detail the processes of judicial rule-making on the appellate level, and, as we shall see, appellate courts are no more value-neutral than the legislatures. In fact the courts necessarily take sides in the constant war between antagonistic interest groups in society. Before we can discuss this fact, however, we must briefly sketch a complex process primarily for the benefit of non-lawyer readers.

7.1 THE COURT STRUCTURE

The judicial process proceeds on two distinct levels: those of the trial court and the appellate court. The functions of the two types of courts, while to some degree overlapping, are in most respects quite different.

A plaintiff having a cause of action against another (or a prosecutor with a criminal action against a defendant) initiates the action in a trial court. He does this by reciting the facts which he believes to be true and which he believes add up to a right for a judgment in his behalf. The paper in which he recites these facts and his claim for judgment, the complaint, is served upon the opponent together with a summons.

The opponent now has two alternatives open to him. He may move to dismiss the complaint for failure to state a cause of action. Such a motion is, in a sense, a "so what?" motion. It says that even if everything said in the complaint be true, so what? The argument implied is that there is no rule of law that subsumes the alleged facts. Or he can answer the complaint by asserting that some or all of the factual allegations are untrue. (In some jurisdictions he can do both simultaneously.)

The motion to dismiss the complaint for failure to state a cause of action raises one sort of issue of *law*. The answer raises issues of *fact*. If the defendant does not move to dismiss the complaint or if the motion is denied, then the case goes to trial. The trial proper is concerned only with the resolution of the issues of fact. In the course of the trial, the judge will have to make a variety of rulings, on evidence and on various procedural motions. These motions, too, raise issues of law. Ultimately the trial results in a judgment for or against the plaintiff.

These events take place in "lower" courts, usually municipal and superior courts. The losing party then has a right to appeal. An appeal in most instances in this country brings before the appellate court only questions of law. It asks the appellate court to review, *not* whether the judge or jury correctly resolved the *factual* issues, but whether the judge properly decided the various questions of law raised by a motion for dismissal or the questions of law raised by the various motions made in the course of the trial.

The role of trial courts is therefore quite different from the role of appellate courts. Trial courts are engaged most of the time in trying issues of fact: listening to witnesses, examining documents, or directing juries in their consideration of these matters. In addition, trial courts engage in a whole group of ancillary activities—the appointment of administrators for decedent's estates and receivers in bankruptcies, the sentencing of convicted criminals, and a host of others.

Of all these variegated activities of the court, only questions involving issues of law come before appellate courts. Every issue of law arises because a litigant has asked the trial judge to do something. In response, the judge either acts or declines to act in accordance with the request. If the aggrieved party believes that the judge has acted wrongly, he may appeal.

To say that the trial judge acted wrongly is to say that he adopted a wrong rule, or norm, to guide his action. What is at issue in the appellate court is the correct statement of the norm or rule which ought to guide the trial judge. The

THE APPELLATE COURTS: INPUTS

statement of the rule by the appellate court, under the case-law system of precedents, becomes the rule for a host of similar cases thereafter.

When we discuss the appellate courts and their work, therefore, we are concerned with their rule-defining function. As we shall see, to define a rule in genuine dispute in fact requires the court to create a new one. We are concerned, therefore, with the scope of discretion of the appellate courts in their rule-creating function.

Whether appellate courts are value-neutral depends in part on whether their role is merely to logically subsume the relevant facts under a preexisting norm, or whether the process of judging on the appellate level requires the exercise of discretion. Before we investigate this general problem, we shall examine two models of government, the one asserting that the rule of law denies official discretion, the other asserting its inevitability.

7.2 THE PERVASIVENESS OF OFFICIAL DISCRETION

Ever since Dicey, it has popularly been supposed that the rule of law requires the absence of discretion in the rule-applying authorities. More modern models, especially those of Hans Kelsen and H. L. A. Hart, yield precisely the opposite conclusion.

Dicey and the Rule of Law

A. V. Dicey (1835–1922) in 1885 wrote an extraordinarily influential book, *The Law of the Constitution*,[1] in which he asserted that law consisted in a body of fixed and ascertainable rules, and by the "rule of law"

We mean . . . that no man is punishable or can be lawfully made to suffer in body or goods except for a distinct breach of law established in the ordinary legal manner before the ordinary courts of the land. In this sense the rule of law is contrasted with every system of government based on the exercise by persons in authority of wide, arbitrary, or discretionary powers of constraint.[2]

Dicey's proposition was a vigorous statement in opposition to the trend of State intervention in economic processes. Inevitably, where the State must make decisions concerning economic affairs, it must exercise some power of choice. Dicey's most influential twentieth century disciple, Friedrich von Hayek,[3] has gone so far as to assert that, since planning implies official discretion impossible for citizens to foresee, it is inconsistent with the rule of law. Hayek defines the rule of law in a radical, Diceyian way: it means "that government in all its actions is bound by rules fixed and announced beforehand—rules which make it possible to foresee with fair certainty which authority will use its coercive powers in given circumstances and to plan one's individual affairs on the basis of this knowledge."[4]

While most jurisprudents and social scientists today would probably deny the Dicey-Hayek notions of what ought to be the case with respect to economic affairs, there is nevertheless a shared sentiment that the rule of law as defined by them surely should apply to at least the courts and the police. Two modern authors, Hans Kelsen and H. L. A. Hart, however, have developed models of law and the legal system based on different principles. These models are worth examining.

Hans Kelsen and the Hierarchy of Norms

Hans Kelsen is an Austrian jurist whose work has had a major impact on modern jurisprudence. A positivist, he apparently began his work in ignorance of Austin's contribution,[5] and his intellectual roots were in Neo-Kantianism. Neo-Kantian idealism, drawing its inspiration from Kant himself, viewed the natural and the cultural sciences as being dominated by different governing principles. The governing principle of the natural sciences was said to be causality, the governing principle of the cultural sciences, volition.

Kelsen fastened on the notion of vioition as the essential characteristic of law. A pure theory of law, therefore, must build on this single principle, carefully cleansed of notions of justice, politics, ethics, or sociology. Since human volition is expressed primarily in norms of conduct, the pure science of law must be concerned with the relationship between norms of conduct. Natural science is concerned with what *is* the case, and how what is the case can be predicted form what came before. Law, in Kelsen's view, is concerned only with what *ought* to be the case.

The effort, therefore, is one of reduction: to reduce the analysis of law to the single irreducible principle of volition. This principle can be explicated only in terms of how it works its way through the legal order; hence what is required is an examination of the formal relationship between norms.

Kelsen thus arrived at the same position as the English positivists, albeit by a totally different route. Just as Austin disregarded what the law ought to be and concentrated his attention on the norms themselves, so did Kelsen. A norm, to be effective, must be sanctioned by an authority. The central formal problem with respect to a legal norm, therefore, is its source. Each norm must find its authority in some higher authority, who in turn must be acting in accordance with a norm. Thus, by a regressive series, one discovers that the source of the norms must be some Original Source, which Kelsen calls the *Grundnorm*, or constitution. The *Grundnorm* possesses the original power to issue norms to subordinate authorities by hypothesis. It cannot be explained without invoking the other social sciences which Kelsen has excluded from his ken. Thus Kelsen, by a consideration only of the inherent characteristics of volition, ends with a hierarchical structure of norms issuing from an Original Source, which resembles Austin's Sovereign in many ways.

The legal order, therefore, in Kelsen's view can be perceived as a hierarchy of norms. The act of a jailer in incarcerating a convicted criminal derives its justification from the convicting judgment of the judge, which in turn derives its validity from statutes enacted by the legislators, who in turn derive their authority from the Constitution itself.

Now the State, as traditionally conceived and, indeed, as conceived by Austin, is an entity distinct from the legal order. Kelsen asserts that this dualistic view of State and law has an essentially ideological function. The essence of the State is popularly thought to be power; the essence of law, is order. By conceiving of the State and law as distinct entities, "the state is transformed from a bare fact of power to a legal institution justifying itself as a community governed by law (Rechtsstaat)."[6] Thus, the dualistic view of the State ends by asserting the primacy of order over power—in popular terms, as the Rule of Law. It ends, therefore, by justifying and strengthening the State's authority, by inducing the layman to view the State as controlled, not by power, but by the values which most men perceive in order—by law.

Kelsen denies that the State and law are different entities. To be a State, says Kelsen, "the legal order must have the character of an organization in the narrower and specific sense of this word, that is, it must establish organs who, in the manner of division of labor, create and apply norms that constitute the legal order; it must display a certain degree of centralization."[7] In sociological language, the State is a set of positions defined by norms, whose function is to create, modify, and sanction the breach of norms. The hierarchy of norms thus is simultaneously the legal order and the State itself.

The hierarchical order of norms is based on a successive concretization of their content. The Constitution lays down norms of the broadest sort for the conduct of the legislators. Legislators lay down rather more concrete, but still very general, laws for the conduct of judges. Judges, in turn, must make these general rules concrete in individual cases. Statutes which delegate power to policemen to make arrests necessarily give them discretion, for they must make determinations about when to apply the general rule. *Thus at every stage in the legal order, there is discretion in the officials who occupy the various positions in it.*

The discretion granted to officials at every level of course is not the same in scope. Legislators have very different roles to play from those of judges, and judges, from those of policemen. In every case, however, there is necessarily room for discretion—a discretion bounded by norms which explicate its limits, but nevertheless a discretionary power.

What Kelsen's model suggests, therefore, is that logically the central characteristic of a legal system cannot be the inflexibility of its rules, but the pervasive existence of discretion. His model suggests that the ideal of a government of law (i.e., in which norms govern every sort of activity in society) rather than of men (in which there exists significant areas of discretion in officials) is a myth properly relegated (at best) to high school textbooks on civics. It tells us to expect that the normative system within which officials operate endows them with wide areas of discretionary activity.

That this is so can be seen in the very nature of modern government. A complex government is a bureaucratic government. As Weber has said, such a government requires the specialization and differentiation of functions. The activities of the persons in different positions are then controlled by a central decision-making structure through rules which lay down general standards for the behavior of the rule-applying bodies.

Hart and the Concept of Law

H. L. A. Hart, like Hans Kelsen and John Austin, is a positivist. He directs our attention to three recurrent issues in jurisprudence: "How does law differ from and how is it related to orders backed by threats? How does legal obligation differ from, and how is it related to, moral obligation? What are rules and to what extent is law an affair of rules?"[8] He first proceeds to demolish Austin's rather simplistic notion that laws are commands to citizens, mainly on the grounds that whatever effect a law may have upon the citizen, it is only rarely a coercive "order" in the sense that the command by an army officer to a subordinate is an "order." Kelsen urged that rules of law had best be considered as hypothetical judgments. The rule, "Thou shalt not kill," according to Kelsen, is best understood as a fragment of a hypothetical judgment addressed to the judge: "If it appears before you that the defendant has killed, then you shall order a sanction to be visited upon the defendant."[9] Hart urges that to so understand the rules of law is to obscure their effect as a form of social control. The rule is the "internal" reason why the citizen does not kill in the first place; only when the norm is breached does it come into play in its second sense.

The fact is that some rules of law are norms in a double sense. In the first place, they are addressed to the ordinary citizen and they describe society's role-expectation for him, under pain of sanction. In the second place, they are role-defining norms for the judge, for they describe the action expected of him if certain conditions come to pass. Such rules may be called (as Hart calls them) "primary" rules.

This dual aspect of the primary rules of law, their being addressed simultaneously to citizen and judge, is of course an essential element of our original model.[10] It is a necessary feature that derives from the fact that rules of law are distinguished from custom primarily in that there are separate enforcement agencies to adjudicate whether most rules of law have been violated, and to assess and enforce the sanction. The dual aspect of the primary rules is in fact expressive of this fact. Custom, on the other hand, which is enforced, not by a special agency, but by the persons affected or by the mass of citizens without official sanction, can be thought of as being a primary norm *simpliciter*, addressed to the citizens and sanctioned directly by the persons or collectivities who believe that the custom has been breached.

Parenthetically, it may be noted that this dual aspect of primary rules of law is the source of many of the problems posed in the sociology of law. Where the norm that the citizen actually regards as controlling his conduct is different from that regarded by the judge as controlling, the judge is called upon to sanction a norm that is rejected by the citizen. In areas where it is deemed desirable to permit citizens to determine their own norms of conduct, e.g. in much of the business and commercial world, the primary rules as invoked by the judges ought to conform to the norms defined by the relevant groups themselves. In other areas of law, where the law-makers regard the rejected legal norms as proper and the privately defined norms as improper, e.g. in the subculture of the homosexual, the disagreement points up the necessity of devising ways to institutionalize the authoritatively approved substantive norms embodied in the primary rules.

Hart then distinguishes a completely different set of rules which can hardly be deemed "commands" in any sense. These are rules typically addressed only to officials. They define the scope of the official's power to create law; they purport to describe to him where he shall look to determine which primary rules are authoritative; and they describe the procedures which the official is to follow in exercising his powers. Usually these rules are supported by sanctions much more diffuse than those which support the primary rules; in many cases, formal sanctions are in fact nonexistent.

The rules defining these sorts of official conduct Hart has labeled "secondary" rules. Most often they are power-conferring rules, which purport to define only the outer limits of official discretion. Hart concludes that the "heart" of a legal system is a "complex union of primary and secondary rules."[11] Obviously, he means by this a legal system which contains institutions with the specialized functions of creating, adjudicating, and enforcing norms. A "legal system" has at its heart the conjunction of the two sets of rules only if by "legal system" one means a system of norms enforced by such specialized institutions. Hart's concept of law is thus ultimately dependent on a definition which reflects the sort of society in which Hart lives.

Hart goes on to point out that the effectiveness of a system of law depends on the "unified or shared official acceptance" of the secondary rules. He says:

What makes "obedience" misleading as a description of what legislators do in conforming to the rules conferring their powers, and of what courts do in applying an accepted ultimate rule of recognition (which defines which primary rules are authoritative), is that obeying a (primary) rule (or an order) *need* involve no thought on the part of the person obeying that what he does is the right thing both for himself and for others to do: he need have no view of what he does as a fulfillment of a standard of behaviour for others of the social group. He need not think of his conforming behaviour as "right," "correct," or "obligatory" . . . Instead, he may think of the rule only as something demanding action from *him* under threat of penalty; he may obey it out of fear of the consequences, or from inertia, without thinking of himself or others as having an obligation to do so and without being disposed to criticize either himself or others for deviations. But this merely personal concern with the rules, which is all the ordinary citizen *may* have in obeying them, cannot characterize the attitude of the courts to the rules with which they operate as courts (and, one might add, most other officials in the law-enforcement system). This is most patently the case with the ultimate rule of recognition in terms of which the validity of other rules is assessed. This, if it is to exist at all, must be regarded from the internal point of view as a public common standard of correct judicial decision, and not as something which each judge merely obeys for his part only . . .[12]

Hart then makes a point seemingly unrelated but which, as we shall see, goes to the heart of the matter. He points out that the nature of language, in which all norms must be cast, is that it has an "open" texture. If one uses the word "table," for example, most people would have little difficulty in identifying with that word a four-legged article of furniture with a flat top standing about thirty inches high and without built-in drawers or cabinets. This meaning of the word Hart calls its "core" meaning. But what happens when we start sawing off the legs, an inch at a time? At some indeterminate point we shall start wondering whether the article of furniture is a "table" or a "bench." This indeterminate area Hart refers to as the "penumbra" of the word.

Lon Fuller has added a significant gloss to Hart's linguistic analysis. He demonstrates that in fact even the core meaning of words varies, depending on the context. Suppose, for example, that an ordinance reads, "Any person who sleeps in a public waiting room of a bus system or railroad shall be convicted of loitering and fined not more than $5.00." That a drunk, sprawling over a bench asleep in a way that offends standards of public decency, is within the core meaning of the offense defined by this ordinance is self-evident. But what of the middle-class commuter who missed his midnight train and perforce must wait for the milk train four hours later, who sits upright, respectable, but dozing? That his case is at best in the penumbra is likewise self-evident. Yet his conduct is within the "core" meaning of "sleeps," viewed as a word abstracted from the context. Thus, Fuller urges, the core meaning of statutes cannot be determined from the words alone, but must be considered in terms of context and purposes.

That there is a "core" meaning, however, seems clear; that there is also a "penumbra" is likewise clear. In any event, there must be a necessarily vague area for the application of any rule. It is evident that every level of the law-application and law-enforcing apparatus must be endowed with discretion to determine the purposes of rules, and whether a given set of facts lies within or without the core meaning of the rules. When a policeman sees our middle-class commuter dozing on the bench, he necessarily must exercise discretion to arrest or not to arrest the man. The discretion which Kelsen thought must exist on every level of the legal order thus arises, not merely through the logical characteristics of a system whose sole principle is volition, but inevitably from the very nature of language and symbols.

In practice, there are additional reasons for the existence of wide discretion on the part of law-applying authorities of which two especially may be identified. First, many of the norms controlling conduct, both primary and secondary, are vague, ambiguous, and contradictory. To a large extent, this is a result of our commitment to a system of laws which finds its roots in the common law. Many of the norms of conduct both for citizens and for officials find their origins, not in statutes, but in case law. The very nature of a case-law system (as opposed to the systems found in many countries where there are systematic codifications of various areas of law) is that the selection of issues to be actually decided follows a hit-or-miss pattern, depending on whether individual litigants choose to initiate a case raising the question. Moreover, the determination of each case is made on the basis of the facts of that particular case, as litigated by particular litigants in a particular lawsuit. The facts of the particular case and the way in which private litigants have chosen to raise them frequently determine the shape of the ruling which emerges. This rule may or may not be the one which a wise legislator would have selected had he had in hand adequate empirical studies of the possible effect of potential alternative rules before deciding the case. The existence of vagueness, ambiguity, and contradiction in the pertinent norms gives the law-applying official a wide discretion in selective enforcement.

A second reason is related especially to the secondary rules. The value-acceptances of those classes who are in control of State power tends to presuppose order, not merely as one of the desirable objectives of a polity, but as the essential value to be achieved. It is only natural for people with that kind of value-set to want to see the agencies of law-enforcement hemmed in by the fewest and most relaxed norms possible. For example, one might refer to the storm of protest that has arisen against the Miranda decision, on the ground that it will permit more criminals to go free than otherwise might have done. This decision, as we shall see below, requires the police to notify a suspect of his right to counsel, and excludes confessions obtained in violation of that rule. To emphasize the objective of punishing criminals means, to these protesters, refraining from defining sharply the permissible scope of police action in searching out, arresting, and interrogating the suspects. It is only to be expected, then, that the very norms defining the scope of power of enforcement agencies will in many, probably most, cases be couched in deliberately vague terms.

The limitations on the use of violence by police in effectuating arrest, for example, is ordinarily defined as the use of "reasonable" force, i.e. the force required by a reasonable man to effectuate the arrest. But the word "reasonable" in this context has no determinate meaning; it is a normative construct made by the judge or jury *ex post facto*. In practice, judges and juries are loath to constrain police in their activities against criminal or dissident elements. Thus the norm which purports to limit police to "reasonable" force in fact gives them a discretion whose boundaries are found to exist rather more in law review articles than in practice.

The Hart model qualifies, but fundamentally is consistent with, what is predicted by the Kelsen model. We can expect to find great areas for discretionary action by law-enforcement officials and, indeed, by officials of the State structure generally. Even those norms which define the limits of discretion we can expect to find cast in vague terms. Finally, we can expect to find that there are very few, if any, sanctions for much of official action. In short, we can expect to find a normative structure that defines the action of law-applying agencies very vaguely indeed, and whose limits depend on sanctions enforced, not by other agencies, but by self-limitation on the part of the agencies themselves, which are supposedly limited by these norms.

7.3 FROM DISPUTE-SETTLEMENT TO RULE-CREATION; THE NORMS OF JUDICIAL DECISION-MAKING; PRIMARY RULES AND SECONDARY RULES

A lawsuit charges that a citizen violated a rule of law. When such a case is brought before a judge, the latter's action is supposedly guided by two different kinds of norms. As we have seen, there are primary rules which may be regarded in one aspect as norms for the conduct of the citizen, and in another respect as norms for the conduct of the judge.[13] A primary rule instructs a judge that if it appears to him that a certain kind of violation was committed by someone, then he shall direct that a sanction of a certain sort be applied.

But there is a vast collection of such primary rules. The mere statement of the statutes of the United States, let alone the tremendous number of decisions construing them and the administrative decisions making them more concrete, occupies thousands of pages of small print. Citizens and judges alike must determine which of this host of primary rules ought to govern conduct in a specific case.

Citizens and judges make this determination in different ways. Citizens usually know the rules relevant to most of their day-to-day actions. Businessmen know business law. Drivers know the traffic rules. They are aware of these norms because at some point they have been told what they are. When in doubt, the citizen ordinarily asks someone whom he believes to be knowledgeable about the rules. For the more affluent members of society, it is the lawyers in the community who advise them on the law; for the less affluent, it is likely to be a "prison-house lawyer" or some counterpart in the local community.

When a lawyer advises a citizen what the law is in a given case, he is aware that his advice may ultimately be tested before a judge. In this sense, therefore, his statement of what the law is can be viewed, as Holmes suggested,[14] as a prophecy of what a judge will do if such a case is presented in court.

The lawyer can only make such a prophecy if he is reasonably confident that the judge will act in an ascertainable manner in determining which primary rule should govern a specific case. That is to say, a lawyer must be able to assume that the judge will follow a norm of conduct of which the lawyer is aware, in the selection of a primary rule. This set of norms Hart has named "rules of recognition." It is on these norms that lawyers rely in advising the citizenry and on which citizens rely in their daily life. They therefore constitute a most important statement of society's role-expectation of judges.

7.4 CLEAR CASE AND TROUBLE CASE

When a petitioner—the State in a criminal case, the plaintiff in a civil suit—brings an action, he recites a set of facts which he believes entitles him to an order of the court ordaining that a particular State sanction be imposed. In a criminal action, the prosecutor asks for a verdict of guilty of the crime charged, on the basis of which specific santions flow: imprisonment, fine, etc. In a civil action, the plaintiff asks for a judgment which (in most cases) states that the defendant ought to pay a sum of money to the plaintiff.

It is up to the judge to determine the primary norm which controls the case. There are secondary rules which are supposed to guide him under these circumstances. The paradox is that while there are two different kinds of cases that come to be decided, there is only one legitimate set of secondary rules.

Cases that come to be decided are of two sorts, which we may call "clear" cases and "trouble" cases. In the clear case, the large majority of the cases that come to court, there is really no issue of law. Every time a defense lawyer and the plaintiff's attorney can agree on the question, whether the defendant is liable in law to the plaintiff, they must be in agreement about the governing norm of law. If the defendant's counsel in a criminal case honestly believes that defendant has no defense in law, he must be in agreement with the prosecution as to the appropriate norm to apply to the case.

But there are also a relatively few cases in which this unanimity of counsel is lacking. In these cases, the parties are sharply at odds as to which rule of law ought to be applicable, and its proper content. It is these cases, the "trouble" cases, which make up the grist of the work for the appellate courts.

The "clear" case does not pose an issue of law because two conditions are met. In the first place, there is a preexisting primary rule of law which can be accurately discovered by following the norms of judicial behavior embodied in the secondary rules. The primary rule may be statutory or it may be embodied in the common law. Not only must the form of words that symbolize the rule be agreed upon, but the concepts to which the words refer, their meaning, must be commonly understood.

More often than not the meaning of words in a rule of law can be understood only in terms of the policy which the rule is designed to promote. The clear case then depends, not merely on the discovery of the form of words in which the primary rule is embodied, but also on a common understanding among lawyers and judges of their contextual meaning. In the second place, as we have seen, every primary rule can be rewritten as though it were an hypothetical judgment, in the form, "if thus-and-so appear to the court to be the case, then the judge shall give judgment for plaintiff." The second condition for a "clear" case is that the facts of the case at hand must so clearly be specific instances of the generalized categories of the primary rule as to be beyond question; i.e., they must lie within the "core meaning" of the rule.[15]

Each of the two conditions for a case to be a "clear" one has been said by some writers of the American realist school of jurisprudence to be illusory. The radical realists argue that at least in a system of case law depending on precedents, a precedent cannot establish a rule of any ascertainable content. Therefore, it is said that any earlier case can have *any* meaning which the judge assigns to it.[16] We shall discuss this objection below when we discuss the role of precedents in our system of judicial decision-making. The second objection grants that there are "relatively precise" rules of law established by precedents which the judge can apply. However, it is argued that these rules

... can only be applied once the case has been characterized as being a member of the class controlled by a given rule. Thus, the decision reached in any particular case will depend not upon the particular rules of the legal system but rather upon the characterization which the judge makes of the particular fact situation. And ... since this process of characterization is not a logical or deductive process, it follows that the judge can characterize the fact situation any way he wishes in order to produce the desired result.[17]

Which of these arguments is true—Hart's linguistic theory that there are "core" cases which are unquestionably within the meaning of a given rule, or the radical realists' claim that every case requires the judge to characterize it as within or without the rule, a process which permits the judge complete freedom to decide the case either way as he chooses—is an empirical question. If there are in fact cases in which every trained lawyer would agree that the case is plainly within the meaning of the rule, then the radical realists' view cannot be accurate.

As we saw earlier, there indeed are such cases. Moreover, any complex society must be run by rules. Lawrence Friedman has stated the case persuasively:

If most of the operating ... rules of the legal system were not well settled ... many of the normal processes and activities of life that people carry on with reference to legal rules would be profoundly altered. In a complex social and economic system, a legal system on the model of law school appellate cases would be insupportable. There are strong needs to know what is lawful, for example, whether we are validly married if we go through certain forms ... We need to know the permissible ranges of speed. Moreover, in business affairs, we need to know that a deed in a certain form executed in a standard manner truly passes title to a piece of land. If every such transaction had to be channeled through a discretionary agency, the economic system could not survive in its present form. A market economy and a free society both impose upon the legal system a high demand for operational certainty in parts of the law which regulate important aspects of the conduct of everyday life and everyday business . . . [D]iscretionary rules are tolerable as operational realities only in those areas of law where the social order or the economy can afford the luxury of slow, individuated justice. If there is a social interest in the mass handling of transactions, a clear-cut framework of non-discretionary rules is vital.[18]

Trouble cases arise because either of the two conditions defining a "clear" case is missing. In the first place, there may be disagreement about the formulation of the rule of law. This disagreement may arise for a variety of reasons. It may arise because the applicable legal norm contains a word which is inherently vague, such as the statutes creating criminal negligence. In *Commonwealth v. Pierce*, [19] for example, the accused was a physician. Being called to attend a sick woman, he, with her consent, kept her in flannels soaked in kerosene for three days, as a result of which she died. The defendant honestly believed that the prescribed cure would be efficacious. Was he guilty of homicide by negligence? That depended on whether the construction of the word "negligence" which the court adopted required that the accused perceive that he was running a risk; and on that question, there was no clear precedent. (Judge O. W. Holmes held that there ought to be no such requirement and held Pierce guilty.)

Dispute over the applicable norm may also arise because, while the act at issue is plainly within the "core" meaning of the words used, the particular act appears to be outside the rationale of the rule. In *People v. Roberts*,[20] for example, the defendant's wife was incurably sick, suffering from multiple sclerosis. She was in great anguish, and desired to end her life. Defendant admitted that, at her request, he mixed a poison and placed it within her reach. She drank it and died. The statute classified murder by poison as murder in the first degree. Ought he be included within the statutory definition? (He was convicted of murder in the first degree and sentenced to life imprisonment.)

Another kind of trouble case arises when the content of the applicable rule is subject to doubt. In *Regina v. Kemp*,[21] for example, three doctors, from both sides, agreed that the accused had killed his wife while he was in a fit of melancholia during a temporary loss of consciousness arising from a physical disease, arteriosclerosis. The applicable common-law rule affecting insanity, which was formulated in *M'Naghten's Case*[22] in 1843, permits defense of insanity only on the ground that the accused was suffering from a "disease of the mind." Was a physical disease affecting the brain a "disease of the mind"? (The court held that it was.) In *Hotema v. United States*,[23] the accused believed in witches and that the Bible taught that one should not suffer a witch to live. He believed that the party he slew was a witch. The applicable common-law rule (also based on *M'Naghten's Case*) held that the defense of insanity was available if the accused was suffering from an insane delusion at the time of the killing. Was the belief in witches an "insane delusion"? (The Court held that if the belief was the result of investigation and belief in the Scriptures, and that he knew it was a violation of human law to kill witches, accused would be guilty; but if the belief was the product of a diseased mind, he would be not guilty by reason of insanity.)

The circumstances in which the rules themselves are vague may be cited almost unendingly. In addition to cases in which the rules themselves lack definition or clarity, however, are cases in which there is doubt as to whether a particular action falls within or without the "core" meaning of the words used. In *McBoyle v. United States*[24] the petitioner was convicted of transporting in interstate commerce an airplane that he knew had been stolen, and he appealed. The statute under which he was convicted, the National Motor Vehicle Theft Act of October, 1919, provided in part: "That when used in this Act: (a) the term 'motor vehicle' shall include any automobile, automobile truck, automobile wagon, motor cycle, or any other self-propelled vehicle not designed for running on rails." Was the stolen airplane included in the phrase "any other self-propelled vehicle not designed for running on rails"? (The Supreme Court held that it was not.) By comparison, in *Taylor v. Goodwin*,[25] the accused was charged under a statute forbidding furiously driving a bicycle. Was the bicycle included in the word "carriage"? (The court held that it was.) Judge Lush[26] concurred in the result. In the following year, Judge Lush held that for purposes of a taxing statute a bicycle was not a "carriage."[27] In these cases, the facts at issue fall within the penumbra of the words used, and a court must resolve whether to extend the core meaning of the word to include the facts at issue.

In any such "trouble" case, there is *ex hypothesi* no preexisting primary rule of law covering the case at hand. Instead, there is a dispute about what the appropriate rule may be. If there is no clearly applicable primary rule, the court is necessarily faced with the problem of choice: It must determine what the appropriate form and content of the rule is to be. Instead of discovering a preexisting norm, the court must actually create a norm. Its range of choice as to what the norm shall contain will usually be limited by the legal materials with which the court must work. Whatever the limitations, however, the choice of law in such a case is a creative act. It is in fact a legislative, i.e. law-making, act.

The same sort of judicial creativity occurs when a court has discovered that there exists a clearly articulated and well-understood legal rule, which arguably but not clearly subsumes the facts of the case at hand—the "penumbra" case. The choice which then faces the court may be viewed as one of whether the facts of the case are to be brought under the rule; i.e., it is a characterization problem. In such a case, the court is actually required to redefine the rule, for by determining that a particular state of facts is *clearly* within the rule, the court is enlarging the scope of the rule's core meaning. By enlarging its meaning, the court is in fact refashioning the rule. Thus, just as in the case where the rule itself is vague or ambiguous, the determination that the rule subsumes a particular set of facts within its penumbra requires the court to create a new rule of law. Again, although the scope of judicial creativity is limited by the received techniques, nevertheless the court is faced with the necessity of making a choice between alternative possible rules of law.[28]

That the court in any "trouble" case must fashion a new rule of law to govern the case at hand suggests an important truth: in every trouble case, the norm to which the actors are being held is formulated *after they have acted*. It is an *ex post facto* norm.[29]

The "clear" case and the "trouble" case therefore present very different problems to the judge. In the clear case, the judge must first discover some preexisting articulated legal rule, within whose core meaning fall the facts of the given case. In the trouble case, on the other hand, the judge must fashion a new rule *ex post facto*, which will simultaneously determine the cause at hand and govern future cases of similar nature.

We can now explain why it is that the process of *applying* rules necessarily involves courts in the process of *making* rules. So long as a case meets the conditions of a "clear" case, the court is indeed only applying the rules; i.e., it determines whether the facts of the case meet the conditions for the invocation of a sanction. If, however, the rule is not clear, or if the facts are not plainly within its core meaning, the court in deciding the case must devise a rule which will include the facts at hand within its core meaning.

7.5 APPELLATE COURTS AS A RULE-MAKING SYSTEM

A variety of materials go into a court decision: the legal material with which the court must work, the values it must take into account, the personality and background of the judge, etc. The court, takes all the "raw" materials and converts them by more or less determinate processes into rules or norms of law.

Thus viewed, appellate courts may be thought of as a rule-making system. Each court has certain inputs, which then go through a conversion process—the judge does something with them. The outputs are the rules that become the norms for the future conduct of citizens and judges. (See Fig. 7.1.) We shall examine in turn the inputs, the conversion processes, and the outputs of appellate courts.

The traditional myth is that the only significant input into the rule-making

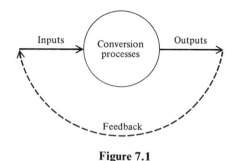

Figure 7.1

process is "the law." In fact, however, as we have already seen, appellate judges are in the business of formulating rules about how men ought to act in certain circumstances; indeed, they articulate the most formal and the most heavily sanctioned norms in society. What a decision-maker decides ought to be the case obviously depends, not only on the various notions of law and policy which are called to his attention, but on a variety of different influences, of which we mention six: (1) the way in which the issues are presented, (2) the sources of theory, (3) the personal attributes of the judge, (4) the professional socialization of the judge, (5) situational pressures on the judge, (6) organizational pressures on him, and (7) the alternative permissible rules of law.

Inputs: Issues

It is self-evident that most issues that call for decision by appellate courts are raised as a result of the choices made by individual litigants to bring the cases before the courts. Judges do not determine those choices. The result is that, on the whole, courts have been particularly active in rule-making in those areas of law which affect litigants who are sufficiently wealthy to be able to activate legal processes. For example, law books are full of cases detailing the rules with regard to the law of trusts. Trusts are a device by which wealthy people place money or property in charge of a responsible person (or, more frequently nowadays, a corporation) to be managed for the benefit of children, widows, or for charitable purposes. The corpus of trust law concerns the norms of conduct for trustees: what investments they may or may not make, what kinds of accounts they must keep, with whom they may deal, the exact line that demarcates fair dealing by trustees from frauds on their part on the beneficiaries, and so on. There are hundreds of appellate cases which define these rules with great detail and relative precision. Yet these cases affect numerically only the tiniest fraction of the population.

By contrast, there are many legal problems affecting the poor which never reach the courts, although the number of persons affected may be very large. Consider, for example, the problem of industrial insurance. As life insurance became an important element in our economic and social life, cases concerning it have come before the courts rather frequently, since most life insurance is carried by relatively affluent persons. Moreover, the amounts of money involved in these cases are frequently relatively substantial, making litigation concerning them ecnomically worthwhile. There is, however, a kind of life insurance called "industrial insurance," which is written in small principal amounts ($100 to $500). No medical examination is required. The premiums are likewise small, and since they are collected weekly, they frequently amount to no more than a few cents a week.

Because the amounts at issue are so small, very few cases concerning industrial insurance have ever reached appellate courts. As a result, the insurance policies tend to favor the insurance companies most unfairly. In 1934, Fuller wrote that there were warranties concerning the health of the insured:

> ... sufficiently inclusive to make most of the policies issued void if these warranties were taken literally... Many of the policies are so worded as to bind the companies to practically nothing. Not infrequently a large portion of the premium is paid for disability insurance *which is cancellable at any time by the company.*[30]

Nevertheless, these abuses have arisen, and, except in those rare instances where the legislature has intervened, they remain as widespread today as they were in 1934. Cases concerning them have simply not been in litigation. As a result, appellate courts have never had an opportunity to lay down rules to control the relationships created by insurance contracts of this sort. The insurance companies, the economically most powerful party to the contracts, largely remain in a position to determine unilaterally the conditions of the contracts.

Perhaps nowhere has the effect of economic constraint on the issues posed to courts for decision and clarification been more significant than in the area of criminal law. One example may suffice: the norms controlling the actions of police in the course of making arrests and interrogating criminal suspects. Proportionately, far more poor people than middle-class people are arrested or interrogated by police. Moreover, the police generally feel fewer restraints on them in treating the poor, for the poor tend to be politically powerless and hence are usually less capable of exerting unpleasant pressures on a policeman, if he treats them in ways not warranted by the norms which are supposed to guide a policeman or if he exercises his discretion in a way adverse to their interests.

As a result, most instances of police malpractice occur with respect to the poor. Only in very, very rare instances are these malpractices brought to the attention of the courts by poor people, for they lack the money to hire lawyers. As a result, if the definition of the norms regulating police conduct vis-à-vis persons suspected of crime depended solely on rules articulated by appellate courts in cases initiated and litigated to the appellate stage by poor persons themselves, the norms would remain vague and ill-defined.

There is one important ameliorating factor in this matter with respect (in recent years) to civil rights and civil liberties. A few private associations, nationwide in scope, have interested themselves in these areas, with respect to which they have acted as moral entrepreneurs. The National Association for the Advancement of Colored People for many years supported litigation affecting the civil rights of black citizens, no one of whom was likely to have been wealthy enough to finance the litigations. The roster of issues which the NAACP has litigated is very long indeed: the white primaries in the South, the provision of equal facilities for higher education, the requirement that juries be selected in a nondiscriminatory manner, the prevention of racial discrimination in interstate commerce, and, most far-reaching of all, the school desegregation cases.[31]

With respect to police practices, the American Civil Liberties Union has been particularly active. Indeed, it is not too much to say that the entire law of police practice has been created through the cases supported by the ACLU.

In recent years a large proportion (perhaps most) of the significant cases that have brought innovations in criminal law have been the result of interested groups serving as moral entrepreneurs to bring about changes in the law. In the preceding chapter we pointed out how law-enforcement agencies act in this capacity. More often than not, however, it is independent groups which have provided the necessary financial backing in bringing a case from lower courts to appellate courts. The important features of the processes are nonetheless the same: the law gets shaped by the efforts of moral entrepreneurs who for whatever reason (personal gain, high moral principle, etc.) are willing to expend the energy and money necessary to seek a change in the law.

This is not to say that appellate courts are altogether powerless to influence the kind of cases which come before them. One important formal exception is the United States Supreme Court's discretionary appellate jurisdiction, defined by means of the exercise of the ancient *writ of certiorari*. Since 1926 the Supreme Court has had the power to decide whether or not to accept most appeals. The statute extending this power to the Supreme Court was enacted because the docket of the Court was becoming seriously overloaded. It was believed that the Court's chief function was not to ensure that justice was done in individual disputes, but to resolve issues of law.

As a consequence of *certiorari*, the Court has at least a veto power over the selection of issues for determination. While it still cannot determine which issues will arise, it can prevent itself from deciding issues which in its opinion ought not be heard at the moment.

Appellate courts can also exercise significant influence over the sort of cases brought before them by the content of their opinions—which is a somewhat less formal, but nevertheless important procedure. The dissenting opinion may play a particularly important function in pointing out a legal path which might win a majority in the court. Such an opinion practically invites new litigation aimed at the point suggested by the dissent.

Inputs: Policy

Whence come the arguments which influence the decision of judges of the appellate courts? Here one must be careful not to assume that the arguments in question are the "real" or "true" determinant of judicial behavior. No doubt they are the overriding determinant in some cases; but many other elements also enter into the conversion process that transforms the inputs of problems, policies, personality, training and social pressures into specific decisions, and among these elements the policies and the arguments of the counsel supporting them are of course not insignificant.

One example of the importance of policies and the arguments in support of them may suffice. In 1860, the first case involving the so-called fellow-servant rule came to the Supreme Court of Wisconsin. The fellow-servant rule was an exception carved by the English common-law courts into the general rule that an employer is liable for the torts (negligent or intentional wrongs) of his employees acting in the course of their employment. For example, when an employee runs over someone in a truck on his employer's business, the employer is liable in damages, although he may be thousands of miles away from the scene. If, however, the person injured is also an employee of the employer, then the fellow-servant rule (in general) barred recovery. When this rule first came to the Wisconsin court, the judges refused to follow precedents from other states, on the ground that the rule lacked sound policy.[32] Two judges voted in favor of the rule, one judge abstained on jurisdictional grounds.

In the very next year, a similar case came before the Wisconsin Supreme Court.[33] Now the court reversed itself. The judge who had earlier abstained, and one of the two judges who had voted with the majority not to be bound by the fellow-servant rule, now voted to adhere to it. In reversing his position, Judge Dixon (who changed his vote) said in part:

In coming to this conclusion [i.e., that his vote ought to be changed] I have no words of apology to offer, and but few observations ... I recede more from that deference and respect which is always due to the enlightened and well considered opinions of others, than from any actual change in my own views. The judgment of a majority in [the first Wisconsin case on the fellow-servant rule] is sustained by weighty and powerful reasons. Like reasons are not wanting on the other side, and that side is sustained by the almost unanimous judgments of all the courts both of England and this country. I think I am bound to yield to this unbroken current of judicial opinion.[34]

The judge who changed his position, therefore, based this shift on deference to the opinions of other judges. This was a policy judgment. To the extent that judges pay deference to the opinions of other judges merely because of the weight of numbers arrayed against a given position, to that extent are idiosyncratic or arbitrary decisions avoided.

The source of this shift in the Wisconsin case can be traced quite distinctly in the brief of the counsel. In the earlier case, counsel for the railroad said only that "... If repeated decisions arising under almost every variety of circumstances can settle and determine the law, then the principle [the fellow-servant rule] cannot be disputed. It has been decided by the highest courts of England, New York, Pennsylvania, Illinois and South Carolina, and the decisions have been numerous ..."[35] In the later case, however, the same counsel for the railroad argued far more vigorously and at much greater length. We quote only a very small portion of the brief:

...The decision in [the earlier Wisconsin fellow-servant rule case] has the merit of standing alone ... We have supposed that when a question had been repeatedly before the Courts, and as often and as repeatedly decided, and the same principle affirmed, not only was it prima facie evidence of the law, but *conclusive* ... In every case in this country, or in England, where the question has been raised, the decision has been directly the reverse of the decision made by this Court! [Citing seven English and twenty-nine American decisions.]

... we submit that where there is found to be such a unanimous and unvarying amount of authority, that this Court ought to hesitate and ponder well before placing itself on record in opposition to all these Courts ... We do ask this Court ... to adhere to the maxim of the law, *stare decisis* [i.e., that precedent should be followed]. And we insist that even if the "reasoning" of some of the judges in giving their opinions is not entirely satisfactory to every member of this Court, that it is more in accordance with the maxims of the law for this Court to abide by former precedents *stare decisis* where the same points come again in litigation, as well to keep the sale of justice even and steady and not liable to waver with every new Judge's opinion, as also because the law in that case, being solemnly declared and determined, what before was uncertain and perhaps indifferent, is not become a permanent rule, which *it is not in the breast of any subsequent Judge to alter or swerve from, according to his own private judgment, but according to the known laws and customs of the land,*—NOT DELEGATED TO PRONOUNCE A NEW LAW, BUT TO MAINTAIN AND EXPOUND THE OLD ONE ... [36]

The arguments of the counsel in a case are, as the Wisconsin cases suggest, a principal source of the policy arguments used by appellate courts.

Not every lawyer, however, carries as much weight with a court as every other. In every court there are counsel who appear before it time and again, more frequently than not representing substantial clients. Judges come to respect some of these men and not others. It is predictable that the arguments of some well-known counsel will be accorded weight that will not be accorded to the arguments of lesser-known lawyers.

Not only are lawyers more or less well known and more or less persuasive, but the lower courts from which the cases come are more or less well respected. So also are the appellate courts whose decisions may be precedents for the cause at hand. In a classic study, Rodney L. Mott received ratings of the various State appellate courts from 259 law school professors. He also determined the relative frequency of cases from the several appellate courts which appeared in law school casebooks. In addition, indices were constructed of the number of times the opinions of the several State appellate courts were cited by other State courts, by the United States Supreme Court, and with approval by the United States Supreme Court. From these various indices he constructed a rank order of State Supreme Courts, which ranged from 25.18 for New York down to 2.12 for New Mexico.[37] Schubert points out that occasionally a higher court will even try to legitimize its opinion by trading on the reputation of a lower court judge,

... as did Chief Justice Vinson in a politically conservative opinion supporting a decision approving the conspiracy convictions ... of the leaders of the American Communist

Party.[38] Vinson attempted to advertise the position of the majority of the Court (for whom he spoke) as being really not illiberal, since the Supreme Court (as he pointed out) merely was approving the decision and supporting rationale that had been adopted in this very case by the Court of Appeals for the Second Circuit. That court had spoken, in turn, through no less august a personage than the great Learned Hand, author of *The Bill of Rights* and (both off and on the bench) of other reputedly liberal writings, and a federal judge whom most lawyers considered to be of much greater ability than all but a handful of the justices who have sat on the Supreme Court during the twentieth century.[39]

The opinions of other lower courts and the arguments of counsel are, of course, the formal inputs of policy arguments. There are a host of informal ones, however, of which the comments of law school professors are perhaps the most important. The relationship between leading law schools and appellate courts is close. Many justices, both of the federal and state appellate courts, choose their clerks from able young members of the graduating class of either their own law school or, if there is only one major law school in the state, from that. Most important of all are the law reviews. These journals constitute a unique institution, being the only major professional journals whose editors are students. In the cases of the major law reviews—those of Harvard, Yale, Columbia, Michigan, Wisconsin, and a few others—faculty control is quite literally nil. These reviews are the major forum for publishing the results of legal research, and their impact on the courts can be very great. For example, the arguments which justified the "one man, one vote" Supreme Court decision in the legislative redistricting case, *Baker v. Carr*, was first put forward in an article in the *Harvard Law Review*.[40]

The policy input deriving from the law schools is unique, for besides the personal attitudes of the judges themselves, it is the only important policy input which is independent both of the institution of the courts themselves and of the economic, moral, or personal interests of the litigants. Moreover, as we have seen, pragmatic decision-making requires empirical studies of the actual effect of the rules. Such studies, to the extent that they are in fact made, appear in the law reviews. The importance of these reviews is attested by the frequency with which they are cited as authority in appellate opinions.

Inputs: The Personal Characteristics of the Judges

Since in many of the trouble cases, the issue turns upon questions of value, it would seem that the personal characteristics of the judges are relevant. To understand properly why judges make the policy choices they do, it is necessary to examine these characteristics in three dimensions: first, their background as individuals; second, their background as lawyers; and third, their situation as appellate judges.

There are judges on many appellate levels in the United States. Our attention here is directed only toward the highest state and federal appellate judges. We shall direct our attention first at the characteristics of judges appointed to the

Supreme Court of the United States in the period 1933–1957. Some of these characteristics are suggested by Table 7.1. From this table (and further data of the same sort concerning all the Supreme Court justices in our history), Schmidhauser concludes that "Throughout American history there has been an overwhelming tendency for presidents to choose nominees for the Supreme Court from the socially advantaged families."[41]

TABLE 7.1   The personal attributes of the Justices appointed to the United States Supreme Court, 1933–1957*

Occupations of fathers	
High social status (proprietors, wealthy farmers, professional men)	13 (81%)
Low social status (mechanics and laborers, small farmers)	3 (19%)
Setting of birth	
United States	
Urban	6 (37.5%)
Small town	8 (50%)
Rural	1 (6.2%)
Europe (Austria)	1 (6.2%)
Ethnic origins	
Western European derivation	15 (93.7%)
Central, eastern, or southern European derivation	1 (6.3%)
Religious Affiliations	
High social status religious affiliations (Episcopalian, Presbyterian, Unitarian)	8 (50%)
Intermediate social status affiliations (Roman Catholic, Jewish)	3 (19%)
Low social status affiliations (Methodist, Baptist)	3 (19%)
"Protestant" (no other information available)	2 (13%)
Nonlegal educational background	
College or university of high standing	10 (61%)
College or university of average standing	4 (26%)
Academy or school of average standing (public or private)	2 (13%)
Legal education	
Law school of high standing	10 (61%)
Private apprenticeship and study under prominent lawyer or judge	1 (6%)
Law school of average standing	5 (32%)
Prior legal or professional experience	
Lawyers who were primarily politicians	10 (62%)
Lawyers who were primarily state or federal judges	1 (6%)
Corporation (primarily) lawyers	2 (13%)
Lawyers by education primarily engaged in academic pursuits	3 (19%)

* J. A. Schmidhauser, "The Justices of the Supreme Court: a collective portrait," *Midwest J. Pol. Sci.*, **3**, 1959, pp. 2–37, 40–49.

The degree to which these personal attributes condition judicial decision-making is rather more difficult to ascertain than the characteristics themselves. Statistically significant relationships have been established between certain personal characteristics and voting tendencies. For example, Nagel established that "Democratic judges were more prone to favor (1) the defense in criminal case, (2) administrative agencies in business regulation cases, (3) the private parties in cases involving the regulation of nonbusiness entities, (4) the claimants in unemployment compensation cases, (5) the libertarian position in free speech cases, (6) the finding of constitutional violation in criminal cases, (7) the government in tax cases, (8) the divorce seeker in divorce cases, (9) the wife in divorce settlement cases, (10) the tenant in landlord-tenant disputes, (11) the labor union in union-management cases, (12) the debtor in debt collection cases, (13) the consumer in sales of goods cases, (14) the injured party in motor vehicle accident cases, and (15) the employee in employee injury cases. Nine of these findings (1,2,4,6,7,10,13,14, and 15) proved to be statistically significant relationships"[42]

Whether these results can be construed to mean that a judge reaches his conclusions *because* he is a Democrat is, of course, subject to serious question. Grossman reports Bowen's finding that none of the variables most significantly associated with judicial decisions explains more than a fraction of the total variance among judges.[43] Grossman concludes that "mere tests of association are inadequate, though useful, and more powerful measures indicate the presence of other intervening variables, between the case and the ultimate decision."[44]

Inputs: The Socialization of Judges

The socialization of appellate judges can best be regarded as involving three stages: that of law student, that of practicing attorney, and that of lower court judge—the usual steps in a judicial career.

The American law school education is a classic example of an education in which the subject matter formally studied is ridiculously simple, but the process of socialization into the profession very difficult. Thurman Arnold once remarked of jurisprudence what is in many respects true as well of the formal part of the study of law. He said that jurisprudence is a tedious subject, tedious not in the way studying a difficult discipline like physics is tedious, but in the way tossing feathers into the air, hour after hour, is tedious. To the extent that the study of law is a study of the universe of norms alone, there is precious little about the law which would challenge a bright junior high school student. By their last year in law school, the better students, those on the law reviews for example, are getting reasonably good grades on the basis of a couple of days' study prior to end-of-term examinations.

The key to an understanding of the socialization of American lawyers in law school is best found through an examination of the outstanding aspect of their educational method, the case method of instruction.[45] Initiated by Langdell at Harvard in 1871, the case method has long since become the dominant form of instruction in every American law school.

This method, in its classic form, has two aspects that are important for our purposes. First, it purports to teach the norms of law by presenting the students, not with textbooks stating in black-letter type what the rules are, but with appellate opinions giving the facts of the cases, the decisions of the Court, and the reasons it gave to justify its opinions. Second, the case-study method is, at least in theory, teaching in the Socratic style.[46]

There can be no doubt that the case method is a thoroughly inefficient way to teach and to learn the rules of substantive law. Its functions are quite different. Two of these functions are especially important in connection with socialization. First, the constant dialogue between professor and students trains most students very rapidly to be tough-minded and independent in thought. At the beginning of the first year, if the professor said that black was white, most law students would carefully make a note of that proposition. By the end of the year, it sometimes seems that if the professor said that "one and one make two," somebody would ask, "Are there no exceptions?" That kind of hard-nosed, sharp questioning of everything is obviously the first essential both to competent counseling and to competent trial practice.

The second function of the case method as originally conceived is perhaps more subtle. The use of decided cases as the basic teaching materials and the concomitant exclusion of an examination of the law in action confines the questions asked to those raised in the cases. Questions that challenge the basis of the system as it exists are thus excluded, except insofar as an imaginative professor raises them. In the latter case, the very use of case materials demonstrates that he is raising an academic question, not an issue with which a hard-nosed, practical lawyer need be concerned.

For example, in times long ago, before automobiles, accidents between horse-drawn vehicles or between vehicles and pedestrians were decided on the basis of which rider or driver acted without due care. The care and skill of the rider of a horse, or that of the man who holds the reins of a stagecoach, plainly is the principal element in determining whether an accident occurs. When the vehicle involved no longer is so simple, but is an enormously complex automobile, traveling at speeds that convert it from an inert mass of metal into a highly dangerous projectile, the original design of the automobile and the design and condition of the roadway probably play an even greater part in determining accident occurrence than the skill of the drivers. Dominated by the perception of the problems derived from earlier cases, however, lawyers and judges have not until very recently begun to question the ancient way of defining the issue.

Hard-nosed independence is necessary if the system is to generate legal advisors who can advise competently, i.e. independently. More important, perhaps, is the necessity, for the continuance of the system, that lawyers and judges define the problems presented within the framework of the existing system. So long as they so define the problems, whether they take a "liberal" or "conservative" tack is relatively unimportant. The early socialization of judges and lawyers, thus, tends paradoxically to make them intellectually independent, but to restrain them from looking for radical solutions, for throughout their law school education they are taught to define problems in the way they have always been defined.[47]

The seeming paradox of intellectual independence combined with acceptance of the existing definition of the situation persists in later practice. The successful lawyer constantly sharpens his wits in situations of conflict. His whole professional career, however, necessarily requires him to take the institutions of American society at any moment as given. One advises a client to act in a particular way because he believes that the system as it is now structured requires him so to do.

Nevertheless, the successful lawyer tends to adopt conservative solutions for a second reason. If he is to be financially successful, his clients must be able to pay fees. In general, rich people and businessmen pay larger fees than poor people and wage earners. Successful lawyers represent successful clients. Inevitably, the successful lawyer, if not already attuned to the value-sets of his client, tends to adopt them.

The successful lawyer who becomes a judge tends to avoid advocating radical solutions for still a third reason. In America, one becomes a judge, in all except a tiny minority of instances, in part because he has been a political animal. The appointee to judgeship more likely than not has already served a period, as a young lawyer in the capacity of prosecutor, city councilman, or the like. He probably is a member on the local political club executive committee, or its analogue. He cannot successfully play the political game by rocking the boat.

The final stage in the socialization of the appellate judge is in most cases a period of time as a trial judge. Judges of all sorts, and trial judges even more than appellate judges, tend to be tied to the existing institutional structure by a myriad of strands of interest and interaction. On their favor turns the careers of many lawyers with whom they were schoolmates and have been professional colleagues, fellow soldiers in political wars, and friends, frequently for many years. It is a rare judge who adopts a value-set markedly different from those of his reference group.

The socialization of lawyers and judges in the past has, therefore, tended to make appellate judges tough-minded and independent people who define situations in ways conformable to the existing institutional structure. In addition, the reference group of most judges can be expected to induce him to select relatively conservative answers to the issues raised.

Inputs: Situational Factors

We recall that H. L. A. Hart asserts that the success of a legal system depends on the fact that judges have internalized the secondary rules which define their positions. Whether this assertion is completely true may be seriously questioned. Hart makes this assumption, however, because of the fact that there are few, if any, formal court-enforced sanctions to support the secondary rules. That is, of course, largely true. There are nevertheless a host of informal sanctions that tend to coerce the appellate judge, not only to conform to the secondary rules, but generally not to challenge the conservative values.

Judges, like everyone else, want increased status, power and privilege. The appellate judiciary is itself a career. The judge who is promoted to an intermediate State appellate bench may yet be promoted to the highest State Court. The judge of a Federal District Court may hope some day to be elevated to the Supreme Court of the United States. Judges cannot but be aware that their decisions will be a principal index used in their promotion. When Judge Burger of the United States Court of Appeals for the District of Columbia was promoted to Chief Justice of the United States, it was quite clear that his conservative stance in judging was a principal consideration in his promotion. Mr. Dooley long ago wrote that "The Supreme Court reads the illiction returns."[48]

Even apart from the potential reward of promotion, there are more immediate situational pressures which tend to make judges more, rather than less, conservative. Judges, especially appellate judges, hold possibly the highest status positions in society. They are invited to join the clubs of the highest elites, they socialize with the powerful and the rich, they meet political leaders at cocktail parties, at political rallies, and in clubhouses. Their power to influence events through informal but critical conversations is enormous. That power bears a direct relationship to their personal prestige among those with whom they socialize. A judge who is anxious to maintain his power in these informal groups cannot permit his opinions to deviate very far from the value-sets held by those with whom his web of life is so closely interwoven.

Finally, it is important to realize that there are other, illicit pressures operating on relatively wide scale on the trial court level, and they are not unknown on the appellate level. Occasionally charges of open corruption are made and sustained against judges. Even more pervasive is the effect of friendship, power, and influence. The young attorney who has tried cases in a local court against older, more established counsel, with a long history of close personal contacts with the trial judge, soon learns that where there is discretion to be exercised— and how pervasive is that discretionary power we have already suggested—it will not often be exercised in his favor.

All the ordinary situational factors tend to operate to ensure that judges will not be radicals. Still a different kind of pressure on the courts is the obvious, but often ignored, bureaucratic pressure of resource allocation.

Inputs: Organizational Interests

A salient characteristic of organizational behavior is that the ongoing policies and activities of organization are those designed to maximize rewards to and minimize strains on the organization. The system of courts is an organization, and it acts in accordance with the general principles applicable to all organizations. Leon Green has said that:

The policies which the courts most clearly articulate are those which concern the administration of the courts themselves. They hesitate to modify the law if the decision will "open the door to a flood of litigation," make it difficult to define definite limits of liability, require an investigation of factual details for which their processes are not well designed, make the re-examination of corollary or subsidiary principles necessary, or threaten to upset an established equilibrium in social conventions, trade practices or property transactions.[49]

We shall discuss two significant organizational pressures to which courts have responded: the volume of litigation and "crises."

The principal source of strain on the courts has been the constantly rising volume of litigation. In the early and middle nineteenth century, this tendency reflected the rising commercial activity of the country. Just as the courts were getting this matter under control through a variety of devices which we shall shortly discuss, there came a wave of litigation by employees against employers arising out of industrial accidents. Ultimately, this problem was largely taken out of the courts by the development of workmen's compensation commissions in the second decade of the twentieth century—just in time to clear a few dockets for the enormous flood of automobile accident cases that engulfed the courts in the nineteen twenties and which have remained the most frequent causes of legal action today.

Yet courts cannot increase their personnel or their physical plant easily. A court cannot expand out of "profits," or by adding a subsidiary or two to meet new problems. It does not control its own purse strings; and those who do have been notably slow in responding to its increased work loads.[50]

The contradiction between a rising volume of litigation and the lag in expanding court structures has been met in a variety of ways.[51] Outside the courtroom, businessmen found it in their interests to adopt form contracts and routine procedures to handle the mass of run-of-the-mill transactions. Once construed by a court, such routine transactions became less likely to soon again require judicial scrutiny.

The principal response, however, was that of the courts themselves. Repetitive, routine sorts of cases, for example, are handled in repetitive, routine ways that obviate formal hearings in most instances on the trial court level, and rarely raise issues for appeal. Most traffic fines are paid by mail, without even the formality of a court appearance.

The courts in fact approve real sanctions against those litigants who do not desire to take advantage of the routine responses. It is a rare parking or speeding offender who will litigate a case, even if he is convinced that he is not guilty, so time consuming are the court appearances required to determine the issues. As a result, only a miniscule percentage of the routine summonses issued ever give rise to any event which consumes a court's time.

Appellate courts have been quick to approve techniques which lower the pressure exerted by the volume of business. In most judicial systems, the Chief Justice is not only the chairman of the appellate bench, but also the chief administrative officer of the courts system. Frequently he and his fellow judges have instituted formalized pretrial conferences, which, although nominally designed to identify the issues, obtain agreement on exhibits, etc. prior to the trial, in fact are primarily glorified bargaining sessions between plaintiff and defense attorneys. In Connecticut, for example, pretrial sessions are held formally for one or two weeks twice a year. During this period all other work of the trial courts stops, and the judges engage in a massive effort to settle every lawsuit on the calendar awaiting trial. Insurance adjusters in automobile accident cases and plaintiffs themselves must be in attendance, so that if a settlement is reached between attorneys, the parties themselves can approve it.

In criminal matters also, appellate courts have been eager to sanction devices designed to reduce the load on the court system. They have frequently placed a stamp of approval on the negotiated plea, asserting that because it saves the State time and money (read: lessens the pressure of business on court dockets) it is a wise and useful device. As a consequence of this approval, over ninety percent of the cases handled in criminal courts are settled by negotiated pleas of guilty by the defendant. In a typical case, the defendant is charged with an offense but agrees to plead guilty to a less serious one to avoid a court trial and the possibility of being found guilty of the more serious charges. Courts encourage such negotiations in part by agreeing to "go along with" the recommended sentence of the prosecuting attorney, the sentence often being an integral part of the negotiation which has previously taken place. This we discuss at length in Chapter 19.

The changing judicial attitude toward arbitration is largely a reflection of the increased volume of judicial business. The earliest cases of arbitration were frowned on as attempts by private parties by contract to "oust the jurisdiction of the court." Responding to the demands of businessmen for quicker and cheaper forms of litigation, as well as to their own desires to reduce the impact of litigation upon the courts as a system, the courts have changed the rules until today not only is arbitration judicially favored, but as a matter of fact there are many more commercial arbitrations than there are commercial lawsuits.

The cost of litigation also has probably been a major factor in cutting down the volume of judicial business. The court fees themselves are relatively low. In many states, they have not changed for nearly a century, so that as little as fifty cents or a dollar may be all that is required in some cases. In other jurisdictions, however, fees may be substantial. Courts have been especially quick to raise the fees for jury trials in noncriminal cases, because that is a particularly slow method of adjudication. In some states, for example, the fee for a jury trial may be as much as sixty dollars or more.

The principal cost of litigation, however, is the cost of paying lawyers. First-class trial lawyers today receive two hundred dollars a day or even more for trial work; and trials can consume an unconscionable amount of time, for procedures are frequently complex, the methods of examining witnesses are slow and cumbersome, and the court calendar is shot with innumerable delays. Appeals are even more expensive, for there are substantial printing bills for briefs to be submitted to the court, and expensive research and writing to be done by counsel. Even so, however, the American system of costs is not so burdensome as the British system. In America, win, lose, or draw, each side usually pays its own counsel (there are a few exceptions). In England, on the other hand, the losing party must pay the fees, not only of his own lawyer, but of the opponent's lawyer as well—a most substantial disincentive to litigation and appeal.

The cost of litigation in commercial matters is, of course, only in part stated in the actual out-of-pocket expenses of court and counsel fees. Litigation is viewed by most businessmen as a hostile act. If a lawsuit is instituted, almost invariably the parties will not continue to do business. A businessman, therefore, will bring an action against a customer or supplier only when he believes that the benefits to be derived from the action will outweigh any hope of future business relationships.[52]

While cost sanctions effectively limit the use of legal process in most cases to those able to afford them, these sanctions typically do not operate very effectively with respect to the largest category of litigation today: automobile accident cases. This is so for two reasons. In the first place, the plaintiff and defendant in automobile accident cases only in the most rare instances have ever had any previous relationship, and do not usually perceive any benefit in maintaining future conditions of amity. The bringing of a lawsuit is not regarded by either as necessarily a hostile act; it is indifferent. The nominal defendant is rarely concerned, since the real defendant, who must pay the judgment, if any, is almost always an insurance company. So the sanction which probably more than any other reason inhibits litigation between businessmen and their customers rarely obtains.

Secondly, there has developed by lawyers' custom over the years a widely used device for paying plaintiff's lawyer's fees: the contingency fee. The lawyer agrees to render all the necessary services in a particular piece of potential or actual litigation in return for a portion of the ultimate return, whether by settlement or judgment. Fees run (as in New York) as high as 40% of the total recovery. If the case is unsuccessful, the lawyer gets nothing and indeed may be out of pocket for court costs. On the other hand, the potential return in most automobile accident cases is sufficiently certain to warrant lawyers who specialize in such claims to take the case of almost any person injured in an automobile accident.

Besides personal injury cases, however, poor people are frequently unable to pay for counsel and for litigation. In some areas, this has meant that the legal remedies theoretically available to everyone have remained a middle-class luxury. Divorce is one example. The standard legal fee for an uncontested divorce in most states is on the order of $300. A poor person cannot afford it. If he or she leaves the spouse, the situation usually remains ambiguous, cloudy, with one or both partners frequently living in adultery (with corresponding insecurity for potential children and susceptibility to criminal arrest) rather than regularizing the relationship with a divorce and a new marriage.

Various devices have been tried to make legal services available to the poor. The small-claims court was designed theoretically to provide a quick and cheap forum in which court processes would be made available, without the need for counsel, to persons making very small claims, which ordinarily would not warrant the cost of a lawyer. In fact, such courts have been used far more frequently by unsecured creditors such as doctors, lawyers, or businessmen to press charges *against* the poor rather than *for* them.[53]

A second method that has been devised is to make available to the poor legal services of certain particular agencies of the government with respect to certain particular recurring sorts of claims. For example, a wage claim by an employee is in most states prosecuted, not by the employee himself, but by the State Department of Labor. The Department first attempts to obtain the wages due by negotiation with the employer. This failing, the Department will most frequently bring a criminal prosecution against the employer for the offense of failing to pay wages when due, a statutory crime in most jurisdictions. Such criminal prosecutions are almost invariably settled by the employer paying the claims under threat of imprisonment if he does not. Similarly, State Departments of Welfare will frequently prosecute claims against husbands and fathers for the benefit of poor or destitute wives and children.

A third device has been the creation of new tribunals, entirely separate from the courts, to service the poor. The outstanding example in this regard, of course, is the Workmen's Compensation Commissions, to which has been turned over the great bulk of industrial accident litigation.

The remaining major area in which the poor are entangled in the law without real legal protection for reasons of costs in hiring attorneys has been the criminal law. This question we shall discuss later in connection with the question of poverty and enforcement of the criminal law.

In addition to these five general responses to the pressures of litigation, appellate courts have devised (or have been given by legislation) certain discretionary powers to decline to accept certain appeals. As we pointed out earlier, this power is most notable in the Supreme Court of the United States. That

Court has the power to decide for itself, on the whole, which appeals to accept for decision, and which to reject, by the granting of a *writ of certiorari*. Only if four Justices affirmatively vote to grant the writ will the Court hear an appeal. In this way, the Court can limit its decision-making to matters calling for significant rule-making: Constitutional issues, matters in which there is a conflict between the rules announced by different Courts of Appeal in the federal system, problems of statutory construction, and the like.

The increasing volume of litigation, therefore, has probably been the single most important variable in determining judicial responses. A second significant variable has been the court's recognition of "crisis" cases. Some cases present issues which are highly charged with political or moral significance. Like all decision-makers, in such instances courts tend to perceive a potential threat to their own legitimacy, for if their decision is not in fact enforced, their whole structure of authority may be undermined.

Such a situation was brought about by the question of legislative apportionment. Some states had for many years increasingly weighted the representation of urban dwellers against rural residency. Instances of complex and absurd gerrymandering were not infrequent. Numerous challenges were made to such imbalances by the initiation of lawsuits directed to the question, whether the equal protection clause of the United States Constitution forbade such gross discrimination. The Supreme Court for many years persistently declined to consider such cases, either by exercise of certiorari powers or by labeling the issue "political" and not "judicial." Finally, it did accept such a case (*Baker v. Carr*), and by deciding it in favor of the plaintiff, worked a major political realignment in the state governments whose effect is only just beginning to be felt.

Crisis cases, as Friedman has suggested,[54] are of two different kinds. Some, like the great Steel Seizure case,[55] are plainly nonrecurrent. Such crisis cases are not nearly so threatening to a court as cases involving deep-seated social conflicts, in which the court *must* in its decision advantage one side or the other. Courts tend to avoid such cases—the reapportionment cases are an excellent example—for as long as they can. When they do face up to the problem, they try to be unanimous (as the Supreme Court was in *Brown v. Board of Education*)[56] in order to legitimize the decision as heavily as possible. The rule is likely to be one whose administration can be delegated to other agencies. It will be as objective and as quantitative as possible, in an effort to end constant probing by litigants for its outermost boundaries. Since the simplest of all rules to administer is one which rejects the case and others like it completely, there is perhaps some tendency to solve crisis cases by rejecting any form of judicial interference.

Inputs: Permissible Rules of Law

As we have seen, the critical question in any trouble case is to formulate a controlling rule of law to govern the case at hand. Yet a court is sharply limited in the range of choice of potential major premises.

The leading—and all-important—rule limiting the range of choice by appellate courts of potential major premises to resolve the trouble case brought before them is that any premise which they adopt (and which therefore becomes a rule of law to control all similar cases in the future) must be "permissible." *It must be arguably consistent with some existing rule of law.*

Consider, for example, a Sudanese case, *Khartoum Municipal Council v. Cotran.*[57] The facts were as follows: In the exercise of powers granted under the Local Government Ordinance 1951 the defendant had dug a drain between $4\frac{1}{2}$ and 5 metres from the side of an unlit road in a residential area in Khartoum. The drain was uncovered, unlit and unguarded, but on the night in question, there was some dim light shed on it from nearby. The plaintiff, a district judge, and his companions arrived in the road by car to attend a party at a nearby embassy, and were obligated to leave the car about 150 yards from their destination. The plaintiff left the road in order to avoid a traffic jam and in attempting to take a short-cut, fell into the drain. As a result he suffered serious injuries to his left foot, involving surgery and considerable pain and suffering. In the event, he was left with a stiff painless foot amounting to a 70 percent loss of the use of the foot.

Under the English common law (which for these purposes we may assume was received in the Sudan), the court held that the defendant was under a duty to take reasonable care to protect the users of the street from the drain it had dug. (In so finding, the Court relied upon a whole gaggle of English precedents, ranging in time from 1842 to 1955). The Court then went on to discuss the standard of care required, and held that the municipality did not take reasonable care to protect the public. It made a judgment of about $5,500 in favor of the plaintiff.

The problem before the Sudanese court was really whether it was wise to expend $5,500 on a single individual who was injured by the local council's negligence. For example, if the money had been spent to hire two nursing sisters for a year, who might have saved the lives of a number of children who otherwise might have died, might it not be a more sensible use of the money? Yet the Sudanese court could not within the limits of the judicial process adopt such a solution. The existing law held that municipalities were under a duty to take reasonable care to protect the users of its street. Any major premises adopted by the court had to be consistent with this rule. So long as the English precedents were deemed applicable, it could not have held, for example, that municipalities were immune from such actions at law, even if in the African circumstance that had been the more sensible and socially useful rule.

Why this sharp limitation upon the creativity of a court in devising solutions to emergent problems? Courts in modern, complex, stratified societies have the primary function of settling disputes by winner-take-all—i.e., by rule-application. They are not primarily rule-creating organizations. The legislature is the primary formal law-maker in every modern country. A court's power to create law arises only incidentally out of its dispute-settling function. It can create law only when it *must* do so in the course of determining the major premise for the law-suit, an inevitable (if relatively infrequent) consequence of dispute-settling by way of norm-enforcement. That is to say, society's role-expectations for judges is that in the first instance, they will decide clear cases according to rules of law, and only when that is impossible will they be forced to create a rule of law to cover the case at hand.

Refer to Kelsen's triangular analysis of the position of courts (Fig. 2.1). In a clear case, a court occupies the position shown in the diagram. There is a norm, in its primary and secondary forms, which clearly subsumes the facts at hand. The court is expected to settle the dispute by applying the norm on a winner-take-all basis. The court is not expected to determine new law to resolve the dispute.

More: The Court's legitimacy depends to a great degree upon its ability to maintain the position that it is not creating law, but only applying it. One can accept the decision of an umpire far more easily if his decision appears to be *compelled* by rules over which he has no discretionary control.

In a trouble case, however, the position of a court is ambiguous. It still is a rule-applier. But it is also a law-maker, for any rule established in this case will be a rule for other similar cases in the future. It must act as a law-maker, while generally appearing to be only a law-applier.

Courts have historically resolved this ambiguity by limiting the scope of their law-making to that which they are *required* to do, and no more. They have achieved this limitation by restricting the range of potential major premises to those which arguably are consistent with existing rules of law. It is a limitation that arises not from choice, but from the imperatives of the court's ambiguous position in a trouble case as a dispute-settler in a system that settles disputes on the basis of winner-take-all and norm-enforcement but where the applicable rule is not clear.

What we can expect, therefore, is a set of rules of two sorts. First, there must be rules which tell a judge that a given rule is in fact an authoritative rule of law. Secondly, there must be rules which tell a judge in a trouble case that a proposed alternative major premise is in fact "permissible"—i.e., that it is arguably consistent with an authoritative rule of law. Since in a trouble case there are invariably at least two such permissible major premises, we must expect the rules in this second category to run at least in pairs, and still be equally authoritative.

In fact, the very nature of precedent suggests that the rules which control the use of a *single* case are susceptible of validating not a single rule, but several rules.[58] The rules of statutory construction run in contradictory pairs.[59] That they do is the best evidence that their function is not to decide cases, but to demonstrate that either of the potential rules of law urged by the opposing parties in a trouble case are at least arguably consistent with existing law. Their function is to demonstrate that the case is indeed a trouble case.

7.6 THE FUNCTIONS OF THE SEVERAL INPUTS

Outputs are a function of inputs and conversion processes. What is the function of these several inputs in limiting the output of appellate courts?

To answer this question, it is convenient to examine a popular paradigm of the process of valuation. As we have seen, every rule of law embodies a policy-choice. John Dewey proposed a model of social inquiry which purports to present a generalized description of the process of valuation. We shall examine that model, and then relate the several inputs to it.

Dewey's Paradigm of Social Inquiry

Dewey urged vigorously that the methods of inquiry that have proven so success-ful in science could and should be adapted to solving the question of what ought to be done. The aim of scientific inquiry, he said, is to discover a connected body of propositions, expressing knowledge about the real world, warranted by experi-mental data. The aim of social inquiry—of determining what ought to be done—is the discovery of propositions expressing knowledge of what ends are better to be achieved. To understand how Dewey proposed that the methods of acquiring knowledge of the first sort, which have been proven so spectacularly successful, might be used to acquire knowledge of the second sort, it is necessary to summarize his notion of inquiry.

"Inquiry," he said, "is the controlled or directed transformation of an in-determinate situation into one that is so determinate in its constituent distinctions and relations as to convert the elements of the original situation into a unified whole."[60] He maintained that the process of inquiry involved four main steps:

1 Inquiry is a response to an *indeterminate situation*. It is the situation itself, he holds, which is troubled, confused, ambiguous, and not merely our perception of it.

2 The first response to the indeterminate situation is to adjudge it to be a *prob-lematic* situation. The definition of the problem—which is a necessary step in perceiving the situation to be problematic—"decides what specific suggestions are entertained and which are dismissed; what data are selected and which rejected; it is the criterion for relevancy and irrelevancy of hypotheses and conceptual structures."[61]

3 The definition of the problem is necessarily a progressive inquiry, precisely be-cause "a problem well stated is on its way to solution."[62] How is the formation of a genuine problem so controlled that further inquiries will move toward a solution?

The first step is to determine the parameters of a given situation. On the cry of "Fire!" in a theater, it is well first to discover the location of the fire and of the exits. Any solution for the problem is apt to be limited by that information.

4 Based upon this preliminary inquiry of the existing constraints in the exis-tential situation, an idea about a possible solution is put forward tentatively. At first, these are merely in the form of suggestions that occur to us. "They may then become stimuli to direct an overt activity but as yet they have no logical status. Every idea originates as a suggestion, but not every suggestion is an idea. The suggestion becomes an idea when it is examined with reference to its functional fitness; its capacity as a means of resolving the given situation."[63]

The *suggestion* is developed into an *idea* through the process of *reasoning*. Reasoning involves the use of symbols (propositions), which are contrasted and compared with the body of accepted knowledge bearing upon the problem at hand.

5   The propositions (hypotheses) thus derived must be tested by a series of operations. It is central to this facet of inquiry that ideas and observed facts are *optional*.

Ideas are operational in that they instigate and direct further operations of observation; they are proposals and plans for acting upon existing conditions to bring new facts to light and to organize all the selected facts into a coherent whole.[64]

Facts are operational, too, in that the facts that are examined are selected and chosen because they are believed to be relevant to the inquiry—i.e., they will assist in a "statement of the problem involved in such a way that its material both indicates a meaning relevant to resolution of the difficulty and serves to test its worth and validity."[65]

Note that Dewey holds that reasoning alone (as he defines it) cannot itself determine whether an hypothesis is warranted. It can direct operations, but only those operations can act upon the indeterminate situation in order to resolve it:

The pre-cognitive unsettled situation can be settled only by modification of its constituents. Experimental operations change existing conditions. Reasoning, as such, can provide means for effecting the change in conditions but by itself cannot effect it. Only execution of existential operations directed by an idea in which ratiocination terminates can bring about the reordering of environing conditions required to produce a settled and unified situation.[66]

The process of social inquiry, he says, may differ in kind but not in principle from scientific inquiry. The central difference is that social inquiry is always involved in an historical situation, for in social inquiry conditions are never fixed.

That conditions are never completely fixed means that they are in process—that, in any case, they are moving toward the production of a state of affairs which is going to be different in *some* respect. The purpose of the operations of observation which differentiate conditions into obstructive factors and positive resources is precisely to indicate the intervening activities which will give the movement (and hence its consequences) a different form from what it would take if it were left to itself; that is, movement toward a proposed unified existential situation.[67]

6   Precisely because social inquiry necessarily concerns a dynamic historical

situation, the purposes of social inquiry *must* be concerned with *consequences*. Any sort of purported justification is silly, other than one phrased in terms of consequences: "Inquiry into social phenomena involves judgments of evaluation, for they can be understood only in terms of eventuations to which they are capable of moving."[68]

Moreover—and also precisely because a social situation is dynamic—it holds the potential of alternative possible ends in the sense of terminating consequences. Thus in social inquiry, to consider alternative modes of changing the existential situation requires the change-agent to consider alternative potential *ends* as well as alternative potential *means*. In any social inquiry, therefore, the ends and the means are alike indeterminate. Hence,

Evaluative judgments, judgments of better or worse about the means to be employed, material and procedural, are required. The evils of current social judgments of ends and policies arise . . . from importations of judgments of value from outside of inquiry. The evils spring from the fact that the values employed are not determined in and by the process of inquiry: for it is assumed that certain ends have an inherent value so unquestionable that they regulate and validate the means employed, instead of ends being determined on the basis of existing conditions as obstacles—resources. Social inquiry, in order to satisfy the conditions of scientific method, must judge certain objective consequences to be the end which is *worth* attaining under the given conditions. But, to repeat, this statement does not mean what it is so often said to mean: Namely, that ends and values can be assumed outside of scientific inquiry so that the latter is then confined to determination of means best calculated to arrive at the realization of such values. On the contrary, it means that ends in their capacity as values can be validly determined only on the basis of the tensions, obstructions and positive potentialities that are found, by controlled observation, to exist in the actual situation.[69]

The surrogate for experiment in the physical sciences is *deliberation*, or reflection upon potential consequences.

. . . . Deliberation is a dramatic rehearsal (in imagination) of various competing possible lines of action. . . . Deliberation is an experiment in finding out what the various lines of possible action are really like. . . .

. . . . All deliberation is a search for a way to act, not for a final terminus. . . .
Hence there is reasonable and unreasonable choice. The object thought of may simply stimulate some impulse or habit to a pitch of intensity which is temporarily irresistible. It then overrides all competitors and secures for itself the solid right of way. The object looms large in imagination; it swells to fill the field. It allows no room for alternatives; it absorbs us, enraptures us, carries us away, sweeps us off our feet by its own attractive forces. Then choice is arbitrary, unreasonable . . . Nothing is more extraordinary than the delicacy, promptness and ingenuity with which deliberation is capable of making eliminations and recombinations in projecting the course of a possible activity. To every shade of imagined circumstances there is a vibrating response; and to every complex situation a sensitiveness to its integrity, a feeling of whether it does justice to all facts, or overrides

some to the advantage of others. Decision is reasonable when deliberation is so conducted. There may be error in the result, but it comes from lack of data, not from ineptitude in handling them.[70]

7   Note that Dewey makes a sharp contrast between "reasoning" and "deliberation." Reasoning is the process of determining whether a particular proposed hypothesis is consistent with the existing body of propositions relating to the given subject-matter. Deliberation is the process of testing the proposed hypothesis in imagination against its potential consequences in activity. *Reasoning alone cannot warrant an hypothesis*. In the history of science, the Aristotelian method of medieval science started from broad generalizations, and purported to validate its propositions by a process of reasoning, demonstrating only that the proposed hypothesis was consistent with the broad generalizations that were taken as given. In modern science, that process is limited to the formulation of the hypothesis. The validation of the hypothesis can only be had through testing it against its consequences in activity. In the social sciences (in most cases), it can only be done in imagination through the process of deliberation. That deliberation will be successful insofar as it is grounded in adequate data on the existing situation, its constraint and resources, and its existing dynamic.

We can summarize by outlining the steps which Dewey urges embody the process of social inquiry:

1   The existence of an undeterminate situation in the real world.

2   The development of an awareness of a problem by the inquirer.

3   The exploration of the constraints and resources available for the solution of the problem.

4   Suggestions arise for the solution of the problem.

5   These suggestions are compared and tested against the body of knowledge concerning the general subject matter by a process of reasoning, and alternative potential courses of action are determined.

6   The probable consequences of these alternatives are viewed in the course of deliberation.

7   The ultimate warrant or proof of the appropriateness of the course of action occurs only when it is actually attempted and its relative success or failure is measured.

Choice and the Inputs to the Appellate Process

Dewey's model suggests that there are a variety of places in the process of inquiry and in the process of making judgments of value in which *selections* must be made, whether consciously or unconsciously. Not *all* indeterminate situations are recognized; not *all* the data defining the problematic situation will be gathered;

only a segment of *all* the potential solutions will occur as ideas; only *some* of the existing body of ideas concerning the subject will be canvassed; and so on.

What is it that determines which of the entire range of data and theories that might be considered are selected for examination? That is a very complex subject indeed, and one with which we shall be concerned at a number of different points in this volume.

One of the ways by which these various considerations are limited lies embedded in the institutional structure of the decision-making process. By that we mean this: In every real-life decision-making process—courts, Ministries, parliaments, executive officials, or what have you—there are rules which define which indeterminate situations are to be recognized and defined as problematic situations, what data are to be collected, what potential solutions may be considered, etc. These rules may act as filters or screens for the decision-maker, imposing on him a narrower range for selection than perhaps he might have wished, or they may act as an aid or guide, directing him to the parts of questions and data which the law-makers who created his position wanted him to take into account.

In examining any real-life decision-making process, there is yet another important input variable that we must consider. That is the value-sets of the decision-makers. For example, many perfectly well-meaning middle-class white Americans, brought up in urban environments, never perceived the black ghettoes as constituting an important social problem until the repeated eruptions of riot and violence there forced them to perceive the problem. In Dewey's vocabulary, they did not perceive the ghettoes and the endemic poverty there as a problematic situation. One can be quite sure that the blacks who lived in the ghettoes knew the conditions of their life were problematical. Why this blindness on the part of otherwise well-meaning, decent whites?

Plainly, there lies in each of us some sort of a mechanism that blocks off certain perceptions of data, theory or alternative potential hypotheses. These internalized filters apparently serve the same function in limiting the range of choice as do the institutional limitations we mentioned above. These internalized filters we shall call "value-sets" or, more simply, "values."

Institutionalized process and the values of the decision-makers combine to limit the inputs to every real-life decisional process. How do they structure the appellate judicial process?

The first steps in Dewey's paradigm, leading to the formulation of hypotheses for testing, are swallowed up by the rules defining the range of potential norms which a court may appropriately use to resolve a law-suit—i.e., the rules of precedent and statutory construction. These overriding institutional limitations restrict the scope for choice of judges to the range of molecular movement.

The values of the judges, and other limiting factors, such as the bureaucratic imperatives of the judicial system, come into play only after the range of choice has been limited by the institutional structure. How these factors operate in the conversion process we examine below.

Conclusion

The principal inputs into the rule-making processes of the appellate courts are issues, policies, the personal attributes of judges, their socialization, situational pressures, the organizational interests of the courts and the permissible rules of law. It is intriguing how these various inputs are necessarily biased in favor of ensuring that courts as institutions are more available to the wealthy than to the poor, and tend to produce solutions in the interests of the wealthy. The single most important variable would seem to be the high cost of litigation, for that one factor alone tends to have the consequences that the issues brought up for decision will be those in which the more advantaged in the community are interested and that the policies urged will be those urged by the more competent or better-known and respected counsel. There are, however, other significant factors pointing in the same direction. The recruitment policies for judges have historically resulted in selection from a thin upper slice of American society. While this factor is not conclusive in determining the outcome of individual cases, it does seem to make the overall policy output of courts politically conservative. The techniques of socialization of judges tend to have the same effect, and their educational and professional experience tend to ensure that judges are loyal adherents to the status quo. The organizational interests of the courts also, especially that of restricting the amount of litigation, tend to restrict litigation to the well-to-do. Perhaps most important of all, the system of precedents and statutory construction limits the choice of judges to relatively small changes in the existing system.

We can generalize our argument in a set of propositions:

1 Every decision-making structure necessarily limits the range of potential inputs with respect to the problems to be considered, the potential hypotheses for their solution, and the data to be examined.

2 By these limitations, decision-making structures necessarily predetermine the range of potential outputs.

3 Every decision-making structure is therefore necessarily biased against a particular set of potential outputs, and in favor of another set of potential outputs.

4 Therefore, every decision-making structure is necessarily value-loaded; it cannot be value-neutral.

These are the inputs for the appellate judges who must respond to the issues by formulating new rules to solve the problems posed. We turn in the next chapter to a consideration of how, given the inputs, the judges and the courts proceed with the "conversion processes," that is the processes which characterize the manipulation of the inputs and which culminate in decisions.

NOTES

1. A. V. Dicey, *Introduction to the Study of the Law of the Constitution*, Macmillan, London, 1959.

2. *Ibid.*, p. 188.

3. Friedrich von Hayek, *The Road to Serfdom*, University of Chicago Press, Chicago, 1944.

4. *Ibid.*, p. 72.

5. Wolfgang Friedmann, *Legal Theory*, Stevens, London, 1967, p. 228.

6. Hans Kelsen, *The Pure Theory of Law*, M. Knight (tr.), University of California Press, Berkeley, 1967, p. 285; translated from the first edition, 1930. Originally published by the University of California Press; reprinted by permission of The Regents of the University of California.

7. *Ibid.*, p. 286. Reprinted by permission.

8. H. L. A. Hart, *The Concept of Law*, Clarendon Press, Oxford, 1961, p. 13. Reprinted by permission of the Clarendon Press.

9. Kelsen, *op. cit.*, p. 7. Reprinted by permission.

10. *Supra*, pp. 11–12; 80–81.

11. Hart, *op. cit.*, p. 111. Reprinted by permission.

12. *Ibid.*, p. 112. Reprinted by permission.

13. *Supra*, p. 80.

14. O. W. Holmes, "The path of the law," *Harvard Law Rev.* **10**, 1897, pp. 457, 458.

15. Cf. Hart, *op. cit.*, pp. 120–132.

16. H. Oliphant, "A return to stare decisis," *A. B. A. J.*, **14**, pp. 71–73.

17. Richard A. Wasserstrom, *The Judicial Decision: Toward a Theory of Logical Justification*, Stanford University Press, Palo Alto, Calif., 1961, p. 19. Reprinted by permission. See also Max Radin, *Law as Logic and Experience*, Yale University Press, New Haven, Conn., 1940, p. 51; H. Oliphant, *op. cit.*, pp. 72–73; Jerome Frank, *Law and the Modern Mind*, Tudor, New York, 1936, p. 268n ("in a profound sense, the unique circumstances of almost any case make it an 'unprovided' case").

18. Lawrence Friedman, "Legal rules and the process of social change," *Stanford Law Rev.* **19**, April 1967, pp. 786–840 at 792. Reprinted by permission.

19. 138 Mass. 165, 52 Am. Rep. 264 (1884).

20. 211 Mich. 187, 178 N.W. 690 (1920).

21. [1957] 1 Q.B. 399, England.

22. 10 C.L.&.F 200 (1843); 8 E.R. 718, House of Lords, England.

23. 186 U.S. 413, 22 S.Ct. 895, 46 L. Ed. 1225 (1901).

24. 283 U.S. 25, 51 S. Ct. 340, 75 L. Ed. 816 (1931).

25. 4 Q.B.D. 228, England (1879).

26. This is *not* a pseudonym.

27. *William v. Ellis*, 5 Q.B.D. 175, England (1880).

28. See R. B. Seidman, "The judicial process reconsidered in light of role theory," *Mod. Law Rev.* **32**, 1969, p. 516.

29. *Ibid.*, p. 523.

30. Lon Fuller, "American legal realism," *U. Pa. Law Rev.*, **82**, 1934, pp. 429, 439n.

31. *Brown v. Board of Education*, 347 U.S. 483 (1954). This was the monumental Supreme Court decision stating that separate or segregated schools were not and could not be equal.

32. *Chamberlain v. Milwaukee and Mississippi Railroad Co.*, 11 Wis. 248 (1860).

33. *Moseley v. Chamberlain*, 18 Wis. 700 (1861).

34. Quoted in C. Auerbach, L. K. Garrison, W. Hurst, and S. Mermin, *The Legal Process: An Introduction to Decision-Making by Judicial, Legislative, Executive, and Administrative Agencies*, Chandler, San Francisco, 1961, pp. 159–161.

35. *Ibid.*

36. *Ibid.*

37. Rodney L. Mott, "Judicial influence," *Am. Pol. Sci. Rev.* **30**, 1936, pp. 295–315.

38. *Dennis v. United States*, 341 U.S. 494, 510 (1951).

39. From *Judicial Policy Making* by Glendon Schubert, p. 110. Copyright © 1965 by Scott, Foresman and Company. Used by permission.

40. A. Lewis, "Legislative apportionment and the federal courts," *Harvard Law Rev.* **71**, 1959, 1057–1098.

41. J. A. Schmidhauser, "The Justices of the Supreme Court: a collective portrait," *Midwest J. Pol. Sci.* **3**, 1959, pp. 2–27, 40–49.

42. J. Grossman, "Political party affiliation and the selection: judges' decisions," *Am. Pol. Sci. Rev.* **55**, 1961, p. 843. Reprinted by permission.

43. R. Bowen, "The explanation of judicial voting behavior from sociological characteristics of judges," unpublished Ph.D. dissertation, Yale University, 1965.

44. J. Grossman, "Social backgrounds and judicial decision-making," *Harvard Law Rev.*, **79**, 1966, pp. 1551–1563.

45. See J. W. Hurst, *The Growth of American Law: The Law Makers*, Little, Brown, Boston, 1950, pp. 256–276.

46. A. P. Blaustein and C. O. Porter, *The American Lawyer*, University of Chicago Press, Chicago, 1954, p. 167.

47. We shall see later that a strange sea change, originated by the American realists, is afoot in the legal world. The essence of the realist movement is to examine, not

only the law in the books, but also the law in action—the way in which the role-occupant actually performs, as well as the way in which he is expected to perform. The confrontation of the pious hopes of American law, with all its high-flown phrases, by the gross reality of the poor, the black, and the Vietnam War, has tended to force many American law students to define the situation in terms of reality rather than the categories received from the conventional wisdom expressed in decided cases. What effect this change will have on the average practicing lawyer remains to be seen. It is sufficient to note here that American law students, in numbers which seem to increase geometrically from year to year, are opting for service programs for their first employment after law school rather than more lucrative private practice.

48. "Mr. Dooley" was the pseudonym of Finley Peter Dunne, a newspaper columnist. E. J. Brander (ed.), *Mr. Dooley and the Choice of Law*, Michie, Charlottesville, Va., 1963, p. 52.

49. Leon Green, "The study and teaching of tort law," *Texas Law Rev.*, **34**, 1956, p. 16. Reprinted by permission.

50. Lawrence Friedman, "Legal rules and the process of social change," Stanford Law *Rev.*, **19**, 1967, pp. 786, 798–799.

51. See generally L. Friedman, *op. cit.*, *passim*, from which this discussion is drawn.

52. See S. Macauley, "Non-contractual relations in business: a preliminary study," *Am. Soc. Rev.* **28**, 1963, p. 55.

53. See I. J. Rapson, "The Dane County small claims court," unpublished thesis in the University of Wisconsin library, 1961.

54. L. Friedman, *op. cit.*, p. 808.

55. *Youngstown Sheet and Tube Co. v. Sawyer*, 343 U.S. 579 (1952).

56. 347 U.S. 483 (1954).

57. (1958) Sud. L. J. R. 85

58. *Infra*, pp. 122–124.

59. *Infra*, p. 125.

60. John Dewey, *Logic, The Theory of Inquiry*, Holt, New York, 1938, pp. 104–105. Excerpts cited in notes 60–69 reprinted by permission of Holt, Rinehart and Winston, Inc.

61. *Ibid.*, p. 108.

62. *Ibid.*

63. *Ibid.*, p. 110.

64. *Ibid.*, pp. 112–113.

65. *Ibid.*

66. *Ibid.*, p. 118.

67. *Ibid.*, p. 500.

68. *Ibid.*, p. 502.

69. *Ibid.*, p. 503.

70. John Dewey, *Human Nature and Conduct: An Introduction to Social Psychology*, Holt, New York, 1922, pp. 190–194.

8

Conversion processes in appellate courts

The inputs discussed in the preceding chapter are converted into decisions by appellate courts. To understand this process of conversion, we must consider two of its principal features. One is the formal reasoning process that judges are supposed to go through in justifying their decision. This process is describable in terms of the norms defining the judge's role in decision-making, and has been the subject probably of more jurisprudential writing than any other single aspect of the legal process. The other is informal: the effect of small-group interactions taking place within the collegiate body of an appellate bench. We shall discuss each of these processes in turn.

8.1 THE NORMS AND PRACTICE OF JUDICAL DECISION-MAKING IN APPELLATE COURTS

To laymen and law professors alike, many American courts seem to fail to adhere to the norms for their position, or to achieve its goals. The layman who rails at the Supreme Court for "legislating" and not "judging" implies that his role-expectation for the court demands that it "find" the preexisting law, and apply it to the facts of the case at hand. The law professor, on the other hand, can easily demonstrate that when an appellate court purports to have found the law, it usually has in fact made a policy judgment, accompanied by unexpressed premises, illicit inferences, and "inevitable" conclusions that are by no means inevitable.

In short, both the layman and the law professor regard judges as deviating from their proper role, although for very different reasons. Why this paradox?

Decisions and Opinions

If one were to believe that judicial opinions describe the process by which decisions are reached, he would be believing that judges are indeed the most patient of men, who carefully and step by step proceed from premises and facts to conclusion. Perhaps some men so organize their thinking. Many, perhaps most, do not. Many judges have told us that in reaching a decision, the conclusion comes in a flash of understanding. Jerome Frank quotes Judge Hutcheson:

He tells us that after canvassing all the available material at his command and duly cogitating on it, he gives his imagination play, and brooding over the cause, waits for the feeling, the hunch—that intuitive flash of understanding that makes the jump-spark connection between question and decision and at the point where the path is darkest for judicial feet, sets its light along the way ... The judge really decides by feeling and not by judgment, by hunching and not by ratiocination, such ratiocination appearing only in the opinion. The vital motivating impulse for the decision is an intuitive sense of what is right or wrong in the particular case; and the astute judge, having so decided, enlists his every faculty and belabors his laggard mind, not only to justify the intuition to himself, but to make it pass muster with his critics.[1]

As a psychological process, however, it has been denied that rules play no importance in the process of decision-making. Edwin W. Patterson probably summed up the matter as well as it could be when he said that:

... judges do not, it seems, formulate complete syllogisms, and the judicial stream of consciousness, one may venture to suppose, contains a good deal of nonlegal flotsam and jetsam. Men are not transformed psychically when they don judicial robes, but they are transformed morally, i.e., in their dominant loyalties. Some judges decide on the whole case first and then proceed to the analysis of reasons; others by analysis build slowly toward a decision. The flash of insight that brings conviction may occur in an instant; yet the preparatory steps are none the less important.[2]

Far more significant than the psychological process by which a decision is reached is the way in which the decision is legitimized. The opinion plays the central role in this process. Opinions sometimes are dismissed by the claim that they are mere rationalizations of previously determined decisions; that they are merely cynical and fictitious statements of how the judge arrived at his decisions.

Whether they are true statements of how judges reach their decisions or not, they do serve the legitimization function and must be understood in that context.

Why is legitimization important to a court, especially an appellate court? Weber has shown that if the norms of an organization are enforced by naked power alone, the subjects are alienated while conforming to these norms. Better by far that a subject conform to the norms established by officials higher in the hierarchy because he believes it is right and proper that he do so. That is to say, if the norms of conduct laid down by higher authority for the conduct of subjects can be shown to be congruent with the values of the subjects, then the latter will find the orders legitimate and will obey without the threat of coercive force. Weber used the word *authority* to refer to power that is viewed as legitimate.

As we saw earlier, the primary rules created and articulated by an appellate court prescribe the conduct of both citizens and judges; to the extent that opinions create secondary rules, they prescribe only the actions of judges. Laymen do not usually read judicial opinions, which must therefore, be addressed, primarily to other judges and to lawyers, to legitimize the decision in their eyes.

But why need appellate judges legitimize their decisions in the eyes of other judges and lawyers? Would it not be enough merely for the appellate courts to announce their decisions? Perhaps the answer is to be found in the fact that typically there are no sanctions for a lower court's erroneous behavior other than reversal upon appeal. The attitude of the public toward the laws is relatively indifferent; an ordinary citizen may internalize the norms, or he may obey merely because it is less unpleasant to obey than to defy the rules.

But this merely personal concern with the rules, which is all the ordinary citizen *may* have in obeying them, cannot characterize the attitude of the courts to the rules with which they operate as courts ... Individual courts of the system though they may, on occasion, deviate from these rules must, in general, be critically concerned with such deviations as lapses from standards, which are essentially common or public. This is not merely a matter of the efficiency or health of the legal system, but is logically a necessary condition of our ability to speak of the existence of a single legal system. If only some of the judges acted "for their part only" on the footing that what the Queen in Parliament enacts is law, and made no criticisms of those who did not respect this rule of recognition, the characteristic unity and continuity of a legal system would have disappeared. For this depends on the acceptance, at this crucial point, of common standards of legal validity ...[3]

The "characteristic unity and continuity" of a legal system which Hart mentions is not automatically won by the mere existence of a hierarchy of courts and secondary rules. Appellate courts must persuade lower courts to adhere to the authoritative rulings laid down.[3a] Lower courts can construe decisions of higher courts creatively, or woodenly. Some federal courts, for example, have been notable in their willingness to advance the desegregation decisions in ways apt to accomplish desegregation. Others have followed the Supreme Court's lead in so wooden, formalistic, and grudging way as to amount to something very close to outright sabotage.

In short, the problem for the appellate court is to ensure that its decision is perceived by lower court judges as congruent to their own values. They must legitimize their decisions. Unless they do, their is no assurance that the new rules announced will be effective.

Opinions have other (hidden) consequences. In order to justify a decision to others, the judge must test his preliminary hypothesis about the case to see if he can construct an argument which will legitimize the decision in the eyes of other judges and lawyers. As Jerome Frank said, "Judging of all sorts begins with a conclusion more or less vaguely formed; a man ordinarily starts with such a conclusion and afterwards tries to find premises which will substantiate it. If he cannot, to his satisfaction, find proper arguments, . . . he will, unless he is arbitrary or mad, reject the conclusion and seek another."[4] The result is that the requirement of an opinion is a guarantee that judges will test their decisions by forcing themselves to justify them. There are other reasons as well.

During an 1879 debate on the article of the California Constitution requiring written opinions from judges, a delegate said:

The importance of requiring the Court to give written opinions cannot be overrated. They not only become the settled law of the State, and are precedents for subsequent cases, but in many cases where the litigation is not ended by the decision of the Supreme Court, and new trials are consequent upon a reversal, the decision of the Supreme Court should be given in writing, and reasons assigned, for they are instructions to the Court below, and are the controlling rule in the subsequent litigation . . . Undoubtedly it [the requirement that there be written opinions] will . . . result in well considered opinions, because they must come before the jurists of the country and be subjected to the severest criticism . . . It tends to purity and honesty in the administration of Justice.[5]

For all these reasons, it is a general custom, now enshrined in some State constitutions and in the Canons of Judicial Ethics of the American Bar Association, that written opinions shall ordinarily be rendered by appellate judges, thus continuing what Edmund Burke held to be the law of the land in England in 1816: "Your Committee do not find any positive law which binds the judges in the courts in Westminster-hall publicly to give a reasoned opinion from the bench, in support of their judgment upon matters that are stated before them. But the course hath prevailed from the oldest times. It hath been so general and so uniform, that it must be considered as the law of the land."[6]

Opinions, therefore, do not even purport to reproduce the processes of reasoning which led to the decision. They do something even more important: they purport to legitimize or justify the decision in terms which the deciding judge believes will be persuasive to his fellow judges and lawyers. *The reasons they embody can best be understood, therefore, as evidence of contemporary notions of what justifies a decision creating a legal norm.* Before we can examine these changing judicial styles, however, we must first analyze how trouble cases are presented to an appellate court, for only then can we comprehend the problem with which the various period styles had to deal.

The Clear Case Rules of Recognition

As we saw above, fact situations present two sorts of cases for decision: clear cases and trouble cases. The first essential condition of the clear case is that there is a preexisting rule of law which is applicable to the facts of the case at hand. The *rules of recognition* appropriate for the clear case must, therefore, be rules which direct the judge and counsel to the appropriate *existing* rule. What are these clear-case rules of recognition—i.e., what are the norms of decision-making which judges must follow to locate the correct rule?

With respect to statutes, these rules are quite clear. Which statutes are valid and existent can in practically all cases be determined by reference to some clearly articulated standard (e.g., that they have been promulgated by the Secretary of State under his seal). The clear case requires only one rule of statutory construction: The judge must start and end with the words used in the statute (with the proviso we mentioned earlier, that the words be understood in their proper context). If the statute is on its face ambiguous—i.e., if the facts at hand are not plainly either within its core meaning or outside the penumbra—it is not a clear case; nor is it a clear case if the statute contradicts some other statute which might also be relevant to the case at hand.

The reason for the rule just mentioned seems to be embedded in deeply felt notions which in Anglo-American legal philosophy ultimately find their source in the reforming efforts of Jeremy Bentham and the Utilitarians, and before them, in the Enlightenment itself. Bentham held that the ends of the civil law ought to be security, subsistence, abundance, and equality; and of these, the greatest is security. The first requirement of security in the law is that it be, in Bentham's word, "cognoscible," i.e., in a form capable of being readily understood by the layman. It is a necessary corollary that judges construe statutes as they would be understood by the layman, i.e., taken on their face meaning. As Roscoe Pound has said concerning codification:

It [the demand for codification of the common law] is a form of the demand for a complete, intelligible, authoritative statement of the precept governing individual relations and individual conduct. It is a phase of the demand that every man shall be assured of knowing what he may do and what he may not do. It is related to the idea behind our bill of rights. It is part of the quest for a government of laws and not of men; it is part of the claim that men be assured that the magistrate shall regulate their conduct and adjust their relations according to pre-established law and not in accordance with his more or less arbitrary will. It has to do with an important aspect of the social interest in the general security in that it is one means of excluding the personal element in the administration of justice and thus of insuring uniformity, equality, and certainty. Indeed, the idea of a written law is urged not to assure these things, but in order to make the lay public believe that they are assured.[7]

The very nature of precedents makes it difficult to derive clear norms from them with as much precision as one can from a statute. This may be explained by example. Suppose that a father wishes to teach his son to remove his hat when inside a church. He may tell him in so many words, which is to give him a rule analogous to a statutory norm. On the other hand, he may choose to teach him by example. He therefore takes his son to the church and, without saying a word, removes his own hat. What inferences can the son draw from this example? That hats are removed (a) every Sunday when indoors, (b) whenever indoors, (c) inside a church on Sunday, (d) whenever inside a church, (e) whenever inside the Episcopalian Church at Twelfth Street and Capitol Avenue on Sunday, March 19, 1967 . . .? The number of possible inferences is not limitless, but nevertheless very great indeed. Each potential rule is based on generalizing from a different set of facts. Thus, the potential rule that hats are removed inside a church on Sunday identifies three facts as material: (1) removal of hats; (2) being inside a church; (3) on Sunday. On the other hand, it is possible to regard every fact so far mentioned as relevant, in which case we get the rule that hats are removed whenever inside the Episcopalian Church at Twelfth Street and Capitol Avenue on Sunday, March 19.

It is impossible to determine which of these potential rules is the rule to be applied in a future case on the basis of the example alone. Rather, it is not until there are a number of similar examples that the boy can infer which is the correct rule. For example, if he observes that his father enters other buildings on Sundays without removing his hat, he must infer that being inside a church is a material fact; on the other hand, if he observes that his father removes his hat when entering the Methodist Church, he will infer that the denomination of the church is immaterial.[8] It is therefore unlikely that one can determine from a single precedent what rule is properly to be inferred from it; the only rule that one can be sure can be drawn from the single case is a rule which generalizes from *every* fact stated in the precedent case.

Despite the inherent vagueness of precedent as compared with statute, there are many case-law rules of substantive law so thoroughly embedded in our jurisprudence that lawyers and judges have little difficulty in agreeing on their content. It is this agreement which accounts for the fact that the general run of cases raise no issue of law, but only issues of fact. This agreement is possible because judges and lawyers are agreed on the norms by which judges discover the rules established by precedents in clear cases.

As in the case of statutes, the clear-case rules of precedent are clearly put and commonly understood. There is one set of rules which determine the relative authority of a precedent, analogous to the rules that determine whether a statute is valid. These rules tell the lawyer or the judge whether the precedent comes from a court above the deciding court in the hierarchy of authority, and whether the report of the judge's opinion is an accurate and authoritative one. Also, just as there is but a single clear-case rule with respect to the construction of statutes, so there is but a single clear-case rule with respect to the inferences to be drawn from precedents: A precedent case cannot stand for any rule that is not necessary to the decision of the case.

This rule is a necessary concomitant of the institutional structure and function of courts which imposes three main requirements upon them:

1 *The court must decide the dispute that is before it.* Courts are the ultimate dispute-deciders and norm-enforcers in the society. A court cannot, therefore, avoid deciding a case (in most instances) because the job is hard, or dubious, or dangerous.

2 *The court may decide only the particular dispute before it.* The requirement that parties whose interests are at issue must be heard before judgment, a necessary aspect of the adversary proceeding, forbids courts from deciding a case not before it.

3 *The court may decide the particular dispute only according to a general rule which covers a whole class of like disputes.* As we saw earlier in our discussion of primitive law and the emergence of rule-application as the goal of dispute-settlement process (rather than the earlier goal of mediation or compromise), modern law is marked by the notion that disputes are to be settled by reference to general rules. This attitude is buttressed by the impact of the doctrines of natural law, to which our legal ancestors paid deference for many centuries and which also suggests that all men are subject to the same rule. It is further reinforced by the democratic ideology that laws (rules) are to be made by the legislature, and that the courts are then bound to apply these general rules in deciding cases.[9]

It follows, therefore, from the very position and function of the courts in society as dispute-settlers and rule-enforcers, that a judicial decision is legitimate only insofar as it refers to the dispute immediately before it. Hence the central rule of recognition with respect to inferring from an opinion or decision the rule which the court has applied: *A precedent case cannot stand for any rule that is not necessary to the decision of the case.*

Today, many cases involve not merely either the clear-case rule of recognition for statutes, or the clear-case rule of recognition for case law, but rather a combination of the two. Statutes have an open texture. If in the past a statute was construed in a precedent case, its meaning can be understood only in the light of the precedent case. Thus, *to decide a succeeding case, a court will have to consider, not only the statute, but also the precedents which construe it.*

These, then, are the clear-case rules of recognition. They presuppose that rules of law which clearly subsume the facts of the present case preexist the case.

The name for these rules (which comes from Professor Hart) implies this condition; the purpose of the rules is to enable the judge and lawyers to "recognize" the primary norm which is applicable to the case at hand.

The Trouble-Case Rules of Decision

Both the lay and professorial criticisms of appellate courts arise with respect to trouble cases—the only cases to reach appellate courts ordinarily, since only trouble cases raise genuine issues of law. The reason that laymen and law professors disagree in their estimates of judicial deviancy is that they hold to different role-expectations for appellate judges.

To explain why laymen tend to have different role-expectations for judges than most American law professors requires a brief excursion into the history and development of the systems of justification of decisions as exemplified by judicial opinions.

In a trouble case, the essential conditions for a clear case are missing. There is no clearly articulated rule preexisting the given case which plainly subsumes the facts of the case at hand. The application of the clear-case rules of recognition, therefore, ends by revealing ambiguity rather than certainty. To resolve this ambiguity, Anglo-American courts have adopted different ways to legitimize their decisions in the opinions. Llewellyn calls these the *grand* (or *classic*) *style* and the *formal style*. He perceives a resurgence of the grand style in modern opinion-writing; we prefer to call it the *realist style*, for while there are similarities to the grand style in some manners of opinion-writing that are now in vogue among some judges and some courts, there are differences as well.

The Grand Style

Prior to the advent of modern democracy in England and the United States, courts not infrequently frankly and plainly made law when cases arose. They tended to do this under the guise of announcing rules of natural law. "Whenever an issue arose which seemed to the judges to call for relief not directly warranted by precedent, the case was apt to be decided on broad and vague grounds of 'natural justice' and an unanalyzed sense of right and wrong, and of what was fair and just from a lay point of view."[10] This practice represented an uncritical acceptance of the aristocratic viewpoint. Coke said in 1628 that:

reason is the life of the law, nay the common law itself is nothing else but reason; which is to be understood of an artificial perfection of reason, gotten by long study, observation, and experience, and not of everyman's natural reason; for *nemo nascitur artifex* [no one is born a craftsman]. This legall reason *est summa ratio* [is the highest reason]. And therefore if all the reason that is dispersed into so many severall heads, were united into one, yet he could not make such a law as the law of England is; because by many successions of ages it hath been fined and refined by an infinite number of grave and learned men, and by long experience growne to such a perfection, for the government of this realme as the old rule may be justly verified of it, *neminem opportet esse sapientiorem legibus*: no man out of his own privite reason ought to be wiser than the law, which is the perfection of reason.[11]

In this view, of course, judges made law. The result is that much of the common law is indeed in the aristocratic style, sure of its own powers, and canny and shrewd in the ways of men rather than elegant and logically sustained. Supremely self-confident, the judges were adroit in fashioning the rules which made effective both their own powers and the good government of the realm as they themselves perceived it. Hence Goodhart concludes, ". . . it is precisely some of those cases which have been decided on incorrect premises or reasoning which have become most important in the law . . . A bad reason may often make a good law."[12]

An excellent example of the grand style at work is the English case, *Priestley v. Fowler.*[13] The plaintiff was an employee of a butcher. In the course of his employment, he was riding on a wagon of the employer's which was driven by a fellow employee. The van failed by reason of the negligence of the fellow employee. The plaintiff then sued the employer for damages arising from the accident, basing himself on the then well-embedded rule that an employer was liable for injuries inflicted on a third person through the negligence of one of his employees.[14]

Lord Abinger delivered the opinion of the court. He was the son of a rich planter in Jamaica, educated at Cambridge, married to the daughter of a country gentleman, and himself a landowner.[15] He once charged a grand jury (in relation to Chartist demands) that ". . . the establishment of any popular Assembly entirely devoted to democratic principles, elected by persons, the vast majority of whom possess no property, but live by means of manual labor, would be inconsistent with the existence of the monarchy and the aristocracy. Its first aim would be the destruction of property and the overthrow of the throne . . ."[16]

The style of his opinion reflects his aristocratic self-confidence. He began his discussion of the applicable law by saying that:

It is admitted that there is no precedent for the present action by a servant against his master. We are therefore to decide the question upon general principles, and in so doing we are at liberty to look at the consequences of a decision the one way or the other.[17]

He then went on to argue that if the master were to be liable to the servant, the consequences would be "alarming." The owner of a carriage would be liable to his coachman for defects in the carriage made by the carriage-maker; to his footman, for want of skill of his coachman; to his servant, for negligence of the chambermaid in putting him into a damp bed, or for negligence of the cook in not properly cleaning the copper vessels used in the kitchen. He then expounded the reason why he felt that "on principle" a rule permitting a recovery would be wrong "in principle": The servant was ordinarily better advised about the state of affairs on the job than the master, and hence could always decline the service if the situation looked unsafe.

That Lord Abinger failed to examine the grim social realities of industrial life in early nineteenth-century England goes without saying. What we are to notice here is not the sufficiency of the reasons given, or the values substantively embodied in the rule announced. What is of interest is his plainly aristocratic sense that judges make law, and are entitled to make law. He legitimizes the decision only by explaining the reasons why he has come to the conclusion embodied in the opinion. These reasons, appropriately enough, he finds in the social reality as he perceives it and to which he has applied his own values.

Abinger's opinion is interesting because of the light it sheds on his values; it is even more interesting because plainly Abinger believed, and no doubt rightly, that his opinion would legitimize the decision in the eyes of his fellow judges. The aristocratic viewpoint reflected in his opinion speaks volumes about the value-acceptance of himself as well as his fellow judges, and, by necessary implication, about the socialization and recruitment processes for the judiciary in early nineteenth-century England.

A similar style was exhibited by Chief Justice Shaw of Massachusetts, who wrote the opinion in *Farwell v. Boston and Worcester Railroad Company*.[18] That too, was an action by an employee against his employer for injuries arising out of the negligence of a fellow-servant; it, too, was a case of first impression in the jurisdiction. Shaw reached the same result as Abinger had done.

The style of his opinion also resembled that of his English counterpart. It, too, frankly appealed to reasons of "policy" as well as of "justice"; and by policy, Shaw, like Abinger, meant a consideration of the rule for the elite of the society. He said that "In considering rights and obligations arising out of particular relations, it is competent for courts of justice to regard considerations of policy and general convenience, and to draw from them such rules as will, in their practical application, best promote the safety and security of all parties concerned."[19] Shaw then argued that other rules demonstrated a general policy of throwing the risk "upon those who can best guard against it"[20] and concluded, as had Abinger, that the employee on the scene could guard against the hazards of employment better than the employer.

Shaw, like Abinger, was an aristocrat—a Boston Back Bay aristocrat, but an aristocrat nonetheless. " . . . He had no more liking for democracy or respect for the common man than Hamilton or Webster."[21] However, his was the aristocracy of the new mercantile and manufacturing classes in America, not the landed English variety. "His conscience was Tory. The constituency to which his sense of obligation was keenest comprised State Street and Beacon Hill, the bankers, the textile manufacturers, the railway builders. . . He agreed with Taney, as against Marshall and Story, that a merely private interest must yield to interests in industrial expansion."[22] And, as the United States Supreme Court said of a related rule (that of "assumption of risk"), the doctrine was "a judicially created rule . . . developed in response to the general impulse of common law courts . . . to insulate the employer as much as possible from bearing the 'human overhead' which is an inevitable part of the cost—to someone—of the doing of industrialized business . . . "[23]

The Formal Style

Abinger and Shaw represented a dying generation. A new style in the writing of opinions and hence a new theory of what was required to persuade judges that appellate decisions were just and right was already developing.

An example is another case involving the fellow-servant rule, *Murray v. South Carolina Railroad Company*.[24] As in *Farwell*, this case involved an action by the employee of a railroad against his employer for injuries arising from the negligence of a fellow employee. The style of the opinion, however, is that of the age to come, not the age of Abinger and Shaw.

The two most interesting opinions are those of Chancellor Johnson, concurring with the majority, and of Judge O'Neall, dissenting. Both opinions begin with a statement of broad "principles" which they assert were embedded in the common law. Johnson said that "The foundation of all legal liability is the omission to do some act which the law commands, the commission of some act which the law forbids, or the violation of some contract by which a party is injured."[25] From this he deduced by logical reasoning that, since the railroad had not done or omitted to do anything within the forbidden categories, it was not liable. O'Neall, on the other hand, started with an equally broad "principle": "It is highly reasonable that (employers) should answer for such substitute [for the employer], at least *civiliter*; and that his acts, being pursuant to the authority given him, should be deemed the acts of the master."[26] From this, he too deduced the answer—precisely the opposite answer, of course, to that which Chancellor Johnson had deduced from *his* principle.

Both judges legitimized their decisions on legalistic grounds. Legalism has been defined as a system of reasoning that draws only from sources within the legal order itself.[27] Both Johnson and O'Neall believed that they had found, underlying the order of legal rules, broad principles which could be appropriately applied to the facts of the case at hand. Consideration of what Abinger called the "consequences" and Shaw called "policy"—i.e., the effect of the rule upon the society which it was presumably designed to serve—or of ethics, morality, or sociology were not only not included, but in many opinions in the formal style expressly rejected.

Reasons for the Shift from Grand Style to Formal Style

Max Weber believed that legalism of a sort represents the highest development of a legal order. He held that the two basic activities in law are *law-making* and *law-finding*.

The methodology of each may be *rational* or *irrational*; and each may proceed either *rationally* or *irrationally* with respect to either *formal* or *substantive* criteria. Substantive irrationality arises when law-finders or law-makers decide, not on the basis of general norms, but on the basis of emotional evaluations of each case. This practice Weber called "khadi Justice," because he believed that the Moslem judge so rendered his decisions. Substantively rational law-making or law-finding occurs when the judge or legislator consciously follows articulated general principles, whether religious, or ethical, or otherwise. Soviet law is an example of substantively rational law insofar as it is designed to bring about the goals conceived and articulated by its leaders.

Law-making and law-finding are formally rational when the legally operative ("material") facts in any case are determined by reference to general rules. These facts may be of two different sorts. They may be purely extrinsic to the merits,— for example, the seal that determines whether a contract is enforceable, or the two signatures at the end of the will that control the validity of the will. They may, on the other hand, be determined by generic rules which in turn are deduced from generic and abstract concepts; i.e., law-making and law-finding are both formally and logically rational if "the legally relevant characteristics of the facts are disclosed through the logical analysis of meaning and where, accordingly, definitely fixed legal concepts in the form of highly abstract rules are formulated and applied."[28]

This typology of legal systems has been conveniently summarized:

1 *Irrational*, i.e., not guided by general rules.
   a. *Formal*: guided by means which are beyond the control of reason (ordeal, oracle, etc.).
   b. *Substantive*: guided by reaction to the individual case.
2 *Rational*, i.e., guided by general rules.
   a. *Substantive*: guided by the principles of an ideological system other than that of the law itself (ethics, religion, power politics, etc.).
   b. *Formal*:
      (1) *Extrinsically*, i.e., ascribing significance to external acts observable by the senses;
      (2) *Logically*, i.e., expressing its rules by the use of abstract concepts created by legal thought itself and constituting a complete system.[29]

The shift from the grand style to the formal style in opinion-writing is a shift, in Weberian terms, from substantively rational law-making to logically, formally rational law-making. When Abinger and Shaw wrote their opinions, they appealed to "policy," i.e. to ideological considerations. (Would the fellow servant rule be more or less helpful in running a great country estate? Would it advantage or disadvantage railroads? Would it lead to more or fewer accidents?) When Johnson and O'Neall wrote their opinions, on the other hand, their appeals were entirely to broad principles which they presumably derived from the legal order itself.

The formal style, in that it purports to justify decisions by the use exclusively of materials drawn from the legal order, masks the patent fact that in such cases judges create law. We know today, both logically and empirically, that in trouble cases judges *do* make the rules which they then proceed to apply to the facts at hand. Why did the shift occur from the grand style, frankly conceding that the judge was engaged in law-making, to the formal style which hides that patent fact?

The shift reflected the great shift in economic and political power, from the aristocratic government of the eighteenth and early nineteenth centuries to the admission of the middle classes into the corridors of power during the fourth decade of the last century. A variety of different social currents carrying the political and economic demands of the new rulers reached confluence in the demand for law of Weber's logically, formally rational sort.

What economic entrepreneurs demand above all else is advance and certain notice of the legal climate in which they hazard their capital. This demand is expressed in various ways. One aspect was Bentham's claim that the law must be "cognoscible."[30] Another was found in Dicey's notion of the "rule of law" as prohibiting the existence of any form of discretion in the enforcement of the law—a notion summed up in the slogan "a government of laws and not of men."[31] As Weber himself puts it, the "bourgeois interests"

had to demand an unambiguous and clear legal system that would be free of irrational administrative arbitrariness as well as of irrational disturbance by concrete privileges, that would also offer firm guarantees of the legally binding nature of contracts, and that, in consequence of all these features, would function in a calculable way.[32]

This demand was met by the five postulates that Weber believed to be immanent in formal, logical, rational law:

first, that every concrete legal decision be the "application" of an abstract legal proposition to a concrete "fact situation"; second, it must be possible in every concrete case to derive the decision from abstract legal propositions by means of legal logic; third, that the law must actually or virtually constitute a "gapless" system of legal propositions, or must, at least, be treated as if it were such a gapless system; fourth, that whatever cannot be "construed" legally in rational terms is also legally irrelevant; and fifth, that every social action of human beings must always be visualized as either an "application" or "execution" of legal propositions, or as an infringement thereof.[33]

The demand that the law be made certain implied, therefore, that the law exist in a "cognoscible" form *prior* to the dispute which the judge must decide. For judges to legitimize their decisions, in this view, they were required to

CONVERSION PROCESSES IN APPELLATE COURTS

demonstrate that that was the case. Hence, they had to demonstrate in their opinions that they did not create the law, but only found it.

Other political and idiological demands of the rising bourgeoisie coincided with this requirement. The new democratic dogma of the separation of power placed the law-making function in a democratically elected legislature, and reserved to the far from democratically selected judiciary the dispute-settling function. As Landis has suggested, "this led to the conception of the judges as impotent agents, impotent to do otherwise then merely 'find' law." Austin's analytical positivism contributed to this development, for it taught the judges that their task was merely to determine what was the "command of the sovereign," i.e. to examine what the law is, not what it ought to be. Dicey's notion of the rule of law married itself happily to the Blackstonian conception of the common law as "a fully matured system" to inhibit judicial notions of creativity. Finally, in England the judges adopted a position of political neutrality and hence of self-limitation in law-making during the two periods of great creativity in social legislation, the Great Depression of the 1930's and the post-war years of the next two decades. Their neutrality with respect to public law inevitably washed over to inhibit their creativity in the area of the common law itself. In addition to the proliferation of democratic political sentiments, the Benthamite and Utilitarian emphasis on the dispute-settlement function of the courts tended to focus on the desirability of certainty in law, rather than on creativity.

To this day, in England, judges tend to deny that they ever create law. Lord Jowitt, at the Australian Law Convention of 1951, said:

Please do not get yourself into the frame of mind of entrusting the judges to working out a whole new set of principle which does accord with the requirements of modern conditions. Leave that to the legislature, and leave us confine ourselves to trying to find out what the law is.[34]

Lord Simonds (also an eminent English judge) has said:

For to me heterodoxy, or, as some might say, heresy, is not more attractive because it is dignified by the name of reform. Nor will I easily be led by an undiscerning zeal for some abstract kind of justice to ignore our first duty, which is to administer justice according to law, the law which is established for us by Act of Parliament or the binding authority of precedent. The law is developed by the application of old principles to new circumstances. Therein lies its genius. Its reform by the abrogation of these principles is the task not of the courts of law but of Parliament.[35]

In this country, this legalistic notion continues to describe how many, perhaps most, courts legitimize most decisions.

The Realist Critique

The difficulty is that the dogma that the law is a gapless web, and the corresponding norm for judicial law-making, that judges must solve trouble cases only with materials drawn from the existent legal order, are of a prescriptive, not descriptive, nature; that is, they tell us what ought to be the case, not what in fact is the case.

Following these prescriptions, judges sought to demonstrate that every case was a clear case. They tried to solve every case, including trouble cases, by the use of the clear-case rules or some variant of them. The results were logically less than satisfying.

The application of the clear-case rules in a clear case produces one, and only one, articulated rule of law which subsumes the case at hand. That is what makes it a clear case. The application of the same rules in a trouble case produces at least two, and sometimes more, potential rules, each as legitimate as the other in terms of provenance. That is what makes the case a trouble case.

The very fact that the clear-case rules of recognition produce two alternative potential rules, each of which subsumes the facts at hand, which lead to contrary results, and each of which is legitimate in terms of the clear-case rules of recognition, suggests that the clear-case rules themselves cannot resolve the very dilemma which they have produced. Yet the dogma to which courts in the nineteenth century, and in many cases, today, bound themselves, required that the dilemma be resolved by those very rules, for the dogma denies the existence of the "trouble" case.

The above argument shows that, while the tradition of invoking clear-case rules in a trouble case affords the court a range of choice from two or more alternatives, all of which are at least arguably supported, and hence can be legitimized, by the clear-case rules of recognition, what the court in fact must do in trouble cases is to make that choice. In so doing, it creates a new rule. This power to create new rules, however, is precisely what the traditional dogma in question denies to the courts in principle (with the sole exception, perhaps, of the Supreme Court of the United States in certain constitutional cases). In contrast, a legislature is permitted to select from a much wider range of alternatives. O. W. Holmes said, "I recognize without hesitation that judges do and must legislate, but they can do so only interstitially; they are confined from molar to molecular motions."[36]

The realists perceived that, in the event, the courts invented new routes around, through, and under the clear-case rules in order to give their results an air of legitimacy according to those very rules which they are actually violating in a variety of ways. They became amazingly adept at playing with the potential of precedents, making "distinctions" for those which seemed to contradict the desired result by identifying factual differences in case, although the difference was not relevant to the original problem. They seized upon statements of judges as authority when they wanted to do so, although the rules plainly forbid them to look at *obiter dicta* (or statements not necessary to the decision of the case). Llewellyn reports that in one day's work of one appellate court he identified twenty-six different ways of dealing with precedents, none of which were legitimate under the clear-case rule, but all of which had an air of deference to those rules. Where statutes are concerned, a variety of rules were devised to explain their meaning. Llewellyn has also pointed out that these "canons" of statutory interpretation run in contradictory pairs, so that it is possible to use whichever of the rules one likes to reach the predetermined result.[37]

For example, suppose that a taxing statute levies a tax on "ordinary or garden variety of peas." Does this statute levy a tax on one kind of pea, or on two kinds of peas? One canon of statutory construction instructs the judge to read words in their ordinary signification. In this view, the language of the statute would seem to refer to only one sort of peas. On the other hand, there is a canon which instructs the judge that since presumably every word is placed in a statute for a purpose, he must give weight and meaning to every word used. This canon would suggest, therefore, that the legislature intended the tax to apply to two sorts of peas. By invoking the one canon or the other, a judge can reach the result desired and at the same time make it appear that in fact the result reached is the only legitimate one within the system. He can create a law under the guise of finding it.

One example from the African experience must suffice. In *Rex v. Edgal*[38] appellants were convicted of violation of a section of the Nigeria Criminal Code which read in part,

Any person who unlawfully supplies to . . . any person anything whatever, knowing that it is intended to be unlawfully used to procure a miscarriage of a woman . . . is guilty of a felony . . .

In the course of appeal, they asserted that at no place in the Criminal Code was it explained when an abortion was "lawful" or "unlawful." Moreover, the Code (which had been adopted in 1916) stated explicitly that a person could be tried and punished only under an express provision of the Code. Therefore, the appellants claimed, their conviction was illegal. The appellate court affirmed the conviction nevertheless.

The argument for conviction runs as follows: (1) When the draftsman of the Criminal Code was writing the section in question in 1916, he must have meant the word "unlawful" to mean "unlawful" as it was under the then existing common law. (2) In a case in England in 1939[39] it was established that the common law held to be lawful only those abortions which were necessary to preserve the life of the mother. (3) Since the common law had always existed, the judges in 1939 were not "creating" law but merely announcing what the common law had always been. (4) Therefore the common law as announced in the 1939 English case was the common law which the draftsman of the Nigerian Code must have had in mind in 1916 when he used the word "unlawfully" in the relevant section of the Criminal Code. (5) Therefore the appellants are guilty since they did not supply the abortifacient for the purpose of saving the mother's life, but merely for the purpose of doing away with the unborn child.

An equally "logical" line of argument to the contrary might have been like this: (1) To find these appellants guilty one had to read the Code section as though it read, "Any person who supplies to . . . any person anything whatever, knowing that it is intended to be used to procure a miscarriage of a woman under such circumstance that the act would have been unlawful at common law, is guilty of a felony." (2) The Code itself states plainly that no person may be convicted under the common law of crimes. (3) Therefore these appellants cannot be convicted of the crime charged.

Why one line of argument and not the other was selected by the court cannot possibly be determined from the arguments themselves. The ambiguity of the Code statute was a function of the ambiguity of the legal order with respect to the crime of abortion. Examination of the legal order itself with the tool of logic alone cannot explain why one rather than the other possible "logical" argument held sway.

It is for this reason that Holmes said long ago that "General propositions do not decide concrete cases. The decision will depend on a judgment or intuition more subtle than any articulate major premise . . ."[40]

Now, as we saw earlier, all legal decisions require a value-judgment. In the Nigerian case cited, the court was really asked to choose between two different and disparate value-sets. On the one hand there were the values which lawyers subsume under the heading of "legality," of which the Latin maxim *nulla crimen sine lege* (no crime without a law) is an important component. On the other hand, there were the values in preventing abortions not necessary to preserve the life of the mother by punishing these appellants (in the hope that others would be deterred by the example of their punishment).

The principal consequence of legalistic reasoning in trouble cases is that the choice of values by the appellate court is hidden behind a façade of logical necessity. By keeping the premises inarticulate, a court tends to place them beyond discussion. Debate is limited to the relatively sterile question, whether the court's argument is "logical." Thus the decision is legitimized within the system.

We can now explain why judges seem deviant to many American academics in their failure to achieve rational results. Deviancy can occur, despite wholly conformist motivation, when the norms to which the role-occupant is supposed to conform are dysfunctional with respect to the problem with which he is faced. Since he cannot follow the norms to solve the problem that is on his agenda, he must deviate from them if he is to solve the problem at all.

Every lawsuit may be regarded as the working out of a syllogism. The rule of law is the major premise, the facts of the case the minor premise, and the verdict or judgment the conclusion. In an appellate case, the facts are almost invariably taken as given by the state of affairs reported as true by the lower court. What is at issue is the scope and content of the major premise. The logical system of thought is a device of deducing, from given major premises and given minor premises, a correct conclusion. It is not functional for purpose of discovering the appropriate major premise. Hence, when courts seek to find the correct major premise, the techniques of logic alone are insufficient.

The formal style of opinion-writing seeks to use the clear-case rules to solve a trouble case. The clear-case rules are appropriate when the major premise, the controlling law, is clearly defined by the use of those rules. The trouble case is troublesome precisely because the application of clear-case rules yields, not one, but two or more potential major premises. The judges cannot help but be deviant if they try in the formal style to justify their decisions, for they cannot by the use of syllogistic reasoning alone determine what ought to be the major premise. That is a question of policy, of the rational exercise of discretion. The *cri de coeur* of the entrepreneurial classes for a world of fixed, clearly determinate norms has failed because such a world does not and cannot exist.

The Realist Justification

The realists in the end suggest an altogether different theory of legitimization of judicial decisions, one which harks back in many ways to the grand style. Although the early aim of the realist's critique was to develop more sophisticated prediction of judicial actions in the interest of entrepreneurial clients, in the history of America this critique has in fact shifted its focus from the process of decision-prediction to that of judicial decision-making; and in the course of this transformation, the critique has generated a reform movement which is still very much alive in our day.

It is intriguing that the probable origins of the realist school lie in the same pressures which led to the legalistic approach. That approach, it may be recalled, was a response to the demands that law be "cognoscible" in the interests of entrepreneurs who risked capital. To the extent that the legalistic approach necessarily relies on inarticulate major premises, it is plainly insufficient to make judicial decision-making predictable. To the extent that the legitimization processes of the formal style are merely prescriptive (since by their very nature they cannot be descriptive in trouble cases), the basic demands of entrepreneurs are not met.

It was to these demands, in essence, that Holmes was responding when he gave the famous definition of what he meant by the word "law":

Take the fundamental question, what constitutes the law . . . You will find some text-writers telling you . . . that it is a system of reason, that it is a deduction from principles of ethics or admitted actions, or what not, which may or may not coincide with the decision. But if we take the point of view of our friend, the bad man, we shall find that he does not care two straws for the action or deduction, but that he does want to know what Massachusetts or English courts are likely to do in fact. I am much of his mind.

The prophecies of what the courts will do in fact and nothing more pretentious are what I mean by the law.[41]

Obviously, this is a definition of law that is useful only to a practicing lawyer who must advise a client; it is useless to the judge, for it tells him to ask himself how he would decide the case which is precisely the question which he is called upon to answer.[42] But the question which Holmes poses on behalf of this bad-man client is just the question whose answer the entrepreneur, above all others, must know if he is to carry on his affairs with a minimum of risk. Holmes' statement presupposes that the central function of law is to provide a fixed and certain framework of norms within which the individual can conduct his affairs making accurate predictions about the consequences of his actions.

How best, then, to discover what courts will do? The realists' critique, as we saw, asserted that legalistic justifications in the formal style could not lead to prediction since they concealed the inarticulate major premise. Rather, the realists held, again in Holmes' words, that "the life of law has not been logic, but experience."[43] To predict how courts are apt to decide cases, one must examine the empirical evidence; "the use of statistics, economics, criminology, etc., is meant to introduce a new certainty into the knowledge of law: a certainty based on scientific experiment instead of fallacious logic."[44] Jerome Frank tried to base prediction on psychoanalytic theory.[45] Llewellyn held that judges respond to the "sense" of the fact situation.[46] Oliphant said that:

There is a constant factor in the cases which is susceptible of sound and satisfying study. The predictable element in it all is what courts have done in response to the stimuli of the facts of the concrete cases before them. Not the judges' opinions, but which way they decide cases will become the dominant subject matter of any truly scientific study of law. This is the field for scholarly work worthy of the best talents because the work to be done is not the study of vague and shifting rationalizations but the study of such taught things as the accumulated wisdom of men taught by immediate experience in contemporary life—the battered experiences of judges among brutal facts . . .

From this viewpoint we see that courts are dominantly coerced not by the essays of their predecessors but by a surer thing—by an intuition of fitness of solution to problem—and a renewed confidence in judicial government is engendered.[47]

Every theory of justification for appellate opinions, concerning the appropriate formulation of a newly created rule of law, implies a theory of justice. The realists were essentially iconoclasts; they denied that the justifications embodied in opinions of the formal style in fact hung together rationally. (As we have seen, an appellate opinion is concerned essentially with the search for a major premise; the formal-style opinion, based as it is on logic alone, assumes the major premise and thus assumes what is to be proven.) Nevertheless, implicit in their iconoclasm was a theory of justice.

If the life of the law is not logic, but experience, then experience should

CONVERSION PROCESSES IN APPELLATE COURTS

be the test of the rightness of the law. The iconoclasm of the realists thus led straight to the varying pragmatic philosophies of Charles Peirce, William James, and John Dewey, who were exploding the logical, positive world of the mind at the same time that Holmes was destroying the logical, positive world of law. "How well will it work?" became the test rather than the arid, conceptual quiddities of the logicians and legalists. What was called for was a "projective orientation, one which insists upon the most rigorous possible testing of prospective courses of action against explicit goal-objectives."[48]

Dewey taught that *reasoning* could do no more than determine whether a proposed hypothesis was consistent with existing knowledge.[49] It is the office of the rules of precedent and statutory construction to ensure that end.[50] He argued that a process of social inquiry which purported to be rational had to test a proposed solution against its probable consequences by a process of deliberation.

The saving grace of the common law system, whether opinions were justified in the Grand or the Formal style, lay in the fact that decision-making always occurred in the context of a concrete case. A judge deciding a case had before him the facts of a case-study. He could not help but be aware of the consequences of the rule he was enunciating upon the cause at hand. To that extent, he could not help but deliberate upon its consequences. What the realists demanded was a more conscious, scientifically controlled sort of deliberation, explicity stated, as the core of the justification process.

How far the Supreme Court has gone in deciding cases according to the course of action delineated in this model can be seen by examining the now famous desegregation case, *Brown v. Board of Education*, [51] which held that segregation in public education did not meet the standards of the equal-protection clause of the United States Constitution. In that case, the facts demonstrated that the plaintiffs, who were the black children, had been segregated in their public school systems from white children according to race, but that they had been provided with facilities substantially equal to those provided to white children in the same system. Two potential rules could have been found by the use of clear-case rules of recognition. One of these rules, first articulated in *Plessy v. Ferguson*,[52] and reiterated many times during the ensuing decades, was that "separate but equal" governmental treatment in public education met the requirement of the Fourteenth Amendment of the Federal Constitution. The other was the plain language of the Constitution itself, which states that no person may be deprived of the equal protection of the laws on the ground of race, creed, or previous condition of servitude, together with the claim that "separate but equal" treatment in public education was inherently discriminatory.

In *Brown v. Board of Education*, the basic value or goal was determined by the Fourteenth Amendment: That State power must not be used against any person to his disadvantage to discriminate on the basis of race, color, or previous condition of servitude. The Court was therefore not faced with a problem of choice of values or goals, which might have made the problem more difficult.

Given the goal, the principal question left to the Court was empirical: Which of the two alternatives proposed—"separate but equal" treatment of the races, or a flat prohibition of this practice—would accomplish the prescribed objective? Had the problem been solved merely in terms of deductive reasoning based on arguments drawn entirely from within the legal system, two possibilities were available. On the one hand, *Plessy v. Ferguson* had been decided fifty-eight years earlier. It would have been simple to rest on that precedent. The language of the opinion would have been predictable: "It is now too late in our constitutional history to turn back the clock. If radical change in the treatment of the races is to come, it must be by legislative action. We hold, in accordance with fifty-eight years of unbroken precedent, that separate but equal facilities meet the Constitutional command." On the other hand, if the Court wanted to resolve the problem the other way, it might have held that "The command of the Constitution is color-blind. It ordains that State action, too, must be color-blind. *Plessy v. Ferguson* was in error, for it overlooked this fundamental command of the Fourteenth Amendment. That case is therefore expressly overruled." Thus the Court might have reached its decision on the basis of premises drawn entirely from within the legal order: On the authority of precedent, or on the basis of the "plain meaning" of the Constitutional provision.

Instead, however, the Court chose to solve the problem by a pragmatic, problem-solving procedure. It perceived that the case raised questions of fact, not of law: "Does segregation of children in public schools solely on the basis of race, even though the physical facilities and other 'tangible' factors may be equal, deprive the children of the minority group of equal educational opportunities?"[53] This is a question which can be answered, if at all, only empirically. Hence the Court turned to the facts supplied by the lower court. The trial court had held that:

Segregation of white and colored children in public schools has a detrimental effect upon the colored children. The impact is greater when it has the sanction of the law; for the policy of separating the races is usually interpreted as denoting the inferiority of the Negro group. A sense of inferiority affects the motivation of a child to learn. Segregation with the sanction of law, therefore, has a tendency to retard the educational and mental development of Negro children and to deprive them of some of the benefits they would receive in a racially integrated school system.[54]

This opinion, the Supreme Court said, "is amply supported by modern authority." Thus the Court resolved the issue by reference to empirical data gathered by social scientists and drawn from evidence and authorities quite outside the formal legal structure.[55]

By so frankly and openly facing the law-making problem with which it was confronted, however, the Court necessarily seemed deviant to the layman, accustomed to the myth that courts only applied fixed and preexistent law to the facts. Most laymen, in short, are still committed to the role-expectations implied in the formal style of opinion-writing. From that position, of course a court that seeks to legitimize its decision in the realist mode will appear deviant.

8.2 VALUES, OPINIONS, AND LEGITIMIZATION

Why do most judges, and probably also most laymen, continue to believe—or act as though they believed—that appellate decisions can be derived from a fixed body of given rules by syllogistic reasoning? Why have most American law teachers, and a few judges (notably of the Supreme Court of the United States) rejected the formal style of opinion-writing and adopted the realist position? To answer this question, we must first examine the function of values in decision-making.

We saw earlier that this problem is obscured by the formal style of opinion-writing, for the question of values is slid over by the assumption of what Holmes called the inarticulate major premises. The realist conception of decision-making, however, requires that these values be explicated. What categories of generalized ends and means ought a court take into account?

The values served by appellate decision-making are on several different levels. There is, of course, the order of social values to be served by the substantive norm itself. But there are also other values which courts must consider in their decision-making. There are the values involved in determining the appropriate deference to be paid by a court to other branches of government.[56] In construing a statute and hence in determining the meaning of words, should a court dredge out the "intent" of the legislature? Or should it give those words the content which seems proper to the court? Ought the court to defer to administrative determinations, and if so, under what circumstances? There are values peculiar to the legal order itself. To what extent is logical consistency in the corpus of norms an appropriate goal? (Even if one agrees that it ought not be the only or the ultimate goal, he may still want to achieve it so far as possible.) To what extent is deference to precedent desirable?

How ought a court to determine the relative priority of these various possible values? That is to say, how ought a court to determine the goals of the legal order?

During the period of the aristocratic constitution in England, the answer was easily furnished. The judges were entitled to determine on their own the goals to be achieved. Sir Edward Coke, Lord Chief Justice of England in the early seventeenth century, once said that the common law was "locked in the breasts of the judges." Judicial choice of the goals for the law, and hence for society, even during this period, however, was legitimized on the ground that the courts were merely announcing the rules of natural law—reflecting the judicial and public uneasiness about judges themselves making the determinations which affected so many people.

After the democratic revolutions, however, the idea that judges should choose the goals of the society at large seemed even more intolerable, as we have seen. But if the judges did not make their decisions by appealing to their own intuition, how should they make decisions?

Historically, this question has been answered principally in two different ways. On the one hand, many philosophers and jurisprudents have urged that values can be determined through invocation of objective criteria of some sort: by discovering the will of the deity, or by considering the nature of man in society and inferring from that nature the qualities of legal order required. Ultimately, such natural-law philosophies end up relying on personal intuitions of the ideal. What one man perceives as the will of God is not necessarily so perceived by another. What one philosopher believes to be the "essential" nature of man in society does not necessarily match another's beliefs.

This is not to say that natural-law theories are not worthy of close study. As Pareto pointed out, in every age men had clothed their ideological demands in the attire of natural law. It has been in one era radical, and in another conservative. The American Revolution was justified by natural-law theories. During the nine-teen-twenties and early thirties, on the other hand, natural law was the claim of the most conservative wing of the Supreme Court in blocking legal and institu-tional changes which a majority of the electorate apparently believed were necessary and desirable.

The formal-style opinion was a means of evading the issue of values by pretending that the web of the law was so seamless that every case was necessarily covered, either by a specific rule or by a broad "principle" which could be inferred from existing law. Since these principles were in fact often contradictory, and the preferences for one or another depended on the subjective tastes of the individual judges, the formal style in effect permitted each judge to make decisions on the basis of his own conception of the ultimate goals to be served by the legal institutions, i.e. to supply his own inarticulate major premise. This state of affairs the realists believed to be intolerable, because it made prediction impossible and because it denied the central hypothesis of the democratic theory, that the goals to be served by the State were to be determined by the people acting through their elected representatives.

Roscoe Pound offered one possible solution built on the pragmatic philosophy of William James. James held that if any human being demanded anything, the only valid reason for refusing to meet that demand was that it interfered with the claims or demands of other human beings. From this doctrine Pound devel-oped his theory of the "jurisprudence of interest," which held that an essential aim of the law was to satisy as many claims or demands of as many people as possible.

Pound's conception of law was radical in the following sense. Instead of viewing the central task of lawyers as one of predicting what judges would do in order to preserve a safe, sane, and stable legal environment for private capital, Pound thought of law as a means of social engineering. State power is, after all, the single most powerful weapon society has for use to make society what its decision-makers want it to be. By his insistence that law was a central device of social control and hence of social engineering, Pound asserted the modern faith that man can consciously change his social as well as his physical environment. But he evaded, rather than answered, the most important difficulty presented by this view.

The difficulty, of course, lies in the way of determining the serial number of payment of the various claims. That is, how are the courts or the law-makers to determine the relative priority of the various claims urged by the various claimants? Pound proposed, therefore to determine these goals by examining the claims or demands made to discover the values, or "jural postulates," implicit in them.

If, as Pound himself believed, there are "national" or community-wide values, held by practically everybody in the polity, the search for overarching jural postulates, while difficult, is at least theoretically possible. But if society is not patterned on the homeostatic, functional model, but rather on a conflict model in which there are antagonistic strata and classes with mutually incompatible sets of value-acceptances, then the search for a uniform set of value-acceptances to subsume all claims and demands can end only in a statement of the researcher's prejudices.

Pound's own statement of the ultimate jural postulates of American society has been subjected precisely to such a criticism. In 1942, Pound announced that these postulates could be stated in five propositions:

1   In civilized society men must be able to assume that others will commit no intentional aggressions upon them.

2   In civilized society men must be able to assume that they may control for beneficial purposes what they have discovered and appropriated to their own use, what they have created by their own labor, and what they have acquired under the existing social and economic order.

3   In civilized society men must be able to assume that those with whom they deal in the general intercourse of society will act in good faith and hence
    (a) will make good reasonable expections which their promises or other conduct will reasonable create;
    (b) will carry out their undertakings according to the expectations which the moral sentiment of the community attaches thereto;
    (c) will restore specifically or by equivalent what comes to them by mistake or unanticipated or not fully intended situation whereby they receive at another's expense what they could not reasonably have expected to receive under the circumstances.

4   In civilized society men must be able to assume that those who are engaged in some course of conduct will act with due care not to cause an unreasonable risk of injury upon others.

5   In civilized society men must be able to assume that those who maintain things likely to get out of hand or to escape and do damage will restrain them or keep them within their proper bounds.[57]

One must immediately ask, at least, whether in a "civilized" society there ought not to be affirmative guarantees of at least a minimum of material well-being.[58] Perhaps this is what Harold Laski had in mind when he said that Pound emerged from his long journey through the vast seas of Jurisprudence with principles that demonstrate primarily Pound's devotion to the society of Lincoln, Nebraska in the last quarter of the nineteenth century, where Pound came of age.[59]

Pound is right, of course, in stating that there are many matters that come before courts which, while they raise questions about values, are not questions about which many people would feel strongly. Much of commercial law is of this sort; what counts is not so much what is the rule, but that there should be a rule as clearly stated as possible. Moreover, many questions that come before a court can be regarded as raising issues about matters of values only in an instrumental, and not in a consummatory sense. *Brown v. Board of Education* was in fact just such a case on its own merits. Both parties agreed that the Constitution held that no person could suffer because of discrimination by the State on account of race, creed, color, or previous condition of servitude—that was a clear-case rule. The only issue was a question of fact: Did black children suffer because of the mere fact of segregation?

On the other hand, there are also a few great cases that come before the courts—in the United States, especially before the Supreme Court—which do raise great issues concerning the ultimate ends of the law. In such cases, if one takes a conflict view of society, then he must hold that there can be no resolution of the conflict which will match the value-acceptances of everyone in the society, for by hypothesis there is no commonly held set of ultimate values. If, then, ultimate values and goals are not in fact determinable in some way independently of personal values and prejudices, then there can be no clearly satisfactory answer which will help the judge decide cases without reference to his personal value-orientation.

It is probably the suspicion of this unavoidable residue of personal value-choice which explains why some judges, and most laymen, continue to deny that judges properly ought to make law. Such value-choice undermines the dispute-settlement function of the courts in a system where disputes must be settled by winner taking all, i.e. by norm enforcement.

Litigation in our system arises because some plaintiff asserts that the defendant has breached a norm of conduct, and the plaintiff beseeches the court that a sanction be applied. The court, then, must appear to stand above the conflict, judging impartially between man and man and, *mirabile dictu*, even between the individual and the very State of which the judicial order is a part. The classical portrait of justice is invariably as a blind goddess.

In a clear case this classical model strikes close to the truth, and the rule of law *is* a preexisting norm of conduct whose existence and content can be empirically determined. The facts can also be determined in the same way. The classical model retains its vitality in part because, as Durkheim pointed out long ago, norms are indeed social facts.

The classical model, however, obscures the reality of the "trouble" case. We have already seen that values of various sorts must be weighed by courts in making policy-choices, and that there must logically be some overriding set of postulates by which to weigh these in turn.

If one subscribes to some sort of natural-law theory, as we noted before, he might find such postulates within his own intuition; or if, as Pound thought, society does have an overarching set of values, common to practically everybody, then they could be discovered empirically. If, however, one conceives of society as inescapably pluralistic, with different sets of value-acceptances, in the critical cases there can be no rationally determined answer to the problem. By his choice of ultimate values, in this view, the judge necessarily places State power on one side or the other in the unending contentions that lurk behind the societal façade. By the very act of choice, the judge no longer sits above the struggles of society; he unavoidably enters the social fray on one side or the other. The ultimate choices are the resultant of power vectors rather than the outcome of rational debate and reasoned consideration. Courts cannot formulate a trouble-case rule of recognition unless they are prepared to admit that in the most difficult, and usually the most important, of such cases, justice cannot be blind, nor the scales fair. The naked thumb of power necessarily intrudes into the weighing.

The primary consequence of the use of clear-case rules of recognition in trouble cases and of the ensuing legalistic reasoning, as we have seen, is to give the judicial decision an aura of inevitability and fairness that obscures the fact that courts do take sides in the great social issues of the day. That most courts continue to legitimize their decisions in this way can only be an indication that it is in the interest of judges and lawyers to maintain the myth that even in a trouble case the court does not create law. That judges and lawyers have such an interest can hardly be doubted, for collectively their power as a unique subculture in the community depends in the final analysis on the legitimation of judicial decisions, and that depends in a large part, not on the coercive power of the state, but on the persuasive power of myth over the minds of men.

More than the interest of judges and lawyers is involved, however. Every existing rule of law, like any norm in society, represents a choice between possible alternatives. Every such choice involved, at some time in the past, a decision between competing values. To admit that judge-made law, like all law, however created, represents the value-choices of the decision-makers in society, is to admit that the entire corpus of the law necessarily represents the values not of "society" in general, but of those strata in society *pro tempore* in control of the decision-making institutions. By placing the judge above the conflicts of society, by purporting to insulate him from taking part in social conflict, by pretending that the judge never makes value-choices, the myth that the judge applies "clearly defined" laws to the facts validates not only the current decisional output, but the entire corpus of the rules of law.

The rules of law are but generalized prescriptions for the use of State power. To formulate a trouble-case rule, therefore, may strike at the central myth sustaining the State—that it, like the judges in applying the "clear-case" rules, stands above social conflicts and provides merely a framework within which such conflicts can be resolved. To the extent that one regards society as pluralistic, with different sets of value-acceptances in the several strata, he must regard the primary function of the myth that judges find the law and do not make it as the protection of the State against attack by the disinherited. In such a view, to formulate rules of recognition for trouble cases is equivalent to rejecting the myth; it would reveal the fact that in the great social issues, the State is not an impartial arbiter, but an active participant on one side or the other.

To attack the myth of the impartiality of the State with respect to social conflict seems to many to be a subversive act. Lawyers and judges are rarely subversives and, even more important, they are no more courageous than others in their willingness to risk being called subversives. That laymen, too, regard the Supreme Court as deviant because it frankly makes law demonstrates that they subscribe to that same myth.

Yet, in America although not in England, the legalistic method of justifying decisions has been abandoned by some judges in favor of pragmatic rule-making procedures. Obviously, one important factor in this development has been the growth of the realist school itself. Once the vulnerability of the formal-style opinions was discovered, the realist school, no more than the scientific method itself, as it were, could be undiscovered. A second factor may have been the development of the case method of instruction in American law schools, beginning with the first case book, published in 1871 at Harvard by Langdell; this is a development in legal education which never took place in England. The case method requires students to study appellate decisions very closely and critically. Any close study of legalistic decision-making by appellate courts is almost bound to lead to a sense of its inadequacies, especially by law students who are already university graduates (as they are not in England, where law is an undergraduate subject) and who have been increasingly trained in scientific and pragmatic methods.

Perhaps the most important reason for this judicial transformation, however, is historical. During the nineteen-twenties and the first part of the nineteen-thirties, the majority of the Supreme Court valiantly resisted efforts to bring about social change through the use of social-welfare legislation. The device that was used was to construe the Constitution in what appeared to be legalistic terms, but in fact could only be construed as decisions based on the economic prejudices of the judges. Holmes once said in dissenting that the due-process clause did not embody Mr. Herbert Spencer's social statics. By this he meant, of course, that under the guise of legalistic reasoning, the Court was smuggling its own economic prejudices into the opinion as what Holmes called the inarticulate major premise.[60] When the Great Revolution on the Supreme Court occurred in 1937 through the process of attrition of the old Guard and the appointment of a number of new Justices by President Roosevelt, the rationale that the new majority turned to for validating the New Deal's social legislation was, naturally enough, the judicial pragmatism which Holmes had espoused in the minority for so long. In so doing, they set a style of judicial decision-making for which American legal education had long been preparing American lawyers.

The major conversion process by which the raw inputs into the decisional processes are worked into a new rule of law by an appellate court is best expressed in terms of the justification embodied in its opinion, which seeks to legitimize the decision to other judges and lawyers. There has been a distinct evolution in opinion style, from the grand style to the formal style, and in recent years, to a degree, toward the pragmatic method of problem-solving advocated by the realist style.

These conversion processes, however, do not take place in *vacuo*. They operate on specific inputs that in part determine the result. The myth about the operation of the courts suggests that the only input is "the law." But appellate courts are made up of individuals in a group. Whatever system of legitimization is adopted, properly to understand how decisions are made by an appellate court, one must examine the courts as a small group, and analyze the interpersonal relations among its members.

Appellate Courts as Small Groups

Appellate courts are institutions, and to some degree judges exhibit the characteristics of persons who work in institutions. That is to say, they interact with one another, and with the clerks, bailiffs, lawyers, and other men who make up the institution. Inevitably, the conversion process is affected by these interpersonal relationships.

Appellate courts in the United States are typically collegiate benches. That is to say, the judges discuss the cases among themselves and ultimately vote upon the result. One or another judge is then assigned to write the majority opinion, which usually is circulated for comment by the other judges and then finally amended by the writer. Dissenting or concurring judges then have an opportunity to write their own opinions.

The traditional legal view has always been that the individual justice on an appellate bench individually studies each case, followed by discussion by the body of justices as a whole, so that the result will represent the mature collective thought of the Court.[61] At the other end of the scale are iconoclastic notions such as that of Thurman Arnold, who insists that there "is no such process" as the "maturing of collective thought." Instead, he argues, "Men of positive views are only hardened in those views by [judicial] conferences ... I have no doubt that longer periods of argument and deliberation, and more time to dissent, would only result in the proliferation of opinions of which we already have too many."[62]

Behind these positions are differing assessments of the role of reason and logical argument in the formulation of institutional opinions by the courts. The orthodox view presents judges as reasonable men, entering the discussions with hypotheses about the solution to cases, but with minds open to argument by dissenting colleagues. It suggests that the central operative force in judicial decision-making is indeed the force of reason. On the other hand, Arnold's position tends to denigrate the role of discussion. It suggests that the principal force in judicial decision-making is the value-set of the justice involved, rather than the rational arguments adduced. This view would obviously make institutional pressures toward conformity and internal politicking the central forces motivating appellate decisions.

The orthodox view accords with the conventional norms which govern our role-expectation of judges. These norms have been adumbrated in opinions without number. Whether in the grand style, the formal style, or the realist style, all judicial opinions assume that the central persuasive force is reason. The heterodox view seems to assert that judges in fact do not reach joint decisions on the basis that the accepted norms would seem to require.

There is a considerable body of direct evidence that judges indeed do argue with each other in rational terms, and that mainly they are persuaded simply by the force of argument. For example, in March 1945, the Supreme Court at first voted to affirm a conviction, under the Sherman Act, of lumber union officials and employers in the lumber business for conspiring to raise prices and wages through monopolizing the lumber business in the San Francisco area. Justice Black, voting with the majority, was assigned the case. He later circulated an opinion to reverse the case, stating that after study he had become convinced that there was error. After hearing reargument, the Court voted 5-3 to reverse the decision.

This example, however, is not alone conclusive. It may be true that in some cases judges are swayed by argument. In many more cases, however, the vote taken before the writing of an opinion remains unchanged after the opinion is written. In such cases, to what extent is the decision based on reason and argument, and to what extent on group and institutional pressures?

One way to examine this question is to inquire into the nature and character of dissent. To the extent that dissent is openly expressed by judges in opinions that seek to legitimize their positions in terms that appeal to reason, one can be sure that nonrational pressures originating in the appellate bench itself have been resisted. On the other hand, the absence of articulated dissent is ambiguous. It may be an indication that the judges are in fact convinced by rational argument, or it may indicate that they have been coerced into uniformity by other pressures.

What is surprising is not that in some courts dissent is a rarity, but rather, that it is as frequent as it is in many courts. In the Supreme Court of the United States, dissent has increased in frequency in recent years. In 1930, 11% of the opinions were accompanied by dissents; the frequency rose to 28% in 1940, 61 % in 1950, and 76 % in 1957.[63] No State Supreme Court approaches this frequency of dissent. The range of frequency of dissent in State Supreme Courts is, however, extremely high, as Table 8.1 indicates.

Small-group sociological theory holds that "An individual is more likely to conform to group opinion in the following cases: if the object to be judged is ambiguous; if he must make his opinion public; if the majority holding a contrary opinion is large; and if the group is especially friendly or close-knit."[64] If this is true, then it would seem that conformity ought to be the rule rather than the exception in appellate decision-making. The subject matter is invariably ambiguous. Dissenting opinion must be made public. Appellate courts have notoriously long-lived members, whose work and past associations tend to make them friendly and close-knit. Moreover, there is a common institutional pressure on all of them to keep dissent at a minimum. As Judge Learned Hand has observed, dissent "is disastrous [to a court] because disunity cancels the impact of monolithic solidarity on which the authority of a bench of judges so largely depends."[65]

Why is dissent so frequent despite the institutional pressures toward conformity? Why the difference in the frequency of dissent between the different courts? Perhaps the reasons can be found in the peculiar nature of the subject

TABLE 8.1   Frequency of dissent in the fifty-one supreme courts: cases with one or more dissenting votes in samples of twenty-five*

Number of cases with dissent	Jurisdiction
0	Ala., Ariz., Del., Md., Mass., Nev., N.C., R.I., S.C., Tenn., W. Va.
1	Ga., Id., Ill., Ky., Md., Minn., Miss., Mo., N.M., N.D., Vt., Wash.
2	Conn., Fla., Ia., Neb., N.J., S.D., Va., Wyo.
3	Ark., N.H., O., Ore.
4	Col., Kans., Mont.
5	Alaska, Okla.
6	Hawaii, Ind., N.Y., Utah. Wis.
7	Calif., La.
8	Mich.
9	Tex.
10	Pa.
17	U.S. Supreme Court.

*   From R. Sickels, "The illusion of judicial consensus: zoning decisions in the Maryland Court of Appeals," *Am. Pol. Sci. Rev.*, **59**, 1965, p. 100.

matter of the several courts, the character of the persons selected to be judges, and the norms defining the judges' roles.

In the first place, it seems evident that there would be an increased tendency not to conform as the individual judge's commitment to a particular solution of the problem increased. This is confirmed by the marked increase in Supreme Court dissents over dissents among the judges of the several State courts. Many of the matters coming before the State Courts involve rules to which only a rare judge could have a deep emotional attachment. It is probably hard to perceive a great social issue in many of the technical problems of property law, or the precise construction of the Uniform Commercial Code. On the other hand, practically all the problems coming before the Supreme Court of the United States involve questions of high policy, about which men not only differ, but differ passionately. In such cases, it seems that group pressures that might be decisive in bringing about conformity in lesser cases are no longer inadequate in ensuring it.

In the second place, judges are not the sort of relatively inexperienced university students who make up the typical subjects for experimental small-group researches. They are members of a highly articulate subculture, that of the lawyers; they are usually among the most successful members in that subculture, and they have been trained for all their professional lives to take independent positions. It is not to be wondered that they tend to resist pressures toward group conformity that might overwhelm others.

Persons chosen for elevation to the United States Supreme Court bench, however, are characterized by a much wider diversity of backgrounds than those chosen for the State courts. For example, the geographical representation is far wider on the Supreme Court of the United States. State Supreme Court judges invariably are local residents. In many States, where a single party has held effective political power for many years, the bench is apt to be colored in political monochrome. Where judges are elected instead of appointed (as they are in the federal system), they are even more active politically than are some Supreme Court judges before elevation. Although there are no complete statistics, it seems probable that most State court judges are drawn primarily from successful practicing "political" lawyers.

Thirdly there seems to be no complete coincidence of the norms of conduct expected of fellow judges between the several courts. The wide difference in the frequency of dissent recorded in Table 8.1 appears to be sufficient evidence for this, for it is not to be believed that the judges in the different State courts are so different from each other, or the issues presented of so wide a range of controversiality, that they could explain the range of the frequency of dissent. Rather, it seems that the several State courts have different norms of conduct for the judges. In some States, we have been told that there is an informal understanding that, except for the most urgent reasons, judges are bound by majority vote in conference. In other States, for example Maryland, in some cases individual judges write the opinions, and the other judges simply assent without real consideration.[66]

In practically every case, at least a majority of the justices in the end achieve a consensus with respect to a single opinion. How is that consensus achieved apart from the use of rational argument? The process can best be understood by conceiving of the collegiate appellate court as basically a political organization and in terms of the interactions between its several members. We shall examine this notion in connection with the United States Supreme Court, on which most research has been done.

The leadership role in a small group is crucial. Small-group theory distinguishes between "task" leadership and "social" leadership. The former is concerned with getting a job done and the latter with maintaining individual self-esteem and group harmony. The role of the Chief Justice has sometimes been exercised in one way, and sometimes in the other. The role itself gives the Chief Justice two important leverages. He presides at the crucial conference, and has the privilege of stating his views first. He is thus in a position to identify the issues in the cases that seem to him to be significant, and thus to shape the entire discussion. Also, if he votes with the majority, he has the privilege of assigning the job of writing the opinion to one of the Justices in the majority. Chief Justices have been known to vote with the majority even when in disagreement in order to be able to name the opinion-writer. Charles Evans Hughes exercised his role as a task leader and dominated the conferences. Harlan Stone, on the other hand, was basically a social leader, and did not dominate the conferences as Hughes had done.[67]

Small-group theory also holds that in most discussion groups where expertise is equal, the person who talks the most generally wins a position as an informal leader.[68] In the Supreme Court, an institutionalized procedure has been adopted which has the effect of reducing the importance of the dominating speaker, for tradition requires that each Justice state his position in turn, beginning with the Justice who is junior on the Bench. On the other hand, expertise in many areas of law is not equally distributed. Justice Douglas, for example, who once served as Chairman of the Securities and Exchange Commission, obviously possesses special knowledge in this area, and almost all the decisions concerning the Securities and Exchange Act have been written by him. It is hard to believe that in specialized areas such as this, individual Justices do not take leadership when they have an expert knowledge of the field. Thus, the Chief Justice by virtue of his official position and other Justices with special expertise exert special influence in deciding cases.

Judges have frequently sought overtly to exert special influence by special salutes to other members of the bench. Effusive compliments on an opinion are not infrequent. Frankfurter, for example, noted on the back of Justice Stone's opinion in *United States v. Darby*,[69] "This is a grand plum pudding. There are so many luscious plums in it that it is invidious to select . . . It's a superb job."[70]

It seems hardly likely that compliments would be very effective in influencing men of as much experience and stature as are most Supreme Court Justices. It appears, however, that they are an important emollient for the crucial process of bargaining over opinions. Stone once wrote to Douglas,

I have gone over your opinion in this case with some care, and I congratulate you on your lucid and penetrating analysis and the great thoroughness with which you have done a difficult job. If Justice Brandeis could read it he would be proud of his successor.[71]

He annexed a single-spaced typwritten sheet of suggested revisions.

It is, of course, the bargaining process which most clearly suggests that opinions of the Supreme Court are in fact the product of the entire Court. A Justice has only two weapons which he can use against a colleague to obtain changes in the majority opinion: his vote and his willingness to express dissent in a written opinion. Except in close cases, the second is probably the more effective. Stone once wrote to Frankfurter,

If you wish to write, placing the case on the ground which I think tenable and desirable, I shall cheerfully join you. If not, I will add a few observations for myself.[72]

Occasionally, in the course of the bargaining process, pressures that go beyond what might seem the legitimate scope of rational argument are used. In *Hirabashyi v. United States*,[73] the majority of the court voted to uphold the conviction of some Nisei for violating a curfew imposed by the military on the West Coast. Murphy was horrified at the racism that he believed to be embodied in the decision and filed a strong dissent. Frankfurter wrote to him:

Of course, I shan't try to dissuade you from filing a dissent in the case—not because I do not think it highly unwise but because I think you are immovable. But I would like to say two things to you about the dissent: (1) it has internal contradictions which you ought not to allow to stand, and (2) do you really think it is conducive to the things you care about, including the great reputation of this Court, to suggest that everybody is out of step except Johnny, and more particularly that the Chief Justice and seven other Justices of this court are behaving like the enemy and thereby playing into the hands of the enemy?[74]

On another occasion during the war, in *Ex Parte Quirin*,[75] the Justices had difficulty in agreeing on whether the Constitution permitted the trial of captured Nazi saboteurs in military tribunals rather than in regularly constituted civilian courts. One Justice (unnamed), wrote to his colleagues:

Some of the very best lawyers I know are now in the Solomon Islands battle, some are seeing service in Australia, some are subchasers in the Atlantic, and some are on the various air fronts ... I can almost hear their voices were they to read more than a single opinion in this case. They would say something like this ... "What in hell do you fellows think you are doing? Haven't we enough of a job trying to lick the Japs and Nazis without having you fellows on the Court dissipate thoughts and feelings and energies of the folks at home by stirring up a nice row as to who has what power . . .? . . . Just relax and don't be too engrossed in your own interests in verbalistic conflicts because the inroads on energy and national unity that such conflict inevitably produces, is a pastime we had better postpone until peacetime."[76]

Ultimately a unanimous opinion was produced.

8.3 SUMMARY

The first function of courts is to resolve specific claims that rules have been breached. Arising out of this function is a second function: In cases in which the rules are obscure, or the facts at hand do not clearly fall within or without the rules, the court must create a new rule, fashioned *ex post facto*, to decide the case. The rules used for deciding a clear case are extracted from the existing legal order on the basis of the clear-case rules of recognition. The same clear-case rules of recognition, however, in some other cases suggest that there are two or more potentially applicable rules. When courts try to resolve such cases exclusively on the ground of the existing legal system itself, i.e. on the basis of legalistic reasoning, the results often merely mask the inarticulate values of the judges. Some American courts, especially the Supreme Court of the United States, have tried to decide trouble cases in a pragmatic way. In this practice, however, they have been limited by the constraints inherent in the structure of the courts in the Anglo-American system.

These rules, however, explain only a part of the decision-making process. A complete understanding of the conversion process which takes place in an appellate court decision requires that the court itself be understood as a small group, acting as small groups act—i.e., making decisions not merely on the basis of the merits of the problem to be solved, but also in terms of the personal relations between the judges themselves.

NOTES

1. Selections from *Law and the Modern Mind* by Jerome Frank, copyright 1930, 1933, 1949 by Coward McCann, Inc., copyright 1930 by Brentano's Inc., are from Anchor Books edition, 1963, p. 103. Copyright renewed in 1958 by Florence K. Frank. Reprinted by arrangement with the estate of Barbara Frank Kristein.

2. E. W. Patterson, *Jurisprudence: Men and Ideas of the Law*, Foundation Press, Brooklyn, 1953, p. 591. Reprinted by permission.

3. H. L. A. Hart, *The Concept of Law*, Clarendon Press, Oxford, 1961, pp. 112–113. Reprinted by permission of the Clarendon Press.

3a. F. Weiler, "Two models of judicial decision-making," *Can. Bar. Rev.* **46**, 406 (1968).

4. Frank, *op. cit.*, p. 110.

5. *The Debates and Proceedings of the Constitutional Convention of the State of California* **2** 1880, pp. 949 ff. Quoted in M. Radin, "The requirement of written opinions," *Cal. Law Reb.*, **18**, 1930, p. 486.

6. *Report of the Committee of Managers on the Causes and Duration of Mr. Hastings' trial*, four speeches of Edmund Burke, pp. 200–201. Quoted in C. Auerbach, L. K. Garrison, W. Hurst, and S. Mermin, *The Legal Process*, Chandler, San Francisco, 1961, p. 355.

7. Roscoe Pound, *Jurisprudence*, West Publishing Co., St. Paul, 1959, p. 679. Reprinted by permission.

8. This example is drawn from Hart, *The Concept of Law*, pp. 121–122.

9. K. N. Llewellyn, *The Bramble Bush*, Oceana, New York, 1951, pp. 41–45.

10. J. Dickinson, "The problem of the unprovided case," *U. Pa. Law Rev.*, **81**, 1932, pp. 115–116.

11. E. Coke, *On Littleton* (1689), f. 97b.

12. A. L. Goodhart, "Determining the ratio decidendi of a case," *Yale Law J.* **40**, 1930, pp. 161–183.

13. 3 Mees. and Wels. 1 (Exchequer, 1837).

14. See W. S. Holdsworth, *History of English Law*, Methuen, London, 1903–1966, **viii**, pp. 473–475.

15. See Roscoe Pound, "The economic interpretation of the law and the law of torts," *Harvard Law Rev.*, **53**, 1940, pp. 365–367.

16. Quoted in H. V. Evatt, "The judges and the teachers of public law," *Harvard Law Rev.* **53**, 1940, p. 1150.

17. 3 Mees. and Wels. 1, 3 (Exchequer, 1837).

18. 4 Metc. 49 (1842).

19. *Ibid.*, p. 53.

20. *Ibid.*

21. W. Nelles, "Commonwealth v. Hunt," *Columbia Law Rev.*, **32**, 1932, pp. 1128, 1152.

22. *Ibid.*

23. *Tiller v. Atlantic Coast Line Railroad*, 318 U.S. 54, pp. 58–59 (1943).

24. 1 McM. 385 (S.C., 1841).

25. *Ibid.*, p. 389.

26. *Ibid.*, p. 391.

27. Lawrence Friedman, "On legalistic reasoning—a footnote to Weber," *Wisc. Law Rev.*, 1966, p. 148. Cf. J. Shklar, *Legalism*, Harvard University Press, Cambridge, Mass., 1964, p. 1. (Legalism is "the ethical attitude that holds moral conduct to be a

matter of rule following and moral relationships to consist of rights and duties determined by rules.") As Friedman points out, Shklar's definition more accurately describes the justification for legalism than legalism itself.

28. Max Rheinstein (ed.), *Max Weber on Law in Economy and Society*, Edward Shils and Max Rheinstein (tr.), Harvard University Press, Cambridge, Mass., 1954, p. 63.

29. *Ibid.*, p. 1. Reprinted by permission.

30. J. Bentham, "Papers on Codification," *The Works of Jeremy Bentham*, Vol. 4, Bowring (ed.), Simpkin, Marshall, London, 1843, pp. 453–530; see also J. Bentham, *Theory of Legislation*, Hildreth (tr.), Kegan Paul, Trench, Truebner, London, 1911, pp. 149–150.

31. A. V. Dicey, *Introduction to the Study of the Law of the Constitution*, Macmillan, London, 1959.

32. Rheinstein, *op. cit.*, p. 267.

33. *Ibid.*, p. 64.

34. Quoted in W. Friedmann, "Limits of judical law-making," *Mod. Law Rev.* **29**, 1966, p. 593.

35. *Scruttons v. Midland Silicones*, [1962] A.C. 446, 467–468.

36. *Southern Pacific Co. v. Jensen*, 244 U.S. 205, 221 (1917).

37. K. N. Llewellyn, "Remarks on the theory of appellate decision and rules or canons about how statutes ought to be construed," *Vand. Law Rev.*, **3**, 1950, pp. 395, 398–406.

38. 4 W.A.C.A. 133 Nigeria (1948).

39. *Rex v. Bourne*, K.B. 687 (1939).

40. Dissenting in *Lochner v. New York* 198 U.S. 45, 74 (1905).

41. O. W. Holmes, "The path of the law," *Harvard Law Rev.*, **10**, 1897, p. 457.

42. Hart, *The Concept of Law*, p. 133.

43. O. W. Holmes, *The Common Law*, Little, Brown, Boston, 1881, p. 1.

44. W. Friedmann, *Legal Theory*, Stevens, London, 1953, p. 258.

45. Frank, *Law and the Modern Mind, passim.*

46. K. N. Llewellyn, *The Common Law Tradition: Deciding Appeals*, Little, Brown, Boston, 1960.

47. H. Oliphant, "A return to stare decisis," *Am. Bar Assoc. J.*, **14**, 1928, p. 7. Reprinted by permission.

48. L. H. Mayo and E. M. Jones, "Legal-policy decision process: alternative thinking and the predictive function," *George Washington Law Rev.*, **33**, 1964, pp. 318–320.

49. *Supra*, pp. 108–111.

50. *Supra*, pp. 105–106.

51. 347 U.S. 483 (1954).

52. 163 U.S. 537 (1896).

53. *Brown v. Board of Education*, 347 U.S. 483 (1954).

54. *Ibid.*, p. 494.

55. See generally E. Cahn, "A dangerous myth in the school desegration cases," *N.Y.U. Law Rev.*, **30**, 1955, p. 150; Garfinkel, "Social science evidence and the school desegregation cases," *J. Politics,* **21**, 1959, p. 37; K. Clark, "The segregation cases: criticism of the social scientists' role," *Villanova Law Rev.*, **5**, 1959, p. 421; H. Wechsler, "Toward neutral principles of constitutional law," *Harvard Law Rev.*, **73**, 1959, p. 1; Pollack, "Racial discrimination and judicial integrity: a reply to Professor Wechsler," *U. Pa. Law Rev.*, **108**, 1959, p. 1.

56. See R. B. Seidman, "The judicial process reconsidered in light of role-theory," *Mod. Law Rev.*, **32**, 1969, p. 516.

57. Roscoe Pound, *Social Control Through Law* (the Powell Lectures), Archon, Hamden, Conn., 1968, pp. 113–114. Reprinted by permission.

58. In the Declaration of Delhi, The International Congress of Jurists stated that the Rule of Law should be employed "not only to safeguard and advance the civil politic rights of the individual" but also "to establish social, economic, educational, and cultural conditions under which his legitimate aspirations and dignity may be realized." International Congress of Jurists, *The Rule of Law in a Free Society: A Report on the International Congress of Jurists*, New Delhi, India, January 5–10, 1959 (no publisher or date).

59. Harold Laski, *American Democracy*, Viking, New York, 1948, p. 443.

60. Dissenting in *Lochner v. New York*, 198 U.S. 45, 74 (1905).

61. See, e.g., Henry Hart, "The Supreme Court, 1958 term. Forward: the time chart of the justices," *Harvard Law Rev.* **73**, 1959, p. 84.

62. Thurman Arnold, "Professor Hart's theology," *Harvard Law Rev.*, **73**, 1960, p. 1313.

63. See K. M. ZoBell, "Division of opinion in the Supreme Court: a history of judicial disintegration," *Cornell Law Quart.*, **44**, 1959, pp. 186–205.

64. A. P. Hare, "Interpersonal relations in the small group," in R. E. L. Faris (ed.), *Handbook of Modern Sociology*, Rand McNally, Chicago, 1964, pp. 217–219.

65. Learned Hand, *The Bill of Rights*, Harvard University Press, Cambridge, 1958, pp. 72–73.

66. R. Sickles, "Illusion of judicial consensus: zoning decisions in the Maryland Court of Appeals," *Amer. Pol. Sci. Rev.*, **59**, pp. 100–104.

67. W. F. Murphy, *Judicial Strategy*, University of Chicago Press, Chicago, 1964, pp. 397–398.

68. Hare, *op cit.*, p. 236.

69. 312 U.S. 100 (1941).

70. Quoted in W. F. Murphy, *op. cit.*, p. 51.

71. *Ibid.*, p. 52.

72. *Ibid.*, p. 59.

73. 320 U.S. 81 (1943).

74. Murphy, *op. cit.*, 47.

75. 317 U.S. 1 (1942).

76. Quoted in W. F. Murphy, *op. cit.*, p. 47.

9

Outputs of appellate courts

Judges of appellate courts, like other role-occupants, behave according to the norms defining their position, the societal, personal, and other forces exerted upon them, and the activity of sanctioning institutions. Formal sanctioning institutions for appellate courts, however, hardly exist. The rule-making activity of these courts responds, therefore, to the inputs as determined by the adversary system, the recruitment institutions which choose the judges, the socialization of judges, the situational imperatives, etc., as well as to the norms of judicial decision-making and the small-group interactions within the appellate court.

We do not, of course, propose to examine the full substance of the innumerable rules created by appellate courts, which is a task beyond the reasonable scope of this or any other single book. We shall confine ourselves to some of the common characteristics of the rules which these courts have produced. We shall first preliminarily discuss possible models for the phenomena under study. We shall then briefly identify the variables that seem to produce the unique shape of the rules that emerge from the appellate structure. And finally, we shall try to develop some propositions concerning those rules.

9.1 MODELS

As we have seen, the position of appellate courts requires that they be agencies of change. Their position requires that they make decisions which change old norms or create new ones for society.

Robert Chin has suggested three different theories of "changing" a system, which he has denoted as a "system model," a "development model," and a "model for changing." The model adopted by the change-agent determines the sort of changes he will bring about.

Chin describes the system model in familiar structural-functionalist terms:

A "system" model emphasizes primarily the details of how stability is achieved, and only derivatively how change evolves out of the incompatibilities and conflict in the system. A system model assumes that organization, interdependency, and integration exist among its parts and that change is a derived consequence of how well the parts of the system fit together, or how well the system fits in with other surrounding and interacting systems. The source of change lies primarily in the structural stress and strain externally produced or internally created. The process of change is a process of tension reduction. The goals and direction are emergent from the structures or from imposed sources. Goals are often analyzed as set by "vested interests" of one part of the system. The confronting symptom of some trouble is a reflection of difficulties of adaptation (reaction to environment) or of the ability for adjustment (internal equilibrium). The levers or handles available for manipulation are in the "inputs" to the system, especially the feedback mechanisms, and in the forces tending to restore the balance to the system . . . [1]

The range of choice which the system model suggests to the change-agent is limited to those choices which the system itself throws up to the decision-maker. Because the change-agent acts only when tensions arise, and then only to reduce and manage the tensions, the changes for which he is responsible tend to be relatively small and discrete, rather than wide-ranging and radical.

It has frequently been urged that the equilibrium structural-functional model is inherently conservative. "The equilibrium model," say the proponents of the conflict theory, "consciously or unwittingly, becomes a support for the status quo. Instead of being a lens which sharpens our perspective and puts social reality in focus, it becomes a pair of rose-colored glasses which distort reality, screening out the harsh facts about conflict of purpose and interest in human affairs."[2]

Structural-functionalists, of course, deny this charge. Merton claims that structural-functionalism is not *inherently* conservative, because it does not necessarily demand a commitment to any particular ideological orientation.[3]

Merton's rejoinder, however, misses the thrust of the ideological attack. The claim made is not that structural-functionalists are bound by conservative, ideological commitments. Rather, it is that the change-agent who follows the structural-functionalist model is limited to tinkering with conventional wisdom in response to emergent tensions. He is precluded by his way of looking at things from considering any more radical potential alternatives. Wilbert Moore says that the structural-functionalist equilibrium model "either forecloses questions about the sources of change, or if discordant elements are brought into the analysis, . . . will predict one direction of change, and one only—change that restores the system to a steady state."[4]

If this be an accurate claim, then we should expect that any court which adopts the structural-functionist view, either voluntarily or by reasons of institutional constraints upon it, will produce rules which do no more than make relatively minor adjustments to existing institutions. Such a court can provide grease and oil for the bearings, but it cannot design a new machine. This conservative cast to their rule output, moreover, will exist regardless of how the individual judges place in the radical-liberal-conservative-reactionary political spectrum.

A second kind of model Chin has called the "developmental" model.

The developmental model assumes constant change and development, and growth and decay of a system over time. Any existing stability is a snapshot of a living process— a stage that will give way to another stage. The supposition seems to be that it is "natural" that change should occur because change is rooted in the very nature of living organisms. The laws of the developmental process are not necessarily fixed, but some effects of the environment are presumably necessary to the developmental process. The direction of change is toward some goal, the fulfillment of its destiny, granting that no major blockage gets in the way. "Trouble" occurs when there is a gap between the system and its goal. Intervention is viewed as the removal of blockage by the change-agent, who then gets out of the way of the growth forces.[5]

Chin's developmental model is closely akin to Moore's "tension-management" model.[6] Of this Moore says:

The view of society as a tension-management rather than as a self-equilibrating system has distinct advantages in making *both* order and change problematical, but also "normal." Tensions—or inconsistencies and strains, if the word "tensions" is too subjective or has too psychological a connotation—are intrinsic to social systems, not simply accidental accompaniments or the products of changes that impinge on the system from external sources . . . Yet the theoretical tension-management model differs from the presumption of equilibrium in several significant respects:

1   To the degree that at least some tensions are really intrinsic, and not simply organizational problems that can be readily resolved, the predicted change will neither restore an equilibrium or static state nor create a new one.

2   The consequences of change will almost certainly be tension-producing as well as possibly tension-reducing.

3   The use of the term "tension" does not imply that change will initially reduce tension . . .

4   The conception of society (or any social structure) as a tension-management system

involves no presumption at all that the management is "successful," or that the system in fact persists . . . One possible course may be destruction."[7]

This model suggests a rather broader range of choice available to the change-agent than that implied in the systems model. In the latter, only solutions which are wholly consistent with the continuation of existing institutions can be considered. According to the development model, the change-agent can remove "blockages" from the ongoing development of the institution in achieving goals which are somehow immanent in the institution itself. The creation of entirely new institutions, however, is not conceived as a possible choice, because the basic institutional structure is taken as given in the case.

If this model describes the role imposed on an appellate court, then one might expect the rule-output of the court to be of the sort conventionally labeled liberal rather than either conservative or radical. There would be no attempt to make large changes in existing institutions, and those changes that are attempted would respond to a single set of values extrapolated from the existing order.

Chin's third model, the "model for changing," is rather different from either of these: It

is a more recent creation. It incorporates some elements of analyses from system models, along with some ideas from the developmental model, in a framework where direct attention is paid to the induced forces producing change. It studies stability in order to unfreeze and move some parts of the system. The direction to be taken is not fixed or "determined," but remains in large measure a matter of "choice" for the client-system. The change-agent is a specialist in the technical processes of facilitating change, a helper to the client-system . . .[8]

This model is the only one of these three paradigms which is consistent with a general conflict model of society. Unlike the other two models, it permits the change-agent a choice as to goals as well as to means. As in the case of the developmental model, it also permits the change-agent wide range of choice as to the means to be used.

Robert Dahl proposed a tripartite typology of change, which has been expanded by Dahl and Lindblom.[9] We may call these incremental change, comprehensive change, and revolutionary change. For our purposes, incremental change occurs when (a) there is no change in power relations, (b) there are minor changes to existing institutions designed to restore them to equilibrium, and (c) the entire structure continues to operate much as it did before. Comprehensive change occurs when (a) there is a change in power relations within a particular institution, (b) particular institutions are changed in a relatively thoroughgoing way, and (c) the overall structure continues to operate much as it did before. Revolutionary change occurs when there is a thoroughgoing shift in power relations, (b) many institutions are changed radically, and (c) the entire structure of society is changed.

Using this typology, we can see that Chin's systems model is compatible with incremental change, his development model is compatible with either incremental or comprehensive change, and his model for changing is compatible with any of the three types of change.

The inputs and conversion processes of appellate courts determine the kinds of change of which they are capable. We can hypothesize that the ordinary appelate court, following the formal style of rule-making in common-law cases, or cases concerning the construction of statutes, is capable only of incremental change, but that a court which (like the Supreme Court of the United States) takes a realistic approach to construing an extremely vague document such as the Constitution, may be capable of producing comprehensive change. No appellate court, however, will be capable of inducing revolutionary change.

9.2 THE RULE OUTPUT OF APPELLATE COURTS

Courts begin as dispute-settling mechanisms. Every rule which is formulated and announced by an appellate court comes into existence because somebody has conceived that he was aggrieved by the action of somebody else, and so instituted a lawsuit of some sort. While the rule articulated by an appellate court must be a generalized rule applicable to all other parties in similar situations, it must also resolve the instant litigation. Moreover, since judges are sworn to uphold the law, they cannot (or ought not) create new laws which are completely unrelated to the existing framework of rules. As we have seen, the law-creating functions of appellate courts is not something that they search out, but which inevitably they *must* fulfill. Nevertheless, theirs is not a law-creating function *de novo*. Their primary job as dispute-settlers and hence as rule-*appliers* limits the scope of their creativity as rule-*makers*. These several constraints, all arising out of the fact that appellate courts do their rule-making in the immediate context of dispute-settlement, account for some of the peculiar characteristics of the rules which they create.

The total rule output in its variety of configurations is shaped by these pressures and processes. The vast proportion of the rule output of appellate courts is inducive of incremental, rather than radical, change; it aims at overall solutions which are relatively conservative, and it is dominated by the courts' own institutional interests over all other interests in society. To the first two of these generalizations, however, a sharp exception must be made for the present Supreme Court of the United States, for reasons which are peculiar to it. We discuss first the output of appellate courts other than the Supreme Court.

Appellate Courts Generally

Long ago Roscoe Pound said that the great paradox of the law is between the need for stability and the need for change. People need and demand predictability in their jural relationships. They want to know that when they act in certain specified ways there will be certain specified consequences. Actors want a world in which at least our most important actions are governed by ascertainable, predictable norms. At the same time, however, the world moves, and not only in the physical way that Galileo had in mind. Constant flux in social relations *is* the human condition. The power of the State expressed through law can no more than Canute hold back the tide. If the law tries to cast society in a rigid mold, the stresses and strains become so great that tension, anomie, incoherence, and violence inevitably result.

But to say that the law must always strike a balance between stability and change is to say nothing very helpful. The choice posed at any given moment to the rule-maker is only very rarely one whose resolution, one way or the other, will result in immediate, deeply rooted unrest. The nature of the institutional constraints, the inputs, and the conversion processes used by most appellate courts dictate that their choice in general will lead only to incremental change; they favor a return to equilibrium without changing existing institutions more than is required to maintain existing power relations.

Interstitial Rules

Most lawsuits are clear cases. They call for the application of preexisting norms. In trouble cases, in which the rules themselves are at issue, the traditional conversion process requires that each party must demonstrate that his claimed rule of law is based on at least one possible reading of existing rules which are accepted as such—i.e., as we have seen, one must start with the clear-case rules. Bound by norms defining such conversion processes, the court's choice is inevitably a narrow one. In a leading New York case on the definition of insanity, for example,[10] the defendant cut the throat of a woman after, he claimed, he had heard the voice of God calling upon him to kill her as a sacrifice and atonement; and after having killed her, he believed that he was in the visible presence of God. The rules then in force in New York provided that a person could plead insanity as a defense to a criminal charge only if he could prove that "at the time of the committing of the act, the party accused was laboring under such defect of reason, from disease of the mind, as not to know the nature or quality of the act he was doing; or if he did know it, that he did not know what he was doing was wrong." These rules go back to M'Naghton's Case.[11] Schmidt knew that what he was doing was illegal, but believed that he was obeying a higher law. The narrow issue was whether the word "wrong" meant "illegal" or "morally wrong," for Schmidt claimed that although he knew what he was doing was illegal, he did not know that what he was doing was morally wrong. (Judge Cardozo decided that the proper construction was "morally wrong.") But the Court was not called upon to consider whether the entire standard of insanity, based as it was on the psychiatric knowledge of 1843, ought to be maintained, as a legislature would at least have considered. The institutional role and structure of the courts, arising from their original purpose of dispute-settlement, forbade them to take so radical a step.

The character of appellate courts as small groups probably also contributes to this inhibition. As we have seen, the decisions of these courts are frequently based on compromises, on the bargaining between members of the courts themselves. The usual result of such bargaining is to ensure that the opinion will justify the decision on grounds that can command the widest agreement among the various members of the court. The narrower the rule is, the more people can agree with it.

Incapacity for Planning

A corollary to the built-in limitation that appellate courts can induce only incremental rather than radical changes is that courts are incapable of laying out an entire area of law in order to plan a total, integrated response to the challenges posed to them. They cannot take on the "big picture." For example, litigation over water rights in the southwestern United States frequently takes the form of disputes between upstream and downstream owners, each of whom claims the right to divert a certain percentage of the river's flow into his own drainage ditches. Many such disputes, of course, can flare up along the course of a river. There have been cases in which, as a result of a number of such individual actions, the judicial system made a series of judgments with the brilliant result that they allocated far more than 100 percent of the river's flowage.

There are those who have urged that the rules devised by appellate courts, despite the apparently fortuitous way in which cases arise, nevertheless do tend to form a complete and harmonious system. Llewellyn argued that since disputes arise out of conflict, and since conflict is most likely in developing or growing areas of social activity, the development of rules is apt to match the dynamics of society itself. As Fuller has pointed out, this is a sort of classical free-market theory of legal rule-making.[12] Nevertheless, Fuller has shown that a whole field of law may be permanently influenced and biased by the special factors present in the first case raising the question. (It is an old principle that widow's and orphan's cases make bad law.) Moreover, the order in which cases arise may shape the law in a way that a law-maker who could assess the entire programme would perceive to be unwise. The movement for the establishment of Law Revision Commissions is in part aimed at rectifying such mistakes; the Commissions are to be specialized agencies with the function of overviewing entire fields of law.

Inability to Create New Organizations

The most pressing social problems of our time can only rarely be solved by general rules alone. There has thus been an increasing reliance on specially created organizations, each presumably dedicated to the execution of certain areas of public policy, for solutions to emergent tensions. Witness the astounding growth of acronymed agencies in the past half century.

In the school desegregation case, for example, the Supreme Court recognized that the social problem to which its decision was directed could not be solved by laying down universal norms of conduct. Instead, the Court in the *Brown* decision articulated a policy. Ideally, there would have been created an agency empowered to use a whole bag of sanctions—education of public officials, increased school aid for conforming school districts, punishment for obdurate school districts, technical assistance in solving specific local questions, etc.—for the institution of that policy. But its institutional structure imposed a sharp limitation on what the Court could do. The best that it was able to do was to send the case back to individual district courts for the latter to use their equity power to bring about desegregation "with all deliberate speed." The absence of adequate specialized agencies to deal with the problem continued for a whole decade after *Brown*, until the Department of Health, Education, and Welfare was given limited authority in the area in the Civil Rights Act of 1964.

Inability to Determine Potential Consequences

The more the proposed change varies from what presently is the case, the greater is the risk that unforeseen consequences will intervene. Dahl and Lindblom expanded this notion into a whole theory which claims that only incremental change is completely rational.[13] The greater the change, therefore, the more risky it is to proceed in the absence of competent empirical data anticipating what the consequences will be. Conversely, the less empirical information is available, the more likely it is that the change-agent will abstain from instituting comprehensive change in favor of incremental change.

Courts suffer from an institutional disability that prevents them from making the sort of empirical studies that might permit them to make comprehensive changes with even a minimum amount of confidence in the result.

Courts depend on the adversary system for the kind of fact-gathering required to determine whether a particular state of affairs occurred at a particular time and place.[14] Legislative-like rule-making, however, requires different kinds of facts, such as are collected, analyzed, and reported by the several social science disciplines. For the purposes of obtaining these types of facts the usual procedures in the courts are largely irrelevant. Occasionally, as in *Brown*, such evidence may be introduced on the trial court level through expert witnesses. Sometimes the social science data are submitted to the appellate court in the form of a "Brandeis brief" (so called because it was first used by Louis Brandeis when he was an attorney). Both these devices, however, are useful only within severe limitations. The expert is hampered by limits imposed by the rules of evidence, which are designed to guard against various sorts of problems that arise when experts testify in cases involving insanity, medical issues, and the like, and which are ill-adapted to the admission and exclusion of social science data. The Brandeis brief is not subject to close scrutiny by the opposing parties. In neither case is there opportunity for persons affected by the potential ruling, but not parties to the lawsuit, to be represented except as they may be able to argue as an *amicus curiae* ("friend of the court").

Increasing Concern with Trivia in Private Law

As Friedman has demonstrated,[15] in the mid-nineteenth century appellate courts were central to the formulation of universalistic rules of contract law—and, one might add, in other areas of private law as well. The Market reigned, largely without restraint; the people saw in the release of individual energy the engine of economic development.[16] Disputes between individuals were readily perceived by courts as specific examples of universal rules which ordered the operations of the market, and they were decided in those terms. By the middle of the twentieth century, however, everything was *toto caelo* different.

Mid-twentieth century society, taken in general, was middle-of-the road. It believed in the sanctity of majority rule and majority opinion; it did not really believe that men held irreconcilable economic goals, but believed rather in the possibilities and values of team-work and compromise; it believed that nobody gained if the farmer suffered, that strong unions and clean employee cafeterias were good for business, and that it would be morally wrong for labor to lack a voice in running an industry. It was fashionable in 1955 to see (and decry) "conformity" in American society; certainly developments in mass communications and transport made cultural and moral homogeneity possible. The use of "fairness" as a criterion for settling contract disputes meant the replacement of inherited legal concepts with current concepts of what was right. Particular disputes were to be judged in terms of current ethical standards. It meant foreswearing the use of general principles applied absolutely; it meant that courts were dispute-settlers, not agencies creating general norms at the impulse of particular occasions.[17]

The search for particularity and fairness impelled the creation of many government agencies concerned with contract performance of various sorts. As Friedman concludes,

In part, the activism of government (in the middle of the twentieth century) was a judgment that the market was a failure; in another sense, it was a judgment that the economy consisted not of a market, but of many markets, each with its appropriate modality of control. In such a context, the law of contract remained alive, not however, as the organic law of the state's economic system—a kind of constitution for business transactions—but as one among many. It was the system of rules applicable to marginal, novel, as yet unregulated, residual and peripheral business, and quasi-business transactions, transactions which might, in exceptional cases, call for problem-solving and dispute-settling. "Contract" stepped in where no other body of law and no agency of law other than the court was appropriate or available.[18]

The sharp diminution in the rule-making output of appellate courts in contract cases was, ultimately, the resultant of their primary commitment to dispute-settlement. Since the rule-making processes of appellate courts are never placed in motion unless there is a dispute to settle, so long as other agencies have original jurisdiction in contract cases, the contract rule-making output of appellate courts is bound to decline and become more and more restricted to trivia.

The same thing has happened in most other areas of private law. Workmen's Compensation Commissions have drained off all but an infinitesimal fraction of industrial accident cases. Better methods of land registration and a wide use of title insurance have reduced the number of litigations arising from real estate transactions. Standardized lease forms have sharply cut down the number of landlord-tenant litigations, and in many places, rent-control agencies have superseded even the use of the standardized lease form. Insurance contracts have their forms laid down by insurance commissioners. When businessmen litigate, they tend to appeal, more often than not, to governmental agencies of all sorts: local planning and zoning commissions with respect to real estate problems, licensing boards, regulating agencies, tax agents, and specialized tax courts.

Only in one area has the courts' rule-making output in private law proliferated: automobile accidents. In the nineteenth century, tort law—the law that purports to regulate disparate activities within a basically nonregulated society— contained an important component which adjusted the relationships between industry and those affected by its activities. The inadequacy of tort law for regulating such activities led in time to its replacement by other sets of rules: zoning, which tried to prevent incompatible land uses from too close contact, Food and Drug Administrations, Public Utility Commissions, and the like. Only with respect to automobiles have the courts retained their control over practically the entire area—a control whose demise is being heralded by the development of national and state legislation laying down safety standards for automobiles, and whose death-knell will be sounded when the States enact legislation assimilating automobile accidents under the absolute liability imposed in Workmen's Compensation cases.

9.3 THE CONSEQUENCES OF INCREMENTAL CHANGE

The institutional constraints upon appellate courts, according to which they can undertake rule-making only in response to particular disputes between particular parties, and cannot plan large areas of law systematically, nor create new organizations, have combined with the sorts of conversion processes which courts traditionally employ and the fact (which may be a result rather than a cause of the courts' limitations) that increasingly they have been concerned with trivia in the rule-making role, to limit the scope of choice available to appellate courts in their rule-making efforts. Consequently, they have been unable to bring about radical institutional changes (again excepting the Supreme Court of the United

States). Whatever the position of a particular bench in the conservative-radical political continuum, its rule output has necessarily been reflective of the blinders of institution, the conversion processes, and attention to trivia.

The examples are legion. The solution of many of our most pressing social problems today requires a radical redistribution of income. Courts, even if they are so inclined, can do only very little about this. No matter how lenient a court may be when a dispute between a wealthy landlord and a poverty-stricken inhabitant of the ghetto comes before it, the rule it articulates must assume the fact that by and large tenants must pay rent to landlords. Courts have no way of subsidizing the rent, or of constructing public low-rent housing for the poor. Another example can be found in our system of compensation for injuries in automobile accidents. Such accidents are as much a concomitant of a highly mobile society in which automobiles are very widely owned, as industrial accidents are in an industrial society. Just as the cost of industrial accidents ultimately became regarded as part of the costs of production, which ought to be borne by the ultimate consumer largely as part of the price of the product, so ought we at least to consider whether part of the general social cost of a highly mobile society is not the cost of automobile accidents. We have no difficulty in seeing that roads are part of the general social cost; the cost of automobile accidents might well be regarded in the same way. By reason of the several constraints we mentioned, however, courts are incapable of adopting so radical a position even if they wanted to do so.

The actual narrowness of the courts' vision precisely matches the narrowness of vision that can be predicted for Chin's systems model. Appellate courts only make rules in response to stresses arising in existing institutions. The changes they can conceivably make are incremental, designed to make the existing structures function smoothly once again, i.e. to return to an equilibrium in which the institution can operate without further intervention by governmental agencies.

When the restricted scope of choice which is available to judges is considered, not from their point of view, but from the point of view according to which society is based on conflict between its various groups and strata, a radical vision results. In the words of Harold Laski,

Every society is the theatre of a conflict between economic classes for a larger material benefit, for, that is, a larger share in the results to be distributed from the productive process. Since the power to produce within any society is dependent upon peace, the state must maintain law and order to that end. But, in so doing, it is necessarily maintaining the law and order implied in the particular system of class relations of which it is the expression. In a feudal society, that is, the law and order which the state maintains is the law and order necessary to the preservation of feudal principles. In a capitalist society, the state maintains the law and order necessary to maintain capitalist principles . . . [19]

It seems improbable that courts will ever be able to accomplish, save by miniscule changes moving with glacial slowness, the sort of revolutionary shifts in power which would be necessary to change the system entirely. It would even seem highly unlikely that any court could accomplish anything more than incremental change.

Yet the fact is that, although most appellate courts in most decisions do no more than make incremental changes, the Supreme Court of the United States has made decisions which have brought about thoroughgoing changes in particular institutions, accompanied by significant shifts in power relations with respect to those institutions. How can we account for this paradox?

9.4 COMPREHENSIVE CHANGE AND THE SUPREME COURT

It is an intriguing fact that over the past few years a new, a radical trend has arisen in the Supreme Court of the United States. In case after case, the Court has quite decisively disconfirmed what we just stated to be the necessary character of court decisions. In *Miranda v. Arizona*,[20] for example, the Court laid down a whole manual delineating the permissible scope of police interrogation on arrests. In *Matter of Gault*,[21] it outlined the required procedures for juvenile courts. In *Baker v. Carr*[22] it ordered far-reaching changes in State electoral laws. In *Brown v. Board of Education*,[23] it laid down a broad rule which has had profound effects on the entire social fabric of most parts of the country. In none of these cases can it fairly be said that the rules laid down were "interstitial" or "molecular." Why this sharp divergence from the traditional form of rule output of appellate courts? The reasons seem to lie in the unique institutional position of the Supreme Court, the role of moral entrepreneurs in Constitutional litigation, and the pragmatic decision-making methods which the Court has come more and more to employ.

Its Institutional Position

The Supreme Court's power of judicial review of legislation or actions by any governmental body in the country to determine if laws or governmental actions square with constitutional norms in effect gives it a limited veto power over every other branch of government. As a result, it is frequently called upon to decide the direction of the central thrust of entire institutions, as our four examples demonstrate. The Court's first duty is to uphold the Constitution, a notoriously ambiguous document which speaks frequently, not to peripheral matters, but to the most important values of government: fairness, protection of the individual from hostile action by the state, the openness of our society, its potential for peaceful social change, the protection of minority interest from majority will. To resolve ambiguities in most statutes requires a court to forge a new rule which effects only interstitial change. To resolve ambiguities in the Constitution frequently requires the Supreme Court to forge new rules which radically change the essence of existing institutions.

In recent years, the Supreme Court has been called upon to answer just such far-ranging questions at a time when other branches of government were deadlocked on the issues involved. For many years the Court had been making small, molecular attempts to solve the problems as they arose in narrow terms. It had tried on a case-by-case basis to curb police interrogations by limiting their admissibility, but to no avail. Legislatures seemed incapable or unwilling to move into the premises. Petitioners had been knocking at the Supreme Court door for years claiming discrimination in representation in the States, and the Court had responded only that the matter was "political" and therefore not justifiable. But the "political" bodies which ought to have remedied the situation, the Congress and the State legislatures, showed no sign of moving to resolve the problems. Similarly, desegregation in public education was regarded by all the members of the Court as a denial of the promise of the American dream, and yet Congress patently did not propose to interfere.

The Court's institutional position and the facts of history therefore determined that many of the constitutional cases that would reach it would call into question, not only the operations of specific public institutions, but the general direction in which the institution was moving. The constitutional position of the Court has required it to test the institutions in question against the values which it perceives to be expressed in the Constitution itself, at a time when it seemed useless to rely upon some other, perhaps more appropriate, agency to reform these institutions. Moreover, a mechanism existed whose operation ensured that even issues primarily of interest to the poor would come up in contexts in which the policy inputs of at least the petitioners would be directed at deep-seated change.

Rules Important to Special Interest Groups

That courts can only consider issues arising in specific disputes is ordinarily a sharp constraint on their rule output. By the same token, however, the courts are almost the only branch of government whose rule-making capacities can be put into motion at the instance of an individual. Legislatures are under no requirement to move at individuals' requests. Administrative agencies in most cases, too, need not respond to the petition of isolated individuals. The courts alone must respond.

As a result, where the issuance of a rule is important to a particular interest group, it is relatively easy (albeit expensive) for a case to be taken to the highest rule-making levels even when the intrinsic importance of the case would not justify such an investment. In State as well as Federal Courts, tax cases have abounded precisely for this reason. Many states have in the past levied taxes on businesses with only transient interests within the states in question. More frequently than not, the amount involved for any particular business in any particular state has been insufficiently large to warrant the costs of appeals through a multitude of administrative agencies and State and Federal Courts. Since, however, a favorable ruling would have an impact far beyond the particular case, business associations of various sorts have litigated such cases in a continuing effort to persuade the appellate courts to announce rules favorable to their interests.

The peculiar position of the Supreme Court of the United States in constitutional matters has made it the special target of such "test cases." Probably no single individual would have litigated the question of prayers by six-year-old children in public schools before the Supreme Court, at a cost of many thousands of dollars. Yet such cases have repeatedly come before the Court. In these cases the litigations are often carried on in the name of particular individuals, but the real interested party is an organization such as the American Civil Liberties Union. *Brown v. Board of Education*, the school desegregation case, whose impact upon the American society has probably been more widespread than any other case in American legal history, was conceived, tried, and appealed by the NAACP. Most of our current rules governing criminal procedure were created upon litigation by civil liberties groups, as were most of the cases involving freedom of expression, loyalty oaths, and the like. Many, perhaps most, of these cases arose in areas where it was plainly hopeless to even try to persuade the Congress to move. Indeed, in many of these cases there have been Congressional efforts to reverse the Court's ruling by statute.

The existence of moral entrepreneurs has been of great significance in alleviating the built-in bias of the appellate court system, and especially of the most expensive of the courts, the Supreme Court, to select issues for decision which are of primary interest to the well-to-do. But the Constitutional position of the Supreme Court, and the fact that there exist moral entrepreneurs to carry the cases to it, would not alone explain why the Court has abandoned incremental change as the core of the judicial technique in so many cases. These factors at best provide the opportunity for more wide-ranging decision-making. It also needs an entirely different method to guide its decision, and this method the court has found in the pragmatic, realist mode of deciding cases which has dominated Surpeme Court constitutional decisional techniques since the late nineteen-thirties.

Pragmatic Decision-Making

We have already seen that as a result of historical progression, the Supreme Court, since the judicial "revolution" of 1937, has adopted as its most usual form of deciding cases the pragmatic method which is associated with the realist school of jurisprudence.[24] In *Miranda*, for example, even the dissenting justices agreed that the general technique of decision-making adopted by the majority was proper, although they disagreed sharply with the results:

That the Court's holding today is neither compelled nor even strongly suggested by the language of the Fifth Amendment is at odds with American and English legal history and involves a departure from a long line of precedent does not prove either that the Court is wrong or unwise in its present reinterpretation of the Fifth Amendment. It does, however, underscore the obvious—that the Court has not discovered or found the law in making today's decision, nor has it derived it from some irrefutable sources; what it has done is to make new law and new public policy in much the same way that it has in the course of interpreting other great clauses of the Constitution. That is what the Court historically has done. Indeed, it is what it must do and will continue to do until and unless there is some fundamental change in the constitutional distribution of governmental powers . . . Decisions like these cannot rest alone on syllogism, metaphysics or some ill-defined notions of natural justice, although each will perhaps play its part. In proceeding to such constructions as it now announces, the Court should also duly consider all the factors and interests bearing upon the cases, at least insofar as the relevant materials are available; and if the necessary considerations are not treated in the record or obtainable from some other reliable source, the Court should not proceed to formulate fundamental policies based on speculation alone.[25]

Endowed as it is with constitutional power to make decisions controlling the direction of institutions, dominated by a philosophy which no longer conceives of the court's role in decision-making as limited to considering existing legal materials, but feeling free to go to many other "nonlegal" sources for empirical data and even for value-judgments; bound only by the broad language and frequently ambiguous history of the Constitution; and now confronted by situations, presented with increasing insistence by moral entrepreneurs, which the Court regards as blocking the substantial achievement of values it deems important and therefore constitutionally enthroned, and which the passage of years demonstrated were not about to be resolved by the legislature, the Court would naturally try to remove those obstructions entirely and in one blow. The alternative was to permit them to continue and then await the cumbersome, slow, and expensive process of case-by-case litigation to resolve the problems over time. The Supreme Court has acted decisively.

This is not to say, however, that there are no limitations on decision-making by the Supreme Court. The Court's institutional role requires that it make decisions in constitutional cases only insofar as it can shore up its decision on some plausible reading of the Constitution. It can only consider solutions which can be accomplished through formulating a universal rule, applicable to all persons in similar situations. Most important of all, it cannot create a new organization to resolve problems, no matter how plainly the solution requires it.

The *Gault* case is an interesting example of this last and perhaps most important constraint on the Court. In that case, a juvenile had been committed as a delinquent to the State Industrial School by an Arizona juvenile court, on the ground that he had violated a state statute in using lewd language over the telephone to a woman neighbor. The commitment was accomplished without notice of hearing, confrontation of witnesses, counsel, or cross-examination; and it was made on the basis of a confession, which under *Miranda* was inadmissible because it violated the privilege against self-incrimination. The traditional justification for permitting such seeming violations of constitutional standards in juvenile cases was that the State stood *in parens patriae*, and that in the exercise of its fatherly care for juveniles, it could quite properly help them develop into well-adjusted, law-abiding citizens. Since these, rather than "punishment," were the purposes of commitment, it was believed that no "rights" were being violated by doing what was thought to be in the child's interest.

The Court swept all these rationalizations aside in large part by undercutting their factual premises. The classification "delinquent" "has come to involve only slightly less stigma than the term 'criminal' applied to adults." The claim of secrecy of records (invoked to justify the denial of procedural protections) "is more rhetoric than reality." The benevolent, fatherly approach in the interests of the child is not in the best interests of the child after all; modern research suggests that "the essentials of due process may be a more impressive and more therapeutic attitude so far as the juvenile is concerned." The very fact of incarceration is enough; "it is of no constitutional importance—and of limited practical meaning—that the institution to which he was committed is called an Industrial School . . ."[26]

In the event, the Court articulated major new rules of procedure for juvenile courts across the nation, in a far-reaching opinion that went well beyond the decisional demands of the case before it. But there were other options, not open to the Court, which might have been used to resolve the problem of the juvenile courts without introducing the very rigidities of procedure against which the juvenile court movement had initially rebelled. Justice Stewart stated, dissenting:

In the past 70 years many dedicated men and women have devoted their professional lives to the enlightened task of bringing us out of the dark world of Charles Dickens in meeting our responsibilities to the child in our society. The result has been the creation of a system of juvenile and family courts in each of the 50 states. There can be no denying that in many areas the performance of these agencies has fallen disappointingly short of the hopes and dreams of the courageous pioneers who first conceived them. For a variety of reasons, the reality has sometimes not even approached the ideal, and much remains to be accomplished in the administration of public juvenile and family agencies—in personnel, in planning, in financing, perhaps in the formulation of wholly new approaches.

I possess neither the specialized experience nor the expert knowledge to predict with certainty where may lie the brightest hope for progress in dealing with the specialized problems of juvenile delinquency. But I am certain that the answer does not lie in the Court's opinion in this case, which serves to convert a juvenile proceeding into a criminal prosecution.[27]

Justice Stewart was stating that he disagreed with the decision in *Gault* because there were undoubtedly other, better solutions available: more money, more personnel, and greater legislative and administrative attention might and probably would find solutions which did not so clearly abandon the desiderata of informality, and a sense of paternal care.

The Supreme Court and the Developmental (or Tension-Management) Model

Just as the ordinary appellate court in most cases finds that its position, inputs, and conversion processes require its role as change-agent be similar to that demanded by the structural-functionalist model, so also the same factors require that the Supreme Court in constitutional cases define its role as change-agent in terms of Chin's "developmental" (or Moore's "tension-management") model. As in the ideal case, the Court conceives of its position as change-agent in much broader terms than most appellate courts. It believes that it can and should sweep away the obstructions to the continuous growth and development of the institutions in question. Its attitude toward precedent in constitutional law reflects the view that institutions are constantly changing, and therefore it should not mechanically apply old precedents to the new situations. On the other hand, its inability to create new structures means that it must in the main accept and rely on the existing institutions. It could not strike down the juvenile court system, for it could not supply some other organization to meet the problem of juvenile delinquency. It could not even contemplate striking down the whole system of State education, and substituting for it a federal, nonsegregated system, even though the desirability of such an alternative should at least be discussed by a change-agent who perceived the entire range of alternatives. But it could and did decree comprehensive changes in these institutions.

The Court could not examine the widest range of possible alternatives. Just as the ordinary appellate court is in most cases bound to find a solution tenable within the meaning of the statute or case-law authorities, so the Supreme Court must find a solution in constitutional cases tenable under the Constitution. The comparatively large scope available to the Supreme Court is a function, in the final analysis, of the fact that the Constitution really is the basic document of the government. The restraints on the Court's scope for choice likewise are a function of the Constitution. Insofar as the Constitution defines the basic institutions of American government, the Court must fit its decisions within the limits defined by the goals of those institutions.

9.5 APPELLATE COURTS: LIBERAL OR CONSERVATIVE CHOICES

We have tried to demonstrate that the institutional position of appellate courts sharply limits their range of choice of a potential rule. They are forced by their position and function to confine their role as change-agent to one similar to that suggested by Chin's system model—i.e., to the introduction of incremental changes with the aim of reducing emergent tensions within a particular institution.

Willy-nilly they are forced to accept the goals for the institution already set by society. In the result, their overall function is inevitably conservative: The appellate courts' law-creating powers are used to maintain the ongoing system, with only the adjustments necessary to accommodate to the new pressures thrown up as society changes. (The Supreme Court of the United States, in constitutional cases at least, may be an exception to this rule, a matter which we discuss below.)

The overall conservative cast of appellate court decisions is therefore built into the institution itself, regardless of the personal biases of the individual judges. The most flaming radical activist, as an appellate judge, could never in his role as appellate judge fashion any of the agencies of the Welfare State—social security, pure food and drug administrations, workmen's compensation, licensing of radio and television stations, and the like—let alone bring about revolutionary changes.

Even within these tight institutional restrictions, however, judges must make choices. Every rule *does* embody a choice. Can it be said that even within their limited scope courts generally make choices agreeable to the economically and politically dominant classes in the community?

It is perhaps useful to recapitulate the various inputs into the system which suggest that the rule output would be warped in favor of the wealthy. The issues which arise for decision are determined by those who bring the lawsuits, and in light of the expenses involved in litigation, obviously the well-to-do will invoke the judicial machinery rather more frequently than most citizens. The major source of policy inputs is the lawyers, and typically the wealthy can employ the prestigious lawyers whose fees they can afford. The general tendency among lawyers employed by the wealthy is to conform to the values and specific views of their clients. The personal attributes of the judges suggest that they are recruited from a very narrow, educated and well-to-do slice of the total population.

From all these considerations Laski concluded that the actual output of the rule-making system was bound to favor the wealthy even within the range permitted by the institution.[28] On this point he was sharply challenged by Roscoe Pound, who said:

With an economic interpretation of the general course of history and so of legal history one can have no quarrel. Nor within limits can one quarrel with such an interpretation of certain types of events in legal history. What must give us pause is making it the sole weapon in the jurist's armory or the sole instrument in his tool chest; the reference of every item in the judicial process, of every single decision and every working out of a legal precept by applying the technique of the law to the received materials of decision, to the operation, conscious or unconscious, of the desires and self-interest of an economically dominant class.[29]

Pound asserted that "What stands out in the history of Anglo-American law is the resistance of the taught tradition in the hands of judges drawn from any class you like, so they have been trained in the tradition, against all manner of economically or politically powerful interests."[30]

What Pound suggested is that the socialization of lawyers and judges is such that they make their choices in each case in accordance with the received rules of recognition and received values. "The strongest single influence born in determining single decisions and in guiding a course of decision is a taught tradition of logically interdependent precepts and of referring cases to principles."[31] He recognized that so legalistic a judicial process could not resolve the issue in trouble cases. But he believed that there was a common set of values, taught to judges and lawyers, which served as standard for resolving ambiguities: "It is here that the ideal element in law comes into play, since the results of choosing one starting point rather than another are measured by the received social ideal, as it has been taught to judges and lawyers. The effect of economic changes upon this ideal is for the most part gradual and slow, no matter what class is affected. The business man and the leader of industry have had quite as much cause for complaint in this respect as the labor leader; and the farmer, long dominant in American politics, no less than either. As Maitland puts it, 'taught law is tough law.'"[32]

Pound's contention, if true, plainly seems to demonstrate not his thesis so much as Laski's. If there is a "received social ideal" in the law, it must be immanent in its vast panoply. The law at any given moment, viewed in its entirety, could not in the nature of things lay down prescriptive rules adapted to the world that is to be. At its very best it might describe as well as prescribe the world that is. Considering the creaks and lack of fit in most human institutions, it is even more likely to include rules mainly adapted to the world that was. By the very nature of law, the social ideal embodied in it tends to look backward, to the past and not forward into the future; it must always retain a strong scent of the nostalgic. Businessmen and leaders of industry do have cause for complaint about much of our body of laws, for even today it contains remnants of feudalism altogether dysfunctional with respect to the demands of contemporary American society, whether viewed from the perspective of the entrepreneur or the working classes.

For all these reasons, it is not surprising that if one is asked to characterize the central thrust of most appellate opinions, the answer will no doubt be that the values expressed are relatively conservative. What is perhaps a more interesting fact, however, is that a substantial number of appellate decisions are not so backward-looking, that often judges have decided in favor of the disinherited. For example, given the rigid framework of the fellow-servant rule in the nineteenth century, judges were adroit in carving exceptions to it in order to protect widows and orphans whose breadwinner had been injured or killed in industrial accidents. Most notably of all, the Supreme Court of the United States since about 1937 has been consistently more liberal than the Congress, at least in certain kinds of cases, especially in tax cases, cases involving freedom of speech, of press, or of religion, and criminal procedure. How is it possible to reconcile such choices with what would seem to be overwhelming bias in inputs toward conservative rulings?

The answer is complex. We shall discuss first the problem of the State appellate courts, and secondly the special problem of the Supreme Court of the United States.

In the first place, all predictions about human activity as a function of class position, socialization, and the like, are based upon probabilities. The verification of such predictions is not that *individuals* will act as forecast, but that the central tendency of the *group* will be as predicted.

Judging is an intensely individual matter. Each judge must, finally, vote for himself. That one predicts that the overall tendency of appellate judging even within the narrow range of choice presented will be relatively conservative therefore does not exclude the probability that there will be a minority of liberal decisions as well. In the same way, to predict that in throwing dice, numbers one through five will show on five-sixths of the rolls, implies that the six-spot will appear one-sixth of the time.

Chief Justice Stone offers a remarkable example of the danger in predicting that a man from a conservative background will invariably be a conservative judge. Stone was primarily a Wall Street lawyer before going to the bench, although he had served in the academic world as well. His appointment was bitterly opposed by trade unions and some others who claimed to speak for "the masses," on the ground that given his background, he could only be expected to let his ingrained class biases intrude upon his judgment. His opponents, however, were very wrong, for Stone distinguished himself as one of the strongest champions of civil liberties, of the poor and underprivileged, that ever sat on the bench. Other examples could be cited.

Also, there has always been a strong tendency among judges and lawyers, fostered by the adherence to precedents, toward placing a high value on consistency and coherence in laying down legal norms. During the period in which the formal style of opinion-writing prevailed, these considerations became the sole criteria of legitimacy. Even the most ardent realist must give some consideration to them. When a sufficient emphasis is put on consistency and coherence in law, there is a tendency for individual value-preferences to be overriden by the urge to conform to already existing laws.

The existing corpus of the law is not colored a monochromatic conservative. It contains elements, the product of historical forces long since deceased, which remain to serve interests other than those for which they were originally intended. For example, the earliest written assertion of the right to trial by a jury of one's peers was made at Runnymede by the feudal barons, asserting their aristocratic interests against the centripetal forces of the Crown. Trial by jury has come through many a sea-change from Magna Charta to its present form. Whatever its contemporary utility, it seems clear enough that its function no longer is to serve the needs of a particularistic feudal class.

The tendency towards coherence in the law favors the continuation of rights already in the corpus of norms. To the extent that these rights exist, conservative judges by remaining faithful to the law as it was may nevertheless in particular cases make choices that are not unfavorable to interests other than those already possessing power and privilege.

In the United States, a third factor has been of importance in procuring "liberal" court rulings, and that is the overarching influence of the United States Supreme Court. The opinions of this Court, especially in constitutional matters, cannot readily be ignored by State appellate courts, and even less by lower appellate courts in the Federal system. Since 1937 the Supreme Court has, with remarkable if not complete consistency, tended to make libertarian rather than conservative decisions in civil rights and civil liberties cases; it has regularly decided in favor of government control of business in cases concerning economic regulations, and in favor of the government in tax cases.

Courts which adhere to the formal style of judicial opinions suppress, as we have seen, the reasons for their choice of major premise on which they base their decisions. Given the conservative single-breasted grey in which the inputs to the decision processes are clothed, the fact that the decisional output is not invariably so clothed testifies to the court response to the ameliorating factors which we have suggested may be operative.

The Supreme Court of the United States poses a special problem. Its judges come from a remarkably select slice of American society. Their values, in terms of naked class interest and socialization, one might think, should have given the Court a more conservative bias than it has in fact displayed. Why this seeming paradox? Why should the Supreme Court have had, since 1937, a remarkably uniform liberal complexion?

The United States Supreme Court and Political Values

If Pound's notion that judges look to the "received social ideal," i.e. the ideal taught to judges and lawyers, be true, then it would be impossible to explain the Court's liberal tendencies, unless the received social ideal of the justices of the Supreme Court were different from that of the judges of other appellate courts. What does seem quite clear is that apparently the social ideal of the majority of the Supreme Court Justices changed markedly between the early 1930's and the early 1940's, a change strikingly demonstrated by the shift in the presumption of constitutionality.

Prior to 1938, it was well established that every statute was presumably constitutional, and would be declared unconstitutional only if the unconstitutionality could be clearly demonstrated. Prior to that date, the Court held unconstitutional as violating the Due Process Clause many statutes purporting to limit the use of property, but only a tiny handful as violating the freedoms expressed in the First Amendment—freedom of speech, press, association and religion. It had, over the years, held the income tax laws unconstitutional, not because they levied a tax on earned income, but because they levied a tax on the rents and profits of property; it had held unconstitutional a statute setting maximum hours for women, a child labor law, and much of the New Deal legislation aimed at curbing what the Roosevelt Administration regarded as abuses of big business. On the other hand, it had upheld convictions for waving a red flag, for stating that the United States' entry into the First World War was a mistake, for drafting a call for a dictatorship of the proletariat.

The "social ideal" implicit in these cases seems clear. The Constitution (in the words of Holmes) was seen as the embodiment of Herbert Spencer's social statics. Property rights were held to have a higher value than human rights. The contract clause and the due-process clause were seen as major protections not for individuals, but for corporations.

If the Court's basic value premises had remained unchanged from those embalmed in these cases, what has happened since 1943 would have been impossible. In that year, Chief Justice Stone, in a famous footnote, said that it might be that the freedoms embodied in the First Amendment—of speech, press, and religion—were so important that legislation abridging any of them was not entitled to the usual presumption of constitutionality.[33] Since then, it has become a decided rarity for the Court to declare unconstitutional a statute involving a limitation on property rights. The "great, the indispensable freedoms secured by the First Amendment,"[33a] on the other hand, have been protected from State infringement over and over again. Far from using its position to defend the economic status quo against attacks by the disadvantaged, the Court has come to see its most important function as the final protector of the channels by which minorities can try to bring about peaceful social change.

If Pound were correct, so radical a shift of position could not have occurred; the idea of "received social ideal" cannot account for so quick a change in the Court from being a protector of the status quo to being the protector of the challengers of the status quo. The new judges who came to the Court after 1937 obviously had a different sort of social ideal than had those whom they replaced.

This historical shift demonstrates that Pound's notion of a *single* "received social ideal" is not empirically valid. There are as many "social ideals" in American life as there are antagonistic interest groups. These contradictory ideals are all simultaneously enshrined in different areas of American law. Our law imposes granite-like protections for private property against State expropriation. In many other areas it favors property rights over human rights. At the same time, in still other segments it elevates human rights and the democratic process to the highest level. Plainly, the judges who came to the Court after 1937 took their received social ideal from the latter tradition.

That they did so was in part a result of the political processes by which judges are selected for the Court. But they were also the product of the new pragmatic methods of decision-making which the Court had increasingly adopted and institutionalized. The judges who since 1937 have represented the majority have tended to believe that their notions of justice are better served by looking to the consequences of the rule in society and making pragmatic choice based on these investigations, rather than by determining the major premise inarticulately, without express regard for its effects on the polity, and justified mainly by a purported logical or elegant relationship to the existing corpus of rules of law.

The more recent judges, therefore, have resorted to a system of justification of the realist type, for the realists see the world in terms of process, not of ideal models. They are in the pragmatic tradition. Dewey held that the only statements about what ought to be the case that were valid were those that could be empirically verified, i.e. those which could be determined to be useful in resolving problems by empirical data. Dewey's philosophy was sharply oriented toward facts; it was scornful of large abstractions and denied the utility of *summa bona* or ideal models as measures of value.

The pragmatic view of decision-making seems to allow alternative conceptions of the role of values. On the one hand, it is sometimes asserted that problems arise from fact situations alone and admit of but a single "best" solution; this is a sort of natural law conception. Even Llewellyn seems to have believed that there is a "right" or "just" solution for every problem. He subscribed to a statement by the German jurist Goldschmidt, that "Every fact-pattern of common life, so far as the legal order can take it, carries within itself its appropriate, natural rules, its right law . . . The highest task of law-giving consists in uncovering and implementing this immanent law."[34] Dewey at times seems to have adhered to much the same view.[35]

On the other hand, at times it seems that Dewey's pragmatism and its legal analogue, realism, lead necessarily to a sort of aimless expediency. Expediency, it is then claimed, permits each Justice's idiosyncratic value-sets full play. Alexander Bickle describes the ultimate result of this viewpoint:

The final fruit of neo-realism—perhaps either arrested realism or surrealism would be more accurate—is a genial, nihilistic attitude of co-existence with the Court and its work, along with a complete lack of interest in the process by which the work is achieved, or in the proper role of that process in a democratic society. The Court itself is interesting as a mountain is said to be to a climber, because it is there. If there is any judgement to be exercised about it, it is a factional, predilectional one about results. The rest is *elegantia juris*, and it couldn't matter less.[36]

Both these positions deny any function to the generalized aims, usually culturally acquired, of the decision-maker. At least in constitutional litigations, the Constitution itself supplies such generalized objectives: due process, equal protection, free speech and assembly, freedom of religion, right to counsel, the privilege against self-incrimination. All these are generalized objectives which the Court is institutionally required to adopt.

If the system of decision-making follows the formal style, how these generalized objectives become ends in view depends not on any assessment of reality, but on the arid requirements of syllogisms. It is equally logical to assert that "separate but equal" facilities in education will help achieve the generalized aim of equal protection, as to assert that only integrated facilities will move education toward that generalized aim. Syllogistic reasoning denies the assignment of values to the alternative means, for those values could only be determined by empirical data.

Empirical evidence showing the various consequences of the utilization of different means makes it impossible to ignore the values of the means used in pursuing specific ends in view. If empirical data show that the consequences of "separate but equal" educational facilities include identifiable psychological bruises inflicted upon the minorities discriminated against, then the decision-makers cannot ignore that fact. The dilemma posed by the exclusive use of syllogistic reasoning is resolved by empirical data.

So long as judges refrain from examining the actual consequences of the means chosen for certain ends, it is possible to assert that the high-flown generalized objectives of the Constitution are achieved by whatever means are logically compatible with them. "Separate but equal" treatment is logically compatible with the equal-protection clause. The test of voluntariness of a confession is logically compatible with the privilege against self-incrimination. Judicial abstinence in requiring equal weighting of votes in State representative assemblies is logically compatible with the notion that a republican form of government requires representative assemblies to determine electoral matters. Entrusting young persons to the uncontrolled discretion of juvenile courts is compatible with a major premise that "we want to do what's good for Johnny." Only when one is confronted with the actual empirical consequences of the means used does he have to place in the balance the values to be assigned to those means.

To articulate the rhetoric of constitutional protection, but to infer through syllogistic reasoning alone the means to be used to promote certain ends, ensures that, save for chance serendipity, the constitutional phraseology will become a mere legitimizing myth that does not reflect the reality of the situation. Only when the empirical consequences of the means used is examined, and the values involved weighed alongside the generalized ends of the constitutional guarantees, is it possible to bring about the concrete realization of the constitutional objectives in the form of specific ends in view. The realist formula for judicial decision-making requires not the relative weighing of a set of prizings, but a process of valuation in which means and ends become analytically indistinguishable.

If the conjunction of commonly accepted values and empirical data invariably points in only one direction, then one should expect the Court to be always unanimous in its decisions. This is far from the case, however; more frequently than not the Court speaks with a divided voice. That divided voice may reflect differing values held by the Justices, which values, however, should not be construed as different notions of the *summum bonum*, or "received social ideal" as postulated by Pound.

In the first place, the Justices may come to differing opinions because of different assessments of the empirical data. In *Miranda*, for example, the majority found the evidence sufficient to show that the police engaged in improper activity in pretrial questioning. That evidence, we recall, was based entirely on the contents of police manuals. Justice Clark dissented from the majority in rejecting the empirical data as "merely writing in the field by professors and some police officers. Not one is shown by the record here to be the official manual of any police department, much less in universal use in crime detection."[37] Why the Justices take such different views of the data may have nothing whatever to do with values of "liberty" as against "authority"; i.e., it is without reference to a received social ideal. In *Miranda* it may have resulted from differing assessments of the weight to be given to manuals against more concrete evidence.

Secondly, the difference may result from the judges' having different ideas as to the proper role of the Court. Justice Frankfurter was noted for the fact that, despite his politically liberal views, his strong adherence to doctrines of judicial self-restraint frequently led him to vote for anti-libertarian positions.

Thirdly, even though the Justices may accept the same set of values, they may differ, as reasonable men will, with respect to the solution. Justice Stewart's dissent in *Gault* was based on the same concern for the welfare of the juvenile defendant as was the majority's. He disagreed only with the method of protection adopted by the majority.

Finally, however, there is a group of cases in which the constitutional doctrine, as construed, itself requires the Court to weigh conflicting goals alike constitutionally protected: freedom v. security; individual rights v. community protection; the national interest v. "State's Rights." All these are recurrent problems. In such cases, it is difficult to avoid the conclusion that the judges are, indeed, required to invoke their own value-sets in making the ultimate decision. That the Court has in the past three decades relatively consistently chosen to pursue a libertarian path with regard to human rights can probably only be attributed to the political processes by which the Justices have been selected.

9.6 SUMMARY

To understand why any role-occupant acts as he does, one must examine the norms defining his position, the social, personal, and other forces operating upon him, and the activities of sanctioning agents. There are no formal sanctioning agents controlling appellate courts (except, in some instances, higher appellate courts).

Courts, more than any other institution in society, are ordinarily regarded as value-neutral institutional frameworks within which conflict can be resolved. The adjudicative function in a winner-takes-all system of justice requires the court in every case to determine the relevant norm. In trouble cases, a court must create that norm. Law-creation inevitably requires a value-choice. By making that choice, an appellate court ceases to be a merely value-free, neutral framework for the resolution of conflicts. It becomes involved in that conflict; it and its decisions become tools in the social struggle.

To view the courts in this way, however, decidedly is not equivalent to adopting the radical realist viewpoint—what Bickle called "a genial, nihilistic attitude." While appellate courts do have discretion, and they do exercise choice, it is a choice made in the context of the legal process. That process is defined by its inputs and the norms of judicial decision-making. The received norms, based on the assumption that judges do not create law, end up by permitting the widest scope to the unexpressed value-choices of the judges, under the mask of adherence to precedent and statutory language. More modern norms for judicial decision-making require judges to look, not to logical, but to empirical justification of their choice of rule. The judges must therefore consider not only the values involved in the generalized objectives, but also those that are implicated in the means. By transforming the question of value-choice from one of the relative priority to be given to specific prizings, to one of valuation in which generalized objectives are to be translated into specific ends in view, judges are unable so easily to mask their value-choices behind an impenetrable fog of syllogistic rhetoric.

We observe that in analyzing the work of the appellate courts, we have given the major emphasis to the effects of norms and roles, and only a relatively minor emphasis to the impact on the judges of their participation in a bureaucratic structure. This relative emphasis, as we shall see, is in marked contrast to the relative emphasis that seems to be operative in determining the activities of the people. Appellate judges are as formally removed as possible from the grubby pressures that coerce other men to respond to social forces. What pressures there are, tend to force the judges to follow the norms laid down for their positions, and to ensure that men selected for judgeships have deeply internalized the rules defining their positions.

To say that appellate courts are not a value-free, neutral framework, therefore, is not to say that appellate judges are free to do what they choose. How they exercise their discretion, and in whose favor, depends on the entire social complex in which they act, which selects issues for their examination, which recruits them for their roles, which defines the small-group interaction of judges, which in turn defines the limits of their choice. This social complex ensures that appellate courts would in the main limit their choices to enhancing incremental changes, occasionally to promoting comprehensive changes, but never to bringing about revolutionary changes. They can never make rules which will bring about sweeping changes in the allocation of power that will alter the entire structure of society. By invoking the power state within a framework that so limits their choices, they become willy-nilly a bastion of the status quo.

NOTES

1. R. Chin, "The utility of systems models and developmental models," in J. L. Finkle and R. W. Grable (eds.), *Political Development and Social Change*, Wiley, New York, 1966, p. 17. Reprinted by permission.

2. A. Inkeles, *What is Sociology?*, Prentice-Hall, Englewood Cliffs. N.J., 1964, p. 39.

3. R. K. Merton, *Social Theory and Social Structure*, Free Press of Glencoe, New York, 1964, p. 39.

4. Wilbert E. Moore, *Social Change*, © 1963, Prentice-Hall, Inc., Englewood Cliffs, N.J., p. 10.

5. Chin, *op. cit.*, p. 17.

6. Moore, *op. cit.*, pp. 10–11.

7. *Ibid.*, p. 11. Reprinted by permission of the publishers.

8. Chin, *op. cit.*, p. 17. Reprinted by permission.

9. R. Dahl and C. Lindblom, *Politics, Economics, and Welfare: Planning and Politico-economic Systems Resolved into Basic Social Processes*, Harper, New York, 1953.

10. *People v. Schmidt*, 216 N.Y. 324, 110 N.E. 945 (1915).

11. 10 Cl. and F. 200 (1843); 8 E.R. 718 (H.L.).

12. Lon Fuller, "American legal realism," *U. Pa. Law Rev.*, **82**, 1934, pp. 428–438.

13. Dahl and Lindblom, *op. cit.*, *passim.*

14. The sufficiency of the processes to gather even these sorts of facts has been vigorously attacked. See, e.g., Jerome Frank, *Courts on Trial: Myth and Reality in American Justice*, Princeton University Press, Princeton, N.J., 1950.

15. Lawrence Friedman, *Contract Law in America* (Madison: The University of Wisconsin Press; © 1967 by the Regents of the University of Wisconsin).

16. See J. W. Hurst, *Law and Conditions of Freedom*, University of Wisconsin Press, Madison, 1956.

17. Friedman, *op. cit.*, pp. 191-192. Reprinted by permission.

18. *Ibid.*, p. 193. Reprinted by permission.

19. Harold Laski, *The State in Theory and Practice*, Allen and Unwin, London, 1935, p. 162. Reprinted by permission.

20. 384 U.S. 436 (1965).

21. 387 U.S. 1 (1967).

22. 369 U.S. 186 (1962).

23. 347 U.S. 483 (1954).

24. *Supra*, pp. 49–52.

25. Justice White, dissenting in *Miranda v. Arizona*, 384 U.S. 436 (1965), pp. 531–532.

26. 387 U.S. 1, 27 (1967).

27. 387 U.S. 1, 78 (1967).

28. Laski, *op. cit.*, p. 151.

29. Roscoe Pound, "The economic interpretation and the law of torts," *Harvard Law Rev.*, **53**, 1940, pp. 365, 366. Reprinted by permission.

30. *Ibid.*, p. 366.

31. *Ibid.*, p. 367.

32. *Ibid.*

33. *Thomas v. Collins*, 323 U.S. 624 (1945).

33a. *United States v. Caroline Products*, 304 U.S. 144 (1938).

34. K. N. Llewellyn, *The Common Law Tradition: Deciding Appeals*, Little, Brown, Boston, 1960, p. 122. Quoted in S. Mermin, "Concerning the ways of courts: reflections induced by the Wisconsin 'internal improvement' and 'public purpose' cases," *Wisc. Law. Rev.* 1963, pp. 192–252. See also V. J. Wilson and T. G. Russell, "Common law and common sense," *Harvard Law Rev.*, **41**, 1939, p. 301.

35. J. Dewey, *Theory of Valuation*, University of Chicago Press, Chicago, 1939.

36. From *The Least Dangerous Branch* by Alexander M. Bickle, p. 81. Copyright © 1962 by The Bobbs-Merrill Company, Inc.; reprinted by permission of the publisher.

37. 384 U.S. at 499.

Part III

General principles of criminal law

10

The substantive criminal law: general principles

In complex societies, appellate courts and legislatures grind out a vast array of rules and statutes, affecting every aspect of the lives of citizens. Because our society is so complex, and because law is after all an instrument which can be used for a variety of ends, it may be doubted that we can make many valid generalizations about law in its entirety which are more than trivial. We shall narrow our field, therefore, and examine only the law of crimes.

Our objective in examining the body of rules which comprise the substantive law of crimes is twofold. In the first place, these rules are the product of the appellate courts and legislatures. They comprise a body of material against which we can test the major conclusions to which we have come. In the second place, we have an interest in examining the scope of discretion granted to officials at every level of the legal order, and the way in which they exercise that discretion. The substantive criminal law is, as it were, the blueprint which describes the metes and bounds of the discretion of policemen, prosecutors, and judges, within which they may act, perhaps unwisely sometimes but at least legally.

"Law and order," it is frequently said, are the very basis of civilized society. The criminal law has traditionally carried a heavy portion of the burden of maintaining an orderly community, and continues to do so.

The phrase "law and order," however, in its common meaning, contains a contradiction. Under conditions of martial law, "order" may be maintained, but the basis of *martial* law is the suspension of "law." We might maintain order in our communities by merely giving to law-enforcement agencies the unlimited discretion to act to prevent disorder, and trust to their discretion in the selection of individuals and actions which they would inhibit or punish.

A community based on Policeman's Discretion, however, would plainly be antithetical to "the rule of law." The ideal of predictability is obviously attractive. Hence it has been said that the "essential element [of the rule of law] is the reduction of arbitrariness by officials—for example, constraints on the activities of the police—and of arbitrariness in positive law by the application of 'rational principles of civic order.'"[1] The sort of order maintained by unlimited discretionary action by the police is not order under "law," but its opposite. It may produce a society without external disorder, but it would not give the citizens a sense of order, for no man could know when some policeman would adjudge as criminal an action that the citizens thought to be innocent.

A regime under which all society is ruled by "law" in the sense of clearly stated rules which do not depend on the discretion of any official for application, on the other hand, is an unattainable ideal. A society based on the principle of Policeman's Discretion would not have a rule of law; but a society in which there are rules which are clearly applicable in every case, i.e., in which every case is a "clear case"—exists only in the never-never land. The very nature of rules requires that they be formulated in general terms; whether a general term subsumes a particular conduct is inevitably a question of discretion, in any case as to the existence of the facts, and (in the trouble cases) as to the scope of the rule.

In any given case, therefore, the problem posed by the tension between "law" and "order"—between Dicey's romantic notion of a State subject entirely to the rule of law,[2] and its contrary, a State of Policeman's Discretion—is one of drawing a line. Discretion *can* be limited, even if it can never be entirely removed. The issues posed are mainly normative: How much discretion ought the law-applying agencies have? What are the tools with which society can set and enforce the limits to that discretion? What are the limits on society's ability to control discretion?

These problems are pervasive in law. They are particularly important in criminal law.

Whatever views one holds about the penal law, no one will question its importance in society. This is the law on which men place their ultimate reliance for protection against all the deepest injuries that human conduct can inflict on individuals and institutions. By the same token, penal law governs the strongest force that we permit official agencies to bring to bear on individuals. Its promise as an instrument of safety is matched only by its power to destroy. If penal law is weak and ineffective, basic human interests are in jeopardy. If it is harsh and arbitrary in its impact, it works a gross injustice on those caught within its toils ... Nowhere in the entire legal field is more at stake for the community and the individual.[3]

The compromise between the twin objectives of order and legality is achieved by two complementary sets of norms: (1) the substantive criminal law, and (2) the procedural criminal law. The latter prescribes the limits within which law-applying authorities must remain in their treatment of citizens. It includes such matters as the law of arrest, the scope of the prosecutor's discretion, the nature of a trial, etc. These we shall discuss in the following chapters.

The substantive criminal law is, in a sense, the more important, for it defines both the law and the order that society wants the policeman, the prosecutors, and the courts respectively to enforce and maintain. In the first place, it prescribes the limits within which the citizen is to conduct himself. It commands him not to kill, to rape, to take narcotics, or to leave off the top of his garbage can. By implication what is not forbidden by the criminal law a citizen is free to do, without fear of criminal sanction. In this way, the substantive criminal law defines the sort of order it deems desirable. If it does not make it a crime for a man to wear long hair and necklaces, then the sort of community which it defines admits such conduct as legal.

A caveat must be added. That the substantive criminal law proscribes specific conduct, of course, does not imply that it will be effective. Our original model[4] suggests that how the individual acts will be a function of the primary norms directed to him, the total "field" of political, social, economic, psychological, and other forces operative upon him, and the sanctioning activities of law-applying agencies. Where these forces so combine as to force a large number of role-occupants into activity defined as illegal, it may be doubted that activity by law-enforcement agencies can ever sufficiently control the illegal activity. In such a case, what may be required, instead of an increase in sanctions and enforcement powers, is a fundamental restructuring of society's institutions to change the overall pattern of forces operating upon the role-occupant. For example, if a large group of civil servants are corrupt, it may be that the only efficient method of controlling the corruption is to increase salaries so that the motive for corruption disappears, rather than to expand the law-enforcement machinery. Similarly, the cure for "crime in the streets" may well be a restructuring of the society which leads to such widespread criminality, rather than an increase in the forces of control.

In the second place, while defining permissible conduct for citizens, the norms of criminal law also prescribe the proper conduct for the law-enforcement agencies. A law against murder, even as it tells the citizen that he may not commit murder, tells the policeman that in the event of a citizen committing murder, he should arrest the latter; it further tells the judge that he should convict the murderer and impose a sanction for the offense. By the same token, the absence of a law making it a crime for a man to wear long hair and beads commands the policeman, the prosecutor, and the judge that they are not to arrest, to prosecute, or to convict him for such behavior. The criminal law thus places gross limitations on the scope of permissible action by the law-enforcement agencies, for unless an official can point to a law which at least arguably purports to proscribe a conduct at issue, the official presumably lacks power to do anything to the accused.

We shall pursue this dual function of the criminal law, first, with respect to the traditional law of crimes, which to this day largely bears the stamp of its origins in judicial rule-making; second, we shall examine how the responses developed in the traditional areas of the criminal law have met the challenges of newer, statutory offenses which make up the bulk of criminal offenses today, and the consequent scope for police discretion in modern criminal law; and lastly, we shall consider the development of a few constitutional doctrines by which courts have tried to limit the scope of policeman's discretion as these doctrines are expressed in the substantive criminal law.

10.1 THE SCOPE AND TECHNIQUE OF THE SUBSTANTIVE CRIMINAL LAW: "ORDINARY" CRIMES

For centuries the central thrust of the criminal law was directed against the perpetrators of what today we tend to think of as "ordinary" crimes—murder, rape, robbery, burglary, and the like—almost all of which are distinguished by being offenses which have identifiable victims. The law of crimes still bears the undisguisable hallmarks of this long history, a history in which the major institution shaping the law was the English judiciary.

Traditionally, courts have maintained the doctrine that *actus facit reum nisi mens sit rea*: "To do the act is itself not criminal unless there be as well a guilty mind." The ancient Latin maxim suggests the two classical elements of crime: the *actus reus* (the "act") and *mens rea* (the guilty state of mind). To these we may add three other broad principles that underlie the common law of crimes: the requirement that there be a *harm*; the requirement of *legality*; and the principle that *punishment* follows an adjudication of guilt—i.e., the breach of norm must be sanctioned.[5]

The criminal law ideally, as we have seen, is the major device by which society draws the line between law and order. It therefore is a system of social control in two complementary senses. On the one hand, it is a system for the social control of the ordinary citizen. The elements of harm, punishment, and *mens rea* are the central devices by which the criminal law defines the harms for which punishments are to be imposed, the sorts of punishment to be imposed, and the kinds of persons who are to be punished. On the other hand, the requirements of *legality* and *act* serve the main burden of defining the scope of policeman's discretion, and verifying the appropriateness of its exercise.

Harm and Punishment: Antisocial Activity and Its Prevention

The substantive criminal law bears the burden of, first, laying down norms of conduct, and second, sanctioning their breach. We shall first consider the sort of harms that are proscribed and the sanctioning system generally. We shall then examine the doctrine of *mens rea*, which is the central identifying device of the traditional criminal law for selecting from among the persons who commit harms those whose breach of the norm is to be sanctioned.

Mala in Se, Mala Prohibita

In some societies (the Shambala for example), if a member of a kinship group is killed, it makes little difference whether the death occurred by accident or through the intentional misconduct of a member. If, therefore, there is an unnatural death, then the kinship group or tribe of the person causing the death must make amends. In Western legal thought a distinction is drawn between intentionally killing someone and accidentally killing him. To cause a pedestrian's death by mere lack of care in driving is seen as justly giving rise to a claim for damages but, it is not regarded as a "criminal" act, unless, of course, the "lack of care" was so gross as to be defined as criminal. The harm done—the death of a human being— is the same whether the case is one of death through a driving accident or of the intentional killing of another person. By the same token, while the law sees such acts as forcible rape, robbery, arson, and theft as clearly criminal, certain offenses proscribed by statute, such as intentional violation of a zoning ordinance, gambling, or selling shares of a corporation in interstate commerce without registration with the Securities and Exchange Commission, are usually considered "criminal" only because they are proscribed by statute, not because of their "inherently" criminal character.

Legal theorists have tried to explain this difference in attitude toward various sorts of offenses in different ways. Perhaps the oldest distinction is that which Blackstone offered, between crimes *mala in se* and crimes *mala prohibita*. He said:

In regard to *natural duties*, and such offences as are *mala in se*: here we are bound in conscience, because we are bound by superior laws, before those human laws were in being, to perform the one and abstain from the other. But in relation to those laws which enjoin only *positive duties* and forbid only such things as are not *mala in se* but *mala prohibita* merely, without any intermixture of moral guilt, annexing a penalty to non-compliance, here I comprehend conscience is not further concerned, than by directing a submission to the penalty, in case of our breach of these laws.[6]

The distinction between crimes *mala in se* and *mala prohibita* falls down, however, as soon as one begins to question whether a particular crime is one or the other. Bentham attacked the entire classificatory scheme in a classical passage:

If any act can with propriety be termed pernicious, it must be so in virtue of some events which are its consequences . . .; therefore no act can strictly speaking, be *mala in se*, in itself pernicious; nor even of, or by itself, any farther than the words *of* or *by* may be understood to exclude the influence of certain laws. Now, then, as to *mala prohibita*. Why is it that any event is prohibited, if prohibited with a good cause? Because the events, which are its consequences, are pernicious, if the law is a good one. The distinction between *mala in se* and *mala prohibita*, therefore, appears but verbal. If the consequences are otherwise than pernicious, the law, and whatever punishment it is sanctioned by, are groundless, and hence improper . . .[7]

Writing in 1907, the sociologist E. A. Ross captured the essence of the problem of differentiating between crimes that are *mala in se* and those that are *mala prohibita* when he pointed to the complexity of modern life as the source of much of the confusion:

Modern sin takes its character from the mutualism of our time. Under our present manner of living how many of my vital interests I must intrust to others! Nowadays the water main is my well, the trolley car my carriage, the banker's safe my old stocking, the policeman's billy my fist. My own eyes and nose and judgment defer to the inspector of food, or drugs, or gas, or factories, or tenements, or insurance companies. I rely upon others to look after my drains, invest my savings, nurse my sick, and teach my children. I let the meat trust butcher my pig, the oil trust mould my candles, the sugar trust boil my sorghum, the coal trust chop my wood, the barb-wire company split my rails.

But this spread out manner of life lays snares for the weak and opens doors for the wicked. Interdependence puts us, as it were, at one another's mercy, and so ushers in a multitude of new forms of wrongdoing.

The sinister opportunities presented in this webbed social life have been seized unhesitatingly, because such treasons have not yet become infamous. The man who picks pockets with a railway rebate, murders with an adulterant instead of a bludgeon, burglarizes with a "rake off" instead of a jimmy, cheats with a company prospectus instead of a deck of cards, or scuttles his town instead of his ship, does not feel on his brow the brand of a malefactor. The shedder of blood, the oppressor of the widow and the fatherless, long ago became odious, but latter-day treacheries fly no skull-and-crossbones flag at the masthead. The qualities which differentiate them from primitive sin and procure them such indulgence may be clearly defined.

1   Modern sin is not superficially repulsive. Today the sacrifice of life incidental to quick success rarely calls for the actual spilling of blood. How decent are the pale slayings of the quack, the adulterator, and bandit or assassin! Even if there is blood-letting, the long-range tentacular nature of modern homicide eleminates all personal collision. What an abyss between the knifeplay of brawlers and the law-defying neglect to fence dangerous machinery in a mill or to furnish cars with safety couplers! The providing of unsuspecting passengers with "cork" life-preservers secretly loaded with bars of iron to make up for their deficiency in weight of cork is spiritually akin to the treachery of Joab, who, taking Amasa by the beard "to kiss him," smote Amasa "in the fifth rib"; but it wears a very different aspect. The current methods of annexing

the property of others are characterized by a pleasing indirectness and refinement. The furtive, apprehensive manner of the till-tapper or the porch-climber would jar disagreeably upon the tax-dodger "swearing off" his property or the city official concealing a "rake-off" in his specifications for a public building. The work of the card sharp and the thimblerigger shocks a type of man that will not stick at the massive "artistic swindling" of the contemporary promoter. A taint of unworthiness, indeed, always attaches to transactions that force the person into humiliating postures. Your petty parasite or your minor delinquent inspires the contempt that used to be felt for the retailer. The confidence man is to the promoter what the small shopkeeper was to the merchant prince.

2 Modern sin lacks the familiar tokens of guilt. The stealings and slayings that lurk in the complexities of our social relations are not deeds of the dive, the dark alley, the lonely road, and the midnight hour. They require no nocturnal prowling with muffled step and bated breath, no weapon or offer of violence. Unlike the old-time villain, the latter-day malefactor does not wear a slouch hat and a comforter, breathe forth curses and an odor of gin, go about his nefarious work with clenched teeth and an evil scowl. In the supreme moment his lineaments are not distorted with rage, or lust, or malevolence. One misses the dramatic setting, the time-honored insignia of turpitude. Fagin and Bill Sykes and Simon Legree are vanishing types. Gamester, murderer, body-snatcher, and kidnapper may appeal to a Hogarth, but what challenge finds his pencil in the countenance of the boodler, the savings-bank wrecker, or the ballot-box stuffer? Among our criminals of greed one begins to meet the "grand style" of the great criminals of ambition, Macbeth or Richard III. The modern high-power dealer of woe wears immaculate linen, carries a silk hat and lighted cigar, sins with a calm countenance and serene soul leagues or months from the evil he causes. Upon his gentlemanly presence the eventual blood and tears do not obtrude themselves.

3 Modern sins are impersonal. The covenant breaker, the suborned witness, the corrupt judge, the oppressor of the fatherless—the old-fashioned sinner, in short—knows his victim, must hearken, perhaps, to bitter upbraidings. But the tropical belt of sin we are sweeping into is largely impersonal. Our iniquity is wireless, and we know not whose withers are wrung by it. The hurt passes into that vague mass, the "public," and is there lost to view. Hence it does not take a Borgia to knead "chalk and alum and plaster" into the loaf, seeing one cannot know just who will eat that loaf or what gripe it will give him. The purveyor of spurious life-preservers need not be a Cain. The owner of a rotten tenement house, whose "pull" enables him to ignore the orders of the health department, foredooms babies, it is true, but for all that he is no Herod.

Often there are no victims. If the crazy hulk sent out for "just one more trip" meets with fair weather, all is well. If no fire breaks out in the theater, the sham "emergency exits" are blameless. The corrupt inspector who O.K.'s low-grade kerosene is chancing it, that is all. Many sins, in fact, simply augment risk. Evil does not dog their footsteps with relentless and heartshaking certainty. When the catastrophe does come, the sinner salves his conscience by blasphemously calling it an "accident" or an "act of God."

Still more impersonal is sin when the immediate harm touches beneficent institutions rather than individuals, when, following his vein of profit, the sinner drives a gallery under some pillar upholding our civilization. The blackguarding editor is really undermining the freedom of the press. The policy kings and saloon keepers who get out to the polls the last vote of the vicious and criminal classes are sapping manhood suffrage. Striking engineers who spitefully desert passenger trains in mid-career are jeopardizing the right of a man to work only when he pleases. The real victim of a lynching mob is not the malefactor, but the law-abiding spirit. School-board grafters who blackmail applicants for a teacher's position are stabbing the free public school. The corrupt bosses and "combines" are murdering representative government. The perpetrators of election frauds unwittingly assail the institution of the ballot. Rarely, however, are such transgressions abominated as are offenses against persons.

The grading of sinners according to badness of character goes on the assumption that the wickedest man is the most dangerous. This would be true if men were abreast in their opportunities to do harm. In that case the blackest villain would be the worst scourge of society. But the fact is that the patent ruffian is confined to the social basement, and enjoys few opportunities. He can assault or molest, to be sure; but he cannot betray. Nobody depends on him, so he cannot commit breach of trust—that arch sin of our time. He does not hold in his hand the safety or welfare or money of the public. He is the clinker, not the live coal; vermin, not beast of prey. Today the villain most in need of curbing is the respectable, exemplary, trusted personage who, strategically placed at the focus of a spider-web of fiduciary relations, is able from his office-chair to pick a thousand pockets, poison a thousand sick, pollute a thousand minds, or imperil a thousand lives. It is the great-scale, high-voltage sinner that needs the shackle. To strike harder at the petty pickpocket than at the prominent and unabashed person who in a large, impressive way sells out his constituents, his followers, his depositors, his stockholders, his policy-holders, his subscribers, or his customers, is to "strain at a gnat and swallow a camel."

No paradox is it, but demonstrable fact, that in a highly articulate society the gravest harms are inflicted not by the worst men, but by those with virtues enough to boost them into some coign of vantage. The boss who sells out the town and delivers the poor over to filth, disease, and the powers that prey owes his chance to his engaging good-fellowship and big-heartedness. Some of the most dazzling careers of fraud have behind them long and reassuring records of probity, which have served to bait the trap of villainy.[8]

If there is no inherent distinction between crimes, then what is the source of the perceived differences? Why are breaches of some norms subject to sanctions backed up by the massive authority of the State, while others are merely torts, giving rise to claims for compensatory damages, and still others no more than bad manners which call forth at most raised eyebrows?

Some writers have pointed to the conscience or moral ethic of the community as the source of this difference. Jerome Hall, for example, has said that:

The moral judgments represented in the criminal law can be defended on the basis of their derivation from a long historical experience, through open discussion, in which many persons have participated in one way or another. They may not validly be contrasted with individual ethics because the individual participates in the group ethics. These are, also, in that sense and for the most part, his ethics ... The process of legislation, viewed broadly to include participation and discussion by the electorate as well as that of the legislature proper, provides additional assurance that the legal valuations are soundly established . . . [I]nasmuch as normal persons in any given culture have common attitudes regarding the elementary interests protected by the criminal law, it is a fair inference that the doer of an objectively wrong act normally knows that his conduct is immoral.[9]

Other writers, like Holmes, find in expediency alone the rationale for sanctioning against certain particular harms and punishing the individuals perpetrating these harms.[10] The difference between these two theories ultimately rests on the difference between the homeostatic and the conflict views of society. The one assumes that, for whatever reasons—a mystical *Volksgeist* or a common acculturation—values are commonly held, and that the penal law embodies such values. The other assumes that the penal law at any given moment, like any other set of legal norms, represents the rules for the application of State power that are desired by or convenient for those *pro tempore* in control of the State machinery.

To a degree, of course, Hall is plainly correct. Part of our cultural heritage is the criminal law itself. As Hall points out,

(a) the criminal law is at least as old as ethics; [and] (b) . . . our ethical principles are in great measure at least the product of positive law . . . [11]

What most people would call "ordinary" crimes are therefore mainly those which were early incorporated into the substantive law. We must refer to history to learn what their general characteristics were, and why they were singled out.

Process and Substance

It is a commonplace that much of the shape of the substantive common law finds its origin not in deliberate choices of substantive issues, but in the expediencies imposed by procedural rules. The procedural rules were developed before the substantive rules because, as our model suggests, the dispute-settling function of courts precedes the rule-enforcement function of courts. Procedural rules first arise through the necessity of settling disputes.

The first procedures for the settlement of the sort of disputes that today we would call "criminal" was, of course, the blood feud. Even before the Norman invasion, it was "the consistent aim of the Wessex dynasty . . . to do away with the blood feud as the basis of private law."[12] When William the Conqueror introduced trial by combat between the injured party and the person he accused, in the appeal of felony, the language used expressly treats the dispute as a form of private war.[13]

That criminal prosecutions should rest on private, not public, initiative was, no doubt, inevitable in an era without police. Devices for ferreting out crimes existed whose operations nominally were initiated by the crown, such as the grand jury. In practice, however, in the period prior to the Stuart ascendency, the justices of the peace accepted private accusations by petition, which they then submitted to the grand jury.[14]

Criminal prosecutions which rest on private prosecutions take place on three preconditions. In the first place, there must be a victim; otherwise, there would be nobody to initiate the prosecution. And given a victim, there must be a high degree of visibility for the crime. Indeed, the requirements for a successful prosecution for some offenses came to depend on the degree of visibility. In rape, for example, it came to be a condition for raising the hue and cry against the rapist that the victim complain early to the nearest citizen, displaying the bloody garments.

In the second place, there must be ascertainable harm done; otherwise there could be no victim. In the third place, an individual cannot initiate prosecution until he has determined that a norm of conduct has been breached; moreover, it must be a norm of conduct which the victim perceives as one for which he is entitled to a remedy through law. In a relatively simple society, the norms are in fact commonly known. They do not need to be reinforced through judicial decision. The function of the courts then becomes, as we have seen, heavily weighted in favor of dispute-settlement rather than norm-enforcement. Indeed, even in the great formative period of the criminal law there were very few statutes defining crimes. Those few that did exist "purported only to mark off (not to create) classes of crime which everybody should have known to be crimes beforehand."[15]

In sharp contrast to the offenses which violated deeply embedded norms of conduct—rape, murder, arson, and the like—there were in every era in English history a wide variety of rules which served economic and political interests. Ordinances punished "idle rogues," forbidding riot, poaching in the King's forests, drunkenness, and gambling. These ordinances were introduced by legislation; they were frequently frankly innovative, instead of merely restating existing norms; most important of all, they were enforced, not by the central criminal courts, but by the justices of the peace, who slowly became the major instrument of governmental control in the countryside.

Whether an offense was triable in the central criminal courts as a felony, or triable before a magistrate as a misdemeanor, depended mainly on historical accident. If the offense found its historical roots in an offense that existed in the simpler society of the early Middle Ages, it was apt to be a felony and hence regarded as part of the traditional common law of crimes. If, on the other hand, it had its origin in legislation, then it was apt to be a misdemeanor, to merit a less severe punishment (all felonies were punishable by death until the early nineteenth century), and to be triable before a justice of the peace.

The above difference is nicely seen in the distinction between the common-law crime of larceny by trick or device, and the statutory misdemeanor of theft by false pretense. As the idea of crime of larceny was developed by the courts from the ancient offenses of burglary and theft, one of the essential characteristics of larceny came to be a wrongful taking of property, marked by an "asportation" or movement of the property out of the possession of its rightful owner against his will. Where the property was taken with the consent of the owner, though this consent was obtained by a false statement, was it a "wrongful taking" on the part of the accused? The line that came to be drawn depended on whether the owner had been tricked into consenting only to a temporary relinquishment of possession, in which case he still retained ownership, or whether he had been induced to agree to a transfer of ownership to the accused. If it were the former, then the original owner remained the owner of the property, and if the accused then kept the property and did not return it, the courts held that the original taking was a wrongful one because it was induced by trick or device. It was, therefore, a common-law larceny and a felony.[16] If, however, the owner agreed to part with title as well as possession in consequence of the fraudulent representation, there was no taking against the will of the owner (even though the consent to the taking was fraudulently induced). Parliament therefore enacted a statute[17] that made it a misdemeanor to obtain property through a false pretense. The one was a felony and the other a misdemeanor only because of the historical development of criminal law, not because of any intrinsic difference between the offenses.

However, not only the specific content, but also the overarching broad principles, of the "traditional criminal law" were forged in this specific historical development. In order to understand these principles and their consequences, in both their rhetorical and their actual functions, we shall examine, first, the problems relating to the selection of persons to be sanctioned from the rank of all those who commit harms, and second, the principles which purport to limit police and prosecutor's discretion.

The Objectives of Punishment

The ultimate function of the system of criminal-law-enforcement is to ensure so far as possible that the order prescribed by norms of the criminal law is maintained. Traditionally, this has been accomplished by identifying specific individuals who are then processed and treated in certain ways by the sanctioning system. In order to understand the sanctioning system, therefore, one must first understand the purposes for which men are sentenced and punished by criminal courts.

The history of the theories of punishment seems to fall into five principal stages. The first stage, beginning in the Middle Ages and continuing through the middle of the eighteenth century, was characterized by extremely severe penalties even for relatively trivial crimes. Apparently there was not any theoretical or philosophical basis for this practice.

The second stage was one in which doctrines of retribution became popular, under the leadership of Immanuel Kant. He urged a mystical connection between

THE SUBSTANTIVE CRIMINAL LAW: GENERAL PRINCIPLES

the harm done to society by the crime and the degree of punishment. He held that a nice balance between the intrinsic evil of the deed and the punishment must be maintained in order to maintain the mystical balance of the social order. At the time, the doctrine had a humanist thrust, for it argued for a scaling of punishments, instead of continuing to impose the punishment of horrible death even for miniscule breaches of trivial rules. It urged the slogan "make the punishment fit the crime."

In the third stage, the eighteenth- and early nineteenth-century rationalists, led by Jeremy Bentham under the banner of Utilitarianism, sought to derive the principles of punishment from human nature, holding that the basic objective of the criminal law was to deter potential criminals by example. These doctrines and their ethical implication are well exemplified in the writings of the Reverend Sydney Smith, editor of the *Edinburgh Review* in the eighteen-thirties:

In prisons which are really meant to keep the multitude in order, and to be a terror to evil-doers, there must be no sharing of profits—no visiting friends—no education but religious education—no freedom of diet—no weavers' looms or carpenters' benches. There must be a great deal of solitude; coarse food . . . a planned and regulated and unrelenting exclusion of happiness and comforts.[18]

This doctrine, called general deterrence, was based on the notion that severe punishment of criminals would serve to deter other potential criminals from engaging in criminal conduct. It was based on the psychological theory developed by Bentham, called the calculus of pleasure and pain, that every man before he acted calculated the pleasure and pain to be derived from the projected act. If, then, punishment were foreseen as the necessary consequence of crime, and the punishment were just slightly more painful than the pleasures to be derived from the crime, the criminal would be deterred. Since pain was perceived as an absolute evil, however, the least pain was to be applied which was consistent with the objective of deterrence.

The ethical theory which sustains the doctrine of general deterrence is well expressed, again, by the Reverend Sydney Smith:

When a man has been proved to have committed a crime, it is expedient that society should make use of that man for the diminution of crime; he belongs to them for that purpose.[19]

Holmes suggested a similar point of view when he wrote to his friend Harold Laski:

If I were having a philosophical talk with a man I was going to have hanged (or electrocuted) I should say, I don't doubt that your act was inevitable for you, but to make it more avoidable by others we propose to sacrifice you for the common good.

You may regard yourself as a soldier dying for your country if you like. But the law must keep its promises.[20]

This is a theory that holds that criminals, at least might be treated, as means to the good of society. Kantian humanism, it should be noted, asserted precisely the opposite: That no man should be treated as a means, but only as an end.

Implicit in the notion of general deterrence is that of special deterrence—i.e., that the purpose of punishing *this* criminal is to ensure that *he* does not repeat the offense. Indeed, Bentham seems quite naïvely to have moved from one to the other notion. Special deterrence implies a very different sort of value-acceptance from that implied by general deterrence, for it limits punishment to that which is necessary to deter *this* criminal from repeating the crime. Since it measures punishment by the needs of the criminal himself, it is not inconsistent with the Kantian imperative.

By 1865, English prison theory crystallized in the Prisons Act of that year, which sought to transform prisons from mere places for the storage of convicted criminals into harsh and indeed cruel instruments of refined torture—without, of course, shedding blood, for that would have been regarded as barbaric. The conditions called for by the Reverend Smith were realized. Hard labor consisted of shot drill, crank drill, and treadmill. Shot drill required the prisoner endlessly to lift heavy cannonballs, keeping the elbows away from the body and the knees straight, moving the balls a few paces and then placing them on the ground, only to repeat the performance endlessly. Solitary confinement became the rule rather than the exception. Diet was reduced to the minimum compatible with the sustenance of life. A typical statement of the period is found in a letter from the Secretary of State to a Mr. Ussher, then the Administrator of the Colony of the Gold Coast, in 1869. Ussher had asked for money to build more prison accommodations. The Secretary answered with advice on how to avoid over-crowding in prisons.

It can be done by resorting to shorter and sharper punishments, by whipping in addition to shorter terms of imprisonment or in total substitution for any imprisonment . . . by substituting in the earlier stages of imprisonment strictly penal labor [i.e., shot drill, crank drill, and treadmill], and by lowering the diet to the minimum required for health. By these means the crowding of prisons becomes less not only by shortening the duration of each prisoner's term but (as experience has shown) by lessening the number of Offenders.[21]

It did not take very many years for the British establishment to realize that the policies established in the Prisons Act of 1865 were self-defeating. After all, prisoners had to be released at some point; and when released, would it not be necessary that they have acquired skills and habits conducive to a law-abiding life? The Gladstone Committee in 1895 urged that prisons serve a dual function, deterrence and rehabilitation. Since that time, the trend of thinking of most penologists has been that the principal function of prisons is to rehabilitate the prisoner.

We have then five goals of punishment inherited from our history. These five potential objectives of punishment for criminal conduct linger on in our law. The prevailing penological theory justifies the multigoal system of sentencing:

When the legislature declares conduct to be criminal, it affirms a purpose to forbid it and to meet defiance of the prohibition by the moral condemnation of conviction and judicious application of the sanctions that the law provides. The least that it demands is that the disposition be so cast that it does not deprecate the gravity of the offense, whatever that may be, and so afford a license to commit it. But how much more than this the prohibition should be taken to imply is obviously indeterminate. Deterrence (both general and special), incapacitation and correction are all possible objectives of the sanctions that may be employed in dealing with offenders; all are means to crime prevention and as such entitled to be weighed. Not even crime prevention is, however, the sole value to be served. The rehabilitation of an individual who has incurred the formal condemnation of the law is in itself a social value of importance, a value it is well to note that is and ought to be the prime goal of correctional administration and that often will be sacrificed unduly if the choice of sanctions is dictated only by deterrence. Finally, it is surely important that the deprivations incident to dispositions not be arbitrary, excessive or disproportionate, measured by the common sense of justice.[22]

The difficulty is that the quantum and quality of sanctions demanded by any one of these several objectives may be sharply different from that demanded by another. For example, in 1961 a federal court convicted several of the nation's highest paid, most prestigious corporate executives of conspiracy in restraint of trade. The defendants were

middle-class men in Ivy League suits—typical businessmen in appearance, men who would never be taken for law-breakers. Over and over their lawyers described them as pillars of their communities.

Several were deacons or vestrymen of their churches. One was president of his local Chamber of Commerce, another a hospital board member, another chief fund raiser for the Community Chest, another a bank director, another director of the taxpayer's association, another an organizer for the Little League.[23]

Presumably, these men did not require a stay in prison to deter them from repeating the offense, or for purposes of rehabilitation. On the other hand, the objectives of retribution and general deterrence arguably demanded a substantial jail sentence; indeed, precisely because the defendants were pillars of their community, the aim of general deterrence would seem to require a greater penalty. (In fact, the sentences handed down were only for 30 days.)

The same ambivalence obtains in many cases involving homosexuals. The objective of rehabilitation in such cases usually demands, at most, psychiatric care. To place a homosexual in a prison would seem counterproductive with respect to that objective; it is roughly analogous to sentencing an alcoholic to serve his sentence in a brewery. Yet there is always the possibility that there may be some marginal homosexuals who might be deterred from engaging in the forbidden acts if they were aware that conviction inevitably meant a long stay in prison—or so the argument goes.

The objectives of general deterrence, as we have seen, imply the value-acceptance that a man may be used as a means for social ends. The notions of special deterrence and of rehabilitation, on the other hand, assert the dignity and value of the individual human being. The values of general deterrence are well expressed in Sydney Smith's eloquent phrase, that prisons—and indeed, the whole structure of the criminal law—ought to be designed "to keep the multitude in order." Whether by increased policeman's discretion, or by harsh punishments designed "to be a terror to evil-doers," the objective remains the same: To maintain the existing social order, and its benefits and privileges, even, if necessary, at the expense of human values.

The substantive criminal law defines not only the harmful actions which are proscribed, but also lays down the identifying characteristics of persons who are to be subject to sanction. What those characteristics ought to be depends on the purposes to be served by the sanctioning process. If general deterrence were the sole objective, then the mere commission of the harm ought to be sufficient to incur a finding of guilt, so that potential criminals would learn that they would have no defense whatever if they were found to have in fact committed the harms. On the other hand, if special deterrence were the sole criterion of sentencing, then whether or not the criminal could have been deterred at the time of the act becomes critical, for if he could not have been deterred, then punishment to deter him from the same act in the future would be pointless. We therefore must examine the strictures by which the substantive criminal law purports to identify persons subject to punishment. Since there is a relationship between the objectives of punishment and those identifying criteria, we would expect that there would be a confusion among the identifying criteria to parallel the confusion in the objectives of sentencing.

Mens Rea

There is no profit in punishment for punishment's sake. On this, practically all modern writers on criminal law are agreed. If punishment is to work to society's advantage, it must operate on persons who are amenable to change. For example, if the sole purpose of punishment were special deterrence, it would be pointless to punish a person who was incapable of change with respect to the characteristics which led him to commit the crime.

Since the express purpose for the finding of guilt in a criminal case is to expose the offender to possible sanction, the detection of guilt must necessarily include a discovery that the accused possesses the personal characteristics which make him amenable to the purposes of punishment. The relevant characteristics depend on the purposes which punishment is designed to serve. If the sole purpose of punishment were the retribution for sin, defined theologically, then the significant factor would be a consciousness of guilt, for in Christian doctrine guilt is a matter of evil intention or motive. If general deterrence is the only reason for punishment, then mere commission of the harm ought to be enough; even the punishment of an insane person warns other potential criminals that there is no escape from punishment if the harm is committed. If special deterrence is the end to be achieved, then the accused must be a person who could take the prospect of further punishment into account in calculating whether or not to commit the offense again. If restraint is the objective, then the critical factor ought to be the total character of the accused. If rehabilitation is the objective, then the criterion for conviction must be a psychiatric judgment that the accused is amenable to treatment.

The theological criteria, as might be expected, were enunciated first in time.

To the ecclesiastics the working of a man's mind was of paramount importance, since their aim was to eradicate sin and wickedness, and it was in the mind of man that these grave faults originated and existed; and in their view that which called for penance and atonement was the evil intention or motive which had prompted the harmful deed. In their own spiritual courts they not only exercised a considerable jurisdiction over laymen, but they also claimed and established an exclusive right to deal with ordained clerks who were charged with serious crimes, and they admitted no impossibility in the investigation of the mental element in wrongdoing . . . [24]

These notions of sin combined with the common ethical conception—itself probably a result of long centuries of Christian influence—that "it was not proper to punish a man criminally unless he had known that he was doing wrong."[25] By the early seventeenth century, the religious and ethical conceptions had crystallized into the maxim *actus non facit reus nisi mens sit rea*. As a result, "It is almost impossible to deny that in popular thought the notion of crime is inextricably bound up with that of moral blameworthiness, in some sense of that phrase . . . The connection between crime and moral guilt is enshrined in the common law."[26]

Benthamite strictures of "cognoscibility" in law gave an additional impetus to the doctrine. If the public policy is to ensure that citizens know the law, its corollary must be that unless a citizen knows that he is doing wrong, he cannot be guilty under the law (unless, of course, his ignorance itself is his own moral delict). The concept of *mens rea* thus reflects not only medieval notions of sin and retribution, but also of middle-class dreams of a universe of pre-existing, cognoscible norms.

It is part of the mythology about the criminal law that *mens rea* in the sense of consciousness of guilt remains a touchstone of criminal liability. It is a myth frequently perpetuated by the comments of judges. Lord Goddard, an English judge, once said that "It is of the utmost importance for the protection of the liberty of the subject that a court should always bear in mind that, unless a statute clearly or by necessary implication rules out *mens rea* as a constituent part of a crime, the court should not find a man guilty of an offense against the criminal law unless he has a guilty mind."[27] Even so careful a judge as Justice Jackson has said:

Crime, as a compound concept, generally constituted only from the concurrence of an evil-meaning mind with an evil-doing hand, was congenial to an intense individualism and took deep and early root in American soil... Courts, with little hesitation or division, found an implication of the requirement as to offenses that were taken over from the common law. The unanimity with which they have adhered to the notion that wrongdoing must be conscious to be criminal is emphasized by the variety, disparity and confusion of their definitions of the requisite but elusive mental element... By use of combination of these various tokens, they have sought to protect those who were not blameworthy in mind from conviction of infamous common-law crimes.[28]

In fact, however, *actual* consciousness of guilt is not today a necessary ingredient for most instances of criminality, even with respect to "infamous common-law crimes." An English judge stated it concisely in 1921: "*Mens rea* means an intention to do an act prohibited by the statute; it has not necessarily a moral connotation."[29] Consciousness of wrongdoing—the very essence of a "guilty mind"—has been abandoned in favor of intentional, or even reckless or negligent conduct.

How did this sea change in the notion of *mens rea* come about? The requirement of consciousness of wrongdoing is consistent with the principle of either retribution or special deterrence as the objective of punishment. It is inconsistent with a broadly applied notion of general deterrence, and it is equally irrelevant to restraint as the goal. As classical Utilitarianism began to dominate British jurisprudential thought, general deterrence as an objective of the law found itself in sharp contradiction to the now deeply embedded doctrine of *mens rea*.

The upshot of the confrontation was a compromise. *Mens rea* as a generalized notion of consciousness of guilt was to disappear from the substantive criminal law except as rhetoric. It was replaced by two different doctrines: the requirement that the act be voluntary, and the so-called general defenses. These two doctrines combine to make the critical question, not whether an individual defendant had consciousness of guilt, but whether a reasonable man in his shoes and with his physical characteristics would have had consciousness of guilt. This is the so-called doctrine of "objective" *mens rea*. If it is thought that the latter would feel guilty, then the predictability of the criminal law is sufficiently definite, and the accused may be found guilty and punished. He has "objective" *mens rea.*

The Voluntary-Act Doctrine

As a minimum, special deterrence demands that the act be voluntary, not merely a muscular spasm.

> The reason for requiring an act is, that an act implies a choice, and that it is felt to be impolitic and unjust to make a man answerable for a crime unless he might have chosen otherwise.[30]

The principle is fixed in a rule that one is not liable for a criminal harm arising from an involuntary act. In *R. v. Nagang*[31] a South African case, for example, the accused was convicted on a charge of assault to do grievous bodily harm. It seems that he was asleep in a room with a number of other men, and stabbed the complainant as the latter was leaving the room. There was no apparent motive for the stabbing. The accused testified that he was asleep, and awoke as a result of a nightmare. In his sleep, he said, he had seen a "tokoloshe," a much-dreaded spirit or demon. He grabbed his knife, put it under his pillow, and went back to sleep. Again he saw the tokoloshe coming; he screamed, and stabbed the "thing" as it came toward him. On appeal, the conviction was reversed, because "the appellant acted involuntarily or automatically and cannot be held criminally responsible for his act which was no more than a purely physical reflex."

The General Defenses and Mens Rea

All the so-called general defenses, i.e. defenses which are available to the accused in any case, describe conditions that affect the accused's consciousness of guilt. Insanity, immaturity, mistake of fact, necessity and coercion, intoxication, and mistake of law are defenses (to the extent that they are defenses at all) only because each of the general defenses describes the circumstances in which, for reasons beyond his conscious control, an ordinary person could not have had consciousness of guilt or capacity to control his actions. We lack space to follow the tedious course of this thread of reasoning as it spins through the web of the common law. Rather, we shall explore it in connection with a rather bizarre group of cases: killings by Africans brought up in a tribal culture of persons whom they believed to be bewitching them, tried under a codified version of the common law of crimes. Before we can examine the issue directly, however, we must say a word about the nature of the African beliefs in witchcraft.[32]

For many Africans, witchcraft belief is an integral part of their Weltanschauung, growing out of indigenous theories about the psyche. The Akan (one of the largest West African tribal groupings), for example, postulate man as tripartite. His physical body, a mere shell, encloses two indwelling souls, the *kra*, or life-soul, and the *sunsum*, or personality-soul.[33] A wicked entity, the *obayi*, on occasion seizes dominion of the *sunsum* of a witch. Without her volition, her *sunsum* makes excursions from her earthly body. Free of physical restraint, it attacks the *kra* or *sunsum* of its victim by sucking it forth secretly from its material shell. As the *kra* is devoured, sometimes by degrees, sometimes in a rush, so the physical body of the victim withers. As the *sunsum* is destroyed, so will the victim's hope of worldly success disappear.[34]

Prior to European overlordship, death, usually in some peculiarly horrible form,[35] was the invariable punishment for proven[36] witches. The colonial governments, having but recently abolished equally barbaric measures against witches in the metropolis, abolished them in the colonies as well. But superstition nevertheless flourished[37] albeit now shorn of institutional protection.

The African who believes in witchcraft is thus faced by a fearful dilemma. He believes in witches to his bones.[38] He knows that they can destroy his *kra* or *sunsum* in sundry mysterious ways, for which there is no defense, so that both his physical existence and his hope for earthly success are endangered as much by witches as by a threatened blow of panga or spear or matchet. He sees nothing in the societal order to which he can appeal for protection. His own tradition approves of capital punishment for witches.

Faced by such dread forces, bereft of societal shield, terrified by the loss of the values at stake, some Africans not surprisingly have struck back in terror and in self-defense. How have the common-law judges treated them when they were charged with murder?[39]

The response of the courts has been practically unvarying: such defendants are guilty of murder. But the verdicts, with their concomitant death sentences, are in both West[40] and East[41] Africa almost invariably leavened with a judicial prayer that the appropriate executive would reverse the decision just made. Such a formalized, indeed institutionalized,[42] reliance on executive clemency at once vitiates any supposed deterrent effect of the death penalty and confesses to a felt inadequacy in the judicial solutions to the problems posed by these cases.

This judicial solution has been an all but unvarying rejection of the various defenses urged, whether they are based on the naked claim that these defendants lack a guilty mind, or whether an attempt is made to fit the actions within the conventional categories of self-defense, or defense of others, mistake, insanity, or provocation.

The visceral response of any lawyer to the killing of a supposed witch in imagined self-defense is that the superstition negates *mens rea*.[43] This claim was rejected in the case of *Kumwaka Wa Malumbi and sixty-nine others* (Kenya).[44] Seventy defendants admitted beating to death an old woman they believed to be a witch. The court overruled a plea that the homicide was *ipso facto* excusable: "For courts to adopt any other attitude in such cases, would be to encourage the belief that an aggrieved party may take the law into his own hands, and no

THE SUBSTANTIVE CRIMINAL LAW: GENERAL PRINCIPLES

belief could well be more mischievous or fraught with greater danger to public peace and tranquillity."[45] Sixty defendants were sentenced to death; ten juveniles were detained.[46]

The more conventional plea of self-defense has not fared better. In *Erika Galikuwa*[47] (Uganda), the defendant was convicted of killing an unscrupulous witch-doctor. The defendant imagined that he had heard the witch-doctor's "spirit voice" repeat a demand for ransom on two occasions, at one point with a threat to kill "by sucking your blood." Terrified, the defendant killed "and saved my life." The court, upholding a conviction for murder, pointed out that a plea of self-defense was not tenable, for "it is difficult to see how an act of witchcraft unaccompanied by some physical attack could be brought within the principles of English Common Law."[48]

The defense that the killing was necessary to save the life of another has been equally unavailing. In *Konkomba* (Gold Coast),[49] the defendant's first brother died, whereupon he consulted a "juju" man, who pointed out the victim of the murder as the guilty witch. Then the defendant's second brother became ill and charged the victim with causing his illness by witchcraft. The defendant slew the supposed witch. He was, of course, found guilty of murder.

The case may fairly be contrasted with *Rex v. Bourne*.[50] There the defendant, a socially prominent doctor, was charged with committing abortion upon a fifteen-year-old victim of a brutal rape. His defense in part was that he had relied upon the advice of a psychiatrist that, if the pregnancy were permitted to continue, severe psychiatric damage to the child might well ensue. The abortion was held justifiable.

The cases are not dissimilar. In each case, the defendant honestly believed that what he did was necessary to save another. Each acted upon the advice of an expert in the relevant field. Yet one man was found guilty, and the other exonerated. The only apparent difference was that the tribunal believed in psychiatry, and not in witchcraft.[51]

Seemingly, the criterion of criminality turns on the validity of the belief under which the defendant acted. Discussion along this line is usually subsumed under the heading of "mistake": to what extent should a misapprehension about the true state of affairs exculpate a criminal defendant?

In *Gadam*[52] (Nigeria), the defendant was convicted of murder. The Crown's case was that the defendant believed that his wife had been bewitched by the deceased, whom he therefore killed. The defendant relied on a section of the Nigerian Code, affording a defense for a mistake which is both "honest and reasonable." The court conceded that witchcraft belief was common among ordinary members of the community, but held that "it would be a dangerous precedent to recognize that because a superstition, which may lead to such a terrible result as is disclosed by the facts of this case, is generally prevalent among the community, it is therefore reasonable."[53]

The critical question is, of course, the standard to be used in determining what is "reasonable." The measure adopted has invariably been, not the average man of the defendant's community, but the reasonable Englishman.

The Attorney General for Nyasaland v. Jackson[54] (Federation) states the rule with unparalleled bluntness. The court held squarely that the standard of reasonableness of the mistake when a supposed witch is killed in imagined self-defense "is what would appear reasonable to the ordinary man in the street in England . . . On this basis, and bearing in mind that the law of England is still the law of England even when it is extended to Nyasaland, I do not see how any court, applying the proper test, could hold that a belief in witchcraft was reasonable so as to form the foundation of a defense that the law could recognize."[55]

If the claim of mistake has not afforded refuge for these defendants, neither has insanity. In *Philip Muswi s/o Musola*[56] (Kenya), the defendant killed his wife by shooting her with an arrow when she was sitting in her kitchen. There had been continual quarrels between them for some time, and the defendant believed that she was practicing witchcraft against him. A psychiatrist testified that there was a history of madness and epilepsy in the family and that the defendant was probably suffering from a mild depression on the night of the killing. The psychiatrist believed that the defendant knew what he was doing; that he could distinguish right from wrong; that what he was doing was not contrary to tribal law; and that the defendant believed that he was justified in doing what he did. A defense of insanity was overruled, for

even if [the defendant] believed that he was justified in killing his wife because she was practicing witchcraft, there is again no evidence that such belief arose from any mental defect; it is a belief sometimes held by entirely sane Africans.[57]

The case in which it was most clearly articulated why beliefs in witchcraft per se did not constitute insanity within the M'Naghten rules arose in, of all unexpected forums, the Supreme Court of the United States. In *Hotema v. United States*,[58] the defendant killed a supposed witch in obedience to the biblical injunction. The court approved a charge which directed that if the defendant's belief in witches was simply the conclusion of a sane mind, he was to be convicted, but if as the result of a disordered mind, acquitted. Insanity as a ground of defense exculpates only when the defect is a mental disease and not merely one of training.[59]

Nor does the defense based on the claim of partial delusion stand on any better ground. Under the traditional rule, the facts imagined must themselves be sufficient to excuse or justify the killing.[60] Since the accused does not imagine himself physically backed to the wall, the claim of delusion is an insufficient defense.[61]

The claim of provocation, with one very narrow exception, has been equally unavailing as a defense.[62] In *Fabiano* (Uganda),[63] defendants believed that the deceased was a wizard who had killed members of their families. They discovered the supposed wizard naked and crawling about their compound at night. The court found that the defendants actually believed that the deceased was then and there practicing witchcraft against them, and allowed a partial defense of provocation.

We think that if the facts proved establish that the victim was performing in the actual presence of the accused some act which an ordinary person of the community did generally believe, to be an act of witchcraft against him or another person under his immediate care (which act would be a criminal offense under the Criminal Law (Witch-craft) Ordinance of Uganda . . .) he might be angered to such an extent as to be deprived of the power of self-control and induced to assault the person doing the act of witchcraft. And if this is to be the case a defense of grave and sudden provocation is open to him.[64]

This is merely a special application of the usual rule which reduces to man-slaughter a killing done in a provoked passion. The standard is always that of the reasonable man of the community to which the accused belongs.[65] And the killing must actually be done in the heat of passion engendered by the provoca-tion.[66]

The plea has been unavailing in most of the witchcraft cases because there is usually time for passion to cool. But the peculiar nature of witchcraft is that it presents an overhanging, omnipresent threat. Time in such a case does not cool the passions; it inflames them. It was inevitable that provocation, like all the other defenses invoked, would not be a useful shield for these defendants.

No doubt, the received conceptual patterns of the common law could have been manipulated to yield more equitable conclusions. The reasonableness of the mistake might readily have been measured against the community from which the accused comes rather than against the "man on the Clapham omnibus"; moreover, there is the serious question whether the common law requires that the mistake be "reasonable."[67] It might have been possible to treat witchcraft beliefs as evidence of insanity.[68] The notion of provocation might have been extended by recognizing that beliefs in witchcraft provide the sort of provocation in which passion may overcome reason even after long brooding. Or, finally, it might be possible to deal with these cases by specific legislation.[69]

The acceptability of these various solutions might be assessed in terms of the ultimate objectives of criminal law. To some extent the criminal law retains a deterrent function. It also serves to identify the defendant as a person who is exceptionally dangerous[70] and hence properly requires rehabilitative treatment or restraining sanctions. But all these proposed solutions suffer from a common shortcoming. The cases cited are only examples of a broad spectrum of prosecu-tions in which what is right and proper in an indigenous African society is criminal in the eyes of the common law.[71] In all these cases the criminal act is intentional, and the defendants cannot, unless the courts ape Procrustes, be fitted up with any recognized defense. It is as though England had been conquered by a nation of Hindus, so that the eating of beef immediately became a high crime.[72] Would the Englishman who ate his usual dinner possess a guilty mind? Can it fairly be said that an African under analogous circumstances possesses *mens rea*?[73]

Now there is a sharp difference between our myths about *mens rea* and the actual requirements of the law. The myth is that the criminal law requires the presence of a "guilty mind" as a precondition to actual guilt,[74] a requirement patently demanded by humanitarian and ethical notions.[75] But the hard-nosed rule of law is that a man is guilty of a crime if he has committed it intentionally,[76] and if the action does not fit into one of a very few prescribed categories: self-defense, mistake, insanity, youth, and the like. *Mens rea* in modern law is wholly objective.[77] Its ethical content is at best limited.

The judges' uneasiness with the results which they reached in the witchcraft cases arises from their feeling that these defendants are without *mens rea* in the mythological, i.e. the moral and subjective, sense, although they plainly have *mens rea* in the legal, i.e. the objective, sense. Can the contradiction be resolved? Is it possible perhaps to generalize from the exceptional defenses to find some new exception that will subsume all these cases? To find such a common denominator, we need a brief excursion into the psychology underlying these defenses.

It is a commonplace that the psychology which provides the foundation for the M'Naghten Rules represents the human psyche in terms of a constant wrestling match between reason and passion.[78] The same psychology underlies our notions of *mens rea*. An American court once described it as the notion that "there is a separate little man in the top of one's head called reason whose function it is to guide another unruly little man called instinct, emotion or impulse the way he should go."[79]

The role of the criminal law, according to both the Benthamite and the neoclassical theory, is to provide by its sanctions an incentive for reason to follow the right road.[80] Sanctions must be imposed, therefore, whenever an intentional criminal act has been committed, unless for one of three exceptional causes, reason understandably failed to guide passion along the road of legality. First, reason may have been withered by inherent infirmity. Insanity and youth are the chief causes. Secondly, reason in choosing to do the act may have been properly exercised, for example for self-defense. Mistakes also fall within this category. Thirdly, reason under all the circumstances of the action may understandably have been temporarily overpowered by passion. Provocation is of course the principal cause of this.

These categories aside, the law punishes a man whose reason does not control his passion. Except perhaps in cases of inherent physical infirmity, the test is invariably that of the reasonable man. If a mistake be one that a reasonable man would not have made, it is not an admissible excuse. If the error be that the defendant failed to act as carefully as a reasonable man should have, then he is guilty, whether or not he actually perceived the risk.[81] If the issue is whether the defendant foresaw the consequences of his conduct, the test is not whether he actually foresaw these consequences, but whether a reasonable man would have foreseen them.[82] In short, the law actually punishes a man for the failure of his reason to control his actions, save where a reasonable man's reason would likewise have failed, or where the defendant is physically incapable of reasoning.[83]

The "reasonable man," however, is a normative concept,[84] which hypostatizes, not the average man, but the ideal man—i.e., a man with some, but not the grosser, human failings. It is a reference to the judge's notion of a standard of conduct which the average man can fairly be expected to achieve. In criminal law, the concept of *mens rea* performs a similarly normative function. It is a statement of a standard of conduct for the little man labelled reason. To state that *mens rea* is present, is merely to say that the defendant's reason failed to act as would a reasonable man's under the circumstances.

The use of the reasonable man as the standard for determining whether a particular accused had *mens rea* resolves the tension between general deterrence and special deterrence, between utilitarianism and humanitarianism. This concept, and the objective *mens rea* which is built upon it, simultaneously furnish a rationale to punish anyone who fails to meet objective norms and an excuse to exonerate someone who failed to meet them when most men would likewise have failed. Like many of the seminal legal concepts, it resolves the pervasive antagonism between social expediency and individual right, between order and law.

The success of the notion of objective *mens rea* in resolving this tension obviously turns on how close a fit there is between the reasonable and the average man. If they are fairly closely congruent, then the criterion of objective *mens rea* could serve its function tolerably well. In most cases, it would protect the morally innocent; in some cases, the morally innocent might be found criminally guilty, but the result would not be shocking; and in the few cases in which moral innocence was distressingly clear, the executive could spring to the rescue with an order of clemency. In short, if there is a value-consensus, there can rarely be a great difference between moral guilt and legal guilt.[85]

A very different state of affairs arises where, as in Africa, the actual consciousness of guilt is cut from one bolt of cloth, but the criminal law is cut from another. There the average man and the reasonable man in colonial days stood continents, and sometimes worlds, apart. Since the humanitarian function of the concept of *mens rea* depends on the narrowness of the gap (although the function of general deterrence is indifferent to it), the result was that colonial law was devoted almost entirely to the objective of deterrence. Put bluntly, in the final analysis, colonial law selected its victims without regard to moral guilt. It imposed its norms upon the indigenous population by sheer terror. Despite the best intentions of judges and administrators, the use of the criterion of objective *mens rea*, based on precedents embodying values drawn from English law, to determine the guilt of defendants with different sets of values, guaranteed that the law would be concerned only with harsh deterrence,[86] with "keeping the multitude in order."

These African cases suggest that our system of criminal law is based on a model which assumes that the morality expressed in the criminal law is in fact the morality of the accused. To the extent that these moralities are identical, it is true that no person can be convicted of "ordinary" crime unless he is conscious of guilt. To that extent, the criminal law serves the function of special deterrence. To that extent, it expresses a set of values consistent with the humanistic ideal.

If ours were a society with a single set of value-acceptances with respect to the subject-matter of the criminal law, the matter might end there, and one might conclude with commiseration for the African's circumstance. On the other hand, if the correct model of American society is one in which there is a sharp conflict between competing strata (as suggested earlier), each with its own set of value-acceptances, then the results of appealing to the concept of objective *mens rea* are not in principle different from what happened in Africa. The criminal law then serves the function of general deterrence, tempered slightly by the alleviating doctrines embodied in the general defenses. It is a system of criminal law which would preserve the existing social order even, if necessary, at the expense of human values.

We find ourselves, therefore, returning to an issue on which is largely based one's view of the criminal law as well as of most other issues relating to American society. Is our society basically a unified, relatively homogeneous order, or is it at bottom, despite a façade of cohesion, a welter of conflict?

10.2 SUMMARY

The harmful actions selected for sanction, the system of punishment used, and the identifying criteria for *mens rea* constitute the core of the substantive law by which the latter defines the sort of order that ought to obtain in society and ordains which general category of individuals the law-applying authorities shall punish in maintaining that order as well as what techniques of punishment shall be used to achieve it. We have seen that the actions selected for sanction by the traditional criminal law are those which have analogues in the norms that control even the simplest society. They have gone through sea changes from age to age to meet the demands of each new group *pro tempore* in control of the judicial apparatus. We have seen that the current concept of *mens rea* is based on the idea of special deterrence to the extent that the accused's perception of wrongdoing matches what the judge thinks he might have perceived had he been in the former's shoes and possessed the same physical (but not acculturated) characteristics. The existing multipurpose system of sentencing ends up by giving the judges the widest possible scope for discretion in handing out punishment.

If judges do participate in a common morality with every accused, then there can be no doubt that the criminal law proceeds upon humanist, i.e. "ethical," grounds. If that be the case, then the norms embodied in the law express every man's morality; objective *mens rea* describes not only the state of consciousness of the reasonable man, but that of any particular defendant as well; and the level of punishment meted out is precisely what is required to deter other reasonable men from committing the same crime. But if the norms described in the criminal law represent the morality of the middle classes and not of the lower depths from which the vast majority of defendants come, if the consciousness of values of the defendant differs from that expressed by that hypostasis of the judge's morality, the reasonable man, then many of the persons convicted of crimes are convicted even though they could not have done otherwise. Their punishment can only be primarily for purposes of general deterrence. As Holmes put it, they are sacrificed for the common good, as judges perceive this good. The "common good" must be translated as good for others of a similar social class as the judge.

The substantive criminal law does more, however, than to define the sort of order in society that will be supported by the strong arm of the State. It also defines the scope of discretion which policemen, prosecutors, and judges are authorized to use in determining who is to be subject to sanctions. It is to this aspect of the criminal law that we turn in the next two chapters.

NOTES

1. Jerome H. Skolnick, *Justice Without Trial: Law-Enforcement in Democratic Society*, Wiley, New York, 1966, p. 8.

2. A. V. Dicey, *Introduction to the Study of the Law of the Constitution*, Macmillan, London, 1959, p. 188.

3. Herbert Wechsler, "The challenge of a model penal code," *Harvard Law Rev.*, **65**, 1952, p. 1095. Copyright 1952 by the Harvard Law Review Association and reprinted by permission.

4. *Supra*, p. 12.

5. Jerome Hall has made a more elegant analysis, by adding to the five elements we have adduced two others: causality and concurrence. In order to ensure legality, and for purposes of identifying the persons subject to penal sanctions, we can analyze the requirements of causality and concurrence separately by showing their respective contributions. So refined an analysis does not seem necessary here. See Hall, *General Principles of Criminal Law*, Bobbs-Merrill, Indianapolis, 1947, p. 11.

6. Sir William Blackstone, *Commentaries on the Laws of England*, Murray, London, 1880, p. 65.

7. J. Bentham, *The Works of Jeremy Bentham*, Vol. 1, Bowring (ed.), Simpkin, Marshall, London, 1843, pp. 192–193.

8. Excerpts from E. A. Ross, *Social Control*, Macmillan, New York, 1922, pp. 1–25 *passim*.

9. Reprinted from Jerome Hall, *General Principles of Criminal Law*, pp. 356–357. Copyright 1947 by The Bobbs-Merrill Company, Inc., Reprinted by permission. All rights reserved.

10. O. W. Holmes, *The Common Law*, Little, Brown, Boston, 1881, Lecture 2 *passim*; see *Commonwealth v. Kentucky*, 170 Mass. 18, 20, 48 N.E. 770 (1897).

11. Hall, *op. cit.*, p. 297. Reprinted by permission.

12. Alan Harding, *A Social History of English Law*, Penguin, Baltimore, 1966, p. 21.

13. J. F. Stephen, *A History of the Criminal Law of England*, Vol. 1, Macmillan, London, 1883, p. 61.

14. Harding, *op. cit.*, p. 76.

15. *Ibid.*, p. 81.

16. *The King v Pear*, 1 Leach 212, 168 E.R. 208 (1779).

17. 30 Geo. II, c. 24 (1575).

18. Quoted in L. Radzinowicz and J. W. C. Turner, "A Study in Punishment I: Introductory Essay," *Can. B. Rev.*, **21**, 1943, pp. 89, 91.

19. *Ibid.*

20. O. W. Holmes, *Holmes-Laski Letters*, Howe (ed.), Harvard University Press, Cambridge, 1953, p. 806.

21. Dispatch no. 95, November, 19, 1869, from Secretary of State to Administrator, Gold Coast, ADM 1/27, quoted in R. B. Seidman, "The Ghana prison system: an historical perspective," *U. Ghana Law J.* **3**, 1966, pp. 89, 95.

22. Herbert Wechsler, "Sentencing correction and the model penal code," *U. Pa Law Rev.*, **109**, p. 469. Copyright 1961 by the University of Pennsylvania Law Review and reprinted by permission.

23. *New York Times*, February 7, 1961; © 1961 by The New York Times Company. Reprinted by permission. Quoted in M. G. Paulsen and S. H. Kadish, *Criminal Law and its Processes*, Little, Brown, Boston, 1962, p. 70.

24. C. S. Kenny, *Outlines of Criminal Law*, Turner (ed.), Cambridge University Press, Cambridge, 1962, pp. 12–13. Reprinted by permission.

25. *Ibid.*, p. 14. Reprinted by permission.

26. Peter Brett, *An Inquiry into Criminal Guilt*, Sweet and Maxwell, London, 1963, pp. 37–38.

27. *Brend v. Wood*, 62 T.L.R., 462–463 (1946).

28. *Morissette v. United States*, 342 U.S. 246, 72 Sup. Ct. 240, 96 L. Ed. 288 (1952).

29. In argument in *Rex. v. Wheat and Stocks* (1921) 15 Cr. App. Rep. 134–135.

30. Holmes, *The Common Law*, p. 54.

31. [1960] 3 S.A. 363 T.P.D.

32. The remainder of this section is based largely on R. B. Seidman, "Witch murder and mens rea: a problem of society under radical social change," *Mod. Law Rev.*, **28**, 1965, pp. 46–61.

33. M. J. Field, *Search for Security*, Northwestern University Press, Evanston, Ill. 1960 p. 36.

34. *Ibid.*; and see Evans-Pritchard, *Witchcraft, Oracles and Magic among the Azande*, Clarendon Press, Oxford, 1937.

35. H. W. Debrunner, *Witchcraft in Ghana*, Presbyterian Book Depot, Accra, 1961; R. S. Rattray, *Religion and Art in Ashanti*, Clarendon Press, Oxford, 1927, p. 29; R. S. Rattray, *Ashanti Law and Constitution*, Clarendon Press, 1929, p. 313; E. S. Haydon, *Law and Justice in Buganda*, Butterworth, London, 1960, p. 283.

36. Typically, the "proof" was by ordeal. Rattray, *Ashanti Law and Constitution*, pp. 392–395; Mary Kingsley, *Travels in West Africa*, Macmillan, London, 1897, p. 464; E. G. Parrinder, *Witchcraft: European* and African, Faber and Faber, London, 1963, pp. 177, 178.

37. In Africa as in Europe, witchcraft superstitution seemingly flourishes in times of social instability. Parrinder, *op. cit.* (n. 36), p. 205; Debrunner, *op. cit.* (n. 35), p. 71. Colonialism made African society even more unstable than it had been.

38. The judges repeatedly find that the defendant genuinely believed that the deceased was a witch who threatened his life. See, e.g., *Galikwa* (1951) 18 E.A.C.A. 175 (Uganda); *Gadam* (1954) 14 W.A.C.A. 422 (Nigeria).

39. All the former British African countries have criminal codes embodying, in most essentials, the common law of crimes.

40. See, e.g., *Maawole Konkombe* (1952) 14 W.A.C.A. 236 (Gold Coast); *Gadam* (1954) 14 W.A.C.A. 442 (Nigeria).

41. See, e.g., *Sitakimatata s/o Kimwage* (1941) 8 E.A.C.A. 57 (Tanganyika); *Akope s/o Karouon* (1947) 14 E.A.C.A. 105 (Kenya).

42. "In dismissing both appeals, we conclude by observing that in all cases such as this we are aware that the element of witchcraft as a mitigating factor is always taken into account by the Governor in Council." *Kajuna s/o Mbake* (1945) 12 E.A.C.A. 104 (Tanganyika).

43. That is, the guilty mind which traditional doctrine insists is a necessary element in murder.

44. (1932) 14 K.L.R. 137.

45. *Ibid.*, p. 139.

46. Cf. A. L. Goodhart, *English Law and the Moral Law*, Stevens, London, 1953, p. 93: "Retribution in punishment is an expression of the community's disapproval of crime, and if this retribution is not given expression that the disapproval may disappear." Which society is expressing its disapproval when a British colonial judge sentences the male population of a Kenya village to death?

47. (1951) 18 E.A.C.A. 175.

48. *Ibid.*, p. 178.

49. (1952) 14 W.A.C.A. 236.

50. [1939] 1 K.B. 687.

51. No less an authority than Lord Hale once charged a jury: "That there are such creatures as witches he has no doubt at all . . ." Trial of the Suffolk Witches, (1665) 6 St. Tr. 687, pp. 700–701. Accord: W. Blackstone, *Commentaries on the Laws of England*, Welsh, Philadelphia, 1897, iv, pp. 60–61.

52. (1954) 14 W.A.C.A. 442.

53. Quoted by the court from *Iferone*, W.A.C.A. selected judgments for July-October-December 1954, p. 79 (cyclostyled).

54. [1957] R. & N. 443.

55. *Ibid.*, p. 447.

56. (1956) 23 E.A.C.A. 622.

57. *Ibid.*, p. 625.

58. 186 U.S. 413 (1901).

59. Cf. J. F. Stephen, *A History of the Criminal Law of England*, Macmillan, Vol. 2, London, 1883, p. 163: "Anyone would fall into the description in question [i.e., insanity] who was deprived by reason of disease affecting the mind of the power of passing a rational judgment on the moral character of the act which he meant to do." Query, whether defendants in the witchcraft cases had the power of passing such a judgment.

60. *M'Naghten's Case* (1943) 10 Cl. & F. at p. 211, 8 E.R. 718 at p. 723.

61. *Skekanja* (1948) 15 E.A.C.A. 158 (Tanganyika).

62. *Mawole Konkomba*, (1952) 14 W.A.C.A. 236 at p. 237 (Gold Coast); *Kumatairraf Mursei* (1939) 16 E.A.C.A. 117.

63. (1941) 8 E.A.C.A. 96.

64. *Ibid.*, p. 101.

65. *Mensah* [1946] A.C. 83 (P.C.); *Atta* [1959] G.L.R.R. 337.

66. *Rothwell* (1891) 12 Cox 145; *Mancini v. D.P.P.* [1942] A.C. 1.

67. G. Williams, *Criminal Law: The General Part*, 2d ed., Stevens, London, 1961, pp. 366–368; G. Williams, "Homicide and the Supernatural" (1940) 65 L.Q.R. 504; J. Lewis, "Outlook for a Devil in the Colonies" [1958] *Crim.* Low Row. 661.

68. C. S. Kenny, *Outlines of Criminal Law*, 17th ed., University Press, Cambridge, 1958, p. 54.

69. G. Williams, *Criminal Law*, p. 488.

70. The defendant in most of these cases *ex hypothesi* is subject to the same super-stitions as most of the members of his community, and therefore is not identifiably more dangerous than they are.

71. See, e.g., *Alpha Kanu* (1959) 16 W.A.C.A. 90 (Sierra Leone) and *Ufuonge Enweonye* (1959) 15 W.A.C.A. 1 (Nigeria) (whole village cooperating to kill trespassers on "their" section of a river); *Akpunono* (1947) 8 W.A.C.A. 107 (Nigeria) (killing of infant twin); *Zanhibe*, 1954 (3) S.A. 597 (woman horribly burned by witch-doctor exorcising a demon); *Kofi Antwi* (1955) 1 W.A.L.R. 29 (Gold Coast) (man shot by elders resisting attempt by malcontents to seize the stool, traditional symbol of chiefly authority).

72. "The gross absurdity of endeavouring to apply the substance but particularly the forms of our law to the people of India may best be conceived by supposing for a moment 12 Conongoes, Moreland and Pundits, taking their seats in Westminster Hall, beginning the administration of justice there and gravely assuring the people of England that it was intended merely for their advantage. In the short space of one term every inhabitant of the metropolis would be capitally convicted for eating his ordinary food, and perhaps it would be no more than a just retaliation for the capital conviction of a Gentoo on the Coventry Act or one of the Statutes of Forgery." Statement of A. MacDonald, Counsel for the East India Company, December 26, 1782, (Ms. Home Misc. No. 411, India Office, London, quoted in J. Michael and H. Wechsler, *Criminal Law and its Administration*, Foundation Press, Chicago, 1940, p. 285, n. 8.)

73. See *Khetso Neghgi* (1948) 23 K.L.R. 36 at p. 37.

74. See Shearman, J., in *Allard v. Selfridge* [1925] 1 K.B. 129 at p. 137.

75. J. W. C. Turner, "The Mental Element in Crimes at Common Law, in L. Radzinowicz and J. W. C. Turner, *The Modern Approach to Criminal Law*, Macmillan, London, 1945, p. 195; Williams, *Criminal Law*, p. 30.

76. Turner, *op. cit.* (n. 75), p. 199; Williams, *Criminal Law*, p. 31; P. A. Devin, "Statutory Offences" (1958) *J. Soc. Pub. Teachers of Law*, **4**, p. 213.

77. "Every man runs the risk that a court may decide that what he has done is a crime or is immoral, but his liability does not depend on his own ability to make that decision; and his risk is the same whether or not he has any idea that what he is doing is immoral, or a civil wrong, or a crime." Turner, *op. cit.* (n. 75), p. 216.

78. See, e.g., J. Biggs, *The Guilty Mind*, Harcourt, Brace, New York, 1955, pp. 203 ff.

79. *Holloway v. United States*, 148 F. (2d) 668, cert. denied 334 U.S. 852 (1948).

80. J. Bentham, *The Works of Jeremy Bentham*, Vol. 1, Bowring (ed.), Simpkin, Marshall, London, 1843, p. 397.

81. *Machekequnabe* (1897) 28 Ont. Rep. 309 (the defendant, an American Indian, was posted as a guard to defend against a Wendigo or man-eating spirit, which had been seen in the area; he shot and killed his foster-father, whom he mistook for the Wendigo; *held*, manslaughter).

82. *D.P.P. v. Smith* [1962] A.C. 290.

83. Drunkenness is not a defense, although it plainly is a sort of physical incapacity of the mind. The objective standard even applies to the ordinary factual knowledge possessed by every "normal" adult in the community. J. Hall, *General Principles of Criminal Law*, 2d ed., Bobbs-Merrill, Indianapolis, 1960, p. 375.

84. G. Williams, "Provocation and the Reasonable Man" [1964] *Crim.* Law Rev. 740, at p. 742.

85. Cf. Hall, *op. cit.* (n. 83), pp. 166–167.

86. *Atma Singh s/o Ghanda Singh* (1942) 9 E.A.C.A. 69 (Kenya) (The defendant, following Sikh custom, cut off the nose and ears of his unfaithful wife. On appeal from sentence, the court said: "When one further considers that one of the most important objects of punishment is deterrence, our view is that a lesser sentence might be misunderstood. If . . . there still exists among the Sikh or any other Indian community a custom of disfiguring deserting or unfaithful wives in the hideous and barbaric fashion exemplified in this case, then the demand for a heavy sentence for such acts would be all the more necessary"); *Zanhibe*, 1954 (3) S.A. 597 (The defendant, a native doctor, had a woman forcibly restrained over a fire to exorcise a demon; the woman died. The court assumed that moral guilt was absent, but said: "It . . . seems to me that even where moral guilt is absent a court may, in a proper case, where a very large section of the community, especially an unenlightened one, requires to be protected against dangerous practices, disregard the existence of that form of mitigation.")

11

Substantive criminal-law principles controlling the acts of law-enforcement agents

Lurking behind the question of where society should draw the line between "law" and "order," between an impossible universe of unambiguous, discrete rules of conduct and one whose outward peace is maintained by unrestricted exercise of policeman's discretion (and, since his discretion not infrequently suggests to him the use of force, of the discretionary use of nightstick, mace, tear gas, blackjack, and gun), lies a value judgment. The more precise the rules are, the more restricted is the police discretion, and also the more predictable are the consequences from the point of view of the individual citizen. Which is more desirable, then: a world in which every individual can be relatively certain that when he acts in a certain way the consequence will be what he anticipates them to be, or a world in which there may be relative uncertainty but less "disorder"?

Certainty and predictability are the major criteria for what Max Weber called "legal rational legitimacy." It is a basic characteristic of bureaucracy that it can legitimize itself only when it is seen to be instrumental. It is instrumental if its activity as carried out by its members proceeds by rule. The more the policeman's discretion is contained by rules, the more likely he will be regarded as acting instrumentally, and hence the more he will be subserving the values of legal rational legitimacy.[1]

Where the line between law and order favors the terminus labeled "law," the policeman's discretion is correspondingly diminished. To diminish policeman's discretion is to reduce the chances that he will use his authority to further, not the official objectives of the criminal law, but his own personal objectives or those of the police as a bureaucracy. Where the citizens are concerned, therefore, the predictability of consequences also has the value of ensuring that socially approved force will not be misused by the policeman, for it is only insofar as such force is used for reasons unrelated to the grant of power that its exercise becomes unpredictable.

To favor a world of Policeman's Discretion, however, is to favor not only the existing relationships between those with power and property, and those without, but their further growth. In any world where policemen exercise uncontrolled discretion, the police will inevitably use their discretion in their own interests. It will never be in their interest to attack those who hold important power and privilege, for they are in a position to retaliate. The policeman's discretion will necessarily be used primarily against the poor and the disinherited. To favor "order" as against "law" is to favor an intensification of existing disparities.

Taking any particular social ordering as given, we see that the tension between the regime of law and the regime of Policeman's Discretion is a reflection of the persistent tension between human rights and property rights, between the protection of individual liberty and the protection of a given social order. Any given regime of law may be more or less equitable, more or less egalitarian, or more or less exploitative. Within any given framework, however, the dichotomy between law and order remains. Its resolution represents the result of a process of valuation.

What groups in society would one expect, then, to advocate wider discretionary power for the police? Plainly, any group which feels that its position in society is threatened by serious disorder, as well as (for bureaucratic reasons) the police themselves. The cry for increased police discretion, that "there is more law at the end of a nightstick than in all your courts," is widely supported among lower-middle-class or blue-collar groups, not infrequently in areas where they are homeowners. Civilian review boards are a device for controlling police discretion, by providing a convenient forum in which citizens who claim to have been injured by the police can have their complaints heard. A proposal for the establishment of a civilian review board in New York City was defeated in a referendum in 1966. That the proposal was widely attacked by precisely the groups just described was noted by every observer.

Why the police themselves are the chief moral entrepreneurs in favor of their own increased discretion is a rather more complex question.[2]

We note that the conflicting values which create the tension between law and order, between the world of the rule of law and the world of Policeman's Discretion, are precisely the values which create the tensions concerning the objectives of punishment. It can be hypothesized that the same group which is constantly demanding a wider scope of discretion for the police would also be in the forefront of advocating harsh punishments without regard to consciousness of guilt.

Before we can discuss the ways in which the substantive criminal law limits the discretion of the law-applying officials, however, we must discuss the central concept in the law generally which serves to control the discretion of administrative officials. This concept is embodied in the doctrine of *ultra vires*, literally "beyond the power." As Kelsen's model suggests, an official acts *qua* official only when the action is in accord with the norms laid down for his conduct by higher authority. If he goes beyond that, the action loses its official character and he acts merely as a private person.

Entick v. Carrington,[3] has rightly been called a cornerstone of the British Constitution; indeed, it represents a rule which is the cornerstone of law *and* order everywhere. The case came up when some representatives of the Secretary of State ransacked the papers and files of a political opponent. There was no law permitting such conduct. The plaintiff sued for trespass. The Secretary of State pleaded that "reasons of State" were sufficient justification. The court held, first, that unless there was a rule of law permitting the search, the officials in question were to be treated merely as private citizens who committed a trespass; and second, that there was no rule of law which gave the Secretary of State or his servants unlimited discretion to search property. It followed that the defendants were liable for trespass.

For the purposes of criminal law, the basic rule of *ultra vires* (governing acts going beyond the permissible discretion of office holders) raises three principal issues: What is the permissible scope of discretion? What methods are available by which superior officials (especially courts) can determine the truth of a policeman's allegations that the factual conditions for official action exist? That is, what methods are there for verifying the allegation by the policeman that the accused committed a crime? What devices are there for ensuring that the police do not exceed their authorized jurisdiction? The first problem is largely subsumed under the doctrines of legality, the second under the requirements of harm and act. The third problem is mainly a problem of procedural criminal law, which we shall discuss in connection with the problems of arrest.

The Doctrine of Legality

Glanville Williams has written:

"Englishmen are ruled by the law, and by the law alone," wrote Dicey. "A man may with us be punished for a breach of law, but he can be punished for nothing else." In its Latin dress of *nullum crimen sine lege, nulla poena sine lege*—that there must be no crime or punishment except in accordance with fixed, predetermined law—this has been regarded by most thinkers as a self-evident principle of justice ever since the French Revolution.[4]

That it has been so regarded is, of course, another aspect of the middle-class legal culture, which demanded certainty in the legal order above all else. It is an important aspect of Weber's legal-rational legitimacy.

The *nulla poena* rule is a rule which demands the minimum amount of discretion in law-enforcement agencies. It demands "law" rather than "order." It expresses the central proposition of the legal culture of the ruling classes in Western, middle-class society since the great democratic revolutions of the late eighteenth and nineteenth centuries.

The detailing of the harms in the criminal law, and the insistence that the sanctions provided by the criminal law be in the main reserved for those who create a harm or who do something tending toward a specific harm, are thus the first and essential step taken toward a society that would have *both* law and order.

It is sometimes argued that the *nulla poena sine lege* rule requires us to wait until after the crime has been committed—the murder accomplished, the woman raped, the householder robbed—or is very close to being committed before we can seize, restrain, and rehabilitate those with clear tendencies toward criminal activity.

The processes of the criminal law ever work after the fact. They are set in motion to bag the offender after he has committed the crime. It is as if we were engaged in a hunting enterprise under the rules of which society must not capture nor shoot until the game has reached a given stage of growth and development. This method of dealing with the criminal misses the essential point. Society wants protection. What are the inhibitions on the state which keep it from entering upon a throughgoing program of crime prevention? . . . If we accept the view that individuals are amenable to guidance and correctional treatment after they have committed anti-social acts, all the more, it would seem clear, would they be amenable to these influences before they have committed them.[5]

A criminal law based upon such a notion, that persons should be arrested before a harm is imminent, would indeed be one which gave the broadest possible discretion to administrative officials; presumably psychiatrists and social workers would wield the influence rather than policemen, to be sure, but nevertheless this is an enormously wide discretion. Obviously, there are, in our present state of knowledge, enormous practical difficulties connected with preventive detention. Even the psychiatrists and the social workers deny that the present state of knowledge is sufficient to permit identification of potential lawbreakers in advance of actual criminal activity with any reasonable accuracy of prediction. Moreover, the argument for preventive detention is based on the premise that our resources for rehabilitation are sufficient to restructure the personalities of most potential offenders after identification. At the present time this is simply not true, in terms either of our knowledge of the way to go about doing this, or of the money and facilities to do it with.

Probably the most important difficulty, however, is not merely practical. Time has taught us through bitter experience that discretion granted to administrative officials to be used for the public good is all too apt to be used for the private good of the official or for the bureaucratic advantage of the administration itself. Since the pay-offs to individuals and to bureaucracies tend to be controlled by the wealthy and the powerful, discretion tends, in the final analysis, to be used for the benefit of the wealthy and the powerful—not, of course, necessarily in each individual case, but necessarily in its general tendency. (The discussion in this book of the application of the law in complex societies demonstrates these propositions.) The broader the granted discretion, the more potential there is for its exercise for dubious purposes under the guise of legitimate exercise of power.

One safeguard against the illegitimate use of a granted discretion is that there be some way by which higher officials—in criminal law, primarily the courts —can *verify* the claims made by administrators. The vaguer the criteria for permissible administrative action are, the more difficult becomes the verification. If psychiatrists or social workers were granted the discretion to incarcerate for "treatment" persons who had a potential for criminal activity, the unlimited possibilities of human condition suggest that there could be no definite criteria for the exercise of judgment, and hence there could be no effective verification. A society in which order is maintained with the principle of Psychiatrist's Discretion is different only in name from a world organized on the basis of Policeman's Discretion. The substantive principle of legality is the legal doctrine which stands in the way of both these kinds of world. The requirement of a perpetrated harm as an element of criminality serves to ensure that at least on this occasion the defendant was not only probably dangerous, but demonstrably so. Significantly, in criminal cases where the defendant is found to be insane and therefore not subject to "criminal" sanctions, the court can in most states have him admitted to a mental institution for an indeterminate period (release being dependent on psychiatric and court approval) *without ever demonstrating that he has in fact committed any offense in the first place.*[6]

The *nulla poena* doctrine, i.e. the doctrine that there is no crime unless there is a law prohibiting the act, not only requires that there be a law under which the accused can be charged, but it demands that ideally there be no scope for discretion at all in administrative officials. As we have seen, however, no rule can be written in such a way as to remove all ambiguities; some discretion must always exist.

Observed that the principle (*of nulla poena*) is not satisfied merely by the fact that the punishment inflicted is technically legal. The Star Chamber was a legal tribunal, but it did not exemplify the rule of law in Dicey's philosophy. "Law" for this purpose means a body of fixed rules; and it excludes wide discretion even though that discretion be exercised by independent judges.[7]

Lacking anything like the American Constitution, the common law could not appeal to some higher legal authority to forbid wide-ranging criminal laws. The judges therefore devised the rule of strict construction of penal statutes. In effect, this rule held that where there was ambiguity about the meaning of a criminal law, the doubt was to be resolved in favor of the accused. In *McBoyle v. United States,*[8] for example, the accused flew an airplane which he knew had been stolen across a state line. The National Motor Vehicle Theft Act provided in part that "when used in this act: (a) the term 'motor vehicle' shall include an automobile, automobile truck, automobile wagon, motorcycle, or any other self-propelled vehicle not designed for running on rails . . . " The statute made into a criminal offense the transportation in interstate commerce of a "motor vehicle," knowing it to have been stolen. Justice Holmes reversed a conviction, on the ground that it was impossible to read the statute "as including airplanes under a term that usage more and more confines to a different class." He continued:

Although it is not likely that a criminal will carefully consider the text of the law before he murders or steals, it is reasonable that a fair warning should be given the world in language that the common world will understand, of what the law intends to do if a certain line is passed. To make the warning fair, so far as possible the line should be clear. When a rule of conduct is laid down that evokes in the common mind only the picture of vehicles moving on land, the statute should not be extended to aircraft simply because it seems to us that a similar policy applies, or upon speculation that, if the legislature had thought of it, very likely broader words would have been used.[9]

Legislatures and the public generally, however, have short patience with rules which they perceive as "technical" or "legalistic." After all, the argument goes, McBoyle had plainly done something wrong; he knew he was flying a stolen airplane. Why should he not be punished? It was to be expected that a contrary rule would be pressed upon the courts, frequently in statutory form. The New York Penal Law is typical:

21. The rule that a penal statute is to be strictly construed does not apply to this chapter or any of the provisions thereof, but all such provisions must be construed according to the fair import of their terms, to promote justice and effect the objects of the law.

That judges should often, and legislatures only rarely, lay special emphasis on the notion of law as opposed to the demands for order arises from the fact that judges and legislators play different roles, and have gone through different socialization processes. Judges have been socialized into the regime of rules. They spend their working days dealing with rules of all sorts. Pound's "received social ideal" embodies the concept of legality to a markedly high degree. In their roles as legislators, legislators are, as we have seen, especially responsive to middle-class demands. The middle class assumes that it is law-abiding, and that order is one of the great goals, perhaps the greatest goal, of society. That judges should tend to perceive values in the rule of strict construction, and legislators should not, is perhaps to be expected.

Judges, however, have had to respond to public pressures for increasing the scope of power for the law-applying authorities. They therefore maintained, during the formative period of the common law, "attempt" and "conspiracy," as inchoate offenses, despite the all-encompassing vagueness of the terms—vagueness which these offenses retain to this day in their statutory form, as we shall discuss below.

Even today judges retain a residual power to create brand new offenses under the guise of construing the common-law offense, or its statutory analogue, of conspiracy to corrupt public morals. In *Commonwealth v. Morgan*,[10] for example, the defendant was indicated and convicted for the common-law misdemeanor of doing "any act which directly injures or tends to injure the public to such an extent as to require the state to intervene and punish the wrongdoer, as in the case of acts which injuriously affect public morality, or obstruct or pervert public justice, or the administration of juctice." The accused had called the complaining witness, a married woman, several times a week for a period of time, suggesting intercourse as well as acts of sexual perversion. There was no statute making such conduct a criminal offense. The Court nevertheless convicted the defendant, although there was no precedent for such a conviction in Pennsylvania. One judge dissented on the ground that "after nearly two hundred years of constitutional government in which the legislature and not the courts have been charged by the people with the responsibility of deciding which acts do and which acts do not injure the public to the extent which warrants punishment," for the court to create a new crime would be "an unwarranted invasion of the legislative field."

The doctrine of legality has largely been a matter of rhetoric of academic textbook-writers, therefore, except so far as it concerns the rule of the *nulla poena*, the *ex post facto* rules, and the strict construction canon. This is perhaps to be expected, considering the very nature of the judicial process. Every time a court cuts down the power of the police, certain vocal middle-class elements in the society subject the court to severe criticism. The widespread criticism of the Supreme Court of the United States for its recent decisions concerning confessions and juvenile delinquents illustrate this fact.

The identification of the harms for which punishments are to be rendered and the correlative rule of legality are the important aspects of the substantive law which limit the scope of the policeman's discretion. The requirements of a completed act, of causality, and of concurrence are the elements of criminal law that make possible the verification of the policeman's claim of rightful exercise of discretion.

The Conditions of Verification of Official Discretion:
The Requirement of an Act

When a policeman or a prosecutor decides to arrest and to charge a person with a crime, he must make a two-fold determination. First, he must decide that there is in fact an existing rule of law, within whose terms the acts done by defendant fall. Secondly, he must make a factual determination concerning the incident in question. Assuming that the facts which the policeman believes to be the case are actually specific instances belonging to the categories of fact identified by the statute or rule as elements of the crime, a question arises as to whether the policeman's opinion of the facts is an accurate or truthful statement of them.

The role of the policeman is to enforce law and preserve order. As we saw earlier, these are frequently antithetical aims. We shall see that the great weight of societal and bureaucratic pressures on the police, their own socialization and their own self-perception, combine to influence policemen to favor order as against law. Inevitably, policemen and prosecutors tend to believe rather more readily than most citizens in each case that an individual in question has done the acts which constitute a crime.

The trial of a criminal case can thus be regarded as a societal device by which the policeman's and prosecutor's opinions about the facts are verified by an independent body. In practice, as we shall see in the following chapters, the number of cases actually tried is exceedingly small. The reason for this is that at every stage in the legal process of prosecution, the public-defender or private-attorney organizational features of the legal system are such that all the officials bring pressure on the client to plead guilty. What might have been an institutionalized mechanism for testing the validity of the policeman's and prosecutor's opinions does not serve that purpose at all in actual operation.

Unless the matters to be verified are actually verifiable, the trial is a sham. Verification requires proof of an act and of causality. Sir James Fitzjames Stephen, an English judge and philosopher of the criminal law, wrote in 1883 that

Criminal law must, from the nature of the case, be far narrower than morality. In no age or nation, at all events, in no age or nation which has any similarity to our own, has the attempt been made to treat every moral defect as a crime. In different ages of the world injuries to individuals, to God, to the gods, or to the community, have been treated as crimes, but I think that in all cases the idea of crime has involved the idea of some definite, gross, undeniable injury to some one. In our country, this is now, and has been from the earliest times, perfectly well established. No temper of mind, no habit of life, however pernicious, has ever been treated as a crime, unless it displayed itself in some overt act. It never entered the head of any English legislator to enact, or of an English court to hold, that a man could be indicted and punished for ingratitude, for hardheartedness, for avarice, sensuality, pride, or, in a word, for any vice whatever as such. Even for purposes of ecclesiastical censure some definite act of immorality was required. Sinful thoughts and dispositions of mind might be the subject of confession and of penance, but they were never punished in this country by ecclesiastical criminal proceedings.

The reasons for imposing this great leading restriction upon the sphere of criminal law are obvious. If it were not so restricted it would be utterly intolerable; all mankind would be criminals, and most of their lives would be passed in trying and punishing each other for offences which could never be proved.[11]

What is external and observable is provable. An assertion by an official that the defendant *did* something is empirically verifiable. On the other hand, the assertion by an official that the accused *thought* something, or is potentially a dangerous person, is—at least in our present state of knowledge—far less verifiable. If officials are permitted to arrest, prosecute, and convict on the basis of thought alone, or on the basis of official prediction of potential danger to be caused by the accused, there would be almost no way for other officials and, ultimately, for society itself, to prevent official exercise of power for reasons unrelated to the goals for which the power was given. Official power could then be used instead with bias or prejudice, and for purposes of personal advancement or political advantage.

In practice, the incumbents in official positions in the legal system operate in ways which reflect their biases as "keepers of the morality." They in fact select for processing those persons in the community who, by their standards, are "bad," and attempt to impose sanctions on them. The dynamics of this process are illustrated in the study, presented in Chapter 16, of a case in which the attempts by the local law-enforcement agencies to rid the community of a member regarded by them as morally corrupt culminated in embarrassment for everyone concerned.

Formally, the requirement that there must be an *actus reus* before there is a crime has the function of ensuring that law-enforcers will *not* act solely from their own intuitive judgment of who has a "guilty mind."

The traditional requirement of an *actus reus* as an element of crimes apparently arose as a necessary consequence of the origins of the criminal law in claims that specific norms of conduct had been violated. Rape, murder, arson, and robbery all require for their accomplishment observable acts by identifiable people. The central issue in a trial thus became whether the accused did commit the act. The early common law of crimes thus had built into it the requirement for verification of the accuser's claim.

The limits of the *actus reus* doctrine are tested, appropriately enough, by efforts of legal officials to discover potential offenders as early as possible. Since thought is conventionally held to precede action, sooner or later a zealous prosecutor or judge is apt to try to convict someone merely for his thought. While nominally the laws of attempts and of conspiracy require an *actus reus*, in fact the vagueness of these doctrines permit wide scope of administrative discretion precisely at the point where precision seems to be needed.

Attempts

The New York Penal Law restated the common-law rule:

2. An act, done with intent to commit a crime, and tending but failing to effect its commission is an attempt to commit that crime.

This definition necessarily lacks the relative specificity in describing the necessary act that defines the substantive crime. The fact of death defines the acts which are relevant to any particular killing; the fact of the removal of property defines the acts which are relevant to any particular taking of property. What defines the act which constitutes the attempt, however, is a tendency to effect the commission of crime.

Where courts draw the line between "mere preparation" and attempt, i.e. between nonculpable and culpable acts "tending but failing to effect" the commission of a crime, is one aspect of the resolution of the tension between law and order. The issue can be set out by contrasting two cases.

In *People v. Miller*,[12] the accused threatened to kill one Jeans, a black man. He came to a field in which Jeans was working, bringing a rifle with him. He stooped and appeared to be loading the rifle. Jeans fled. A third party took the gun from the accused. It was found to be loaded. The Supreme Court of California reversed a conviction for attempt to commit murder, on the ground that this was "mere preparation."

In *McQuirter v. State*,[13] the complainant, a white woman, walked past the truck in which the accused, a black man, was sitting. He got out of the truck and followed her down the street. She stopped in at a friend's house. When she proceeded on her way again, the accused came toward her from behind a telephone pole. The complainant told her children to ask a friend to come and meet her. When the accused saw her friend coming, he went back down the street and leaned on a stop sign across the street from complainant's home. After half an hour he left. A sheriff testified that the accused had said he planned to rape the complainant. On appeal after a conviction for assault with intent to commit rape, the Alabama Court of Appeals affirmed the conviction, on the ground that there was sufficient evidence from which a jury might infer that the accused intended to rape the complainant. The Court added that "in determining the question of intention the jury may consider social conditions and customs founded on racial difference, such as that the prosecutrix was a white woman and the defendant was a Negro man."

It is the vagueness of the articulated rules with respect to attempt that permits the law-applying officials to exercise the wide scope of discretion exemplified in these two cases. As Hall says,

The present vagueness of the rules, as compared with those on "ultimate" crimes, is not an essential characteristic of the crime, nor is it a result of the generality of the attempt doctrine. For there is no reason why the rules on criminal attempts can not be formulated as precisely as any rules . . . It could be provided, e.g., that an attempt to poison consisted in handing a deadly dose to the intended victim; or that, to have an attempt to commit arson, a lighted match must have reached the distance of two inches from combustible materials in a dwelling-house. In relation to every "ultimate" crime, a series of very specific attempts could be formulated. The lack of such specificity is the result of history and, especially, of the policy underlying the present rules, i.e., the desirability of maintaining an area of vagueness because of the variety of potential fact-situations. The major qualification of that policy is the principle of legality . . ."[14]

The fact that the vagueness is maintained in the law of attempts suggests that with respect to attempts, at least, courts have been prone to retain as much discretion as possible or, at least, have not discovered a way to get around the vagueness.

Conspiracy

The same pervasive vagueness that persists in the law of attempts exists also in the law of conspiracy. The gist of the offense is said to be the agreement to commit a crime; "a conspiracy is a partnership in criminal purposes."[15] This vagueness thus serves a dual purpose:

In the first place, it is an inchoate crime, complementing the provisions dealing with attempt and solicitation in reaching preparatory conduct before it has matured into commission of a substantive offense. Secondly, it is a means of striking against the special danger incident to group activity, facilitating prosecution of the group and yielding a basis for imposing added penalties when combination is involved.[16]

At common law, there was no requirement that any action be taken pursuant to the agreement. Quite commonly, a condition for conviction was added to statutes that it should be alleged and proven that an overt act, however slight, had taken place in pursuit of the criminal purpose. The overt-act requirement, however, was in fact usually satisfied by acts which would fall far short of satisfying most courts today even to the effect that an attempt had been proven to have taken place under the vagueness of the rules defining that offense.

Since conspiracy is "predominantly mental in composition,"[17] the offense suffers from the lack of identifiable acts which must be proven to have taken place by the prosecution in order to verify the opinions of policeman and prosecutor that the defendants in fact did commit the offense. As a result, "even when appropriately invoked, the looseness and pliability of the doctrine present inherent dangers . . ."[18]

The specified harms against which the criminal law warns, combined with the requirement of an act which causes them, thus make possible the verification of policemen's opinions of guilt, although, as we have seen, at critical points in the law of harms (for example, the crime of conspiracy against public morals) and in the definition of the required act (the law of attempts and the law of conspiracy), great legal escape hatches have been retained for the exercise of police and judicial discretion, the claims resulting from which are largely unverifiable despite the strictures of the principle of legality.

Summary

The way in which the traditional criminal law resolved the tension between law and order was not the result of conscious, dramatic choice of harms to be sanctioned, or of principles of punishment and devices to curb police discretion. Rather, it was the result of judicial law-making that proceeds by slow, incremental changes in existing institutions over many centuries.

The basic shape of the institution of the criminal law came from the original function of the law to resolve disputes arising from overt breaches of the norms of conduct deeply embedded in a relatively simple society. The harms which were important in those days—murder, rape, arson—remain in name the harms to which a part of the criminal law is addressed today, although the legal content defining these wrongs has vastly changed.

Of perhaps more lasting importance has been the fact that these early crimes were all crimes with victims, arising out of specific acts. When the philosophical and political ideal of legality became significant, the requirements of harm and of act were available as devices by which courts and juries could verify the policeman's and prosecutor's opinions about guilt.

Historical reasons also explain the principle of *mens rea*. Arising from theological considerations which were largely unconnected with notions of punishment, the principle fitted well with the developing utilitarian concept of deterrence, and now finds itself in many ways the principal touchstone on which to find guilt in the classical crimes.

Finally, the idea of legality, having rapidly become an important conceptual element since the early nineteenth century, was developed amidst an already well-established body of criminal law. The doctrine of *nulla poena sine lege* married itself happily with the new democratic dogmas of the separation of powers to limit judicial law-making in the area of crime. There remained, however, the extraordinarily vague crimes of attempt and conspiracy, whose criminal status was sanctified by age. Since judicially initiated change in the law is bound to be incremental rather than radical (a point elaborated in Chapter 9), it is not surprising that these two crimes have remained as vaguely defined as they are.

In short, the historical elements of the criminal law have largely determined its main organizing principles. These principles have provided it with an ethical content, and tended to ensure that only those who might have been deterred would be punished. They have provided a technique for verifying the policeman's accusatory claims, have ensured that crimes would be highly visible and hence have visibly reduced the opportunities for discretionary actions by police or prosecutors. They have supplied, in their long history, at least limited guarantees of legality.

Since relatively early days in the history of law, however, there have been a set of crimes which do not conveniently fit into the well-defined categories. These are political crimes, offenses against administrative regulations, crimes of status, and crimes without victims.

NOTES

1. The discussion here parallels that found in Albert Camus, *The Rebel*, when the argument is joined to a conflict between "justice" and "freedom."

2. See J. H. Skolnick, *Justice Without Trial: Law-Enforcement in Democratic Society*. Wiley, New York, 1966.

3. (1760) 19 St. Tr. 1030.

4. Glanville Williams. *Criminal Law: The General Part*, 2nd ed., Stevens, London, 1961, p. 575. Reprinted by permission.

5. A. J. Harno, "Rationale of a criminal code," *U. Pa. Law Rev.*, **85**, 1937, p. 549. Copyright by the University of Pennsylvania Law Review and reprinted by permission.

6. See A. S. Goldstein, *The Insanity Defense*, Yale University Press, New Haven, Conn.

7. Williams, *op. cit.*, p. 578. Reprinted by permission.

8. 283 U.S. 25, 51 Sup. Ct. 340, 75 L. Ed. 816 (1931).

9. *Ibid.*

10. 177 Pa. Super. 454, 110 A 2d 688 (1955). Reference is to Pennsylvania.

11. J. F. Stephen, *A History of the Criminal Law of England*, Macmillan, London, 1883, iii, p. 78.

12. 2 Cal. (2d) 527, 42 P. (2d) 308 (1935).

13. 36 Ala. App. 707, 63 So. 2d 388 (1953).

14. Reprinted from Jerome Hall, *General Principles of Criminal Law*, p. 94. Copyright 1947 by The Bobbs-Merrill Company, Inc., Reprinted by permission. All rights reserved.

15. O. W. Holmes in *United States v. Kissel*, 218 U.S. 601, 608 (1910).

16. *Model Penal Code*, tentative Draft No. 10 (1960), comments to 5.03, 96–97.

17. A. J. Harno, "Intent in criminal conspiracy," *U. Pa. Law Rev.*, **89**, pp. 624–632.

18. R. Jackson, concurring in *Krulewitch v. United States*, 336 U.S. 440, 69 Sup. Ct. 716, 93, L. Ed. 790 (1949).

12

The scope and technique of the substantive criminal law: statutory offenses

To the traditional offenses (rape, murder, robbery, etc.), modern legislatures have added a host of new ones. While of many differing sorts, these offenses may conveniently be classified into four major groups: crimes without victims, political crimes, regulatory offenses, and crimes of status. In point of fact, many more arrests, prosecutions, and convictions are made today for crimes belonging to these categories than for the conventional offenses of the traditional criminal law. It is a common characteristic of these newer offenses that, in one way or the other, the laws defining most of them have abandoned some or all of the devices by which the common law placed restrictions on policeman's discretion. These laws have in fact increased the policeman's opportunity to replace law with "order."

12.1 THE ABANDONMENT OF THE CONCEPT OF HARM

The early law of crimes depended upon the initiative of a private prosecutor. It was therefore a condition that for there to be a crime there had to be a recognizable victim, a recognizable harm, and an act performed by the accused which caused the harm. Many of the newer categories of crimes lack one or all of these criteria.

Crimes without victims have been defined as offenses arising in "situations in which one person obtains from another, in a fairly direct exchange, a commodity or personal service which is socially disapproved and legally proscribed."[1] The transfer of dope or marijuana, abortion, gambling, prostitution, and homosexual practices are leading examples of such crimes. In every case, far from there being any harm done by the accused to someone which the latter readily perceives as harmful, the accused does something which the latter wants him to do; the latter is even willing, frequently enough, to pay a price for the service.

Regulatory offenses, also are usually cases where nobody has specifically been injured. If one leaves the tops of garbage cans in the street, or drives above the speed limit, or fails to register a securities issue with the Securities and Exchange Commission, nobody is injured, except perhaps potentially, by the failure of one's conduct to conform to the law. There is at the instant that the offense is committed no ascertainable individual who is a victim. Crimes of status, of which vagrancy is the most important example, obviously do not have a specific victim.

Unlike the traditional crimes, these offenses do not generate specific complainants who initiate police action. When a person is robbed or assaulted or raped, a specific individual is aggrieved and makes complaint. As a result, police investigation and prosecution of these offenses depend on specific pressures from identifiable injured victims on the police. Lacking a victim, crimes without victims, regulatory offenses, and crimes of status depend for their prosecution upon police initiative in commencing the prosecution.

Since these offenses largely occur in private, they bring in another dimension: their relative lack of visibility. "Murder will out" is an old folk saying but drug traffic, homosexuality, and breach of regulatory offenses will rarely "out." They "surface" only when (on rare occasions) moral entrepreneurs or newspaper reporters force them into daylight, or the police themselves search them out.

The lack of complainants and low visibility combine to make it possible for police to decide whether to prosecute or not to prosecute specific instances which come to their attention. The absence of specific injuries to specific persons necessarily vastly increases the potential scope of police discretion.

12.2 THE ABANDONMENT OF THE *ACTUS REUS*

Some of these newer offenses tend to involve neither *actus reus* nor harm. This is especially clear with crimes of status. A narcotics addict has not committed an *act* of addiction. A vagrant *is* a vagrant; he has not *done* it. Other regulations purport to attack what are called "continuing offenses." For example, many zoning statutes make it a "continuing offense" to permit a zoning violation to remain in existence, with each day constituting a separate offense. Again, after the original violation, surely it is a misnomer to say that the accused *does* anything in permitting the offending use to remain.

The legal abandonment of the *actus reus* in these cases has the primary result of eliminating the requirement that the accused must have made a *choice* before he can be subject to penal sanctions. In the absence of a choice on the part of the accused, his punishment can only serve the end of general deterrence, for it cannot deter him or others similarly situated.

The abandonment of the *actus reus* condition in practice is also suggested in the increased use of the conspiracy statute. As we have suggested, this statute has always held within itself the seeds of abuse, for there is precious little about the prosecutor's allegations (of the existence of an agreement) which the court can verify. As a result, the accused is under the mercy of the jury's surmise about his intentions, which is precisely the kind of result which the *actus reus* provisions would prevent.

A special problem arises with respect to political crimes. In statutory seditious libels or conspiracies, very frequently the construction placed on the applicable statute has required the proof of the existence of an agreement to bring down the government through force and violence. For example, the essence of the crime under the Smith Act was defined in the charge to the jury (which the Supreme Court approved):

... you cannot find the defendants or any of them guilty of the crime charged unless you are satisfied beyond a reasonable doubt that they conspired to organize a society, group and assembly of persons who teach and advocated the overthrow or destruction of the Government of the United States by force and violence and to advocate and teach the duty and necessity of overthrowing or destroying the Government of the United States, with the intent that such teaching and advocacy be a rule or principle of action and by language reasonably calculated to incite persons to such action, all with the intent to cause the overthrow or destruction of the Government of the United States by force and violence as speedily as circumstances would permit.[2]

If the reader has difficulty in understanding this charge, how well could the jury have understood it?

In fact, in criminal offenses, this extraordinarily vague charge of seditious intention is generally proven by the speeches made by the accused, and by the books and pamphlets that they have circulated. The fact that the speech was made is ordinarily not disputed, nor that the books and pamphlets have been circulated. What is at issue is not the fact that something was done, an *actus reus*, but rather, the meaning intended by the writers or speakers, for the books and pamphlets and speeches have no relevant meaning except as to evidence of the disputed intent.

Except in rare cases of verbal clarity, words cannot serve in the absence of such intent. Political tracts only rarely plainly reveal a seditious intention. Like most other writings, they rarely suffer from the fortune of indisputable precision of expression. Usually the central contention comes to concern the meaning intended by the writer—a matter about which men can frequently speculate endlessly and without hope of empirical verification.

The absence of an *actus reus* as the principal fact to be proven undercuts the procedural basis for a trial. Trials at law are significantly called "trials of an issue of fact." The process of trial is one in which one party tries to verify the allegations of fact contained in his complaint, and the other party tries to demonstrate that the allegations contained in the complaint have not been verified. The rules of evidence and procedure are designed for these purposes.

These rules are reasonably functional when what is to be proven is whether a particular event took place at a certain time and place. The verification depends on witnesses who mainly state their elementary sense impressions: what they saw, heard, smelled, felt, or tasted. From these testimonies the jury need only determine whether what the witnesses report having seen, felt, heard, smelled, or tasted were in fact the qualities sensed. This determination is dependent on an inference whose only debatable component is usually whether the witnesses are accurately reporting what they observed.

In cases in which there is no *actus reus*, however, the situation is totally different. The "act" itself, the trivial overt act required—in the case of a conspiracy indictment, the making of the speech or circulation of the literature in a seditious conspiracy—is generally hardly contested, if at all. What is at issue is the inference to be drawn concerning the intent of the accused. What inference is drawn does not depend primarily on a witness' veracity; rather, it depends on the general hypothesis which the jury chooses to use in making the inference suggested by the testimony. If the defendant sold sugar and a third person used the sugar illicitly to make whiskey, did the defendant know that the latter intended to put the sugar to this use? That depends on the hypothesis used by the jury. Should this hypothesis be "When a person sells a commodity to another person which the buyer intends to use for criminal purposes, the seller probably knows the uses to which the commodity will be put," or should it be the converse? On this issue there is no way for empirical evidence to guide the decision-maker. There is, therefore, no way to verify the prosecutor's allegation, and the accused is subject to the prejudices of the trier of fact.

The scope of discretion that has been left to the police, prosecutors, and judges through the abandonment of the *actus reus* provision in vagrancy cases is suggested by the official practices that are on record. For example, Mayor La Guardia of New York at the graduation exercises of the "World's Fair" class of the New York police department said in 1939:

Now, I give notice that certain individuals are not wanted in New York City, and I want your full cooperation in driving them out. I want you all to read section 887 of the Code of Criminal Procedure. There are certain individuals who are indexed and marked and fingerprinted as vagrants, gamblers, confidence men, pickpockets, men engaged in commercial immorality—they all come under the definition of vagrants...

Out West where I was raised we called those people tinhorns and we drove them out of town. Some of those tinhorns and vagrants have political influence with some politicians. Don't be afraid of them. You've got them on the run now. You will not be censured or transferred for picking up these vagrants in tailor-made, up to the minute fashion clothes. When you pick up any of these tailored punks and you have a suspicion that they'll flash a roll, you may take them to the Health Department for a physical examination.[3]

In *Levine v. State*,[4] the accused was convicted under a New Jersey statute which declared that "all runaway servants or apprentices, and all vagrants or vagabonds, common drunkards, common thieves, burglars or pickpockets, common night-walkers, and common prostitutes, shall be deemed and adjudged to be disorderly persons." He had been three times convicted of burglary in New York; and he and a co-defendant were found loitering and peering into store windows, apparently making observations of buildings in the neighborhood. When questioned, he was evasive in his answers and gave a false address. He gave what was subsequently discovered to be an untrue explanation of their reasons for being in Jersey City, where they were apprehended. The court especially emphasized that the crimes of which both men were convicted were of the sorts that ordinarily are committed by persons acting in concert. Their conviction and sentence were upheld on appeal.

The scope of police and judicial discretion afforded by the vagrancy laws has frequently been aimed at political dissenters. For example,

Martin Duchan, Alexander Ivanhoff, Joseph Migilacano, and Joseph Madoxin were arrested in Jersey City and tried on September 20, 1933 on a charge of "having no legitimate business in Jersey City, and not giving a good account of themselves to the arresting officer." Bail pending trial on this charge was fixed at $10,000 each.

The defendants were organizers of the Shoe and Leather Workers' Industrial Union who had come to Jersey City from Brooklyn to talk to a meeting of the strikers. The arresting officer testified at the trial that they had come for this purpose and that he did not consider that a good account. The trial was held before Judge McGovern of the Second Criminal Court of Jersey City, who found the defendants guilty and sentenced them to six months in the county penitentiary. The charges were brought under a supplement to the Disorderly Persons Act, passed by the legislature in June, 1933.[5]

12.3 THE ABANDONMENT OF *MENS REA*

As we have seen, the requirement of *mens rea* in the statement of the criminal law is supposed to ensure that a man knew, before he acted, that what he was doing was wrong; and, knowing this, he would be able to calculate whether the game was worth the candle—whether the potential gain from the crime was overbalanced by the punishment threatened. Even in its attenuated form of "objective" *mens rea*, there is the requirement to decide whether a reasonable man in the shoes of the defendant (and with his relevant physical characteristics) would have known that what he was doing was wrong. To the extent that the defendant in question matches the characteristics of the reasonable man, the law serves simultaneously the ends of special as well as general deterrence.

The peculiar fact is that the extent to which *mens rea*, whether subjective or objective, is a necessary element of any particular statutory crime is a matter more frequently unclear than not. Remington and Rosenblum, for example, report that "A careful study of all the criminal statutes in Wisconsin a few years ago disclosed that the dominant characteristics of those statutes was their ambiguity on the issue of whether fault is a prerequisite of liability."[6]

In the absence of an express statement in a statute that fault is a prerequisite to liability, one is thrown back to conflicting notions of statutory construction. On the one hand, it may be argued that the function of courts is to apply statutes as written; without a specific requirement of *mens rea*, no such requirement is to be inferred. On the other hand, it is argued equally cogently that,

Every criminal statute is expressed elliptically. It is not possible in drafting to state all the qualifications and exceptions that are intended. One does not, for example, when creating a new offence, enact that persons under eight years of age cannot be convicted. Nor does one enact the defence of insanity or duress. The exemptions belong to the general part of the criminal law, which is implied into specific offenses . . . [W]here the criminal law is codified . . . this general part is placed itself in the code and is not repeated for each individual crime. Now the law of *mens rea* belongs to the general part of the criminal law, and it is not reasonable to expect [the legislature] every time it creates a new crime to enact it or even to make reference to it.[7]

The particular canon of construction adopted—plain meaning on the one hand, or the presumption that the legislature intends a crime to require a *mens rea* even if unexpressed—is therefore a conclusion rather than a reason. The way in which courts legitimize their invocation of the one or the other canon of construction is in fact the "reason" for the decision.

In point of fact, courts have tended to reach a compromise solution to this problem, as they do in so many other areas. With respect to most statutory regulatory offenses, courts have tended to enforce strict liability, however with the proviso that where *mens rea* is in fact lacking, the penalty shall not include prison or other serious sanctions. In *Commonwealth v. Koczwara*,[8] for example, the defendant was sentenced to pay a $500 fine and to serve three months in jail. He was the owner and licensee of a tavern, the bartender of which had sold liquor to minors in violation of the applicable statute. The defendant was not present when the sales were made, nor had he participated in them in any way, nor had he even any knowledge of the sales. The court upheld the conviction, but modified the judgment by remitting the three-months jail sentence. Such regulatory statutes as that which was at issue in this case

are generally enforceable by light penalties and, although violations, are labelled crimes, the considerations applicable to true crimes, which involve moral delinquency and which are punishable by imprisonment or other serious penalty. Such so-called crimes are in reality an attempt to utilize the machinery of criminal administration, as an enforcing arm for social regulations of a purely civil nature, with the punishment totally unrelated to questions of moral wrongdoing or guilt.[9]

The reason, it has been suggested, that such a compromise solution has been reached in most of the regulatory crimes in which *mens rea* is not required, is complex. Sanford Kadish has urged that it is because these statutes are "morally neutral" that we intuitively feel that men ought not to be punished severely for their breach.[10] Harry Ball and Lawrence Friedman point out that this view is an oversimplification, if not an error. In the first place, they say, there is no sharp classification of "economic crimes" which can be marked off from other offenses with respect to morality. What of laws concerning the hours of work of children and women, for example? Or laws requiring barbers to keep their instruments clean and sanitary, which (in Wisconsin at least) is in the same statute as a section making it equally unlawful to "advertise a definite price for any barbering service by means of displaying a sign containing such prices so that the same is visible to persons outside the barbershop."[11]

They conclude that the argument that business crimes are not "immoral" is circular. The reason why traditional categories of crimes are regarded as immoral is precisely (as Hall suggested) that they have long been included in the traditional categories of crime. The "business offenses" are not perceived as immoral because they are newly added to the catalogue of criminal offenses. They are not immoral because they have not been included among the traditional crimes, and they have not been included among the traditional crimes because they are not immoral.

Instead of the "moral neutrality" which Kadish identifies as the reason for the compromise solutions, Ball and Friedman point to a variety of other factors. Just because the stigma of criminality is so great, public pressure and judicial identification with men of their own class and status lead judges to identify with the businessman gone wrong: "There but for the grace of God go I." The consistent failure to invoke criminal sanctions for many of the economic crimes, even when they are on the books, adds to the sense of injustice in those exceptional cases where penal sanctions are levied. These factors may be especially important where, as is frequently the case, the initiation of the criminal prosecution rests in fact not with the police, nor with the district attorney, but with a regulatory agency whose members over the years have developed a symbiotic relationship with the regulated industry.

12.4 AMBIGUITY OF LAW

One of the most striking facts about the penal laws is their pervasive ambiguity. The resultant scope of discretion by officials is remarkable with respect to sentencing provisions; but ambiguity is also present elsewhere in the criminal law.

Probably there is no place in the entire field of the operations of the State in which administrative officials have the scope for discretion that is given to judges in setting sentences. Typically, criminal statutes provide for a maximum sentence or, in some states, a minimum and a maximum sentence. The Court has complete freedom to set the sentence anywhere between the stated limits—in the case of a crime with a maximum sentence of ten years, any place from no sentence at all to ten years in the penitentiary. In the United States, in most jurisdictions there can be no appealing the sentence alone. Even the provisions for minimum and maximum sentences can frequently be circumvented. A court ordinarily has authority to sentence a person and then suspend the sentence in the event of good behavior. From the point of view of the accused, a suspended sentence is far less a penalty than a sentence to be served.

On the other hand, very frequently a person is charged in the same proceedings with more than one offense. For example, the police may catch a burglar stealing from a locked automobile service station at night. In the police station, they question him about three other similar "breaks" in the vicinity, and he confesses to these as well. He is then charged with all four offenses, the one for which he was originally arrested and the three others to which he confessed.

On conviction for all four offenses, it is entirely within the court's discretion to order the sentences to be served concurrently or consecutively. If the court sentences the accused to, let us say, three years imprisonment on each count, then, if served concurrently, the effective sentence will be three years; but if served consecutively, the effective sentence will be twelve years.

The result of this extraordinarily broad scope for discretion in sentencing, combined with the ambiguity in the purposes of punishment, has been a wide discrepancy in the punishments imposed by judges. We discuss this below. (See Chapter 21.)

Efforts have been made to find institutional devices to achieve greater uniformity in sentencing. In Connecticut, for example, a three-judge division of the Superior Court sits on appeal from sentence. The theory is that at least this arrangement will promote uniformity. As of 1960, the Connecticut Sentencing Review Division had heard 256 appeals from sentence, reducing fifteen and increasing seven.[12] A similar panel in Massachusetts between 1943 and 1956 acted on more than 1200 appeals, decreasing approximately 350 sentences while increasing fewer than twenty.

The difficulty is that, while appellate review of sentences, especially with appeals to a single appellate body, may provide uniformity, it does not and cannot limit the scope of judicial discretion granted by the statutes, nor can it change the central ambiguity of sentencing philosophy. Wisconsin has therefore tried another method. It now provides by statute that whatever the sentence imposed, the minimum sentence is invariably no more than one year. The accused may be released on pardon at any time after that by action of the prison authorities. While not providing any better substantive limits for the discretion of the prison authorities, those officials seem in Wisconsin to be motivated by notions of rehabilitation. Moreover, their judgment with respect to rehabilitation is not a judgment *in futuro*, but in fact: Has the prisoner demonstrated sufficient improvement to warrant his release?

The statutory penal law suffers from pervasive ambiguity in many other areas besides sentencing provisions. Remington and Rosenblum have identified five sources for this ambiguity. In the first place, there is ambiguity by default. Legislative draftsmanship has simply been of a regrettably low quality. "The majority of criminal statutes exist outside the criminal code in the typical state. These have been given little or no attention . . ." The reason, they say, is that on the whole legislators are probably not dissatisfied with the way ambiguous criminal statutes are being administered in practice, and "the advantage of flexibility may well outweigh the desire for clarity and certainty."[13]

Secondly, there are, as we have seen, inherent limitations to language. Thirdly, the ambiguity in certain statutes is deliberate. Clarity is particularly difficult in procedural areas, for example in formulating a defensible statute permitting the police to detain a suspect for investigation, an area hedged by constitutional restrictions.

The issue can and has been dodged in many states by utilizing existing vagrancy statutes as a basis for detaining and investigating suspicious characters. The vagrancy statutes serve this purpose precisely because of their ambiguity.[14]

Fourthly, there is another sort of designed ambiguity. The more explicit the criminal law and the sharper the boundaries of the crimes described by statute, the more chance there is that a person may come close to violating the statute and not be caught in its net. To law-enforcement agencies, such laws frequently appear to permit the "guilty" to slip through a "loophole"; i.e., law-enforcement agencies prefer ambiguity in order to maintain "order." Remington and Rosenblum quote the draftsmen of the Model Gambling Act:

The Commission has also had great difficulty with this problem of finding a formula which would exclude the social or casual gambler from prosecution and punishment, yet which would not result in opening a large breach in the statute for the benefit of professional gamblers and their patrons. The Commission recognizes that it is unrealistic to promulgate a law literally making a criminal offense of the friendly election bet, the private, social card game among friends, etc. Nevertheless, it is imperative to confront the professional gambler with a statutory facade that is wholly devoid of loopholes.[15]

In addition, there is a third kind of designed ambiguity, involving deliberate delegation of authority to administrative agencies. This practice has had the Supreme Court's approval with respect to economic regulations.[16] The authors suggest that "a careful study of legislative attitude in relation to certain kinds of criminal conduct might well disclose a legislative willingness to delegate a measure of discretion to an enforcement agency thought to be expert in the matter involved."[17] Of course, legislators are apt to think that the police are experts in the enforcement of the criminal law.

Finally, some criminal statutes reflect a community ideal. Statutes against fornication and adultery, for example, are practically never repealed even if they are rarely enforced in practice. They express a community ideal; but so long as they exist, they stand as an overhanging threat to otherwise law-abiding citizens. Remington and Rosenblum refer to "a recent Wisconsin case in which a woman was charged and convicted of fornication. It appears quite clearly that the prosecution resulted primarily because she had agreed, and then refused, to testify against her boy friend."[18]

Remington and Rosenblum make it quite clear that, in the final analysis, there are ambiguities in the statutory criminal law because that is the way the legislators want it. They must want it that way because the wide descretion granted to police, prosecutors, and judges to arrest, prosecute, and convict leads to results that the legislators want; that is to say, the empirical consequences of granting broad discretion to the law-applying agencies conform to the legislators' desires. At least, the way in which the law is applied does not result in pressures on the legislature for change. We examine below what those consequences are.

12.5 THE CONSEQUENCES OF DISCRETION

The progressive abandonment of the devices by which the common law limited the scope of administrative and judicial discretion, and demanded that *mens rea* be a necessary concomitant of crime, has tended to expand the effective scope of police discretion in prosecuting the newer statutory crimes; it has also tended to lift general deterrence above special deterrence as the primary legal aim. This whole development has been aided by the pervasive vagueness of our criminal statutes. The line between law and order, therefore, has been pushed progressively towards the side of order and away from the controls implied in the concept of law.

The value-acceptance that lurks behind the expansion of the discretion of the law-applying authorities, and those that emphasize general as opposed to special deterrence, are, as we have seen, identical. They emphasize the requirements of society conceived as a corporate body as against the protection of individual freedoms; they favor social stability and freedom from violence as against the stability that individuals find in the ability to predict accurately the legal effects of their actions. In short, they tend to emphasize the very opposite of the Kantian dictate; they tend to treat the individuals as means for the protection of society rather than as ends in themselves.

It is evident that the demand for maintenance of the existing order of things will come most heavily from classes which enjoy the benefits and privileges of the status quo. That the legislature should respond to the demands of the middle classes is exactly what our model of legislative behavior would predict. It is to be expected, therefore, that the legislature would enact statutes which are consistent with the value-acceptances of the privileged in the society. Legislatures have reacted to the problem of violence in the ghettos in the main not by enacting the ameliorative measures with respect to employment, education, housing, and reduction of police mistreatment and white intolerance, which are almost unanimously regarded as the long-run solutions, but by granting ever wider powers to the police, both by enacting substantive laws of ever-increasing reach[19] and by decreasing even the relatively ineffective controls on police discretion that presently exist.

The response of the courts to the legislative development has been predictable. On the whole, the problems at issue have not been judicially considered in detail. Criminals are rarely wealthy and rarely have the funds to finance lengthy appeals. The issues simply have not been presented to most State appellate courts. When they have been presented, usually the response has been confined to marginal adjustments to existing institutions as defined by precedents or statutes. Rather than striking down a vagrancy statute as unconstitutional, the courts have been inclined at most to narrow the reading of the statute.

State v. Grenz,[20] for example, was a case arising from prosecution under the Washington vagrancy statute, which provides in part that every "(8) person who wanders about the streets at late or unusual hours of the night without visible or lawful business . . . is a vagrant, and shall be punished by imprisonment in the county jail for not more than six months, or by a fine of not more than five hundred dollars." A chicken farm in Spokane had lost more than 300 chickens from theft between January and June of 1945. A deputy sheriff noticed a car parked in a wooded area off the highway. On inspection, he found that it contained a number of gunny sacks, some with chicken feathers in them. He and some other deputies watched the car until about 1:30 a.m., when the accused came running toward it, and drove off on the highway. The deputies followed for a few blocks. Then they stopped to discuss their next move. When they started up again, they saw the defendant stoop over with one hand outstretched toward the wires of a fence. The officers then flashed their lights for the first time. The defendant ran, but stopped on command. He was dressed in dark overalls, buttoned to the neck, wearing sneakers and dark gloves despite the balmy night. He carried a flashlight, two gunny sacks, strings, and clothespins. At the trial, the accused, who himself operated a chicken farm, claimed that he had been to a picnic; he had seen the police car following him without lights and, afraid of being robbed, had taken the action which the officers had observed.

After conviction, the accused appealed. He claimed that there was no evidence he was wandering about the streets without any "visible and lawful" business, and that a single instance of wandering about the streets did not constitute "vagrancy." The court overruled both claims. It was argued that, in the first place, since there was evidence from which a jury might infer a criminal intent, the claim that the accused was "there without any visible or lawful business" was sustained. Second, "a continuous or habitual wandering about the streets at late or unusual hours of the night is not required to constitute vagrancy . . . The obvious intent of the legislature in enacting subdivision 8 of the vagrancy statute was to enable law-enforcement officers to keep the streets clear, at late and unusual hours of the night, of those persons who, by reason of being bent upon serious mischief, theft, or burglary, have no visible or lawful business or mission in the locality."[21]

The court might have found the statute unconstitutional, as did a dissenting judge. It might have held, as the accused had urged, that "with mere guilty intention, divorced from overt act or outward manifestation thereof, the law does not concern itself."[22] To hold this position, however, would require the court to invalidate the whole institutional restriction on vagrancy and thus eliminate the functions which it served. Instead, the court supplied by interpretation the elements vaguely stated in the statutory language itself.

If the response of the State appellate courts has, in the main, been to accommodate and to preserve the newer statutory offenses, trying at best to make their language more precise, the Supreme Court of the United States, taking advantage of its special position in the framework of government, has managed in a variety of cases to set out limitations on the abandonment of *actus reus* and *mens rea*, as well as insisted on at least a minimum level of statutory precision. It is to the work of the Supreme Court that we now turn.

The Reaction: The Constitutional Defenses

As we might have expected, the Supreme Court of the United States has stood outside the mainstream of judicial development, and has asserted a variety of constitutional objections to the modern abandonment of legality, of *actus reus* and *mens rea*.

The Constitution and the concept of legality. To say that a criminal statute is vague or ambiguous is to say that its penumbra is very broad. The common-law answer to the problem of ambiguity (since a common-law court could not declare a statute unconstitutional) was the doctrine of the strict construction of penal statutes. But this was not the only plausible solution. It was equally possible to say that if a statute was broad, it gave notice that the whole area of conduct was of dubious propriety and hence should be avoided by anyone except at his peril. So Holmes held in *Nash v. United States* in 1912.[23] That was a case of indictment under the Sherman Anti-Trust Act, for a conspiracy in restraint of trade and to monopolize trade. The statute had been held earlier as prohibiting only combinations that "unduly" restricted competition or "unduly" obstructed the course of trade. Hence, it was argued that the Act as construed was unconstitutionally vague as a criminal statute. Holmes rejected the argument, stating that "the law is full of instances where a man's fate depends upon his estimating rightly, that is, as the jury subsequently estimates it, some matter of degree."[24] He quoted East's Pleas of the Crown (1803) that "the criterion in such cases is to examine whether common social duty would, under the circumstances, have suggested a more circumspect conduct."[25]

It soon arose that there were some "offenses" which were not at all improper, and involved activities which were regarded by businessmen and judges as altogether appropriate. In these cases, the doctrine of vagueness came into play to forbid invoking a statute whose penumbra was unconscionably broad. In *International Harvester Co. v. Kentucky*,[26] the statute at issue forbade the raising or lowering of price above or below the "real value" of an article, which was taken to mean its market value under fair competition and under normal market conditions. Holmes invalidated the statute, on grounds of impermissible vagueness; how to determine the "real value" of an article, he said, was a problem "that no human ingenuity could solve. The reason is not the general uncertainties of a jury trial, but that the elements necessary to determine the imaginary ideal are uncertain both in nature and degree of effect to the acutest commercial mind . . ."[27]

After the great shift in the Supreme Court in 1937, the problem came to be regarded in a somewhat different way. Now the area of protected activity outside the penumbra was taken to be, not economic activity, but the sort of activity protected by the First Amendment—especially, freedom of expression. The leading case was *Winters v. New York*,[28] in which a New York statute had been construed by the highest state court to forbid publications that "so massed their collection of pictures and stories of bloodshed and lust 'as to become vehicle for inciting violent and depraved crimes against the person.'" This statute was held to be unconstitutionally vague. The test of precision in statutory drafting was said to be whether it was of such a character "that men of common intelligence must necessarily guess at its meaning." Since it would be utterly impossible for the actor ever to know with any precision when he had massed sufficient stories of bloodshed and lust to place himself within the statute's condemnation, the law in question was unconstitutionally broad.

The distinction between the economic cases and the First Amendment cases was made in *United States v. National Dairy Products Corp.*[29] There the Court upheld, against constitutional attack, Section 3 of the Robinson-Patman Act, making it a crime to sell goods at "unreasonably low prices for the purpose of destroying competition or eliminating a competitor." The Court said:

the approach to "vagueness" governing a case like this is different from that followed in cases arising under the First Amendment. There we are concerned with the vagueness of the statute "on its face" because such vagueness may in itself deter constitutionally protected and socially desirable conduct . . . No such actor is present here where the statute is directed only at conduct designed to destroy competition, activity which is neither constitutionally protected nor socially desirable.[30]

The Court seemingly had dropped the classical notion that one function of the criminal law simultaneously was to make it possible for citizens reasonably to anticipate the action of authorities, in criminal matters, by limiting the permissible scope for official discretion. However, the very next year it reasserted this position. In *Bouie v. Columbia*,[31] the Court assimilated the *ex post facto* provision of the federal Constitution (which applies by its terms only to the federal Congress) to the due-process clause of the Fourteenth Amendment (which applies to the States). In *Bouie*, the defendants were convicted of criminal trespass for entering a drugstore which they were invited to enter, and then sitting-in at a segregated lunch counter in the store. The South Carolina statute under which they were convicted made criminal "entry upon the lands of another . . . after notice from the owner or tenant prohibiting such entry." The Supreme Court of South Carolina had, in this very case, construed the word "entry" to mean also "remaining after notice to leave." The federal Supreme Court found this an unconstitutional *ex post facto* construction of the statute, and in so doing, it discussed the basis of the doctrines of legality:

When a statute on its face is vague or overbroad, it at least gives the potential defendant some notice, by virtue of this very characteristic, that a question may arise as to its coverage, and that it may be held to cover his contemplated conduct . . . There can be no doubt that a deprivation of the right of fair warning can result not only from vague statutory language but also from an unforeseeable and retroactive judicial expansion of narrow and precise statutory language . . . "[J]udicial enlargement of a criminal act by interpretation is at war with a fundamental concept of the common law that crimes must be defined with appropriate definiteness." Even where vague statutes are concerned, it has been pointed out that the vice in such an enactment is twofold: inadequate guidance to the individual whose guidance is regulated, and inadequate guidance to the triers of fact.[32]

The Court therefore assimilated the *nulla poena* rule to the Constitution. It may be expected to resist any attempts, covert or overt, to enforce a penal statute *ex post facto*. In the present state of the authorities, it draws a distinction between vagueness in cases involving First Amendment rights and other offenses. Whether it will continue to draw this distinction, however, may be doubted, for the value-acceptances which are implied in its attitude toward the discretion of police and prosecutors, and demonstrated in the cases concerning the power to arrest, seem inconsistent with this distinction.

The Constitution and the *actus reus*.   A host of attacks had been made on statutes making mere status a crime, but it was not until 1962 that the Supreme Court met the problem directly. When the court did meet the problem, however, it rested its decision, not on the due-process clause, but on a heretofore little used Constitutional provision, the prohibition on cruel and unusual punishments.[33]

A California statute made it an offense for a person to "be addicted to the use of narcotics."[34] The accused was convicted of violating this statute. The trial judge (whose construction of the statute was binding on the Supreme Court for purposes of this case) charged the jury that "That portion of the statute referring to 'addicted to the use of' narcotics is based on a condition or status ... To be addicted to the use of narcotics is said to be a status and not an act. It is a continuing offense and differs from most other offenses in the fact that [it] is chronic rather than acute; that it continues after it is complete and subjects the offender to arrest at any time before he reforms."[35]

The Court fastened on the inability of the accused to do anything about his condition as the key to determining the unconstitutionality of the statute, although its appeal was rhetorical rather than coldly analytical:

It is unlikely that any State at this moment in history would attempt to make it a criminal offense for a person to be mentally ill, or a leper, or to be afflicted with a venereal disease. A State might determine that the general health and welfare require that the victims of these and other human afflictions be dealt with by compulsory treatment, involving quarantine, confinement, or sequestration. But, in the light of contemporary human knowledge, a law which made a criminal offense of such a disease would universally be thought to be an infliction of cruel and unusual punishment in violation of the Eighth and Fourteenth Amendments ....

We cannot but consider the statute before us as of the same category ...[36]

Justice Douglas, in a concurring opinion, added a significant gloss. He pointed out that "Cruel and unusual punishment results not from confinement, but from convicting the addict of a crime ... The purpose of Section 11721 is not to cure, but to penalize ... A prosecution for addiction, with its resulting stigma and irreparable damage to the good name of the accused, cannot be justified as a means of protecting society, where a civil commitment would do as well ... We would forget the teachings of the Eighth Amendment if we allowed sickness to be made a crime and permitted sick people to be punished for being sick."[37]

The impact of *Robinson* has not yet reached its full potential. Already pursuant to this decision, it has been held that it is a defense to a charge of being "drunk and intoxicated in any street, alley, park or parking" to prove that the accused is a chronic alcoholic.[38] Two states have held that vagrancy laws are unconstitutional. The reach of the Eighth Amendment has not yet been felt.

The Constitution and *mens rea*. The Supreme Court for many years treated with relative complacency the development of a body of criminal law in which *mens rea* was not an identifying characteristic of guilt.[39] It did so in reliance on the familiar distinction between crimes *mala prohibita* and *mala in se*, for in the former class of offenses, "the emphasis of the statute is evidently upon achievement of some social betterment rather than the punishment of crimes as in cases of *mala in se.*"[40]

The Court has, however, refused to permit the *mens rea* requirement to be eviscerated entirely from conventional crimes. In *Morisette v. United States,*[41] the accused took some shell casings apparently rusting in a refuse pile on U.S. Government property and sold them as scrap metal. He was charged with the conversion of Government property. It was admitted that he had taken the shell casings knowing that they were on the Government reservation, but that he believed that they had been abandoned. The trial court and Circuit Court of Appeals agreed that he was guilty, holding that the statute required only that he had intended to sell property belonging to the Government; his knowledge that to do so was unlawful was irrelevant. In rendering this decision, the Court of Appeals relied on *Shevlin-Carpenter* and *Balint.*

The Supreme Court reserved the decision. It reaffirmed the Balint decision, but said that it was very different from the case at bar. It made the distinction on historical grounds:

Stealing, larceny and its variants and equivalents, were among the earliest offenses known to the law that existed before legislation; they are invasions of rights of property which stir a sense of insecurity in the whole community and arouse public demand for retribution; the penalty is high and, when a sufficient amount is involved, the infamy is that of a felony, which, says Maitland, is "as bad a word as you can give a man or thing." State courts of last resort, on whom fall the heaviest burden of interpreting criminal law in this country, have consistently retained the requirement of intent in larceny-type offenses . . .

Congress, therefore, omitted any express prescription of criminal intent from the enactment before us in the light of an unbroken course of judicial decision in all constituent states of the Union holding intent inherent in this class of offense, even when not expressed in a statute . . .[42]

12.6 SUMMARY

In the last three chapters we have examined a few selected aspects of the law of crimes, viewing it both as a product of the discretion given to courts and to legislatures to create rules, and as a set of rules defining the scope of discretion of policemen, prosecutors, and judges. We have seen that the historical antecedents of the common-law crimes demanded a harm, an act, and a *mens rea.* The nineteenth-century brought into the forefront of ideology the notions of legality and of deterrence as the core of the criminal law. The concepts of harm and of the *actus reus* served well the concept of legality, providing assurance that there was a reasonably definite rule preexisting the crime, and that there would be some means of verifying the policeman's suspicion. Even in the common law, however, there were built-in exceptions, of which attempts and conspiracies were the most apparent. The notion of *mens rea* served the newer notions of deterrence as the objective of punishment.

The vast expansion of statutory crimes rapidly eroded many of these guarantees. Crimes without victims, some regulatory offenses, and crimes of status frequently do not require an *actus reus* or even a harm to an identifiable victim. Their corresponding low visibility effectively extends the policeman's discretion. Applied to crimes of expression, and indeed to many modern group crimes generally, the law of conspiracy tends to undercut the requirement of verification of the policeman's opinion of guilt. Lastly, the progressive deterioration of the notion of *mens rea*, first in the older group of crimes where it has increasingly come to be interpreted as a mere intent to do the act forbidden by law, and secondly, with respect to regulatory offenses, where the requirement has frequently been dropped altogether, has tended to lay ever heavier emphasis on general deterrence over special deterrence.

This trend away from the classical concepts which limited the scope of discretion of policemen has been largely the result of legislative action. Ever attentive to their role, appellate courts in general have not resisted this trend, despite its apparent deviation from the central principles of the traditional criminal law.

In recent years, however, there has been a significant development of resistance in the Supreme Court, which has emphasized the doctrine of legality, resisted the tendency to create crimes of status, and refused to join the movement toward abolishing the *mens rea* requirement in traditional offenses.

In the event, however, legislative ambiguity and the tendency toward ever broader policeman's discretion have made the substantive criminal law a poor reed on which to lean for adequate controls. Increasingly, the court has turned to procedural devices to control the discretion by law-applying officials. As Remington and Rosenblum conclude:

The substantive criminal law must inevitably leave broad scope for the exercise of discretion as to what conduct is to be subjected to the criminal process. If this is so, then it seems obvious that concern ought to relate to who is to exercise this discretion, how it is to be exercised, and how it is to be controlled to prevent its abuse. On these central issues, too little has been said.[43]

The difficulty, however, is that procedural devices at best can enforce only the boundaries of the discretionary area defined by the substantive criminal law. Given the broad scope for police discretion, vague criteria for its use, and ambiguous conditions for verification, the devices for controlling police discretion are incapable of narrowing the scope granted. The substantive criminal law defines society's objectives with respect to both law and order. Procedural devices can be used to ensure that a given definition is the line which is observed in practice, but they cannot by themselves narrow the area defined.

NOTES

1. E. M. Schur, *Crimes Without Victims*, Prentice-Hall, Englewood Cliffs, N.J., 1965, p. 170.

2. *Dennis v. United States*, 341 U.S. 494 (1950), 511–512.

3. *New York Times*, April 19, 1939; © 1939 by The New York Times Company. Reprinted by permission. Quoted in J. Michael and H. Wechsler, *Criminal Law and Its Administration*, Foundation Press, Chicago, 1940, p. 1016.

4. 110 N.J.L. 467, 166 ATL. 300 (1933).

5. *Int. Jurid. Assoc. Bull.*, 1933, **2**, No. 5, p. 3. Quoted in Michael and Wechsler, *op. cit.*, p. 1035.

6. Frank Remington and Victor Rosenblum, "The criminal law and the legislative process." *Ill. Law Forum*, 1960, p. 481, reprinted by permission; referring to F. J. Remington, R. R. Robinson, and W. J. Zwick, "Liability without fault criminal statutes," *Wis. Law Rev.*, 1956, p. 625.

7. G. Williams, *Criminal Law: The General Part*, Stevens, London, 1960, pp. 259–260. Reprinted by permission. See generally C. Howard, *Strict Responsibility*, Sweet and Maxwell, London, 1963.

8. 397 Pa. 575, 155A 2d 825, (1959).

9. 155A. 2d at 827; but see H. V. Ball and L. M. Friedman, "The use of criminal sanctions in the enforcement of economic legislation: a sociological view," *Stanford Law Rev.*, **17**, 1965, p. 197.

10. Sanford H. Kadish, "Some observations on the use of criminal sanctions in enforcing economic regulations," *U. Chicago Law Rev.*, **30**, 1963, p. 423.

11. Wis. Stat. 148.04(A), (14), (1961)

12. Comment, "Appellate review of primary sentencing decisions: a Connecticut case study," *Yale Law Rev.*, **69**, 1960, p. 1453.

13. Remington and Rosenblum, *op. cit.*, p. 481. Reprinted by permission.

14. *Ibid.*, pp. 489–490. Reprinted by permission.

15. *Ibid.*, pp. 491. Printed by permission.

16. *Ibid.*, pp. 492–493.

17. *Ibid.*, p. 493. Reprinted by permission.

18. *Ibid.*, pp. 493–494. Reprinted by permission.

19. See, for example, the "Anti-Riot Act" recently enacted by Congress.

20. 26 Wash. 2d 764, 175 P. 2d 633 (1946).

21. 26 Wash. at 770, 175 P. 2d at 637.

22. 26 Wash. 2d at 770, 175 P. 2d at 637, quoting *People v. Belcastro*, 356, Ill. 144, 190 N.E. 301, 392 A.L.R. 1223.

23. 229 U.S. 373, 33 Sup. Ct. 780, 57 L. Ed. 1232 (1912).

24. *Ibid.*

25. *Ibid.*

26. 234 U.S. 216, 34 S. Ct. 853, 58 L. Ed. 1284 (1914).

27. *Ibid.*

28. 333 U.S. 507, 68 Sup. Ct. 665, 92 L. Ed. 840 (1948).

29. 372 U.S. 29, 83 S. Ct. 594, 9 L. Ed. 561 (1963).

30. *Ibid.*

31. 378 U.S. 347 84 S. Ct. 1697, 12 L. Ed. 894 (1964).

32. 378 U.S. 347 at 352–353, quoting *Pierce v. U.S.* [314 U.S. 306 at 311] and Paul A. Freund, "The Supreme Court and civil liberties," *Vanderbilt Law Rev.*, **4** (1951), pp. 533, 541.

33. The Eighth Amendment to the Federal Constitution.

34. California Health and Safety Code, §11721.

35. *Robinson v. California*, 370 U.S. 660, 82 S. Ct. 1417, 8 L. Ed. 2d 758 (1962).

36. *Ibid.*

37. *Ibid.*

38. *Easter v. District of Columbia*, 361, F. 2d 50 (App. D. C., 1966).

39. *Shevlin-Carpenter Co. v. Minnesota*, 218 U.S. 57, 30 S. Ct. 663, 54 L. Ed. 930 (1910); *U.S. v. Balint*, 258 U.S. 250, 42 S. Ct. 301, 66 L. Ed. 604 (1922).

40. *U.S. v. Balint*, 258 U.S. 250, 42 S. Ct. 301, 66 L. Ed. 604 (1922).

41. 342 U.S. 246, 72 S. Ct. 240, 96 L. Ed. 288 (1952).

42. *Ibid.*

43. Remington and Rosenblum, *op. cit.*, p. 481. Reprinted by permission.

Part IV

The implementation of law

13

The implementation of law in stateless societies

The creation of rules is only a part of the legal process. As our basic model suggests, the laws usually must be sanctioned to be effective. In complex societies, this is done by specially designated agencies. Before we turn to consider the sanctioning process, however, it may be useful, by way of contrast, to examine dispute-settlement and law-enforcement in stateless societies.

13.1 "STATELESS" SOCIETIES DEFINED

Two British anthropologists, M. Fortes and E. E. Evans-Pritchard, edited an influential little book, *African Political Systems*, published in 1940. The book consisted of seven brief monographs by various authors, each concerning a specific African tribal society. In their Introduction, the editors drew a distinction between two different kinds of political systems.

It will be noted that the political systems described in this book fall into two main categories. One group, which we refer to as Group A, consists of those societies which have centralized authority, administrative machinery, and judicial institutions—in short, a government—and in which cleavages of wealth, privilege and status correspond to the distribution of power and authority ... The other group, which we refer to as Group B, consists of those societies which lack centralized authority, administrative machinery, and constituted judicial institutions—in short, which lack government—and in which there are no sharp divisions of rank, status and wealth ... Those who consider that a state should be defined by the presence of governmental institutions will regard the first group as primitive states and the second group as stateless societies.[1]

The word "state," like the word "law," is probably incapable of any but a stipulative definition. For the purposes of this book, we mean by the phrase "stateless societies" what Fortes and Evans-Pritchard would include in their "Class B" societies. We shall consider the maintenance of public order and dispute-settlement in two such societies, the Nuer and the Arusha in Africa.

13.2 THE NUER

The Nuer live in a flat savannah country on both banks of the White Nile as it flows northerly from northern Uganda across the southern Sudan toward Khartoum and Egypt. The land is clayey, parched and bare during drought, and flooded and verdant when the rivers overflow their banks during the rainy season from June through December of each year. When it rains, the villages, which are built on sandy ridges rising out of the water, are separated by flooded, swampy areas. People and cattle are relatively isolated on these ridges, along which the villages stretch for a mile or two. In the dry season, all is dry and sere; great cracks open up in the hard clay soil, and the villagers must set forth to find water for their cattle. Then the villagers burn the grass to provide for new pasture. They live in small camps near water holes. When the rains set in, they return to the safety of their ridge-top villages, to begin again the eternal, unchanging cycle of their lives.

The harsh environment and the very simple technological level which the Nuer have achieved demand that the members of the community work cooperatively against the ever-present threat of famine. Evans-Pritchard, whose work on the Nuer forms the basis for most of our knowledge about them, says that the Nuer

are generally on the verge of want and that every few years they face more or less severe famine. Under these conditions, it is understandable that there is much sharing of food in the same village, especially among members of adjacent homesteads and hamlets ... [Moreover, the] paucity of raw materials, together with a meagre food supply, contracts social ties, drawing the people of village or camp closer, in a moral sense, for they are in consequence highly interdependent and their pastoral hunting, fishing and, to a lesser degree, their agricultural activities are necessarily joint undertakings.

He concludes:

Thus, while in a narrow sense the economic unit is the household, the larger local communities are, directly or indirectly, cooperative groups combining to maintain existence, and corporations owning natural resources and sharing in their exploitations. In the smaller local groups the co-operative functions are more direct and evident than in the larger ones, but the collective function of obtaining for themselves the necessities of life from the same resources is in some degree common to all local communities from the household to the tribe.[2]

Nuer society faces two rather different problems in the maintenance of public order arising out of the two different conditions of life. During the rainy season, the principal problem is to maintain order within the isolated village—a close-knit community in which practically everybody is related to everybody else, and everyone is dependent on the corporate cohesiveness of the village as an economic unit and for mutual welfare. During the dry season, the same requirements obtain, but in addition it is important that the herdsmen be able to move safely through the countryside without fear of attack by other Nuer from other villages moving through the same country.[3]

In order to understand how the Nuer meet these two different kinds of problems in maintaining public order, one must examine briefly the systems of organization of Nuer society. The Nuer are organized into tribes, each of which is further divided and subdivided and subsubdivided on a territorial basis into primary, secondary, and tertiary tribal sections. A tertiary section is divided into villages, and villages into domestic groups.[4] While these tribal segments are territorial in nature, they are also related through common lineage in a complex way, so that each segment of the tribe, while including persons not of the same lineage, nevertheless often regards itself as connected to a particular agnatic group ("agnatic" means related through the male line).

As a result of this system of division and subdivision, every Nuer is a member of a host of corporate groups. He is a member of his own village; and vis-à-vis another village, even one within his own tertiary tribal section, he considers himself an outsider. Vis-à-vis another tertiary tribal section, however, he considers himself to be a member of his own tertiary section, and thus allied for these purposes with every village in it; and so goes the association with respect to all the tribal divisions up to the tribe itself.

Public order is maintained among the Nuer, first, by the norms of conduct determining who is to join, and on whose side, in any situation involving the resort to force. In the event of violence between two persons, others are supposed to support whichever of the two persons is in their smallest corporate group. Thus if a member of Village A kills a member of Village B, all the other members of Village B are supposed to support the aggrieved parties (the family of the deceased) against the killer; and Village A's members are supposed to support the killer. On the other hand, if both Village A and Village B are members of the Z tertiary section, in a similar case between any member of Z tertiary section and X tertiary section, then all the village members of both A and B will unite behind the member of their tertiary section.

What outsiders might regard as a simple mad anarchy centered about the "barbaric" and "primitive" concept of blood feud is thus the significant regulating force of the society. A man hesitates to violate the norms of peaceful conduct for fear of visiting upon his head the wrath, not only of his victim, but of all those within the relevant corporate group of the victim as well. While no doubt this fear is somewhat offset by the expectation that one's own in-group will support him in such an event, the expectation of support depends on whether one is aware that one has or has not complied with socially approved norms. Whether as victim or as aggressor, the amount of opposition one stirs up and the amount of effective support he can expect are functions of whether the conduct involved does or does not match the role-expectation of others in the community.

Such a system of maintaining public order provides no way of resolving *bona fide* disputes concerning the question whether the norm was in fact violated, or what was the appropriate applicable norm. It is reasonably appropriate for maintaining order, however, among relative strangers, for the fear of setting off serious group conflict, with all its dangers to oneself and to one's close relatives and associates, tends to deter breach of the acceptable rules of conflict.

But these rules are far less satisfactory either within the village community or between villages which are close neighbors. When there is a killing, mystical sanctions operate which forbid persons between whom there is a blood feud to eat and drink from the same vessels. Were they to do so, they believe, they would die.

Yet within the same village and between adjacent villages there is a common economic and familial bond. Women from one lineage or village may marry men from another lineage or village. A feud may place a man and his sister's children, who are supposed to be particularly close relations—on opposite sides. The cooperation on which Nuer existence depends may be seriously threatened.

The Nuer do have an official of sorts, a man who is, rather loosely, called a leopard-skin chief because he has the right to wear a leopard-skin. His title notwithstanding, the leopard-skin chief is not a chief in the sense of having any authority over anybody else. Within the village, if a man's action is resisted— for example, if a farmer claims that another man owes him a bullock and he proceeds to take it by self-help, with resistance on the part of the owner—others will try to persuade the disputants to ask the leopard-skin chief to mediate the dispute in an effort to avoid the difficulties which unresolved fued will bring about.

The leopard-skin chief has more than a merely passive role, however. When a man has killed another man, he may neither eat nor drink until he has gone to a leopard-skin chief for the latter to cut his arm until the blood flows. Moreover, the hut of the chief is a sanctuary. A killer usually stays in that hut to avoid vengeance. Meanwhile, the leopard-skin chief actively tries to persuade the kin of the deceased to accept cattle in compensation for the killing. But he has no authority to impose any decision.

The chief is not asked to deliver a judgment: it would not occur to Nuer that one was required. He appears to force the kin of the dead man to accept compensation by his insistence, even to the point of threatening to curse them, but it is an established convention that he shall do so, in order that the bereaved relatives may retain their prestige. What seems really to have counted were the acknowledgment of community tie between the parties concerned, and hence of the moral obligation to settle the affair by the acceptance of a traditional payment, and the wish, on both sides, to avoid, for the time being at any rate, further hostilities.[5]

Thus "the leopard-skin chief does not rule and judge, but acts as mediator through whom communities desirous of ending open hostility can conclude an active state of feud."[6]

There is a fixed scale of compensation—said to have been forty to fifty heads of cattle until recently—to be paid regardless of the actual status or position of the deceased, or of the number of persons dependent on him. The payment is accompanied by a ritual cleansing and atonement, performed by the leopard-skin chief.

In lesser disputes than homicide, usually over ownership of cattle, the leopard-skin chief and the elders act as mediators. The chief does not, however, act as judge in this instance either; he has no power to summon the parties or to compel compliance with his decision. His only power is to visit the defendant with the plaintiff and some elders and inquire whether the former and his kinsmen are prepared to settle the matter. If the defendant agrees, it is possible to submit the matter to arbitration by the chief in consultation with the elders. Even this decision, however, is reached by general agreement and "in a large measure, therefore, arises from an acknowledgement by the defendant's or plaintiff's party that the other party has justice on its side."[7]

The seeming anarchy of Nuer life is an illusion. The Nuer society is able to maintain order because there is a social structure consisting of a set of positions defined by norms.

Nuer society is extremely simple, homogeneous, and unstratified. The norms are simple, widely known, and internalized. The intangible and largely unconscious sanctions and rewards of ordinary social intercourse are sufficient to enforce these norms. At the same time, harsh environment and simple technology combine to teach that compromise, with the concommitant restoration of social cohesion, is a more pressing social imperative by far than the winner-takes-all solution, along with norm-enforcement. As a result, the dispute-settlement mechanism is a device, not for imposing punishment for the breach of norms, but for the restoration of social cohesion. There are no special agencies for norm-enforcement; the feud, in which the whole society is involved, is the sanctioning institution.

13.3 THE ARUSHA OF TANZANIA

The Arusha live on the lower slopes of Mt. Meru, an extinct volcano in northern Tanzania. They are an agricultural people, cultivating bananas, maize, beans, millet, and garden vegetables. The mountain fields are fresh and verdant, with ample rainfall. Population pressure, however, has been great, and has forced some to settle on the peripheral lands around the base of the mountain—lands which are relatively dry and infertile. On the mountain slopes, the Arusha are as crowded as are any African people, and land scarcity is the central problem of the economy. There is little economic stratification.

Arusha society is organized around two complementary principles, lineage and age-set. The patrilineal system is divided into a series of units of descending order: tribe, moiety, clan, clan-section, subclan, maximal lineage, inner lineage, and family. Each of these is divided into two mutually exclusive sets of *ilwashata* (sing.: *olwashe*) so that every individual can be categorized as a member of any specific unit in the lineage system, and of a specific *olwashe* in that unit. Allegiance to an *olwashe* within a specific unit of the lineage system is by birth, by marriage, or by timing of circumcision in the age-set pattern. For example, within the family, the *olwashe* of a wife is the same as the *olwashe* of the wife who "sponsors" her. Her adult male children form part of the same *olwashe*. The norms of conduct require that members of one *olwashe* in any given unit support the other members of the same *olwashe* who may be in disputes with other members of the same unit.

The age-group system for males is divided into six grades: youths (prior to circumcision), junior *murran* (warriors), senior *murran*, junior elder, senior elder, and retired elders. Each age-group consists of all those from a single parish (the smallest political unit) who were initiated during a single period of four to six years. Ideally each age-group constitutes a corporate entity, the members of which are conscious of their unity and indeed often act as a single body; they recognize common rights and obligations and acknowledge their own selected leaders.[8] So close is the relationship between age-mates in a particular age-group that it even extends to rights of sexual access to the wife of an age-mate, so long as this right is not used excessively. In all matters, members of the same age-group act together: they drink together, work together, fight together. The age-set includes all the age-groups of the same grade from the different parishes; but the basic allegiance is not to the age-set—it is to the smaller age-group.

Each age-group is linked with alternate age-groups above and below its own level. Young men are sponsored during the circumcision rites by patrons of the senior murran level, who in turn were sponsored by older men who now are of the senior elder level. Thus at any given time, youths, senior murran, and senior elders are linked by the relationship of patron and ward, as are junior murran and junior elders.

Each of these two subsystems of Arusha society, the patrilineal subsystem, and the parish age-group subsystem, has its own special influence and leadership, and its own special public assemblies in which to hear disputes. The leaders of the patrilineal descent system are called counsellors; those of the age-group system are called spokesmen. Disputes arising within the patrilineal system are heard in moots, at which only members of the descent subsystem are present. Disputes within the parish between members of different patrilineal systems are heard by the parish assembly. Conclaves of single age-groups, or of single inner lineages, are held in minor matters.

The Arusha are essentially a peaceful people. Violence is viewed as tantamount to an admission of weakness in a man's argument; it is viewed as an "inequitable and immoral act."[9]

The course such a dispute may take can be studied in the Kadume case reported by P. H. Gulliver.[10] Makara, father of the petitioner Kadume, died. On his death, his land was occupied by his neighbor and half-brother, Soine. After four or five seasons had come and gone, Kadume laid claim to the land which Soine was using; Soine refused to surrender it.

Soine went to the lineage counsellor, who convened a conclave of the inner lineage. At this conclave, Soine remained obdurate: Kadume's mother, he said, had abandoned Kadume's father some ten years before the dispute arose, and left Makara unwived and uncared-for. Only Soine and his wife had concerned themselves with his welfare. Soine himself had only a small farm, while Kadume had a piece of land on his mother's brother's farm, which he was already cultivating. The counsellor suggested that Kadume graze some animals in Soine's paddock (as he had been doing earlier), but Kadume rejected the suggestion.

The counsellor, at Kadume's request, then convened an internal moot of the inner lineage, consisting of the counsellor himself and nine members of the larger maximal lineage who lived nearby. Kadume was then only a senior murran, not an elder, so he asked a lineage notable, Kirevi, to be his spokesman.

Kirevi stated the applicable norm: sons inherit the land of their fathers. Soine asserted the same arguments he had used earlier. He denied that sons, rather than brothers, always inherit fathers' lands. Kirevi's response stressed the unity of the lineage, and he urged Soine not to disrupt it. Lokure, a member of the lineage, then urged that Kadume be permitted to occupy some of the land.

Silence followed Lokure's speech, indicating general agreement, whereupon Soine began immediately to discuss what portion of the land Kadume should have. Kadume interrupted Soine to claim all the land, but the latter rejoined effectively with a reminder of the amount of land that Kadume already had in his mother's brother's farm.

The dispute was settled on this basis. The members of the moot walked over the land and established a boundary between the land which Soine was to retain, and that which Kadume was to have. The whole moot then concluded by drinking beer at Soine's house—a customary ceremony formalizing the amicable settlement of the dispute.

There now exist local magistrate's courts in Arushaland, organized and directed by the new national government. These courts operate basically in the

English tradition, although they are required to apply "customary law." They must, therefore, decide on the basis of "winner taking all," but using the norms of the traditional society to decide who ought to be the winner.

In the case just cited, Kadume decided not to appeal. The pressure of community solidarity, expressed by the unanimous silent approval of the proposed compromise, and the ceremonial beer-drinking which solemnized the settlement of the dispute and the restoration of social harmony, deterred him even if he had not believed that he ought to accept the community-sponsored compromise. If he had appealed, there can be little doubt that the magistrate, operating under a set of norms derived not from African but from English society and legal tradition, would have had to decide on the basis of "winner taking all." It would have awarded all the land to Kadume in accordance with the applicable norm. One magistrate, an Arusha himself, told Dr. Gulliver that he hated to try cases such as Kadume's, because he was aware that the judgment of his court was not and could not be the same as the judgment of the moot or conclave.

Arusha society, like Nuer society, is simple, relatively unstratified and homogeneous. The traditional dispute-settlement system, as in the case of the Nuer and for the same reasons, need not and does not direct itself primarily toward winner-takes-all kind of settlement and norm-enforcement. In Kadume's case, the norm in question was agreed on by all: sons inherit the father's land. The overriding value, however, was the restoration of communal harmony. The dispute was therefore settled on the basis of compromise, enforced by unanimous agreement in the moot. The pressure of the entire society was therefore exerted to persuade the disputants to accept the result, and to drink beer and return to social harmony.

In the absence of a system of dispute-settlement based on "winner taking all" and of norm-enforcement, no specialized agency to judge, to enforce the judgment, and hence to sanction the breach of norm is required. The magistrate's court, operating on a very different set of norms which require it to decide on the basis of "winner taking all" and of norm-enforcement, does require such a specialized agency.

13.4 CONCLUSIONS

These brief studies of folk societies and their order-maintaining and dispute-settlement procedures show that such societies can be compared with our own with respect to the three dimensions corresponding to the adjudicative, legislative, and executive functions of government. The norms that define these functions H. L. A. Hart has named, collectively, the "secondary" rules.[11]

First, even in these relatively simple societies, there exist officials—the leopard-skin chief among the Nuer, the counsellors and spokesmen among the Arusha—whose roles require them to perform certain duties in connection with dispute-settlement. The entire dispute-settlement mechanism rests on these officials performing their duties either voluntarily or on demand. Unless the leopard-skin chief seeks out the parties and begins the mediation process, or unless the lineage counsellor calls the appropriate moot or conclave, there is no recourse but to raw violence as the means for resolving the conflict.

The nature of the norms which define the roles of these officials are in some respects similar to, but in other respects significantly different from, the norms defining the roles of adjudicative officials in a society with a centralized monopoly of violence inhering in the State structure. In the first place, in these simple societies the knowledge of norms is assumed to be part of the common socialization of the members of the community. The maxim that "every man is presumed to know the law," so transparently a legal fiction in modern society, seems to correspond to the reality. It can do so only because the societies are simple, the corpus of norms is neither great nor complex, and the socialization is commonly shared and relatively homogeneous. There is, therefore, no need for specialized agencies or institutions claiming expertise in the business of discovering laws under the guidance of the rules of recognition, as there is in the case in our own society. Rules so important in our own society that Hart has asserted that their existence is the *sine qua non* of the existence of "law."

A second distinction concerns what Hart calls rules of change. Whether there are rules for changing the norms in Nuer and Arusha societies is not clear. We are told by anthropologists[12] that legislation does exist in some tribal societies. One would expect it to appear only in more complex and sophisticated societies.[13] As Robert Redfield puts it in describing an ideal type:

In folk society the moral rules bend, but men cannot make them afresh. In civilization the old moral orders suffer, but new states of mind are developed by which the moral order is, to some significant degree, taken in charge.[14]

This fact suggests one of the more important distinctions between primitive and modern societies. Again Redfield puts it aptly:

The important statement that is generally true and relevant here is that in primitive societies uninfluenced by civilization the future is seen as a reproduction of the immediate past. Men see their children doing on the whole what they did themselves and are satisfied to see them doing so. The fortunes of individual men and women may rise and fall; calamity may strike one man or everybody, and success may or may not come; but the ways of life, the things to try for and to realize, remain the same . . .

On the whole, I think that neither the primitive societies nor the ancient civilized societies show us, except rarely, the phenomenon of conscious reform in their institutions . . . An announced purpose to change things in such a way as to make society different from what had ever been before is probably unimportant in Western history until quite modern times . . .[15]

Men cannot consciously desire to change the norms of their society unless there are means available to effectuate their desires. There must be institutions through whose activities the norms can be changed and enforced. The development of institutions for the enforcement of the traditional normative system is a precondition to the perception that men could, by changing the normative system, transform society. Courts, judges, and the whole sanctioning apparatus which depends on them arose to perform an inherently conservative function, but their existence is the precondition for the use of law as a tool for induced social change.

The third distinction between the two types of societies relates to the existence of distinct rule-sanctioning agencies. No such institutions exist in either Nuer or Arusha society, where norms are enforced by the agreement of the whole community and by the requirement of mutual support among members of corporate groups. Whether, in societies so clearly based on common acceptance of norms and value-consensus, the State is value-neutral or not, is a question which does not arise. There is no State precisely because the societies are so homogeneous.

In complex societies, there are enforcement agencies. In the ensuing chapters we shall examine these agencies to determine whether they are, as their principal sustaining myth maintains—a value-neutral framework for the containment of conflict, or whether they are, as conflict theorists insist, instruments for the enforcement of domination by the powerful and the privileged.

NOTES

1. E. E. Evans-Pritchard and M. Fortes, *African Political Systems*, Oxford University Press, London, 1940, p. 5. Copyright 1940 by the International African Institute. Reprinted by permission.

2. *Ibid.*, pp. 273–274. Reprinted by permission.

3. L. P. Mair, *Primitive Government*, Penguin, New York, 1964, p. 23.

4. Evans-Pritchard and Fortes, *op. cit.*, pp. 278–283.

5. *Ibid.*, pp. 291–292. Reprinted by permission.

6. *Ibid.*, p. 293. Reprinted by permission.

7. *Ibid.*, p. 293. Reprinted by permission.

8. P. H. Gulliver, *Social Control in an African Society*, Boston University Press, Boston, 1963, p. 25.

9. *Ibid.*, p. 220.

10. *Ibid.*, pp. 255–258.

11. H. L. A. Hart, *The Concept of Law*, Clarendon Press, Oxford, 1961, p. 91.

12. See R. Redfield, *The Primitive World and Its Transformations,* Cornell University Press, Ithaca, N.Y., 1953.

13. *Ibid.*, p. 14.

14. *Ibid.*, p. 25.

15. Reprinted from Robert Redfield, *The Primitive World and its Transformations*, pp. 120–123. Copyright 1953 by Cornell University. Used by permission of Cornell University Press.

14

The implementation of law in complex societies: introduction

In an earlier chapter, we raised the question which seems to us to be central to the understanding of the legal system in America: Is it a neutral, value-free structure within which the conflicts of our society can peaceably work themselves out, or is it in fact an integral part of the social conflict itself? Is the legal system value-neutral, or is it value-loaded?

We have examined this question with respect to two of the most important rule-making institutions—legislatures and the appellate courts—emphasizing the functions of the appellate courts. We have seen that the way in which the appellate courts make rules and the sorts of rules which they produce tend to be functions of the norms creating and defining the activities of the courts, and of the social pressures upon the decision-makers. In this and subsequent chapters we shall examine the same question with respect to the process of criminal law-enforcement, starting with arrest, and proceeding through prosecution and trial, ending with sentencing.

14.1 THE CRIMINAL PROCESS IN AMERICA: AN OVERVIEW

Each year in the United States approximately four million persons are arrested. Most of these arrests are for relatively minor offenses. In 1965, for example, police departments reporting to the Federal Bureau of Investigation reported 4,955,047 arrests, of which only 834,296 (17%) were for offenses which are categorized by the FBI as "Type I" or "major" offenses. Even this figure distorts somewhat the seriousness of most of the offenses for which arrests are made. It is clear, however, that well over 80% of the arrests made by police are for minor, albeit not necessarily inconsequential, offenses. This in part accounts for the fact that, of the over four million arrests made each year, fewer than one hundred thousand persons (2 or 3%) are sent to prison. Most of the persons arrested never appear in court, many are released after booking, some are held in jail for only a short time, and still others appear in court but spend only a short time in a city or county jail.

The President's Crime Commission conducted a national survey to locate the number of persons in the population who had been victims of crime and to see what subsequently happened to their cases.[1] The findings illustrate the sifting process of the legal system in macrocosm (see Table 14.1). Of the 2077 cases of victimization reported in the survey, only 120, or just 5% culminated in trials. The major single cause of legal inaction was a failure on the part of the victims to report the crimes to the police: 51% of the victims reported not having told the police about the incident. The reduction of the over 1000 cases that remained to 120 ending in trials is largely accomplished by the discretionary powers of the various legal processing agencies.

A more detailed accounting, which will further illuminate the role of official discretion in criminal-law procedures, shows a still more dramatic reduction in the number of persons who make their way through the legal process and move from arrest to conviction. A recent survey of law-enforcement activities in Washington, D.C. provides data that are fairly representative[2] (see Table 14.2). In Washington, D.C. in 1965 there were 25,648 felonies known to the police, and there were 6266 arrests. We do not know, unfortunately, what percentage of the felonies known were accounted for by these 6266 arrests (since one arrest might

TABLE 14.1

Total cases	2007	Arrest made	120
Police notified	1024	Trial	50
Police came	787	"Proper" conviction*	27
Police called incident a crime	593		

* As characterized by the victim.

Source: P. H. Ennis, "Criminal victimization in the United States: a report of a national survey." A report of a research study submitted to the President's Commission on Law Enforcement and Administration of Justice, Field Surveys II, U. S. Government Printing Office, 1967, p. 49.

TABLE 14.2   Disposition of adults arrested for felonies in Washington, D.C., during 1965.

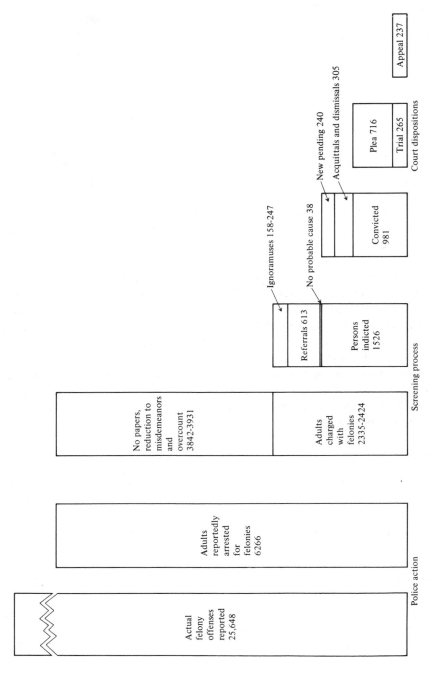

From President's Commission on Crime and Law Enforcement in Washington, D.C., U.S. Government Printing Office, 1967.

account for fifteen felonies), nor do we know how many persons might have been arrested but turned loose by police at the time of initial contact or after screening at police headquarters. We do know, however, that of these 6266 arrests over 50% were released from felony charges. After screening by the prosecutor's office there remained an estimated 2379 adults charged with felonies by the prosecutor. The remaining cases were either dismissed or had charges reduced to misdemeanor offenses. Later in the process, after grand jury hearings, 1526 persons were indicted and convictions were obtained in 981 cases. Of these convictions, 237 were appealed and no final disposition was available at the time of the report. However, in the appeals court of the District of Columbia, the number of appeals granted averages around 20% of the cases appealed, so it is a fair estimate that around forty-five of the appeals were granted. Thus, during the course of legal process approximately 85% of the persons arrested for felonies avoided a felony conviction or, conversely, of the persons arrested for felonies only 15% were ultimately convicted.

The majority of those arrested are released from criminal prosecution; the remainder are charged with lesser (misdemeanor) offenses. Even the figure of 15% is an underestimate of the impact of the legal process on the distribution of persons arrested, since it does not include those persons who are released by the police and never come to the attention of the prosecutor.

With nothing save these raw statistics to judge the legal process by, the picture that emerges is nonetheless quite revealing. First it is clear that the bulk of the criminal law enforcement effort is directed towards minor infractions of the law—drunkenness, vagrancy, disorderly conduct, and the like. Second, even within the small proportion of the serious offenses (which at most accounts for only twenty percent of the total arrests) the vast majority of these offenses never culminate in a criminal conviction. To understand the process we must know in some detail precisely what takes place in the organizations responsible for "enforcing the law."

14.2 THE ORGANIZATION OF LAW ENFORCEMENT

Next to the courts themselves, the criminal-law-enforcement agencies are popularly considered the most impartial and value-neutral of all the institutions of the State. In this view, we rely on the police as the embodiment of the State's monopoly on instruments of organized violence, to represent all of us, and to be neutral in the face of social conflict. We rely on prosecutors to be just and deliberate, and the trial procedures and sentencing to be neutral and immune from the pressures of society. So they are nominally. But how actually do they function? And why?

To answer these questions, we can adopt our original model and place in the position of the object of the normative injunction the particular role-occupant whose behavior we want to understand: the police, the prosecutor, the trial judge.

The problem, then, is to understand the norms that define these positions, the social and other forces operating on the role-occupants, and the activity of whatever enforcement agencies may exist.

It is our hypothesis that the agencies involved in criminal procedures, like the appellate courts, do have wide areas of discretion, they do exercise this discretion, and in general this discretion is exercised in favor of the advantaged and powerful groups in the society. In the case of the appellate courts, we saw that the reason for the generally conservative tinge of their work-product was a function of the structuring of the court inputs, including the recruitment process for the judges and the generally dysfunctional norms of decision-making, which permitted the unexpressed values of the judges to take a dominant place in the decision-making process. In the case of the criminal-law-enforcing agencies, however, a far more significant factor is the pressures of the bureaucratic structure into which these agencies are shaped.

Complex societies differ from primitive and transitional societies in many salient ways. Of all the differences perhaps none is more important for an understanding of the legal system than the fact that modern societies function through formal, bureaucratically structured organizations. We are born in bureaucratically organized hospitals, educated in bureaucratically organized schools and universities, attend bureaucratically organized churches, work in bureaucratically organized corporations and businesses, buy our food and clothing from bureaucratically organized stores, draw retirement pensions and insurance from bureaucratically organized government agencies, and we die and are buried by bureaucratically organized funeral homes in bureaucratically organized cemeteries. And these bureaucratic institutions function upon a permit granted by the largest bureaucratically organized institution of all, the Government itself.[3]

The organizational motif which dominates complex societies is the bureaucracy, which is modern societies' solution to the problem of making decisions with the maximal rationality, of making efficiency automatic and the smooth functioning of society a matter of routine decisions and ready solutions. The law is no exception to this organizational tendency toward bureaucratization.

Through the differentiation of functions characteristic of bureaucracies different organizations emerge, and in the legal system such organizations develop special skills in handling various aspects of the legal procedures. Complex normative structures prescribe the various roles of these organizations. Police departments are charged with the responsibility of detecting law violations, arresting suspected offenders, and gathering the necessary information to enable others to decide whether the case should be brought to trial and, if tried, on the guilt of the offender. The prosecutor is assigned the task of preparing the case for trial and presenting the case of "the State" in court. The judge presumably acts as a disinterested party who decides on guilt or innocence—when a jury is not present—and on the appropriate punishment. A lawyer presumably independent of all the others involved in this procedure is supposed to act on behalf of the accused.

This description of what *is supposed* to happen tells us almost nothing about what *in fact* takes place. None of the functionaries actually perform their tasks in a way wholly conforming to this prescriptive description. Where they are presumed to look objectively at the events around them, they in fact look selectively and subjectively at the events through the lenses of their organizational and bureaucratic perspectives. What we must look at, then, is not only the "blueprint" of the legal system but the actual activity of its role-occupants from day to day, and from year to year.

Every organization is goal-directed. The official goals are expressed in the formal normative structure which defines the positions making up the organization. The goals of the organizations involved in criminal-legal procedures are those expressed in the prescriptions for the operations of these organizations.

Every organization, however, is subject to goal-substitution. Organizations exist in a social context in which both an organization and the individuals who staff its positions find some activities and policies rewarding and others productive of strain. Ever responsive to these inducements and penalties, an *organization and its members tend to substitute for the official goals and norms of the organization, ongoing policies and activities which will maximize the rewards and minimize the strains for the organization.* The activities and policies of law-enforcement agencies which sometimes appear irrational and whimsical to outside observers are in fact quite rational (albeit not necessarily desirable) activities which are designed to maximize organizational rewards and minimize organizational strains. This general principle is reflected in the fact that in the administration of the criminal law *persons are arrested, tried, and sentenced who can offer the fewest rewards for nonenforcement of the laws and who can be processed without creating any undue strain for the organizations which comprise the legal system.* The remainder of this chapter is an elaboration on this general principle.

The most important characteristic which service organizations, such as law-enforcement agencies, share with one another is that they do not produce their own resources. They depend instead on someone else to procure the resources for them. This dependence leads to the organizations' developing a very special relationship with those responsible for the allocation of resources. The organizations must, therefore, take into account the latter's wishes.

In complex societies, the central government allocates resources to its various subsidiary agencies. The political organizations which constitute the government are manned by persons recruited in a variety of ways: in some countries, by direct appointment by those who hold power; in others, by more or less open and fair elections. In the United States, the "power of the purse" is specifically delegated to the legislature. It is *there* that the allocation of resources to law-enforcement agencies is made.

The primary responsibility of the law-enforcement agencies, then, is regarded by them to be a responsibility to those groups that control their resources: at the state level, the governor and the legislators; at the municipal level, the mayor and the city council. Since legislatures are themselves bureaucratically structured, it not infrequently happens that the major source of funds for the law-enforcement agencies is in fact a small handful of legislators manning those legislative committees which make recommendations on law-enforcement funds.

Another important characteristic of service organizations which is shared by law-enforcement agencies is the powerlessness of the client. This powerlessness is both a cause and a consequence of organizational procedures. If the client is unable to muster sufficient support from individuals outside the organization who could cause "trouble" or "strain," then the decision of how to handle him will likely be determined, not according to the official goals of the organization, but solely on the grounds of what is organizationally efficient and (therefore) "right." It thus becomes important for the organization to select as clients those who are unable to cause any particular trouble.

Organizations can do this for two reasons. First, the role-occupants are granted wide areas of discretion. The omnipresence of discretion flows from the necessarily ambiguous nature of rules, or the logical impossibility of having rules that explicitly cover all contingencies. Second, members of organizations invariably work out ways to "beat the system" in order to avoid applying the rules where they do not want them applied. The consequence of this state of affairs is that in most organizations there is sufficient discretion, either authorized or unauthorized, placed in the hands of functionaries at every bureaucratic level, so that most of the decisions made are not predictable simply from knowledge of the rules. Rather, a full understanding of what actually takes place requires the knowledge of how resources are allocated within the organization and how this increases the likelihood of some kinds of decisions being made while decreasing the likelihood of others.

For example, it is a safe bet that, other things being equal, the client's conception of legitimate needs will take second place to making a decision which is likely to be approved by persons at higher levels:

Sensitivity to the Client may often be disadvantageous for the organization man. If, when confronted with an irregular case, he rigidly sticks to organization's norms, he usually fares better than if he tries to bend the norms of the organization to the client's needs or if he bothers his superiors with the case. Furthermore, contact with clients is usually relatively concentrated on the lower levels of the organizations: those who are successful in their relations with clients may find it more difficult to attain promotion than those who prepare themselves for the next, less client-oriented stage by being more organization- than client-minded. To sum up: to be overly client-oriented and to transmit clients' demands upward is a relatively unrewarding experience in any organizations.[4]

14.3 THE MEANS OF GOAL-DISPLACEMENT

We speak of goal-displacement as having occurred when the expressed and agreed-upon goals of the organization are neglected in favor of some other goals. In the context of the present discussion this means usually that some unstated goals of bureaucratic efficiency or smooth functioning displace such goals as serving the client or impartially enforcing the law.

Pervasive pressures towards goal-displacement can succeed only if the persons occupying roles in the organization respond to them. Goal-displacement is thus most likely to take place when one or more of the following conditions are present: first, that the role-occupants are not motivated to resist pressures towards goal-displacement; second, that there exists sufficient uncontrolled discretion to permit goal-displacement to occur; and third, that the norms governing adherence to the explicit goals of the organization are not enforced by the imposition of sanctions.

In point of fact, in most law enforcement agencies all three of these conditions obtain. To begin with, the role-occupants are not motivated to resist the pressures of bureaucracy towards goal-substitution; on the contrary, there is a pervasive subculture (particularly among the police) which explicitly denies the legitimacy of the expressed goals of due process of law which is supposed to govern the behavior of law enforcement personnel (see Chapters 15–17).

Second, discretion is pervasive in the administration of American criminal law: rules are inherently fuzzy in the penumbra, the newer statutory crimes omit entirely the traditionally normative protections against the misuse of discretion by law enforcement officers, and the pluralistic value system of American society encourages the police to be calculating.

Finally, as we shall see in the following chapters, there is a complete and total lack of effective sanctions governing the behavior of police. Although occasionally a police officer, prosecuting attorney or a judge may be prosecuted and censured for violating the official goals of the law, these occurrences are exceedingly rare. The more typical situation is that these officials are protected from exposure of misdeeds and rarely are sanctions imposed.

Given that bureaucratic forces tend to warp the official goals, and given the absence of motivation to resist, the existence of wide areas of discretion, and the absence of effective sanctions, what can one expect? Rarely explicitly formulated, there is a very simple rule which will explain most of the actions of the law-enforcement agencies in complex societies, and which can be derived from the general characteristics of organizational bureaucratization discussed above. The rule is that discretion at every level of law-enforcement will be so exercised as to bring mainly those who are politically powerless into the purview of the law. Whilst the particular groups that are politically powerless vary from society to society, in general the lower classes are the most powerless. They are, therefore, the groups which receive the brunt of the law-enforcement effort and provide the necessary raw materials for keeping the law-enforcement agencies functioning.

In the next two chapters we shall demonstrate the validity of this general proposition by presenting some empirical evidence concerning the legal process. The survey of these data will be best accomplished by examining the various "steps" involved in the legal process: arrest, prosecution, trial, and sentencing.

14.4 SUMMARY

In this chapter, we have outlined a model which provides a framework within which to view the process of law enforcement in complex societies. By way of summary, it is convenient to conceive of this model in terms of the following propositions:

1 The agencies of law-enforcement are bureaucratic organizations.

2 An organization and its members tend to substitute for the official goals and norms of the organization ongoing policies and activities which will maximize rewards and minimize the strains on the organization.

3 This goal-substitution is made possible by:
   a) the absence of motivation on the part of the role-occupants to resist pressures towards goal-substitution;
   b) the pervasiveness of discretionary choice permitted by the substantive criminal law, and the norms defining the roles of the members of the enforcement agencies; and
   c) the absence of effective sanctions for the norms defining the roles in those agencies.

4 Law enforcement agencies depend for resource allocation on political organizations.

5 It will maximize rewards and minimize strains for the organization to process those who are politically weak and powerless, and to refrain from processing those who are politically powerful.

6 Therefore it may be expected that the law-enforcement agencies will process a disproportionately high number of the politically weak and powerless, while ignoring the violations of those with power.

NOTES

1. President's Commission on Law Enforcement and Administration of Justice, *The Challenge of Crime in a Free Society*, U.S. Government Printing Office, 1967.

2. *Report of the President's Commission of Crime in the District of Columbia*, U.S.

Government Printing Office, 1966, p. 241. See also T. G. Russell, "Dylan and the oriental arrest statutes," unpublished manuscript, Cuesta College.

3. See Amitai Etzioni, *Modern Organization*, Prentice-Hall, Englewood Cliffs, N.J., 1964, p. 1.

4. *Ibid.*, p. 100. Reprinted by permission.

15

The investigation and control of criminal activity by the police

A principal identifying characteristic of the State is that it alone can legitimately exercise violence within the polity. The State not only possesses the only legitimate power of violence, but it is required in the interests of the polity to exercise violence from time to time to prevent private parties from exercising violence in *their* private interest.

The State is not a mystical entity, but an enormous, sprawling bureaucratic structure constituted by a vast variety of positions which are defined by different sorts of norms and statuses, and occupied by individual human beings who are subject to the frailties that beset the human condition. Like all bureaucratic structures, the State is theoretically goal-directed; it exists for a set of purposes. The power of violence over which it has a legal monopoly is supposed to be wielded for the purpose of attaining these goals rather than the private goals of the individuals who occupy positions within its structure, or even the organizational goals of the subsystems within it.

Two major questions therefore arise: (1) What are the goals for which this monopoly of violence is to be used, and how are these goals to be translated into norms defining the roles of the individuals occupying official positions? (2) How can the State itself ensure that the role-performance of the individuals occupying these positions will conform to the official norms and goals? In this chapter we discuss the norms which define the role of the policeman, who embodies one of the two significant centers of legitimate power of violence in the State (the other is the military forces).

15.1 THE CONCEPTUAL FRAMEWORK

The value-choice between "law" and "order" implied in the relative specificity of the substantive law is equivalent to a choice between two alternative models of the criminal process, named by Herbert L. Packer the crime-control model and the due-process model.[1] Each of these models entails its own set of value-acceptances.

The crime-control model "is based on the proposition that the repression of criminal conduct is by far the most important function to be performed by the criminal process,"[2] for only by guaranteeing order can individuals in a society be guaranteed social freedom. This model demands that a high proportion of criminal activity be sanctioned. Since the resources allocated to crime-detection and punishment are small, the efficiency of the system must be very high. To achieve such a high efficiency, according to this model, there must be a reliance on the expertise of the police to discover the criminal and weed out the innocent at an early stage in the process. This model is also based on the factual assumption that among the persons whom the police suspect of crime, a relatively high proportion—far higher than the number of criminals in the population—are in fact guilty of criminal activity. There flows from this assumed probability a presumption of guilt—a factual presumption that it is more probable than not that a person suspected by the police is guilty of crime, a presumption whose probability grows constantly higher as the accused passes through the system from stage to stage without being rejected at one point or another.

The due-process model, on the other hand, takes as its central value the protection of noncriminals from physical restraint by agents of the State. Where subscribers to the crime-control model are prepared necessarily to tolerate a certain level of error in determining who is guilty, those who subscribe to the due-process model are not. The central value in the due-process model might be stated in terms of the proposition that it is better that a hundred guilty men go free than that one innocent man be found guilty.

The *presumption of innocence*, which enforces this value-judgment, is in fact not a factual presumption at all. Rather, it is a procedural device which says, in effect, that the coercive power of the State is not to be used until certain procedures have been followed. These are procedures which are designed so far as possible to ensure that the policeman's suspicions of guilt have been independently validated by another and quite distinct agent, the trial court with or without a jury.

If the criminal procedures follow the crime-control model, than it is highly probable that the police will treat various groups in the population in a discriminatory manner. Suspicion is based on probabilities. Every police handbook emphasizes that a competent policeman is always suspicious. The basis of his suspicion must be those characteristics and situations which his experience teaches him are most apt to indicate criminality. Thus a policeman has written in an article on field interrogation:

A. Be suspicious. This is a healthy police attitude, but it should be controlled and not too obvious.
B. Look for the unusual.
  1. Persons who do not "belong" where they are observed.
  2. Automobiles which do not "look right."
  3. Businesses opened at odd hours, or not according to routine or custom.
C. Subjects who should be subjected to field interrogation.
  1. Suspicious persons known to the officer from previous arrests, field interrogations, and observations.
  2. Emaciated appearing alcoholics and narcotics users who invariably turn to crime to pay for the cost of habit.
  3. Persons who fit description as wanted suspect . . .
  4. Any person observed in the immediate vicinity of a crime very recently committed or reported as "in progress."
  5. Known trouble-makers near large gatherings.
  6. Persons who attempt to avoid or evade the officer.
  7. Exaggerated unconcern over contact with the officer.
  8. Visibly "rattled" when near the policeman . . .
  9. Many others. How about your own personal experience?[3]

Certain minority groups, notably blacks, have crime rates that are higher than those for the population at large. (The reasons for this—the extent to which this is the result of poverty forced on them by the white world, and the extent to which it is the result of the policeman's self-fulfilling prophecy—are discussed elsewhere.) Evidently, if the police rely on their experience in determining the characteristics of persons more likely than the average to have committed crime, inevitably they will tend to suspect those who have the characteristics of the people most frequently involved in crime. Since high crime rates are demonstrably intimately connected with poverty, the police will tend to be suspicious of the poor and disinherited minority groups: the blacks, Mexican-Americans, Indians, and Puerto Ricans. The crime-control model, which is based upon the presumption of guilt arising out of the statistical probabilities of policeman's suspicion being correct, thus provides the police will probably operate with extra severity against these groups.

The ideal of due process is protected against this potential for discrimination by two closely connected procedural devices: the presumption of innocence and the requirement that guilt be proven at the trial *beyond a reasonable doubt*. The presumption of innocence requires that at every stage, until the final determination of guilt, every accused person be treated as though he were innocent. It thus purports to guarantee that all of the requisite steps designed to vindicate the policeman's suspicions will be employed, for otherwise, there can be no final determination of guilt. The requirement that proof of guilt be beyond a reasonable doubt is, of course, the precise converse of the presumption of guilt upon which the crime-control model of the criminal process is based.

What is intriguing about these two models is that, while courts, legislatures, and even policemen give lip service to the ideals of due process, in fact they operate largely according to the crime-control model. We shall examine briefly three areas of critical importance in criminal proceedings: the legitimate use of force by policemen to prevent crime or to effectuate arrest, the use of force in determining whether an investigation ought to proceed, and the use of force during the investigation itself.

15.2 THE LIMITS ON THE USE OF VIOLENCE BY THE POLICE

The American policeman regards himself as the embodiment of society's legitimate power of violence. When in uniform, he carries a billyclub, he wears an ammunition belt and a holster with a gun in it, his handcuffs dangle from the belt, he frequently sports a crash helmet, and he carries mace and other incapacitating chemicals. The tools of his trade are instruments of violence.

Society equips the police with the capacity for violence not for the individual benefit of the policeman, but for its own benefit. The result, however, has a dual thrust. Sometimes violence must be used to accomplish society's immediate purposes, e.g. to subdue a violent robber in order to arrest him and make him amenable to the criminal proceedings. Sometimes, however, it must be used by the policeman in his own defense. It is the nature of a policeman's day-to-day work, that he may occasionally come in contact with the most violent elements in society. Police work is probably the only peacetime occupation in which sudden death by knifing or gunshot constitutes a significant occupational hazard. The society therefore equips the policeman with instruments of violence for his own protection, because it is in society's interest that he be able to protect himself; and the police are generally regarded as having a job which is infinitely more dangerous than any other occupation. This conception is in part due to the stereotyped image of police work as consisting in the arrest and pursuit of persons who commit crimes of violence and destruction such as rape, arson, murder, armed robbery, and the like. In point of fact, the policeman is only rarely called upon to arrest or pursue persons engaged in crimes where violence is even remotely possible. The bulk of his day-to-day activities consists in "peace-keeping"— settling domestic quarrels, watching people come and go on streets where crimes rarely occur, arresting a drunk, or rescuing a cat from an ice floe in the local river. Eighty percent of the arrests made by the police every year are for very minor

offenses; over fifty percent of the arrests are for drunkenness alone. Few policemen are threatened with severe bodily harm in any year, and even fewer are
actually killed. Table 15.1 shows a comparison between the number of policemen
killed every year and the number of persons killed by policemen every year. There
are, on the average, four times as many people killed by policemen as there are
policemen killed in the line of duty. Further, given that many of the seventy-odd
policemen killed each year die in automobile accidents and other noncriminal
events, it is clear that the number of police killed each year by "criminals" is
much smaller than the impression given to the public in law-enforcement propaganda. Indeed, firemen, who are generally regarded as having a relatively safe
occupation, are more likely to be killed in the line of duty than are policemen.

These facts notwithstanding, the policeman's job is regarded as a highly
dangerous one. That some policemen are killed is sufficiently impressive to underscore the dangerous nature of the job, although the public image and the image
of the police themselves exaggerate the real danger considerably.

Police in other countries are even less likely to meet with violence than are
the police in the United States. In England it is an extremely rare event when a
police officer is killed in the line of duty. Police work in England is generally
regarded as an exceedingly safe occupation. Certainly streetcar conductors and
bus drivers are in much greater danger of being maimed or killed in the line of
duty than are British police officers. The same holds true in most Scandinavian
and European countries.

The norms which define the permissible use of violence by a policeman are
appropriate to the purposes for which he is given the instruments of violence.
He is permitted to use force either to effectuate the official purposes of taking

TABLE 15.1   Comparison of the number of policemen killed in the line of duty with the
number of persons killed by the police[4]

Year	Persons killed by police				Police killed in line of duty
	Total	*White*	*Black*	*Other*	
1956	226	123	101	2	46
1957	228	119	106	3	45
1958	229	111	116	2	49
1959	227	110	115	2	49
1960	245	125	119	1	48
1961	237	134	100	3	71
1962	187	89	93	2	78
1963	246	111	129	2	88
1964	278	134	141	3	88
1965	271	154	114	3	83
Average per year	237	109	103	2	64

certain categories of criminals into custody or preventing certain sorts of crimes, or to defend himself. The law provides, however, that he use only the minimum amount of force necessary to effectuate these purposes.

The laws which specify the norms for the policeman's role, therefore, do not give him any general license to apply force. Instead, they give him a limited privilege. It is a defense to any charge of police hitting or wounding or killing that the police officer was acting within the scope of his duties or in self-defense. The Wisconsin Criminal Code, for example, provides in part:

939.45. *Privilege.* The fact that the actor's conduct is privileged, although otherwise criminal, is a defense to a prosecution for any crime based on that conduct. The defense of privilege can be claimed under any of the following circumstances: . . .

2 When the actor's conduct is in defense of persons or property under any of the circumstances described in s. 939.48 (relating to self-defense and the defense of others) or 939.49 (relating to the defense of property). While reasonable force can be used to prevent or terminate an unlawful interference with property, "it is not reasonable to intentionally use force intended or likely to cause death or great bodily harm for the sole purpose of defense of one's property," or

3 When the actor's conduct is in good faith and is an apparently authorized and reasonable fulfillment of any duties of a public office; or

4 When the actor's conduct is a reasonable accomplishment of a lawful arrest . . .

The critical question concerning the content of these norms, of course, is the word "reasonable." This is a concept frequently used in law. It has a dual aspect. In the first place, all of us use the question of "reasonableness" as a test of truth. If John claims that he agreed to sell to Mark a ten-year-old Ford sedan in poor condition for an agreed price of $3000, and Mark agrees that he promised to buy the car, but claims that the agreed price was $250, and there is evidence that the market price of such a used car was $250, most of us would tend to believe Mark rather than John. Here we are using the concept of what is "reasonable" in a factual sense, for that report of conduct is more likely to be true, which matches our knowledge of the everyday conduct of most of us.

More frequently, however, the word "reasonable" is used in law to mask a normative concept. It is used by courts and legislatures to cover a variety of cases too wide for precise definition. A legislature cannot be expected to lay out with precision for all possible cases the amount of force which one is entitled to use in effecting an arrest. Instead, in the Wisconsin statute, the legislature says only that the use of force is not criminal when part of a "reasonable accomplishment" of a lawful arrest, leaving for courts and juries to give the word "reasonable" specific contents in specific situations.

Appellate courts have given some content to the term through their decisions. In general, the word "reasonable" has come to mean "necessary." Was the force used no more than was necessary to accomplish the purpose for which the privilege to use force was given? The Wisconsin statute with respect to self-defense codifies the rule which has been evolved in most common-law jurisdictions:

939.48. *Self-Defense and Defense of Others.* (1) A person is privileged to threaten or intentionally use force against another for the purpose of preventing or terminating what he reasonably believes to be an unlawful interference with his person by such other person. The actor may intentionally use only such force or threat thereof as he reasonably believes is necessary to prevent or terminate the interference. He may not intentionally use force which is intended or likely to cause death or great bodily harm unless he reasonably believes that such force is necessary to prevent imminent death or great bodily harm to himself.

The same rule applies in matters of arrest: The police officer is entitled to use only so much force as is necessary to accomplish the arrest.

That the police in general have not internalized the norms defining the permissible use of violence seems quite clear from numerous studies. In a survey[5] of policemen in a midwestern city in 1951, officers were asked to respond to this question: "When do you think a policeman is justified in roughing a man up?" They responded as follows:

Reason	Percentage
Disrespect for police	37
To obtain information	19
For the hardened criminal	7
When you know the man is guilty	3
For sex criminals	3
When impossible to avoid	23
To make an arrest	8

The officers believed that "the only way to treat certain groups of people including Negroes and the poor, is to treat them roughly."[6]

A more recent study conducted for the President's Commission on Crime and Law Enforcement documented through observations the frequency and severity of violence by police as they carried out the routines of their jobs. Researchers recorded their observations in the cities of Boston, Chicago, and Washington, D.C., which were gathered by sitting in patrol cars and monitoring booking and lockup procedures in high-crime precincts for seven weeks, seven days a week. They divided the use of physical force by the police into two categories:[7] First, force was considered undue, unreasonable or unwarranted "only in those cases in which a policeman struck the citizen with his hands, fist, feet or body, or where he used a weapon of some kind—such as a nightstick or a pistol." Secondly,

a physical assault on a citizen was judged to be "improper" or "unnecessary" only when force was used in one or more of the following ways:

1   If a policeman physically assaulted a citizen and then failed to make an arrest; proper use involves an arrest.

2   If the citizen being arrested did not, by word or deed, resist the policeman; force should be used if it is necessary to make an arrest.

3   If the policeman, even though there was resistance to the arrest, could easily have restrained the citizen in other ways.

4   If a large number of policemen were present and could have assisted in subduing the citizen in the station, in lockup, and in the interrogation room.

5   If an offender was handcuffed and made no attempt to flee or offer violent resistance.

6   If the citizen resisted arrest, but the use of force continued even after the citizen was subdued.

This survey of police methods disclosed thirty-seven cases during the period of investigation in which force was used improperly. Forty-four citizens were assaulted by the police during this period. In thirteen of these cases the use of force occurred in the station house when at least four other policemen were present. In about half of these cases the person assaulted by the police was bruised but not seriously hurt; in three cases the person assaulted required hospitalization. The following case was reported, not as necessarily representative, but at least as an indication of the way in which undue force is sometimes used by the police:

The watch began rather routinely as the policemen cruised the district. Their first radio dispatch came at about 5:30 p.m. They were told to investigate two drunks in a cemetery. On arriving they found two white men "sleeping one off." Without questioning the men, the older policeman began to search one of them, ripping his shirt and hitting him in the groin with a nightstick. The younger policeman, as he searched the second, ripped away the seat of his trousers, exposing his buttocks. The policemen then prodded the men toward the cemetery fence and forced them to climb it, laughing at the plight of the drunk with the exposed buttocks. As the drunks went over the fence, one policeman shouted, "I ought to run you fuckers in." The other remarked to the observer, "Those assholes won't be back; a bunch of shitty winos."[8]

Not long after they returned to their car, the policemen stopped a woman who had made a left turn improperly. She was treated very politely, and the younger policeman, who wrote the ticket, later commented to the observer "Nice lady." At 7:30 they were dispatched to check a suspicious auto. After a quick check, the car was marked abandoned.

Shortly after a 30-minute break for a 7:30 "lunch" the two policemen received a dispatch to take a burglary report. Arriving at a slum walkup, the police entered a room where an obviously drunk white man in his late 40's insisted that someone had entered and stolen his food and liquor. He kept insisting that it had been taken and that he had been forced to borrow money to buy beer. The younger policeman, who took the report, kept harassing the man, alternating between mocking and badgering him with rhetorical questions. "You say your name is Half-A-Wit (for Hathaway)? Do you sleep with niggers? How did you vote on the bond issue? Are you sure that's all that's missing? Are you a virgin yet?" The man responded to all of this with the seeming vagueness and joviality of the intoxicated, expressing gratitude for the policemen's help as they left. The older policeman remarked to the observer as they left, "Ain't drunks funny?"

For the next little happened, but as the two were moving across the precinct shortly after 10 p.m., a white man and a woman in their 50's flagged them down. Since they were obviously "substantial" middle-class citizens of the district, the policemen listened to their complaints that a Negro man was causing trouble inside the public-transport station from which they had just emerged. The woman said that he had sworn at her. The older policeman remarked, "What's a nigger doing up here? He should be down on Franklin Road."

With that, they ran into the station and grabbed the Negro man who was inside. Without questioning him, they shoved him into a phone booth and began beating him with their fists and a flashlight. They also hit him in the groin. Then they dragged him out and kept him on his knees. He pleaded that he had just been released from a mental hospital that day and, begging not to be hit again, asked them to let him return to the hospital. One policeman said: "Don't you like us, nigger? I like to beat niggers and rip out their eyes." They took him outside to their patrol car. Then they decided to put him on a bus, telling him that he was returning to the hospital; they deliberately put him on a bus going in the opposite direction. Just before the Negro boarded the bus, he said, "You police just like to shoot and beat people." The first policeman replied, "Get moving, nigger, or I'll shoot you." The man was crying and bleeding as he was put on the bus. Leaving the scene, the younger policeman commented, "He won't be back."[9]

For the rest of the evening, the two policemen kept looking for drunks and harassing any they found. They concluded the evening by being dispatched to an address where, they were told, a man was being held for the police. No one answered their knock. They left.

Another case is also illustrative:

White officers responded to a man with a gun ... and heard three shots fired. Then the white man with the gun got a drop on the officer—somehow they got the gun away and handcuffed him (gun was a 12 gauge 1905 musket). When they got him to the station garage, they kicked him all over, but the principal one was the officer who had been in danger when the man had the drop on him. He beat him as the others held him up. I got to the scene and the lockup man whistled for them to stop but they didn't. The Lieutenant arrived with everyone else and said there's going to be a beef on this one so cover it up and go find the empty shells. Someone call an ambulance (he needed it badly). Then the Lieutenant took complete control. They got the shells, got a complainant who said the three shots were an attempt to kill the officer, and he would sign a complaint, said he called an ambulance, etc. They wrote a cover for the incident. The officer who beat the man most was shaken by then but the others gave him support, telling him how brave he was and how wise he had been not to kill the guy at the scene, etc. They then set about to put all the stories in order and I was carefully notified of it in detail so I would have it straight. I had enough rapport with these officers that they talked about it even after. The man was in pretty bad shape when he got to the hospital.[10]

The researcher also observed assaults on suspects in lockups and station houses.

It is important to keep in mind that in many of these cases the police were well aware that they were being observed. One can only understand their willing-ness to behave in such a manner despite the presence of observers by realizing that from the perspective of the police their actions were completely justified. Indeed, it is standard police rhetoric to refer to anyone who objects to such practices as "bleeding hearts"—an expression reminiscent of President Johnson's comment about "nervous nellies" who opposed the escalation of the Viet Nam War. The police respond to criticisms of their tactics with rhetorical questions about the desire of some "softheaded fools" who want them to treat everyone with "TLC" (tender loving care).

It is undoubtedly the case, however, that in the presence of observers the police are more reticent in the use of undue force than they would be otherwise. If violence is a common pattern of police behavior even in the presence of observers, then such violence is bound to occur when the police are not under observation, if only because we all have the tendency to rely on established patterns of actions, and also because of the aroused emotions of the moment. But in all likelihood the observed frequency of violence represents a sizeable reduction over what routinely takes place. Thus it seems safe to assume that however much violence was discovered in this study, it was an underestimate of the actual amount of violence taking place.

Although the estimate of the overall frequency of undue police violence is undoubtedly conservative, nonetheless, the frequency is quite high. Using as a base the 643 white suspects encountered by the police during the period of study, the researchers report a rate of police abuse of 41.9 per 1000 suspects. This rate is much higher, incidentally, than the rates of crimes of violence among the population, and almost one thousand times as high as the murder rate in the United States. For black defendants, the abuse rate is lower but still of some con-sequence. Of 751 black suspects 17 experienced undue use of force—a rate of 22.6 per 1000.

There is no ready explanation for the unusual finding that blacks experience less violence at the hands of the police than whites of the same social class. Indeed, the data reported earlier on the number of persons killed by police indicated that blacks were much more likely to be killed than whites, considering their proportion in the population. The two findings, then, are in conflict. It would be premature to conclude from these observations that the blacks are less likely to be the recipient of police violence than whites are, and much other impressionistic evidence suggests just the reverse of this is the case. It seems likely that this dis-crepancy has something to do with the characteristics of this particular study rather than reflecting a general tendency in the police departments. Certainly if the cities studied were in the south, it would have been most surprising if the same results were obtained. Until more data become available, we should hold this question in abeyance.

The important finding for the analysis at hand is that the poor are much more likely to be on the receiving end of illegal police violence than other groups in the society. Black or white, the likelihood of being a victim of police brutality is highly correlated with being poor. It is the poor man in the slums, be he a white wino or a black teenager, who faces the prospect of being brutalized by the police. In the words of the report, "the lower class bears the brunt of victimization by the police."

As was the case in the responses to the questionnaire mentioned earlier in this chapter, a frequent reason for the use of unwarranted force and violence by the police was the attempt to "instill respect" in the citizens for the police. One policeman commented to the observer: "On the street you can't beat them. But when you get them to the station, you can instill some respect in them." The research team found that open defiance of police authority was present in 39% of the cases where the police used undue force. It is important to realize, however, that:

Open defiance of police authority . . . is what the policeman defines as *his* authority, not necessarily "official" authority. Indeed in 40% of the cases that the police considered open defiance, the policeman never executed an arrest.[11]

There are indications that the tendency of police to be overly quick in reacting with violence has increased dramatically since the onset of urban riots in the black ghettos, the increased frequency of peace demonstrations, and the emergence of militant and quasimilitary groups of blacks advocating self-protection for the black community. The police response to these changes in the American scene has generally been repressive and intimidating. The consequence has been that police are more likely to use undue force when arresting or questioning blacks than they have been previously, though the tendency has always been strong. When the police attempt to exert total control over the situation, it often means that they would resort to violence at the slightest provocation or perhaps when no provocation is forthcoming save the appearance of "the man." The following case is illustrative:

A black man was stopped for making an illegal left turn. He was a large man with a beard and semi-hippie attire. The police officer approached the car and pushed the man up against the side; when the black man objected to the treatment the officer and his partner beat the man to the ground. A further beating was administered at the station-house.[12]

The police in this particular city reported that they were "very wary" of black men with beards and Afro-style clothing. It was the feeling of the police that all such men were potentially dangerous to the policeman's safety and that therefore the latter had to keep the upper hand at all times, even to the point of using violence *before* any was used toward him.

In several cities the police and prosecuting attorneys' offices have gone on open campaigns to harass and intimidate members of the Black Panthers. In Oakland,

California, off-duty policemen once entered the offices of the Black Panther Party and shot holes in a picture of Huey Newton which was hanging on the wall. In New York City, off-duty policemen once attacked and beat up blacks in a courtroom. In Seattle, the police, at the direction of a prosecuting attorney, have indiscriminately arrested and unnecessarily used force against members of the Black Panther Party.

The use of force in cases of crowd and riot control is another problem entirely. In the case of brutality or excessive violence by an individual officer, it is traditionally argued by police apologists that the problem is not systemic but individual to the officers involved. In many cases involving crowd control, however, the excessive use of violence by the police involved seems to be on such a wide scale that it is hard to believe that the incident was not officially encouraged or condoned. For example, a national news magazine described how the police ejected students conducting a sit-in at Columbia University in 1968: At one building,

police threw dozens of students from inside the building to rows of policemen and plainclothesmen outside, where some were punched, kicked and hit with clubs and handcuffs. One blond girl was thrown to the brick sidewalk and beaten unconscious... In some areas (of the campus) the police behaved with restraint; in others they were vicious. [13]

Similar stories could be quoted of police action at a substantial number of civil rights demonstrations, student demonstrations, and riots. Since in every case there are well-documented stories and even motion pictures showing policemen beating citizens even after they had fallen to the ground, there can be little doubt that the police in such a case had gone beyond the legitimate use of force provided for by the statutes.

The best-investigated instance of police violence during demonstrations is provided by the "Walker Report," which is an analysis of the riot that occurred during the Democratic National Convention in Chicago in 1968. During the convention large numbers of demonstrators gathered in the city to protest against the war in Vietnam, the method of selecting presidential candidates, and the "establishment." The response of the police, according to the report prepared for the National Commission on the Causes and Prevention of Violence, was to employ large-scale force and violence. The report termed the disturbance in Chicago a "police riot."

The control of the police power completely broke down. Demonstrators, reporters, passers-by, and onlookers were indiscriminately attacked, beaten, and assaulted by policemen:

police action was not confined... to necessary force even in clearing the park: A young man and his girl friend were both grabbed by officers. He screamed "We're going, we're going," but they threw him into the pond. The officers grabbed the girl, knocked her to the ground, dragged her along the embankment and hit her with their batons on her head, arms, back and legs. The boy tried to scramble up the embankment to her, but police shoved him back in the water at least twice. He finally got to her and tried to pull her in the water, away from the police. He was clubbed on the head five or six times. An officer shouted, "Let's get the fucking bastards," but the boy pulled her in the water and the police left.

Like the incident described above, much of the violence witnessed in Old Town that night seems malicious or mindless:

There were pedestrians. People who were not part of the demonstration were coming out of a tavern to see what the demonstration was . . . and the officers indiscriminately started beating everybody on the street who was not a policeman.

Another scene:

There was a group of about six police officers that moved in and started beating two youths. When one of the officers pulled back his nightstick to swing, one of the youths grabbed it from behind and started beating on the officer. At this point about ten officers left everybody else and ran after this youth, who turned down Wells and ran to the left.

But the officers went to the right, picked up another youth, assuming he was the one they were chasing, and took him into an empty lot and beat him. And when they got him to the ground, they just kicked him ten times—the wrong youth, the innocent youth who had been standing there.

A federal legal official relates an experience of Tuesday evening.

"I then walked one block north where I met a group of 12–15 policemen. I showed them my identification and they permitted me to walk with them. The police walked one block west. Numerous people were watching us from their windows and balconies. The police yelled profanities at them, taunting them to come down where the police would beat them up. The police stopped a number of people on the street demanding identification. They verbally abused each pedestrian and pushed one or two without hurting them. We walked back to Clark Street and began to walk north where the police stopped a number of people who appeared to be protesters, and ordered them out of the area in a very abusive way. One protester who was walking in the opposite direction was kneed in the groin by a policeman who was walking towards him. The boy fell to the ground and swore at the policeman who picked him up and threw him to the ground. We continued to walk toward the command post. A derelict who appeared to be very intoxicated, walked up to the policeman and mumbled something that was incoherent. The policeman pulled from his belt a tin container and sprayed its contents into the eyes of the derelict, who stumbled around and fell on his face.

"It was on these nights that the police violence against media representatives reached its peak. Much of it was plainly deliberate. A newsman was pulled aside on Monday by a detective acquaintance of his who said: 'The word is being passed to get newsmen.' Individual newsmen were warned, 'You take my picture tonight and I'm going to get you.' Cries of 'get the camera' preceded individual attacks on photographers."

A newspaper photographer describes Old Town on Monday at about 9:00 P.M.:

"When the people arrived at the intersection of Wells and Division, they were not standing in the streets. Suddenly a column of policemen ran out from the alley. They were reinforcements. They were under control but there seemed to be no direction. One man was yelling, 'Get them up on the sidewalks, turn them around.' Very suddenly the police charged the people on the sidewalks and began beating their heads. A line of cameramen was 'trapped' along with the crowd along the sidewalks, and the police went down the line chopping away at the cameras."

A network cameraman reports that on the same night:

"I just saw this guy coming at me with his nightstick and I had the camera up. The tip of his stick hit me right in the mouth, then I put my tongue up there and I noticed that my tooth was gone. I turned around then to try to leave and then this cop came up behind me with his stick and he jabbed me in the back.

"All of a sudden these cops jumped out of the police cars and started just beating the hell out of people. And before anything else happened to me, I saw a man holding a Bell & Howell camera with big wide letters on it, saying 'CBS.' He apparently had been hit by a cop. And cops were standing around and there was blood streaming down his face. Another policeman was running after me and saying, 'Get the fuck out of here.' And I heard another guy scream, 'Get their fucking cameras.' And the next thing I know I was being hit on the head, and I think on the back, and I was forced down on the ground at the corner of Division and Wells."[14]

After the "police riot" in Chicago, 101 demonstrators were hospitalized for injuries sustained in attacks by policemen. An additional 425 persons were treated at seven medical facilities set up by the Medical Committee for Human Rights. Over 200 more persons were treated by the Committee's mobile medical teams, and the committee estimated that over 400 persons were given first aid for tear gas or mace.[15]

Reports of police actions in cities that have experienced riots in the black ghettos are similar. The number of civilians killed is difficult to estimate because of the police effort to suppress such statistics, but reliable estimates for the riot in Newark, New Jersey, alone range from thirty-five to well over fifty. Of these civilians killed, according to one of the participants, only a very small handful were shot while breaking the law; almost all the rest were shot while they were in the area but not engaged in any illegal activity.[16]

The typical response of police departments to public criticism of such behavior by large groups of officers is to close ranks in defense. The standard excuse is that the police met with "resistance." For example, after the Columbia incident referred to above, the New York Commissioner of Police is reported to have said that "his men encountered 'a good deal of resistance' when they entered the buildings (to eject the demonstrators)."[17] Sometimes the fact that demonstrators used vile and abusive language at the police or spat at them is given as the excuse: "After all, the police are human." However, a policeman's privilege of using violence, as the Wisconsin statute states, extends to self-defense only in cases of "unreasonable interference with his person." The use of abusive language is not an interference with the person. Similarly, during the Democratic Convention in Chicago in 1968, the police were shown on television screens across the country swinging night sticks and beating numerous demonstrators. In this case, the police and the mayor of the city defended the police action by arguing that they had had advance knowledge of the potential violence of some of the demonstrators, including the fact that some of the demonstrators were armed with lethal weapons. The police and public officials in this instance justified the excessive use of violence by the police on the grounds that the police were potentially endangered.

The use of violence *in excess* of the amount necessary to accomplish the purposes for which the right to use violence is granted is the limiting case of crime-control, where the police are in fact themselves punishing the suspect for the claimed misconduct, basing the punishment entirely on their own perceptions of guilt and, frequently, their own conception of what constitutes criminal behavior, and where all the procedural protections of accusation, hearing, and sentencing are abandoned.

It must be stressed that the tendency for the police to use violence is not a necessary outcome of police organization in complex societies. In England large peace demonstrations have apparently met with cooperative and patient police reaction. Indeed, policemen have even been attacked by demonstrators and refused to respond with violence. In a recent British demonstration where thousands of people were marching, where the police had been forewarned that some of the marchers were planning to destroy public buildings and physically attack the police, where rumors had reached the police that "outside agitators" were coming to stir the crowd to riot, the police responded with great restraint and a general unwillingness to use violence even in the face of violence being used against them. Reports have it that by the end of the day, the demonstrators who remained into the night eventually joined hands with the policemen and concluded the day's march with song—with the policemen joining in.

Although systematic data are not available, what evidence there is suggests that the police in the United States are among the most violent in the world. However, even in the United States there are wide variations in the propensity of different law-enforcement agencies to resort to violence in the treatment of suspects. What little evidence there is suggests that federal prisoners are less likely to be the victims of violence than state prisoners. Arnold Trebach interviewed inmates in penitentiaries in New Jersey, Pennsylvania, and in a federal prison and found 54% of the New Jersey prisoners claiming that the police had either used or threatened to use violence, 41% of the Philadelphia prisoners making the same claim (and this was mainly the threat of violence), and 22% of the federal prisoners making this claim. Furthermore, 70% of the federal prisoners responded that they had been "treated well" by the federal police.[18]

The reasons for the police violence also vary. In the study cited above, 70% of the New Jersey prisoners who had been subjected to violence maintained that this was done to coerce confessions, whereas there were very few such claims either in Philadelphia or among federal prisoners. Indeed, among the New Jersey prisoners 22% claimed that they had signed confessions as a consequence of police violence, but none of the Philadelphia prisoners and only 5% of the federal prisoners made similar claims.

Is police brutality a recent phenomenon? If not, why has it suddenly been pressed into public concern?

There can be little doubt that police brutality is as American as apple pie and has almost as long a history. It has been hidden for generations, along with the Other America, by the walls that separate the middle class and the urban poor. In recent years, the growing loss of legitimacy of the American government has led to wide-spread civil rights demonstrations, anti-war demonstrations, and campus protests. Police brutality could no longer be hidden. Urban riots have frequently been diagnosed as having been triggered by police violence, and urban riots cannot be concealed. The same militancy which has brought about civil rights demonstrations has induced blacks to challenge police brutality on a variety of levels. The long-continued pressure of moral entrepreneurs, such as the American Civil Liberties Union, has succeeded in casting some light on the dark shadows of police station back rooms.

15.3 THE INITIATION OF A CRIMINAL INVESTIGATION

The Norms of Search and Arrest: Historical Background

Perhaps nowhere in the entire range of police activities is there a greater disparity between the "law in the books" and the "law in action" than with respect to police activity in determining whether or not to initiate an investigation. In order to understand the disparity between the norm and the practice, we must look into the history of the problem.

As the Supreme Court noted in *United States v. Wade,*

When the Bill of Rights was adopted, there were no organized police forces as we know them today. The accused confronted the prosecutor, and the evidence against him was marshalled, largely at the trial itself.[19]

The Founding Fathers had been taught the lessons of oppression by both the British and their own colonial government. They therefore incorporated a variety of guarantees that trials would be truly adversary proceedings in which the accused were protected from the start of the investigation by the presumption of innocence until actually found guilty. They incorporated into the Bill of Rights guarantees against unlawful searches, seizures, and self-incrimination, and for due process of law; they instituted requirements for jury trials, indictments, and right to counsel in criminal cases.

These guaranteed rights originated in the great English State trials; that is, they arose from political cases. They were incorporated into the Constitution not as devices to protect the poor and the impoverished from indiscriminate police harassment, but as means to protect citizens against governmental suppression of dissent.[20] They arose in a social context in which there was no systematic policing of urban areas by an organized body of armed men charged with the specific responsibility of deterring or preventing crime.

The police role today, at least as frequently conceived of by members of polite middle-class society, and certainly as conceived of by the police themselves, requires them not merely to arrest men for crimes, but also to actively patrol the streets in order to suppress incipient wrong-doing. A prominent spokesman for the police point of view has said:

To prevent crime, the police must either stand guard at every point of possible attack, which is a physical and economic impossibility, or intercept the person with criminal intent before he robs, rapes or kills. It is better to have an alert police force that prevents crime than one that devotes its time in seeking to identify the assailant after the life has been taken, the daughter ravished, or the pedestrian slugged and robbed . . .

The typical citizen would feel that the police were remiss in their duty should they fail on their own initiative, or refuse on legal grounds, to investigate by questioning a person who was lurking in the neighborhood for no apparent reason. The disturbed citizen would expect the police to discover whether the suspect was armed, and if so to disarm him and prosecute him should it be discovered that he was carrying the weapon illegally. Should the suspect refuse to explain what he was doing in the neighborhood, and the policeman apologized for questioning him and then went about his duties leaving the suspect to continue his lurking, the citizen would consider that he was not receiving adequate protection . . . [21]

Before the existence of organized police forces, however, the question of the policeman's powers to stop a citizen and detain him for questioning did not arise. Constables and other colonial peace officers did not have the responsibility of patrolling the neighborhood with general authority to maintain peace and good order. Their responsibilities were heavy enough,[22] but with respect to crime their principal duty was the service of process. In that simpler time (circa 1768, in New York),

The engines of the law were usually set in motion against persons accused of minor and sometimes serious offenses when the injured person would appear before a committing magistrate alleging the commission of a crime. The accusing witness would then enter his accusation in the form of an affidavit which was in the nature of an information on oath. The accused very often was called into court by the constable or sheriff, perhaps at the behest of the accuser, and the committing magistrate would then take an "examination" of the accused.[23]

In the case of more serious crimes, unless the offender was caught red-handed, a warrant of arrest would be issued by a magistrate on application of an official, either before or after indictment by a grand jury.[24] Moreover, it was apparently already a settled law that ordinarily there could be no search without a warrant.[25]

The institutions of colonial society were therefore so structured that criminal process was almost invariably initiated by the action of a magistrate in issuing a warrant, either of arrest or of search. There was no other way for the process to begin, unless the decision to arrest were to be made by the constable himself, the mere "spit-dog of the treadmill of government."[26]

The governments of eighteenth-century England and the American colonies circumvented the settled law governing search and arrest, not by abandoning the formalities of the warrant procedure, but by obtaining warrants on little or no specific information, and by the issuance of writs of assistance and general warrants. As a result, the governments could arrest persons on warrants which did not name them and which did not contain accusations charging them with specific offenses; they could search premises on mere suspicion, although protected by the form of a warrant. The practice was denounced by James Otis in 1761 as exemplifying "the worst instruments of arbitrary power," placing "the liberty of every man in the hands of every petty officer."

It was toward these evils that the Fourth Amendment to the Constitution was directed[27]:

The right of the people to be secure in their persons, houses, papers and effects, against unreasonable searches and seizures, shall not be violated, and no Warrants shall issue, but upon probable cause, supported by Oath or affirmation, and particularly describing the place to be searched, and the persons or things to be searched.

Search Warrants

The problem which we face today is the extent to which the Fourth Amendment, drawn to meet a different problem in a different social context, expresses a central policy of law-enforcement which should be transmuted through the course of judicial decision-making into norms applicable to police activity in a very different age and a very different sort of society. The Fourth Amendment might have been interpreted narrowly, according to its plain meaning, as merely prohibiting the specific actions cited. On the other hand, it may be regarded as a concrete embodiment of a significant aspect of the ideal of due process, for it requires that neither citizens nor their property may be taken into custody without the arresting officer's having met the standards set forth in the Amendment, and those standards are obviously higher than mere suspicion.

In fact, the Supreme Court has identified two central criteria for the issuance of warrants: that the evidence described in the oath or affirmation be sufficiently weighty that it can be fairly characterized as constituting "probable cause," and that it be issued only on the independent and presumably disinterested determination by a magistrate that the evidence disclosed meets that standard.[28]

Actually, however, the requirements for a warrant are almost entirely nullified by the development of other rules lending constitutional sanction to arrests and searches without warrant—primarily the rule permitting a search that accompanies a valid arrest without warrant. In Philadelphia, a sample of 770 arrests made in 1952 showed that only about 3% of them were authorized by arrest warrants and "the use of search warrants in the cases examined was virtually non-existent," although searches were involved.[29] In Detroit, from 1956 through 1963, only a total of 288 search warrants were issued.[30] They were used mainly for vice crimes: gambling, narcotics, and traffic in pornographic or obscene materials.[31] Even where courts stringently apply the rules governing the admissibility of evidence gathered without a warrant, the police frequently circumvent the intent of the rule by first making an illegal search and then, if evidence of criminal activity is found, obtaining a warrant to make a "legal" search.

Arrest

The rules which were originally developed for governing the issuance of warrants have come to be assimilated to the law of arrest by a curious route. According to common law and by statute today in many jurisdictions, a police officer is permitted to make an arrest without warrant if he has reasonable grounds to believe that a felony was committed and that the accused committed the crime.[32] Arrests for misdemeanors typically may be made only if the misdemeanor was committed in the presence of the officer and he has reasonable grounds to believe that the accused committed the offense. Since warrants for arrest may be issued only if a probable cause has been presented, the concept of "reasonable grounds" for arrest has been equated to the requirement of probable cause.

That it would be intolerable if the police had the power to detain persons at random is evident. The question that arises is the degree of probability that must be shown before the awesome power of the State could be exercised coercively against the individual. As we suggested earlier, the very nature of the law of probabilities makes it likely that persons who belong to a minority group with a high crime rate will be subject to police suspicion rather more easily than others simply because of their group identity. To permit an arrest on that basis alone necessarily builds into the law of arrest the objective fact of discrimination.

By the very nature of the crimes involved and the required process by which arrests were ordered, the common-law tradition tended to make the probabilities of discrimination in arrest relatively low. Where the crime involved has an identifiable complaining victim, as in colonial America, the dual requirements that there be a probable cause for believing that a crime was committed and for believing that the accused committed the crime are usually both fulfilled. The fact that a crime was committed is demonstrated almost invariably in the story of the complainant, and the central issue is whether there is sufficient evidence to focus the probabilities of guilt upon the named individual. Once it is certain or at least highly probable that a felony was committed at a specific time and place, the circle of possible suspects is reduced sharply. While innocents may still be falsely suspected because they possess some of the characteristics of the accused criminal, the population of possible suspects is limited by temporal and geographical circumstances.

In *Mallory v. United States*,[33] for example, a woman reported that while in the basement of an apartment house she had been raped by a masked Negro of a certain build, which she was able to describe. The Negro janitor, his wife, and their two grown sons, a younger son, and the janitor's half-brother lived in a basement apartment. The two grown sons and the half-brother all fitted the general description. There were no others in the neighborhood who fitted the description. While the Supreme Court expressed some doubt that probable cause existed for the arrest of any of the three, at least the evidence which existed for a specific crime drew a circle limiting the persons subject to suspicion.

Where the crime is one without a victim and hence without a visible harm, and officers are to search out the criminal activity, the problem posed is quite different. In lieu of an individual with no apparent motive to lie about the commission of the crime, the police must necessarily depend heavily on informants, in many cases persons with criminal records themselves with strong motivations to obtain police favors.[34] In the absence of an informer, and pressed to "prevent crime," police are then apt to be suspicious of criminal activity on the basis of very slight evidence indeed.

It is possible to capture addicts by cruising in an unmarked car in certain neighborhoods and looking for what the police call "furtive" movements—a shuffling that indicates to the eye of the skilled narcotics policeman that his suspect is trying to dispose of a "joint of weed" (marijuana cigarette) or a "dime paper" (ten-dollar package of heroin).[35]

While the observation of such furtive movements undoubtedly leads to a substantial number of valid arrests, as demonstrated by the number of cases in which convictions have been obtained on the basis of marijuana or heroin seized at the time of the arrest, there is no information about how many persons have been stopped and searched on the basis of movements which, although furtive, were innocent. Such cases remain beneath the visibility line. They embody the principle of the crime-control model, for the decision regarding the invocation of State power in these cases is dependent on the policeman's suspicion of criminal activity.

Stop and Frisk

The extreme practice prescribed by such a model is the "stopping and frisking" by the police of every person of whom they are "suspicious." Police call this "field interrogation." Almost without exception, they believe that the practice is essential to adequate crime-control.[36]

Whether this practice falls within the constitutional prohibition of "unreasonable searches and seizures" is debatable. A policeman, like anyone else, no doubt has the privilege of asking a question of a person in the street.[37] What is most obscure is whether the police officer has the power to search the person stopped, or to hold him against his will even for a brief period.

Two arguments have been suggested. In the first place, the word "arrest" has sometimes been limited to mean "taking into custody that he may be held to answer for a crime."[38] By assimilating the constitutional word "seizure" to "arrest," as so construed, therefore, some courts have made relatively brief detentions for field interrogation immune from constitutional attack. This argument was rejected by the Supreme Court in *Terry v. Ohio*. There the Court said:

It is quite plain that the Fourth Amendment governs "seizures" of the person which do not eventuate in a trip to the station house and prosecution for crime—"arrests" in traditional terminology. It must be recognized that whenever a police officer accosts an individual and restrains his freedom to walk away he has "seized" that person.[39]

Hence even a field interrogation must be subject to the constitutional requirement that the "seizure" not be "unreasonable."

The second argument that has been made is that the degree of probability required for stopping and frisking is a variable one, depending on time, place, and circumstances. In *Terry*, the Court said that to assess the reasonableness of the police conduct there at issue,

it is necessary "first to focus upon the governmental interest which allegedly justifies official intrusion upon the constitutionally protected interests of the private citizen," for there is "no ready test for determining reasonableness other than by balancing the need to search [or seize] against the invasion which the search [or seizure] entails." Camara v. Municipal Court, 387 U.S. 523, 87 S. Ct. 1727, 18 L. Ed. 2d 930 (1967). And in justifying the particular intrusion the police officer must be able to point to specific and articulable facts which, taken together, with rational inferences from those facts, reasonably warrant that intrusion. The scheme of the Fourth Amendment becomes meaningful only when it is assured that at some point the conduct of those charged with enforcing the laws can be subjected to the more detached, neutral scrutiny of a judge who must evaluate the reasonableness of a particular search or seizure in light of particular circumstances.[40]

Mr. Justice Douglas dissented from this holding. He argued that before a warrant for arrest could be issued by a magistrate there must be facts sufficient to warrant a finding of "probable cause" that a crime had been committed, was in the process of being committed, or was about to be committed. To permit a policeman to stop-and-frisk on a lesser factual basis effectively permits the police officer to make an arrest and a search on grounds substantially less than those upon which a magistrate would constitutionally be permitted to order an arrest.[41]

A number of states, following the lead of New York, have enacted "stop-and-frisk" laws. These laws in general purport to authorize police officers to detain a person for a limited time where he "reasonably suspects" that the detainee has been, is committing, or is about to commit a felony, and may search the person of a detainee when he has "reasonable ground to *believe* that he is in danger of life or limb."[42] The constitutionality of the New York statute fell for decision in *Sibron v. New York* and *Peters v. New York*.[43] The Court, however, declined to consider the constitutionality of these statutes on their face. Instead, the Court rested on the standards of *Terry v. Ohio*, and proceeded to adjudge in each case whether there were constitutionally sufficient grounds for the search and seizure.

The current doctrine, therefore, leaves the norms of stop-and-frisk very vague indeed. To make the reasonableness of a particular field interrogation depend on a "balancing" of the need to stop-and-frisk against the invasion thereby entailed, leaves an extraordinarily wide scope for police discretion. To require "specific and articulable facts" which "reasonably warrant" the intrusion at least makes it clear that mere suspicion not generated on some observable activity by the suspect will not suffice to pluck a stop-and-frisk out from under the constitutional umbrella.

15.4 SEARCH AND ARREST PRACTICE

Searches

In practice, the police engage in wholesale violations of the norms laid down for their conduct. Illegal searches without warrants are made daily. A study of the "racket court" in Chicago for the year 1950, for example, revealed that in 4673 out of 6649 cases, the defendant raised an objection to the legality of the search by the police. In 4593 of these cases, the court granted a motion to suppress the evidence on the ground that the search was illegal.

Arrests

The record with respect to arrests is, if anything, even more formidable. Police make arrests knowing that the arrests are improper, using the detention incident to arrest as a form of sanction. An arrest made without the purpose of taking the person arrested before a court is plainly illegal.[44] Yet it is done daily. Drunks are continually being arrested, allegedly for their own safety. Year after year, in the United States, drunkenness and disorderly-conduct arrests account for over 50% of all the arrests made in the country.[45] The Detroit *Police Manual* recognizes two categories of drunks: so-called "golden-rule" drunks, who are released after reaching sobriety, and others. In 1956, for example, 5865 intoxicated persons arrested were treated as "golden-rule" drunks and released; 8665 were prosecuted. Wayne R. LaFave reports that:

The golden rule procedure is normally confined to non-habitual drunks and is regularly applied to this class . . . Because the procedure is thus limited, it is more commonly applied to those found outside the "skid row" area . . . [46]

Suspected prostitutes are also arrested, without any "probable cause," as part of a calculated system of harassment of prostitutes which the police employ because they are dissatisfied with the difficulty of obtaining convictions in soliciting cases. In a prostitution case, most courts require the prosecution to establish before a conviction that the woman accosted the officer, not vice versa; that the woman suggested an immoral act, and its nature; and that the woman set the price for her favors.[47] Since these matters are frequently difficult to establish, police "do something" about prostitution by making arrests which they know cannot result in successful prosecutions, i.e., without probable cause. A Detroit police official stated candidly that such arrests were made for several reasons:

First, to get them off the street; second, as a means of harassment. It's a deterrent. They know when certain officers are on the job they are very likely to be picked up and they won't go over on that corner. These particular women I referred to are not only prostitutes but they are decoys for the so-called Murphy game. There have been persons murdered who came into contact with them. As a general rule, in fact almost invariably, these women are out there at two o'clock when the saloons close, when the prospective customers have a lot of liquor in them. They don't want to go home; they are looking for strange experiences. And we've had murders. We had one fellow that was found in an ashcan. There's our problem—we have no crimes committed in the presence of the police, nothing that legally warrants the arrest. Shall we say "Well, now because our hands are tied, we are going to let these women alone?"[48]

In Detroit, one precinct in the heart of the district where prostitution is common reported 2942 arrests in a six-month period for "disorderly persons investigation"—a euphuism for arresting a prostitute without sufficient evidence for a prosecution—and only 56 arrests for soliciting, in the same period. Many of these arrests were made when the woman was not even "on the street." One prostitute brought before a station lieutenant asked, "Is it fair to take us out of a restaurant while we are eating?"[49] Some arrests were made of women who were not prostitutes, and some precinct lieutenants in Detroit try to discover this by questioning. Others, however, simply lock up for the night all women arrested as prostitutes without investigation. LaFave states that "even with the most cautious lieutenant on duty, it is presumed that the girl brought in is a prostitute, and she is released only if it is quite definitely shown that she is not"[50]—a remarkably clear example of the operative presumption of guilt that obtains when the law-enforcement agencies aim primarily at crime-control.

A third important category of persons who are habitually arrested by police without a whisper of probable cause is the transvestite. Transvestitism is not a crime, although it is doubtless offensive to many citizens. The arrest is apparently made both to control the practice and to try to extract information about homosexuals from the transvestite. "Like the streetwalking prostitute, they can be observed by the general public. Their presence is likely to be an affront to the ordinary citizen, and the failure of the police to do something may be interpreted as an indication of lax enforcement."[51]

The final significant category of formal but unlawful arrests, made for purposes other than prosecution, are for gambling and liquor-law violations. This type of arrest frequently goes hand-in-hand with "searches" made, not for the purpose of discovering evidence, but for the purpose of destroying evidence. For example, the Boston *Globe* of March 19, 1961 reported:

Slattery's Spoilers—taking a tip from Eliot Ness—struck in East Boston yesterday and arrested 31 men in a scene straight out of the Roaring Twenties.

Gambling raids by Police Deputy John J. Slattery and his special squad have become so commonplace that almost every bookie in town can see them coming. But yesterday, Slattery added a new wrinkle as he swooped down on the New Deal Associates clubhouse at 978 Saratoga St. First, he rented a panel truck. Then, he ordered his men to dress in battered hats and caps. The 12 officers in plainer than plain clothes piled into the closed truck. They carried sledgehammers in case they had to smash down the door. The rest was almost automatic. When the truck pulled up in front of the converted stores, two men were coming out the door. The raiders promptly hustled them back in. Slattery told the 31 men inside that if the Bookie would step forward he would release all the rest. No one volunteered. All were taken to East Boston police station and charged with being present where gaming implements were found.

Slattery said that some of the men had horse play slips in their pockets. In all, more than $3000 was taken from the suspects, police said. The raid followed many complaints from wives that their husbands were losing too much money, Slattery said. He said that the establishment was averaging $30,000 a week.

His squad literally took the place apart—removing window mouldings, floorboards and the like in search for playing pads and other gambling equipment.[52]

Persons believed by the police to be members of gambling rings—runners, bookmakers, and others—and liquor-law violators are subjected to punitive arrests without intention to prosecute just as are prostitutes. In such cases, the cash, automobiles, and telephones in the places raided are usually confiscated even when, as usually happens, the owners are not prosecuted for the offense. In six months, in one precinct in Detroit, the police confiscated $8810.31 from 582 individuals, only 24 of whom were prosecuted.[53]

The purposes of the arrests in these cases are explicitly punitive. An assistant prosecutor in Detroit told Wayne LaFave.

The laws in Michigan with respect to gambling are most inadequate. This is equally true of the punishment feature of the law . . . The Detroit gamblers and numbers men confidently feel that the odds are in their favor. If they operate for six months or a year, and accumulate untold thousands of dollars from the illegal activity, then the meager punishment imposed upon them if they are caught is well worth it. Then, too, because of the search and seizure laws in Michigan, especially in regard to gambling and the numbers game, the hands of the police are tied. Unless a search can be made prior to an arrest, so that the defendant can be caught in the act of violating the gambling laws, there is no earthly way of apprehending such people along with evidence sufficient to convict them that is admissible in court. Because of these two inadequacies of the law the prosecutor's office and the police department are forced to find other means of punishing, harassing, and generally making life uneasy for the gamblers.[54]

Police also use their power of arrest to hold the arrested person while an investigation is in process—that is to say, the arrest is made in order that some probable cause can be found later to justify the arrest. In 1960, the Washington, D.C. Police Department made 4684 arrests for investigation, of which only 257 (5.5%) ever resulted in charges with specific offense.[55] In Detroit, from 1947 through 1956, out of a total of 658,808 nontraffic arrests, 219,053 were listed as arrests for investigation.[56]

Occasionally, the police engage in dragnet arrests, usually under pressure from a particularly notorious or bloody crime or a crime in which a police officer has been killed. In Detroit, in December 1960 and January 1961, after a series of rapes and murders of young women, about 1000 persons were arrested. In 1965, the FBI reported 76,346 arrests on suspicion, in an area covering about 70% of the nation's population.[57] The task force of the President's Commission on Crime reports that "these statistics almost certainly understate the number of investigative arrests in the country."[58] Similar arrests are frequently made under the guise of a specific charge, either for vagrancy, drunkenness, or other petty offenses. After all, as an instructor in a training session said, "It is a poor policeman who cannot find a description to fit the suspect, as you officers have at least thirty days of bulletins in your notebooks."[59]

Stop and Frisk

By far the greatest number of individual contacts between the police and citizens occur in field interrogations. In San Diego in 1965, written reports were made of over 200,000 field interrogations, and there probably were as many stops which were unrecorded.[60]

These interrogations plainly occur in many cases where there is no basis for suspicion. In the most extensive study of actual police practices in the matter,[61] Laurence P. Tiffany et al. classify the reasons why the policemen they observed conducted field interrogations: (1) generally suspicious circumstances (males are stopped more frequently than females, young persons more frequently than old, blacks more frequently than whites, poor-looking people more frequently than the affluent-looking, in the nighttime more frequently than in daylight, persons in high-crime-rate areas more frequently than in low-crime-rate areas); (2) criminal conviction or arrest record; (3) association with a suspect (usually suspected because of a record; but typically white males in the company of a black male who is interrogated will also be interrogated, although if alone, they probably would not have been); (4) suspicious activity with respect to property; (5) loitering or otherwise suspicious activity; (6) citizen reports of a suspicious person. A person having any of these requisite characteristics may be stopped and interrogated—and detained, if necessary against his will, during the interrogation—even when there is no report of a crime having been committed in the area.

15.5 THE CONSEQUENCES

As might be expected, the fact that the police regularly ignore the rules of due process with respect to the initiation of an investigation—rules summed up in the requirement of probable cause—means that they operate on the crime-control model of the legal system. As we have seen, a necessary characteristic of a legal system based on the crime-control model, which allows a world of Policeman's Discretion, is that it discriminates against persons living in high-crime areas and members of minority groups who tend to live in those areas.

The facts of this discrimination have been extensively documented. They are reflected in the hostility felt by many blacks toward the police. The task force on police of the President's Crime Commission gave many examples:

Race has an undue influence on who is stopped . . .

Practice is o.k., but the way it was carried out was unfriendly, abusive, etc. Not against method, but how it is used.

Personally, I found it offensive and was affronted on occasions of its use in New York.

Spanish-Americans are picked up sooner.

Many Negroes stopped in other neighborhoods and questioned. Happens more to Negroes than to others.

When they stop everybody, they say, well, they haven't seen you around, you know, they want to get to know your name, and all this. I can see them stopping you one time, but the same police stopping you every other day, and asking you the same old questions.[62]

Black juveniles in particular are stopped and questioned more frequently than white juveniles.[63] A study in San Francisco found that juveniles were frequently stopped when they traveled outside their own neighborhoods:

If we go someplace, they tell us to go on home. Because every time we go somewhere we mostly go in big groups and they don't want us. One time we was talking on Steiner Street. Some cop drove up and he say, "Hey. Hanky and Panky. Come here." And he say, "You all out of bounds get back on the other side of Steiner Street."

If boys from Hunter's Point or Fillmore (Negro neighborhoods in San Francisco) go in all white districts, the police will stop you and ask you where you from. If you say Fillmore or Hunter's Point, they'll take you down to the station and run checks on you. Any burglaries, any purse snatchings, anything.[64]

Persons with particular hair styles or clothing are especially subject to the stop-and-frisk treatment:

Why do they pick us up? They don't pick everybody up. They just pick up the ones with the hats on and trench coats and conks (a Negro hair style). If you got long hair and hats on, something like this one, you gonna get picked up. Especially a conk. And the way you dress. Sometimes, like if you've got on black pants, better not have on no black pants or bends (a kind of trouser) or levis. They think you going to rob somebody. And don't have a head scarf on your head. They'll bust you for having a head scarf.

The way you walk sometimes . . . Don't try to be cool. You know. They'll bust you for that . . . Last night a cop picked me up. He told me I had a bad walk. He say, "You think you're bad."[65]

The Commission reported that white youths who wear the type of clothes popular among delinquents are also apt to be stopped without evidence of criminality.[66]

That minority groups have come to believe that the illegal activities of the police tend to be concentrated on them has been recognized by courts. In *Lankford v. Gelston*[67] several persons committed an armed robbery of a liquor store in Baltimore, in the course of which a police lieutenant was seriously wounded. That same night, a police sergeant, who was a member of a party of police searching nearby homes, was fatally shot. The police, on information, obtained warrants for the arrest of two brothers named Veney. During the next two and a half weeks, they searched 300 private residences looking for the Veneys. The accused were blacks, and most of the dwellings searched were occupied by blacks. In many of these searches, the police acted on the basis of anonymous telephone tips and nothing more, and, of course, without warrants. The court described one such search:

Mr. and Mrs. Wallace have made their home at 2408 Huron Street for 21 years. They live with a three-year old son, three daughters, Lucinda (a Baltimore public school teacher), Harrietta (a college student) and Sharon (a high school student), and two other relatives. At 8:30 p.m. on December 30, 1964, Lieutenant Coll of the Southwest District was told by a clerk at another police station that she had received an anonymous call from a man who said the Veneys were sheltered at this address. Lieutenant Coll testified that since this was the first time that the Veneys had been placed in this neighborhood, he felt that an investigation was in order. A little after 9:00 p.m. Lieutenant Coll led about 14 officers to the house. When the officers arrived, Lucinda was showing slides to a group of her family and guests. Mr. and Mrs. Wallace were both out, Mrs. Wallace at a beauty shop she operated four doors away. Six officers armed with shotguns and rifles entered and searched the home; others who were stationed outside would not allow Mrs.

Wallace to enter and refused to explain to her what was happening. Reduced to tears, she was finally admitted to her home, where she was joined by her children, all crying hysterically. As the policemen were departing, they told Lucinda and her mother that they had received an anonymous call that the Veneys were in the house.[68]

An action was brought for an injunction restraining further searches of this kind. On appeal, the court granted the requested injunction.

The plaintiffs had argued that the searches were racially discriminatory. The trial court had rejected the argument, reasoning that "the police concentrated on Negro residences because the Veneys are Negroes and most of the information received related to their supposed presence in Negro neighborhoods."[69] The appellate court rejected the District Court's reasoning:

The invasions so graphically depicted in this case "could" happen in prosperous suburban neighborhoods, but the innocent victims know only that wholesale raids do not happen elsewhere and did happen to them. Understandably they feel that such illegal treatment is reserved for those elements who the police believe cannot or will not challenge them. It is of the highest importance to community morale that the courts shall give firm and effective reassurance, especially to those who feel that they have been harassed by reason of their color or poverty.[70]

If the police activity according to the crime-control model effectively imposes the heavy hand of the police on minority groups and the poor rather more than it does on others, it also succeeds in discovering a certain number of criminals who otherwise might never have been caught. As we shall see, the entire body of law concerning searches and arrests has been developed through cases in which suspects were searched or arrested, frequently illegally, but where the searches disclosed evidence of criminality on the basis of which the accused were later prosecuted. The President's Commission reported that a survey in several large cities showed that one out of every five persons frisked upon field interrogations carried dangerous weapons—10% were carrying guns and another 10% knives.[71] Moreover, the fact that responsible police officers believe very firmly that the right to stop and frisk is essential to keeping down crime rates is evidence for the importance of continuing this practice which is not lightly disregarded.

Illegal arrests for the purpose of harassment of prostitutes, gamblers, and the like, also arguably serve the purpose of lowering the level of vice offenses to one which is more nearly tolerable to the "decent elements" (translated: some white middle class) in the community. By the very nature of the problem, however, it is difficult or impossible to discover empirically whether in fact this is so, or whether the effect of such illegal arrests is merely to impose a tax on the activities involved.

Two interesting paradoxes stand out. First, the rhetoric with which the police defend their illegal search and their field interrogations is invariably in terms of the prevention of serious felonies and crimes of violence. They constantly warn the citizenry that without the police having this power, the murderer will escape, the robber perpetrate his crime, the rapist go unpunished. In fact, however, as the vast majority of the reported cases suggest, the crimes that are in fact discovered are crimes without victims: gambling, prostitution, narcotics offenses. The extent to which field interrogations and illegal arrests can or do curb the commission of serious felonies by the person who the police and their supporters assert is the target of the illegal practices remains unknown. What is evident is that the most frequent cases by far that are discovered or prevented are precisely those offenses which do not threaten individual citizens directly.

It is also clear that the price paid in terms of loss of respect for the law and general disdain for the law-enforcement agents is a very high one indeed. The police are not referred to as "pigs" simply because they enforce the laws against the blacks and the poor. They have received this appellation because in the mind of the blacks they are thoroughly corrupt and slovenly. Certainly a substantial amount of this attitude can be traced to the fact that the police harass persons who from their own perspectives have "done nothing." The police engage in these harassments despite the facts that such harassments are against the law. It is foolhardy to suppose that a group of people can be coerced into abiding by the law by a group of policemen who refuse to abide by it themselves. It is clearly no more justified for a policeman to refuse to obey the laws restricting his right to stop and frisk, tell people to move away from a corner or search dwellings, than it is for a ghetto resident to refuse to obey the laws against looting or rioting. Indeed, it is likely that the refusal of the police to obey those laws which they see as unjustified contributes to the willingness of others to violate laws which *they* think are unjustified.

The second paradox lies in the complete inversion of the purposes for which the due-process provisions were devised, in the way in which they are actually followed. In those cases which the police know beforehand will culminate in formal prosecutions, they are careful to observe the norms which define their powers. A narcotics squad which seeks to make an arrest of a suspect on whom they have acquired considerable evidence will obtain a search warrant and sometimes even an arrest warrant before searching and arresting. The more important the criminal, the more serious the crime, the more careful are the police in abiding by the formalities laid down by law.

The result is that the due-process provisions are followed in precisely those cases with respect to which the aim of these provisions is relatively indifferent. That aim, we recall, is the maximum protection, not for the criminal, but for the innocent who may be harassed by police activity. The crime-control model, on the other hand, focuses on the desirability of deterring and apprehending criminals. It presupposes the value-judgment that the inconvenience to the law-abiding citizen incidentally harassed is to be borne in the interests of the control of crime.

The actual operation of the rules, however, exchanges these priorities. The police in fact operate accordingly to the crime-control model in most of their contacts with the population. As a result, the ordinary innocent citizen is subjected to interrogation, search, and perhaps illegal arrest based on policemen's suspicion. The "big-time" criminal, however, is protected by the police interest in making their charges stick in court. He is therefore surrounded with all the protections laid down by the courts with respect to police conduct. The ordinary citizen is subjected to the crime-control model's presumption of guilt; the criminal, of whose activities the police already have significant evidence, is protected by a presumption of innocence. The more innocent the citizen, the more he lives in the world of policeman's discretion; the more guilty, the more he is afforded the protections of the law.

15.6 THE INVESTIGATION OF CRIMINAL ACTIVITY

The pattern of systematic contradiction between the norms of the due-process model and the facts of police conduct in accordance with the crime-control model can be discerned in a variety of police practices in their investigation of crime. Of these practices, which include such activities as wiretapping and entrapment, we shall discuss only one: in-custody interrogation.

The Problem of Pretrial Interrogation

The fact that the critical procedures of the criminal law in colonial America and its contemporary England were, by reason of the nonexistence of the police, almost entirely focused on the trial itself, resulted in a set of constitutional guarantees which also were focused on the procedures of trial. Three such guarantees have become extremely important in the current social scene. The Fifth Amendment contains guarantees of due process and against self-incrimination:

No person shall be . . . compelled in any criminal case to be a witness against himself, nor be deprived of life, liberty or property, without due process of law . . .

The Sixth Amendment contains a variety of guarantees, of which the right to counsel has today become the most significant:

In all criminal prosecutions, the accused shall enjoy the right to a speedy and public trial, by an impartial jury of the State and district wherein the crime shall have been committed, which district shall have been previously ascertained by law, and to be informed of the nature and cause of the accusation; to be confronted with the witnesses against him; to have compulsory process for obtaining witnesses in his favor, and to have the Assistance of Counsel for his defense.

These several guarantees were intended to embody the aim of due process as conceived in the late eighteenth century. By guaranteeing the several rights which they mention, these constitutional Amendments ensured that trial proceedings would be based on the notion of presumption of innocence. The Fourth Amendment ensured that the limited scope of pretrial proceedings in the America of that day *would* be limited; the Fifth and Sixth Amendments focused on the trial itself.

As the Supreme Court has said in 1967, however, in contrast to be eighteenth-century practice, in which the confrontation of the accuser and the accused was largely limited to formal in-court proceedings,

today's law-enforcement machinery involves critical confrontations of the accused by the prosecution at pretrial proceedings where the results might well settle the accused's fate and reduce the trial itself to a mere formality.[72]

The police today regularly seek to interrogate every suspect. Whether under arrest or voluntarily, the suspect is brought to the station house and questioned, usually under a formal police department rule requiring interrogation. In effect, he is subjected to a preliminary proceeding in what Yale Kamisar has called the "gatehouse" to American criminal procedure:

The courtroom is a splendid place where defense attorneys bellow and strut and prosecuting attorneys are hemmed in at many turns. But what happens before the accused reaches the safety and enjoys the comforts of this veritable mansion? Ay, there's the rub. Typically he must pass through a much less pretentious edifice, the police station with bare back rooms and locked doors.

In this "gatehouse" of American criminal procedure—through which most defendants journey and beyond which many never get—the enemy of the state is a depersonalized "subject" to be "sized up" and subjected to "interrogation tactics and techniques most appropriate for the occasion"; he is "game" to be stalked and cornered. Here ideals are checked at the door, "realities" faced, and the prestige of law enforcement vindicated. Once he leaves the gatehouse and enters the "mansion"—if he ever gets there—the enemy of the state is repersonalized, even dignified, the public invited, and a stirring ceremony in honor of individual freedom from law enforcement celebrated.[73]

In fact, as we shall see, between 85% and 95% of criminal defendants never make it to this "mansion." They plead guilty, and by that plea foreclose themselves from most of the advantages that they might enjoy in the relative comfort of the "mansion." Moreover, for every accused who is interrogated and is charged, there are many, many more who are arrested, interrogated, and freed. In Washington, D.C. in 1960, of 1356 persons "arrested for investigation" and held for eight hours or more—during which time it can be assumed that practically all of them were questioned—only 1.2% were ever formally charged.[74] In Chicago in 1956, "50% of the felony prisoners produced in Felony Court (were) held without charge for 17 hours or longer," and another 30% could not be accounted for in terms of pre-booking detention because of police failure to complete the arrest slips.[75] The "gatehouse" proceedings are not confined to the guilty, but reach out to many more who are innocent but nevertheless subjected to the same treatment as the guilty. And at times the interrogation succeeds in getting innocent men to plead guilty.

The Rules and Their Development: The Provenance of *Miranda*

The problem with the Fourth Amendment has been to maintain its guarantees in the face of the challenge posed by the very existence of a police force whose operation has a built-in bias toward the crime-control model of law. The problem with the other Amendments has been to extend the reach of their underlying principle into the gatehouse.

The latter problem has arisen in a number of contexts, but none more pervasive then with respect to the admissibility of confessions obtained by the police while the accused was in custody. A common law of evidence holds that a confession is inadmissible against a defendant where it is not voluntary, i.e. when it is induced by any promise or threat relating to the charge, and made by or with the sanction of a person in authority.[76] The ground for rejecting such confessions is said to be that, if induced by hope or fear, their validity cannot be assured.[77] Since a person convicted on the basis of an unreliable confession can hardly be said to have been convicted by due process of law, the use of confessions tainted by fear of sanction or hope of reward was early held to violate constitutional guarantees.

The first case, in which this principle was upheld was *Brown v. Mississippi.*[78] The Supreme Court described the facts as set forth in a dissenting opinion before the Supreme Court of Mississippi:

The crime with which these defendants, all ignorant negroes, are charged (murder), was discovered about 1 o'clock p.m. on Friday, March 30, 1934. On that night one Dial, a deputy sheriff, accompanied by others, came to the home of Ellington, one of the defendants, and requested him to accompany them to the house of the deceased, and there a number of white men were gathered, who began to accuse the defendant of the crime. Upon his denial they seized him, and with the participation of the deputy they hanged him by a rope to the limb of a tree, and, having let him down, they hung him up again, and when he was let down a second time and he still protested his innocence, he was tied to a tree and whipped, and, still declining to accede to the demands that he confess, he was finally released and he returned with some difficulty to his home, suffering intense pain and agony. The record of the testimony shows that the sign of the rope of his neck were plainly visible during the so-called trial. A day or two thereafter the said deputy, accompanied by another, returned to the home of the said defendant and arrested him, and departed with the prisoner towards the jail in an adjoining county, but went by a route which led into the state of Alabama; and while on the way, in that state, the deputy stopped and again severely whipped the defendant, declaring that he would continue the whipping until he confessed, and the defendant then agreed to confess to such a statement as the deputy would dictate, and he did so, after which he was delivered to jail.

The other two defendants, Ed Brown and Henry Shields, were also arrested and taken to the same jail. On Sunday night, April 1, 1934, the same deputy, accompanied by a number of white men, one of whom was also an officer, and by the jailer, came to the jail, and the two last named defendants were made to strip and they were laid over chairs and their backs were cut to pieces with a leather strap with buckles on it, and they were likewise made by the same deputy definitely to understand that the whipping would be continued unless and until they confessed, and not only confessed, but confessed in every matter of detail as demanded by those present; and in this manner the defendants confessed in all particulars of detail so as to conform to the demands of their torturers . . .[79]

The decision of the Supreme Court of Mississippi confirming the convictions for murder was appealed. At the hearing, the State argued, first, that the privilege against self-incrimination had earlier been held to be inapplicable to the States, and second, that the claim of the denial of due process had been improperly asserted according to the State procedural rules. The Supreme Court reversed the decision on the ground of the denial of due process of law in extorting the confessions, for

the trial is . . . a mere pretense where the state authorities have contrived a conviction resting solely upon confessions obtained by violence. The due process clause requires "that state action, whether through one agency or another, shall be consistent with the fundamental principles of liberty and justice which lie at the base of all our civil and political institutions."[80] It would be difficult to conceive of methods more revolting to the sense of justice than those taken to procure the confessions of these petitioners, and the use of confessions thus obtained as the basis for the conviction and sentence was a clear denial of due process.[81]

Seven years later, in *Ashcraft v. Tennessee*,[82] the Supreme Court took a second giant step. Here, the accused confessed to the murder of his wife after having been steadily and relentlessly questioned by relays of skilled interrogators from 7:00 p.m. on a Saturday to 9:30 a.m. on Monday, with five minutes of respite, faced by a blinding electric light, although the officers swore that throughout the proceedings they had been "kind and considerate." The Supreme Court held that the uncontradicted evidence described a situation "inherently coercive." It said in a pregnant passage that

It is inconceivable that any court of justice in the land, conducted as our courts are, open to the public, would permit prosecutors serving in relays to keep a defendant witness under continuous cross-examination for thirty-six hours without rest or sleep in an effort to extract a "voluntary" confession. Nor can we, consistently with Constitutional due process of law, hold voluntary a confession where prosecutors do the same thing away from the restraining influences of a public trial in an open court room.[83]

This is apparently the first statement by the Supreme Court which started the long process by which the constitutional guarantees originally applicable only to the trial proceedings began to be assimilated to rules governing pretrial investigative proceedings.

The Court, in *Ashcraft*, staked out the position that whether or not a confession was "voluntary" and hence consistent with due process raised a federal question, an independent examination of which had to be made by the federal courts. In a long succession of cases, the federal courts faced a variety of issues arising out of pretrial interrogation by the police, all requiring the court to determine, long after the occurrence of the facts and frequently with less than adequate records, whether or not the conditions under which the confession had been obtained were such that the confession was not wholly "voluntary."

The practice of basing criminal convictions on involuntary confessions is plainly compatible only with the crime-control model of criminal proceedings. It is based on the notion that the officers *know* the accused to be guilty, and that he is merely being stubborn when he resists their urgings that he confess. The principal difficulty with using voluntariness as the test of admissibility is that this test can be used only when, someplace along the line, through some unusual happenstance, the case of the confessed criminal is shunted into proceedings where the due-process provisions are complied to. It is impossible to determine how many of the vast number of convictions obtained by use of a guilty plea are based on coerced confessions. In any case, the very existence of a confession, whether coerced or not, is a trump card in the hands of a prosecutor in bargaining over a plea. Every practicing criminal lawyer knows that the first question to ask a prisoner on being retained is whether the latter has made a statement concerning the crime. If he has, it is a rare case indeed that will end in a trial. Without a trial, there is no place at which the accused can raise the issue of voluntariness of the confession.

What is required is a set of norms governing police conduct during pretrial in-custody interrogations. Without precise norms and without a full trial, there is no way of telling whether the police have acted properly. As so often happens, when a great bulk of cases are judged by a vague standard requiring individual weighing in every case, there was bound to appear in place of the existing standard a relatively precise set of rules.

Before such rules could be formulated, however, it was necessary to extend the constitutional guarantees to cover the pretrial investigations. The essential first step in this direction seems to have been taken in *Watts v. Indiana*,[84] where in-custody interrogation was perceived as posing an outright challenge to the basic premises of due process.

To turn the detention of an accused into a process of wrenching from him evidence which could not be extorted in open court with all its safeguards, is so grave an abuse of the arrest power as to offend the procedural standards of due process.

This is so because it violates the underlying principle in our enforcement of the criminal law. Ours is an accusatorial as opposed to the inquisitorial system . . . Under our system society carries the burden of proving its charge against the accused not out of his own mouth . . . The requirement of specific charges, their proof beyond a reasonable doubt, the protection of the accused from confessions extorted through whatever form of police pressure, the right to a prompt hearing before a magistrate, the right to assistance of counsel, to be supplied by government when circumstances make it necessary, the duty to advise the accused of his constitutional rights—these are all characteristics of the accusatorial system and manifestations of its demands.[85]

The nature of an accusatorial system of law is that the burden of proof rests on the government. The system requires that the accused be clothed with a presumption of innocence from the time he is first suspected until final judgment of guilt, not as a presumption of fact but as a procedural device to ensure that the due process model does not slip over into the crime control model. This is the essential condition for guaranteeing that we live in a world of law, not one in which policeman's discretion can go unchecked.

To conceive of the problem presented by coerced confessions in terms of due process tends to direct the attention of the court to the formulation of norms for police conduct, whereas in its traditional formulation in terms of the voluntariness of the confession, the problem is focused on the guilt or innocence of a particular defendant with respect to a particular crime. The justification for this shift of emphasis is found in a redefinition of the principles supporting the right to counsel and the privilege against self-incrimination.

Right to Counsel

Of these two principles, the extension of the right to counsel from post-indictment to the preindictment investigation was the first to appear. That the federal guarantee of the right to counsel extended to state courts at least in cases where the death sentence might be imposed was early decided.[86] Moreover, it was held that in any given case the defendant had an absolute right to insist that his own retained counsel participate fully in the trial and in preparation for the trial.[87] This right was slowly pushed back to cover the arraignment itself.[88]

There were two essential questions to be answered. In the first place, to what extent did the federal guarantee of the right to counsel in noncapital cases require the State to provide counsel for the indigent? In the second place, did the right to counsel apply to prearraignment interrogations which customarily took place in the police station?

The question of counsel for the indigent accused in noncapital cases was answered in one way in 1942, only to suffer slow evisceration and ultimately complete reversal in 1963. In *Betts v. Brady*[89] a divided Supreme Court held that an indigent prisoner was not entitled to counsel provided by the State except where he could demonstrate that the absence of counsel made his trial fundamentally unfair and hence a denial of due process. This decision was slowly destroyed by exceptions, until it was overturned in the great case of *Gideon v.*

Wainwright[90] in 1963, where the Court held that a State court during the trial of any crime must provide counsel to an indigent defendant. The Court put the issue in terms of the requirements of due process:

Reason and reflection require us to recognize that in our adversary system of criminal justice, any person hauled into court, who is too poor to hire a lawyer, cannot be assured a fair trial unless counsel is provided for him. This seems to us to be an obvious truth. Governments, both state and federal, quite properly spend vast sums of money to try defendants accused of crime. Lawyers to prosecute are everywhere deemed essential to protect the public's interest in an orderly society. Similarly, there are a few defendants charged with crime, few indeed, who fail to hire the best lawyer they can get to prepare and present their defense. That government hires lawyers to prosecute and defendants who have the money hire lawyers to defend are the strongest indications of a widespread belief that lawyers in criminal courts are necessities, not luxuries ... From the very beginning, our state and national constitutions and laws have laid great emphasis on procedural and substantive safeguards designed to assure fair trials before impartial tribunals in which every defendant stands equal before the law. This noble ideal cannot be realized if the poor man charged with crime has to face his accusers without a lawyer to assist him.[91]

The due-process conception of the criminal process, if carried out in all its rigor, demands that the State proceed by accusatory proceedings. It demands, as we have seen, that such proceedings begin not merely in the mansion of the formal trial, but also in the gatehouse of the preliminary interrogations.

Without a counsel to assist him, the ordinary suspect in police interrogations is helpless in resisting the police effort to extract from him the information which may later be used for convicting him. More important, however, than the cases of the guilty man are the much larger number of cases in which citizens are interrogated without any formal proceeding ever being instituted against them. Since the cases called to the attention of the court are always those in which the persons interrogated have been formally charged, the problem was to shift the focus of attention from the fairness of the particular conviction at hand, to the conduct of the police generally. The device by which this shift of emphasis was accomplished was the development of the privilege against self-incrimination, of which the right to counsel was ultimately perceived as an essential element.

The Privilege Against Self-Incrimination

The privilege against self-incrimination finds its origins in English history. It was urged in ancient times, but the critical historical event raising it to the level of a legal principle was the trial of "Long John" Lilburne, an anti-Stuart Leveler, who declined to take the Star Chamber oath in 1637. The oath would have bound him to answer all questions asked. He declaimed,

Another fundamental right I then contended for, was, that no man's conscience ought to be racked by oaths imposed, to answer to questions concerning himself in matters criminal or pretended to be so.[92]

It should be noted that Lilburne made this assertion at a time when torture was in common use in England to extort confessions, not only in Star Chamber, but "as a matter of course in all grave accusations, at the mere discretion of the King and the Privy Council, and uncontrolled by any law besides the prerogative of the Sovereign."[93] A contemporary remarked,

The Racke is us'd no where as in England. In other Countries tis us'd in Judicature, when there is a *semi-plena probatio*, a halfe proofe against a man, then to see if they can make it full, they racke him to try if hee will Confess. But here in England, they take a man and racke him, I doe not know why, nor when, not in time of judicature, but when some body bids.[94]

The Puritan Parliament abolished Star Chamber and made reparation to John Lilburne. The sentiments thus nurtured were brought over by the immigrants to America, and finally found their place in the Bill of Rights.

The use of torture as a device to aid interrogation is, like police brutality, a limiting case of the crime-control practice. It assumes that the interrogators *know* the accused to be guilty, and that it is only his obduracy which prevents a confession and a clean, neat, and professional conclusion to the case. This practice is apt to be taken up in any age where the legal system operates on the crime-control model. In 1965 in New York City, the police "brutally beat, kicked, and placed cigarette butts in the back of a potential witness under interrogation for the purpose of securing a statement incriminating a third party.[95]

The privilege against self-incrimination is a more secure foundation for developing a prohibition against the use of coercively obtained confessions than the due-process clause. After all, the tortures inflicted on Brown or Ashcraft were little different from the rack and inquisition of Star Chamber, to defend against which the privilege was originally forged. The privilege was not invoked in State trials because between 1908 and 1964 it was held inapplicable to the States. To understand why it was held to be inapplicable requires a soupçon of constitutional history.

The ten Amendments to the federal Constitution apply only to the federal government. It was the Fourteenth Amendment to the federal Constitution that for the first time imposed a specific limitation on the judicial process of the States, for it prohibits the States for infringing the privileges and immunities of a citizen of the United States, or depriving them of due process of law. Earlier, in *Twining v. New Jersey*,[96] the Supreme Court squarely held that the privilege against self-incrimination was not a privilege or immunity of the United States, nor was its denial by a state a violation of due process of law. The Court held that the privilege "came into existence not as an essential part of due process, but as a wise and beneficent rule of evidence developed in the course of judicial decision."[97] While the principle is no doubt "salutary," the Court said that "it cannot be ranked with the right of hearing before condemnation, the immunity from arbitrary power not acting by general laws, and the inviolability of private property."[98]

The *Twining* doctrine proved an exceptionally hardy one, but it could not withstand the pressures for creating rules which would embody the ideals of due process. It finally collapsed in 1964 when the Court held that *Twining* had been erroneously decided. The Court stated that the confession cases based on due process had led to the principle that a confession was inadmissible unless it was "free and voluntary." This the Court held to be equivalent to saying that a person could not be forced or compelled to incriminate himself. It summed up the tendency of the cases:

The shift (in the requirement that the federal standard of voluntariness in confessions be imposed upon the states) reflects recognition that the American system of criminal prosecution is accusatorial, not inquisitorial, and that the Fifth Amendment privilege is its essential mainstay... Governments, state and federal, are thus constitutionally compelled to establish guilt by evidence independently and freely secured, and may not by coercion prove a charge against an accused out of his own mouth. Since the Fourteenth Amendment forbids the States from inducing a person to confess "through sympathy falsely aroused" ... or other like inducement far short of "compulsion by torture" ... it followes *a fortiori* that it also forbids the States to resort to imprisonment, as here, to compel him to answer questions that might incriminate him.[99]

The floodgates having been opened, the privilege against self-incrimination was rapidly elevated to the highest rung of the constitutional ladder. Combined with the newly affirmed right to counsel, it formed the pattern for a whole new system of norms for the conduct of pretrial interrogations.

The *Miranda* Rule

The stage was now set for the full incorporation of the ideals of due process into the norms laid down by the Court for police practices in interrogation. This was done on the conceptual level by the discovery that the privilege against self-incrimination was far more than a mere procedural device to produce against a defendant's being compelled to testify against himself.

As a "noble principle often transcends its origins," the privilege has come rightfully to be recognized in part as an individual's substantive right, a "right to a private enclave where he may lead a private life. That right is the hallmark of our democracy." ... We have recently noted that the privilege against self-incrimination—the essential mainstay of our adversary system—is founded on a complex of values ... All these policies point to one overriding thought: the constitutional foundation underlying the privilege is the respect a government—state or federal—must accord the dignity and integrity of its citizens. To maintain a "fair state-individual balance," to require the government "to shoulder the entire load" ... to respect the inviolability of the human personality, our accusatory system demands that the government seeking to punish an individual produce the evidence against him by its own independent labors, rather than by the cruel, simple expedient of compelling it from his own mouth . . . In sum, the privilege is fulfilled only when the person is guaranteed the right "to remain silent unless he chooses to speak in the unfettered exercise of his own will."[100]

That the central issue concerned the difference between law and order, between crime control and due process, was nowhere more clearly set forth than in an exchange in the Supreme Court between William I. Siegel, arguing for the State in *Vignera v. New York* (one of the companion cases to *Miranda*), and Justice Fortas:

Mr. Justice Fortas: "Mr. Siegel, I suppose it is at least arguable that prior to Magna Charta and prior to the adoption of our own Bill of Rights most people who were convicted were guilty. Nevertheless, it has been the wisdom of the ages that some safeguards are necessary. Isn't that so?"

Mr. Siegel: "I agree with that."

Mr. Justice Fortas: "I suppose that when you look at this philosophically and morally in terms of the great human adventure towards some kind of truly civilized order, these great provisions of the Magna Charta and our own Bill of Rights were designed to do two things: one, to eliminate even the unusual case of an unjustified conviction; and two, to lay out a standard for the relationship between the state vis-à-vis the individual. Would you think that that observation is justified?"

Mr. Siegel: "Undoubtedly, sir."

Mr. Justice Fortas: " . . . So, the point upon which I am asking you to comment is . . . not to take a look at this problem from the point of view of facilitating the task of putting people in jail, if they commit the crime. In other words, the problem really affects the basic relationship of the individual and the state. It really goes beyond the administration of justice, and that is the history of mankind.

" . . . You can say, 'Well, the police secured a conviction in 90% of the cases and it is all right.' That is a very sensible attitude, from one point of view, but perhaps, it is the point of view that has been rejected by history."

Mr. Siegel: " . . . there is an immediate objective, also, and the immediate objective is to protect society; because, if society isn't protected, it in one degree or another, lapses into anarchy because of crime and then the opportunity to reach this beautiful ideal is gone . . . The problem that is before this court, it seems to me, is just how to keep the balance between the ultimate necessity of the civilized, peaceful society and the constitutional rights of a specific defendant."

Mr. Justice Black: "Don't you think that the Bill of Rights has something to do with making that balance?"

Mr. Siegel: "Yes, sir."[101]

The precise issue in *Miranda* was the one with which we began this discussion: The extent to which the police may interrogate in the station house without counsel, without advising the accused of his right to counsel or his right to keep silent. In *Escobedo v. Illinois*,[102] in 1964, the Court had held that a statement elicited through police interrogation was inadmissible in the trial of the accused solely on the ground that the statement was elicited before indictment, but after the investigation had focused on the accused, and after the police had refused to honor his request to consult his lawyer during the course of the interrogation. In *Miranda*, the police had interrogated the accused for two hours in private without advising him of his constitutional rights; and that fact alone was held to be sufficient to make the statement inadmissible.

The basis of the decision was not philosophical, but empirical. The Court quoted *in extenso*, as we have seen above (p. 180), from police manuals of instruction, in lieu of specific observations of what actually goes on in police interrogation rooms. These manuals made it clear that the basis for successful pretrial interrogation is the overpowering of the will of the accused by the interrogator. The Court concluded that

Even without employing brutality, the "third degree" or the specific stratagems described (in the police instruction manuals), the very fact of custodial interrogation exacts a heavy toll on individual liberty and trades on the weakness of individuals . . .[103]

The protection was woven from the dual strands of the privilege against self-incrimination and of the right to counsel. The privilege prohibited the extraction of confessions, and the right to counsel ensured that the privilege would be observed. Indeed, as Justice Jackson once observed many years before,

Under our systems [a lawyer] deems that his sole duty is to protect his client—guilty or innocent—and that in such a capacity he owes no duty whatever to help society solve its crime problems. Under this conception of criminal procedure, any lawyer worth his salt will tell the suspect in no uncertain terms to make no statement to the police under any circumstances.[104]

The thrust of the new ruling concerning the privilege against self-incrimination was that it defined the line between the policeman's use of discretion and the rule of law. Yet the Court was left with a practical problem. Over the years, it had repeatedly defined that line in terms of the "voluntariness" of confession. Repeatedly, it had had to examine the facts involved in specific cases to determine in terms of the results of police conduct whether that conduct had overreached the line of demarcation. Neither legislatures nor public officials had seen fit to lay down precise codes of behavior for the police which might sharpen the definition of impermissible conduct.

The Court therefore laid down a set of norms for police conduct. The test now became, not whether the confession or statement of the accused was "voluntary," but whether the police had acted in a certain precisely defined way:

To summarize, we hold that when an individual is taken into custody or otherwise deprived of his freedom by the authorities and is subjected to questioning, the privilege against self-incrimination is jeopardized. Procedural safeguards must be employed to protect the privilege, and unless other fully effective means are adopted to notify the person of his right to silence and to assure that the exercise of the right will be scrupulously honored, the following measures are required. He must be warned prior to any questioning that he has the right to remain silent, that anything he says can be used against him in a court of law, that he has the right to the presence of an attorney, and that if he cannot afford an attorney one will be appointed for him prior to any questioning if he so desires. Opportunity to exercise these rights must be afforded to him throughout the interrogation. After such warnings have been given, and such opportunity afforded him, the individual may knowingly and intelligently waive these rights and agree to answer questions or make a statement. But unless and until such warnings and waiver are demonstrated by the prosecution at trial, no evidence obtained as a result of interrogation can be used against him.[105]

The movement begun long ago finally came to fruition. The guarantees of due process moved forward from the mansion to the gatehouse of the law. But, as we have seen so often, this has had little significant effect on actual police practice.

The Consequence of *Miranda*

The most complete investigation of station house interrogations yet published appears to be that conducted by members of the *Yale Law Review* staff in New Haven, Connecticut, during the summer of 1966.[106] An analogous investigation was conducted by the Institute of Criminal Law and Procedure in Washington, D.C.[107]

The principal conclusion both in New Haven and in Washington is that *Miranda* seems to have changed the practice of the police very little. In New Haven, the police appeared to be seriously interested in interrogating 61% of the suspects.[108] In Washington, the number of suspects interrogated by the police fell from 55% to 48% between the period just before the *Miranda* decision and the period just after it. The New Haven Police Department regulations require that the detective attempt an interrogation of every suspect arrested.

As we just saw, the *Miranda* opinion used information concerning coercive techniques of interrogation contained in police instruction manuals as surrogate for empirical data about what actually went on during such interrogations. The New Haven police did not use any of the tactics described in these manuals on 44 out of 127 suspects, but on 38 of the suspects they used three or more of these tactics. Threats as well as feigned sympathy for the suspect were used. The Yale students making the observations reported that from other evidence they had it appeared that the level of police coercive treatment had been especially subdued while, and because, they were present. Both before and after the period of observation, "the detectives frequently displayed a more hostile air ... The police told suspects more often that they would be 'worse off' if they did not talk, played down the seriousness of the crime, swore at the suspects, and made promises of leniency."[109]

In neither New Haven nor Washington, apparently, did the police in even the majority of cases give the accused the *full* warnings spelled out in the *Miranda* decision. In Washington, 29% of the suspects said that they had not been given any warning, and 62% said that they had not been given the full warning. In New Haven, only 25 out of 118 suspects were given the full *Miranda* warning.

Even when given, however, the warning was hardly effective. Most of the detectives, even when they gave the warning, "incorporated into their tactical repertoirs some sort of hedging on the warnings . . ." Some changed the warning slightly: "Whatever you say may be used *for* or against you in a court of law." Often, the detectives advised the suspect with some inconsistent qualifying remark, such as "You don't have to say a word, but you ought to get everything cleared up," or "You don't have to say anything, of course, *but* can you explain how . . ."[110]

In some of the New Haven cases the police went even further:

Even when the detective advised the suspect of his rights without these undercutting devices, he commonly de-fused the advice by implying that the suspect had better not exercise his rights, or by delivering this statement in a formalized, bureaucratic tone to indicate that his remarks were simply a routine, meaningless legalism. Often they would bring the flow of conversation of a halt and preface their remarks with "Now I am going to warn you of your rights." After they had finished the advice they would solemnly intone, "Now you have been warned of your rights," then immediately shift into a conversational tone to ask, "Now, would you like to tell me what happened?"

In the few cases where a suspect showed an interest in finding a lawyer and did not already know one, the police usually managed to head him off simply by not helping him locate one. Sometimes they refused to advise the suspect whether he should have a lawyer with him during questioning; more often they merely offered him a telephone book without further comment, and that was enough to deter him from calling a lawyer.[111]

In New Haven, the only constant factor affecting the detectives' giving or withholding of the full warning was the seriousness of the crime. The more serious the crime, the greater was the probability that the full *Miranda* warning would be given.[112] Moreover, the suspect was even more likely to get the warning in those cases of serious crime where the police had already enough evidence for trial, but not enough for conviction, i.e. in precisely those cases where, as we shall see, the exclusionary rule might make the difference between conviction and acquittal.

Both in Washington and in New Haven the warnings, even when given, apparently had little effect on the suspects' behavior. Many simply do not understand the serious implications of the decision to call a lawyer. In Washington, only one out of fourteen suspects asked for a lawyer. Over four out of ten gave statements to the police. In New Haven, the observers concluded that in only 6% of the cases did the *Miranda* warning affect the result.

The New Haven observers attributed the ineffectiveness of the warning to a variety of reasons. The accused persons frequently did not seem to be able to grasp the significance of making a statement, even when the warning was given, either because the warning was given in such a way as to minimize its effectiveness or because "since most suspects had little education—many could not even read— and appeared both ill-at-ease and dazed at the process," the warning had little impact. A very high proportion of those arrested by the police were in fact guilty of the crimes charged. When presented by the evidence in the possession of the police, the accused tended to try to exculpate themselves—and sank deeper into the morass.[113] A number of them gave statements which they believed exculpated them—for example, that in an assault case, the victim began the affray—when in fact the statements were incriminating.

In short, the *Miranda* rules, despite the great amount of controversy they have caused, seemingly have not significantly changed the conduct of either the police or the accused persons. However, it must be noted that the New Haven data were gathered in the first few months after the *Miranda* decision had been handed down. It is possible, though doubtful, that it takes a long time for rules of this sort to be internalized by the police and hence to affect police activity.

An example of slow change can perhaps be seen in the development of the confessions rule. In 1931, the Wickersham Commission reported that police used the third degree with remarkable frequency.[114] That police brutality continues to be a factor was documented by a footnote to the *Miranda* decision itself:

see *People v. Wakat*, 415 111.610, 114 N.E. 2d 706 (1953); *Wakat v. Harlib*, 253 F. 2d 59 (C.A. 7th Cir. 1958) (Defendant suffering from broken bones, multiple bruises and injuries sufficiently serious to require eight months' medical treatment after being manhandled by five policemen); *Kier v. State*, 213 Md. 556, 132 A. 2d 494 (1957) (police doctor told accused, who was strapped to a chair completely naked, that he proposed to take hair and skin scrapings from anything that looked like blood or sperm from various parts of his body); *Bruner v. People*, 113 Colo. 114, 156 P. 2d 111 (1945) (defendant held in custody over two months, deprived of food for 15 hours, forced to submit to lie detector test when he wanted to go to the toilet); *People v. Matlock*, 51 Cal. 2d 682, 336 P. 2d 505 (defendant questioned incessantly over an evening's time, made to lie on cold board and to answer questions whenever it appeared he was getting sleepy.)[115]

Despite the continuation of such practices today, the level of their incidence seems to have declined. In New Haven, the observers learned from interviews both with detectives and with suspects that

there seemingly has been a substantial change in police attitudes and practices from 1960 to 1966. Both groups believe the interrogation process has become considerably less hostile; detectives are unwilling to use tactics approved seven years ago. For example, we found several instances where detectives stopped an interrogation when the letter of *Miranda* did not require them to do so. This change is probably attributable both to court decisions on the criminal law and to change in administration within the department.[116]

The President's Commission on Law Enforcement and the Administration of Justice came to the same conclusion:

In 1931, the Wickersham Commission reported that the extraction of confessions through physical brutality was a widespread, almost universal, police practice. During the next several years the Supreme Court issued a number of rulings that excluded such confessions as admissible evidence in court. There can be no doubt that these rulings had much to do with the fact that today the third degree is almost nonexistent.[117]

How the rulings of the Supreme Court in the confession cases contributed to the lowering of the level of violence during in-custody interrogation, of course, is difficult or impossible to assess. They might have contributed to it through an educative process involving the police officers generally. They might have contributed to it by offering support to a general community sentiment against brutality, and thus providing by way of community disapproval a sanction for officers who violated the norm. They might have contributed to it by creating a community climate of opinion in which the officers, as members of the community, participated.

Nevertheless, the precise *Miranda* warnings and the sort of conduct which the rulings prescribed do not seem significantly to have solved the problems with which the Court was primarily concerned. Suspects are still interrogated under conditions of severe psychological coercion and, occasionally, physical coercion. The prescribed warnings either are not given at all, or given incompletely, or are incomprehensible as given. Suspects are still subjected to precisely the sort of grilling which the Supreme Court has held to be over the line between questioning and coercion as drawn by the privilege against self-incrimination. We must consider, first, the reasons for this discrepancy between role-expectation and role-performance, between the "law in the books" and the "law in action," and second, what remedies are available to bring about a greater conformity between the two. This second consideration will form the subject-matter of the next chapter.

A similar pattern of discrepancy is to be found with respect to the relationship between court decisions and the juvenile-court practices in handling juveniles charged with delinquency. For years juveniles had not been extended the same constitutional rights as adults even in principle. (As we have seen, in practice the benefits deriving from the constitutional guarantees have largely fallen on the prosperous members of the community, both criminal and noncriminal). But the juvenile was not even potentially protected by these guarantees. In a recent decision,[118] the Supreme Court extended the right to counsel, freedom from self-incrimination, right to notification of charges, and right to confrontation and countercharges to juveniles as well as adults. Interestingly, the crime-control model of legal process has heretofore dominated the perspective of those working in juvenile courts as well as that of the police. There is, of course, an important difference in terminology: the juvenile probation officer or social worker is concerned with the "problems" (meaning personality-adjustment problems) of those juveniles brought before them; the question of guilt or innocence with respect to the charged criminal offense is really irrelevant. Yet the attitude involved is strikingly similar to that of the police when they arrest, harass, or "keep moving" persons "known" by them to *be* problems. For the social worker the concern is to intervene (harass, keep moving, have arrested, or detain) persons who *have* problems; for the police the task is to arrest, or deal with in other ways, persons who *are* problems. In both instances, the assumption is that the person is "guilty" and that something official must be done to modify his behavior pattern whether or not the person is *legally* guilty of having committed a punishable offense. The *Gault* decision is designed to change this set of operating procedures in dealing with juveniles just as the aforementioned decisions are designed to change the operating procedures for handling adults.

But the results of the *Gault* decision are almost identical to the results of *Miranda*; that is, little has changed in actual practice. A study of the effect of the *Gault* decision on the practices in juvenile courts in three "urban centers" disclosed wide variations from one city to another in the courts' compliance with the rulings stemming from *Gault*. In no case, however, were the requirements of *Gault* strictly followed. In one city 56% of the defendants were advised of their right to counsel, in another city only 3% were so advised, and in the third city there was not a single case where the juveniles or their parents were adequately advised of the child's right to counsel. In some cases (18% in one city, 65% in the second, and 18% in the third) the juveniles or their parent were given partial advice on the right to counsel. For example, the judge said to the parent in one case:

"Mrs. C., did you know you have the right to have a lawyer?"

The authors of the study comment:

The warning, phrased in the form of a question, was directed solely at the parent, and the judge failed to state that the boy and his parent were entitled to appointed counsel if they were indigent.

That this omission was of considerable importance can be gleaned from the remainder of the conversation between the judge and the parent. In response to the question "Did you know you have the right to a lawyer?"

she replied that she "didn't know." She paused, then she said, "Well Mr. O——(the probation officer) said that it was up to me, and I said that I didn't have any money." The Judge said, "Well, one thing you have here is all kinds of lawyers." He said that they could get some at the Legal Aid Society. The mother replied, "Well, I have one, but he's so expensive." And the judge left it at this, and they went ahead and heard the case.[119]

Why this discrepancy between the role and role-performance? Given the model outlined in Chapter 14, which points out the tendency of organizations responsible for the administration of justice to operate in ways that minimize the strains and maximize the rewards for the organizations, the organizational disregard for the Supreme Court decisions such as *Miranda*, *Gideon*, and *Gault* is quite predictable. Obviously the courts, the prosecuting attorneys, and the police will be infinitely more burdened by the cases they handle—the bureaucratic strains will vastly increase—with no concomitant increase in reward if the Supreme Court rulings are implemented. For one way or another such decisions, no matter what their authority may be, will be circumvented through bureaucratic procedures. There is no cure for this tendency. The higher courts may continue to refine the decisions for the implementation of the due-process ideals; but so long as crime control remains the organizationally more viable aim, it will dominate the legal operation. It is possible, of course, to create a legal system in which failure of the processing agencies such as the police to live up to the requirements of due process will create more strain on them than can be compensated for by organizational efficiency gained from ignoring due process. To accomplish this, however, necessitates the creation of an organizational body or bodies capable of opposing the perspectives dominant in the processing agencies at the lowest level. As the administration of justice currently stands, only the appellate courts, and then frequently only the highest federal courts, systemically attempt to force the lower courts, prosecuting attorneys' offices, and police departments to observe due process. Since the higher-court decisions do not much affect the day-to-day operations of the said agencies, the strain created by these decisions is minimal.

An adequate system of legal representation for the poor would go a long way to solve the problem in the United States. Lawyers representing indigents could theoretically create sufficient strain for the processing agencies so as to reduce the organizational viability of the aim of crime control and increase the organizational viability of the due-process ideal. Short of such an overall change in the organizations dealing with criminal justice, however, it is obvious that higher-court decisions will have little if any effect on the day-to-day practices of the police or the lower courts.

NOTES

1. Herbert L. Packer, "Two models of the criminal process," *U. Pa. Law Rev.*, **113**, 1964, p. 1. Copyright 1964 by the University of Pennsylvania Law Review.

2. *Ibid.*, p. 9. Reprinted by permission.

3. Thomas F. Adams, "Field interrogation, originally published in *Police*, Vol. 7, No. 4, March–April 1963, p. 23, by Charles C. Thomas, Publisher. Reprinted by permission.

4. *Vital Statistics of the United States*, Vol. 2, Part A, "Mortality," U.S. Public Health Service, HA203 U6, National Center for Health Statistics, Section 1.

5. William A. Westley, "Violence and the Police," *Am. J. Soc.*, **59**, 1951, pp. 34–38; quoted in the President's Commission on Law Enforcement and Administration of Justice, *Task Force Report: The Police*, U.S. Government Printing Office, 1967, p. 183.

6. *Ibid.*, p. 40 (Commission report, *ibid.* p. 183).

7. All unacknowledged quotations and conclusions in the following discussion (through page 280) are from Albert J. Reiss, Jr., "The use of physical force in police work," report prepared for the President's Commission on Law Enforcement and Administration of Justice, University of Michigan, Ann Arbor, 1966, pp. 16 ff.

8. Also quoted in the Commission's *Task Force Report: The Police*, p. 182.

9. *Ibid.*, p. 182.

10. *Ibid.*, p. 182.

11. Reiss, *op. cit.*, pp. 16 ff.

12. William J. Chambliss, field notes.

13. *Newsweek*, May 13, 1968, p. 60.

14. *The Walker Report: Violence in Chicago*, "Rights in conflict," Bantam, New York, 1968, pp. 5–8.

15. *Ibid.*, pp. 353–354.

16. Thomas Hayden, *Rebellion in Newark*, Random House, New York, 1967.

17. *Time*, May 17, 1968, p. 59.

18. Arnold S. Trebach, *The Rationing of Justice*, Rutgers University Press, New Brunswick, N. J., 1964, pp. 40–41.

19. *United States v. Wade*, 388 U.S. 218, 87 S. Ct. 1926, 18 L. Ed. 2d 1149 (1967).

20. See generally Irving Brant, *The Bill of Rights: Its Origin and Meaning*, Bobbs-Merrill, Indianapolis, 1965.

21. Orlando W. Wilson, "Police arrest privilege in a free society," *J. Criminal Law, Criminology, and Police Science*, **51**, No. 4, 1960, pp. 395–398. Reprinted by special permission of the Journal of Criminal Law, Criminology and Police Science (Northwestern University School of Law), © 1960.

22. See Julius Goebel, Jr., and Thomas R. Naughton, *Law Enforcement in Colonial New York: A Study in Criminal Procedure (1664–1776)*, Commonwealth Fund, New York, 1944, pp. 401–402.

23. *Ibid.*, pp. 339–340. Reprinted by permission.

24. *Ibid.*, pp. 424–425.

25. *Ibid.*, p. 394.

26. *Ibid.*, p. 401.

27. Leon R. Yankwich, "The background of the American Bill of Rights," *Geo. Law Journal*, **37**, 1948, pp. 1, 14–17.

28. See generally Lawrence P. Tiffany, Donald M. McIntyre, and Daniel L. Rotenberg, *Detection of Crime*, Little, Brown, Boston, 1967.

29. Paula R. Markowitz and Walter I. Summerfield, Jr., "Philadelphia police practice and the law of arrest," *U. Pa. Law Rev.,* **100**, 1952, pp. 1182–1217.

30. Tiffany *et al., op. cit.,* p. 101.

31. *Ibid.,* pp. 101–104.

32. Ronald A. Anderson, *Wharton's Criminal Law and Procedure,* Lawyer's Co-op, Rochester, N.Y., 1957, p. 1596.

33. 354 U.S. 449, 77 S. Ct. 1356, 1 L. Ed. 2d 1459, (1957).

34. Jerome H. Skolnick, *Justice Without Trial,* Wiley, New York, 1966, p. 112.

35. *Ibid.,* pp. 120–121. Reprinted by permission.

36. The President's Commission on Law Enforcement and Administration of Justice, *Task Force Report: The Police,* U.S. Government Printing Office, 1967, pp. 183–184.

37. B. J. White, concurring in *Terry v. Ohio,* 392 U.S. 1, 885 S. Ct. 1868, 20 L. Ed. 889 (1968) at 392 U.S.

38. *United States v. Ponanno,* 180 F. Supp. 71 (S.D.N.Y., 1960).

39. *Terry v. Ohio* (cited in note 37).

40. *Ibid.*

41. W. O. Douglas, dissenting in *Terry v. Ohio* (cited in note 37).

42. N. Y. Code Crime Proc. sec. 180a (McKinney Supp. 1967).

43. 392 U.S. 41, 88 S. Ct. 1889, 20 L. Ed. 2d 917 (1968).

44. Fowler V. Harper and Fleming James, *The Law of Torts,* Little, Brown, Boston, 1956, Section 3.18, pp. 275–286.

45. William J. Chambliss, "Types of deviance and the effectiveness of legal sanctions," *Wisc. Law Rev.,* 1967, p. 703.

46. Wayne R. LaFave, *Arrest: The Decision to take a Suspect into Custody,* Little, Brown, Boston, 1965, p. 441. Reprinted by permission.

47. *Ibid.,* pp. 453–454.

48. *Ibid.,* p. 456. Reprinted by permission.

49. *Ibid.,* p. 454.

50. *Ibid.,* p. 456. Reprinted by permission.

51. *Ibid.,* p. 468. Reprinted by permission.

52. Quoted in Monrad G. Paulsen and Sanford M. Kadish, *Criminal Law and Its Processes: Cases and Materials,* Little, Brown, Boston, 1962, pp. 801–802.

53. Detroit Police Department 90th Stat. Annual Report, 1955, p. 65.

54. LaFave, *op. cit.,* p. 478. Reprinted by permission.

55. *Task Force Report: The Police,* p. 186.

56. *Ibid.,* p. 186.

57. *Ibid.*, p. 186.

58. *Ibid.*, p. 186.

59. LaFave, *op. cit.*, p. 297.

60. *Task Force Report: The Police*, p. 184.

61. Tiffany *et al., op. cit.*

62. *Task Force Report: The Police*, p. 184.

63. Irving Piliavin and Scott Briar, "Police encounters with juveniles," *Am. J. Soc.*, **70**, pp. 206–212.

64. Carl Werthman and Irving Piliavin, "Gang members and the police," in David Bordua (ed.), *The Police*, Wiley, New York, 1967, pp. 56, 77, 79. Reprinted by permission.

65. Quoted in *Task Force Report: The Police*, p. 185.

66. Ibid., p. 185.

67. *Lankford v. Gelston*, 364 F. 2d 197 (4th Cir, 1966).

68. 364 F. 2d at 200.

69. 364 F. 2d at 203.

70. 364 F. 2d at 204.

71. *Task Force Report: The Police*, p. 185.

72. *United States v. Wade*, 388 U.S. 218, 87 S. Ct. 1926, 18 L. Ed. 2d 1149 (1967).

73. Yale Kamisar, "Equal justice in the gatehouses and mansions of American criminal procedure," in Yale Kamisar, Fred E. Inbau, and Thurman Arnold, *Criminal Justice in Our Time*, University of Virginia Press, Charlottesville, 1965. Reprinted by permission.

74. The Report and Recommendations of the Commissioner's Committee on Police Arrests for Investigation, Washington, D.C., July, 1962.

75. A.C.L.U. (Ill. Div.), Secret Detention by the Chicago Police 25 (1959).

76. *The Queen v. Thompson* [1893] 2 Q.B. 12, 14; *Ibrahim v. The King* [1914] A.C. 599, 610–611.

77. *Regina v. Baldry* (1852) 2 Den. 430, 169 E.R. 568.

78. 297 U.S. 278, 56 S. Ct. 461, 80 L. Ed. 682 (1936).

79. 297 U.S. at 281.

80. *Herbert v. Louisiana*, 272, U.S. 312 at 316, 47 S. Ct. 103, 71 L. Ed. 270, 48 ALR 1102 (1926).

81. 297 U.S. at 286.

82. 322 U.S. 143, 64 S. Ct. 921, 88 L. Ed. 1192 (1943).

83. 322 U.S. at 154.

84. 338 U.S. 49, 69 S. Ct. 1347, 1357, 93 L. Ed. 1801 (1949).

85. 338 U.S. at 54.

86. *Powell v. Alabama*, 287 U.S. 45, 53 S. Ct. 55, 77 L. Ed. 150 (1932).

87. *Chandler v. Fretag*, 348 U.S. 3, 75 S. Ct. 1, 99 L. Ed. 4 (1954).

88. *Hamilton v. Alabama*, 368 U.S. 52 at 55, 82 S. Ct. 157, 7 L. Ed. 2d 114, (1961).

89. 316 U.S. 455, 62 S. Ct. 1252, 86 L. Ed. 1595 (1942).

90. 372 U.S. 335, 83 S. Ct. 792, 9 L. Ed. 799 (1963).

91. 372 U.S. at 344.

92. William Haller and Godfrey Davies, *The Leveller Tracts, 1647–1653*, Columbia University Press, New York, 1944, p. 454; quoted in *Miranda v. Arizona*, 384 U.S. 436, 86 S. Ct. 1602, 16 L. Ed. 2d 694 (1966).

93. Jardine, *A Reading on the Use of Torture in the Criminal Law of England* (1837) 17; quoted in Morris Ploscowe, "The development of present-day criminal procedures in Europe and America," *Harvard Law Rev.*, **48**, 1935, p. 433, 458n.

94. *Table Talk of John Selden* (Pollock ed., 1927), p. 133; quoted in Ploscowe, *op. cit.*, p. 458n.

95. *People v. Portelli*, 15 N.Y. 2d 235, 205 N.E. 2d 857, 257 N.Y.S. 2d 931 (1965); summarized in *Miranda v. Arizona*, 384 U.S. 436, 446 (1965).

96. 211 U.S. 78, 29 S. Ct. 14, 53 L. Ed. 97 (1908).

97. 211 U.S. at 106.

98. 211 U.S. at 113.

99. *Malloy v. Hogan*, 378 U.S. 1, 84 S. Ct. 1489, 12 L. Ed. 2d 653 (1964).

100. *Miranda v. Arizona*, 384 U.S. 436, 86 S. Ct. 1602, 16 L. Ed. 2d 694 (1966); see also Sanford H. Kadish, "Methodology and criteria in due process adjudication—a survey and criticism," *Yale Law J.*, **66**, 1957, pp. 319, 346–347.

101. Quoted in L. Hall and Y. Kamisar, *Modern Criminal Procedure*, 2d. ed., West, St. Paul, 1966, pp. 411–412.

102. 378 U.S. 478, 84 S. Ct. 1758, 12 L. Ed. 2d 977 (1964).

103. 384 U.S. at 448–454.

104. R. Jackson, concurring in *Watts v. Indiana*, 338 U.S. 49, 57. 69 S. Ct. 1347, 93 L. Ed. 1801 (1949).

105. 384 U.S. at 478–479.

106. Michael Wald, Richard Ayres, David W. Hess, Mark Schantz, and Charles H. Whitehead, Jr., "Interrogations in New Haven: the impact of Miranda," *Yale Law J.*, **76**, 1967, p. 1519.

107. Richard J. Medalie, Leonard Zeitz, and Paul Alexander, "Custodial police interrogation in our nation's capital: the attempt to implement Miranda," *Mich. Law Rev.*, **66**, 1968, p. 1347.

108. Wald, *et al.*, *op cit.*, p. 1539.

109. *Ibid.*, p. 1531. Reprinted by permission of The Yale Law Journal Company and Fred B. Rothman and Company.

110. *Ibid.*, p. 1552. Reprinted by permission.

111. *Ibid.*, p. 1552. Reprinted by permission.

112. *Ibid.*, p. 1552.

113. *Ibid.*, p. 1572.

114. National Commission on Law Observance and Enforcement, Report on Lawlessness in Law Enforcement, **4**, 1931; see Bates Booth, "Confessions, and methods employed in procuring them," *So. Cal. Law Review*, 4, 1930, p. 83; Paul G. Kauper, "Judicial examination of the accused — a remedy for the third degree," *Mich. Law Rev.* **30**, 1932, p. 1224.

115. *Miranda v. Arizona*, 384 U.S. at 446 n7.

116. Wald *et al., op. cit.*, p. 1574. Reprinted by permission.

117. Report by the President's Commission on Law Enforcement and Administration of Justice, *The Challenge of Crime in a Free Society*, U.S. Government Printing Office, 1967, p. 93.

118. *In re Gault*, 387 U.S. 1. 87 S. Ct. 1428, 18 L. Ed. 2d 527 (1967).

119. *Ibid.*

16

The implementation of law in complex societies: arrest

The police having determined that there is probable cause for arrest, they are empowered to take the accused into custody, to prepare a case for prosecution, and to advise the prosecutor of their evidence. In this chapter we shall discuss the formal framework of norms determining which of the persons for whom probable cause exists the police are supposed to arrest and suggest the reasons why these norms are widely ignored.

A. THE FORMAL FRAMEWORK

The typical formal rule concerning the authority of police to arrest requires that they arrest *all* offenders. The Wisconsin statute, for example, states that

the chief [of police] and every policeman . . . shall arrest with or without process and with reasonable diligence take before the municipal justice or other proper court every person found in the city in a state of intoxication or engaged in any disturbance of the peace or violating any law of the state or ordinance of such city . . . .[1]

While there is a variation in the wording of the various statutes, with relatively few exceptions the plain meaning of almost all State statutes have a similar thrust.[2]

Courts have, in the main construed these statutes as imposing a ministerial, non-discretionary duty upon police officers. As we have already seen, in the nature of things any official charged with enforcing a general rule necessarily must make a determination, whether a particular set of facts fits within or without the rule, a decision that in penumbral cases calls for an exercise of discretion.[3] What the courts must mean, therefore, is that when it is a "clear case"—i.e., when the facts of the case at hand beyond argument place it within the core meaning of the rule— the policeman has no alternative: He *must* make the arrest. A Kansas court said that "There is a discretion to be exercised, but that discretion is reposed in [the legislature and the city council]. They have left no room for the exercise of discretion on the part of officials charged especially with the duty of seeing that the laws are enforced."[4] A Wisconsin court sustained the conviction of a Wisconsin sheriff under a statute punishing a public official who "intentionally fails or refuses to perform a known mandatory, nondiscretionary, ministerial duty of his office."[5] The sheriff had failed to prosecute a father for assault upon his son after the son had told the sheriff he did not want to sign a complaint against his father[6]—a situation in which only a rare policeman would arrest.

This non-discretionary standard is one which matches the normative expectations of some academic writers, much of the public, and probably the police themselves. In the philosophic perspective, it is said, "one of the standards of the police in a democratic society is the sharp demarcation of the police job from judicial functions, and the restriction of the police to the so-called ministerial work."[7] The reason has been explicated:

To have police arrest on reasonable grounds and then to provide a prompt, fair trial with all the legal and constitutional safeguards of democratic law is one thing. To allow the police to act not only as officers but also as prosecutors, judges, jury and administrators of penal institutions, substituting crude, sometimes barbaric methods for the rational, fair procedures and treatment symbolized as "due process" is the complete antithesis of democratic law.[8]

This requirement is a reflection of the ingrained notion that the State must be impartial in its dealings with citizens, and in no place more significantly than with respect to the invocation of the ultimate sanctions embodied in the criminal law, an objective attained primarily through the use of general rules,[9] but also through a variety of other devices, such as the insistence upon the independence of the judiciary.

The non-discretionary standard embodies the central value-system of a democratic society, in which, as popular mythology has it, the representative body, the legislature, creates the norms of conduct, and the executive enforces them.

The criminal process ordinarily ought to be invoked by those charged with the responsibility of doing so when it appears that a crime has been committed and that there is a reasonable prospect of apprehending and convicting its perpetrator. Although the area of police and prosecutorial discretion not to invoke the criminal process is demonstrably broad, it is common ground that these officials have no general dispensing power. If the legislature has decided that certain conduct is to be treated as criminal, the decision-makers at every level of the criminal process are expected to accept that basic decision as a premise for action . . . . This assumption may be viewed as the other side of the ex post facto coin. Just as conduct that is not proscribed as criminal may not be dealt with in the criminal process, so must conduct that has been denominated as criminal be so treated by the participants in the process.[10]

This notion that the executive should not exercise discretion, but merely apply clear existing norms without fear or favor may have deep psychological roots. Alexander and Staub assert that

when a criminal escapes his supposedly well-deserved punishment, we feel aroused. In the case of miscarriage of justice, we feel that we ourselves might some day fall victims of the same type of injustice; in the case of escape from justice, however, every member of the community feels that he was wronged, for a man who violated the law escaped punishment; he was forgiven, as it were, for a transgression which is forbidden the righteous member of the community. We deal in both cases with the struggle for freedom of one's instinctual drives; it is a protest against the restriction of these drives. It is as if the individual member of the community said to himself: "If other people are punished unjustly, then *my* personal freedom is also in danger, or if *another* escapes the punishment he deserves, why should *I* continue to conform?"[11]

This demand that the police exercise a narrow ministerial function, applying the rules of criminal law in every case, is a demand in the nature of things that can only be asserted by people not customarily subject to police involvement in their affairs. From the point of view of a population that lives much of its lives in the streets, in which the policeman looms large in every day affairs because of the high visibility of slum life, equality of treatment can never mean blind application of rules. Every case is different. Every case involves different people, with different motives, different circumstances, different pressures operating upon them. Hence it is perhaps to be expected that

There are prevalent in society two general conceptions of the duties of the police officer. Middle-class people feel that he should enforce the law without fear or favor. Cornerville [a slum district in an Eastern city inhabited almost exclusively by Italian immigrants and their children] people and many of the officers themselves believe that the policeman should have the confidence of the people in his area so that he can settle many difficulties in a personal manner without making arrests.[12]

The average police administrator, whatever his private feelings, assiduously cultivates the image that he and his department are committed to the policy of full enforcement. Herman Goldstein asserts that " . . . the mere suggestion that a police administrator exercises discretion in fulfilling his job may be taken as an affront—an attack upon the objective and sacrosanct nature of his job—that of enforcing the law without fear or favor."[13] It is an image that is expressed by the ideal embodied in the usual policeman's oath, and the manuals of police practice.

Why policemen so frequently deny that they ought or even do exercise discretion is a complicated manner. They recognize that the population—at least the dominant middle-class segment—expects them to be impartial. Impartiality is, of course, inevitable when rules are applied strictly in every case. It is not impossible to achieve when discretion is invoked, so long as there are consistent standards by which discretion is to be exercised. It is, however, far more difficult to ensure impartiality in such a case, and even harder to ensure that the police will be *seen* to be impartial. Moreover, any such guidelines to discretion, if formally stated, would be highly controversial. Finally, the most pervasive reason is probably that the police themselves are not aware of the extent to which they in fact exercise discretion and thus make policy.[14]

Whatever the reasons, the consequence is that the police project an image that comports with the values held by middle-class Americans and middle-class expectations for the policeman's role. In so doing, the police legitimize their use of power, for "when the exercise of power is seen as legitimate by those subject to it—that is, when the orders issued or rules set conform to the values to which the subjects are committed—compliance will be much deeper and effective."[15]

In fact, of course, the police exercise discretion every day as to whether or not to arrest even in the event of clear violations of law—as every motorist knows who has sweet-talked a policeman out of issuing a well-deserved traffic ticket.

Discretion exists when the occupant of a position may, consistently with the norms expressing the role-expectations for that position, adopt one of several courses of action. The role-occupant is granted this discretion in order to carry out certain purposes or goals of the bureaucratic structure of which he is a part. The difficulty is to ensure that the discretion is exercised in ways that will carry out those purposes, rather than some private, non-public or non-official purposes. For example, suppose that a traffic ordinance states that the offense of speeding is committed when the driver of a car travels "at a rate of speed faster than reasonable under the circumstances, taking into account the condition of the highway, traffic conditions, weather conditions, and visibility." This is a norm for a policeman, for it instructs him that he is to arrest an offender when the policeman possesses evidence that he drove at a rate of speed faster than reasonable under the circumstances, taking into account the four elements stated. If the policeman considers those four elements, and none other, and decides that the rate of speed is not unreasonable, and hence makes no arrest, his decision may be not the decision that another would have made. It is, however, within limits, a decision which is within the formal structuring of the role: It is made by the person to whom the legislature has (at least by implication) given the authority to make the initial determination, and he has considered only those factors which the legislature has instructed him to take into account. If the policeman considers not the factors the ordinance requires him to take into account, but only that the driver has given him a ten dollar bribe, on the other hand, the public goals for the position have been pro tanto defeated.

The danger is that of goal displacement or distortion, a phenomenon that arises "when an organization displaces its goal—that is, substitutes for its legitimate goal some other goal for which it was not created, for which resources were not allocated to it, and which it is not known to serve."[16] Goal displacement is always a potential result when discretion exists in a bureaucratic organization—and discretion necessarily exists in every stage of a rule-governed structure.

The principal doctrine which has been invoked to control the exercise of the de facto discretion which policemen exercise in determining whom to arrest has been constitutional.

The Fourteenth Amendment forbids any State official from practising discrimination— that is, from discriminating between classes of persons except by reason of differences which are germane to the purposes for which the discretion is granted. As the Supreme Court said long ago,

Though the law itself be fair on its face and impartial in appearance, yet if it is applied and administered by public authority with an evil eye and an unequal hand, so as practically to make unjust and illegal discriminations between persons in similar circumstances material to their rights, the denial of equal justice is still within the prohibition of the constitution.[17]

Courts have been required to face this issue in a series of cases in which an accused seeks to defend against a criminal charge on the ground that others are not prosecuted although equally guilty, or where a person who has been prosecuted seeks an order of the court to compel the prosecution of others. The traditional rule has always been that non-enforcement against others is not a defense in a particular action, on the theory that if the accused is guilty of the offense, that others are also guilty cannot relieve him of penal liability. In *Society of Good Neighbors v. Van Antwerp*,[18] for example, the petitioner brought a suit for an injunction to restrain the officials of Detroit from prosecuting it for operating a bingo game in plain violation of the statutes, on the ground that many other religious, charitable, service, patriotic and other non-profit organizations were operating similar bingo games without prosecution. The court denied the relief sought, on the ground that "a right to violate the law can never be conferred by laxity in its enforcement as to others. The very foundation of a court of equity is good conscience, and it will not lend its aid by way of the extraordinary writ of injunction to assist law violators. He who hath committed inequity shall not have equity." By asserting that it would only take into account the dogma of full enforcement, the court refused to recognize that the prescriptive norm was not in the least descriptive of actual practice.[19]

Other courts have been, perhaps, more realistic, and have admitted the defense where the pattern of discrimination has been shown to be not merely discriminatory, but intentionally so, and based upon reasons not germane to the purposes for which the discretion was granted. The defense has been allowed in cases involving intentional discrimination against black gamblers.[20] Perhaps the clearest statement of the rule appears in *Peo. v. Utica Daw's Drug Company*.[21] There the defendant, a "cut-rate" drugstore, claimed as a defense to a prosecution for selling goods on Sunday that the prosecution was intentionally discriminatory, since it was aimed only at "cut-rate" drugstores and not at many other stores selling the same sorts of goods. The Court sustained the validity of the constitutional claim, saying in part:

Selective enforcement may be justified when the meaning or constitutionality of the law is in doubt and a test case is needed to clarify the law or to establish its validity. Selective enforcement may also be justified when a striking example or a few examples are sought in order to deter other violators, as part of a bona fide rational pattern of general enforcement, in the expectation that general compliance will follow and that further prosecutions will be unnecessary. It is only when the selective enforcement is designed to discriminate against the persons prosecuted, without any intention to follow it up by general enforcement against others, that a constitutional violation may be found.

In addition to the grounds suggested, other cases have indicated that full enforcement is not to be required when the statute has in fact become a dead letter, or when the resources of the police are insufficient to meet all the demands for full enforcement, so that some method of rationing them is required.

None of these cases do more than scratch the very surface of the problem of selective enforcement. What to do when a gambling statute on its face applies to *every* game of chance—even a social game of pennyante poker in a private house between close friends? What to do when a husband assaults a wife, who after calling the police, changes her mind; is it better to enforce the law or to save the family? Is it wise policy to arrest every traffic violator, or is justice sufficiently served by warning some whose offenses seem less serious although clearly violations of the applicable ordinance?

It is interesting that the sorts of problems in which these issues arise rarely include the traditional felonies. Police in fact do arrest every person who seems to them to have violated a major criminal statute. There is complete enforcement of the traditional crimes; murderers, rapists and robbers do not get the benefit of any de facto police discretion not to arrest. The only exception to this rule is probably the case in which the information which lays the basis for the proposed arrest comes from an informer whose identity the police feel it is more important to protect than to arrest the person identified. Beyond this, however, all the cases in which the problem arises are in those areas of the substantive law which our analysis suggested had abandoned the ancient guarantees of harm, *mens rea*, or *actus reus*, or any of them.

At any rate, only in these very limited cases have there been authoritative guidelines laid down to guide the police discretion to arrest or not. The prevalent ideology of full enforcement has prevented any further development.

Without guidelines for discretion, without even an admission that discretion is in fact used, it is not to be wondered that the actual pattern of arrest suggests that the consequence of the invocation of police power has not in fact been the sort of impartial application of an even-handed justice that our democratic ideology demands. It is to this subject that we now turn.

B. THE SOCIAL ORGANIZATION OF POLICE WORK

In the history of Anglo-American criminal law, Sir Robert Peel stands out as having made a most significant contribution which has had profound effects. It was principally through Peel's efforts that in 1829 the British Parliament passed the bill establishing the first police force in England or the United States. It was a limited force, with jurisdiction over most, but not all, of London and certainly not the entire nation.

The police force was established for a variety of reasons. Peel, like J. Edgar Hoover and most police officers after him, pointed to the "alarming rate" at which crime was increasing. His statistical analyses, like those of police advocates to follow, were rather narrow in their perspective, but nonetheless the argument swayed some to support the establishment of a police organization. Another reason for establishing the police in 1829 was that the onerously poor population of the London slums was rioting. The police were seen as a means of controlling the rioters and keeping them from destroying property and life in the "respectable" sections of the community.

Since their emergence in 1829, the police have become a mainstay of the criminal-legal system. Criminal proceedings are initiated in almost every instance by an arrest made by policemen. Although originally the policeman was supposed to be simply a citizen in uniform performing the responsibilities of all citizens,[22] modern industrialized societies have long since given up this notion (although some people, such as the British, still pay lip service to the idea). They are in fact recognized as playing a distinct social role, and their principal job is to control crime and keep the peace.

16.1 POLICING AS AN ORGANIZATIONAL PHENOMENON

In Chapter 14 we set forth a model showing why the criminal process takes the shape it does. We stressed the bureaucratic nature of the agencies which comprise the legal order and argued that this bureaucratic character leads them to operate in ways that will maximize the resources of and minimize the strains on the organizations. In the last chapter we showed how this emphasis on the part of the police leads to their adoption of the crime-control model of operation at the expense of due process, the aim of which dominates the blueprint of the legal system and, in the main, the decisions of appellate courts. We want now to discuss in detail the process of arrest and its effect on the day-to-day events which comprise the criminal process in action. To do this we must discuss at greater length than we have thus far what it means for the police to "maximize resources" and what "sources of strain" they must control if they are to have a smooth-functioning bureaucracy.

There is a strong feeling (expressed in some states by statute) that the police should not be the subject of political manipulation by public officials. Recently the mayor of Lackawanna, New York, was publicly chastised for attempting to control the local police through political appointments, in violation of state statutes. In point of fact, however, even with statutes prevailing and occasional enforcement of these statutes, the police are nonetheless highly dependent on the support of elected politicians. It is the politicians through the city council, and in the form of county supervisors, mayors, city managers, governors, and legislators, who control the resources of the police department because, as publicly elected officials, they hold the public purse strings. Moreover, usually the chief of police is appointed by political leaders. Under these circumstances the police must satisfy the demands of these various groups, or their resources will be reduced. At the same time, if they are to avoid strain, the police must avoid at all costs aggravating persons who can influence the views of the legislators, councilmen, mayor, or governor. Just as "public arousal" is one of the phenomena that elected officials seek to prevent, so its avoidance is one of the guiding principles that dictate the activities of police departments.

What is "public arousal"? Is it the anger and hostility of minority groups who live in the slums and have little or no effective voice with which to speak their antipathy to the police? Is it the cry of the prostitute who must pay a "tithe" to the cop in order to work her block? Is it the cry of the skid-row derelict who is arrested at the whim of the patrolman? Obviously not. These and other cries of dissatisfaction with the police go unheard. Politicians do not view such shouts of antipathy as having any meaning. Indeed, in the logic of the white middle- and upper-class politicians who dominate the governments of the cities and states, these cries serve as some kind of evidence that the police are doing what they are supposed to. As "everyone knows"—every middle-class white politician, that is—it is in the festering sores of the city, the slums and ghettos, that crime is rampant. The policeman who responded to demands from *those people* would only invite criticism from white middle-class citizens.

"Public arousal" means essentially the hostility of white middle-class persons with political clout. These people do not necessarily have to be brothers of the mayor. They may be no more politically involved than the typical suburbanite who contributes seventeen dollars to the Republican campaign every September. They have at their command, however, the ears of persons who can express "public arousal." Potentially they are in the position to get the press to air their grievances. They can contact someone "who knows someone in city hall." Any "respectable" member of the community can, if he chooses to, create a "stink" which will cause strain for the organization and will ultimately influence the distribution of resources to the organization.

"Public arousal," then, has a very special meaning. In the day-to-day operations of the police force, the avoidance of public arousal requires that organizational procedures be developed that will minimize the likelihood of the police being criticized or chastised for their actions. It does not mean that every citizen receives the same consideration. Middle-class persons suspected or accused of a crime will receive "TLC" from the police. But the same treatment need not be given to the typical arrestee from the ghetto or skid row. *Their* treatment will not become public, hence will not arouse the public. Mistakes occur, of course (and we shall detail one such instance later in this chapter). For the most part, however, the standard procedure of having special units to deal with "respectable" citizens and using "crime-control" methods with slum and ghetto residents is sufficient to ensure that "public arousal" and criticism will occur only rarely.

This dominating theme in the social organization of police work has all-encompassing consequences. It dictates where the police will look for (and therefore find) crime; what kinds of persons will be arrested for what kinds of offenses; how those arrested are treated when they are arrested, and the degree to which due-process rather than crime-control procedures is followed. We shall cover each of these various consequences in turn.

16.2 THE LOCATION OF CRIMINAL BEHAVIOR

We pointed out earlier that there are innumerable, one might almost say an infinite number of, criminal offenses that could be uncovered by the police. The startling ones of rape, robbery, murder, and grand theft occur only rarely and command but a minute investment of police work out of their whole organizational enterprise. Eighty percent of the arrests in the United States each year are for minor offenses. On a typical day the police make arrests for drunkenness, disorderly conduct and petty grievances.[23] The decision that these offenses rather than others call for arrests is made by the police departments and in the prosecuting attorney's offices. By contrast, other offenses which could also invite arrests, such as discrimination in jobs or housing, unfair advertising, excessively high interest rates on loans, and the like, for all practical purposes never do. When the laws governing them are enforced, the enforcement is through special administrative boards (such as the Pure Food and Drug Administration) whose sole function is to administer these laws, and rarely through the criminal process.

Typically the police limit their search for potential crimes to lower-class sections of the city. Even in police-state societies, there are not enough policemen to permit the constant surveillance of every citizen or every square mile of the territory. Where, then, should the police be distributed so that they would be likely to detect crime? The answer is as simple as the question: where the largest number of crimes occur. But the answer to the question of where most crimes occur may not be as simple as it looks. Generally, the evidence for where the crimes occur most frequently consists of past records. If the central district of the city had the highest crime rates in years past, then that is where the police must focus their attention today. But lying behind this simple logic is a potentially dangerous cycle. It is possible that the only reason the central section, or any other section, has shown a higher crime rate in the past is that the police were there to look. Thus it is quite possible that the police, by this apparently simple directional decision as to where to look for crime, may well contribute to the maintenance of a self-fulfilling prophecy. Crime will be prevalent where we look for it, not because of the inherent criminality of the areas surveyed, but merely because so many of the things that people do in their daily lives are against the law that any area inundated with policemen will show a correspondingly high crime rate.

Weight is added to this interpretation when it is realized that a "high crime rate" does not mean that there are large numbers of rapes, murders, assaults, and robberies committed in that area. Most of the law-enforcement effort, as mentioned before, consists in arresting and processing persons accused of very minor offenses: drunkenness, vagrancy, street-walking, and the like. We mentioned earlier that in 1965 the police in the United States reported making 4,955,047 arrests of which only 834,296 (approximately 20%) were for "Type I" or what the Federal Bureau of Investigation considers "major" crimes.[24] There is good reason to question the degree to which even this proportion of the total arrests might not be an overestimate of the number of serious offenses that take place. For example, two categories of major crimes include offenses that are relatively inconsequential. Over 10% (101,763) of the "major crimes" were accounted for by auto theft. Yet the vast majority (over 90%) of the auto thieves are more accurately described as "joy riders"—adolescents taking an automobile for a short period of time just for a ride in it.[25] In most of these cases, the automobile is found within twenty-four hours being abandoned by the "thieves." Another category which characteristically includes a number of offenses whose seriousness is questionable is that of "larceny over fifty dollars." While thirty or forty years ago, to steal something valued at "over fifty dollars" might have meant stealing a rather expensive commodity, this is certainly no longer true. Indeed, one hub cap from a new automobile or a headlamp from a motorcycle may be valued at over fifty dollars. To place such offenses in the same category as crimes against person and burglary is to distort their seriousness. Much of the alleged increases in serious crimes in recent years is attributable to an increase in the number of autos taken for a joy ride rather than to an increase in other types of serious offenses.

Another equally important source of "increase in serious crimes" is the organizational decision on the part of many police departments and prosecuting attorney's offices to charge defendants with the most serious crimes possible in order to have a better position from which to bargain. Thus someone who is arrested for drunkenness will be charged with "battery against a police officer" if he has in any way been violent. Since "battery against a police officer" is a felony, it is easier to coerce a bargain with the defendant as that if he pleads guilty to public intoxication, a misdemeanor, then the prosecutor will drop the felony charge. The "serious-crime rate" nonetheless still reflects the arrest for the felony.

No systematic research has been done to indicate the degree to which these practices affect the officially reported crime rate, and some is certainly badly needed. It does seem clear, however, that much of even the small proportion of "serious" crimes reported by the police itself consists really of quite minor crimes. In view of all the temptations to inflate the number of serious offenses handled by the police, it is probably quite conservative to estimate that no more than 10% of the arrests made every year by police are for serious crimes against person or property. Furthermore, even among the major crimes, most (roughly 80%) are crimes against property. These data contrast rather sharply with the widespread belief that most police activities center around crimes against the person, such as assault, murder, and rape.

16.3 VISIBILITY OF OFFENSES

The facts just noted make it clear that the largest contribution to the arrest rate in any area derives from the police making arrests for relatively minor offenses. Although no data are available for an accurate assessment, casual observation would suggest that the frequency of drunkenness, gambling, and numerous other offenses is probably as great in the middle-class, "respectable" neighborhoods as it is in the lower-class "slums." The middle-class transgressions are invisible, however, not just because the police do not as thoroughly survey the areas in search of transgressions, but also because middle-class wrongdoings (as defined by law) typically take place in private and privacy is an effective barrier against scrutiny.[26] James Wilson has captured this point and the essence of its implications when he writes:

In a slum neighborhood, personal and family privacy is at a premium. The doors, walls, windows, and locks which provide for most of us the legally-defined privacy which it is the policeman's duty to protect are much less meaningful to people who must share their rooms with other persons and their apartments with other families. Particularly in warm weather, such people move outside, sit on their front steps, lean out their windows, and loiter in the streets. The street is, in effect, every man's front room.[27]

In a word, all behavior, including transgressions of varying degrees of seriousness, are much more visible in the slums than anywhere else in the city. Their increased visibility moves the police to scrutinize with considerably more care the activities which take place. And in scrutinizing, they find. Thus is created the self-fulfilling prophecy of high crime rates in slum areas.

Crowded living conditions create an environment in which most behavior, even what occurs in one's own home, is susceptible to screening by the neighbors and by law-enforcement officials. Domestic disputes, exessive drinking, and other quasi-illegal acts are much more likely to be seen in the lower classes than in the middle classes. Even the delinquent acts of the juveniles are more visible among lower-class than among middle-class youths.[28] Middle-class adolescents generally have access to automobiles; many of them have their own car. The automobile provides a means of escape from the scrutiny of law-enforcers: drinking can be done in out-of-the-way places, delinquent acts can be committed in neighboring communities rather than near one's own home. The lower-class adolescent, by contrast, will find such mobility difficult to manage. If he drinks, he must do so in an alley; when he gambles, he is not protected by the security of his parents' home; indeed, with the urban lower-class adolescent even so private behavior as the sexual act is likely to be carried out in relatively more public arenas than is the case with the middle-class adolescent, who has the privacy at least of his car.

Gambling is an excellent example where there is a sharp difference in visibility between lower- and middle-class practices. In a large house, there is always a room where a group of middle-class men wishing to gamble can do so without disturbing other members of the family. The lower-class male, however, has less opportunity to gamble in his own home, which usually consists of a small apartment which he shares with a large number of other people. He is more likely to find an alleyway or the backroom of a public establishment a more convenient place to gamble. Thus, middle-class gambling is protected from police scrutiny by the privacy of a home,[29] whereas a lower-class gambler must expose himself to the sanctions of the legal system by gambling in public.

The deviancy of the poor suffers from a multitude of other subtle visibilities. Being more frequently involved with governmental agencies, such as those dispensing welfare, vastly increases the chances of having one's deviancy officially discovered. From their study of a police department's morals detail, J. H. Skolnick and J. R. Woodworth found that the discovery of statutory-rape cases by the police was largely dependent on referrals from welfare agencies:

The influence of poverty on the discovery of statutory rapes is obvious: the largest single source of reports is from the family support division (40%). At the time of the study ADC aid could be given to a mother only if her real property was worth less than $5,000 and her personal property less than $600. One social worker reported that most applicants possessed no real property; those who had originally owned such property had exhausted its value prior to applying for aid. *Thus, statutory rape is punished mainly among the poor who become visible by applying for maternity aid from welfare authorities.*[30] (Italics added.)

The official statistics furnish evidence that problems of drinking, fighting, and gambling are concentrated in lower-class areas. Yet these statistics are not informative as to differences, either in frequency or seriousness of these acts, between lower and middle classes. They simply reflect the fact that middle-class affluence affords a shield against public scrutiny that is not enjoyed by members of the lower class. The weight of the evidence indicates that to a significant degree the legal system's processing of law violators involves the arrest and prosecution of lower-class persons for doing in public what middle- and upper-class persons do in private.

The fact that the availability of privacy affects the process of arrest can be misleading, however. It is certainly *not* the case, as Arthur L. Stinchcombe has argued, that the institution of privacy is such a strongly held value that the police are kept from intervening in private places thereby.[31] Indeed, it is perfectly clear that police practices in the slums and ghettos systematically ignore the right to privacy of these people. Take, for example, the case of the welfare workers who invade unannounced the homes of mothers receiving aid to dependent children in order to see if there are any "unauthorized men" living on the premises. The following case may be unusual, but it nonetheless illustrates the point:

One family . . . complained of repeated harassment . . . The family consisted of a mother, her teenage son and younger daughter. The mother and daughter slept in the combination living room, dining room and bedroom, and the son slept in a small converted closet off the bedroom. One night they were awakened at three o'clock in the morning by loud knocking at their door. The son went to the door, which opened into the bedroom occupied by the mother and daughter. Two men pushed past him without identifying themselves as investigators from the Department of Public Aid, and said they were looking for the father who was reported to have returned home. Without apology they left, but returned several weeks later at one o'clock in the morning, repeating the same performance, again without finding their man.[32]

The failure of the legal system to deal with the middle- and upper-class law-violators does not derive from the strength of the institution of privacy. It derives instead from the very rational choice on the part of the legal system to pursue those violators that the community will reward them for pursuing, and to ignore those violators who have the capability of causing trouble for the agencies.

The police invade the privacy of the home of slum and ghetto dwellers without much reticence. They also establish a string of informers to let them know where illegal activities, such as gambling and prostitution, are taking place even when these activities are confined to private dwellings. Police have never been known to plant informers among middle-class suburbanites to locate the weekly floating poker game. They do not use the same techniques for getting around the privacy of middle-class businessmen who charge exhorbitant interest rates and illegally garnishee wages of the poor. But the police do use extremely subtle and complicated techniques for locating lower-class persons who are selling, buying, or simply possessing marijuana or other drugs.

The institution of privacy, then, is a convenient value for the police to espouse as explanation of laxity in the enforcement of laws against middle-class persons. It is, however, convenient for them to ignore it when they are trying to locate criminal activities among the lower classes. The phenomenon to be explained is why the police let privacy shield middle-class illegality, but not lower-class illegality. The answer, we suggest, is that in the one instance it is organizationally wise to let the offenses pass, while in the other it is not.

16.4 VISIBILITY OF OFFENSE AND LAW-ENFORCEMENT

A study of delinquency in a large city, where there is a densely populated area inhabited by Japanese as well as a more typically urban black ghetto, provides data on the relationship between the visibility of deviant acts and the legal process. The official statistics show that black youth have the highest delinquency rate of any racial group in the city, whites the next highest. The Japanese have virtually no delinquency at all as shown in official statistics. The police believe, as do most of the people in the community who are in any way connected with youth and problems, that the Japanese youth are of a different cut than most groups. Families have more solidarity; adults form a more homogeneous and tight-knit community. As a consequence, youthful delinquency is exceedingly rare. Believing this, the police devote little time to surveying the Japanese community. Patrolmen are assigned in large numbers to the black ghetto and to the skid-row area, but are only sparsely assigned to survey the area encompassing the Japanese community. Furthermore, the Japanese socio-economic level is considerably higher than that of the blacks, and consequently the residences are more likely to be private, thus affording an added barrier to the visibility of transgressions.

William Chambliss and Richard Nagasawa, utilizing a self-reported delinquency index, obtained responses on involvement in delinquency from a sample of Japanese, black, and white youth attending high school in the area that has the highest delinquency rate of the city.[33] Their findings (see Table 16.1) suggest that,

TABLE 16.1   Comparison of arrests (for 1963) and self-reported delinquency involvement by racial groups[34]

	Percent of each group arrested during 1963	Percent of each group classified as having high delinquent involvement on the basis of self-reported delinquency*
White	11%	53%
Black	36%	52%
Japanese	2%	36%

*   A self-reported delinquency scale was developed and the respondents were divided so that 50% of the sample was categorized as having high and 50% as having low delinquent involvement.

while the Japanese youth do have a somewhat lower rate of delinquency than white or black juveniles, they are scarcely "delinquency free" as is generally assumed. The really striking difference which emerges between the official rates of delinquency (as given in police statistics) and the self-reported rates of the three groups is quite predictable from the difference in visibility of the acts; it is certainly not predictable from the relative propensity of the youths in the various groups to commit transgressions, as judged from their self-reported involvement.

In short, police decisions have an important "self-fulfilling" quality. Precisely how many more offenses could be uncovered in areas of more sparse and more affluent populations it is impossible to guess. We should, however, look rather carefully at the assumption that previous crime rates are an adequate index of the propensity of one group to commit more crimes as compared with some other group. Statistics and legal action concerning even apparently obvious offenses, such as murder and rape, are likely to be very biased against lower-class areas for much the same reason that statistics on minor offenses are. Murder is one of the more difficult crimes to hide; yet it is proportionately more difficult for someone in a lower-class area to hide than it is for someone in a middle-class area. In addition, the police are understandably more reticent about bringing charges of murder against a "respectable" member of the community then they are against someone who is viewed with suspicion to begin with. Arnold Trebach, in his investigation of police practices in Pennsylvania and New Jersey described a case where the police arrested a black man for a knife attack and beat him until he confessed to the crime.[35] Later investigation disclosed that the man could not possibly have committed the crime, and he was completely exonerated. It is almost impossible to imagine the police using similar tactics against anyone who is "respectable." To coerce a confession from a middle-class white man in this way would risk bringing down the wrath of the entire politically powerful white community on the police department. Such an action would be far too risky even if the police were thoroughly convinced that they had arrested the right man.

Data on forcible rape are probably similarly biased. There are doubtlessly many more rapes committed than are reported because of the reticence of victims to publicize the rape. If a rape occurs in an automobile or in the privacy of a home, then the likelihood of the event's becoming public is totally dependent on the victim's taking action. If, on the other hand, the rape occurs in an alley or in an apartment where shouts are easily heard by neighbors, then the probabilities are highly dependent on other factors. Rather than being ashamed to report the crime, under these circumstances the offended person may feel compelled to file a complaint in order to demonstrate publicly that she was not a willing partner.

Once the policeman goes out on a beat (or into a patrol car) the process of seeing more crimes among the poor continues. Even if he is committed to arresting all violators of the law (which virtually no policeman can do), there is considerable discretion called for. How does a policeman decide, for example, that something is amiss and should be looked into? Where policemen are assigned the same beat for some period of time, one of the most often used techniques for making such a decision is to look for "unusual" events. To the uninitiated, things which appear as unusual events may not be so at all. A policeman may, for example, ignore the fact that a woman comes running out of her house screaming that someone is going to kill her. If this has happened every Friday night at approximately the same time for a year, the policeman may well decide to ignore it. Or, if the same shop-keeper is always engaged in an apparently violent argument with the same customer every week, the policeman may continue on his appointed rounds without so much as a second look into the store. In fact, what may stand out in his routine as an unusual event is the absence of a shouting argument or the absence of a drunk at a street corner. This process of finding the unusual is also a highly selective one, and is yet another series of sociologically significant factors which shape the legal process.

16.5 OFFENDER'S DEMEANOR AND ARREST

Discovering someone who is suspected of a crime is but the initial step of a long process. The policeman must decide whether or not a suspect should be "brought to the station."[36] If he is "brought to the station," then the sergeant or some other police officer must decide whether or not to hold him for charges or release him. In this game of decision-making the lower-class suspect is once again at a dis-advantage compared to a middle-class suspect. The police take the suspect's demeanor as exceedingly important. If he is, in the eyes of the police, contrite, apologetic, and respectful, then he "deserves a break." If, by contrast, he is hostile, belligerent, and defiant, then he deserves to be punished—to be "taught a lesson." If he is violent or abusive toward the police, he must be taught to respect law and order—even if creating this respect requires the policeman himself to break the law.

Irving Piliavin and Scott Briar made extensive observations on the criteria used by policemen to help them decide how to dispose of juveniles whom they had arrested or were considering arresting. The first criterion was the nature of the offense. If the juvenile was suspected of having committed an offense such as robbery, homicide, aggravated assault, grand theft, auto theft, or rape, then the officer would take him to the station. There was, however, some discretion even in these cases.

In most cases where the offense was relatively minor, discretion played a major role in the arresting process. The criterion used by the police more than any other was an assessment of the boy's "character": if the policemen making the decision viewed the boy as basically "all right" or "good," then he would be inclined to "give him a break" and release him. On the other hand, if the boy were seen as basically "bad," then he would be detained. The assessment of "goodness" in turn was determined principally by the demeanor of the youth.

Older juveniles, members of known delinquent gangs, Negroes, youths with well-oiled hair, black jackets and soiled denims or jeans (the presumed uniform of "tough" boys), and boys who in their interactions with officers did not manifest what were considered appropriate signs of respect tended to receive more severe dispositions.[37]

Table 16.2, taken from the study by Piliavin and Briar, shows the influence of a youth's demeanor on the severity of police disposition.

The correlation drawn by the police between demeanor and deviant behavior has very little factual basis. Cultural factors, more than deviancy, tend to determine demeanor toward the police. Black culture in urban America, for example, places strong emphasis on the expression of a "cool" demeanor for the male black.[38]

On the other hand, middle-class white culture teaches its young that the policeman is "your friend in blue," the man who extends the helping hand to lost kiddies and pregnant ladies. Middle-class white youths, whatever their true thoughts, rapidly learn the techniques of displaying respect for authority, and they do not lose status among their peers by doing so. Black youths are treated more harshly, not because they are necessarily more deviant than white middle-class youths, but because they have been raised in the black culture—because they are black.

The demeanor of the offender frequently has other consequences besides the incurrence of more severe sanctions. Frequently, though perhaps not as often as some polemicists have insisted, the police resort to the illegal use of violence in order to see that someone whom they "know" is guilty is adequately punished. The violence may be used as a means of obtaining a confession[39] or it may simply be used to "bring the person in line." In either case, the demeanor of the offender is a crucial factor in determining whether or not the police will resort to illegal violence in the course of arresting or incarcerating a suspect.[40]

TABLE 16.2 Severity of police disposition and youth's demeanor

Severity of police disposition	Youth's demeanor		Total
	Cooperative	Uncooperative	
Arrest (most severe)	2	14	16
Citation or official reprimand	4	5	9
Informal reprimand	15	1	16
Admonish and release (least severe)	24	1	25
Total	45	21	66

Since one's dress as well as his associations are also used as criteria to determine the appropriateness of making an arrest, the likelihood of arrest is vastly increased for persons whose appearance is unconventional. In recent years, in urban areas throughout the United States, youths who have adopted the long hair and shabby dress fashions which characterize the "hippies" have found themselves a frequent target of police harassment.[41] While in some of these cases the police have insisted that the arrests are justified because of the "well-known" prevalence of drug use among these groups, the fact remains that it is probably the unusual demeanor of the offenders more than any other single factor which accounts for the extent of police activity directed at them.

16.6 BIAS

The final variable that must be discussed before we can understand the shape of the police activities is the prevailing biases in the policing organizations. Just as the police must decide where to send patrolmen to look for crime, so they must also decide what kinds of acts to police in the first place. Police departments typically have "vice squads," which utilize innumerable ingenious techniques such as the use of informers and entrapment to discover the use of drugs, the presence of prostitution and homosexuality, or the distribution of pornography. Police departments never have divisions for investigating crimes of corporations, such as collusion, false advertising, or charging excessive interest rates.

The effect of institutionalized bias operates in other equally important ways. It is striking to note the degree to which the delinquencies of lower-class youth are generally viewed as "serious," while the delinquencies of middle- and upper-class youth are likely to be viewed as simply "fun" or, at worst, youthful "hell raising."

It may be that such a biased perspective is organizationally rational, but that does not mean that it is justified. Lower-class youths typically engage in *delinquencies* such as fighting, sexual relations, and petty theft. Middle-class youths, by contrast, typically engage in *activities* such as drinking, vandalism, and truancy.[42] No doubt the dominant middle-class perspective is similar to the view of the police about the relative seriousness of these respective offenses. Legally and sociologically, however, such an assumption is quite questionable. Drinking, the characteristic middle-class delinquency, frequently leads to drunken driving. Save for those relatively rare occasions when two hard-core urban juvenile gangs engage in open warfare, the fights that lower-class youths engage in are rarely capable of causing high risk of the serious physical harm that probably ensues whenever a middle-class youth indulges in drunken driving. Similarly, with respect to property damage, the frequent vandalism of middle-class youths in all likelihood is more costly to the community than is the theft behavior of even the most active and successful of lower-class youths.

An intensive study of department store shoplifters has revealed the operation of policing agencies' biases in the handling of various types of shoplifters. The department store detective is particularly vulnerable to charges of false arrests, which can have serious consequences for the store. A "bad pinch" may well involve the arrest of someone from the middle or upper class. As a consequence, the department store detective must take considerable caution in making an arrest. In essence, what this means in day-to-day terms is that the store detective must actually see the act of shoplifting before he can make an arrest. Since "seeing" depends on "looking," only those persons will be seen and subject to arrest who are watched. According to Mary Owen Cameron, persons who appear suspicious to store detectives include those who appear to be looking around to see if they are watched, unaccompanied adolescents, and blacks.[43]

Once a person is apprehended, the store must decide whether or not to notify the city police. The most important single criterion used by store detectives in making this decision is whether the person was engaged in commercial or consumptive theft. If the shoplifter is believed to have been stealing for refund or resale, then he will certainly be charged with the offense. If, on the other hand, the detective decides that the person was merely stealing for his own use, then other characteristics of the offender will determine whether or not he will be processed beyond the store detective's office. It is at this point that racial bias plays an exceedingly important role. Cameron found that while 6.5% of all adults arrested were black, 24% of all prosecutions were of blacks. Whereas the store tended to charge most whites with "lesser offenses," 50% of all blacks were charged with larceny.[44] Cameron also demonstrates that this differential treatment of whites and blacks could not be accounted for on the grounds that the blacks stole more expensive merchandise or that they were more likely to have prior records of theft. In short, a differential of over 40% in the proportion of persons prosecuted for serious offenses was a function of police bias, rather than a function of real differences in the seriousness of offense or the likelihood of recidivism.

In the last few years in America we have begun to see the manifestation of a categorical bias against juveniles quite similar to the bias which has characterized police treatment of blacks and other minority group members in the past. It is probably safe to say that until fairly recently the police were very reticent about arresting and processing youths from middle- and upper-class families. Recently, however, the police seem to have become more aggressive in enforcing the laws against the children of "respectable" parents as they have always enforced them against children of the poor. A principal reason for the change is the growing alienation between the "younger generation" and the adult world. This alienation stems in large part from the different reaction of the adult world and youth to the use of stimulants and depressants, particularly marijuana and the "mind expanding" drugs such as LSD. It is less easy for middle- and upper-class parents to dismiss a youth's experimenting with or taking periodically one of these depressants or stimulants than it was for a parent a generation ago to dismiss the drinking and "hell raising" of his children as merely a phase of "growing up."

The police, for their part, have responded to the request for enforcement of laws prohibiting the taking of all kinds of artificial stimulants and drugs by arresting and processing middle- and upper-class youths as they have traditionally arrested the less affluent. As the drugs have spread from the slums to the suburbs, the parents and teachers in the suburbs have asked for help from law-enforcement agents. The response has been to place informers in the schools (colleges as well as high schools), to crash parties, and develop informants to help the police make arrests.

The "respectable" community got more than it bargained for. Instead of reducing the propensity of youth to partake of the drugs, the intervention by law-enforcement agents has probably contributed to the rapid dissemination of drug use throughout the middle- and upper-class strata. It has probably also contributed to the willingness of youth to experiment widely with different kinds of drugs. It has certainly contributed to the breakdown of traditional patterns of dealing with norm-violations by middle- and upper-class youth. As it slowly became clear to the parents of these youths what the consequences of intervention by the law-enforcement agencies means in terms of prison sentences, jail sentences, interrupted education, etc., and as the younger generation conducted a successful campaign to "educate" their parents as to the "facts" of "pot," law-enforcement agencies have begun to feel the sting of community criticism for their processing of middle- and upper-class youthful law-violators. The response is predictable. Characteristically, police departments and prosecuting attorneys' offices have begun to withdraw from the all-out campaign of only a few years ago against pot in the high schools and colleges. The effort at drug control is, once again, being focused on the use of drugs in the slums, where arrests can be made and convictions obtained without creating the kind of organizational strains that have burgeoned with the arrest of middle- and upper-class youths.

16.7 OPERATIONAL IMPLICATIONS OF THE CRIME-CONTROL MODEL

We have dealt substantially in the last few chapters with the implications for police work of adopting the crime-control model of legal activity. We need only add here some of the systemically introduced patterns of police work which stem from subscribing to the crime-control model of legal operations. Essentially what this model prescribes is for the police in their routine activities to locate potential criminals or sources of trouble in the community and act to eliminate them from the community. More often than not, the policeman's operating procedures involve a host of techniques for accomplishing these goals: harassment by arrest, threats of violence, a show of force, and in some instances the creation of a case against a person where there is no case. The case of Edward Lamb, a well-known and highly successful industrialist and broadcaster, is illustrative of the tactics that may be employed by police departments (in this case an investigative branch of the Federal government) in order to punish and control a person defined within the organization as a threat to the community.

The case of Edward Lamb, who in the 1950's was accused by the FCC of being a communist,[45] illustrates the "getting the criminal, regardless" philosophy is working to its logical extreme. The entire story is too long to tell, but the broad outline is as follows. Edward Lamb was an affluent and generous backer of liberal democrats for many years. During the era of Joseph McCarthy when communist witch-hunting was at its peak, Lamb was a financial and public supporter of Adlai Stevenson. The Federal Communications Commission became convinced that Edward Lamb was a threat to the American way of life. Whether this fear arose from the antipathy of a Republican-dominated organization attempting to control the Democrats or from a more acceptable (but no more justifiable) fear that Edward Lamb was in fact a communist and therefore a threat to America will never be known. For whichever reason—and there may have been others as well—the FCC attempted to take away television and radio station licenses for Mr. Lamb's station.

During the FCC hearings, at which the federal government attempted to prove that Mr. Lamb had been a member of the communist party from 1944 to 1948, a string of witnesses testified against Mr. Lamb. These informants were paid by the FCC with money and given immunity from other sanctions. One, for example, was subject to deportation and testified persumably to ensure postpone-ment or cancellation of his deportation. Another witness, a former prostitute, testified that she was a former wealthy socialite who had lost her fortune during the depression and met Edward Lamb when she joined the communist party after the disillusionment that came with impoverishment. Her entire story, including her testimony that someone (allegedly acting for Edward Lamb) had offered her $50,000 *not* to testify against Lamb, was shown to be a complete lie. She was later indicted for perjury. Other witnesses were equally tainted; one went so far as to admit that the questions of the prosecutor and his answers had all been carefully rehearsed prior to his coming to the trial. While it is of course impossible to obtain unbiased analyses of this case, the transcripts from the court records and the analysis by Edward Lamb make it quite clear that the law-enforcement agents involved were willing to go to almost any length to "get" Edward Lamb. From the perspective of the law-enforcement agencies, "getting him" was precisely what they were supposed to do. His guilt was predetermined by their investigations, and if the evidence they could provide for that position could not stand up in court then it was their task to create the kind of evidence that would.

A less dramatic case, but one that illustrates the same general principle, occurred in a small midwestern town where the law-enforcement agents of the community decided to maintain public order by ridding the town of one Joe Lord.[46]

Joe Lord (this is not his real name) arrived in town, a small midwestern community, inconspicuously enough. The police were not forewarned and, at the time of his arrival, he did not, to the best of their knowledge, have a criminal record. Shortly afterward, however, a series of incidents brought him to the attention of officials and culminated in their defining him as a deviant.

In the course of a few years Lord had purchased several taverns, all of them catering primarily to a lower-class clientele. He also purchased and resold some property in a transaction described by one official as "shady," apparently because Lord had somehow received advance knowledge that this piece of property was going to be sought by a local bank and that this would raise its price considerably. The town officials did not understand where Lord could have obtained financing for these enterprises; they assumed he was "not the type" to have either investments or enough capital to pay for these "deals." The prosecuting attorney, in an interview, hinted that Lord was being financed by a group of "outsiders."

In addition to the three taverns, Lord also purchased what came to be known as the 713 Club. (This building, located in a lower-class deteriorating area, was two doors away from a home owned by the university in the town and occupied by the university's vice-president. Despite the fact that it was several miles from the campus, this home was of considerable sentimental value to the university, because it had once been the home of the university's president.)

Shortly after this purchase, Joe Lord applied for a liquor license for the 713 Club. At the hearing he was opposed by the university, and by several persons who lived near the club. The secretary of the Board of Trustees was one of three university officials who appeared at the hearing to voice the university's opposition, which was strenuous, organized, and effective. As a result, Joe Lord's application was refused.

Officers of the university were convinced that Joe Lord's taverns frequently served liquor to minors and allowed them to drink to excess on the premises. Other local officials had even more serious reservations about Lord's character. The mayor stated that he first became aware of his activities several years before when Joe Lord was sued by his former wife for failure to pay alimony, a fact also commented upon by one of the deans at the university. The town officials also thought that Joe Lord at times rented rooms for purposes of prostitution, and they suspected him of somehow being involved in selling drugs. Both university and town officials said there was evidence that Lord was involved with a known distributor of drugs from a nearby large city. The information supporting this suspicion was tenuous at best; it was, however, sufficient to arouse fear among the officials, who perceived Joe Lord as a person always "walking a tightrope between legal and illegal activities."

As a result of these suspicions and fears the local officials tacitly agreed, apparently with the complicity of the university, to "do something" about Joe Lord. But "doing something" about him involved some risk. His known activities were, at the worst, minor transgressions (selling liquor to college students), and, at best, describable only as "shady" or "on the fringe" of legality. Furthermore, his suspected illegal activities took place in privacy. And finally, Lord had at least a modicum of esteem in the community. He did not enjoy membership in the upper enchelons of the community's social life, but he was not readily defined as intrinsically "bad." Thus the officials were faced with the problem of "doing something" about a case that could become a source of trouble for the police themselves. They chose, not surprisingly, to engage in what amounted to a campaign of harassment.

Lord was accused of "keeping a gaming device" (a punch board on which the winning number received a fifth of whiskey) in one of his taverns; he was tried, found guilty, and fined. Next came the refusal of his application for a liquor license for the 713 Club. Then some girls were arrested in a hotel (which was partly owned by Lord) on a charge of "keeping a dive" when they sold a drink of whiskey to a plain-clothes policeman. And finally, some underage students were arrested at Lord's 713 Club, where they were having a private party at which alcoholic drinks were served. This last offense might have been serious enough to drive Lord from town had it not been for some events which were unanticipated by the officials and which, in fact, almost culminated in their own undoing.

One of the fraternities at the university had rented the second floor of the 713 Club for a private party for the night of the Coronation Ball. At eleven o'clock that night, when the party was in progress, the police received a phone call from an unknown person stating that a woman who occupied a third-floor apartment above the 713 Club had had a heart attack. When the police arrived to investigate, they were seen by the students, who thereupon assumed that their party was about to be raided and proceeded to leave the premises by every available means—windows, fire escapes, and stairs.

The mayor, on his way home from visiting friends, heard, on the police radio in his car, the call instructing the police to make the investigation. Recognizing the address as that of Joe Lord's club, the mayor speeded there, parked his car in the adjoining alley, and went into the building just as the students were scurrying from it. (One fleeing student dashing down the alley opened the door of the mayor's car and said to the mayor's wife: "You'd better get the hell out of here fast. The cops are here.")

The police, occupied upstairs, had paid no attention to the students' party. The mayor however, insisted that the police "stake out" the building. The prosecutor and the police chief were notified that the place was about to be raided.

At 1:00 a.m. ten students joined the party. They danced and had a "couple of drinks." At 1:30 six plain-clothes policemen came into the room and informed the students they were under arrest and that they would all have to "come down to headquarters." The male students were handcuffed (a procedure described by the dean of students as "highly irregular"), taken to the sheriff's office, booked, and held in custody. The boys were placed in cells upstairs in the jail; the girls, one of whom was the Coronation Queen, were put into one large room. A phone call by the girls alerted their sorority and the university to their arrest. Bond was scraped together from the sorority and from a university fund specifically set aside for such purposes. Within a few hours the students were released on bail.

The story of the mass arrested was headlined the next morning in several towns where the students were residents. Special attention was given to the arrest of the Coronation Queen, ironically enough because her father, a well-known public relations man in the state, had previously arranged for national coverage of her coronation. The papers, of course, quickly switched the emphasis away from a routine story to one that featured her arrest at a party described by the police as a "drinking orgy."

The following day her father came down to the university and informed the dean of students and the police that there had been a grievous error. He also informed the local police that if they did not drop the charges he would sue them for false arrest. The local police, the mayor, and the country prosecutor had, of course, not anticipated such a reaction; in fact, they were all somewhat stunned by the publicity. Some rather uncomplimentary remarks were exchanged publicly between university officials and the mayor and between the mayor and the prosecutor.

The mayor was the only one to come out of the fracas apparently unscathed. He consistently maintained that the students should be prosecuted and that they should receive their deserved punishment. The prosecutor, on the other hand, maintained that the police would not sign an affidavit showing that they had evidence against the students and that therefore he could not prosecute the case. He even went so far as to place a statement in the local paper for one week that if anyone, citizen or policeman, would sign a complaint and thereby commit himself to testify against the students, he would prosecute.

By this time the university was trying to be as quiet as possible.

There were numerous letters to the editor of the local newspaper, most of which were uncomplimentary to the university and to the prosecutor.

Of the ten students involved, four (those who were not befriended by the Coronation Queen's vociferous and influential father) were placed on probation by the university. All of the girls were placed on probation by their national sorority. The father protested to the sorority headquarters that its action was not justified since "no crime" had been committed by the students.

The whole series of events was described by the dean of students as a "comedy of errors," a most accurate caricature.

More routinely, policemen harass persons who need to be controlled: "bums" on skid row, black youths who gather on street corners, prostitutes, homosexuals, and any other group or individual who the police feel needs to be controlled and who are also incapable of effectively entering a complaint against them. The case reported in Chapter 13 where the police beat and placed on an out-of-town bus a black man who had presumably "caused trouble" illustrates this procedure of harassment as a mechanism of control. Significantly, the police ended this encounter with the comment "He won't be back," suggesting that in their mind they had done their job satisfactorily.

Occasionally a police department may attempt to use the same methods for controlling persons usually placed "beyond the pale" of police work. A professor of English at an eastern university was arrested and charged with having marijuana in his home. He argued, in what became a nationally publicized case, that the marijuana had been placed in his home at the suggestion of the police by an informant (a young girl whom the professor had befriended and taken into his home) in order to harass him. The professor was, in the eyes of the police, a radical trouble-maker without whom the community would be better off. But the police rarely utilize these practices against persons of the legitimate community precisely because the risks are too great. No bureaucracy is willing to risk alienating large segments of the community in order to accomplish its goals when it must have the support of the community in order to thrive and survive. The cases of Edward Lamb, the English professor from the east, and the beauty queen from the midwest are informative particularly because they represent cases where standard police practices which work so effectively for the organization when employed against the lower classes do not work at all well when transferred to the more well-to-do and the politically powerful. The upshot, of course, is that the police realize this and practice their crime-control activities with the poor. By contrast, nonenforcement characterizes their dealings with the politically and economically powerful members of the community—unless enforcement is absolutely necessary, in which case due process is observed.

16.8 SUMMARY

The formal norms defining the policeman's obligation to arrest do not give him any discretion to arrest or not to arrest whenever there is probable cause. He is nominally bound by the dogma of full enforcement. In fact, however, discretion to exercise the power of arrest necessarily exists de facto. The Fourteenth Amendment of the federal Constitution has been invoked to prevent police from exercising their descretion in a discriminatory manner. Actually, a number of variables—the fact that middle-class persons can create greater tensions and provide greater rewards for the police as an organization, the relative visibility of criminal activity in slum areas compared with middle-class areas, the self-fulfilling prophecy that slums have higher crime rates (which lead to increased policing in the central city), the "cool" culture of black youth compared with the ingrained middle-class politeness of middle-class youth, and systematic racial biases of policemen—combine to ensure that the crime-control model will in fact dominate police activity with respect of the poor. By contrast, in dealing with the politically and economically powerful members of the community, the police are apt to observe the due-process model. The dogmas of full enforcement cannot be fulfilled, and the doctrines of constitutional law tend to be reduced to the rhetoric of appellate courts.

NOTES

1. Wis. Stats. §62.09(12)(A).

2. See Wayne R. LaFave, *Arrest: The Decision to Take a Suspect into Custody,* Little, Brown, Boston, 1965, pp. 76–79.

3. See *State ex rel Pacific American Fisheries v. Darwin*, 81 Wash 1, 13, 142 Pac. 441, 444 (1914).

4. *State ex rel Parker v. McKnaught*, 152 Kan. 689, 107 P. 2d 694 (1940).

5. Wis. Stats. §946.12(1) (1955).

6. *State v. Lombardi*, 8 Wis. 2d 421, 99 N.W. 2d 829 (1959).

7. Jerome Hall, "Police and law in a democratic society," *Indiana Law J.*, **28**, 1953, pp. 133, 155. Reprinted by permission.

8. *Ibid.*, pp. 155–156. Reprinted by permission.

9. Lon L. Fuller, *The Morality of Law*, Yale University Press, New Haven, Conn., 1964, p. 46.

10. Herbert L. Packer, "Two models of the criminal process," *U. of Pa. Law Rev.*, **113**, 1964, pp. 1, 7–8. Reprinted by permission.

11. Franz Alexander and Hugo Staub, *The Criminal, the Judge and the Public*, Free Press, New York, 1956, pp. 212–214. Copyright 1956 by The Macmillan Company. Reprinted by permission.

12. William F. Whyte, *Street Corner Society*, University of Chicago Press, Chicago, 1943, p. 136. Reprinted by permission.

13. Herman Goldstein, "Police discretion: the ideal versus the real," *Pub. Admin. Rev.* **23**, 1963, p. 140.

14. President's Commission on Law Enforcement and Administration of Justice, *The Challenge of Crime in a Free Society*, U.S. Government Printing Office, 1967, pp. 103–104.

15. Amitai Etzioni, *Modern Organizations*, Prentice-Hall, Englewood Cliffs, N.J., 1964, p. 51.

16. *Ibid.*, p. 10.

17. *Yick Wo v. Hopkins*, 118 U.S. 356, 6 S. Ct. 1064, 30 L. Ed. 220 (1886).

18. 324 Mich. 22, 36 N.W. 2d 308 (1949).

19. See also *Bargain City v. Dilworth*, 29 U.S. Law Week 2002 (Pa. Ct. Com. Pl. 1960).

20. *People v. Harris*, 182 Cal. App. 2d Supp. 837, 5 Cal. Rptr. 852 (1960); see *People v. Winters*, 171 Cal. App. 2d Supp. 876, 342 P. 2d 538 (1959).

21. 16 App. Div. 2d 12, 225 N.Y.S. 2d 128 (1962).

22. Michael Banton, *The Policeman in the Community*, Tavistock, London, 1964.

23. William J. Chambliss, *Crime and the Legal Process*, McGraw-Hill, New York, 1969, pp. 457–458.

24. *Uniform Crime Reports*, U.S. Government Printing Office, 1965. These offenses include murder, rape, aggravated assault, burglary, larceny over fifty dollars, and auto theft.

25. See Jerome Hall, *Theft, Law and Society*, Bobbs-Merrill, Indianapolis, 1935, Chapter 6.

26. Arthur Stinchcombe, "Institutions of privacy in the determination of police administrative practices," *Am. J. Soc.*, **69**, September 1963, pp. 150–160.

27. James Q. Wilson, "The police and their problems: a theory," *Public Policy*, **12**, 1963, p. 195. Reprinted by permission.

28. William J. Chambliss, "Law in action: inquiries of the criminal law process," unpublished manuscript, Chapter 5.

29. Stinchcombe, *op. cit.*, pp. 150–160.

30. Jerome H. Skolnick and J. Richard Woodworth, "Bureaucracy, information and

social control: a study of a morals detail," in David J. Bordua (ed.), *The Police,* Wiley, New York, 1967, p. 109. Reprinted by permission.

31. Stinchcombe, *op. cit.*, pp. 150–160.

32. Greenleigh Associates, Inc., "Facts, fallacies and the future: a study of Aid to Dependent Children of Cook County," 1960, p. 64; as quoted in Charles A. Reich, "The new property," *Yale Law J.*, **63**, 1964, p. 767. Reprinted by permission of The Yale Law Journal Company and Fred B. Rothman and Company.

33. William J. Chambliss and Richard I. Nagasawa, "On the validity of official statistics," *J. Research on Crime and Delinquency*, January 1969; see also Richard I. Nagasawa, thesis cited in note 34.

34. Richard I. Nagasawa, "Delinquency and non-delinquency: a study of status problems and perceived opportunity," unpublished master's thesis, Department of Sociology, University of Washington, 1965, p. 35. Reprinted by permission.

35. Arnold S. Trebach, *The Rationing of Justice*, Rutgers University Press, New Brunswick, N. J., 1964, pp. 32–36.

36. Interestingly, one way in which the police avoid the possibility of being sanctioned for making an illegal arrest is to tell a suspect that he must "come down to the station" rather than to place him "under arrest." Only when he says the latter does the policeman become subject to counteraction by a suspect for false arrest. If he says the former, there is no legal recourse for the suspect.

37. Irving Piliavin and Scott Briar, "Police encounters with juveniles," *Am. J. Soc.*, September 1964, pp. 216–229. Copyright © 1964, University of Chicago Press. Reprinted by permission.

38. Malcolm X and Charles Kiel, *Urban Blues*, University of Chicago Press, Chicago, 1966. See also *The Autobiography of Malcolm X*, Grove Press, 1967.

39. Trebach, *op. cit.*, pp. 32–36.

40. Chambliss, "Law in action," Chapter 7.

41. *Ibid.*, Chapter 5.

42. William J. Chambliss, "Two gangs," (in press).

43. Mary Owen Cameron, *The Booster and the Snitch*, Free Press of Glencoe, New York, 1964, pp. 30–31.

44. *Ibid.*

45. Edward Lamb, "Trial by battle: a case history of a Washington witch-hunt," occasional paper, Center for the Study of Democratic Institutions, 1964.

46. William J. Chambliss and John T. Liell, "The legal process in the community setting," *Crime and Delinquency*, October 1966, pp. 310–317. Reprinted by permission.

17

Police deviancy

Not everyone is agreed that the existing divergence between the norms for police activity embodied in the due-process model and their actual activity in accordance with the crime-control model, is unacceptable. Some argue that all is well, that the norms of due process satisfy the middle class conscience, and the actual practice of crime-control meets the necessity of reducing crime. In the best functionalist tradition, one might argue that every institution continues to exist because it serves a function necessary to the existence of society as a whole; the continued existence of society is a shared value; therefore, the existing police institutions, despite their contradictions, ought to be left alone.

It is easy in reading such a book as this to fall into the trap of assuming that everybody believes that the police should abide by the law. A glance at the morning's headlines would dispel this notion. There is a constant stream of speeches, of letters to the newspapers, of public comment of all sorts, urging the police to "get tough" with criminals, with dissident students, with riotous ghetto blacks, with peace advocates. To urge the police to "get tough," in this context, means to urge them to brutalize the objects of the attack in order to deter further activities of the sort in question. Since the police do not by law have any authority themselves to punish offenders, the proponents of a "get tough" policy are in fact urging the police to act illegally. Even the most generous construction of the "get tough" policy cannot be less than that the police are to exercise their discretion in ways uniformly adverse to individuals whom they suspect of crime.

The decision by the police to abide or not to abide by the law, to abide by the norms of due process or to respond to the demand that they "get tough," has incalculable consequences for society. During the past decade, local disorders of unprecedented scale and frequency in our recent history have troubled the United States. Urban riots and student unrest, some of which are marked by open warfare between the police and substantial groups in the population, are the daily diet of the newspaper reader. The police find it necessary to prepare for even worse incidents. Throughout the country, police forces are stocking unprecedented quantities of the new hardware of suppression: mace, tear gas, pepper gas, armored troop carriers, shotguns, machine guns, field artillery, special riot uniforms—the whole arsenal of violence.

What we see is, of course, a vast and fearsome decline in the legitimacy of our government, and specifically the legitimacy of the police as an institution. A government that cannot govern significant groups in the population except by terror and violence can, by definition, no longer rule by authority alone. Naked power must act as surrogate for legitimacy.

To understand the relationship between the ideal of due process and the imperative that the police abide by it, we shall examine, first, the demands of legitimacy. We shall then examine the causes of police deviance. Finally, we shall examine the various institutions that have been devised in an attempt to police the police.

17.1 THE DICTATES OF LEGITIMACY

Legitimacy is not a matter of taste like a preference for strawberry over chocolate ice cream, or lavender over lemon scent. There are usually few important consequences for the consumer in making the latter kind of choices. But whether a government maintains its legitimacy determines whether it can rule as well as its style of exercising its power.

We have already mentioned Max Weber's distinction between *power* and *authority*. Power refers to the ability to coerce the subject. A government, on the other hand, has authority when its subject adheres to the rules laid down by the government because he believes it right and proper that he should do so. The extent to which the citizen follows the rules because he thinks it right and proper is the measure of the government's legitimacy. The greater its legitimacy, the less coercion will be required to enforce the rules.

Weber spoke in terms of the legitimacy of a government in general. It is to be doubted whether one can fruitfully speak in this way, as a brief reference to the way things work out will make clear. A law commanding the citizen not voluntarily to stop his heartbeat needs little bureaucracy to enforce. In the United States

POLICE DEVIANCY

(as compared with many other countries), state laws commanding the citizen to pay income tax are relatively easy to administer. The same state governments, however, find it quite impossible to enforce laws prohibiting adultery. The concept of legitimacy as applied to a government *in general* thus seems to paint with too broad a brush, for legitimacy may vary significantly between different governmental institutions and their specific activities.

Even with respect to a particular institution, legitimacy may be an overly general concept. The same police who, as finders of lost children, aid to the travelling stranger, and guardian angels of campers, are perceived as kind, gentle, and friendly, may be simultaneously regarded by the same public as insensitive disrupters of friendly poker games, nosy Grundys interfering with a more or less innocent caper in Lover's Lane, or brutal oppressors of the poor.

Despite its limitations, the concept of legitimacy is useful, for governments do find it more or less difficult to enforce their rules. A government in wartime, fighting a popularly supported war against a ruthless invader, can impose stringent controls with far less enforcement machinery than might be necessary in peacetime. A government headed by a charismatic leader, a George Washington or a Lenin, can achieve far greater compliance to innovating laws with less costs of enforcement than some other governments. In this sense, relative legitimacy of government is one among many factors influencing conformity to official norms by a role-occupant.

Legitimacy is an absolute necessity for successful government. No government has the resources to compel citizens to do what, on a large scale, they are determined not to do. As many cities and universities have discovered, when even a relatively small proportion of their populations withdraws its consent and refuses to abide by the rules prescribing its conduct, all the police available are insufficient to ensure the continued operation of the city or university. A city patrolled by National Guardsman and under strict curfew may have no riots, but this calm is not the same as that of another city which conducts its day-to-day activity without the presence of the forces of coercion. A university campus garrisoned by police is incapable of carrying out its normal educational functions. Legitimacy is not a tasty luxury. It is a necessity if the enterprise of government is to be even moderately successful.

How is legitimacy to be achieved? Weber created a typology of various kinds of legitimacy. He held that there were three ideal types: charismatic legitimacy, sacred or traditional legitimacy, and legal-rational legitimacy. Charismatic legitimacy is obtained when a leader manages to bathe the entire government in the charisma of his personality. Sacred or traditional legitimacy exists because government is supported by long-continued tradition and myths which have been accepted by the people as part of their value-sets. Legal-rational, or bureaucratic, legitimacy is derived from the subjects' acceptance of a set of more abstract propositions and hence their acceptance of the government's ruling is, in a sense "derived" from these propositions as justified.[1]

One might object that this typology is not exhaustive. British imperial rule in Africa, for example, for a time and with certain specific publics seems to have legitimized itself by acting paternalistically, i.e. in an authoritarian way which some of the subjects were persuaded served their substantive interests. It is difficult to subsume this sort of government under the Weberian categories.

We need not argue the issue. Neither traditional nor charismatic legitimization can sustain a police force. The police are not ordinarily supported by beliefs in their sacerdotal character, and few police chiefs are charismatic vis-à-vis the ghetto. There remains only legal-rational legitimacy.

Legitimacy in any of Weber's three varieties ultimately is designed to make government possible in a society in which power and privilege are not equitably distributed. This state of inequality is clearly characteristic of charismatic and traditional authority. These types of authority rest on the irrational and super-stitious beliefs of the subjects in the revered character and personality of a great leader, or the extraordinary sanctification brought about by prolonged existence. Rational-legal legitimization, however, occurs when the exercise of power is perceived by the subjects to be responsive to *their* claims, demands, and interests. Does not this sort of legitimacy depend on government's acting in the subjects' interests? If so, does it not imply that a government based on legal-rational legitimacy ensures equality?

The claims, demands, and interests of people in a society are always of two sorts: substantive and procedural. On the substantive side, most people in our society demand for themselves as large a share of the goods, power, and privileges of this world as they can get. Since in the nature of this imperfect society goods, power, and privileges are unequally distributed, the ruling elites (who by definition have more than their equitable share) must find a way to legitimize inequality. Charisma and tradition served in the past. Legal-rational legitimacy, however, can be achieved only by making it appear that substantive inequality in the distribution of wealth, power, and privilege is a function of relative contribution to the on-going collective enterprise involving all of us, that is the whole society. A State relying on legal-rational legitimacy does this by purporting to establish a social order in which *opportunity* to obtain wealth, power, and privilege is equally shared, for if opportunity is truly equally shared, then the actual distribution must be related to the success in taking advantage of equal opportunity. The demand for substantive equality is thus transferred to that for procedural equality.

Equality of opportunity is formally achieved through a set of laws which supposedly apply equally to everyone. "Since legal statutes are stated in general and impersonal terms, they appear to support abstract principles of justice rather than the special interests of particular men or classes of men."

This requirement that government act through apparently universal rules, ensuring the equal treatment of all citizens, is deeply embedded in the Constitution, although historically this doctrine is based on reasons related to but analyti-cally different from the demand for equality. The historical origin of the doctrine lies in the middle-class opposition to the aristocratic government of eighteenth-century England. That required them to oppose the traditional legitimacy of the aristocracy—after all, no one could accuse George III of being charismatic. The middle-class demanded, above all else, certainty and predictability in the doings of the government. Albert Cohen sums up the middle-class ethic:

After all, each participant in a collective enterprise has committed some resources, foregone some alternatives, made an investment in the future. He had done this on the assumption that, if he plays by the rules, so will others. His effort, whether it be chasing a ball in a baseball game, doing his homework assignment, or showing up on time, makes sense only if complemented by appropriate and expected behavior on the part of others. Distrust, even if it is unfounded, weakens organization by undermining motivation; to distrust others is to see one's own effort as pointless, wasted and foolish, and the future as hazardous and uncertain. One is then inclined to "pull out of the game" if he can, and to invest his resources with those whom he can trust . . .[2]

Society is the largest of all collective enterprises. The middle class above all is unwilling to invest its capital unless the rules of the game are "cognoscible," predictable in advance.

The Constitution meets the demands for predictability of governmental action in a variety of ways: by prohibiting *ex post facto* laws and bills of attainder; by the due-process requirement that substantive criminal statutes be stated in as narrow terms as possible in order to prevent the police from having too broad an area of discretion; by prohibiting cruel and unusual punishments; by the due-process requirements of fair hearing and the assistance of counsel; by prohibiting enforced self-incrimination; and, above all, by the due-process requirement that only an official expressly authorized by law to act coercively against a citizen may so act. All these constitutional guarantees add up to but two basic principles: That no official may act against a citizen except in accordance with a rule that was in existence before the citizen took the action which has been called into question; and that when he does have to determine whether the citizen committed certain acts which are the preconditions for the official action, the official will make as rational a decision as possible, free from any bias and prejudice and arbitrariness. Procedurally in the criminal law, these guarantees rest in the presumption of innocence and in the accusatory system of legal action.

These constitutional guarantees met the demands of the middle class for predictability; they also meet the demands for equality of treatment. It is the great accomplishment of the Supreme Court to have extracted from these specific guarantees, aimed at specific eighteenth-century governmental practices, broader principles expressing the essence of legal-rational legitimization.

Legal-rational legitimacy exists when rulings are accepted as derived from higher-level propositions which are themselves accepted as legitimate. In other words, the rulings of the organization (and hence the organization itself) must be seen as *instrumental* to the proper goals. If the rulings are derived from the higher-level propositions, they must be somehow conducive to the ends expressed in those propositions. Alvin W. Gouldner writes that

the organization is conceived as an "instrument"—that is, as a rationally conceived means to the realization of expressly announced group goals. Its structures are understood as tools deliberately established for the realization of these group purposes.[3]

If there is equality of treatment, then the State may be regarded as an impartial framework within which the struggle for power and privilege takes place. That the State is in fact such an impartial framework is the central myth that supports government in the United States. For this myth to be true, the police as an organization must be wholly impartial. Their task is ministerial, they connot exercise discretion. They must not determine guilt or innocence; these decisions must be left to the courts. The police must not choose which criminal to arrest and which not to arrest; they must merely enforce the laws. They must not exercise violence as punishment; they must use only the minimum force necessary to carry out their ministerial ideal.

The norms of due process are thus necessary concomitants to the myth of the liberal democratic State. The due process guarantees were placed in the Constitution to ensure that the instruments of government remained instrumental and therefore their operation predictable. The Supreme Court, by insisting on compliance to due process, does more than merely bring out the implications of the words in the Constitution; it is laying down the conditions for the maintenance of the legitimacy of government.

The objectives defined for the police by the imperatives of government legitimacy are therefore the ideals of due process. The only kind of formal legitimacy the police can achieve is legal-rational: they must be seen as acting instrumentally.

Max Weber lists seven characteristics common to bureaucratic organizations, and hence to legal-rational legitimacy. Each of these characteristics serves several functions, but all have this much in common: they serve to ensure that the organization retains its instrumental character. They do so by ensuring that the activities of the individuals making up the organization, in their capacity as members of the organization, are directed toward achieving the organizational goals.

First, an organization must be "a continuous organization bound by *rules*."[4] Goal-achievement requires continuity in organizational effort. Rules are general statements describing how individuals are to act in specific sets of circumstances. If the rules are relevant to the goals of the organization, and if no individual in the organization acts except in accordance with the rules, then the role-occupants within the organization will only act instrumentally.

Rules also ensure equality of treatment, "the dominance of a spirit of informal impersonality, '*sine ira et studio*,' without hatred or passion, and hence without affection or enthusiasm. The dominant norms are concepts of straightforward duty without regard to personal considerations. Everyone is subject to formal equality of treatment; that is, everyone in the same empirical situation. This is the spirit in which the ideal official conducts his office."[5]

Government by rules also ensures that rationality will be the objective of the decision-making process. Individual cases can be decided occasionally by whim, without the main thrust of the organization being significantly deflected. A rule which is to control, not a single case, but many such cases, however, must be adopted with some rational effort, i.e., with some effort at relating the purposes entertained with the probable consequences of the rule. Thus, rational methods of rule-creation and rule-application become part of the requirements of legal-rational legitimacy.

Second, each role-occupant must have "a specific sphere of competence. This involves (a) a sphere of obligations to perform functions which have been marked off as part of a systematic division of labor; (b) the provision of the incumbent with necessary authority to carry out these functions; and (c) that the necessary means of compulsion are clearly defined and their use is subject to definite conditions." Unless each role is related to the others, the cooperation necessary to achieve the common goals is improbable. Without authority to carry out his function, the role-occupant will not succeed in moving the organization towards those goals. Without rules defining permissible use of compulsion, force is apt to be used for selfish purposes.

Third, "The organization of offices follows the principle of hierarchy; that is, each lower office is under the control and supervision of a higher one." Without a built-in system of supervision and control, there is a high probability that substitution of personal and unofficial goals for the official organizational goals will take place.[6]

Fourth, "The rules which regulate the conduct of an office may be *technical* rules or norms. In both cases, if their application is to be fully rational, specialized training is necessary. It is thus normally true that only a person who has demonstrated an adequate *technical* training is qualified to be a member of the administrative staff."

Fifth, "It is a matter of principle that the members of the administrative staff should be completely separated from the ownership of the means of production or administration... There exists, furthermore, in principle, complete separation of the property belonging to the organization, which is controlled within the spheres of the office, and the personal property of the official." Without such separation, official decisions may be influenced by personal interest in property.

Sixth, "there is also a complete absence of appropriation of his official position by the incumbent. Where 'rights' to an office exist, as in the case of judges, they do not normally serve the purpose of appropriation by the official, but of securing the purely objective and independent character of the conduct of the office so that it is oriented only to the relevant norms."

Seventh, "Administrative acts, decisions, and rules are formulated and recorded in writing . . . This applies at least to preliminary discussions and proposals, to final decisions, and to all sorts of orders and rules." Some writers have tended to regard this requirement as secondary. It serves, however, to ensure continuity, impartiality, and governance by rule, and hence the instrumentality of the organization.

These requirements of course represent an ideal type. No organization has ever realized these conditions completely, nor in principle could one ever do so. Every one of Weber's seven characteristics of bureaucracy carries exceptions. Rules cannot control every activity of officials; and as we saw earlier, rules by nature must admit of some discretion in their application. Specific spheres of competence must be described by rule. Since rules are fuzzy at the edges, the spheres of competence are always only more or less specific. It is the nature of organizations that personal relationships develop between superiors and inferiors— what we mean by *krugovaya poruka*. One way to inhibit *krugovaya poruka* is to set up inspectorships outside the administrative hierarchy to guard against any hierarchal breakdown. The hierarchal principle itself, therefore, demands in some cases that it be violated to preserve it. Technical training may produce narrow specialists unable to grasp "the big picture"; the efficient use of specialists may require "generalists." Similar exceptions could be enumerated for the remaining requirements.

It is apparent that Weber's ideal characteristics for legal-rational legitimacy match the demand for predictability and certainty which underlie the due-process model. Complete or absolute fulfillment of this demand is impossible. Kenneth Culp Davis writes that:

Every governmental and legal system in world history has involved both rules and discretion. No government has ever been a government of laws and not of men in the sense of eliminating all discretionary power. Every government has always been *a government of laws and of men.*[7]

Weber's model therefore is not of an actual, existent government. It refers to an ideal which conforms to a set of values which Weber believes are held by the majority of the population. If a government realizes these values, Weber tells us, it will have achieved legal-rational legitimacy. Therefore, Weber's model tends to denigrate the place of discretion, and elevate the importance of rules and of decisions made *sine ira et studio* (without regard for personal considerations). The only considerations that should be taken into account in making official decisions are the goals of the organization; only in this way can the organization retain its instrumental character.

Are the values of the legal-rational bureaucracy—the values expressed both in Weber's seven characteristics of bureaucracy and in the norms of due process—in fact held by the population at large? In general, it would seem highly likely that they are. Ours is an exceedingly complex society, with an incredibly high degree of division of labor. The bureaucratic organization is in many ways man's most important invention, more important than the wheel, the secrets of flight, or the discovery of the atomic nucleus. Bureaucracy as the dominant system of modern social organization was inevitable if modern technology was to be used effectively. Without bureaucratic organization in industry, in schools and universities, in government, in every sphere of life, it would be impossible to accomplish the tasks of industrialized society.

Social organization determines values. Society does not stop at our skins, but penetrates our consciousness. Living in a bureaucratic society, we absorb its values.

To say that we all absorb the values of a bureaucratic society is not to say that its values are the *summum bonum* (the highest good) for all of us. How a blackman in the ghetto or a poor white in a rural wasteland weighs the predictability of governmental action (the chief value involved in legal-rational legitimacy) against the predictability of the next meal, may be quite different from the way in which a member of the Long Island polo-playing set driving his convertible Lincoln Continental weighs the same considerations. To say that we absorb the values of the bureaucratic society is only to say that they shape our consciousness enough so that we commonly do regard the maintenance of legality and regularity as a generalized, culturally acquired objective.

Shaped as we are by the society in which we live, our acceptance of the values of bureaucracy, therefore, implies that the values of regularity, of legal-rational legitimacy, will have some weight in our evaluation of the government. For this reason, the legitimacy of the police is not a pleasant luxury for the government; it is a necessity. Herbert Packer says:

In today's crisis of confidence, the question of sanctions is *the* central question. The main source of hostility to the police among minorities is the helpless frustration engendered by the certain knowledge that, whatever the police do, there is no way by which they can be called to account for it...No code of police practices that does not provide effective sanctions for police lawlessness can so much as begin the long repair job that will be required to win minority group acceptance of even the most necessary police functions.[8]

The crisis of legitimacy that intrudes daily into our consciousness with television pictures of students defying the police, of ghettos which must be patrolled as though they were occupied enemy territory, of open warfare between police and significant elements in the society, demands that the police begin to act instrumentally, according to due process. Yet the demands of the middle classes with respect to criminal law and the legitimacy of the police are shot with contradictions. On the one hand, the middle-class citizens, perhaps more than any others, require predictability in their daily lives, for property interests are meaningless unless the legal climate affecting them is relatively stable. They therefore insist that, so far as *they* are concerned, the police must adhere to due process. On the other hand, the same people of the middle classes, more than others, demand that the police do more than merely arrest wrongdoers for disposition by the courts. They demand that the police *prevent* crime. Effective crime-prevention, however, is not conducive to police observance of due process. Hence the two demands of the middle classes are essentially incompatible.

That the courts would devise rules promoting due process is thus necessary in view of our Constitution. This demand for a cloak of legal-rational legitimacy for the police is derived from those demands embodied in the Constitution which resulted in its guarantees, however these guarantees may have been generated in the context of eighteenth-century aspirations. That the courts should promote due process is also a necessary consequence of the inputs and conversion processes of the appellate courts viewed as decision-making structures.

That the police would perceive their role according to the crime-control model is, however, equally a necessary consequence of their position in society. We examine next the reasons for the deviant motivation of the police.

17.2 A THEORY OF POLICE DEVIANCY

In accounting for the fact that the functionaries of the criminal-law system will organize themselves in such a way as to (a) enforce certain laws and ignore others and (b) enforce laws against the powerless and not against the powerful, we pointed out how these organizational decisions were tied to the (1) bureaucratic structure of the enforcement agencies and (2) the position of the police vis-à-vis the power and interest groups in the society. To understand why the police adopt the crime-control model instead of the constitutionally prescribed due-process model, we must look in more detail at the role of the police.

The deviant motivation of police—their internalization of the crime-control model rather than the due-process model—does not arise because the police are inherently bad or evil. Its source lies in the ways in which the police force as an institution comes to shape the world view of the individual. The police must cope with conflicting demands of the community and they must define their job and the common features of their relationship to the "civilian" population.

Just as there is no consensus in society as to what constitutes criminal behavior, so there is no consensus as to what should be done about what is regarded as criminal. The unequal distribution of property, power, and privilege in society leads to demands from the socially disinherited for greater equality. These demands sometimes culminate in these people's insistence on their right to expropriate property, seize power, and confiscate privileges which they have previously been denied. At the same time, the privileged members of the society, especially the middle-class property owners, demand that their ownership and persons be secure from hostile or arbitrary acts. They want to be secure from such acts which are "criminal" as well as the same kind of actions that stem from the behavior of officials.

The police are thus put squarely in the middle. The control of the dis-inherited, who are regarded as potentially dangerous, from the perspective of the police can be most efficiently accomplished through the arbitrary use of force and coercion. But these methods, when applied to the privileged, bring forth public criticism and censure.

The simple and most often practiced solution is to adopt a dual standard. Crime-control practices prevail in dealings with the poor, and due process is observed in dealings with the privileged. In sophisticated police departments there are special details whose principal task is to answer calls and when necessary to make arrests in the "well-to-do" sections of the city. Typically the investigations, contacts, and arrests in such cases are handled with great care and attention to the due-process requirements of criminal law and to the public-relations concerns of the police. Similar practices are discouraged when dealing with the disinherited.

To complicate the picture further, there are important groups among the privileged, the moral entrepreneurs, who insist that due process also be observed in handling the poor. Thus the police are never able to please everyone by adopting a particular procedure. While in general the invisibility of police actions in the ghettos and slums keeps the hue and cry opposing the use of crime-control techniques to a limited number of "respectable" citizens, the fact that there is any opposition at all means that the police are never entirely free from cross pressures no matter what procedures they adopt.

How the police respond to the contradictory pressures to which they are subject is a function of their motivation and of the sanctions which support the formal rules. We turn first to the question of motivation.

Jerome Skolnick has contributed an analysis of the policeman's "working personality"—the "cognitive lenses through which" they "see situations and events."[9] These lenses are ground to a prescription whose central measurements are derived from two peculiar characteristics of the policeman's role, *danger* and *authority*.

The policeman's "personality" is forged in his elemental role, that of a man on the beat. With rare exceptions, all policemen come up through the ranks. They all serve a period of apprenticeship as a patrolman on the beat.

The primary responsibility for which police forces were developed, and to which they even today respond, is the control and prevention of violence in city streets.

The *raison d'être* of the policeman and the criminal law, the underlying collectively held moral sentiments which justify penal sanctions, arises ultimately and most clearly from the threat of violence and the possibility of danger to the community.[10]

The belief that he is in constant physical danger from unknown and mysterious forces necessarily makes the policeman suspicious. Indeed, he is trained to be suspicious, as we pointed out earlier.[11]

There is some evidence (see p. 275) that the belief that the policeman is in constant danger is not altogether consonant with reality. This divergence of belief from reality is not hard to understand. If the professors in universities were outfitted with guns, mace, and night sticks and were authorized to use them on "trouble-makers on campus," doubtless they would regard their job as dangerous as well. To some extent, the perception of danger is a function of the policeman's role as agent of legitimate violence. Also, of course, the job of policeman *is* more dangerous than that of the average citizen in the working-class suburb where the policeman is likely to live. Thus, even though his job may not be as dangerous as he thinks it is and even though the possibility of experiencing serious physical harm may be greater for the average slum dweller victimized by police brutality than it is for the average policeman, there is nonetheless ample comparative evidence to convince the policeman that danger abounds in his occupation.

Secondly, the police are required constantly to exercise authority over the ordinary citizen. They are told to write traffic tickets, order citizens to "move on," control public morality in lovers' lanes and beer halls, restrain citizens from engaging in the beloved but illegal pleasures of prostitution, gambling, and smoking marijuana.

There are three principal correlatives to the role-imposed conditions of danger and authority. First, the police are isolated from the ordinary citizenry. They perceive themselves as being hated by the average citizen whom they believed themselves to be protecting; their friends tend to be other policemen. Second, they develop a high degree of professional solidarity as a consequence of the professional need to cooperate in moments of danger and because of their common social isolation. Finally, they tend toward a notably conservative outlook, both politically and emotionally.[12] "The fact that a man is engaged in enforcing a set of rules implies that he also becomes implicated in *affirming* them."[13] In affirming the rules which control the actions of citizens, he becomes emotionally committed to the maintenance of the status quo which is supported by the rules he is enforcing.

These built-in pressures conditioning the policeman's role and the correlative conditions necessarily tend to make him see the world through lenses that will show the crime-control model in more agreeable light than the due-process model. Skolnick concludes,

Danger typically yields self-defensive conduct, conduct that must strain to be impulsive

POLICE DEVIANCY

because danger arouses fear and anxiety so easily. Authority under such conditions becomes a resource to reduce perceived threats rather than a series of reflective judgments arrived at calmly . . . As a result, procedural requirements take on a "frilly" character, or at least tend to be reduced to a secondary position in the face of circumstances seen as threatening.[14]

In sum, the policeman's habits and cast of mind derive from continuous self-perception as being physically threatened, and as the very embodiment of protection for a particular social order. They are bound to make him responsive to demands that he protect the social order rather than demands that he abide by procedural limitations which makes it more difficult for him to control those persons whom he sees as a threat to that order.

That practically all policemen have been socialized into the profession through the job of the foot patrolman, which is subject to the dual conditions of danger and authority, explains why the higher authorities in police bureaucracies have the same conceptions about the world as the foot patrolman. Hence, "if a policeman can give some reason to his *organizational superiors* (including the district attorney) for conducting a search, in practice the worst punishment he can suffer is loss of a conviction."[15] Similarly, with every police violation of the norms of the due-process model, the critical question becomes not whether the policeman violated the norm, but whether he acted in an "administratively reasonable" way.[16]

The norms of due process met the demands for the control of crime sufficiently in the rural colonial society in which they were originally shaped. Colonial society, for all its variety and fluctuations, was relatively homogeneous, at least when compared to the sharp stratification of twentieth-century urban communities. It was basically rural, not urban. Strangers were highly visible. The community policed itself. Crimes were reported by their victims, and suspects by the populace at large. The sense of community ensured that the night was watched by a thousand neighborly eyes.

Modern urban society is altogether different. The alienation of the city-dweller from his neighbor is proverbial; the easiest place to lose oneself is in the impersonal coldness of the city. Far from being pervasively observed with concern, as the eighteenth-century community was, a city street body is watched, if at all, by unseeing or uncaring eyes. A famous case in New York where thirty-eight people saw or heard a young woman being stabbed to death without any one of them bothering to call the police lest he "get involved" is only an especially spectacular example of the community's unconcern over crime that does not affect it directly.

The inability of the police to rely on the cooperation of the urban population for crime control is especially severe in the slum and ghetto areas with high crime rates. It is in these areas that alienation from the society is the greatest, and it is here that the loss of legitimacy of the law and the police is at its highest.

The ghetto is, after all, the product of white middle-class society. The National Advisory Commission on Civil Disorders said

What white Americans have never fully understood—what the Negro can never forget—is that white society is deeply implicated in the ghetto. White institutions created it, white institutions maintain it, and white society condones it.[17]

Gerhard Lenski has described five kinds of reaction to the monopolization of power and privilege by the elite, of which three are relevant to the criminal law.

Every system of power and privilege also sets in motion a deadly *struggle for survival among the offspring of the common people* ... From the standpoint of the elite, the struggles which developed among the common people have been a matter of little concern ...

Another reaction

is one which usually annoys elites but represents no serious threat to their security or status. This is the response of *petty thievery* by those in subordinate positions ...

A third reaction

manifests itself in *crimes of violence directed against members of the elite and their agents* ... The severity of the punishments undoubtedly reflects a recognition of the existence of widespread, latent hostility toward the holders of power and the realization that anything less than prompt and severe punishment may encourage more widespread violence. Furthermore, when crimes of this sort occur, the interests of the elite and the middle classes coincide and all the holders of power line up on the same side, thus making for a very unequal contest.[18]

All of these reactions are common in the ghettos and slums of urban America. To the dwellers in these areas, white middle-class America sees the criminal law, as did Sydney Smith a century and more ago, as a device "to keep the multitude in order."

James Baldwin writes eloquently:

The only way to police the ghetto is to be oppressive. None of the Police Commissioner's men, even with the best will in the world, have any way of understanding the lives led by the people they swagger about in twos and threes controlling. Their very presence is an insult, and it would be, even if they spent their entire day feeding gumdrops to children. They represent the force of the white world, and that world's criminal profit and ease, to keep the black man corralled up here, in his place. The badge, the gun in the holster, and the swinging club make vivid what will happen should his rebellion become overt ...

It is hard, on the other hand, to blame the policeman, blank, good-natured, thoughtless, and insuperably innocent, for being such a perfect representative of the people he serves. He too, believes in good intentions and is astounded and offended when they are not taken for the deed. He has never, himself, done anything for which to be hated— which of us has? And yet he is facing, daily and nightly, people who would gladly see him dead, and he knows it. There is no way for him not to know it: there are few things under heaven more unnerving than the silent, accumulating contempt and hatred of a people. He moves through Harlem, therefore, like an occupying soldier in a bitterly hostile country; which is precisely what, and where he is, and the reason he walks in twos and threes.[19]

In the absence of community cooperation, it may be that the police *require* interrogative powers. The New Haven project found that

In New Haven there is ample room for improved investigative techniques and abilities. The police do little "scientific" investigation . . . The detectives receive no special training for their work . . . Even if some physical evidence is left at the scene of a crime, New Haven's Detective Division probably has neither the manpower nor the skills and equipment to analyze it . . . For the most common crimes—burglary and larceny—investigation is especially perfunctory. In some instances it amounted to little more than cataloging the losses, noting the method employed, and assuring the victim that the Department is working on the case . . . In sum, improved investigative techniques might make some of the interrogations now considered "necessary" inessential. But substantial budgetary increases and organizational changes would have to come first. Facilities must be improved, manpower increased and trained. Until such changes are made there is little possibility that investigation efforts will contribute significantly to law enforcement.[20]

Fred Inbau tends to deny that improvement in techniques or manpower would lessen the necessity for interrogation of accused persons in many cases:

Many criminal cases, even when investigated by the best qualified police departments, are capable of solution only by means of an admission or confession from the guilty individual or upon the basis of information obtained from the questioning of other criminal suspects.[21]

In colonial society, given the cooperation of the community and a relatively low level of violence, due process did not interfere with the control of crime. Given the impersonality of the city and the consequent lack of community cooperation in the apprehension of criminals, the poor training, low budgets, and consequently insufficient police manpower to meet all the manifold demands on the police, the observance of due process is incompatible with the middle-class demands for order imposed on the police officer.

The common police socialization and its concomitant set of values are reinforced by the bureaucratic organization of police work. For the average policeman, as we saw, the critical reference group is the body of policemen with whom he almost exclusively associates. Policemen are dependent on each other in crucial ways for the successful accomplishment of their jobs. Cohen writes:

Successful deviance usually requires the active assistance or the acquiescence of others, both in its performance and in the evasion of detection and punishment. But others must be motivated to render this assistance. This is likely to occur: when a number of people depend upon one another in important ways to begin with, such as the proper completion of their respective tasks in the division of labour; when, at any given time, several of them have burdens which could be lightened or problems that could be solved by violating the rules; and when it is probable that, sooner or later, almost anybody *might* find himself with such burdens or problems.[22]

Cohen describes the Russian version, "krugovaya poruka," which may loosely be translated as "group support." It is not a Soviet invention; it is common in every organization. He writes:

Krugovaya poruka often comes to embrace those very individuals whose office it is to prevent and expose it. This is because those individuals, by virtue of *their* job, are thrown into interaction with those they are supposed to police, and in various degrees often become dependent upon them.[23]

The police, whether patrolmen or administrators, are precisely in such a relationship of *krugovaya poruka* with one another. Understandably, the police administrator can only support his men. He cannot be expected to discipline them for carrying out departmental policy against "the enemy" any more than the ordinary officer can be expected to testify against his brother officers.

The police as a group, after all, have a cohesion only found among the military and paramilitary, supported in the case of the police by the common sense of community antagonism. Every complaint against an individual policeman tends to be translated into an accusation against the police as an institution. As a result, "an almost inflexible code develops that prevents any officer from testifying as to the actions of another that might be considered improper or illegal."[24]

One of the authors of this book vividly remembers an experience he had while practicing law in New York City. Having graduated from law school only a year before, he was employed at a firm that specialized in representing labor unions, and was sent by the firm to post station-house bail for a client who had been arrested on a picketline. The police station was in a brownstone building with high stoops, over which hung the traditional green lights. Having seen to it that bail was posted for his client, he was walking out with the latter when they passed at the entrance a burly officer pulling along a slight, obviously drunken black man. An instant later they heard a scream and turned to look.

The officer had knocked the black man to the ground, and was beating him bloodily and unmercifully around the head, shoulders, and body with a heavy nightstick. Other officers, lounging about the desk, were laughing and calling to the attacking officer to "lay off." Finally, a lieutenant went around the desk, smiling and joking, took the policeman by the arm and gently led him away with the victim lying bloodied on the floor. At that point another officer noticed the author and his companion watching. He hurried over and none too gently ushered them out.

What is notable about the event is not the mere fact of the brutality, although that was harsh enough. It is the common acceptance by all the police present that the unmerciful beating the author witnessed was plainly within the permissible range of police behavior, and clearly protected by group camaraderie.

A useful way of conceiving of what we have been describing as the working world of the policeman is to see this world as a subculture. It is a subculture in which deviancy—the violation of the constituted rules of due process and the imposition of a set of deviant rules stressing crime-control—is given high value among the members. The police subculture emphasizes the characteristic of aggressiveness and insists on "respect" from outsiders. The justification to which the police resort is that they are carrying out the job of "preserving society," oftentimes against society's own wishes. It is to be expected that a large number of policemen will feel that their own position requires them to adopt the crime-control attitude, with special emphasis on aggressiveness, fearlessness, and being prepared to go to any limits to achieve the objective of "defeating crime."

Given these common factors—the conflict between the official goals and the norms as perceived by the police, the interdependence of police on one another, their common self-perception as heroes fighting crime—it is not to be wondered that common group values emerge that justify deviancy with respect to formal due-process rules of police conduct. The sharing of deviant motivation leads in time to a subculture in which the deviant motivation is the normal one, and deviant conduct is expected conduct.

Such a sub-culture is self-perpetuating. The new recruit is socialized into the subculture and taught to be deviant. E. R. Stoddard concluded from a careful study of a particular police department:

From data furnished by a participant informant, an informal "code" of illegal activities within one police department was documented. The group processes which encouraged and maintained the "code" were identified. It was found that the new recruits were socialized into "code" participation by "old timers" and group acceptance was withheld from those who attempted to remain completely honest and not be implicated. When formal police regulations were in conflict with "code" demands upon its practitioners, the latter took precedence. Since the "code" operates under conditions of secrecy, only those who participate in it have access to evidence enough to reveal its methods of operation. By their very participation they are implicated and this binds them to secrecy as well . . .

Although some individual factors must be considered in explaining police deviancy, in the present study the sanction of group acceptance was paramount. This study clearly demonstrates the social genesis of the "code," the breeding ground for individual unlawful behavior. From evidence contained herein, an individualistic orientation to police deviancy may discover the "spoiled fruit" but only when the "code" is rooted out can the "seedbed" of deviancy be destroyed.[25]

Stoddard was talking primarily about graft. His observations, however, are obviously equally true about the failure of the police to adhere to the norms of due process.

The courts lay down due-process norms for the police to follow. The police are deviantly motivated with respect to these rules. In that confrontation, whether the police adhere to the norms of due process or act according to their own deviant motivation depends in large part on the sanctioning processes available. It is to a consideration of devices to control the police that we now turn.

NOTES

1. Amitai Etzioni, *Complex Organizations, A. Sociological Reader*, Holt, Rinehart, and Winston, New York, 1961, p. 1; see also Max Weber, *The Theory of Social and Economic Organization*, Alexander M. Henderson (tr.) and Talcott Parsons (ed.), Oxford University Press, New York, 1947, p. 328.

2. Albert K. Cohen, *Deviance and Control*, © 1961, Prentice-Hall, Englewood Cliffs, N.J., p. 5. By permission of the publishers.

3. Alvin W. Gouldner, *Patterns of Industrial Bureaucracy*, Free Press of Glencoe, New York, 1954, p. 404.

4. Max Weber, *The Theory of Social and Economic Organization*, Talcott Parsons (ed.), Oxford University Press, New York, 1947, pp. 329–330.

5. *Ibid.*, p. 340.

6. Hans Kelsen, working from very different premises, concluded that it was this hierarchical character of the order of legal norms that made it expressly "legal." In Kelsen's model, the hierarchy of norms is derived from the *Grundnorm*, or constitution—i.e., the embodiment of what myth defines as the formal statement of government goals.

7. Kenneth Culp Davis, *Discretionary Justice: A Preliminary Inquiry*, Louisiana State University Press, Baton Rouge, 1969, p. 17.

8. Herbert L. Packer, "Policing the police: nine men are not enough," *The New Republic*, September 4, 1965, p. 17. Reprinted by permission of *The New Republic*, © 1965, Harrison-Blaine of New Jersey, Inc.

9. Jerome H. Skolnick, *Justice Without Trial*, Wiley, New York, 1966, p. 42. Reprinted by permission.

10. *Ibid.*, p. 45. Reprinted by permission.

11. Thomas F. Adams, "Field interrogation," *Police*, Vol. 7, No. 4, March–April, 1963, p. 28.

12. Skolnick, *op. cit.*, p. 59.

13. *Ibid.*, p. 59. Reprinted by permission.

14. *Ibid.*, p. 67. Reprinted by permission.

15. *Ibid.*, p. 221. Reprinted by permission.

16. *Ibid.*, p. 223.

17. *Report of the National Advisory Commission on Civil Disorders*, Bantam, New York, 1968, p. 2.

18. Gerhard E. Lenski, *Power and Privilege: A Theory of Social Stratification*, McGraw-Hill, New York, 1966, pp. 64–66. Used with permission of McGraw-Hill Book Company.

19. James Baldwin, *Nobody Knows My Name*, Dell, New York, 1962, pp. 65–67. Copyright © 1960 by James Baldwin. Reprinted by permission of the publisher, The Dial Press.

20. Michael Wald, Richard Ayres, David W. Hess, Mark Schantz, and Charles H. Whitehead II (eds.), "Interrogations in New Haven: the impact of Miranda," *Yale Law J.*, **76**, 1967, pp. 1519, 1597–1599. Reprinted by permission of the Yale Law Journal Company and Fred B. Rothman and Company.

21. Fred E. Inbau, "Police interrogation—a practical necessity," *J. Criminal Law, Criminology, and Police Science*, **52**, 1961, p. 16.

22. Albert K. Cohen, *Deviance and Control*, © 1966, Prentice-Hall, Inc., Englewood Cliffs, N.J., p. 88. By permission of the publishers.

23. *Ibid.*, p. 89. Reprinted by permission.

24. Herman Goldstein, "Administrative problems in controlling the exercise of police authority," *J. Criminal Law, Criminology, and Police Science*, **58**, No. 2, 1967, pp. 160–167. Reprinted by special permission of the Journal of Criminal Law, Criminology, and Police Science (Northwestern University School of Law) © 1967.

25. E. R. Stoddard, "The informal 'code' of police deviancy: group approach to 'blue-coat' crime," *J. Criminal Law, Criminology, and Police Science*, **59**, No. 2, 1968, pp. 201, 212–213. Reprinted by special permission of the Journal of Criminal Law, Criminology, and Police Science (Northwestern University School of Law) © 1968.

18

The control of police illegality
and police discretion

Our general model suggests that where role-performance fails to match role-expectation as defined by the operative norms, it does so because the total "field" within which the individual operates is insufficient to induce or compel him to conform. That "field" is defined by two kinds of elements: first, the entire spectrum of social, political, economic, and other societal and personal forces exerted on the role-occupant, which can be assumed for our present purposes as given; second, the sanctioning activities of the various sanctioning agencies, which can be controlled, but only to a degree, by the policy-makers.

The fact that the police do in fact act illegally suggests not only that the societal and personal forces operating on the police are conducive to deviancy, but also that the various sanctioning agencies do not interact with the police in a way that would inhibit the deviant tendency and produce conformity. Before we can discuss the actual influence that sanctioning institutions have on the police, however, we must analyze the notion of "sanctions."

18.1 THE MEANING OF "SANCTIONS"

Two rather different concepts of "sanctions" may be dredged up from the legal literature. The traditional notion limits the word to mean penalties attendant on the breach of a norm.[1] A penalty, of course, may be conceived of as a reward. It makes little difference analytically (although it may make a great deal of difference psychologically) whether a sanction, in this sense, is conceived of in one way or the other. For example, suppose that we want to persuade merchants to remove overhanging signs from their properties. It makes no difference except psychologically whether we stipulate that "Merchants without overhanging signs will receive a $100 annual reduction in their local tax assessment" or "Merchants with an overhanging sign shall pay a $100 tax therefore."

The traditional notion of sanctions assumes that the social, political, economic, and personal forces operating upon the role-occupant are for the time being incapable of change; they are given in the circumstances. The operation of the sanction is conceived of as that of a single additional element to the "field" within which the role-occupant operates. This element is in the form of a specific detriment or reward which is thought to be decisive in influencing the calculating role-occupant to see that his net advantage lies in conformity rather than deviancy.

The sanction enters into this calculation in terms of two variables: the relative certainty of receiving the penalty or reward, and the severity of punishment involved. The effectiveness of the sanctioning institutions, in the traditional view, depends on the role-occupant's calculation of the probabilities of punishment.

More sophisticated theories of sanctions endow the concept with a wider meaning. The problem is understood as one of restructuring of the "field" within which the role-occupant operates.[2] The use of the traditional negative sanctions is only one element in that process. Other forms of sanctions might include changing the motivation of individuals by education or socialization, reforming the institutional climate within which he operates, or even the physical conditions governing his role. "Sanctions" become whatever rules the law-making authority lays down to restructure the "field" of the role-occupant in an effort to produce conforming behavior.

Negative sanctions of the traditional sort invariably occupy a large part of whatever sanctions (in the more modern sense) are used. In this more modern view, however, they are not simply conceived of, however, as mechanically appealing to the narrow calculational sense of the role-occupant, but dialectically. Traditional sanctions have a multiple effect. The fact of conviction for breaching a norm puts the stigma of deviancy on a role-occupant. If he exists in a subculture which accepts deviancy as normal, however, that very fact may be a reward, not a punishment. The policeman who "loses" a case because he extorted a confession by beating a black man may be glamorized and admired by his fellow police officers for the act, and sympathized with, not abhorred, for the failure of the prosecution. His reference group will reward him precisely because he was sanctioned by the court. This of course is a consequence of the subculture of the police which supports deviancy.

It seems apparent, therefore, that sanctions, as traditionally conceived, are effective only when the norm for which the sanction is applied represents the internalized norm of the majority of the role-occupant's subculture. Where the primary purpose of the sanctioning agency is directed at affecting the activity of only a few persons who are deviant for psychological reasons specific to themselves as individuals, it may be that negative sanctions are sufficient. Where, as is the case of police departments, the sort of activity which the sanctions are nominally aimed at inhibiting in fact are encouraged by the other members of the reference group and indeed by the entire subculture, it may be doubted that negative sanctions aimed at the individual policeman will produce significantly changed behavior. Our hypothesis is thus that existing sanctioning institutions at best aim at modifying individual acts and not at removing the underlying causes of police deviancy.

18.2 CONTROLS ON POLICE ILLEGALITY

The problem of sanctioning the breaches of norms by a member of the very bureaucratic structure responsible for sanctioning such deviancy presents a paradox. On the one hand, only internal controls can, in the last analysis, be wholly effective. Highly placed officials within the hierarchy control the promotion, conditions of work, and other rewards of lower placed members. Sanctions imposed by institutions external to the hierarchy can readily be offset by the activities of the officials of the bureaucracy itself. On the other hand, the officials within the bureaucracy are bound by a variety of constraints which inhibit disciplining the bureaucracy's own members for the violation of rules laid down by an outside agency.

Given this paradox, it is obvious that only when the higher officials of the police have themselves internalized the norms of due process can it be expected that the lower ranks of the police department will conform. It seems obvious that when the higher officials really want to enforce a norm of conduct within the ranks, they can do so. Rules relating to the cleanness of uniforms, sleeping on duty, and (in some police forces) public demeanor are sanctioned, and observed by the majority of the force. The aim of control must be, therefore, to impose sufficient sanctions on the higher officials of the police force that they will in turn sanction breaches of the law by the ranks.

18.3 INTERNAL CONTROLS

Internal control by the police resulting from citizen complaints has not achieved the desired results. Two reasons explain the failures: inherent obstacles to a useful complaint procedure, and inherent contradictions in the position of the police force as an institution when presented by a complaint against an individual officer.

Internal police controls have traditionally been initiated by citizen complaint. Herman Goldstein explains the limitations of this procedure:

Individuals most subject to abuse [by the police] are those with the least competence and the least standing to complain. Ghetto residents, for example, are generally unaware of the limitations on police powers. But even if they were aware that a given action was illegal and they are made familiar with the processes by which complaints may be filed, aggrieved parties may not choose to file a complaint. Persons residing in such areas are fearful of possible reprisal. They fear that their future conduct might be subject to special scrutiny. And they fear endangering a relationship with the police which they depend upon should the need for a variety of emergency services arise. Even when mechanisms are established to facilitate the filing of grievances, the percentage of complaints arising from ghetto areas is small in relation to the density of population and the probability that abuses occur.[3]

Moreover, the complaint process is costly to the complainant. It requires time, travel, the reimbursement of witnesses, and frequently the employment of an attorney. "A common awareness of the inconvenience one is caused and the degree to which one is placed in an accusatory position serves as a major deterrent."[4]

The institutional limitations on police self-regulation are even greater than those the complaint process imposes on the individual. In the first place, the internal cohesion of the police—the very factor which gives rise to much police deviancy—makes it difficult to properly process citizen complaints. The officials in the higher echelons are torn by the contradiction of their own positions. Great pressure is put on individual patrolman to prevent crime; it is difficult for the executive, having thus responded to public pressure for crime-prevention, to fault a policeman whose only offense is a somewhat aggressive attitude in carrying out departmental policy. This contradiction becomes especially acute when the department is regarded, as all policemen tend to regard it, as being in a "war" against crime. After all, in war there are no rules, and it is the community which pushes the police into the "war." Finally, the police administrators, like all administrators, are dependent on the support of their inferiors for their own successful accomplishment of their jobs. *Krugovaya poruka* operates at every level. As a result, writes Goldstein,

Chiefs respond to this kind of a situation [i.e., when there is public criticism of an officer for clearly illegal activity by the officer] in different ways. There are those who place a higher value on maintaining a good relationship with their subordinates than upon being responsive to well-founded public criticism. Such chiefs are prepared to defend the actions of their officers, however illegal and improper they may have been; or they are, as a minimum, prepared to resolve all questionable cases in favor of their personnel. The chief who attemps to balance, in a judicious manner, the interests of his men with the public's interest undertakes the more difficult chore, for he must be prepared to incur the wrath of either his many subordinates or his public or both in borderline cases. His conclusions may lead to his punishing an officer who, in the eyes of his fellow officers, acted heroically. Or he may, in weighing the evidence, find it necessary to dismiss charges against an officer who appears, in the minds of the public, to be clearly guilty of the alleged charge.[5]

Indeed, some police departments gather ranks so closely against complainants that they automatically institute charges of "false reporting to the police" against the complainant. Sometimes the complainant is required to support his charges by an oath, with a threat, explicit or implicit, of a charge of false swearing if he be unable to substantiate his charges.[6] It is a bold complainant who will carry through charges under such circumstances.

The internal cohesion of the police is probably the reason why police departments do not commonly have their own investigative units to "police the police," save in the limited area of corruption, and not very frequently even there. The same pressures on police officials which tend to make them support their personnel when charged by outsiders with improper activity, operate to prevent an official from instituting independent investigative efforts. The National Advisory Commission on Civil Disorders (The Kerner Commission) reported:

In Milwaukee, Wisconsin and Plainfield, New Jersey, . . . ghetto residents complained that police chiefs reject all complaints out of hand. In New Haven, a Negro citizens' group characterized a police review board as "worthless." In Detroit, the Michigan Civil Rights Commission found that, despite well-intentioned leadership, no real sanctions are imposed on offending officers. In Newark, the Mayor referred complaints to the FBI, which had limited jurisdiction over them . . ."[7]

In the second place, all attempts to devise a method of sanctioning deviant police activities suffer from the limitations imposed by the conditions in which police infractions of the regulatory rules occur. The infractions frequently arise in situations of high emotional tensions where the police are regarded both by the citizen and by themselves as being adversary to the citizen. The police suspect the citizen of antagonism to them; the citizen suspects the police of prejudice. In such situations, witnesses are apt to be involved and committed to one side or the other. It is peculiarly difficult to ascertain what in fact took place.

This difficulty is compounded by the fact that police illegality takes place most frequently at times and places chosen by the police. In some cities, the practice has been to beat prisoners while in police cars, or in elevators in criminal courts buildings—places where the isolation is complete. Police in many situations where they anticipate the use of excessive force remove their badges, thus making indentification almost impossible. After the notorious riots in Chicago at the time of the Democratic National Convention in 1968, most of the small handful of officers actually subjected to disciplinary hearings were charged not with the substantive crime of assaulting citizens, but with the relatively minor

CONTROL OF POLICE ILLEGALITY AND POLICE DISCRETION

breach of regulations involved in removing badges before the "action" took place.

The circumstances in which many arrests are made are, by their very nature, ones in which an individual is isolated from other citizens: the lone black at night in a white area, the lower-class individual wandering in a middle-class neighborhood are most likely to be accosted by the police. Any friction that arises can readily result in police misconduct without any witnesses save, perhaps, other officers, who are bound by the informal "code" not to testify against a fellow officer.

These varying pressures and conditions combine to ensure that few police departments maintain effective units to investigate citizen complaints effectively. In 70% of all departments, complaints are processed by the district unit to which the officer belongs.[8] The President's Task Force on the Police found these investigations to be haphazard and dependent on the attitude of the particular line commander. Records were inadequate. Regulations were either not followed or so unclear as to be impossible to follow.

The processes of internal departmental hearings and the penalties assessed were found by the Task Force to be largely inadequate. There might or might not be formal hearings. The hearings might be held in secret.[9] The complainant was sometimes not allowed to examine witnesses. He might not be entitled to see the investigative report or to counsel. The punishments were light or non-existent: "seldom is meaningful disciplinary action taken against officers guilty of one or more forms of brutality."[10] Finally, the results of the disciplinary hearings were made public in less than half of the departments surveyed by Michigan State University in its study of police practices.

These inadequacies of internal policing by the police have a circular effect. Distrust of the police is compounded by distrust of the remedies granted to the complainants. Repeated failures of complainants to get satisfaction in their complaints lead them to decline to file complaints. Without complaints, the internal police disciplinary procedure never is triggered into action.

The ineffectiveness of the complaint procedure is therefore built-in. Complaints against individual officers set off all the forces which solidify the police hierarchy against outsiders. The pressures which they create encourage the cover-up of individual delinquency. To cover-up individual delinquency is to ensure that the deviancy from the official norms will be regarded as approved by higher ranks. The subculture of police deviancy is thus reinforced.

18.4 THE COURTS AS SANCTIONING INSTITUTIONS

As we saw earlier, the legal concept that confines authority to that defined by law is that of *ultra vires*. So long as the police—or any government officials, for that matter—act within the norms defining their roles, their actions are protected by law, even if the same action by a private citizen would be an offense.

And from a legal point of view, as soon as the police step out of their role by violating the norms defining it, they become mere private citizens, subject to legal sanctions and penalties. The *ultra vires* doctrine is thus a principal device of the administrative law for enforcing Weber's criteria of legal-rational legitimacy. It purports to ensure, first, that the officers act according to rules; second, that the role-occupants are confined to their specific functions, as part of the bureaucratic division of labor; and, third, that the necessary use of compulsion is used only under the defined circumstances.

The courts and legislatures have devised four principal means for sanctioning breaches of rules laid down for the police in their treatment of citizens: criminal prosecutions, civil actions, injunctions, and the exclusionary rules.

Criminal Actions

A policeman's use of force against a citizen is criminal when the force used exceeds the minimum amount necessary to accomplish the objectives for which the privilege of using force is granted. Force in excess of the minimum necessary for these purposes is criminal, even if the actor is clothed in a blue uniform.

The difficulty with the use of the criminal law against the police, however, is that the prosecutors and the police closely depend on each other's cooperation in performing their jobs. *Krugovaya poruka* is operative once again; so much so that in many jurisdictions it is a matter of course that in any case where there is a claim of police misconduct, the prosecutor will not agree to a reduced charge or a *nolle prosequi* in the course of plea bargaining, unless the accused executes a general release of liability in favor of the police officers. It is difficult to reconcile the prosecutorial concern for police immunity from civil suit with the purposes for which prosecutors are granted the discretion on which plea bargaining depends. In at least one Eastern jurisdiction, the police invariably arrest those whom they brutalize, with or without evidence, knowing that, under pressure from the prosecutor, the accused will invariably release them from civil liability for the fake arrest and beating in order to escape the criminal charge.

The inability or unwillingness of prosecutors to bring criminal charges against the police was clearly demonstrated after the Chicago riots during the Democratic National Convention in 1968. There were innumerable well-documented cases of police assaults. A national news magazine, for example, carried a photograph of a police officer, whose face appeared large and clear in the photograph, spraying mace at the photographer; the stream of mace was very clear. In the nature of things, a photographer cannot be committing assault while taking a photograph. The picture was solid evidence of an assault by the officer. There were many other cases equally clearly documented. Not a single criminal prosecution was instituted against any police officer, although, of course, hundreds of citizens were arrested. In Madison, Wisconsin, a riot took place in 1969, involving students and the police. The local newspapers were full of stories of police mis-

conduct: throwing tear gas bombs into private homes, beatings, throwing pop
bottles and rocks at crowds of people. (The fact that someone in a crowd throws
rocks at the police does not justify the police in throwing rocks, let alone throwing them indiscriminately into the crowd.) A County Board member was assaulted
while walking peaceably down a street. A city alderman sympathetic to the
students, arrested on a traffic offense, was forced to submit to a haircut while
being booked by a sheriff's deputy who did not like his haircut. Over a hundred
civilian arrests were made. Not a single arrest, not a single prosecution of a
police officer was instituted.

The ineffectiveness of criminal proceedings against the police has been even
more blatant when the victims are blacks. Repeatedly in the South, those charged
with police brutality and even killings of blacks have been exonorated by local
grand juries. The Federal Civil Rights Statute has sometimes played a useful
function in such circumstances. That statute[11] makes it a crime to deprive any
person "under the color of any law ... of any rights, privileges and immunities
secured or protected by the Constitution or laws of the United States ... on
account of such inhabitant being an alien or by reason of his color or race."
Federal officers, responsive to national rather than local political pressures, have
invoked the Civil Rights Statute in some cases in which local authorities have
refused to prosecute, with the ludicrous result that sometimes a police officer
who has killed a citizen is tried, not for murder, but for depriving his victim of
his civil rights.

The ineffectiveness of the criminal law in controlling police activity is
again evident when we come to the two federal statutes which prohibit searches
in excess of a warrant[12] or without a warrant.[13] These statutes were enacted in
1921. During the forty-eight years since the enactment of these statutes not a
single violation of these statutes has appeared in the appellate reports. There
have been innumerable cases reaching the federal courts in that period in which
judicial findings have revealed either searches in excess of authority or without
warrant.[14]

Civil Actions

Legal actions by injured parties against police officers for damages, for false
imprisonment or assault have not been any more successful than criminal actions
as a deterrent against police illegality. Such an action may be based on the
common law of torts or the Federal Civil Rights Statute,[15] which gives a right to
an aggrieved person for damages against "every person who, under the color of
any statute, ordinance, regulation, custom or usage, of any State or Territory,
subjects, or causes to be subjected, any citizen of the United States or other
person within the jurisdiction thereof to the deprivation of any rights, privileges,
or immunities secured by the Constitution and its laws ... " This statute was
originally part of the Ku Klux Klan Act of 1871. In *Monroe v. Pape*,[16] it was held

to comprehend an action against police officers who, in that case, allegedly broke into the plaintiffs' Chicago home in the early morning, routed them from bed, made them stand naked in the living room while they ransacked the house, emptying drawers, and ripping mattresses. They detained one petitioner for ten hours in the police station on an "open" charge, without taking him before a magistrate or permitting him to call an attorney or his family.

While civil actions do not depend on the intitiative of a prosecuting official, they suffer from formidable practical difficulties that deter potential plaintiffs, make the actions themselves infrequent, and even less often successful. The potential plaintiffs are usually from lower-class backgrounds, frequently with criminal records. Juries, whose members are usually middle class, are notoriously unsympathetic. We have already mentioned the difficult evidential problems that hamper any action against individual police officers. In addition, in most states the doctrine of sovereign immunity (deriving historically from the immunity of the English crown from suit) protects the governmental body involved, and individual police officers rarely have the assets to pay a substantial judgment.

Miscellaneous Forms of Relief

In a few cases, injunctive power has been used by courts to restrain improper police practices. In *Wirin v. Horral*,[17] it was held possible for a taxpayer to enjoin the authorities from using public funds to blockade areas of Los Angeles to facilitate an unconstitutional "dragnet" of the area. We have already referred to *Lankford v. Gelston*,[18] in which an injunction was granted to prohibit the Baltimore police from engaging in searches without warrants based on anonymous tips.

The Exclusionary Rule

Criminal actions, civil suits, and injunctive relief are plainly little, if any, more effective than internal organizational controls by the police themselves. The courts have, as a last resort, turned to the rules of evidence as a device to sanction the breaches of the various rules of police conduct which relate to arrest and the collection of evidence.

The exclusionary rule holds that evidence seized in violation of law is inadmissible in a subsequent criminal prosecution. We have seen how the rule governing confessions was extended from its original concern with voluntariness to the *Miranda* rules, which condition admissibility of in-custody statements upon police compliance with norms laid down in that case.[19] The federal standard, and that of a minority of states, always excluded evidence seized in an illegal search and seizure, although a majority of the states did not observe the same criteria. The Supreme Court in 1960, in *Mapp v. Ohio*[20] incorporated the exclusionary rule with respect to searches and seizures into the constitutional guarantee. The consequence was to make the exclusionary rule applicable in all proceedings, federal or state.

There is little doubt that, if this were the best of all possible worlds, the exclusionary rule would make little sense, for it imposes no direct sanction against the police wrong-doer. The implication of this rule, as Cardozo puts it eloquently, is that "The criminal is to go free because the constable has blundered."[21] The startling consequences are:

The pettiest police officer would have it in his power, through overzeal or indiscretion, to confer immunity upon an offender for crimes the most flagitious. A room is searched against the law, and the body of a murdered man is found. If the place of discovery may not be proved, the other circumstances may be insufficient to connect the defendant with the crime. The privacy of the home has been infringed, and the murderer goes free. Another search, once more against the law, discloses counterfeit money or the implements of forgery. The absence of a warrant means the freedom of the forger.[22]

The California court, in summarizing the argument, said that "allowing ... criminals to escape punishment is not appropriate recompense for the invasion of their constitutional rights; it does not punish the officers who violated the constitutional provisions; and it fails to protect society from known criminals who should be punished."[23]

The Supreme Court rejected these arguments in *Mapp v. Ohio*. In that case, seven Cleveland police officers forced entry into Mr. Mapp's house, claiming to have information that "a person [was] hiding out in the home, who was wanted for questioning in connection with a recent bombing, and that there was a large amount of policy paraphernalia being hidden in the house." After forcing their entry and without a warrant (although they falsely told Mrs. Mapp that they had a warrant), they searched the house thoroughly. They found neither the wanted witness nor policy paraphernalia, but they did turn up what Justice Douglas, in concurring with the decision, described as "four little pamphlets, a couple of photographs, and a little pencil doodle." These were allegedly pornographic. Mrs. Mapp was tried and convicted of the knowing possession of pornographic material. She appealed in part on the ground that the pamphlets, photographs, and doodle were improperly admitted into evidence. The Supreme Court of Ohio, operating under a state doctrine that admitted illegally obtained evidence, upheld the conviction. On further appeal, the United States Supreme Court reversed the decision.[24]

The reversal was based on pragmatic reasoning. The Court was "compelled to reach that conclusion because other remedies have completely failed to secure compliance with the constitutional provision."[25] The rule was a "deterrent safeguard";[26] and was "calculated to prevent, not to repair."[27]

The effectiveness of the exclusionary rule with respect to police searches and seizures, like the effectiveness of the exclusionary rule with regard to the

Miranda strictures upon police behavior, may well be doubted.[28] It is not likely to be effective for a variety of reasons. Four structural reasons suggest themselves. In the first place, the exclusionary rule reaches into only a very small part of police activity. Brutality or offensive behavior not related to the extraction of confessions, for example, are unaffected by the exclusionary rule.

Secondly, it is argued that the rule will persuade officers in all searches and interrogations to act lawfully, because only with properly obtained evidence can the suspect be convicted. This argument assumes that the police will feel "punished" if their accusations fail to stick. In fact, the police are far more concerned with "clearing" then with conviction. A police officer who clears a reported crime is rewarded by the system. He is not sanctioned by his superiors for not being able to sustain the charge in court. Thus, the potential inadmissibility of illegally obtained evidence does not deter him in most cases from using illegal methods to "clear" the crime in the books.

Thirdly, if the courts' rulings are to be effective guides for police action, they must be effectively communicated to the police.[29] The effective rulings governing police actions are those of the local trial court. But these rulings are rarely published and may vary between the local judges. Appellate-court decisions are usually phrased in arcane language not readily understood by the ordinary policeman. LaFave and Remington ask rhetorically what an average policeman is supposed to make of this key sentence in *Escobedo v. Illinois*:[30]

> We hold, therefore, that where, as here, the investigation is no longer a general inquiry into an unsolved crime but has begun to focus on a particular suspect, the suspect has been taken into police custody, the police carry out a process of interrogations that lends itself to eliciting incriminating statements, the suspect has requested and been denied an opportunity to consult with his lawyer, and the police have effectively warned him of his absolute constitutional right to remain silent, the accused has been denied "the Assistance of Counsel" . . . and that no statement elicited by the police during interrogation may be used against him at a criminal trial.[31]

Finally, the sanctions of the exclusionary rule, whatever they may be, simply do not reach the 90-odd percent of cases which do not go to trial, but are settled by a plea of guilty—let alone the even greater proportion of cases that do not reach the court at all. It is a commonplace of punishment theory that the effectiveness of enforcement is a greater deterrent than the degree of punishment. The motorist who knows that he can exceed the speed limit with only about one chance in a hundred of being caught is very apt to exceed the speed limit. A policeman who knows that less than one investigation out of a hundred will ever have to stand the glare of public examination at a trial, is apt to ignore the possibility of losing the exceptional case.

In addition to these structural reasons for the failure of the exclusionary rule to lead to conformity by the police, there is another, perhaps even deeper, reason,

CONTROL OF POLICE ILLEGALITY AND POLICE DISCRETION

which is independent of the initial cause of police deviancy. Police deviancy arises because their roles within a bureaucracy of a certain sort, positioned in a stratified society, are subject to certain pressures. On the other hand, the policeman's self-perception as the ruthless, implacable avenger of crime, and the subculture of the police that nurtures police behavior according to this self-perception, will not be affected by a court's refusal to convict a criminal, despite evidence against him, on the ground that "the constable blundered." Such an action on the part of a court will, indeed, tend to reinforce the policeman's judgment that the courts are fighting "dangerous criminals" with cream puffs. More likely than compelling the police to abide by the norms of due process, it will persuade him to evade these norms more adroitly.

18.5 OTHER SANCTIONING AGENCIES

The joint failure of internal police discipline and of the courts to effectively sanction deviant police officers has occasioned the development of a variety of alternative sanctioning institutions, most of which, however, have not received wide acceptance. We discuss, in turn, the traditional control institutions (city council, mayor, police commissioners or board), the civilian review boards, and the Ombudsman.

18.6 TRADITIONAL EXTERNAL CONTROL INSTITUTIONS

The democratic blueprint of government calls for the police to be under more or less direct control of elected representatives of the people. If this control is too direct, however, it may paradoxically threaten the maintenance of the police as an effective institution. Too many temptations exist to use the bureaucracy of the police itself as a weapon in political conflict. "Early efforts to assure popular control of the police did include provisions in some cities for the chief of police to be elected. In others, the police were made responsible to the local legislative body. It became quickly apparent, however, that such direct control led to a pattern of incompetence, lax enforcement, and the improper use of police authority. Elected officeholders dictated the appointment and assignment of personnel, exchanged immunity from enforcement for political favors, and, in some cities, made use of the police to assist in winning elections."[32]

As a reaction to this development, communities sought to immunize the police from political influence. As part of a nationwide "good government" movement to make local government not a matter of politics but of administrative efficiency, so-called "weak mayor" forms of government developed. Most of the city's administrative authority was delegated to appointed boards, usually immune from any but fiscal controls by the elected government, and in some cases even from that. Typically, the police came to be controlled by a board of police commissioners, appointed by the mayor but holding office for relatively long and staggered terms. Sometimes even these boards have no control over internal police discipline.

The boards have not been noticeably more useful than the professional police hierarchy in sanctioning breaches of the rules. They are manned almost entirely by untrained civilians. Like most part-time amateurs trying to control a bureaucracy, these men are at the mercy of the professionals. More often than not, the only qualification for board membership is political regularity. In addition, their administrative position forces the board members to perceive themselves as part of the police structure. To criticize a policeman is to attack the police force. They are thus in no better position than higher police officers to process complaints against individual officers.

18.7 CIVILIAN REVIEW BOARDS

A common device for ensuring regularity in bureaucratic structures is to put the enforcement agency formally outside the bureaucracy. In the armed forces, the inspector general's role lies external to the formal chain of command. His job is to ensure that Army units abide by the overall rules laid down for their government. Large corporations frequently have roving "trouble-shooters" with an analogous function.

Similar arrangements have been proposed to help "police the police." Thus civilian review boards are in part to play a role for the police not unlike that of inspector general for the armed forces. "A review board procedure serves two basic functions: maintaining discipline within the Department and satisfying civilian complainants. A procedure that satisfactorily performs one function does not necessarily discharge the other."[33]

In fact, however, most of the proposed civilian review boards have been primarily assigned the latter function, i.e. "to provide citizens—especially those members of minority groups residing within ghetto areas—an opportunity to air their grievances regarding the exercise of police authority."[34] The established boards—there are only two with any significant body of experience—have power to recommend disciplinary action by the police force itself but they cannot themselves impose punishment. As a result, while useful as a communications channel, their actual impact upon police deviancy in those cities where they have existed does not seem to have been very great. Keeping open the channels of communication helps, no doubt, to maintain legitimacy. It alone, however, cannot long substitute for the requirements of legal-rational legitimacy.

The Philadelphia Board has had the longest existence. From 1958 through 1965 it received 725 complaints, 333 of which were dealt with to the satisfaction of the complainants without resorting to formal hearings. In 38 cases disciplinary action was recommended; 15 of these recommendations resulted in suspensions of up to 30 days, and 23 of them led to official reprimands. The president of the NAACP in Philadelphia is reported as having said, "It ain't worth a damn!"[35]

The reason for the Philadelphia Board's relative ineffectiveness appears to be built into the procedural structures of the Board and its place relative to the police department and city government. The Board relies on the police themselves for its investigation.[36] It has not successfully publicized its findings. It has no power of imposing punishment, although its recommendations are usually followed. Perhaps as a result of its insecure position, its recommended punishments have been regarded by civil rights leaders as perhaps even less severe than what the police themselves would have imposed.[37]

Perhaps the most important reason that the potential effectiveness of a civilian review board is to be suspected lies in its weak structural position. As the recipient of complaints against individual officers who have frequently done no more than what the department explicitly or implicitly encouraged him to do, and without final power to impose punishment, the board will inevitably come to act mainly as a buffer between the citizen and the police, whatever other functions it may claim to have. It will permit the citizens to "blow off steam" while insulating the individual policemen from serious punishment. It seems inevitable that a civilian review board structured like the Philadelphia Board will become not the outside disciplinarian and inspector that is required, but part of the existing system.

18.8 OMBUDSMEN AND OTHERS

The Ombudsman as presently conceived is an independent public official with power to investigate allegations of impropriety or illegality in the operations of government, and to make recommendations to the head of the relevant agency to correct any illegality found. Historically, the first Ombudsmen in Scandinavia served the functions of inspectors general of the armed forces; only later did they begin to oversee other functions of the government. Varying forms of ombudsmen exist in many countries. In the Soviet Union and other Eastern European countries the State Procurator exercises even greater powers of control over the operations of the bureaucracy than does the Scandinavian Ombudsman. In these countries, the Procurator has power directly to order agencies to change their practices, reverse decisions, or discipline functionaries. His office is sufficiently independent and powerful to be fairly called a fourth branch of the government.

The Ombudsman seems to hold some potential for removing police deviancy. First, while he deals with individual complaints, the Ombudsman will not impose specific sanctions upon a deviant officer. Instead, he reports the matter to the head of the agency, who is held strictly accountable for the correction and disciplining of the offender. Since the Ombudsman's success as a public official does not depend on the cooperation of individual policemen, he is not apt to be absorbed into the system. His success does not even depend on the cooperation of the head of the police department. The Ombudsman has various ways of dealing with him: through publicity, recommendation to the legislature or the executive, or, in some systems, by direct intervention. Second, if the Ombudsman is to function at all, he must have his own investigative services, with the power of subpoena. Third, his function is primarily not to resolve individual complaints, but to ensure that the government agency involved functions legally as an institution. He is supposed to be interested not so much in the individual case as in the ongoing, repetitive activity of the agency. There is less chance, therefore, that he will become a mere lightning rod to deflect complaints from citizens against the police.

For all these reasons, Herman Goldstein, perhaps the most thoughtful of the academics concerned with the internal operations of the police (and also with wide practical experience in the field), concludes:

The mere presence of a detached, independent critic would serve, in a very important way, to support a police administrator anxious to make the right choice when confronted with strong pressures that move him in the other direction. Application of this form of control to all agencies of government would lessen the defensive posture that the police assume when singled out from other agencies for special scrutiny. And the transfer in emphasis from exclusively negative criticism—in the form of recommendations for disciplinary action or in the form of dismissal of criminal charges because of the way in which evidence was acquired—to constructive suggestions for change and improvement would afford the opportunity for making the complaint process serve as an effective method for strengthening administration.[38]

The hoped for success of the operation of an Ombudsman, however, must be considered in the light of the problems of internal control which we discussed earlier. A police official, however much he may be convinced of the necessity of abiding by the rules of due process, must in the last analysis discipline individual policemen who break the rules. He must promulgate a strict policy prohibiting violations of due process, he must educate his officers in the necessity of observing the law, he must sensitize his officers to minority-group problems. Unless he disciplines those officers who break the law, however, other supervisory programs will be largely fruitless. An unsanctioned rule is not a norm; it is a mere hortatory statement. Furthermore, only by sanctioning men for specific breaches can higher officials teach those in the ranks that they really do intend the latter to abide by the due-process rules. And only by so doing can the higher officials slowly transform the subculture that nurtures police deviancy.

The Ombudsman is thus faced, in the end, with many of the same constraints that limit the effectiveness of the individual complaint system and internal police controls. His major advantage is that by exerting pressure on the head of the agency, he can hopefully begin to induce policy changes that reach beyond the individual officers to the whole style of the police department.

He can induce those changes only in a political climate in which higher police officers understand that they must obtain compliance to the norms of due process from their subordinates in order to avoid being themselves sanctioned by higher political authorities. Such sanctions seem relatively improbable. The same pressures by the groups in the population who favor order over law affect political officials as well as the police. As Walter Gellhorn remarks,

The critic can isolate aberrations; he can suggest better ways of reaching agreed ends; he can point out new applications of previously accepted concepts ... What he cannot do is to force resistant officials to embrace a philosophy newly created by him. Rather, he shares tenets whose validity the great mass of officials readily acknowledge. If administrators' objectives and his, their conceptions of honorable service and his, fundamentally conflicted, the external critic could achieve little.[39]

The fundamental conflict between due process and crime control reflects fundamental dichotomies and antogonisms in society. So long as these exist, it seems doubtful that police violations of due process can be effectively sanctioned, although no doubt increased pressures toward conformity can be generated by the use of better internal complaint systems, civilian review boards, and Ombudsmen. Until the police are effectively sanctioned, substantial adherence to the rules laid down for their conduct is unlikely. Until the police adhere to these rules, the achievement of formal legitimacy for the police seems equally unlikely.

18.9 THE CONTROL OF DISCRETION

The Weberian criteria for legal-rational legitimacy require (1) that discretion be limited so far as possible in order that decisions be made according to rules, and (2) that discretion be exercised only on the basis of considerations relevant to the official goals of the organization, *sine ira et studio.*

Many of the formal norms of American administrative law are aimed at realizing these conditions. They help protect legal-rational legitimacy in those areas of the government to which they apply. To understand why these rules do not promote police legitimacy, we shall have to examine, first, the existing norms embodied in the administrative law and the situations to which they apply; second, their inapplicability to problems involving the police; and third, suggestions for surrogate controls over police discretion.

18.10 THE CONTROL OF DISCRETION IN AMERICAN ADMINISTRATIVE LAW

American administrative law developed historically in the context of governmental efforts to regulate business. The earliest administrative-law cases relating to the problem of discretion concerned the licensing of taverns and public houses during the nineteenth century. The great federal administrative agencies—the Interstate Commerce Commission, the Federal Communications Commission, and the rest—have been the source of most of the litigations out of which have emerged the federal administrative laws. In the states, public utility commissions' rate-setting and questions concerning zoning have frequently been the wellsprings of administrative-law rulings.

Administrative laws have been forged mainly in these contexts rather than with respect to police activities or welfare problems because of the inherent limitations of the adversary system. The government's attempt to regulate business generated deliberate decisions which were subject to challenge. The persons aggrieved were mainly businessmen, with money and lawyers to invoke judicial review. And there was a set of common-law procedures, more or less poorly adapted to the problem, but nevertheless available, for the control of administrators.

This context in which the administrative law has developed consistently limited the scope in which the problems were conceived. Thus the tendency was to put the questions involved in terms of "individual rights" (represented by the private litigant) as against "the interests of society" (represented by the agency). The legislature invariably gave the power to make substantive decisions to the agency. The courts were hard put to find some device by which they could limit the agency's discretion without substituting judicial for administrative discretion.

The result was a set of rules which as a body require the agency to conform to the Weberian standards. We can see the purpose of these rules by examining the rules with respect to the scope of discretion, the rules with respect to fair procedure, the rules with the respect to the elements that may be taken into account in decision-making, and the remedies available for violations of the norms of administrative law.

Scope of Discretion

The question of the permissible scope of discretion has largely been formulated in this country in terms of the delegation of legislative power. The rhetoric is drawn from the federal (and state) constitutions, in which "legislative power" is said to be "vested" in the legislature. The power to exercise discretion was originally seen as a "legislative power." Operating under nineteenth-century notions, drawn ultimately from Dicey and *laissez-faire* dogmas, courts early held that Congress could not delegate any part of its legislative power. This doctrine was clearly unworkable. The Supreme Court therefore held that "Congress cannot delegate any part of its legislative power except under the limitation of a prescribed standard."[40]

The problem became one of determining what sorts of standards were constitutionally permissible. Two factors have received consideration. On the one hand, without standards meaningful judicial review of an administrative decision is as plausible as the shrimp's whistle, for it is impossible to determine the relevance of evidence, or even whether only public-viewing considerations have entered a decision, apart from some standards. On the other hand, experience suggests that for a variety of reasons the development of standards is frequently best left with the administrative agency, not the Congress. Consequently, increasingly in recent years very vague legislative standards have been upheld by the courts: "just and reasonable," "public interest," "unreasonable obstruction to navigation," "public convenience, interest or necessity," "unfair methods of competition," "reasonable variations," and others.[41] "Delegation by Congress," the Court said, "has long been recognized as necessary in order that the exertion of legislative power does not become a futility.[42]

Despite its increasing vagueness, the delegation doctrine still retains some vitality. It lies largely quiescent on the federal level, although it is occasionally invoked by state courts to strike down legislation that grants power far wider than that required by the necessities of the situation. Insofar as it continues to have vitality, this doctrine tends to ensure that government will be run according to rules so far as the legislature can oversee its operation.

The weakness of the delegation doctrine has been somewhat remedied by the custom of the better-run agencies to limit their own discretion by rules issued in advance. By so doing, they can ensure uniformity against the multifarious pulls by lower-ranking bureaucrats. The Internal Revenue Service is outstanding in this respect, although not typical. The 1968 version of its Federal Tax Regulations fill 4400 double-columned pages, which Kenneth Culp Davis characterizes as "a truly magnificent body of law."[43]

Procedural Fairness

The decision-making process involves inputs, conversion processes, outputs, and feedbacks. Much of American administrative law is devoted to ensuring that the inputs to the decisional process will include everything that the decision-maker should take into account to make wise decisions, and nothing that might sway his decisions toward unofficial goals. They thus tend to promote decisions which are instrumental to the official goals of the institution, *sine ira et studio*.

In response to the rhetoric of "individual rights" and the procedural imperatives of the adversary system, therefore, methods have been developed to ensure that the decision-makers get the necessary information. Principal among these methods are those which may be subsumed under the general rubric of "fair hearing." An administrative decision adjudicating individual rights must be made, according to the Federal Administrative Procedure Act, after the agency has afforded "all interested parties opportunity for . . . the submission and considerations of facts, arguments, offers of settlement or proposals of adjustment where time, the nature of the proceeding, and the public interest permit . . ."[44] Indeed, unless there is a hearing at some point in the administrative process, it is likely that the decision would be set aside for violation of the due-process clause of the federal Constitution.[45]

The hearing procedure legitimizes a decision in two ways: It satisfies the litigant that his claim and evidence have been heard by the deciding authority; and it increases the probability (since the litigant usually has special knowledge of the facts and the incentive to bring them forward) that the decision-maker will have all the necessary factual and theoretical inputs, so that a decision will not fail for lack of information.

Rules of evidence limit the matters to be proved to those which are (in the words of the Administrative Procedure Act) not "irrelevant, immaterial, or unduly repetitious."[46] Thus the input of evidence is specifically related to the conversion processes. An administrative agency, in accordance with the Administrative Procedure Act, may impose a sanction, or issue a rule or order, only "as supported by and in accordance with the reliable, probative and substantial evidence."

The key words are "irrelevant" and "probative," which are the opposite sides of the same coin. An item of evidence is relevant or probative only if in conjunction with a general proposition, either commonly accepted or proven by expert testimony, it can lead to an inference (or, more likely, a series of inferences) directed toward the proof or disproof of the proposition of a matter of fact ultimately in question. If the agency must determine whether a given drug is sufficiently safe to the sold on the open market, for example, a witness may testify that he tried the drug experimentally on a particular sample of ten thousand patients. This testimony can be conjoined with a general proposition (assuming it to be true) that "a sample of ten thousand patients chosen as the sample in the experiment has an 'extremely high degree' of probability of having the same reaction to the drug in question as the population at large." Hence it can be inferred that the drug in question will be safe for the population at large.

Evidence must be probative *of something*; it cannot be merely probative in general. It is in connection with this criterion that the requirement of narrowly defined scope of discretion is so important. It is impossible to determine what evidence is relevant, and whether the agency made its decision on the basis of relevant evidence, unless one can identify the criteria which make it probative. If a statute gives discretion to an administrator without stating (explicitly or implicitly) the criteria under which discretion may be exercised, it is impossible to determine what evidence is relevant or probative.

American administrative law also includes rules governing the process by which the decision is to be reached. Of these rules, we have already mentioned the most important: That a decision must be based on probative evidence. A decision based on evidence which is not relevant to the official criteria cannot be instrumental to the goals of the agency, but to some personal or subjective goals of the administrator. Suppose, for example, that a statute gives the administrator the right to control prices during war time. If the statute requires the administrator to set the price so that the seller can make a "reasonable" profit, or something similar to this, no doubt there will be dispute over how much profit is reasonable, but at least a general sort of criterion is set. Suppose, on the other hand, that a statute merely stated that the administrator be given the right to "set retail prices" of commodities. Would the administrator, then, be acting *ultra vires* if he were a devoted teetotaler and therefore set the price of Scotch whiskey of any brand so that it does not exceed five cents a quart, knowing full well that such a price would simply drive Scotch whiskey off the market? The conversion processes, like the input processes, are dependent on the rules defining the range of discretion of the administrator.

Finally, American administrative law provides for a sanctioning process over administrators, primarily in the form of an appeal to the courts and, if the administrators have acted in violation of the norms defining their scope of discretion, a reversal of the decision by the court. The process of sanctioning defines its principal inherent limitation: It is dependent, in the main, upon the initiative of the individual who has been harmed. It therefore suffers from all the built-in constraints of the adversary system. Far more discretionary decisions are made by policemen about the poor than are made by regulatory agencies about the activities of businessmen. American administrative law has been forged, however, in the context of the latter, not the former.

Summary

The scope of the norms embodied in administrative law is extremely large and cannot here be further adumbrated. It is sufficient to point out (1) that these rules were developed in the context of problems concerning administrative control over business activities, where there were specific decisions to be made affecting particular businessmen, and (2) that the rules are reasonably well adapted to that context to ensure that the rulings of the administrative agency as they affect the individual are instrumental to the official goal of the agency as declared in its governing statutes.

18.11 ADMINISTRATIVE LAW AND THE CONTROL OF POLICE DISCRETION

As we have seen, the police have vast areas of concern in which to exercise their discretion. Kenneth Culp Davis points out that the police

make far more discretionary determinations in individual cases than any other class of administrator; I know of no close second . . . The amount of governmental activity through the police, measured by man-hours, is more than forty times as much as the amount of governmental activity through all seven of the independent federal regulatory agencies; those agencies in the aggregate have about 10,0000 employees but the nation has about 420,000 policemen, exclusive of supporting personnel.[47]

It is startling to realize that, this fact nothwithstanding, the institutions of administrative law which serve to maintain the legal-rational legitimacy of other branches of American government are simply inapplicable to the police. And the persons affected by police activity most frequently are not businessmen with the resources and lawyers to challenge the police exercise of discretion. Most important of all, the constant denial of the police that they have any discretion makes it difficult to control the discretion which they in fact exercise. Denying that they exercise any discretion, they do not issue any rules on their own; and, as we have seen, there are no court-developed rules to limit their discretion. As a result, police discretion is exercised in ways that almost ensure its incompatibility with the government objectives. It is exercised by the very lowest ranks of the police, usually without any kind of general rule to guide it, and without any forum in which it can be tested and an abuse sanctioned. The President's Task Force on the Police comments:

Direct confrontation of policy issues would inevitably require the police administrator to face the fact that some police practices, although considered effective, do not conform to constitutional, legislative, or judicial standards. By adopting a "let sleeping dogs lie" approach, the administrator avoids a direct confrontation and thus is able to support "effective" practices without having to decide whether they meet the requirements of law.[48]

Police practices in fact involve the extensive use of discretion. In fact, any repetitive activity involves some rule, however obscure. By failing to make the rule explicit, indeed by denying that discretion exists, rules which are thoroughly illegal are in fact implicitly approved. Kennett Culp Davis has given an example of such an implicit rule, and how it might read if made explicit:

Whereas, various statutes make the distribution of narcotics a crime; whereas, the federal and state constitutions guaranteed equal protection of the laws; and whereas, the Police Department of the City of X finds that law enforcement with the resources at its disposal is inadequate when the statutes and constitutions are complied with; now, therefore, the Police Department of the City of X, pursuant to power which it necessarily assumes but which no statute or ordinance has granted to it, does hereby promulgate the following rules, which shall supercede all constitutional provisions, statutes and ordinances to the contrary:

1 The arresting officer may release a violator of a narcotics statute no matter how clear the evidence is against him, upon making a finding that he may become an informer.

2 Upon releasing such a violator, no officer shall interfere with his further purchase or sale of narcotics, so long as a finding is made that he is supplying information to the police or may be about to do so.

3 All transactions by which an officer trades nonenforcement for information shall be kept secret, so that the absolute discretion of the officer will be immune from check or review by any other governmental authority and immune from criticism by the public.

4 When two violators of the narcotics laws have committed the same offense in the same circumstances, no principle concerning equal justice under law or equal protection of the laws shall control when an officer chooses to trade nonenforcement for information; all provisions of constitutions, statutes and ordinances to the contrary are hereby superseded.

5 Whenever an informer becomes recognized as such by the underworld, the officer who has made promises of immunity from arrest shall request another officer to arrest and prosecute the informer, and such second officer shall falsely pretend to have no knowledge of such promises of immunity; as soon as an informer's effectiveness has been spent, considerations of decency and fairness about keeping promises shall be given no weight.[49]

Similar *de facto* rules could be written about stopping and frisking blacks and not others; the arrest of the poor or minority-group members for minor crimes, and more lenient treatment of middle-class persons committing the same offenses; entering private premises without warrant; the enforcement of gambling laws against social gambling games; and a hundred others.

In short, police practices are immune from the surveillance of those institutions which elsewhere in American law are the primary means of keeping the governmental operations legitimate. What can be done about controlling the discretionary power of the police so as to ensure that police decisions remain instrumental to the officially established objectives of the police department?

18.12 SUGGESTIONS FOR THE CONTROL OF POLICE DISCRETION

If the police are to exercise the discretion which they undoubtedly do exercise in a manner consistent with the requirements of legal-rational legitimacy, they must exercise it in accordance with rules which are regarded by the relevant public sectors as conductive to the official purposes of the police as defined by law, and they must be subject to sanctions which will ensure that these new rules are obeyed. We have already discussed the difficulties involved in developing sanctioning agencies that will work. It is generally agreed, however, that it is both possible and desirable for the police to make rules concerning the exercise of discretion which will have binding force on the lower ranks.

Consider, for example, the problems posed to the police by public civil rights demonstrations or other similar demonstrations, sometimes involving mass civil disobedience. In the South, many police departments simply acted illegally. The United States Commission or Civil Rights reported in 1965 that

local officials in a number of Southern communities suppressed constitutionally protected public protests by arrest and prosecution ... Local officials in communities studied by the Commission in Mississippi, Alabama, Florida and Georgia did not permit persons to exercise the right to assemble peacefully to make known their grievances. Civil Rights demonstrators were repeatedly arrested, dispersed or left unprotected before angry crowds, without regard for the right to public protest assured by the Constitution.[50]

Other police officials simply chose to assert the "full enforcement" policy J. E. Towler asserts

The racial demonstrators on the move are seeking to go to jail . . . To arrest them is the only honorable thing to do . . . The policeman has a sworn duty to perform. When he is aware that a law is being violated, he must take the necessary action to stop it . . . If the law is on the books, he is sworn to enforce it.[51]

A third position is taken by the St. Louis Police Department. It has ruled:

It is the policy of the Department regarding racial disturbances that no direct police actions will be taken in the absence of violence, orders of the court or emergency situations wherein life or property is endangered . . . Generally in such instances the officers assigned on the scene will be plainclothes personnel . . . In the absence of violence or emergency, no action will be taken unless warrants are issued. Under these circumstances the officer shall only observe and report existing conditions.[52]

As a result of this ruling, St. Louis has had approximately 170 demonstrations between 1963 and 1967, with only very few arrests. The administrative ruling, made in advance, reduced the scope of discretion for the officer on the spot.

A striking example of the danger of permitting the officer on the spot to exercise his personal discretion without guidelines is an occurrence in Madison, Wisconsin, in May 1969. For over thirty years, block parties had been held informally in many parts of Madison, with the police cooperating in blocking off the area from traffic. The week before the incident in question, a student community (largely fraternity members) had held precisely such a party. A large group of students living in the area in which there were a number of relatively long-haired "hippy" student and nonstudent types decided to hold a similar party. The party was peaceful and pleasant, and confined to a block that had relatively light traffic. A single police inspector, apparently acting on his own initiative, decided to "enforce the law." He insisted that the students not use the street for their party. The situation grew increasingly tense. Finally, the tension exploded (whether it was the police or the students who exploded first it is difficult to say). Three days of violence ensued in which the police carried on open warfare against the students. The out-of-pocket cost to the city alone exceeded $28,000, more than a hundred students and nonstudents were arrested, and the loss of legitimacy by the police was enormous. A rule published in advance defining the circumstances in which block parties were permitted might have avoided the entire affair.

Without rules, without checkup by superiors, without sanctions supporting the rules already developed, the police could hardly be expected to do other than what they now do—namely, permit the lowest ranks unlimited discretion to make policy. Davis asks: "Can unconfined, unstructured and unchecked discretionary power of an individual officer be good government?"[53]

18.13 SUMMARY

Our hypothesis was that, given the absence of motivation to resist pressures on the bureaucracy, and given the wide discretion and the absence of effective sanctions, police organizations and individual police officers are apt to conform not to the requirements of due process but, rather, to the pressures of the politically powerful. We have seen that there is both according to law and in fact wide discretion available to the police. Far from being motivated to resist the pressures toward the crime-control model, the police and the whole police subculture are deviant on a wide scale in terms of the norms which the police have pledged to obey. Finally, those institutions of American law which in other areas of public life serve to bolster the legitimacy of government agencies by maintaining their instrumental nature with respect to official institutional objectives, are inoperative where the police are concerned, and no other institution has yet been developed which is likely to produce the desired result.

The police are thus deviant. They act illegally, breaching the norms of due process at every point: in committing brutality, in their searches and seizures, in arrests and interrogation.

The consequences of police deviancy touch on the very foundations of American government. Without legitimacy the government can rule by force alone. It can do so in a sense and for a time. But when it does, the quality of community life will suffer, as it already has suffered. When ghettos and universities must be garrisoned lest they become battlegrounds for guerilla wars, life elsewhere in the community is similarly transformed and it has already become less appealing than it ever was before in the nation's history.

Legitimacy is not a luxury. It is a necessity. A government that subscribes to due process meets the requirements of legal-rational legitimacy. The crime-control model of government, however, is self-defeating. Police deviance does not threaten only the blacks, the dissenting students, or the poor and the politically weak. It threatens everyone, including the privileged members of the society who put pressure on the police to adopt the crime-control model; it can and it already has drastically transformed their world.

The problem of controlling the deviant actions of the police is precisely the same, though on a smaller scale, as the problem of controlling deviant tendencies in the polity at large. If the rules are regarded as legitimate by a high proportion of the members of the polity and if the rule-enforcers are looked upon with respect, then compliance is likely to be high. By contrast, if the rules are denigrated and the rule-enforcers are seen as "outsiders' working in the interests of "others," then no amount of coercion is likely to successfully bring about compliance. It may create an uneasy and unstable truce, but lasting compliance with the rules and social harmony is an absolute impossibility under such circumstances.

By the same logic, the modification of the rules governing police activity will be unsuccessful so long as the rule-changes are seen as illegitimate by many policeman. The rules are most likely to be seen by the policemen as illegitimate if they conflict with the demands made on them and with the view of the world emanating from the policeman's role. Ultimately, the economic, political, and social structure which creates the propensities to violate the norms of police work must be altered if we are to successfully alter the patterns of police behavior. Short of that, some progress can be made by improving the recruitment and socialization of police officers, formulating rules for the control of their discretion, and changing distribution of rewards in the bureaucracy. A more nearly complete solution to the problem will not so easy, however; it would require more drastic changes in the social structure itself.

NOTES

1. Edwin W. Patterson, *Jurisprudence—Men and Ideas of Law*, Foundations Press, Brooklyn, 1953, pp. 159–165.

2. See generally Robert A. Dahl and Charles E. Lindblom, *Politics, Economics, and Welfare: Planning and Politico-Economic Systems Resolved into Basic Social Precesses*, Harper and Row, New York, 1953, pp. 87–115.

3. Herman Goldstein, "Administrative problems in controlling the exercise of police authority," *J. Criminal Law, Criminology, and Police Science*, **58**, 1967, pp. 160–167, from which much of the material in this and succeeding sections of this chapter is drawn. Reprinted by special permission of the Journal of Criminal Law, Criminology, and Police Science (Northwestern University School of Law) © 1967.

4. *Ibid.*, p. 168. Reprinted by permission.

5. *Ibid.*, p. 167. Reprinted by permission.

6. President's Commission on Law Enforcement and Administration of Justice, *Task Force Report: The Police*, U.S. Government Printing Office, Washington, 1967, p. 195.

7. *Report of the National Advisory Commission on Civil Disorders*, Bantam, New York, 1968, p. 310.

8. *Task Force Report: The Police*, p. 194.

9. Harold Beral and Marcus Sisk, "The administration of complaints against the police," *Harvard Law Rev.*, **77**, 1964, pp. 499–505.

10. *Task Force Report: The Police*, p. 197.

11. 18 U.S.C.A. §242.

12. 18 U.S.C.A. §2234.

13. 18. U.S.C.A. §2236.

14. Caleb Foote, "Tort remedies for police violations of individual rights," *Minn. Law Rev.*, **39**, 1955, pp. 493–497.

15. 42 U.S.C.A. 1938.

16. 365 U.S. 167, 81 S. Ct. 473, 5 L. Ed. 2d 492 (1961).

17. 85 Cal. App. 2d 497, 193, P. 2d 470 (1948).

18. 364 F. 2d 197, (4th Cir., 1966).

19. *Supra*, Chapter 15. *Miranda v. Arizona*, 384 U.S. 436, 86 S. Ct. 1602, 16 L. Ed. 2d 662 (1965).

20. 367 U.S. 643, 81 S. Ct. 1684, 6 L. Ed. 2d 1081 (1960).

21. *People v. Defore*. 242 N.Y. 13, 150 N.E. 585 (1926), at 587.

22. 150 N.E. 585 at 488.

23. *People v. Cahan*, 44 Cal. 2d 434, 282 P. 2d 905 (1955).

24. 367 U.S. 643 at 644.

25. 367 U.S. 643 at 648.

26. 397 U.S. 643 at 648.

27. *Elkins v. United States*, 364 U.S. 206 at 217, 80 S. Ct. 1437, 4 L. Ed. 2d 1669 (1960).

28. Wayne R. LaFave and Frank J. Remington, "Controlling the police: the judge's role in making and reviewing law enforcement decisions," *Mich. Law Rev.*, **63**, 1965, pp. 987–1003.

29. *Ibid*.

30. 378 U.S. 478, 84 S. Ct. 1758, 12 L. Ed. 2d 977 (1964).

31. LaFave and Remington, *op. cit.*, pp. 990–991.

32. *Task Force Report: The Police*, p. 30.

33. *Report to Mayor-Elect John V. Lindsay by the Law Enforcement Task Force Appointed for the Period of Governmental Transition*, quoted in *The New York Times*, December 31, 1965, p. 15.

34. Goldstein, *op. cit.*, p. 160. Reprinted by permission.

35. Fred E. Inbau, "Democratic restraints upon the police," *J. Criminal Law, Criminology, and Police Science*, **57**, 1966, pp. 265–270.

36. Beral and Sisk, *op. cit.*, p. 515.

37. *Ibid*.

38. Goldstein, *op. cit.*, p. 170. Reprinted by permission.

39. Walter Gellhorn, *Ombudsmen and Others: Citizens' Protectors in Nine Countries*, Harvard University Press, Cambridge, 1966. Reprinted by permission.

40. *United States v. Chicago, M., St. Paul and P. R. Co.*, 282 U.S. 311 at 324, 51 S. Ct. 159, 75 L. Ed. 359 (1931).

41. Kenneth C. Davis, *Handbook on Administrative Law*, West, St. Paul, 1951, p. 45.

42. *Fahey v. Mallonee*, 332 U.S. 245, 67 S. Ct. 1552, 91 L. Ed. 2030 (1947).

43. Kenneth C. Davis, *Discretionary Justice: A Preliminary Inquiry*, Louisiana State University Press, Baton Rouge, 1969, p. 223.

44. Administrative Procedure Act, 5 U.S.C.A. §1001 *et seq.*, §5 (b).

45. See, e.g., *Peters v. Hobby*, 349 U.S. 331 75 S. Ct. 790, 99 L. Ed. 1159 (1955).

46. Administrative Procedure Act, 5 U.S.C.A. §1001 *et seq.*, §7(c).

47. Davis, *Discretionary Justice*, pp. 222–223. Reprinted by permission.

48. *Task Force Report: The Police*, p. 17.

49. Davis, *Discretionary Justice*, p. 96. Reprinted by permission.

50. United States Commission on Civil Rights, "Law enforcement: a report on equal protection in the South," U.S. Government Printing Office, 1965, pp. 173–175.

51. Juby E. Towler, *The Police Role in Racial Conflicts*, Thomas, Springfield, Ill., 1964, pp. 3–10.

52. Quoted in J. L. LeGrande, "Nonviolent civil disobedience and police enforcement policy," *J. Criminal Law, Criminology, and Police Science*, **58**, 1967, p. 403.

53. Davis, *Discretionary Justice*, p. 89. Reprinted by permission.

19

Prosecution

The typical situation surrounding criminal prosecution is characterized by Wayne LaFave as

one in which the police make an arrest without a warrant and then bring the suspect to the prosecutor with a request that he approve the issuance of a warrant. The decision to arrest is clearly made by the police. The decision as to whether to charge the suspect and the selection of the charge are the responsibility of the prosecutor. The prosecutor's charging decision is manifested by his approval or refusal of the issuance of the warrant.[1]

For an offense to move from arrest to consideration by a court it must pass through intermediary processing by the prosecutor's office. At this stage of the legal process it is determined in which of essentially three possible ways the case is to move from arrest to court proceedings: indictment, information, and complaint.

In general, all three possibilities hinge on prosecutorial willingness to proceed. An indictment is a finding by a grand jury that there is probable cause to believe that the accused committed the crime charged. Since there is no defense before a grand jury, the grand jury considers only the evidence presented by the prosecutor. It is a rare grand jury that defies the prosecutor. An information is a charge of criminal offense filed by the prosecutor on the basis of his own determination of probable cause. A complaint by a citizen charging a man of criminal offense in most states cannot be heard in court, but must be made to the prosecutor. The prosecutor stands astride the criminal process, controlling the gates that lead to the trial court.

As we have seen, the articulated norms for police conduct require the police to enforce every violation of the law. Judges, too, formally are not in the position to dismiss a charge or, if the accused is proven guilty, to find the accused not guilty, although they are given vast powers of discretion in the choice of sentence. Of the three principal actors in a criminal prosecution, the prosecutor alone is formally to decide whether or not to enforce the law, and the degree of crime with which to charge the offender.

What is the scope of the discretion lodged in the prosecutor's office? How in fact is this discretion used? What are the consequences of the prosecutor's having discretion and his use of it in particular ways? It is to these questions that we now turn.

19.1 THE SCOPE OF THE PROSECUTOR'S DISCRETION

In England, the power of prosecuting criminal cases was originally, and remains in theory today, largely lodged in the hands of private persons, who are not compelled by law to initiate such prosecutions.[2] When initiated, the action still resembles a private lawsuit between private parties rather than a prosecution initiated and carried on by the sovereign power.

In the United States, the office of the public prosecutor was grafted on the traditional system of private criminal litigation.[3] The public prosecutor thus assimilated the functions of the private prosecutor, and just as the private prosecutor had discretion whether or not to prosecute, so the public prosecutor was endowed with the same discretion.

In actuality, the prosecutor's discretion is almost unlimited. As the court said in *Brack v. Wells*,[4] a Maryland case,

As a general rule, whether the State's Attorney does or does not institute a particular prosecution is a matter which rests in his discretion. Unless the discretion is grossly abused or such duty is compelled by statute or there is a clear showing that such duty exists, mandamus will not lie.

That is, a court will not issue a writ compelling the prosecutor to prosecute. It is true that if the power to prosecute is used in a discriminatory manner, its use may be enjoined,[5] but that is nearly the only grounds for interference with the prosecutor's discretion. Occasionally, a court has removed a prosecutor from office for failing to prosecute manifest and flagrant violations of crime within the court's jurisdiction.[6] However, such occasions have been rare. In practice, the prosecutor's decision to initiate a prosecution, and the degree of crime to be charged, lie entirely in his discretion. That discretion is, for all practical purposes, unreviewable.

His discretion is almost as broad if he wants to decline to prosecute a charge already laid. In some states, there are no limits placed upon the prosecutor's discretion to stop a prosecution *in media res*. In most states, however, a small element of judical control is inserted into the process by permitting the prosecutor to initiate prosecution, but requiring judicial approval for a withdrawal of the charges.[7] In fact, however, as in the case of the decision to prosecute, "the prosecutor's discretion in the use of nol pros (*nolle prosequi*, or decision not to prosecute) is an enormous power in the hands of one public official. Its use is generally not subject to publicity and public scrutiny . . ."[8]

The scope of the prosecutor's discretion to prosecute or not to do so can be justified in terms of the due-process model. Even within the framework of full enforcement, somebody must make preliminary decisions concerning the probability of success of a prosecution—to decide whether the evidence is sufficient for conviction or whether the facts as claimed fall within or without a rule of law. Moreover, there are numerous cases in which considerations individual to a defendant suggest that invocation of the awful machinery of the criminal law is unnecessary or undesirable:

There are many legitimate reasons for a prosecutor's failure to prosecute: where the alleged criminal act may be the result of some quarrel between neighbours and all parties are equally at fault; where the alleged criminal act may be the result of some minor domestic dispute; where an overzealous creditor may be attempting to pervert the criminal process for the purpose of collecting a civil debt; where the expense of extradition might not justify the spending of public funds to bring back a person accused of a petty crime; where a person may have committed a technical violation of the law, and a warning may be sufficient to prevent further infractions; where the evidence is so slim that it would be unfair to subject a person to the ordeal and notoriety of a prosecution—these are some of the considerations that a prosecutor must weigh before proceeding in any particular case.[9]

In fact, as might be predicted, the decision to prosecute at all tends to be a function of the sorts of pressure to which the prosecutor is subject. That white-collar crime is treated with exceptional leniency by prosecutors has been often documented. They are crimes that frequently do not carry deep social stigmas, and hence the prosecutor rarely feels much animus toward the criminals. His values not being involved, it is easy for him to agree not to prosecute, and to leave to civil action or to the noncriminal action of a regulatory agency the sanctioning of the individuals involved. Ferdinand Lundberg writes:

In the case of white-collar crimes of corporations, if any individual is punished (usually none is) it is only one or very few. The authorities do not dig pertinaciously with a view to ferreting out every last person who had anything to do with the case. But . . . it is different with crimes of the lower classes. In kidnapping, for example, the FBI, in addition to seizing the kidnappers, flushes to the surface anyone who (1) rented them quarters to conceal the kidnapped person or to hide in; (2) acted as unwitting agents for them in conveying messages or collecting ransom; (3) transported them; (4) in any way innocently gave aid and assistance; or (5) was a witness to any of these separate acts. The government men do such a splendid job that almost everyone except the obstreticians who brought the various parties into the world are brought to bar, where the aroused judge "breaks the book over their heads" in the course of sentencing.[10]

Prosecutorial discretion is notoriously gentle with the moneyed rich. Cleveland Amory says that in at least seven notorious "society" murders since 1920, the investigations were dropped "for the sake of the families."[11] Lundberg writes:

The mechanics of these affairs are, in general, as follows: After the crime, with the police beginning to set up their lines of investigation, prominent individuals in the same social set, with at least the consent of the family . . . get in touch with the leading politician or politicians upon whom the police are dependent for their jobs. The right politician, responsive to the halo of money, tells the chief of police, "Drop this investigation, for the sake of the grief-ridden family. The guy got what he deserved anyhow, and the family knows it."[12]

It is a rare community in which it is not common knowledge that there is strong evidence that a member of the local elite once committed manslaughter while driving in a drunken state, or something even worse, and escaped prosecution.

In practice, of course, the prosecutor's discretion is not so frequently invoked for the determination of whether or not to prosecute as for the determination of the degree of crime with which the accused is to be charged. According to the due-process model, the considerations to be taken into account in determining the degree of crime to be charged are not different from those to be taken into account in determining whether to prosecute at all. One would expect, therefore, that prosecutors would usually charge less than the maximum conceivable crime, which logically should be reserved only for the most heinous offender. *In fact, however, prosecutors invariably initiate prosecutions for the highest degree of crime that the evidence can sustain.* Before this phenomenon can be explained, however, we must first explain the significance of the negotiated plea of guilty in American criminal procedure.

19.2 THE USE OF GUILTY PLEAS IN THE LEGAL PROCESS

If due process is to be followed, criminal proceedings must clothe the accused with the presumption of innocence until he is proved guilty in an adversary proceeding. As we saw at several points, the adversary proceeding is supposed to be the sovereign remedy for earlier ills. It is in the courtroom, at the trial itself, that the majestic rights enshrined in the Constitution are upheld; it is there that evidence illegitimately obtained will be suppressed; it is there that the prosecution will be required to keep the high standards to which it is held; and it is there that the presence of counsel and judge will prevent oppression or overreaching by police or prosecutor, however weak, humble, or lowly the accused may be.

In fact, these things do happen in many, probably most, cases that actually reach adversary, public hearings. But in the United States, it is an abnormal criminal proceeding that ends up in public hearings. *At least ninety percent of all criminal prosecutions result in guilty pleas*, most of them after negotiations between the accused (or his counsel) and the prosecuting attorney. To understand the nature of criminal prosecution, therefore, it is essential to understand the process by which guilty pleas are reached in so high a proportion of the cases, and to see the consequences.

The norms which formally control the processes by which guilty pleas are reached are consistent with due process. The adversary system allows that there must be some cases in which the proof of guilt is so overwhelming that it is a waste of time for a defendant to insist on a trial when the result is obvious. In such cases, a plea of guilty is not an abridgement of due process.

The principal requirement is that there be some guarantee that the plea is reached not as a result of improper coercion, trickery, promise of lenient treatment, but is the genuine expression of the defendant's free will.

A plea of guilty is of course, frequently the result of a "bargain," but there is no bargain if the defendant is told that, if he does not plead guilty, he will suffer consequences that would otherwise not be visited upon him. To capitulate and enter a plea under a threat of an "or else" can hardly be regarded as the result of the voluntary bargaining process between the defendant and the people sanctioned by propriety and practice.[13]

Hence in most states there is a formal ceremony when a plea of guilty is accepted. Donald Newman reports a typical case, in which a defendant was originally charged with armed robbery. The charge was reduced, after negotiation, to unarmed robbery, a much less serious offense. The following dialogue occurred in open court:

Judge: You want to plead guilty to robbery unarmed?
Defendant: Yes, Sir.
Judge: Your plea is free and voluntary?
Defendant: Yes, Sir.
Judge: No one has promised you anything?
Defendant: No.
Judge: You're pleading guilty because you are guilty?
Defendant: Yes.
Judge: I'll accept your plea of guilty to robbery unarmed and refer it to the probation department for a report and for sentencing December 28.[14]

Indeed, the formal rules frequently require the judge to make such an inquiry. Rule 11 of the Federal Rules of Criminal Procedure provides: "A defendant may plead not guilty, guilty, or, with the consent of the court, *nolo contendere*. The court may refuse to accept a plea of guilty, and shall not accept a plea of guilty without first determining that the plea is made voluntarily with understanding of the nature of the charge. If the defendant refuses to plead or if the court refuses to accept a plea of guilty or if a defendant corporation fails to appear, the court shall enter a plea of not guilty." Under a federal statute[15] a conviction based on a plea of guilty may be set aside after sentencing if the plea proved to have been involuntary, obtained through promises of leniency, or entered without knowledge of the defendant's rights.

Apart from these grounds, however, a plea of guilty is beyond review. Whatever may have preceded the plea is forever painted out. No court will ever have an opportunity, save in the most extraordinary and unusual cases, to examine the conduct of officials which led to the arrest, the charge, or the plea itself. Thus the guilty plea is at once an admission of guilt by the accused and a cover of obscurity for prior police and prosecutorial activities.

The seemingly mindless ritual by which a defendant assures the court that what everyone present knows is not the case, is the case, is, therefore, not a meaningless little ceremony that does not differ from a host of other seemingly mindless ceremonials in the law. It is the significant act by which the accused surrenders himself voluntarily to the forces of the State; he signifies his cooperation and acquiescence. Those acts of cooperation and acquiescence are the very contrary of the adversary posture which lies at the heart of the due-process proceedings. The assurance that the plea is the genuine expression of the accused man's free will, which is the necessary validation of the plea under the due-process requirements, becomes the instrument by which the defendant voluntarily and finally abandons claims for protection under the due-process guarantees.

As might be expected, a plea of guilty is a source of considerable psychological satisfaction to many of the participants in the law-enforcement agencies. To the police, it is an assurance that their suspicions were accurate.[16] To the prosecutor, it is another case expeditiously handled. To the judge, it places his conduct beyond any possibility of appeal (for sentences are not ordinarily appealable). To the correctional authorities, it suggests that the accused can be rehabilitated, for without recognition of wrongdoing, it is believed, rehabilitation cannot succeed.[17]

The defense counsel, under the due-process model, has a significant role to play in the process of negotiating with the prosecutor for a guilty plea. A federal court has commented:

In a sense, it can be said that most guilty pleas are the result of a "bargain" with the prosecutor. But this standing alone, does not vitiate such pleas. A guilty defendant must always weigh the possibility of his conviction on all counts, and the possibility of his getting the maximum sentence, against the possibility that he can plead guilty to fewer, or lesser, offenses, and perhaps receive a lighter sentence. The latter possibility exists if he pleads guilty . . . to the whole charge against him.

No competent lawyer, discussing a possible guilty plea with a client, could fail to canvass these possible alternatives with him. Nor would he fail to ascertain the willingness of the prosecutor to "go along." Moreover, if a codefendant is involved, and if the client is anxious to help that codefendant, a competent lawyer would be derelict in his duty if he did not assist in that regard. At the same time, the lawyer is bound to advise his client fully as to his rights, and to the alternatives available to him, and of the fact that neither the lawyer nor the prosecutor nor anyone else can bargain for the court. There is nothing wrong, however, with a lawyer's giving the client the benefit of his judgment as to what the court is likely to do, always making it clear that he is giving advice, not making a promise.

The important thing is that there shall be no "deal" or "bargain" but that the plea shall be a genuine one, by a defendant who is guilty; one who understands his situation, his rights, and the consequences of the plea, and is neither deceived nor coerced.[18]

It can be argued that even the negotiated guilty plea is consistent with due process. It is said to be an essential safety valve to permit the softening of the impersonal general commands of the law.

The negotiated plea is a way in which prosecutors can make value judgments. They can take some of the inhumanity out of the law in certain situations. The law, for example, might in a given case require the death penalty and yet the prosecutor may believe that the death penalty would be unfair, because of the defendant's age, lack of education, drunkenness, or other factors. Our sentencing laws are exceedingly severe and, if they were strictly applied, they would be great breeders of disrespect for the law.[19]

Newman reports a variety of other reasons for charge-reduction in order to humanize criminal justice. The personal characteristics of the accused may suggest the desirability of a reduction—for example, the youth and inexperience of the violator; the "respectability" of the defendant; the disrepute of the victim, complainant, or witnesses; the low mentality of the accused; and the fact that the conduct in question is viewed as normal within the subculture of the defendant (probably the most frequently invoked reason to reduce the charges in cases of blacks involved in violence within the ghetto). Charges are frequently reduced because of mitigating circumstances: violence arising out of a mutual affray; the prior illegal relationship of victim and defendant (it is difficult to press a charge of theft against a prostitute who takes the customer's money without accomplishing the promised act), and the like.

In practice, there are heavy institutional pressures on the prosecutor to obtain guilty pleas. His own office is, at least in urban centers, invariably over-worked. Trials are arduous. They require that witnesses be interviewed and their statements taken, the law researched, motions drawn and filed, and perhaps an appeal briefed and argued. To the overworked prosecutor, a short hearing on plea and sentence is a welcome respite.

The police reward the prosecutor when he succeeds in obtaining a guilty plea by praise and good will. Courtroom time for many police is not paid; even when it is paid, it frequently comes in the policeman's off hours. Trials call for putting in extra time by the police, not only in court but in the preparation of testimony as well. If there was police misconduct in the gathering of evidence, a trial risks its exposure.

Judges, too, place enormous pressure on prosecutors to process the criminal docket expeditiously. In every State, there is a chronic shortage of trial judges. Dockets, both civil and criminal, get longer every year as society becomes more complex and more sophisticated, and as the number of automobile accidents continues to mount. Criminal actions take precedence over civil actions. In every civil action, however, there is a hungry lawyer with channels for placing heavy pressure on trial courts through professional associations and personal contact. Moreover courts are always under heavy political and public pressure simply to reduce costs. Perhaps the single most frequent reason given for imposing a relatively light sentence on a guilty plea is that the accused should be rewarded for saving the State the expenses of a trial. Pressures to save money, and to expedite the criminal docket so that lawyers can get their much more lucrative civil cases tried, combine. The higher judiciary (which in most states are responsible for judicial administration) constantly place enormous pressure on lower courts to speed up the docket.

This pressure can be extremely heavy on occasion. The lawyer author remembers a young and relatively inexperienced Public Defender who took his position seriously. Instead of pleading practically everybody guilty (as his predecessor had done), he began to try a relatively high proportion of his cases. The docket in the local trial court immediately slowed up. Out of three judges assigned to that particular bench, one began to spend all his time on criminal trials instead of a third of that time. Since there are a variety of matters—not only criminal cases, but injunctions, receivership matters, cases with elderly defendants, etc.—which have priority, every bit of the delay tended to operate to the detriment of the ordinary civil docket, especially the jury docket. After some six months, this young Public Defender received a peremptory order to come to the state capitol to see the Chief Justice. The Chief Justice read him the riot act in terms of the need to avoid "frivolous" trials and the like, warning him of the necessity of "cooperating" with the prosecution and the judges. The Chief Justice was successful; the Public Defender resigned in disgust.

The trial judge feels very sharply the pressure of the higher judiciary to expedite the docket. This pressure comes in the form of constant judicial pressure to settle civil lawsuits without trial. In criminal cases, there is constant pressure on both the prosecutors and the defense counsel to negotiate guilty pleas. So strong is this interest of the trial judge to expedite the cases that not infrequently either the defense counsel or the prosecutor will find a way to include the judge directly in the plea-bargaining session, knowing that almost invariably the judge will put pressure on whichever party seems most willing to go to trial.

Finally, there are political incentives working on the prosecutor to obtain guilty pleas. A conviction is a conviction. In the election wars, the only measure of a prosecutor's efficiency that the public seems to understand is the gross number of convictions he has obtained. Whether the convictions are for very minor offenses or for major felonies, whether they are obtained by way of guilty pleas or trials, whether they are of the highest or lowest possible charge—no matter; the essential figure is the gross number of convictions. The more trials there are, the lower will be the number of convictions.

There are, therefore, heavy institutional and bureaucratic pressures on the prosecutor to obtain guilty pleas and avert a trial. How widespread bargaining with defendants for guilty pleas has become is indicated in a *University of Pennsylvania Law Review* survey which disclosed that eighty-six percent of the prosecutors responding to the questionnaire had answered "yes" to the question: "Is it the practice of your office to make arrangements with criminal defendants (or their counsel) when appropriate, in order to obtain a plea of guilty?"[20] The same survey revealed that these guilty pleas were obtained through bargaining with the accused. Three types of bargains most often used were promise of sentence-reduction made by the prosecutor, acceptance of pleas to lesser offenses which were included in the charge, and dismissal of some counts or of other indictments. The most prevalent practice was the use of less serious charges by the prosecutors.

Donald Newman investigated the use of bargaining to obtain guilty pleas in one medium-size county in the midwest. His investigation disclosed that of the felons convicted by one particular court ninety-three percent were disposed of by guilty pleas. Newman's findings from this one court in a midwestern community are generally confirmed by Blumberg's study of the use of guilty pleas in a large metropolitan court. Blumberg concludes:

The overwhelming majority of convictions in criminal cases (usually over 90%) are not the product of a combative trial-by-jury process at all, but instead merely involve the sentencing of the individual after a negotiated, bargained-for plea of guilty has been entered.[21]

For the most part, then, the day-to-day activities of a prosecuting attorney in processing criminal cases is to use his office to obtain guilty pleas. The evidence indicates that in a sizeable proportion of the cases processed plea-bargaining is completed between the prosecutor and the defendant without a lawyer or public defender intervening on the part of the defendant. Newman found, for example, that fifty percent of the defendants who pleaded guilty did so without the advice of or consultation with counsel.[22]

Judges, too, recognize that without a high proportion of guilty pleas, the whole court administration of criminal law would break down. Newman quotes a judge:[23] "The truth is, that a criminal court can operate only by inducing the great mass of actually guilty defendants to plead guilty, paying in leniency the price for the pleas."[24] In fact, however, as we have seen, the excessive case loads of the courts are themselves a function of decisions within the legal system.

If there is so much pressure to expedite the docket, why do law-enforcement agencies expend so much of their resources in the repeated arrest of drunkards, only to release them after a short confinement in jail and return them to their old habits?[25] There is, it would seem no particular public pressure on the police or the courts to persist in this mockery of the legal system. The explanation for its continuance seems to be in the bureaucratic structure of the legal system. The arrest of "drunken," "disorderly," and "suspicious" persons provides a source of continuing evidence for the necessity to increase the size of the law-enforcement agencies. It also serves as a constant reminder to "the public" indirectly and the resource allocators directly of the "crime problem" and of the law-enforcement agencies' efforts to "do something" about it. The fact that, by their own admission, what they are doing is not really solving the problem—it is in all likelihood aggravating it—seems to be of little consequence. In the absence of any other solution—and no acceptable alternative has been found—the resource allocators must choose between supporting the present policies, with all their shortcomings, or doing nothing. Doing nothing may well be politically disastrous. The decision to "take the line of least resistance" is inevitable. The politicians support the law-enforcement agencies' requests for bigger and presumably better bureaucracies to cope with the problem, by arresting more drunks.

19.3 THE CONSEQUENCES OF THE GUILTY PLEA SYSTEM

As a result of these pressures on the prosecutors and the courts, the negotiated plea becomes, not the exception, but the rule. Negotiations between prosecutors and defense counsel become institutionalized. In Detroit, for example, there is one assistant prosecutor whose only job is to screen cases just prior to arraignment with the express purpose of singling out those cases in which guilty pleas are to be obtained for reduced charges.[26] In a typical trial court in Connecticut, the prosecutor has regular office hours in which to confer with defense counsel for plea-bargaining.

All the legal roles involved change radically as plea-negotiation becomes institutionalized. The police, knowing that a negotiation will take place and in order to enhance the prosecution's bargaining position, will tack on numerous charges where one charge might have sufficed as the cause of an arrest. For example, a man arrested for disorderly conduct will be charged with public intoxication, disorderly conduct, resisting arrest, and assaulting a police officer. While there may be some evidence that the additional charges can be sustained, the primary purpose of adding them to the information is to increase the pressure on the defendant to plead guilty to a "lesser" charge—namely, one of the alleged crimes, rather than standing trial for all four.

The prosecutor's discretion is no longer used primarily for independent determination of the appropriate charges. Instead, aware that a bargaining session with a defense counsel is ahead, prosecutors invariably bring the highest charge that the facts will permit. In Detroit, an assistant prosecutor whose job is to file the original charges explained to Newman:

> The other day the bargaining prosecutor came in and told us: "For God's sake, give me something to work with over there. Don't reduce these cases over here; let me do it over there or many of these guys will be tried on a misdemeanor." What he was referring to is, if we had graded a case at the lowest charge in the class of offenses in which it logically belonged, a defense attorney could conceivably get his man to plead to even a lower crime, a misdemeanor, for example. We will limit to the highest possible charge because we expect a reduction in court for a plea.[27]

It is, of course, the pervasive vagueness of the substantive criminal law that makes such flexibility possible. As we saw, that vagueness is an important source of prosecutorial discretion. This discretion is supposed to be used, on the due-process model, to humanize the application of the rules so as to achieve "substantial justice." In fact, however, the charges as originally brought are not shaped by these considerations, but by the expectation of bargaining before trial.

The judge's role becomes warped as well. Despite the strictures of the due-process rules, the judges are completely aware that the pleas which are solemnly asserted by defendants to be free and voluntary, made without coercion or promise of benefit, are almost invariably the result of a bargain struck in the hallways. In fact, sometimes one sees a judge solemnly approving a defendant's statement that his plea was not induced by threat or promise, when the plea bargain was actually struck in the judge's chambers!

That plea bargaining warps the judicial process from its ostensible functions is evident in those cases in which the judges approve a change in plea to a charge which the accused could not possibly have committed. For example, one of the authors of this book represented a defendant on a speeding charge in Connecticut many years ago. A conviction of speeding then resulted in an automatic loss of license for thirty days, which the defendant was loath to incur. There was considerable doubt that the prosecution could prove the speeding charge. The prosecutor offered to reduce the charge to the very minor offense of crossing a white line, usually subject to a $5 fine. The charge was appropriately reduced, and the plea solemnly recorded, although on the street in question there was no white line.

Appellate courts have condoned the practices of plea-bargaining even to the point of refusing to overturn decisions where there was no logical connection between the defendant's acts, and the crime to which he pleaded guilty. A defendant in a New York court who had been charged with manslaughter was permitted to plead guilty to "attempted manslaughter in the second degree."[28] (An attempt at a crime is usually subject to more lenient punishment than the crime itself.) The New York penal code defines manslaughter as a homicide committed "without a design to effect death"; i.e., it is an accident. In his appeal the defendant insisted that one could not be guilty of "attempted manslaughter." One could not "attempt" an accident. The appellate court was well aware that the reduction in charge from "manslaughter" to "attempted manslaughter" which had been made in a lower court was a result of bargaining for a guilty plea between the defendant and the prosecutor. The court upheld the plea, despite the patently illogical nature of the reduced charge:

The question on this appeal is whether this definition which includes an "intent to commit a crime" renders the plea taken by the defendant inoperative, illogical or repugnant and, therefore, invalid. We hold that it does not when a defendant knowingly accepts a plea to attempted manslaughter as was done in this case in satisfaction of an indictment charging a crime carrying a heavier penalty. In such a case, there is no violation of defendant's right to due process. The defendant declined to risk his chances with a jury. He induced the proceeding of which he now complains. He made no objection or complaint when asked in the presence of his counsel whether he had any legal cause to show why judgment should not be pronounced against him, and judgment was thereafter pronounced. As a result, the range of sentence which the court could impose was cut in half—a substantial benefit to the defendant ... While there may be question whether a plea to attempted manslaughter is technically and logically consistent, such a plea should be sustained on the ground that it was sought by the defendant and freely taken as part of a bargain which was struck for the defendant's benefit.[29]

Of all the roles involved in the criminal process, it is defense counsel's which is most deeply affected by the plea-bargaining system. The guilty plea represents the final submission of the accused to the crime-control model. In the very process of striking it, the defense counsel is ensnared in that model. He is transformed from an adversary upholding the values of due process to a cooperator in crime control. This transformation can be seen by examining the roles of the public defenders and the "courthouse regulars" who handle the bulk of criminal matters.

A few states have established public defender's offices. Ordinarily, a public defender is to assist only indigent defendants. The theory on which the role is built is that due process requires an adversary system, the operations of which become a sham when a defendant is without the benefit of counsel. The formal role of the public defender thus places him in perpetual and uncompromising opposition to the public prosecutor.

In fact, it does not work that way, however. Gresham Sykes has shown that even in a maximum-security penitentiary, in which guards and inmates are nominally in completely antagonistic positions, in fact the "society of captives" functions by way of successive bargains struck between guards and prisoners.[30] The bargaining process itself demands that the guards adopt, to a degree, the values of the convicts. In the same way, the bargaining process that is the daily business of the public defender and prosecutor ensnares the defender in the prosecutorial and police culture, the culture upholding the crime-control model of legal system. David Sudnow writes from his study of a public defender's office in California:

In the course of routinely encountering persons charged with "petty theft," "burglary," "assault with a deadly weapon," "rape," "possession of marijuana," etc., the Public Defender gains knowledge of the typical manner in which offenses of given classes are committed, the social characteristics of the persons who regularly commit them, the features of the settings in which they occur, the types of victims often involved, and the like. He learns to speak knowledgeably of "burglars," "petty thieves," "drunks," "rapists," "narcos," etc., and to attribute to them personal biographies, modes of usual criminal activity, criminal histories, psychological characteristics, and social backgrounds.[31]

As the public defender learns the faces of crime, the personal characteristics and typical behavior patterns of criminals, he comes to adopt the perspective of the prosecutor's office. He adopts this perspective in part because the public defender is dependent on the prosecutor for defining the situation for him. More significantly, the public defender's office must in fact accept the view of the defendant adopted by the prosecutor's office if it is to operate with maximum efficiency as an organization. There will be essentially no rewards (save perhaps the vague and intangible one of serving the clients) for the public defender who too vigorously opposes the view of the prosecuting attorney. Indeed, such a stance would so effectively interrupt the "normal processes" of the organizations concerned to such a degree, that it would simply not be tolerated, as the young public-defender friend of Seidman discovered. On the other hand, a public defender who cooperates with the prosecuting attorney's office in securing guilty pleas from defendants will find that everything, including his superior's assessment of the quality of his work, runs in his favor.

Blumberg, on the basis of an investigation of criminal lawyers practicing in criminal courts, argues that a similar process corrupts criminal lawyers generally:

The institutional setting of the court defines a role for the defense counsel in a criminal case radically different from the one traditionally depicted. Sociologists and others have focused their attention on the deprivations and social disabilities of such variables as race, ethnicity, and social class as being the source of an accused person's defeat in a criminal court. Largely overlooked is the variable of the court organization itself, which possesses a thrust, purpose and direction of its own. It is grounded in pragmatic values, bureaucratic priorities, and administrative instruments. These exalt maximum production and the particularistic career designs of organizational incumbents, whose occupational and career commitments tend to generate a set of priorities. These priorities exert a higher claim than the stated ideological goals of "due process of law," and are often inconsistent with them.[32]

The defense attorney, even when he is a private attorney with no formal organizational ties to the court (such as those of the public defender or court appointed lawyer, for example) is nonetheless dependent on the organization of the court and the prosecutor's office if he is to be in any way effective. Frequently the defense attorney is maximally rewarded when his case is quickly disposed of. If there is only a limited source of pay for the defense, then the attorney will not receive adequate compensation for his efforts unless he manages to obtain a plea of guilty from his client and a "deal" with the prosecutor. Indeed, the pressure to obtain a plea of guilty from the defendant or to arrange a deal rather than go to trial is omnipresent, even when the defendant has moderate financial resources. The expense of an extended trial is sufficiently great so that only the most affluent defendants can really adequately compensate a lawyer who tries his case rather than obtaining from him a plea of guilty.

In addition to this very lowly economic factor is the fact that most private attorneys who handle criminal cases become court "regulars." They appear repeatedly before the same judges, and work with the same prosecuting attorneys and the same court staff on a large number of cases. As a consequence, the attorney must operate in each case in ways that increase the likelihood of co-operation from the court and the prosecuting personnel on future cases. The court can confer many favors: low bail, easy sentences, generous continuances to permit the client to find the lawyer's fee. Judges are well aware of the importance of these favors to the private attorneys. Not infrequently, after striking a plea bargain in the judge's presence and with his approval, a judge will say, in effect, "Well, let's go out and put on the show. We must allow the defense counsel to show his client that he is earning his fee." A lawyer who can acquire the reputation that he has "the hex" on a particular judge will attract more clients than one against whom it is believed the judge constantly exercises his discretion adversely.

Prosecutors, too, can give favors to defense counsel. A reputation of having close and favorable relationships with a prosecutor more than any other single factor can built the practice, and hence the income and prestige, of a criminal lawyer. To reach such a position, the lawyer cannot cause difficulties for the prosecutor. Most important of all, he must be "reasonable" in his plea-bargaining—that is to say, he must keep his demands within the accepted range within which prosecutors exercise their discretion.

Because of the prospective continuing relationship between the prosecutor and the "courthouse regular," the personal interests of the attorney intrude into the plea-bargaining process. A continuing relationship requires good-natured compromise. What the attorney has to compromise, however, is not his personal interests but those of his client. Frequently in a plea-bargaining session in which the same defense counsel represents several clients in different and unrelated cases, at some point one or the other party will try to bargain one case against another: "You give me that one, and I'll give you this other one." The process of bargaining itself corrupts the defense counsel and lures him into the system.

The criminal defense of a client is especially amenable to this type of corruptive influence largely because once the sentence has been imposed, there are rarely any objective criteria by which the defense attorney's performance can be judged. If a man accused of grand larceny is sentenced to only three years in prison, the sentence may represent something of a victory for the defense. Indeed, if the defense attorney can convince the defendant and his relatives that things would have been much worse if they did not enter into a bargain with the prosecutor, then such a turn of events will be viewed as a successful defense. The issue of guilt or innocence takes second place to the fact that it is almost always possible for the defense attorney, trading on his claimed professional expertise, to convince the defendant that things could have been much worse. Since the maximum punishment is rarely imposed, in fact things could generally have been worse. The plea-bargain is well adapted to clothing in an appearance of client-protection a transaction that in fact protects the interests of the defense counsel, and through him the organizational interests of the prosecutor and trial court.

The consequences of the plea-negotiation system of criminal justice is in many, probably most, cases to warp the due-process model of legal system into its very opposite. Any system that depends primarily on pleas of guilty for so high a proportion of the ultimate convictions is hardly an adversary system. Equally important, however, is the effect that the guilty-plea procedures have on the preceding activities in the criminal process.

As we have already seen, the principal sanction that has been devised to control police activities is the exclusionary rule. This rule, however, can control police illegality in collecting evidence only if the police fear that the evidence so collected will not be admissible in a later trial. On the other hand, if, as is the case, ninety percent of all criminal charges end in pleas of guilty, then the police need not abstain from illegal methods for fear of a trial. The guilty plea effectively validates all that has gone before.

Indeed, the possibility of the plea-bargaining actually creates an incentive for the police to act illegally. Faced with an illegally extracted confession or evidence obtained in an illegal search, and with the prosecutor bringing the highest degree of charges which the evidence (including the illegal evidence) might sustain, it is a bold and self-confident defendant or defense counsel who will hazard a maximum penalty against the chances of having a judge or jury find that the evidence was in fact illegally obtained. Instead, when a prosecutor asserts that he will insist on trying the accused for the highest possible degree of the crime and that he will seek to validate the evidence obtained, most accused persons will accept a reduced charge in exchange for a plea of guilty. Under such circumstances, the police are acting rationally when they act illegally in obtaining evidence.

In sum, the plea-bargaining system inevitably leads the legal system down the road of crime control and makes a mockery of due process. The intriguing fact, however, is that this result is the consequence of the inherent contradictions in the due-process model itself.

The aim of the due process model is that the criminal process be governed by rules rather than by the discretion of the police, the prosecutors, or the judges. The realization of this aim demands sharply defined substantive norms, and the dogma of a full enforcement of the laws. It demands that the police be inhibited from acting merely on their own suspicion.

The government of men by rules, and not by discretion, however, is inevitably an impossible dream. Rules are necessarily vague; discretion in fact must exist at all legal stages—those of creation, application, and adjudication of rules. Moreover, if indeed it were possible to have a world of crystal-clear norms, it would be an intolerable world. Every legal system must have some flexibility to provide for the manifold differences between the persons who are subject to the rules.

The rules even in an ideal due-process system, therefore, must be flexible somewhere; and that is where the prosecutor's discretion comes in. Even in the best of all possible worlds where due process is observed, there is a place for lawyers to engage in plea-bargaining.

This is not the best of all possible worlds, and there are a variety of forces ready to sanction a lawyer at the expense of his client if he does not plead guilty. The pressures on judges and prosecutors to dispose of criminal matters expeditiously, the vagueness of the criminal law generally and hence its unpredictability, the general unpredictability of trial results, and the practice of increasing the seriousness of charges and sentence if a case came to trial—all these combine to make it rational for the lawyer who wants to play the adversary role and represent the best interests of his client to engage in plea-bargaining. By so doing, however, he puts himself into a position where all the pressures we discussed earlier tend to convert his aims into crime control.

In a way, the juvenile-court system is the limiting case of the crime-control model. It had (until *Gault*) formally abandoned due process in the belief that a system benevolently motivated "to do what's good for Johnny" would serve an offender's interests better than the adversary system and due process. Decisions to prosecute were made, not by lawyers presumably interested in convictions, but by social workers interested in the offender's well-being. What patterns can be discerned in their processing decisions?

19.4 THE PROSECUTION OF JUVENILES

It is rare for prosecutions of juveniles to be determined by the prosecuting attorney's office. Since the early part of the twentieth century the juvenile-court movement has come into full flower. Juveniles are handled in specialized courts by "professionally trained" personnel (frequently social workers), whose professed aim is "to help the child." Not infrequently the juvenile court in fact operates very much like an adult court, save that the juvenile is deprived of his civil liberties. From the perspective of the prosecution, however, the important feature of juvenile justice is that the decision to prosecute is made by the police and court personnel rather than the prosecuting attorney.

In one of the few systematic studies of the selection of juveniles for court appearance, Nathan Goldman investigated the selection process in four Pennsylvania communities.[33] Goldman concentrated on juvenile offenders. He discovered that of all the persons arrested, sixty-four percent were released without charge and thirty-six percent were referred to the court by the police. There were some significant differences in the types of offenses for which the offenders were typically released and those for which the offenders were generally referred to the court. Of juveniles arrested for robbery, larceny, riding in a stolen car, committing sex offenses, and being "incorrigible," the rate of referral to the court exceeded eighty percent. By contrast, fewer than fifteen percent of the arrests made for drunkenness, violating a borough ordinance, disorderly conduct, violating a motor vehicle code, mischief, and property damage culminated in referral to the juvenile court.

On first glance these differences in percentage appear to follow quite reasonably from the "common-sense" interpretation of the relative seriousness of the offenses. Closer scrutiny, however, calls this common-sense interpretation into question. Chambliss' investigation into the activities of two delinquent gangs (a lower-class and a middle-class gang) disclosed different types of behavior.[34] Typically the middle-class gang engaged in drinking, truancy (albeit with some semblance of legitimate excuse), gambling, and the destruction of property (vandalism). The lower-class gang typically engaged in sexual offenses (mostly heterosexual intercourse), fighting (incorrigibility), and theft. As in the case of Goldman's data, the response of the police to these different patterns of delinquency was quite different. The police were generally unaware of the middle-class gang's delinquency but quite aware of the delinquency of the lower-class gang. Even when aware of the delinquency of both gangs, the police responded with much more severity against the activities of the lower-class gang.

From Chambliss' description of the activities of these two gangs it is quite clear that the common-sense interpretation of the differential response of the authorities as a reflection of the difference in the seriousness of the two types of offenses is erroneous. Indeed, on balance, the activities of the middle-class gang were in some ways more serious than those of the lower-class gang in terms of either economic costs or threat to personal safety.

The differential response to different types of delinquency on the part of the police in fact is best understood as reflecting essentially the same kind of organizational decision-making that characterizes so many other decisions in the legal system. The police refer to court those offenders whose referral to court will bring rewards to the police organization. Concomitantly, the police will refrain from referring to court those persons whose referral is likely to bring forth the wrath of citizens capable of making "trouble" for the organization. It is essentially in this way that the police come to see those offenses of lower-class minority-group juveniles as more serious than the offenses of middle-class juveniles.

The above interpretation is quite consistent with other findings from the Goldman study. Blacks generally have low social status, and by virtue of the additional stigma of being black, are doubtless one of the "best" (i.e., organizationally safest) groups of persons to treat with severe punishment. It follows, therefore, that if the police are making the decision as to whom to send to court primarily on organizational grounds, then the blacks who are arrested should have a higher incidence of court referral than the whites. This is precisely what Goldman found. In his sample, thirty-four percent of the whites arrested were sent to court as contrasted with sixty-five percent of the blacks.

19.5 CONCLUSION

The decision to prosecute and whom to prosecute for alleged offenses, whether made by the prosecuting attorney's office or, in the case of juveniles, by the police, is one which takes its distinctive character from the bureaucratic features of this phase of law-enforcement. The prosecutor will engage in bargaining with defendants whenever possible in order to make certain that he is able to achieve a high proportion of convictions without jeopardizing the efficient operations of the office by prosecuting problematic cases (i.e., politically powerful persons). When the decision to prosecute rests in the hands of the police, their decisions will reflect essentially the same perspective.

As a consequence, given the social organization of most complex societies, it is the politically powerless who are most likely to be prosecuted for alleged crimes. How favorable a "bargain" one can strike with the prosecutor in the pretrial confrontations is a direct function of how politically and economically powerful the defendant is. In terms of day-to-day prosecutorial activities, what this comes down to is that the lower-class, indigent, and minority-group member is most likely to be prosecuted for his offenses, while the more well-to-do members of the society retain considerable immunity. The crime-control model of the legal system in fact described how the prosecutors exercise their discretion. The character of law-enforcement is thus shaped more by the organizational features of the legal system than by the rules and procedures which comprise the "written" though not the "real" law.

NOTES

1. Wayne R. LaFave, *Arrest: The Decision to Take a Suspect into Custody*, Little, Brown, Boston, 1965, p. 53. Reprinted by permission.

2. Pendleton Howard, *Criminal Justice in England: A Study in Law Administration*, Macmillan, New York, 1931, p. 3.

3. *Ibid.*, p. 5.

4. 184 Md. 86, 40 A 2d 319 (1944).

5. LaFave, *op. cit.*, p. 8.

6. *State ex rel McKittrick v. Graves*, 346 Mo. 990, 144 S.W. 2d 91 (1940); see also *State v. Winnem*, 12 N.J. 152, 96 A 2d 63 (1953); *Wilbur v. Howard*, 70 F. Supp. 930 (E.D. Ky 1947).

7. See Note, "Prosecutor's discretion," *U. Pa. Law Rev.*, **103**, 1955, p. 1057.

8. *Ibid.*, p. 1071.

9. Douglas B. Wright, "Duties of a prosecutor," *Conn. Bar J.*, **33**, 1959, p. 293. Reprinted by permission.

10. Ferdinand Lundberg, *The Rich and the Super-Rich: A Study in the Power of Money Today*, Lyle Stuart, New York, 1968, p. 135. Reprinted by permission.

11. Cleveland Amory, *Who Killed Society?*, Harper, New York, 1960, pp. 544–551.

12. Lundberg, *op. cit.*, p. 376. Reprinted by permission.

13. *People v. Picciotti*, 4 N.Y. 2d 340, 151 N.E. 2d 191 (1958).

14. Donald J. Newman, *Conviction: The Determination of Guilt or Innocence Without Trial*, Little, Brown, Boston, 1966, p. 83. Reprinted by permission.

15. 28 U.S.C. §2255.

16. Jerome H. Skolnick, *Justice Without Trial*, Wiley, New York, 1966.

17. Newman, *op. cit.*, p. 96.

18. *Cortez v. United States*, 337 F. 2d 699, 701 C.A. 9 (1964).

19. Harris B. Steinberg and Monrad G. Paulsen, "A conversation with defense counsel on problems of a criminal defense," *The Practical Lawyer*, 7, No. 5, 1961, pp. 25–43. Reproduced with the permission of *The Practical Lawyer*, Philadelphia.

20. Dominick R. Vetri, "Guilty plea bargaining: compromise by prosecutors to secure guilty pleas," *U. Pa. Law Rev.*, **112**, 1964, pp. 896–908.

21. Abraham S. Blumberg, "The practice of law as a confidence game: organizational co-optation of a profession," *Law and Society Rev.*, Vol. 1, No. 2, 1967, p. 18. Reprinted by permission.

22. Donald J. Newman, "Pleading guilty for considerations: a study of bargain justice," *J. Criminal Law, Criminology, and Police Science*, **46**, 1956, p. 780 at 782.

23. Justice Henry T. Lummus.

24. Newman, *Conviction*, p. 76.

25. LaFave, *op. cit.*, pp. 439–440.

26. Newman, *Conviction*, p. 80.

27. *Ibid.*, p. 81. Reprinted by permission.

28. Cited in Donald R. Cressey, "Negotiated justice," *Criminologica*, February 1968.

29. *Ibid.*

30. Gresham M'Cready Sykes, *The Society of Captives: A Study of a Maximum Security Prison*, Princeton University Press, Princeton, N.J., 1958, pp. 56–57.

31. David D. Sudnow, "Normal crimes: sociological features of the penal code in a public defender's office," Social Problems, **12**, 1965, pp. 255–276. Reprinted by permission of The Society for the Study of Social Problems.

32. Blumberg, *op. cit.*, p. 19. Reprinted by permission.

33. Nathan Goldman, *The Differential Selection of Juveniles for Court Appearance*, National Research and Information Center, National Council on Crime and Delinquency, 1963.

34. William J. Chambliss, *Two Gangs*, unpublished manuscript.

20

The trial

The trial judge performs a variety of functions, of which we shall discuss the trial and the sentencing processes only. His most spectacular duty is to conduct the trial itself. It is in a trial that all the excitement and tension that epitomize the popular conception of the criminal process are found: the crusading district attorney brings to public justice the wicked and the corrupt, the powerful and the evil alike; the bold defense attorney, aided by the resourceful (if not always completely legal) private eye, confounds villainy, tears off the veil of suspicious circumstances, and justice invariably emerges triumphant.

In fact, the trial of an issue of fact to a jury is statistically a tiny wart on the end of the criminal process. At least ninety percent of all accused persons plead guilty. Of the remainder, only a small fraction elect a jury trial.

It is intriguing that despite the tiny number of persons who actually are tried by a jury, every person who is convicted must in one way or another affirmatively waive his right to a jury trial; and, having waived his right to a jury trial, he must, as we have already seen, equally formally waive his right to any trial at all. Viewed in gross, therefore, trials generally and the jury trial in particular must play a significant role beyond the actual determination of guilt and innocence. The formal waiver, so carefully required in every case—the failure to waive is the decided exception—must have a function in the entire process. Before we can understand the function of the trial, however, we must examine in some detail the conduct of the trial itself.

We have continually emphasized that the idealized concept of the criminal process, as embodied in most of the formal norms which structure it, is that of the due-process model, whose leading characteristics are the presumption of innocence and the adversary system. We have found, however, that in some areas of the criminal process this idealized version has in practice, more frequently than not been converted into its very opposite by reason of the ambiguity in the applicable norms, the lack of sanctioning devices, and the bureaucratic pressures largely generated by the bureaucracy's conception of what is best for itself. In the trial, however, which is the very paradigm of due process, the adversary system largely works according to the norms laid down for its conduct. In this case, the law in action on the whole matches the law in the books because of the unique characteristic that here the bureaucratic pressures reinforce rather than undercut the norms. The question that arises is whether due process as practiced in this one area of the criminal process realizes its ostensible goals.

We recall that every action at law can be viewed in terms of an analogy to a syllogism, in which the rule of law is the major premise, the facts of the case are the minor premise, and the verdict or judgment the conclusion. For example, suppose that a statute provides the following:

If the operator of a motor vehicle operates the vehicle on any highway in this State at a speed in excess of 60 miles per hour, he shall be guilty of speeding and fined not less than $10.00 nor more that $100.00.

This statute would then become the major premise of a syllogism, whose minor premise might be:

The accused, on the 15th day of July, 1968, on Highway 19, three miles north of the Town of Stamford, within this State did operate a motor vehicle at the speed of 72 miles per hour.

The conclusion would be that the accused is guilty of speeding, and liable to a fine of not less than $10.00 nor more than $100.00.

If the accused person disputes that the rule of law as claimed by the prosecution or adopted by the court is not a valid and subsisting rule (i.e., that it is not the rule laid down in statute or case law), he can raise an issue of law. It is such cases which provide the bulk of the work for appellate courts, as we have already discussed. A trial of an issue of fact arises when the accused person disputes the factual allegations contained in the minor premise. Assuming that the major premise is not at issue, there remain two further tests to determine the guilt or innocence of the accused: the question whether the factual allegations contained in the minor premise are (for purposes of the proceeding) true, and the question whether the inference leading to the verdict or judgment is valid.

20.1 THE FORMULATION OF THE ISSUES OF FACT

The major premise of any lawsuit specifies several classes of facts. The prosecution must prove its factual allegations which must contain a fact corresponding to each of the classes of facts specified in the major premise before the accused can be found guilty. Thus, in our example, the accused must be proved to have been: (1) the operator of a motor vehicle, (2) operating the vehicle, (3) on a highway, (4) within the State, (5) at a speed in excess of 60 miles per hour. These facts are set forth in the minor premise of the information, indictment, or complaint.

By pleading not guilty, a defendant in effect requires the prosecution to persuade the jury to hold as true each of the specific facts set forth in the minor premise. That it is the prosecution which must persuade the jury that these facts are true, rather than the defendant's having to persuade the jury that they are false, is the central procedural function of the presumption of innocence, the keystone of the accusatory system of criminal process.

20.2 THE ADVERSARY SYSTEM

Our system of criminal process developed out of the adversary system, which had developed primarily as a device by which issues of fact could be litigated. In order to show how and why this system became deeply entrenched, and its implications, we must serve up a soupçon of legal history.

As we have seen, criminal actions were, until relatively recently, primarily a matter of private prosecution. They therefore tended to resemble private civil litigations. The origin of the accusatorial system of criminal law is thus to be found in the adversary system as it operated in noncriminal cases.

The petit or trial jury probably developed from the grand jury, the jury which made the original accusation, whose origins are to be found in the Norman inquest. The Norman inquest consisted in a body of local citizens who from time to time reported to the Crown on local matters; it was the device used notably in the compilation of the *Domesday Book*. At first, the grand jury was representative of every township in the relevant administrative unit, but in time the sheriffs fell into the habit of summoning citizens at large to compose the body. This body heard complaints by private individuals and charged accused persons with offenses.

In the beginning, trials were by ordeal and by battle; but manifest injustices, especially in disputes over land, the all-important asset in feudal society, led to more rational methods of deciding cases. In criminal cases, at first the deciding body was the very same body which had brought the accusation. But during the fourteenth century the custom arose of adding other jurors to bring in fresh opinions on the matter.[1] In 1352, a statute allowed the accused to challenge any members of the indicting jury who were also sitting on the petit (or trial) jury.

The older forms of trial, by ordeal, compurgation, or battle, were all as inscrutable in their process as in their result. The newer method of trial by jury was at first equally inscrutable, for the jurors decided the cases on the basis of their own knowledge. It was a tolerable method of procedure in a closely knit rural society, where one person's business was everyone else's business. Gradually, as society and the cases brought to the jury became more complicated, the juries heard witnesses to the facts. In time, what had earlier been the principal qualification for the juror—personal knowledge of the case—became a ground for disqualification.

That the jury procedure became adversary in nature, in criminal as in civil actions, was a natural development out of the older modes of trial. Before the fourteenth century, criminals were apprehended primarily by devices rooted in the corporate nature of English rural life. The arrest of persons not yet indicted was a responsibility of the community. In the thirteenth century, for example, a vill—the smallest administrative unit—might be liable for failure to arrest those who had committed homicide; or, if the vill could not pay, the hundred was liable.[2] As these older institutions decayed, between the fourteenth and early sixteenth centuries the law came to rely on the individual action of the citizen —a natural outgrowth of the earlier modes of trial, which all depended ultimately on individual action for which the community had once been responsible. Sir William Holdsworth says that "Just as in the older law, all these rules [of pleading and trial] must be put in motion and strictly obeyed by the parties at their own risk, so now the parties must put in motion the machinery of process, and define with the same verbal accuracy as before, and with the same formal words, the crime with which the accused was charged."[3] Just as in the older forms of trial, where the judge merely was an umpire of ordeal, compurgation, or trial by battle, so now he became merely the umpire who ensured that the battle before the jury was played by the appropriate rules.

The mere fact that a proceeding is adversary in nature does not guarantee that it will produce rational or just results. Whether it does so depends on the relative ability of the parties to prosecute their case, the relative rationality of the procedures by which the decision is made, and the relative impartiality of the triers. All of these factors are controlled by the rules under which the adversary proceeding is conducted. These rules may be relatively weighted on the side of the prosecution or the side of the defense. The rules adopted by any given society at any given time are a function of the relative strength of the social forces involved, the historical development of the institutions, and the dominant ideologies of the period.

The sixteenth century in England saw the development of the modern nation-state out of the incubator of feudalism. This development was the result of the battles of townsmen against feudatories, Protestants against Catholics, and the Crown against the barons, led by the Tudor monarchs, Henry VII, Henry VIII, and

Elizabeth, and supported by the ruling oligarchies of the towns and especially of London.

That was a time of great and constant danger for the State. There was no standing army and no police force. The maintenance of public peace depended on the life of the sovereign. Those who supported the Crown and the centralized State in the long and bloody battles against the forces of the old ways demanded that order be maintained at all costs. That public opinion would and did support the progressive weighting of the scales in favor of the prosecution was inevitable. This development reached its height in the notorious proceedings of the Star Chamber; but it was decidedly noticeable also in the common-law trials.

The list of limitations on the ability of the accused to protect himself during the period between the sixteenth and mid-eighteenth centuries makes long and— to our values—painful reading. To make sure that the jurors felt the weight of the evidence, witnesses were allowed to be called by the Crown, but not by the defense; the defendant, unsworn, had to reply as best he could from memory to the evidence against him. In *Throckmorton's Case*,[4] a trial for high treason, for example, a witness referred to some statements made by a man called Arnold. Throckmorton, seeing a friend, Fitz Williams, in the audience, called upon him to be sworn as a witness to rebut the testimony. One of the commissioners trying the case said: "Go your ways, Fitz Williams, the court hath nothing to do with you. Peradventure you would not be so ready in a good cause."[5] When this kind of tactics proved too harsh for the public sensibilities, the accused was permitted to call witnesses. Statutes were enacted in 1589 and 1607 allowing witnesses for the defense, but, illogically enough, prohibiting their being sworn.

Statutes were passed making it more difficult for accused persons to get bail.[6] In the absence of bail, an accused person remained incarcerated before trial, making it more difficult for him to prepare his case. Inquisitorial proceedings against suspects were permitted by justices of the peace, the Privy Council, or the judges.[7]

The magistrates interpreted their powers widely. They actively got up the case against the prisoner, not only by questioning him and the witnesses against him, but also by searching for evidence against him . . . These examinations were conducted secretly, and the evidence was communicated to the prosecutor and the judge, but not to the prisoner.[8]

In addition, the Council used torture to extract confessions, and in important cases simply disregarded all the procedural rules.[9]

In charges of felony and treason the defendant was at first not allowed to have counsel. Indeed, he was not even permitted a copy of the statute under which he was being tried.[10] Slowly, counsel were admitted to argue points of law for the accused. Not until the later part of the eighteenth century was defense counsel permitted to cross-examine witnesses, and it was 1836 before defense counsel was permitted to address the jury.[11]

The judges did not regard themselves as impartial arbiters between the individual and the State; their commitment to their royal masters was more frequently than not made quite clear. In *Elwes Case*,[12] for example, Coke, the presiding judge, cross-examined the accused closely, and finally produced against him a "confession" made by a man named Franklin which had been made privately and not even upon oath before Coke himself, at five o'clock in the morning, before the court sat.[13]

Nor was the conduct of the prosecutors above reproach. The great Lord Coke himself, acting as prosecutor of Raleigh, abused the latter unmercifully before the jury:

Att: Thou art the most vile and execrable traitor that ever lived.
Raleigh: You speak indiscreetly, barbarously and uncivilly.
Att: I want words sufficient to express thy viperous treasons.
Raleigh: I think you want words, indeed, for you have spoken one thing half a dozen times.
Att: Thou are an odious fellow. Thy name is hateful to all the realm of England for thy pride.
Raleigh: It will go hard to prove a measuring cast between you and me, Mr. Attorney.
Att: Well, I will now make it appear that there never lived a viler viper upon the face of the earth than thou.[14]

The judges' feeling that they were part of the governing arm is perhaps nowhere made clearer than in Raleigh's case. The accused insisted on the right to call as witness Cobham, who had confessed to treason implicating Raleigh, but who had retracted his confession. Justice Warburton said:

I marvel, Sir Walter, that you, being of such experience, and wit, should stand on this point: for so many horse stealers may escape, if they may not be condemned without witnesses.[15]

Even that hallowed palladium of English liberty, the jury, did not remain immune from tampering. After Throckmorton had defended himself so brilliantly that the jury acquitted him, they were committed to prison for their verdict. Four submitted and apologised, but eight were haled before the Star Chamber some six months and more after the trial. They were discharged only after payment of £250 in fines (three, who were not worth so much, were fined £60). The foreman forfeited £2000. "'This rigour was fatal to Sir John Throckmorton, who was found guilty (and therefore was executed) upon the same evidence on which his brother had been acquitted.'"

The unflagging support which the towns had given the Tudors withered shortly after the defeat of the Spanish Armada, and feudal reaction's last hope for power in England. Almost immediately, the townsmen began to oppose the new Tudor aristocracy, an opposition that broke into open rebellion under Cromwell. As might have been expected, the weighted scales in criminal trials did not reach a better balance during this period, but remained largely as before.

Following the Glorious Revolution in 1688, however, a relatively long period of tranquillity in British government ensued, which was the century and a half during which reigned the aristocratic constitution. Active threat of revolution disappeared. The aristocracy were firmly in control of the machinery of government, without significant challenge. The machinery of justice in the countryside centered around the Justice of the Peace, almost invariably a member of the landed gentry who acted both as local administrator and as magistrate. The initiation of criminal prosecutions, in this relatively calm epoch, fell more and more on private persons. The notion of the independence of the judiciary, first clearly identified as a significant political fact in 1688, was more easily entrenched as political stability became less closely entwined with the criminal process.

Then the Industrial Revolution brought into existence the new entrepreneurial class which ultimately was to force the aristocrats to share the reins of power. The entrepreneurial opposition to the existing order was expressed in part in a movement toward a more balanced criminal procedure, as part of the middle-class demand for rationality, order, and clarity in law.

In this opposition they were greatly helped by the intellectual revolution that was taking place all over Europe. In the criminal law, the most important consequence of this revolution was the developing notion of *nulla crimens sine lege* and *nulla poena sine lege*—no crime without a law and no punishment without a law. The concept of *nulla poena* embodied the middle-class ideals of rationality, order, and clarity, on which their entire economic enterprise rested. In short, the middle class demanded law in preference to order. They demanded law because they regarded it as a means of limiting the powers of the aristocratic government, which excluded them and used its powers indiscriminately through the courts to put down the organizations of the middle class. They demanded law as a central institution to guarantee legal-rational legitimacy.

They saw in the adversary system a device by which rational and sensible decisions in the legal order could be made, in which the prosecutor's suspicions could be challenged, and in which the State could be compelled to submit suspicions to verification. The individualistic nature of the adversary process was conducive to these ends; and the middle class found it congenial just as in the economic realm they relied on individual enterprise. "Everyman must fend for himself."

The result of middle-class pressure was a system of litigation in which formal differentiation on the basis of birth or wealth was abolished. Just as in the newly developing substantive rules of contract and commercial law, the rhetoric was that all men are equal before the law. In an old saw, the law is magnificently impartial: Both rich and poor may sleep under bridges. In the same sense, the adversary system provides a paper equality. Without affirmative aid to the poor or ignorant, however, such protections become meaningless.

The private prosecution of offenses was one of the advantages of the criminal law system as perceived by the new ruling groups in England. The costs of prosecution were at first borne by the private prosecutor entirely. By 1861, however, as a result of almost a century of piecemeal legislation, the private prosecutor obtained the right to recover, after conviction, the costs of the prosecution, which in England included not merely relatively trivial court costs, but counsel fees as well. Conversely, in case of an acquittal, the prosecutor must pay the costs incurred by the accused. Even as amended in 1861, the law still obviously favored the wealthy, for they could better take the risk of losing the prosecution than a poor one.

Private prosecution, moreover, met the wishes of the new middle class in another way. By making the enforcement of criminal law, like the enforcement of the civil law, a matter of litigation between private parties, the State as represented by the judge became a mere arbiter between private interests. The State was made to appear as providing a neutral framework within which conflict and struggle could take place according to rules, thus ensuring that private initiative would be allowed the fullest play. As James Fitzjames Stephen, L.J., said in his spirited defense of nineteenth-century English criminal procedure,

No stronger or more effectual guarantee can be provided for the due observance of the law of the land, by all persons under all circumstances, than is given by the power, conceded by the English system, of testing the legality of any conduct of which he disapproves, either on private or public grounds, by a criminal prosecution. Many such prosecutions, both in our days and in earlier times, have given legal vent to feelings in every way entitled to respect, and have decided peaceably, and in an authentic manner, many questions of great constitutional importance.[17]

These reforms in criminal procedure were not easily won. The statute of 1836 which finally gave the accused person full right to counsel, for example, was strongly opposed by twelve of the fifteen judges; Justice Park even threatened to resign if the bill were passed. (He reconsidered after the enactment.)[18] But in time the elements of what in this country we call due process became entrenched in English law.

The adversary system was thus an ideal arrangement which met the demands of the new masters of industry and commerce. They demanded and in time achieved a system of litigation that at once gave them a defense against the old aristocratic government and guaranteed their advantage over all lower classes.

In the United States, the Bill of Rights was framed while the great sea change was underway in English criminal procedure. The Founding Fathers, having just rebelled against precisely the same aristocratic government against which the new English middle class was still struggling, like their English counterparts demanded legal-rational legitimacy. They wrote into the new Constitution most of the significant reforms which were still being incubated in England: due process of law; the independence of the judiciary; the right to a jury; *habeas corpus*; the right to counsel; the right to summon witnesses in defense; the right to bail; indictment by grand jury; the privilege against self-incrimination. In short, due process ensures the institution of the adversary system. At the base of this system lies the notion of criminal trial as an accusatory proceeding, guaranteed by the presumption of innocence.

But, as we have already suggested, the legal-rational legitimization of bureaucratic government embodied in the due-process model has an appeal far beyond the narrow confines of class interest or bourgeois ideology. The adversary system and the presumption of innocence provide a device for making decisions about issues of fact which satisfy tolerably well reasonable standards of rational decision-making. Given a powerful impetus by the deeply ingrained socialization of individual justices into the central values of due process, and freed from the confining fetters of a rigid deference to precedent by the heady wine of legal realism, the Supreme Court of the United States has, perhaps not unexpectedly, made a series of decisions which tend further to equalize the scales between the accuser and the accused. Counsel must be supplied if the accused cannot afford to employ his own. Bail provisions have been liberalized. In case of an appeal, the State must supply a copy of the record to the poor appellant. The police must give the *Miranda* warnings.

Serious imbalances between the relative positions of the prosecution and the defense remain. The prosecution still has resources for investigation far beyond that available to most defendants. The criminal bar, servicing as it does mainly very poor people, does not attract the most able practitioners. And, as we saw, the "courthouse regulars" too often become auxiliaries to "the system." Most important of all, despite whatever rules are designed to protect the poor and ignorant, in the final analysis the adversary system demands that the individual defendant must invoke on his own the measures designed to protect him; they are not automatically provided.

The actual trial, however, apart from the difference between the resources available for the prosecution and the defense to prepare for trial, has for a long time been controlled by rules which make it the very epitome of due process. In order to understand due process as practiced at the trial of an issue of fact, it is necessary to look closely at the rules governing the trial, especially those rules relating to the admission and exclusion of evidence.

20.3 THE TRIAL OF AN ISSUE OF FACT

As we discussed earlier, the indictment or information charges the accused of certain specific acts at a certain time and place. By pleading not guilty, the defendant serves notice that he wants the prosecution to persuade the trier—the judge or jury, as the case may be—of the truth of those allegations about matters of fact.

Facts are never true or false; they either exist or do not exist. Our knowledge about facts can never be true or false; it can only be more or less probable. The prosecution's burden, therefore, is to persuade the jury that the truth of the propositions alleged is sufficiently probable that it should, for the purposes of the litigation, assert that they are true.

The entire process of proof in a trial is thus aimed at establishing probabilities. The rules of evidence which control the procedures of proof, if they are properly fashioned, ought to contribute to the correct determination of the probabilities.

The first, and most important rule in a trial, therefore, must be one which limits the admissible evidence to what is relevant to the material issues in question. That is, the defendant is charged with a particular crime, and the proofs must be addressed to showing whether he committed or did not commit this, and not any other, crime, and not whether he was, in general, a good or a bad man.

Two other policies tend to limit the overriding criterion of relevance: to prevent decisions based on prejudice and to reduce confusion of issues and the length of trial. There are many bits of evidence which have little probative value, but will go far to sway a jury's passions. For example, that a defendant has committed other crimes of the same sort suggests that he is *the kind of man* likely to commit such a crime, and hence that it is more probable that *he* committed *this* crime rather than an ordinary citizen. The fact that an accused had an earlier criminal conviction almost ensures his conviction before most juries, regardless of the probabilities as suggested by the rest of the testimony. To admit testimony on a man's past character or past misdeeds not directly associated with the crime charged means in practice that the accused person is being tried not for his conduct on the occasion in question, but for his general bad character.

In general, therefore, testimony which has a high rhetorical or emotive content, but relatively low probative value, is excluded, in the interest of ensuring that the decision will be based on evidence that is directly relevant, and not on emotional bias. Thus, testimony of an accused person's bad character, of his past convictions, or of specific acts of impropriety, is not ordinarily admissible.

In addition, considerations of administrative efficiency of the trial create a set of constraints of their own. There are two principal dangers in this connection: The issues may become too complex and hence divert the attention of the jury from the material facts to be proved; and the trial may become overly long.

Problems arise chiefly with respect to the credibility of witnesses. The trier of fact usually cannot be shown a motion picture of the incident. Rather, he is almost always in the position of trying to discover whether an incident which is now history in fact took place as alleged in the charge. The information relevant to that inquiry can be acquired only through the testimony of witnesses who claim to have knowledge about the facts to be proved, or through pieces of "real evidence"—objects (documents such as letters, deeds, etc., are the most important kind) which can be brought physically into the courtroom for the examination of the trier.

Every time a witness testifies, however, the probability that what he reports to the tribunal is true depends on his credibility, which is a function of five factors: his opportunity to observe the event he is reporting; his capacity to observe; his capacity to remember; his capacity to report it to the tribunal; and his veracity. If any of these factors is called into question, his whole testimony becomes suspect, and hence the probability of the propositions about matters of fact which he reports is reduced.

Since the credibility of the witness is a central factor in determining the probability which the jury will attach to his testimony, it is always at issue. The veracity component of credibility is largely a matter of character. There is, therefore, a great temptation for the opponent to introduce every adverse incident in the witness' past in order to blacken his character in the eyes of the jury, and thus to reduce the probability to be attached to his testimony.

The danger of converting the trial of the accused into a trial of the character of the witnesses, therefore, lurks behind every trial. A host of rules have been devised to reduce this possibility (and with it, the concomitant danger of prolonging the trial unduly). The most important of these rules is embodied in the right to cross-examine witnesses.

Cross-examination—the questioning of a witness by the opponent—has been described as "the greatest legal engine ever invented for the discovery of truth . . . If we omit political considerations of broader range, then cross-examination, not trial by jury, is the great and permanent contribution of the Anglo-American system of law to improved methods of trial procedure."[19] In the Anglo-American system, cross-examination is the principle means of testing credibility. The idea is that by questioning the witness and shrewdly confronting him with other, conflicting evidence, the opposing counsel could force the witness to demonstrate his credibility in court in a way that cannot otherwise be accomplished.

This critical dependence on cross-examination in court procedure has many consequences. Of these, perhaps the limitation on the introduction of hearsay testimony is the most important. Hearsay testimony is testimony in which a witness in court (who is subject to cross-examination and thus to credibility test) reports what some person outside the courtroom (the extrajudicial declarant) told him about a particular matter, in order to persuade the jury of the fact as reported by the extrajudicial declarant. The value of such a report made to the jury thus is a function of the credibility of two persons: the witness and the extrajudicial declarant. Since extrajudicial declarants are not available for cross-examination, hearsay testimony is ordinarily inadmissible. A large number of exceptions exist, mainly in cases in which it is thought that the extrajudicial declarant would be unlikely to make the report in question unless it were true, such as a statement which is against his own economic interest. In such a case, circumstantial guarantees of the credibility of the extrajudicial declarant are deemed surrogate for cross-examination.

Cross-examination has been crowned with a halo in the ideology of Anglo-

American legal culture. Empirical data suggest that it may be a misplaced canonization. Opposing counsel use it as a device to discredit testimony which they know is accurate. Witnesses are confused by cross-examination; and some data suggest that, with some witnesses, the attack on their credibility makes them more stubborn and more sure of what at first was only tentatively stated. In one experimentally staged kidnapping scene, for example, cross-examination on the lapse of time resulted in errors in testimony being doubled or trebled.[20]

Cross-examination has also been regarded as the primary means of avoiding confusion of issues and undue prolongation of trials. With few exceptions, evidence of specific acts by a witness tending to discredit him is admissible only when it can be questioned in cross-examination. Further evidence concerning his credibility introduced solely to contradict the response elicited in cross-examination is ordinarily not permitted. Thus cross-examination has become practically the only way in which a witness' credibility can be attacked.

In a criminal trial, the prosecution, obedient to the command of the presumption of innocence, must first display its evidence, usually through witnesses. Each witness is subject to cross-examination as soon as he has completed his direct testimony. After the prosecution has furnished all its evidence, ordinarily the defense counsel will move for a judgment of dismissal, i.e. a judgment of not guilty on the ground that the prosecution has failed to prove each of the material elements as charged, even assuming the truth of the prosecution testimony. When this motion is denied, the defense will then go forward with its own testimony, each of its witnesses in turn being subject to cross-examination by the prosecution.

In a civil case, at the close of the evidence, either side may move for a directed verdict. That motion is usually granted by the judge when "reasonable men" could not possibly differ about the result—i.e., when all the evidence points conclusively in one direction. In criminal trials, the tradition that juries may act perversely prevents the judge from granting a motion for a directed verdict of conviction, but he may grant a directed verdict of acquittal, meaning that "reasonable men" could not possibly differ in their judgment that the accused has not been proved guilty beyond a reasonable doubt. By contrast, a jury in a civil case, therefore, considers the case only when reasonable men could differ as to the conclusion to be drawn from the evidence presented.

20.4 THE POSITION OF THE JUDGE AND JURY

To what extent are the rules governing the trial of an issue of fact conducive to rational decision-making? Before we can consider this question, and to explicate how the trial processes are the product of social forces, it is necessary to consider the positions of the judge and the jury in an adversary system.

Rational decision-making requires that the decision-maker, before coming to a determination, carefully examine the alternative possible positions. By permitting each side to bring forward whatever testimony is favorable to it, and exposing the testimony of the other side openly to criticism, the trial makes possible this careful consideration of alternatives. The position has been nicely summed up elsewhere:

[A]ny arbiter who attempts to decide a dispute without the aid of partisan advocacy . . . must undertake not only the role of judge, but that of representative for both of the litigants. Each of these roles must be played to the full without being muted by qualifications derived from the others. When he is developing for each side the most effective statement of its case, the arbiter must put aside his neutrality and permit himself to be moved by sympathetic identification sufficiently intense to draw from his mind all that it is capable of giving—in analysis, patience and creative power. When he resumes his neutral position, he must be able to view with distrust the fruits of this identification and be ready to reject the products of his own best mental efforts. The difficulties of this undertaking are obvious. If it is true that man in his time must play many parts, it is scarcely given to him to play them all at once.

It is small wonder, then, that failure generally attends the attempts to dispense with the distinct roles traditionally implied in adjudication. What generally occurs is that at some early point a familiar pattern will seem to emerge from the evidence; an accustomed label is waiting for the case and, without awaiting further proofs, this label is promptly assigned to it. . . . [W]hat starts as a preliminary diagnosis designed to direct the inquiry tends, quickly and imperceptibly, to become a fixed conclusion, as all that confirms the diagnosis makes a strong imprint on the mind, while all that runs counter to it is received with diverted attention.

The adversary system seems the only effective means for combatting this natural human tendency to judge too swiftly in terms of the familiar that which is not yet fully known. The arguments of counsel hold the case, as it were, in suspension between two opposing interpretations of it. While the proper classification of the case is thus kept unresolved, there is time to explore all of its peculiarities and nuances.[21]

Judge Jerome Frank, a leading critic of the adversary system, has identified a variety of weaknesses in the theoretical perfection of the adversary model. His principal criticism is that, far from ensuring that all the facts are developed for the trier's consideration, the system tends to ensure that some facts will not be developed. He identifies seven reasons for this: (1) The whole atmosphere of the courtroom bewilders witnesses. (2) Lawyers, before trial, coach the witnesses who will appear for their clients. In Austrian practice, by contrast, it is the height of unethical practice for a lawyer even to talk to a potential witness before the trial. (3) Dishonest lawyers use this practice to encourage perjury. (4) Cross-examination is a device to discredit honest witnesses. (5) Lawyers refuse to concede facts which they know are true, but which they believe the opposing party cannot prove. Indeed, the Bar Association's Committee on Ethics has held that it is proper professional conduct for a lawyer in the trial of a case not to disclose to the court such facts (although he may have a professional responsibility to try to persuade his client to disclose it, and if the latter does not, to withdraw from the case).

(6) Lawyers rely on surprise as a tactic. (7) Financial weakness may prevent proper investigation of the facts by one or both parties.[22]

The implications of the adversary system for the conduct of judge and jury is that they play relatively passive roles. The role of the judge has been transformed in the course of time, as we have already suggested. In the Middle Ages, he was indeed an umpire in a decision-making process that was frequently enough literally trial by combat. In the Tudor period and the years that followed, judges took on an active role in questioning witnesses and in prosecution, although the form of the adversary proceedings was nominally maintained. The advent of the modern era, with its emphasis on free private action, saw the return of the judge to his passive role of administering the rules of conflict rather than engaging in the conflict itself.

The jurors' role has likewise undergone a radical change over the centuries. From being the source of information about the proceeding they have become more and more the impartial triers of the facts, who listen to the proofs adduced by the two warring parties.

20.5 THE RATIONALITY OF A TRIAL

We can see that the central theme which has dominated theorizing about the trial process has been to make it as rational a method of determining the facts as possible. It may be seriously doubted, however, whether the trial of an issue of fact can ever eliminate irrational elements in reaching a decision.

Trials of issues of fact more frequently than not, especially in criminal cases, are decided on the basis of the testimony of witnesses, unaccompanied by documentary or other types of evidence to strengthen their testimony. The long and lamentable history of innocent men paying severely for the mistakes or malicious designs of witnesses against them bears frightening testimony to the dangers inherent in the whole enterprise.

A variety of experiments have been performed which demonstrate the remarkable inability of ordinary persons to remember accurately, and to report accurately their observations, even laying aside knowingly dishonest or lying testimony. When an incident is staged before an audience, such as a sudden interruption of a calm lecture, only about ten percent of the observers can report accurately even the number of persons involved.[23] The recollection of the sequence of events is likely to be faulty—in one experiment, seven of twenty recollections turned out to be inaccurate.[24] Glanville Williams describes one experiment performed during a law lecture by L. C. B. Gower at the London School of Economics:

There was an altercation between an Englishman and a Welshman; each drew weapons and the Englishman "shot" the Welshman. When members of the audience were examined as to what had happened, they said that the Welshman had brandished his weapon first, whereas in actual fact both drew weapons at the same time. The reason for the mistake was that at the dramatic moment the situation was such that all eyes were on the Welshman. The mistake might be disastrous in a legal case if the question of self-defense were at issue.[25]

Estimates of time intervals are generally little better than guesses.[26] When witnesses are asked to repeat the words used by an actor, "accuracy of reproduction, in a literal sense, is the rare exception and not the rule."[27] As Williams comments, "A witness generally reports not the precise words but his understanding of the purport of what was said, and his understanding may not at all coincide with what was intended to be expressed."[28]

The possibility of misremembering and misreporting what actually took place is greatly enchanced by suggestive or leading questions. The rules of evidence prevent putting such questions to one's own witness, presumably a sympathetic one, save in extraordinary cases. The universal custom of interviewing witnesses before trial, however, permits such questions to be asked prior to the formal trial. In this way the memory of a witness can be warped even by the most scrupulously honest of lawyers.

Identification of evidence and its inaccuracy have produced some of the most spectacular miscarriages of justice. Experiments have repeatedly shown that witnesses are largely incapable of remembering or describing a face—an incapacity that is made worse under the actual circumstances of a criminal incident where the witness may have only a fleeting glance at the criminal. Moreover, once a witness has made an identification, he tends to become more and more positive in his identification as the proceedings move from police line-up to trial. In the experiment at the London School of Economics, nine members of the audience were asked to identify the two actors at an identification parade held a week after the event. The parade consisted of thirteen persons. Only two students out of nine were able to identify the Englishman, and four the Welshman. The other participants identified completely innocent men; one innocent man was identified twice.[29]

Trial proceedings, despite their stated aim of seeking a rational judgment, implicitly recognize that there is a large element of chance and luck in the process. Jerome Michael put it concisely: The court

is supposed to submit an issue to the jury if, as the judges say, the jury can decide reasonably either way. But to say that I can decide an issue of fact reasonably either way is to say, I submit, that I cannot, by the exercise of reason, decide the question. That means that the issue we typically submit to juries is an issue which the jury cannot decide by the exercise of its reason.

The decision of an issue of fact in cases of closely balanced probabilities, therefore, must in the nature of things, be an emotional rather than a rational act.[30]

That this fact is implicitly recognized by the creators of the procedural rules which control the trials of issues of fact is indicated by three of these rules. One is that to which Michael referred: A judge is supposed to grant a motion for directed verdict in a civil case (or for a directed verdict of not guilty in a criminal case) whenever "reasonable men could not differ" about the verdict. The others are the important position assigned to so-called "demeanor evidence," and the broad scope permitted counsel in his address to the jury.

It has frequently been stated by appellate courts that, in assessing the credibility of witnesses, the trier of fact can observe the demeanor of the witnesses, which is something that cannot appear in the cold written records. This increment of evidence, which is available to the jury and the trial judge but not to the appellate court, is the reason usually given to explain why the jury's estimate of credibility is beyond correction or change by an appellate court.

Yet it is self-evident that demeanor evidence is, of all evidence, the most unreliable. The accomplished liar is said to be accomplished precisely because of his ability to control his demeanor and thus to conceal his true emotions. Conversely, it is common currency that honest men frequently shift their eyes, stutter, lick their lips nervously, or otherwise have mannerisms that the standard stereotype suggests are habitual not with honest men, but with prevaricators.

Whenever the importance of demeanor evidence has been urged in matters on which an appellate court wished to act, it has not usually stood in bar. For example, when a trial judge in New Jersey declined to grant an uncontested divorce because he disbelieved the unopposed witnesses for the plaintiff, the appellate court held squarely that, despite the importance of demeanor evidence, he could not refuse to grant the divorce. That appellate courts must justify their deference to the trial judge or jury's assessment of the evidence on grounds so flimsy as the jury's opportunity to observe the witnesses' demeanor, demonstrates that the decision of the trier of fact in a closely contested case cannot be a rational decision.

The ultimate irrationality of a jury's decision in a closely contested case is recognized, finally, by the norms which control the counsel's final address to the jury. Where before everything which might sway emotions was systematically excluded (save where its logical value plainly exceeds its emotive content), in the address to the jury the norm not only permits but demands that counsel make every emotional appeal that he can. The common lore of trials is full of examples of counsel who wept tears in behalf of their clients, staked the decision on Ireland, motherhood, and the flag, appealed to gross racial prejudices, or otherwise startlingly violated the purported goal of rationality in decision-making.

These three leading rules make it clear that at the bottom of every case as to which there might be genuine doubt, the final decision depends not on rational but on irrational factors. On first examination, however, it would seem that the emotive factor, while plainly existent in civil cases, has been excluded from criminal cases by the requirement of proof beyond a reasonable doubt.

In civil cases, the trier of fact is supposed to decide the case in favor of whichever party has adduced the preponderant weight of evidence, no matter by how little it overweighs the countervailing evidence. This rule suggests that in a civil case it is more important to put an end to the conflict than to insist on a higher degree of rationality in the decisional process.

In a criminal case, however, the standard of proof is higher: No man may be convicted unless his guilt is proven "beyond a reasonable doubt." At first blush, it would appear that the jury is therefore prevented from convicting a man unless no reasonable man could disagree. It would therefore appear that the possibility of an irrational or emotional factor holding the balance of the jury's verdict is eliminated, so far as instructions to the jury can do so.

The high standard of proof nominally required in a criminal case, as compared with the lower standard for a civil case, would seem on paper to reflect the different functions and consequences of civil and criminal trials. The one has as its principal purpose the settling of disputes. The other subjects the accused to a degredation in status accompanying a judgment of guilty, and to penal sanctions. The controversy which leads to a civil action is between private parties, and hence its resolution theoretically has wider consequences only in the relatively rare case in which the courts use the occasion to formulate new norms. In a criminal case, however, the controversy is nominally between the State and a subject. Such a controversy does not require resolution in the interests of continued integration of the body politic so much as it demands a display by the State of impartiality and of concern for the individual, for only in this way can the State legitimize itself rationally-legally.

Hence the nominal rule which controls the jury's decision is "proof beyond a reasonable doubt." This rule at least in appearance purports to preserve the essential values of due process. It says that no man can be sanctioned by the penal law unless his guilt could not be doubted by any reasonable man. It provides assurance to the citizen that if he obeys the criminal law, he will not be found guilty merely because of suspicious circumstances beyond his control. It provides for an overriding concern with law rather than order.

The difficulty is that the rule is rather more subtle than it appears in its usual stated form. A jury has the right to find an accused guilty only if he is proved guilty beyond a reasonable doubt *as based on the testimony which the jury regards as credible*. Since it is precisely the credibility component which is least subject to rational determination, in any closely contested case the jury is still thrown back on emotional and subjective judgments as the basis of their decision, even if the decision is made according to the rules. One "credible" witness, opposed by dozens of witnesses which the jury chooses to disbelieve, can therefore provide proof beyond a reasonable doubt.

As a result of the rules with respect to the assessment of credibility, therefore, the verdict of a jury or a trial judge sitting alone is virtually beyond direct attack on appeal. It is beyond direct attack for still another reason: The inscrutability of the jury's verdict.

20.6 THE INSCRUTABILITY OF THE VERDICT

Ordinarily the jury returns what is called a general verdict—in a criminal case, guilty or not guilty. In the privacy of the jury room, theoretically the jury must determine the facts and then, treating the law constituting the major premise as laid down by the judge make the inference leading to the verdict by applying the major premise to the minor premise (propositions about matters of fact the jury chooses to accept as true).

The nature of a general verdict, however, makes it impossible for anybody to know whether the verdict resulted because the jury actually found the facts to be what the verdict implies, or whether they made a logical error in applying the law to the facts, or whether, perversely, they simply disregarded the law or the facts and permitted themselves the luxury of deciding whether they wanted this accused to be punished or released. There is a great deal of data to suggest that in many instances the last case obtains.

Judge Jerome Frank put it sharply:

The general verdict enhances, to the maximum, the power of appeal to the bias and prejudices of the jurors, and usually converts into a futile ritual the use of stock phrases about dispassionateness almost always included in judges' charges. Many books on trial tactics, written by experienced trial lawyers, which give advice as to how to rouse the jury's emotions, make the point that the jury tries the lawyers rather than the case, and that the lawyers, in jury trials, must recognize themselves as actors or stagemanagers engaged in theatrical performances . . . A court has solemnly decided that "tears have always been considered legitimate arguments before the jury," that such use of tears is "one of the natural rights of counsel which no court or constitutions could take away," and that "indeed, if counsel has them at his command, it may be seriously questioned whether it is not his professional duty to shed them whenever the occasion arises.[31]

The problem does not exist so sharply in cases tried by a judge sitting without a jury, since on the appeal, trial judges are usually required to spell out the facts as found and the law they regarded as operative to reach the conclusion they did. The appellate court thus has before it the necessary information to check the processes of inference by which the trial judge reached his conclusion. The same matters, however, are effectively beyond the reach of an appellate court when the trial is by a jury.

It is not that there are no adequate ways by which the jury verdict could be exposed to analysis and correction. The most commonly urged device is the special verdict. Where a special verdict is requested, the jury is required to answer specific questions about the facts at issue. The process of applying the law to the facts thus found is done by the judge on the record. In such cases, both the special verdict and the judge's reasoning are open to appellate-court scrutiny.

Despite the availability of this device, the special verdict is virtually unknown in criminal cases, although it has a limited use in civil cases. Why the jury continues to be allowed to place its verdict beyond the realm of correction is a question that cuts to the heart of the nature of trials of issues of fact, and the entire role of the aims of due process.

20.7 TRIALS: RHETORIC AND CONSEQUENCES

The rhetoric of due process demands the adversary system, the presumption of innocence, and the proof of guilt beyond a reasonable doubt. The value-set which subsumes due process is that of legal-rational legitimization. The State is regarded as an impartial framework, laying down the rules for conflict, and making impartial adjudications. Every man knows in advance what is criminal and what is not criminal; the demands of legality are satisfied—law, not order, presides over social interaction. According to this model, every effort is made, with the rules controlling the admission and exclusion of evidence, to prevent material reaching the trier of fact which will sway his emotions rather than help him decide the case as objectively and rationally as possible. Hearsay, proof of the accused man's bad character or previous criminal record, evidence of other similar crimes by the accused—all of which may logically tend to add to the probabilities of guilt— are nevertheless excluded save in exceptional circumstances.

Yet the rules with respect to directed verdict, the assessment of credibility, and arguments of counsel suggest that there lies at bottom an element of irrationality in any closely contested trial of an issue of fact. Plainly, the rules viewed as a whole suggest that insofar as possible, emotion and bias are to be put aside by the triers; but there still is an irreducible nugget of irrationality that lies at the very core of the trial process.

It is conceivable that the law might have taken the position that, whenever the matter is so much in doubt that prejudice and irrationality had to enter into the process, the accused person ought to be found not guilty. As we have seen, this is at least the supposed thrust of the requirement that guilt be proved beyond a reasonable doubt. It seems plain enough, however, that such a high standard of proof could hardly meet the demands on the criminal law, since it would require the discharge of everyone who might conceivably swear that he was innocent and persuade a few witnesses to swear to the same effect. So long as there is a conflict in testimony, someone must decide whether the conflict is genuine or fictitious, i.e. whether it is sufficient to raise a reasonable doubt. Since the truth-probability of evidence is inevitably a function of credibility, someone must make a preliminary determination of credibility. That determination, we have suggested, in some cases at least is beyond rational decision.

20.8 THE RATIONALE OF JURY TRIALS

It is in light of this residual hard nugget of irrationality that one must consider the consequences of the retention of the jury system. We have already traced briefly the history of the jury from a body of neighbors with personal knowledge of the facts to a group drawn from total strangers. As originally constituted, it was a body responsive to the demands of a folk society; as presently constituted, it reflects the anonymity and alienation of urban living. This change in the composition of the jury reflects the great movement that Tonnies describes as from *Gemeinschaft* to *Gesellschaft*.

In the course of this social transformation the jury's function has obviously changed equally. Instead of being the source of information about the incident, the jury has come to be the arbiter between conflicting sets of witnesses.

Obviously, lay jurors do not have any special expertise in assessing evidence, or in making the sort of skilled and complex judgments that sometimes must be made in a trial. Increasingly in commercial litigation, the parties tend to waive jury trials in favor of trials by a judge alone. In some jurisdictions, "blue ribbon" panels are formed of exceptionally well-educated (and hence middle-class) citizens to sit on complex commercial cases and even in important criminal cases. The very existence of such panels, and the reluctance of litigants in commercial cases to be tried by a jury are plain evidence of the inadequacy of the jury-trial system to cope with complex financial and business issues.

Yet juries have staunch defenders even today with respect to at least two areas of litigation: automobile accident cases and criminal cases. The warmth of support is sometimes extravagant. Sir William Blackstone wrote

Trial by jury ever has been, and I trust ever will be, looked upon as the glory of the English law ... The liberties of England cannot but subsist so long as this palladium of liberty remains sacred and inviolate, not only from all open attacks (which none will be so hardy as to make), but also from all secret machinations, which may sap and undermine it by introducing new and arbitrary methods of trial, by justices of the peace, commissioners of the revenue, and courts of conscience.[32]

What is the source of this extraordinary fervor in support of the jury system?

The wellsprings of enthusiasm for the jury system have been different in different epochs. As we saw, during the Middle Ages the jury was primarily an instrument of the Crown; through the judges and the jury the Crown sought to invade the particularistic jurisdictions of the great feudatories. As the alliance between the Crown and the towns disintegrated, the judges assumed more and more the posture of being mere instruments of the royal will. Occasionally, a bold jury would then disregard a judge's too biased instructions and find a verdict contrary to his wishes (as they did in *Throckmorton's Case*). By 1670 the ancient habit of the judges intimidating jurors by fining them for their obduracy came to an end in *Bushell's Case*,[33] in which it was held that the jury must not be punished for its verdict.

To say that jurors may not be punished for their verdict, especially when the verdict is general and therefore inscrutable, is to say that jurors have the power to disregard the judge's instructions on the law as well as his advice on the facts; no one can tell why the verdict turns out as it does. Toward the end of the eighteenth century, the British Government sought to smother middle-class sentiments and organization for radical democratic reforms in a series of criminal trials for seditious libel. (In one of these cases, the bookseller who sold Tom Paine's *Rights of Man* was defended by the great Lord Erskine, later Chancellor of England). In a few of these trials, the jury brought in a verdict of not guilty, against both law and evidence. It is not to be wondered that the middle-class ideology, while on the one hand urging that laws must be clear, written, and sharply defined, nevertheless simultaneously embraced the jury's uncontrollable discretion with equal fervor. "In times of difficulty and danger," wrote Blackstone, "more is to be apprehended from the violence and partiality of judges appointed by the Crown, in suits between the king and the subject, than in disputes between one individual and another.[34]

The power of juries to decide, and perhaps to defy, the law as well as the facts came to be enshrined in the anticolonial American tradition as well. John Adams expressed this sentiment when he wrote:

The general rules of law and common regulations of society, under which ordinary transactions arrange themselves, are well enough known to ordinary jurors. The great principles of the constitution are intimately known; they are sensibly felt by every Briton; it is scarcely extravagant to say that they are drawn in and imbibed with the nurse's milk and first air. Now, should the melancholy case arise that the judges should give their opinions to the jury against one of these fundamental principles, is a juror obliged to give his verdict generally, according to this direction, or even to find the fact specially, and submit the law to the court? Every man, of any feeling or conscience, will answer, No.[35]

In Rhode Island, judges held office "not for the purpose of deciding causes, for the jury decided all questions of law and fact; but merely to preserve order, and see that the parties had a fair chance with the jury."[36] The antipathy to royal officials expressed in the fervent support of the jury against the judge was aided by the fact that the judges in colonial America were not infrequently laymen and thus had not the status bestowed by expertise.

In the period following independence, the right of juries to decide the law and the facts became part of the democratic myth. The conflict between the British view that the jury had the power perhaps, but not the right, to disregard the judge's instructions and the contrary view came to reflect "the conflict between democratic hopes and English common-law traditions, between a frontier concept of popular justice and an old-world fact of King's law."[37] Jefferson built this idea into an entire philosophy of the role of the people in government:

Were I called upon to decide, whether the people had best be omitted in the legislative or judiciary department, I would say it is better to leave them out of the legislature. The execution of the laws is more important than the making of them.[38]

Federal lower-court judges and even Supreme Court judges sitting on circuit charged juries that they were "the judges both of the law and the fact in a criminal case, and are not bound by the opinion of the court."[39] State courts, too, held the same doctrine until the closing years of the nineteenth century. Howe remarks that "it is not surprising that . . . the jury's independence in criminal cases was vigorously defended. Here the citizen was directly confronted by the force of government; his lively suspicion of all public officials might be somewhat alleviated if he could be assured that his guilt or innocence would be determined by his fellow-citizens."[40]

The deep contradiction within a middle-class ideology that simultaneously regarded clarity, precision, and certainty in law as its highest aim and nevertheless maintained the doctrine of jury lawlessness could not long endure. The simple society of the colonial era rapidly disappeared. A complex society emerged, with a high degree of division of labor, and the complexity of the laws vastly increased. The naïve belief that every man knew the Constitution and the laws became patently untrue.

The complexity of society increased along with the size and sophistication of the legal community. The bar had, of course, its own set of values, one of which, necessary for its own protection, status, and self-esteem, was that the law was a difficult and complex body of rules, not readily understood by those not initiated into its mysteries.

The issue of jury lawlessness was met head-on by the Supreme Court of the United States in *Sparf v. United States*[41] in 1895. In that case the defendants, charged with murder of the second mate of a bark cruising in the Pacific, were found guilty of murder after the trial judge had told the jury in no uncertain terms "as one of the tribunals of the country, a jury is expected to be governed by law, and the law it should receive from the court." An appeal was made on the ground that the charge was erroneous in that it did not inform the jurors that they were judges of the law as well as the facts.

The majority (three judges dissented) upheld the conviction. The opinion based the decision on the principle of legality.

Public and private safety alike would be in peril if the principle be established that juries in criminal cases may, of right, disregard the law as expounded to them by the court and become a law unto themselves. Under such a system . . . jurymen, untrained in the law, would determine questions affecting life, liberty and property according to such legal principles as in their judgment were applicable to the case being tried . . . [T]he result would be that the enforcement of the law against criminals and for the protection of citizens would depend entirely upon juries uncontrolled by any settled, fixed legal principles . . .

Under any other system, the courts, although established to declare the law, would for every practical purpose be eliminated from our system as instrumentalities devised for the protection equally of society and of individuals in their essential rights. When that occurs our own government will cease to be a government of law and become a government of men. Liberty regulated by law is the underlying principle of our institutions.[42]

The State courts had either preceded the Supreme Court in its decision or rapidly followed suit, so that today the rule is unanimously held in this country, that the jury is bound to follow the law as laid down by the court—although, as we saw, the inscrutability of the general verdict makes it impossible to determine whether in fact they did so in any particular case.

The tradition of jury trials does not die easily. It remains as an institution in the law, used in most serious cases and a few that are not so serious. The support for it comes today, however, strangely enough from the very judges who have done so much to strengthen and advance the norms of due process and the concept of legality.

It is here as much as anywhere that the conception of society as based on conflict or on harmonious adjustment seems to determine the arguments advanced. On the one hand, it seems clear enough that, values aside, better educated and better trained persons will make better judges of fact and more intelligent inferences from the law as laid down for them. The facts of even a short case are difficult to remember; in a long case, lasting not infrequently many weeks, it is impossible to remember them accurately.[43] The judge's charge is frequently almost incomprehensible even to appellate judges who come later to analyze it. Judge Curtis Bok has said that "juries have the disadvantage of being treated like children while the testimony is going on, but then being doused with a kettleful of law during the charge that would make a third-year law student blanch.[44] To expect untrained jurors to handle the problems of fact and law in even a simple criminal case with even a modicum of rationality probably is to defy reality.

The difficulty lies in that residue of uncertainty that is built into any trial involving witnesses. If one perceives society in terms of conflicting strata and groups with different value-sets, then the decisions in close cases will necessarily turn on values, not rationality, since they cannot depend on rationality. Juries chosen from a limited slice of society, therefore, must necessarily reflect not the values of society as a whole—there are no such values—but the values of their particular segment of the whole.

That this is so has been ascertained empirically. In an extensive study of juries made at the University of Chicago, it was reported that "persons with German and British backgrounds were more likely to favor the government, whereas Negroes and persons of Slavic and Italian descent were more likely to vote for acquittal." Moreover, "blue ribbon jurors"—jurors chosen because of their higher social, economic, and educational status—were "considerably more prone to convict."[45]

The Supreme Court has expressly recognized these facts in its many decisions insisting that juries be chosen, so far as possible, from an unbiased population sample. Local rules which excuse workingmen from jury duties have been disapproved for use in the federal courts. Convictions obtained from jury panels from which black men were systematically excluded have been upset. The Supreme Court has even gone so far as to reverse a conviction in a capital case in which persons opposed to capital punishment were excluded from the jury.

The rationale of insisting that a jury be chosen from a fair cross section of the community rests on the notion that if a person from the same social stratum as the accused is on the jury, he can, by holding firm to his opinions, deny unanimity to the jury's decision and thus prevent a conviction in a case in which acculturated values may determine the result. It is, however, a rationale that makes sense only in the abstract. Small-group sociology teaches that it is very difficult for one member of a jury to hold out against the group. In the Chicago Jury Project, it was found that hung juries occurred in only six percent of the cases studied. Not a single jury hung with a minority of less than three.[46] A jury will meaningfully judge a defendant from the viewpoint of his group or class, therefore, must include more than mere token representation. A single black man on a jury in the South, for example, does not mean that an accused black will be tried by a jury which is a cross section of the community in any meaningful sense of "cross section."

Moreover, the rules which require that the jury panel be drawn from a fair cross section of the community do not by any means require that the jury which actually makes the decision represent a cross section. The Supreme Court has never required that a jury panel, much less the jury itself, be statistically representative of the community, for such a requirement might prove administratively impossible to enforce. So long as the panel of jurors is chosen by some reasonably nondiscriminatory method, e.g. by selecting them at random from a voting list, the constitutional requirements are satisfied. The luck of the draw thus determines both the composition of the panel and the particular members of the panel who are called to serve on a particular jury. Moreover, the prosecution has certain rights or arbitrary challenges to jurors (as has the defense), that is, to challenge them without giving any reason. It is not unusual in the South, for example, for the prosecution simply to challenge peremptorily every black juror who happens to be chosen by lot, so that the juries which actually try black defendants more often than not exclude all black members, even though the jury cannot be regarded as constitutionally exceptionable.

That the rules laid down by the Supreme Court demand a fair cross section of the community to be represented on the panel does not, of course, mean that every jury clerk or sheriff follows the rules. The continuing stream of cases in which convictions are challenged successfully for failure to follow the rules indicates that the contrary is the case. Indeed, in an adversary system, the method of drawing jurors is likely to be what is convenient for the jury clerks, not what is laid down by the Supreme Court; for, in this system, malpractices can be corrected only upon challenge, and not every case will be challenged.

For example, in Connecticut, at least as late as 1962, each town was assigned a quota of jurors to be supplied to the trial courts. This quota had to be filled by the town clerks. Rather than calling people arbitrarily to jury duty, thus incurring unpopularity for themselves among those selected against their will (and frequently to their financial detriment), most town clerks simply published a call for volunteers. The result was that the jury panel invariably consisted of a very high proportion of middle-class housewives, retired persons, and the employees of public utilities (whose employers continued to pay them as a gesture of public service). Moreover, persons who wanted to sit on juries were usually more conviction-minded than the average citizen. Thus, without any town clerk's consciously wanting to discriminate against blacks and working people, the jury panels in fact contained far fewer members from these groups than their proportion in the population would warrant.

Even if the actual trial juries comprised a fair cross section of the community, however, it may be doubted that the result would be the ideal of rational decision-making, for reasons not connected with the inherent incapacity of laymen. In every society, even though there are certainly different value-sets, there is, nevertheless, a dominant culture—the culture of those who have command of the means of the propagation of culture. As a result, the possibility of minority groups receiving a fair and sympathetic trial even by members of their own group is drastically reduced. The problem becomes even worse when passions run high in the community. Judge Amidon, who tried a number of Sedition Act cases during the first World War, has remarked:

I have tried war cases before jurymen who were candid, sober, intelligent business men, whom I have known for thirty years, and who under ordinary circumstances would have had the highest respect for my declarations of law, but during that period they looked back into my eyes with the savagery of wild animals, saying by their manner, "away with this twiddling, let us get at him." Men believed during that period that the only verdict in a war case, which could show loyalty, was a verdict of guilty.[47]

The reverse reaction has been even more frequent, especially in the South, where juries that are largely white would not convict those who attack blacks or civil rights workers, whatever the evidence.

It might be argued that, in view of these difficulties, trial by a judge alone would produce a higher standard of justice. The difficulty lies in the fact that judges, too, possess a set of values, which are of their own class and group and culture.

In general, juries tend to be less conviction-minded than judges in criminal cases. In the Chicago Jury Project, 500 trial judges throughout the nation were asked to say how they would have decided some 1500 criminal cases which had already been decided by a jury. They disagreed with the jury in 19% of the cases and were found to be considerably more prone to convict. If all the defendants in the 1500 cases had been tried by judges alone, the number of acquittals—actually about one-third, or 500 cases—could have been cut in half.

The differences between judge and jury varied with the cases. In narcotics cases, for example, there was no divergence at all. The maximum divergence was in statutory-rape and drunken-driving cases, in both of which juries were considerably more prone to acquit than the judges.

Why judges are more prone to convict than juries is not easy to ascertain precisely. Dale Broeder says that "in criminal cases, judges often acquire a vested interest in law enforcement; continuance in office often turns on the number of convictions which can be paraded before an electorate. The judge's friend and fellow political worker is often the prosecuting attorney or one of his subordinates, or, on the other hand, the defendant's attorney..."[48] Whatever the reason, that there is not infrequently a broad range of difference between judge and jury is an established fact. It is to the nature of this difference, and the devices that judges have invented with which to control juries, that we now turn.

20.9 OF JUDGES AND JURIES

The whole change of function of the judiciary in the United States could be explained in terms of their sustained interest in controlling juries. Chief Justice Hughes is reported to have said that "An unscrupulous administrator might be tempted to say, 'Let me find the facts for the people of my country and I care little who lays down the general principles.'"[49] So the reasons for the control are to be sought not merely in technical problems involved in the pursuit of a rational technique of fact-finding, but also in the larger policies at issue.

In the early history of this country, when juries claimed and exercised the right to determine law as well as fact, judges had, if nothing more, a narrow professional interest in asserting their control in matters as to which they claimed a special expertise. At the end of the nineteenth century, as we saw, they finally imposed the greatest limitation of all upon the jury when they reclaimed for themselves the power to lay down the law. By then, however, far more was at issue than a merely professional interest.

The latter part of the nineteenth century saw the development in American law of a constitutional doctrine according to which the essence of American government was the constitutional protection of the rights of property. The progressive revelation of this doctrine came in a variety of ways. For example, the first income tax law was declared unconstitutional, not because it taxed wages and salaries, but because it taxed the income and profits from property. State regulations of all sorts were struck down because they were deemed to interfere with the rights of contract. Property could not be hazarded at the whim of a jury. The assertion of judicial control over the jury was perhaps an inevitable development. In particular, the judges found in the doctrine that constitutional issues were issues of law to be decided by the judge, a handy device to remove the most critical issues from a jury's decision.

With the revolution on the Supreme Court that started in 1937, that doctrine became a central device used to protect from a jury's vagaries the constitutional interests, not of property, but of minorities generally. A host of rules were created which took the central issue out of the jury's hands: the voluntariness of a confession; the likelihood that speech or writing created a clear and present danger, (thus permitting its suppression consistently with the first amendment); whether pornographic writing was constitutionally obscene; whether a search and seizure was reasonable; and many others.

In the course of these judicial decisions, the relative positions of the judge and the jury were reversed. In the early days of the Republic, the jury represented the interests of democratic government against the judges who, it was feared, represented an autocratic interest. Today some judges fear the jury as representative of an intolerant and repressive majority.

The methods by which judges can control juries are innumerable. They can control the verdict itself by directing the verdict of acquittal, or by setting aside a verdict after conviction as against the weight of the evidence. They can influence the jury through the terms of the charge. They can declare specific issues to be issues of law, not of fact. For example, the issue whether a plaintiff is contributorily negligent is usually decided by the jury as a question of fact (although a decision on such an issue plainly includes a judgment by the jury that the plaintiff did or did not act in accordance with a standard of conduct which is determined by the jury). In many cases, however, judges have taken that issue from the jury and laid down a specific norm which the jury is supposed to take as the law. In Pennsylvania, for example, it was the rule that a plaintiff had acted unreasonably and therefore negligently if he did not stop, look, and listen before crossing a railroad track—a rule which made it more difficult for a jury to find against the railroad in case of a crossing accident.

How, in view of this decided antagonism of the judges as a class toward the jury, has the jury survived? To answer this question, we must look for the hidden functions served by the jury system in the United States as well as the myths and ideologies which support the institution.

20.10 THE FUNCTION OF THE JURY

In the first place, despite the tremendous volume of literature about the jury, the jury trial actually is invoked in a desperately small proportion of the cases. At least ninety percent—in some jurisdictions, even a greater percentage—of all criminal trials end with a plea of guilty. Of the remainder, many are relatively minor matters customarily tried summarily by a magistrate. Of those still remaining, many are tried by consent by a judge. In Chicago, for example, two-thirds of the felony trials are held before a lone judge. Thus, altogether not more than one or two percent—probably a smaller percentage—of all persons accused of crime are tried by a jury. These statistics notwithstanding, the paradigm of the criminal trial, in the eyes of the public at least, is the trial by jury. This is the residual right which is invariably extolled by orators on the Fourth of July and on occasions marking the Bar Association's annual Law Day celebrations. Jury trial therefore must occupy a symbolic role whose importance far exceeds the frequency with which it is actually invoked.

Part of the reason for this curious support for what appears to be a withering tradition lies in the fact that our legal system is still one of adversary proceedings, whose very model, the due-process model, is the public trial before a judge and jury. At the trial, it is thought, the truth will come out; the innocent need not fear. There illegality in the process of arrest or investigation will be brought to light; there judicial control over the police can be exercised; and there the accused will be defended by counsel trained in the mystique of courtroom procedure.

The very possibility of a trial in any criminal case, no matter how little it is resorted to in fact, thus serves to legitimize the entire criminal process, for it can always be argued that, had the accused's rights been infringed, he would have wanted a trial to prove his innocence. On the potential of a trial, therefore, rests the legitimacy of the treatment of the great mass of criminals who never have a trial at all. It is thus to be expected that the rules governing trials of issues of fact will be fairly rational; and the rules of evidence are as expected. That the decisions made at a trial must in the end contain a hard core of irrationality arises from the nature of the problem of discovering what took place in the past through the use of evidence—and evidence is, after all, the only means by which we can find out about the past.

Since the legitimacy of the criminal process depends on the legitimacy of the trial, it is to be expected that at least in this phase of the process the imbalance between the forces of prosecution and those of the defense will be rectified. As we saw, this has been precisely the thrust of the rules articulated by the Supreme Court. These rules have set out standards aimed at making trials more fair, more rational, more equally balanced between prosecution and defense. Thus the very existence of the rules which the Court has articulated legitimize not only the trial itself but the entire process—even that part of it which manifestly ignores due process.

The legal-rational legitimacy of the entire criminal process thus rests on the ultimate availability of a rational means by which guilt or innocence can be tested. Why, then, has the jury been retained when, by common consensus, it is the antithesis of a rational arbiter of facts?

Part of the answer, no doubt, lies in the tradition of the jury as a protector of the oppressed. Broeder brands this notion as a mere myth:

Probably society does not take with any great degree of seriousness the claim that juries can successfully counteract judicial bias. In criminal cases, the judge's bias is most frequently reflected in the severity of his sentences, not in the manner he conducts the trial. A jury wishing to counteract this severity can only acquit ... Yet we are afraid to vest sentencing powers upon juries, both for fear of their abuse and of the jury's inability to consider questions of punishment apart from those involving guilt. It is only in a very narrow area in which the jury can function as a device for thwarting judicial bias or corruption.[50]

Indeed, if juries were in the habit of not convicting those who are specifically the targets of governmental action—the Communists, the large-scale criminals, the urban rioters—one would seriously doubt whether the jury as an institution would long survive.

It may be that the heart of the matter lies in people's feeling that the determination of issues of fact does, in the final analysis, have a core of irrationality. To leave such decisions with the trial judge is to force him to shoulder the burden of applying his values in the decision. Judge Botein says that "just like jurors, I suppose judges labor under psychological blocks ... When I was a practising attorney I recall that the bar employed a rough psychology in seeking or avoiding assignments before certain judges. Lawyers representing wives in matrimonial matters shunned a judge who had borne a heavy domestic cross for many years. And lawyers representing husbands avoided a judge who had a reputation as a ladies' man. Some judges were labelled 'plaintiff's judges.' Presumably their sympathies were drawn to plaintiffs in accident cases. Other judges were labelled 'defendant's judges,' especially if they had represented casualty insurance companies before ascending the bench."[51] If the judge must decide the case, he cannot avoid exposing his biases. And even without the specific biases Judge Botein mentions, there remains the fact, so startlingly revealed in the Chicago Jury Project, that judges as a class are more prone to convict than juries.

The due-process model and the adversary system depend on the notion that the contest between the prosecution and the defense will be conducted by fair rules that forbid either side to gain an unreasonable advantage over the other, and that are fairly administered by an impartial judge. This image of the trial, so essential to the maintenance of the power of the judiciary and its successful functioning in the society, can easily be destroyed if judges are regarded as prejudiced. The existence of the jury makes it possible for the judge and the whole judicial system to appear to be above the struggle, making judgments fairly in the event of conflicts between the State and its subjects.

Moreover, it is not the frequency of jury trials that is important, it is the existence of the possibility of requiring trial by jury that legitimizes the whole process. When a defendant waives the jury and elects trial by court, he is in effect expressing his belief that the judge will be fair and impartial; the act of waiver legitimizes the judge's decision and reduces the likelihood of a later charge of bias.

Trial by jury is therefore the final legitimization of the due-process model.

The adversary system actually works in the jury trial, at least insofar as the two sides can be made equal in resources and competence. It is in the jury trial that the rules of evidence are honed to a fine edge to excise the false, the irrelevant, and the prejudicial, without taking away the residue of truth in the testimony. It is in it also that the irreducible minimum of emotional or irrational content to the decision-making process is exercised not by the bureaucracy, but by a representative cross section of the community. So long as jury trial exists in potential, and so long as it can be made to appear at an early stage that an accused has voluntarily waived such a trial, every other official in the criminal process can claim that any assertion that he acted unfairly or improperly is demonstrably untrue, for otherwise the accused would have chosen to be tried.

The trouble with this picture given to the public lies in the final irrationality of the fact-finding process in a society rent by class and group conflict. Knowing that the jury's verdict is in fact inscrutable, and that there is no appeal from the verdict, knowing that in a close case the jury is more apt than not to invoke middle-class values to adjudge the matter, and faced by all the institutional pressures we mentioned earlier, it is a bold poor or minority-group defendant who is prepared to hazard a longer and more severe sentence against the chances of a verdict of innocence by the jury. In plain, gambling terms, the game is rarely worth the candle.

The consequence of the persistent failure to introduce reforms in the jury system that would reduce the hazard of a lawless jury now becomes obvious: The jury trial in criminal cases is the final threat with which to drive defendants to accept a negotiated plea. If every accused person were sure that every jury would find him guilty or innocent exactly to the extent that he was, no more and no less, there would be little incentive for him to accept a negotiated plea, unless the offered plea was to a crime of less importance than that of which he knew the trier of fact would find him guilty. The failure to reduce the uncertainty about a jury's verdict results in yet increased pressure on the accused to negotiate a plea.

Thus, it is the very existence of the trial by jury which legitimizes the criminal process as it exists in fact. It is the built-in hazards of the jury trial, however, which exert the greatest pressure on accused persons to plead guilty. A guilty plea makes it impossible to discover whether the process leading to the plea was conducted according to the norms of due process. In the final analysis, the existence of the right to trial by jury simultaneously legitimizes the criminal process' claim to due process, but it also paradoxically, ensures that, to a large extent, the actual practice will be closer to the very opposite norms.

NOTES

1. Glanville L. Williams, *The Proof of Guilt: A Study of the English Criminal Trial,* Stevens, London, 1963, p. 5.

2. Sir William S. Holdworth, *A History of English Law*, Vol. 3, Little, Brown, Boston, 1934, p. 598.

3. *Ibid.*, p. 612. Reprinted by permission.

4. 1 St. Tr. 869 (1554).

5. 1 St. Tr. at 885; see Williams, *op. cit.*, p. 5.

6. 31 Eliz c. 4.

7. 4 James 1 c. 1 sec. 6.

8. Holdsworth, *op. cit.*, Vol. 5, p. 191. Reprinted by permission.

9. *Ibid.*

10. *Ibid.*, p. 192.

11. Williams, *op. cit.*, pp. 7–8.

12. 2 St. Tr. 936.

13. J. F. Stephen, *A History of the Criminal Law of England*, Vol. 1, Macmillan, London, 1883, p. 332.

14. 2 St. Tr. 25 at 26; quoted in Stephen, *op. cit.*, p. 333, n.2.

15. Stephen, *op. cit.*, pp. 334–335.

16. *Ibid.*, p. 329, quoting the reporter of the trial.

17. *Ibid.*, p. 496.

18. Williams *op. cit.*, p. 8.

19. John H. Wigmore, *A Treatise on the Anglo-American System of Evidence in Trial at Common Law*, Vol. 5, Little, Brown, Boston, 1940 [3rd ed.], §1367.

20. Cited in Williams, *op. cit.*, p. 86.

21. Report of the Joint Conference on Professional Responsibility of the Association of American Law Schools and the American Bar Association, Lon L. Fuller and John D. Randall, co-chairmen, *American Bar Association Journal*, **44**, 1958, pp. 1159, 1160. Reprinted by permission.

22. Jerome Frank, *Courts on Trial*, Princeton University Press, Princeton, N.J., 1949, pp. 81–85, 94–96.

23. Horace C. Levinson, *The Science of Chance: From Probability to Statistics*, Faber, London, 1952, p. 235.

24. Frederic C. Bartlett, *Remembering: A Study in Experimental and Social Psychology*, University Press, London, 1932.

25. Williams, *op. cit.*, p. 88, to which we are largely indebted for this section.

26. M. Hunter, *Memory: Facts and Fallacies*, Penguin, London, 1957, p. 99.

27. Bartlett, *op. cit.*, p. 93.

28. Williams, *op. cit.*, p. 89.

29. *Ibid.*, p. 110.

30. Jerome Michael, "The basic rules of pleading," *Record of the Association of the Bar of the City of New York*, **5**, 1950, pp. 175, 199–200. Reprinted by permission.

31. Jerome Frank, concurring in *Skidmore v. Baltimore and O.R. Co.*, 167 F. 2d 54 (2nd Cir., 1948); quotations from *Furgeson v. Moore*, 98 Tenn. 342, 39 S.W. (1897) 341 at 343.

32. Sir William Blackstone, *Commentaries on the Laws of England*, Murray, London, 1880, Vol. III, p. 379.

33. 6 How. St. Tr. 999.

34. Blackstone, *op. cit.*, Vol. IV, p. 349.

35. John Adams, *Works*, Vol. 2, Little, Brown, Boston, 1850–1856, pp. 253–255.

36. Amasa M. Eaton, "The development of the judicial system in Rhode Island," *Yale Law J.*, **14**, 1905, pp. 148–153.

37. Mark D. Howe, "Juries as judges of criminal law," *Harvard Law Rev.*, **52**, 1939, pp. 582–584.

38. Thomas Jefferson to L'Abbé Amends, July 19, 1789; *Works of Thomas Jefferson*, Vol. 3, Washington, 1854, pp. 81–82; quoted in Howe, *op. cit.*, p. 582.

39. J. Baldwin in *U. S. v. Wilson*, Fed. Cas. No. 16, 730, C.C.E.D. Pa. (1830).

40. Howe, *op. cit.*, pp. 591–592.

41. 156 U.S. 51, 15 S. Ct. 273, 39 L. Ed. 343 (1895).

42. 156 U.S. at 101–103.

43. Stephen, *op. cit.*, Vol. 1, pp. 571–572.

44. Curtis Bok, *I, Too, Nicodemus*, Knopf, New York, 1946.

45. Dale W. Broeder, "The University of Chicago jury project," *Neb. Law. Rev.*, **38**, 1959, p. 744.

46. *Ibid.*, pp. 746–747.

47. Quoted in Zechariah Chafee, *Free Speech in the United States*, Harvard University Press, Cambridge, 1948, p. 70.

48. Dale W. Broeder, "The function of the jury: facts or fictions?" *U. Chicago Law Rev.*, **21**, 1954, pp. 386–421. Reprinted by permission.

49. *New York Times*, February 13, 1931, p. 18, cols. 1,2; quoted in Broeder, "The function of the jury," p. 387, n.6.

50. Broeder, "The function of the jury," p. 421. Reprinted by permission.

51. Bernard Botein, *Trial Judge: The Candid, Behind-the-Bench Story of Justice Bernard Botein*, Simon and Schuster, New York, 1952, pp. 182 ff. Reprinted by permission.

21

Sentencing and sentences

Once the plea or verdict of guilty has been recorded, the whole thrust of the procedures of criminal trial changes. Instead of following a set of norms conforming to the ideal of due process, the sentencing is controlled by norms which are frankly incompatible with the ideal. The central fact in the actual procedure, which is carefully protected by the normative structure itself, is the unbelievably wide, almost totally uncontrolled discretion of the trial judge. To understand the sentencing process, we shall consider it as a system, with its inputs, conversion processes, and outputs.

21.1 SENTENCING: INPUTS

A wide variety of inputs enter the sentencing process: information concerning the offense, information concerning the offender, pressures from public and from the police and prosecuting authorities, the personality, training, and value-set of the sentencing judge, the ability and status of the defense counsel, and the personal relationships between the counsel and the court.

The information concerning the offense is derived from a variety of sources. If there has been a trial, of course the trial judge is well aware of the facts of the particular case. In most cases, however, where there is a plea of guilty, the judge's information must come from other sources. There are always the bare facts set forth in the information to which the accused has pleaded guilty. Especially in the case of minor offenses, this is more often than not the only information which the judge will have about the matter. For example, every morning in some police or magistrate's courts one can see a long queue of landlords charged with suffering garbage cans to stand without a cover, each dutifully paying a few dollars—a standard fine set for the charge—to a clerk who has no knowledge of the circumstances of the offense other than the fact of the charge. In traffic offenses, too, a similar procedure frequently obtains. In fact, this procedure is so regularized in traffic cases that in many communities it is possible to plead guilty by mail to certain minor offenses and enclose a standard fine set forth in the policeman's ticket, which is also designed as an envelope to be used for mailing purpose.

Such routine assessment of fines occurs when two conditions are present: there is a great number of such cases so that the court cannot consider each one individually because of the constraints of time and manpower; and the offense does not touch seriously the value-set of the judge.

In more serious cases, on a plea of guilty, the prosecutor will briefly detail the facts out of which the case arose. Such a statement, which may be slanted, sometimes presents the defense counsel with Hobson's choice. If he permits the statement of the prosecutor to stand without challenge, the court may sentence on the basis of information more damaging to the accused than the defense counsel believes the facts to warrant. On the other hand, the legitimacy of the guilty plea depends on the claim that the accused acknowledges that he is in fact guilty. That acknowledgement and the repentence which it implies is the theoretical justification for the leniency which the defendant hopes to earn by his plea. To challenge the facts as set forth by the prosecutor thus places in jeopardy the entire plea, frequently carefully negotiated and delicately balanced. Accordingly, far more often than not the defense dares not challenge the prosecution's statement of the facts, so that it is only a prosecution's view of the offense that the judge ever hears. This view is of course basically the policeman's suspicions put forward as facts, since the prosecutor derives his information in almost all cases from examining the police file on the case.

In practice, however, the prosecutor only rarely presents Hobson's choice to counsel. The prosecutor, perhaps more than any other official in the criminal process, has an enormous stake in the plea-bargaining system. It is in his interest to ensure that adequate inducements are held out to defendants to plead guilty. Some of these inducements are within his power to provide. The act of sentencing, however, even after the reduction of charge, is nominally at least in the hands of the judge. It is to be expected, therefore, that prosecutors will cooperate in presenting the facts of the offense and the character of the accused in as favorable light as possible after the plea of guilty has been recorded. The *Yale Law Journal*, from 140 replies to a questionnaire sent to all federal district judges in 1956, reported that a number of judges gave as a reason for the lighter sentences delivered after guilty pleas, that frequently brutal aspects of the crime emerge during a trial (thus leading to more severe sentences) that are not brought to light by a prosecutor's statement of the facts.[1]

Finally, the judge may learn the details of the offense from a presentence report. This report has much more significance, however, as a source of information about the offender, which is the second of the significant inputs into the sentencing process that we consider here.

As we saw in our discussion of the principles of sentencing, among the elements to be taken into account is the amenability of the accused to rehabilitative treatment. It follows that if the sentence is to fit not merely the crime but also the criminal, the judge must have some information about the accused person.

In the case of many minor crimes, practically the only information the judge can have about the accused is his superficial appearance in court. More than half the cases dealt with in the courts, even excluding traffic offenses, are relatively minor: drunkenness, disorderly conduct, vagrancy. Typically, sentences for such offenders are meted out quickly if not necessarily justly. Caleb Foote reports that the Municipal Court in Philadelphia disposed of 55 cases in 15 minutes.[2] The offenders in such cases almost invariably are persons who are regarded by the judge as having a degraded status—"winos," beggers, prostitutes, in short the "dregs of the society"—and hence so summary a method of dealing with their fates does not usually seriously disturb the middle-class conscience of the judge. Moreover, the bureaucratic pressures for efficiency, speed, and routine are again at work in subverting the individualized sentencing that is the ideal.

In more serious cases, the burden of describing the accused to the court tends to fall on the defense counsel or the presentence investigation and report. In most jurisdictions, whether or not there is a presentence report, the defense counsel will plead for his client prior to the sentencing, at least when the offenses are serious. Frequently he will introduce letters or affidavits from "respectable" members of the community attesting to the good reputation and work habits of the accused, especially if he is a first offender. Witnesses may even be called—a minister, a teacher, or a doctor—to testify to the defendant's previous good character. The purpose of the defense counsel is to persuade the judge that the accused is basically a person of fine character, who committed the theft or assault in question through a temporary, regrettable, but most unlikely aberration.

The prosecutor's role in presenting information about the character of the accused is generally far more limited. Invariably, he will supply the most weighty bit of information relating to the accused—his previous criminal record—contained in the police files. Beyond that, however, he will only rarely oppose the defense counsel's description of the accused, and that is when he is pressed by the police or adverse publicity to obtain a heavy sentence.

Perhaps the most important source of information about the criminal is the presentence report, now increasingly common in most states. This is a report prepared by a social worker, usually attached to the Probation Department. A typical suggested form requires the case worker to supply information under the following headings: (1) offenses, (2) prior record, (3) family history, (4) home and neighborhood, (5) education, (6) religion, (7) interests and activities, (8) health (physical and mental), (9) employment, (10) resources, (11) summary, (12) plan, and (13) agencies interested.[3] Since the argument and evidence put forward by the defense counsel is obviously and admittedly biased in favor of the accused, it is inevitable that the judge will give great weight to the presentence report, prepared as it is by a professional worker presumably without a personal interest in the case. For example, for the years between 1959 and 1965, the Superior Courts of California followed the probation officer's recommendation of probation between 95.6% to 97.3% of the time. In ten judicial circuits of the United States in 1964, the trial courts followed those recommendations in 94.1% of the cases. The California courts between 1959 and 1965 failed to follow the probation officer's recommendation against probation between 12.8% and 21.6% of the time; and in the ten federal judicial circuits in 1964, the recommendations were not followed in an average of 19.7% of the cases.[4]

Public pressures constitute a significant input into the sentencing system, but one which is difficult to evaluate. That local newspapers have undertaken a campaign against a particular category of crime, or have given special publicity to a particular crime in question, plainly has some effect upon the judge's attitude toward the sentence. The Advisory Council of Judges to the National Probation and Parole Association has formally stated that:

the judge must use public opinion constructively as an aid in sentencing, but not be dominated by it; he must respect it, but not be enslaved by it; he must lead the community toward higher standards of justice and treatment, but not be so far ahead of it that it will lose sight of him.[5]

What this Delphic statement may mean in practice, of course, is anybody's guess, but it does demonstrate that judges do take public opinion into account.

The difficulty, of course, is in determining what is "public opinion." For example, following a serious outbreak of violence in the Chicago ghetto, Mayor Daley issued a statement urging the police to shoot looters. It is only to be expected that judges, in looting cases, would respond to such a statement by imposing relatively heavier sentences in Chicago than in New York, where Mayor Lindsay stated that he did not believe it proper to shoot a teen-ager for stealing a six-pack of beer. In either case, the judge is apt to assume that the mayor's statement *is* public opinion. That there may be substantial elements of the public that disagree with either statement may be disregarded.

In fact, the "public opinion" which a judge will follow is likely to be the public opinion of those whose respect and admiration he regards as important.

An English lawyer (later Lord Chancellor of England) put it nicely in a different context:

The majority of us need the approval of their fellow citizens. Consciously or unconsciously, we spend a good deal of time looking over our shoulder to those whose esteem we value. The Conservative looks to Conservatives, the Socialist to Socialists, the lawyer to lawyers, the husband to his wife . . .[6]

Judges look to the approbation of those in their own reference group—other judges and lawyers first of all, and the upper classes generally. So the "public" opinion to which judges are most apt to defer is in fact middle-class opinion, largely as stated in the public press.

As we have suggested, in cases of pleas of guilty prosecutors rarely seek to put pressure on the court to deliver a particularly heavy sentence, for it is in their interest on such pleas to cooperate with the defense counsel to keep sentences low. They will regularly recommend relatively heavy sentences under two circumstances: at a trial and when the police insist on it. In general, the police measure their success in terms of the clearance rate, which is related to arrest and conviction, not to the severity of the sentence. As a result, they are not usually very much interested in the sentence.[7]

The police do interest themselves in the sentence in three situations. In the first place, when they have bargained for a lower sentence with an accused in exchange for a guilty plea or a confession to other unrelated crimes to help the clearance rate, they will try to persuade the prosecutor, and through him the judge, to act leniently.[8] Secondly, the police will try to obtain a heavier sentence where the arrest has been made by a highly specialized unit dealing with a specific problem, and the offender is an habitual offender who has caused the unit a great deal of trouble.[9] Finally, the police will press for a heavy sentence when the accused has been "fresh," or resisted arrest, or otherwise demonstrated a low opinion of the force.

Most prosecutors take the same position. They must cooperate with the police, for without the latter's cooperation the prosecutor's job is impossible. Many prosecutors will not agree to a reduced charge or promise to recommend a specific sentence to the trial judge without substantial agreement by the police. It is not infrequent for the prosecutor to ask the police if the accused had been properly respectful. In cases in which there are allegations of police misconduct— a false arrest or unnecessary violence—it is quite common for the prosecutor to insist on the defendant's executing a release of the arresting officer personally from liability as a condition for *nolle prosequi* or even for an agreement to permit the accused to plead guilty to a lesser charge.

The personality and value-sets of the trial judge form a most important group of inputs into the sentencing process. In most states the personality of the trial judge has been shaped by the fact that he is likely to have spent a good part of his prejudgeship training as a prosecuting attorney. He is therefore conditioned to a pro-police viewpoint and most likely will adopt the crime-control attitude.

The final significant input into the system is the ability and status of the defense counsel, and the personal relationship between the counsel and the judge. The most important aspect of this input is the character of the defense counsel as a member of the "courthouse regulars" or as a little-known outsider. Judges are interested in clearing their dockets; they, too, must meet the demands of bureaucratic efficiency. They are well aware that the lawyer's livelihood depends on the appearance that he is better able to persuade judges to impose lower sentences than others. Moreover, lawyers and judges are members of the same profession; more likely than not, they are both involved in political activities and, especially in smaller communities, may be connected by a hundred professional ties of cases handled together, and favors given and taken.

21.2 SENTENCING: CONVERSION PROCESSES

All these inputs go into the sentencing process. Out of these various bits of information (or perhaps misinformation), pressures, and interpersonal relationships, the judge must fashion a specific sentence. What are the norms which determine the appropriate elements which the judge ought to take into account and which determine the nature of the decision-making process?

As we saw earlier, in fact there are *no* standards or norms which instruct the judge which elements are to be taken into account in sentencing, and what weight they are to be given. He is presented only with a statute which typically provides very broad limits within which he must set the sentence. In New York, for example, robbery in the first degree is punishable by imprisonment of not "less than ten years" nor "more than thirty years."[10] Rape in the first degree is "punishable by imprisonment for not more than twenty years."[11] Burglary in the first degree is punishable by imprisonment from ten to thirty years, burglary in the second degree "for a term not exceeding fifteen years."[12]

So long as a trial judge stays within such limits in his sentences, and in the absence of a specific statute permitting appeal of sentence (which exists in only a very few jurisdictions), an appellate court will not reduce the sentence merely because it is, in the opinion of the appellate court, excessive.[13] Even where a judge uses multiple successive sentences to increase the statutory maximum, an appellate court will not intervene, however much they may deplore the practice.[14] Nor will they intervene when the trial judge uses evidence of a crime not charged to increase the sentence. For example, in *Peterson v. United States*,[15] the defendant was convicted of the theft of a forty-cent postage stamp. The trial judge imposed the maximum penalty under the statute, stating that "the offense for which the defendant was formally found guilty" was "rather trifling." He continued, however, to say that he believed that Peterson was also guilty of subornation of perjury—a crime not charged—"which was the main reason for the severe sentence imposed." The appellate court refused to intervene in the sentence. In *U.S. v. Sacher*,[16] the federal Court of Appeals went so far as to hold that a trial court's "reason for the length of sentence would not affect its validity and should be ignored on appeal."

The origin of this sweeping and almost unchecked power of the trial judge seemingly lies embedded in the history of punishments in the common law. During the great formative period of the common law, death was the only penalty for crimes of any seriousness and for many that were not serious at all. In 1819, Sir Thomas Fowell Buxton put the number of capital offenses at 223 in England. Leon Radzinowicz maintains that, since many of the statutes in fact covered a variety of crimes, the number ought to be three or four times as much.[17] They made a crazy patchwork without rhyme, plan, or reason, as successive Parliaments mindlessly added felonies without end, each punishable by death without benefit of clergy. Arson of a dwelling house was a capital offense. So was burning a cock of hay or a threat to commit arson. But burning down a field of standing ripened wheat was not even a crime. Serious crimes and frivolous ones intermingled without distinction. If murder was a capital offense, so was the heinous conduct involved in maliciously cutting the hop-binds on the poles holding the hops on any plantation of hops.[18] On the other hand, through some weird oversight it was not even a misdemeanor to steal from a furnished house let as a whole.[19]

This intolerably broad definition of capital offenses came to be cut down by the concurrence of three factors: the frequent commutation of the death sentence by the Crown, the arbitrary understating of the value of stolen property by juries (so that there are cases reported in which juries solemnly held that the value of a £100 note was but 39 shillings, thus preventing the crime from being capital, since capital punishment began at theft of property of a value of 40 shillings); and a series of restrictive interpretations by the judges. It is from the first of these, the exercise of the royal prerogative, that the judges derived their power to assess sentence.

The royal prerogative was always entirely discretionary; it remains so to this day. In practice, punishment by death came to be inflicted on smaller and smaller numbers of those convicted by the courts, the royal prerogative being increasingly used to commute the sentences to transportation. (Indeed, many Americans today are the direct descendants of those thus freed and transported.[20]) The custom arose that judges would send a memorial to the Crown recommending transportation, which came to be followed as a matter of course by the King.[21] In 1768 the judges were in effect given the power to order any person convicted of capital offenses without benefit of clergy to be transported for any term they thought proper, or for fourteen years if no term was specially mentioned.[22] The extent of punishment for clergyable offenses, at the beginning of the eighteenth century usually nothing or at the most imprisonment for a year without hard labor,[23] was slowly increased until in the reign of George IV it included imprisonment not exceeding a year or, in some cases, a whipping, and in cases of petty larceny (and some cases of grand larceny), seven years' transportation.[24]

The power given to the judges to commute death sentences was exercised with increasing frequency. In 1805, in England and Wales, 4605 accused persons were admitted for trial; no bills were found in 730 cases; 1092 were acquitted; of the remaining 2783, 350 were sentenced to death, of whom 68 were executed, 595 were transported, 1680 were imprisoned, and 180 were sentenced to a whipping or a fine.[25]

A great wave of reform of English criminal law, led by Sir John Romilly and Jeremy Bentham, in the course of years worked a seachange over the harshness and virtual anarchy of the earlier English criminal law.[26] The result was that by 1883 (when Stephen wrote), capital punishment no longer existed in England save for a very small number of crimes: treason, murder, etc. The reform did not achieve significant rationalization of the structure of punishments, however. For example, in 1883 it was impossible to sentence a man to more than two years of hard labor or to transportation for less than five years; there was simply no sentence available which would remove anyone from society for a period of between two to five years.[27]

The tradition, however, that any punishment short of death was a matter of grace appeared to have been firmly established. The reformers regarded this extraordinary scope of discretion for the judge as part of the evil of a discretionary criminal law which they sought to change. The cardinal aim of the middle-class reformers was a world of law rather than one run at the discretion of either judges or the aristocracy in general. Romilly urged that judges should not have unlimited discretion as to punishment.[28] Bentham tried to lay down rules for punishment based on his utilitarian calculus of pleasure and pain.[29] This movement received impetus from the continent, where the revolutionary dogma of *nulla poena sine lege* had been developed precisely to eliminate the autocratic system of "arbitrary punishment" imposed by the judges.

The drive to formalize the sentencing structure and the opposing tradition that punishment was a matter of judicial discretion resolved themselves in the practice, eventually established in both England and the United States, that the legislature lays down the maximum (and sometimes minimum) punishment for the crime and within the given ranges the judges have discretion to assess the penalty. This development had a powerful ally in the modern penological principle that punishment should be adjusted to the criminal and not to the crime. The doctrine of giving the judges discretion is thus justified today, not on the ground that it is an outgrowth of the royal prerogative, which was its origin, but on ground of the new principles of penology.

The result is the sharp line drawn between the proof of a criminal act, which is subject to all the requirements of due process, and the factual basis of sentencing.

Tribunals passing upon the guilt of a defendant always have been hedged in by strict evidentiary procedural limitations. But both before and since the American colonies became a nation, courts in this country and in England practiced a policy under which a sentencing judge could exercise a wide discretion in the sources and types of evidence used to assist him in determining the kind and extent of punishment to be imposed within limits fixed by law . . .[30]

As we saw,[31] however, the dominant principle is that sentences serve multiple purposes. Retribution, general deterrence, special deterrence, incapacitation, and rehabilitation are all permissible objectives of correctional treatment. The issue to which the discretion of the sentencing judge must be directed in the first place is how much weight to give to each objective in the case at hand. Where this issue is concerned, neither case law nor statutes provide a guide. As a result, judges can work with their own notions of penological theory without even nominal control by an authoritative principle. Since most judges come to the bench without training in penology either in law school or in their subsequent practice—usually a civil practice—they tend to respond, not to penological theory, but to the popular pressures on them.

The absence of appellate review of sentences has meant that no body of norms for sentencing has been developed.[32] In a rare American opinion discussing the question of sentencing, the court said:

What then should be the punishment inflicted upon the defendant in this particular case? What considerations should weigh in the matter? It must be assumed that the discretion given by the (statute in question) is to be exercised by the jury or the court, as the case may be, on some rational basis, and not in an arbitrary, capricious or whimsical manner. The law, however, furnishes no precedents upon which any theory of determination of the question is to be sought.[33]

It may be doubted, however, that even if appellate courts had the power of review, as they have in a few states and in England, they would develop a coherent body of norms for sentencing. Livingston Hall concludes that

with a few exceptions, the machinery of appellate review of sentences has not been employed by the courts which possess it as a means of establishing any general sentencing policy. The case method of the common law has been rarely applied to sentencing; the courts do not often admit that any two sentences must bear a rational relation to each other, or are specific illustrations of general principles which may be deduced from them.[34]

The English Court of Criminal Appeal has had for a long time the power to alter sentences where it is evident that the judge acted on some wrong principle or overlooked some material factor, or that the sentence is manifestly excessive in view of the circumstances of the case.[35] The most that the Court has done, however, is to articulate a string of maxims of sentencing that, like the rubrics of statutory construction, constitute a handy grab bag from which "principles" can be chosen to justify any given sentence.

A few examples from cases in England and British Africa (where judges follow the English rules) will suffice. The leading case is *Rex v. Ball*.[36] In this case, the court made the following often quoted statement:

In deciding the appropriate sentence a court should always be guided by certain considerations. The first and foremost is the public interest. The criminal law is publicly enforced not only with the object of punishing crime, but also in the hope of preventing it. A proper sentence passed in public can serve the public interest in two days. It may deter others who might be tempted to try crime as seeming to offer easy money on the supposition that if the offender is caught and brought to justice, the punishment will be negligible. Such a sentence may also deter the particular criminal from committing a crime again, or induce him to turn from a criminal to an honest life . . . Our law does not, therefore, fix the sentence for a particular crime, but fixes a maximum sentence and leaves it to the court to decide what is, within that maximum, the appropriate sentence for each criminal in the particular circumstances of each case. Not only with regard to each crime, but in regard to each criminal, the court has the right and duty to decide whether to be lenient or severe.[37]

The difficulty is that when "punishing the crime" (a retributive concept), general deterrence, and special deterrence are both regarded as proper considerations to be weighed, and when there is no standard of appropriate weight to be attached to each, the courts inevitably made decisions which are in principle incompatible.

In *Rex v. Petero Mukasa*,[38] the East African Court of Appeals reduced the sentences for manslaughter pronounced on some peasants who had killed some herdsmen believing that they were thieves, on the ground that there was an indigenous Uganda custom permitting people to kill thieves caught in the act (special deterrence). Two years earlier, the same court in *Rex v. Atma Singh s/o Chanda Singh*[39] had refused to reduce the sentence of a Sikh who had not killed an adulterous wife, but had cut off her nose and ears in accordance with a claimed Sikh custom of thus dealing with unfaithful wives. The court said that the existence of so barbarous a custom demanded not a lighter sentence, but a heavier sentence (general deterrence).

In *Rex v. Ball*,[40] as we saw, the court said squarely that "the first and foremost" interest to be served is the public interest. In *Rex v. Reeves*,[41] the Court of Criminal Appeal in England reduced a sentence so that, because a codefendant had received a much lighter sentence, the accused would not suffer "a strong sense of grievance," which was hardly the primary "public interest."

In *Rex v. Schoenfield*,[42] the English court reduced a 30-year disqualification for a first offender for driving while drunk to five years, "which was a more normal period for this type of offense" (retribution). In *Rex v. Walton*,[43] the same court

SENTENCING AND SENTENCES

reduced a 3-year disqualification for a first offender for driving while drunk to 12 months.

In *Rex v. Kyle*,[44] the court said that it was proper to place an accused, otherwise a fit subject for punishment, on probation where great interest in helping him was shown by a residential community (special deterrence). In *Rex v. Mild and Reynolds*,[45] heavy sentences were upheld in a hire purchase fraud, because "hire purchase frauds are rife at present" (general deterrence).

In *Dowling v. Inspector-General of Police*,[46] the accused was convicted of sodomy. The Nigerian court said that a sentence of six months "cannot be considered excessive" when the maximum sentence for the offense was fourteen years imprisonment. Sodomy, whatever its incidence in England, is rare in Nigeria. In *Queen v. Princewell*[47] another Nigerian court sentenced the accused to one month's imprisonment for bigamy where the statute provided a maximum of seven years, remarking that the fact that polygamy was common in Nigeria distinguished the situation from one in England. The court did not mention the maximum statutory sentence as a guide to the seriousness of the offense.

The list could be increased to enormous length. Given precedents of this sort, even where, as in England and Africa, an appellate court has sought to create a body of norms for sentencing, a trial judge can always unearth a shibboleth sanctified by precedent to justify whatever sentence he wishes to impose. If he believes that a severe sentence is required, he can point to the prevalence of crime in the neighborhood, or the "intrinsic gravity" of the offense, or the past bad record of the accused, or "the normal period for this type of offense." If he wishes to justify a lenient sentence, he can invoke a possible "strong sense of grievance" by the accused, or his personal characteristics, or the relation between his sentence and the maximum sentence proposed by the statute. In sum, appellate review has failed to produce a coherent set of principles for the guidance of judicial sentencing. That it has not done so even in those jurisdictions where appeal of sentence is possible reflects not the incapacity or perverseness of judges, but the inherent ambiguity in our approach to crime and punishment.

In the absence of any norms prescribing what factors are legally significant in sentencing and what weight they are to be given, it is to be expected that the sentencing process has come to resemble not a trial of an issue of fact, but an administrative process.[48]

The essence of due process lies in the concept of an adversary proceeding. The principal consequence of the adversary proceeding is that every assertion made by one side which is subject to challenge will be examined critically before the judge. As a result, the judge will have had called to his attention all the relevant factual information and theoretical material which either side can adduce, so that there is at least a built-in assurance that his decision will not be made in ignorance. The sentencing process, however, is nowhere regarded as an adversary process. A few states do have old statutes which seek to assimilate the sentencing process to trial proceedings. For example, an old Utah statute provides that:

When discretion is conferred upon the court as to the extent of punishment, the court, at the time of pronouncing judgment, may take into consideration any circumstances, either in aggravation or mitigation of the punishment, which may be presented to it by either party.[49]

The circumstances must be presented by the testimony of witnesses examined in open court, except that when a witness is so ill or infirm as to be unable to attend, his deposition may be taken by a magistrate of the county, out of court, upon such notice to the adverse party as the court may direct. No affidavit or testimony or representation of any kind, verbal or written, shall be offered to or received by the court or judge thereof in aggravation or mitigation of the punishment, except as provided by this section.[50]

In most states, however, either judges are expressly authorized to receive evidence of any sort on sentencing, or no prescription at all is made concerning the matter. Even in the states which do require evidence, statutes authorizing presentence investigations and reports are treated in practice as creating an exception to the rule.

The Supreme Court, which has so assiduously constructed a due-process framework for other areas of the criminal law, has nevertheless not extended the constitutional vision of the criminal process into the posttrial proceedings as it has the pretrial proceedings. It did make an abortive excursion into the area, however. In *Townsend v. Burke*,[51] in 1948, the Court was presented with an appellant who had been sentenced to ten to twenty years imprisonment after the following enlightening dialogue:

By the Court (addressing Townsend):
Q. Townsend, how old are you?
A. Twenty-nine.
Q. You have been here before, haven't you?
A. Yes, sir.
Q. *1933, larceny of an automobile*. 1934, larceny of produce. 1930, larceny of a bicycle. 1931, entering to steal and larceny. *1938, entering to steal and larceny in Doylestown.* Were you tried up there? No, no, arrested in Doylestown. That was up on Germantown Avenue, wasn't it? You robbed a paint store. [Italics as in Supreme Court Report.]
A. No. That was my brother.
Q. You were tried for it, weren't you?
A. Yes, but I was not guilty.
Q. And 1945, this. 1936, entering to steal and larceny, 1350 Ridge Avenue. Is that your brother too?
A. No.
Q. *1937, receiving stolen goods, a saxophone.* What did you want with a saxophone? Didn't hope to play in the prison band, did you?
The Court: Ten to twenty in the Penitentiary.[52]

SENTENCING AND SENTENCES

The three italicized charges had in fact all resulted in verdicts or judgments of not guilty. The Supreme Court held that to take these into account, whether by design or carelessness, was "inconsistent with due process of law, and such a conviction cannot stand."

A year later, in 1949, however, the Court decided *Williams v. New York.*[53] In that case, a jury found the accused guilty of first-degree murder, recommending life imprisonment. The trial judge, under a New York statute permitting him to ignore the jury's recommendation, nevertheless sentenced Williams to death. In giving his reasons for imposing the death sentence the judge discussed in open court the evidence upon which the jury had convicted. He added that this evidence had been considered in the light of additional information obtained through the court's "Probation Department, and through other sources." After the accused protested his innocence once again, the trial judge stated that the presentence report had disclosed many material facts concerning the accused's background which could not properly have been brought before the jury in its consideration of the question of guilt. He referred to some thirty burglaries which the accused was said to have committed (although he had been convicted of none of these, and had according to the presentence report, confessed to only some of them). The judge also referred to certain activities of the accused as shown by the probation report, which indicated that the appellant possessed a "morbid sexuality," and classified him as a "menace to society." The accuracy of these statements made by the judge was not challenged by the defense counsel. The Supreme Court of the United States held that the proceeding did not violate the due-process clause because the problems of sentencing were such as to make inappropriate to it the adversary procedures used in a trial.

This is a surprising result in the light of *Townsend*. If a judge chooses not to disclose the contents of a presentence report, there is no knowing whether or not he relied on precisely the sort of information that *Townsend* held it wrong to use as grounds for sentence. (The Court did nod its head in Townsend's direction by a sibylline footnote, that "What we have said is not to be accepted as a holding that the sentencing procedure is immune from scrutiny under the due-process clause," citing *Townsend.*)

The reason for the decision was the manifest conflict between modern notions of sentencing and the concept of due process:

Modern changes in the treatment of offenders make it more necessary now than a century ago for the observance of the distinctions in the evidentiary procedure in the trial and sentencing process. For indeterminate sentences and probation have resulted in an increase in the discretionary powers exercised in fixing punishments.

Under the practice of individualizing punishments, investigational techniques have been given an important role. Probation workers making reports of their investigations have not been trained to prosecute but to aid offenders. Their reports have been given a high value by conscientious judges who want to sentence persons on the best available information rather than on guesswork and inadequate information. To deprive sentencing judges of this kind of information would undermine modern penological policies that have been cautiously adopted throughout the nation after careful consideration and experimentation. We must recognize that most of the information now relied upon by the judges to guide them in the intelligent imposition of sentences would not be available if information were restricted to that given in open court by witnesses subject to cross-examination...[54]

The central reason why the adversary system is thought to provide a legal-rational legitimization for the decision-making process is that a rational decisional process requires that the judge be aware of all the potential alternatives for decision, their possible consequences, and the relevant theories and values, before making a decision. The *Townsend* case demonstrated the real danger that a judge, through error or design, might take into account matters that ought not be taken into account. The judges cannot deny that the minimum requirements of a rational decision in sentencing are that the defendant be at least apprised of the factual matters on which the judge proposes to base his sentence, and that the defendant be permitted to argue against the judge's understanding of these facts. Why have the judges decided that in this one activity of sentencing the procedures which have proved in other contexts to be so attractive to them are not to be used?

The fact that the present sentencing procedure developed in a historical context based on prerogative is not a sufficient explanation. Time and time again we have seen judges impose on the criminal process new norms more closely approximating the due-process ideal. Juries have lost their power to decide the law. The accused was first permitted to have counsel and now must be supplied with one. The rules of evidence have been sharpened to exclude the irrelevant. The courts could readily have decreed a change in the traditional norms controlling sentencing.

Nor is the breadth of the investigation demanded by the newer notions of penology a sufficient explanation. In administrative proceedings requiring a far broader investigation the Constitution has been held to require a hearing, despite the difficulty of proof. In setting the rates for an electric generating company, for example, all three parties involved—the company requesting the increase, the Commission staff, and interested members of the public—customarily introduce testimony on such abstruse and complex subjects as the probable increase in the demand for power over the next decade or more, which involves predictions of population increase, the rate of family formation, the migrations into and away from the area, the probable increase in the use of electrical appliances (such as air-conditioning), the projected increase of industry in the area, the sectoral composition of the industrial expansion expected and hence its relative demand for power, the projected movement of prices in fuel, labor, and equipment, and a myriad of other factors. By contrast, the matters at issue in criminal sentencing are relatively simple.

Part of the reason may lie in the fixed pattern of evidence in a judicial proceeding. In *Williams,* the Court rested its decision in part on this ground:

In addition to the historical basis for different evidentiary rules governing trial and sentencing procedures there are sound practical reasons for the distinction. In a trial before verdict the issue is whether a defendant is guilty of having engaged in certain criminal conduct of which he has been specifically accused. Rules of evidence have been fashioned for criminal trials which narrowly confine the trial contest to evidence that is strictly relevant to the particular offense charged. These rules rest in part on a necessity to prevent a time consuming and confusing trial of collateral issues. They were also designed to prevent tribunals concerned solely with the issue of guilt of a particular offense from being influenced to convict for that offense by evidence that the defendant had habitually engaged in other misconduct. A sentencing judge, however, is not confined to the narrow issue of guilt. His task within fixed statutory or constitutional limits is to determine the type and extent of punishment after the issue of guilt has been determined. Highly relevant—if not essential—to his selection of an appropriate sentence is the possession of the fullest information possible concerning the defendant's life and characteristics. And modern concepts individualizing punishment have made it all the more necessary that a sentencing judge not be denied an opportunity to obtain pertinent information by a requirement of rigid adherence to restrictive rules of evidence properly applicable to the trial.[55]

But this reason is hardly convincing, although this set of mind no doubt contributed to the decision in the *Williams* case itself. After all, judges have been adept at fashioning rules of evidence different from those applicable at a trial to suit the demands of administrative proceedings of all sorts, without holding that the inadequacy of the rules of evidence appropriate to a trial disqualified the hearings or required a complete abandonment of due-process standards.

One of the reasons given by the Supreme Court in *Williams* was, as might have been predicted, the now familiar bureaucratic reason of judicial efficiency. "[T]he modern probation report draws on information concerning every aspect of a defendant's life. The type and extent of this information makes totally impractical if not impossible open court testimony with cross-examination. Such a procedure could endlessly delay criminal administration in a retrial of collateral issues."[56]

Yet even this simple reason hardly explains the sharp contradiction between the due-process standard operative elsewhere in the criminal trial (as in *Townsend*), even in sentencing, and in the actual decision in *Williams.* Whatever the reason may be, however, the consequences of the decision are plain: it leaves the judge wholly in command of the overwhelming majority of criminal cases which end in pleas of guilty, and the majority of the few cases which do go to trial and end in convictions. In all these cases, the discretion of the trial judge is essentially unfettered by norms of decision-making, exposure to public examination, or appellate review. Probably no place in the entire universe of State actions (save, perhaps, in the determinations of local Selective Service Boards) are administrative officers endowed with such wide discretion in the invocation of such awesome powers.

The contradictions that exist in endowing sentencing judges with so much power are very sharp. Due process is still the ideal to which lip service is paid. Some minimal due-process requirements are now usually held sacred. If the defendant has a counsel, he must ordinarily be present on sentencing.[57] Sentences imposed in the absence of the defendant are void.[58] The accused must be heard if he affirmatively requests a hearing, but there is no necessity that he be heard unless he makes the request.[59] Rule 32(a) of the Federal Rules of Criminal Procedure provides that the judge should ask the accused if he has anything to say before imposing the sentence, but it has been held that failure to comply with this rule by a judge does not void the sentence unless the accused has affirmatively requested to be heard and has been refused.[60]

The contradiction is well expressed in *U.S.* ex rel. *Collins v. Claudy.*[61] In that case, the court was presented with the question whether due process required a hearing on the issue of prior convictions in order for the trial judge to impose a sentence, under a recidivist statute, in excess of the maximum ordinarily permissible for the crime charged. In holding that it was, the court said:

Such post-conviction consideration of the question of recidivism serves two important purposes. It is as essential to the establishment of the legal basis of the enhanced sentence as proof of premeditation is in many states for capital punishment for murder . . . At the same time it also enables the court to employ informed judgment in the exercise of its far-reaching discretion whether to impose additional punishment, and how much, on account of such prior conviction and attendant circumstances as the inquiry may reveal. Essential fairness dictates that the disposition of any issue thus determinative of the legal power of the tribunal and thereafter influential upon its discretion to punish a defendant must be after some notice to the accused that the issue is before the court followed by some opportunity to be heard.[62]

A hearing at which the accused is not notified of the evidence against him contained in the presentence report is, of course, hardly a hearing at which the accused can adequately present his case. Nevertheless, the suggestion that rational decision-making requires some sort of a hearing before decision suggests that the continuing requirement to legitimize every phase of the judicial process will at some point in the future resolve the existing contradiction between ideal and practice in favor of the due-process ideal.

At present, however, there are no such curbs on the sentencing judge. What are the consequences of permitting basically middle-class judges, socialized into a profession which in most of its functions serves a middle-class clientele, working within a bureaucratic framework where efficiency and smooth functioning are seen as critically important and where informed cooperation with other bureaucrats (e.g., prosecutors and police officers) are essential to efficient functioning, to have unfettered discretion in the sentencing of criminals who are mainly from the poor and minority groups?

21.3 SENTENCING: OUTPUT

The literature on sentencing is replete with examples of discriminatory, prejudiced, and highly idiosyncratic practices. Judges may develop an attitude of indifference and unconcern for the opinions of others, express highly personal and idiosyncratic values and force these values on persons who come before them.[63]

More than half the cases dealt with in the courts are of minor offenses: drunkenness, disorderly conduct, and vagrancy. The typical procedure for handling such cases is to summarily dispense with the normal legal procedures and to simply mete out sentences as quickly and efficiently as possible. Caleb Foote reports the following observations from the municipal court in Philadelphia:

that morning 56 cases were awaiting when the magistrate opened the daily divisional police court for the district which included the "skid row" and the central city area. These cases were the last items on the morning's docket, and the magistrate did not reach them until 11:04 a.m. In one of the cases there was a private prosecutor, and the hearing of evidence consumed five minutes. As court adjourned at 11:24, this left 15 minutes in which to hear the remaining 55 cases. During that time the magistrate discharged 40 defendants and found 15 guilty and sentenced them to three months terms in the House of Correction.

Four of these committed defendants were tried, found guilty and sentenced in the elapsed time of seventeen seconds from the time that the first man's name was called by the magistrate through the pronouncing of sentence upon the fourth defendant. In each of these cases the magistrate merely read off the name of the defendant, took one look at him and said, "Three months in the House of Correction." As the third man was being led out he objected, stating, "But I'm working...," to which the magistrate replied, "Aw, go on."

The magistrate then called the name of one defendant several times and got no answer. Finally he said, "Where are you, Martin?" The defendant raised his hand and answered, "Right here." "You aren't going to be 'right here' for long," the magistrate said. "Three months in Correction." Another defendant was called. The magistrate stated: "I'm going to send you up for a medical examination—three months in the House of Correction."

A number of defendants were discharged with orders to get out of Philadelphia or to get out of the particular section of Philadelphia where they were arrested. "What are you doing in Philadelphia?" the magistrate asked one of these. "Just passing through." "You get back to Norristown. We've got enough bums here without you." Another defendant whose defense was that he was passing through town added, "I was in the bus station when they arrested me." "Let me see your bus ticket," the magistrate said. "The only thing that's going to save you this morning is if you have that bus ticket. Otherwise you're going to Correction for sure." After considerable fumbling the defendant produced a Philadelphia to New York ticket. "You better get on that bus quick," said the magistrate, "because if you're picked up between here and the bus station, you're a dead duck."

In discharging defendants with out-of-the-central-city addresses, the magistrate made comments such as the following:

"You stay out in West Philadelphia."

"Stay up in the fifteenth ward; I'll take care of you up there."

"What are you doing in this part of town? You stay where you belong; we've got enough bums down here without you."

Near the end of the line the magistrate called a name, and after taking a quick look said, "You're too clean to be here. You're discharged."[64]

Among judges presiding over the Chicago Women's Court during a three-year period, Mary Owen Cameron found wide variation in different judges' propensity to use different kinds of sanctions for persons brought before the court for shoplifting.[65] The proportion of cases found "not guilty" ranged from five percent for one judge to twenty percent of the cases tried by another. One judge gave no "token sentences," while another judge meted out token sentences in fifty-five percent of the cases he handled over this period. The proportions of probation sentences ranged from a low of three percent of the jail sentences in the case of one judge to thirty-one percent of the jail sentences in the case of another judge.

Edward Green's study of sentencing practices in Philadelphia courts revealed similar differences.[66] Green categorized cases by the seriousness of the crime and compared the sentences received. He concludes: "at each level of gravity there are statistically significant differences among the judges in the severity of the sentences imposed."

Inquiries into judicial decision-making have also consistently demonstrated the operation of racial and social-class biases in the decisions of judges. Cameron's findings from the sentencing of women for shoplifting illustrate this. Judges found sixteen percent of the white women brought before them on charges of shoplifting to be "not guilty," but only four percent of the black women were found innocent. In addition, twenty-two percent of the black women as compared to four percent of the white women were sent to jail. Finally, of the twenty-one white women sentenced to jail, only two (ten percent) were to be jailed for thirty days or more; of the seventy-six black women sentenced to jail, twenty (twenty-six percent) were to be jailed for thirty days or more.

Green's Philadelphia study showed similar tendencies of judges to impose sanctions more often and more severely on blacks than on whites. Green notes, however, that in his sample this differential treatment is obviated when prior criminal record is taken into account. Green interprets this to mean that the differential severity with which blacks are treated in the courts does not stem from racial discrimination, but rather, it stems from the fact that blacks are more likely to have a past criminal record. We have already seen in previous sections that at the time of arrest and arraignment, the organization of law-enforcement is such that a black man is much more likely to have a "record" than a white person is. In view of this fact, Green's discovery that past criminal records account for the higher rate and severity of black convictions may indicate no more than persistently biased processing. Nevertheless, if Green's findings are generally applicable, they suggest that at least the sentencing practices of judges are nondiscriminatory. It seems more likely, however, that Philadelphia is unique since these findings contradict the results of other investigations. We cannot answer this question with a great deal of confidence, however, since the other inquiries into sentencing practices were not controlled for seriousness of offenses. We can certainly conclude that blacks receive harsher treatment before the courts than do whites, but we must await further research before we can adequately assess the influence of race as contrasted with other variables such as prior arrest records.

The greater severity of treatment accorded the blacks continues after the sentencing has taken place. Between 1930 and 1964, 3849 persons were executed in the United States (see Table 21.1). Of these, forty-five percent (1743) were

TABLE 21.1   Prisoners executed under civil authority, by offense and race (1930–1964)

Type of offense and race	1930 to 1939	1940 to 1949	1950 to 1959	1958	1959	1960	1961	1962	1963	1964	All years
Total	1667	1284	717	49	49	56	42	47	21	15	3849
White	827	490	336	20	16	21	20	28	13	8	1743
Black	816	781	376	28	33	35	22	19	8	7	2064
Other	24	13	5	1	—	—	—	—	—	—	42
Murder	1515	1064	601	41	41	44	33	41	18	9	3325
White*	804	458	316	20	15	18	18	26	12	5	1657
Black*	687	595	280	20	26	26	15	15	6	4	1628
Other	24	11	5	1	—	—	—	—	—	—	40
Rape	125	200	102	7	8	8	8	4	2	6	455
White	10	19	13	—	1	—	1	2	—	3	48
Black	115	179	89	7	7	8	7	2	2	3	405
Other	—	2	—	—	—	—	—	—	—	—	2
All other offenses†	27	20	14	1	—	4	1	2	1	—	69
White‡	13	13	7	—	—	3	1	—	1	—	38
Black	14	7	7	1	—	1	—	2	—	—	31

*   White includes 18 females, black, 12 females.
†   24 armed robberies, 20 kidnappings, 11 burglaries, 8 espionage (6 in 1942 and 2 in 1953), and 6 aggravated assaults.
‡   Includes two females, both executed in 1953, one for kidnapping and one for espionage.

white and fifty-four percent (2064) were black. Blacks constitute less than thirteen percent of the population; yet they contribute over fifty percent of the persons executed. Blacks are more often arrested for all kinds of capitally punishable offense than are whites, and this may account for the higher frequency of executions. For example, in 1965 there were 6509 arrests for murder and nonnegligent manslaughter in the United States, and fifty-seven percent (3704) of those arrested for murder were blacks. To what extent these arrests are a function of discrimination against the blacks is only a guess at this point. It is pertinent to note, however, that there are many more whites than blacks arrested for "manslaughter due to negligence." (In 1965 there were 1833 whites arrested for this offence and 541 blacks.) The practice of prosecutors to bargain for guilty pleas suggests that this differential in the proportion of arrests for manslaughter by neglicence may in part reflect the propensity of prosecutors to file lesser charges against whites more often than against blacks.

That such an interpretation is plausible receives indirect support from a study by Wolfgang, Kelly, and Nolde, who report that among persons awaiting execution on "death row" in Pennsylvania, twenty percent of the whites, as compared with twelve percent of the blacks, had their death sentences commuted. The difference is even greater for felony-murders than for nonfelony-murders.[67]

It is the black felony-murderers more than any other type of offender who suffer the death penalty. This finding is especially striking when we note that nearly three times more white than black felony-murderers have their sentences commuted.

Regional differences are rather striking. A higher proportion of blacks are convicted and executed in the South than any other section of the country, and they are convicted there for a greater variety of crimes. Between 1930 and 1964, North Carolina executed 263 persons: 207 for murder, 47 for rape, and 9 for "other offenses."[68] Of the 263 persons executed, 199 were blacks and 59 were whites. Thus seventy-six percent of the persons executed in North Carolina during that period were blacks. Execution for rape is an almost exclusively Southern phenomenon. Between 1930 and 1964, there were 455 executions for rape in the United States, and all but twelve of these occurred in the South; ten of the exceptions took place in Missouri, and two in Nevada. Of the 455 persons executed for rape, 405 were blacks, 48 were whites, and 2 were of "other races."

21.4 GUILTY PLEAS AND THE COURT

The discussion of the use of guilty pleas in Section 21.2 was focused on the role of the prosecutor. It is obvious from that discussion that the prosecutor's use of the guilty plea could not work without the complicity of the judges on the bench. If the prosecutor's recommendation for leniency was only occasionally adhered to by the judge, then the ability of the prosecutor to keep his bargain would be undermined. Or if the prosecutor's recommendation that the court impose a minimum sentence on the defendant were given only very cursory consideration by the court, the bargain would fall apart. In actual practice the judge and his decisions are highly influenced by the prosecutors; and thus the ability of the prosecutor to "deliver his promises" is assured. The fact that prosecutors have so much influence on the judges partly reflects the formal organization of the court. The judge is highly dependent on the information provided by the prosecutor and his staff. More important, however, is the fact that the judge will find his end of the legal system functions most effectively and efficiently if he does not interfere with the policies and programs of the prosecutor. Occasionally the close relationship between the prosecutor and the judge involves the joint sharing of graft and payoffs. More typically the cooperative relationship evolves out of the shared interests of the judge and the prosecution in seeing that cases are dealt with expeditiously and with a minimum of strain for the court. This view was succinctly put by Justice Henry T. Lummus when he observed:

a criminal court can operate only by inducing the great mass of actually guilty defendants to plead guilty, paying in leniency the price for the pleas.[69]

Donald Newman has estimated that ninety percent of all criminal convictions are the result of a guilty plea.[70] For the most part these guilty pleas are obtained by promises of less severe sanctioning than what the defendant can anticipate if he pleads not guilty. More often than not, judges take into account the guilty plea and apply less severe sanctions. The *Yale Law Journal* sent questionnaires to 240 federal judges and received responses from 140 of them. Sixty-six percent of the respondents reported that the defendant's plea was "a relevant factor in local sentencing procedure,"[71] and the majority of the judges rewarded the defendant pleading guilty with a less severe sentence than his counterpart who had a trial.

There are any number of reasons why courts and prosecutors look with favor on guilty pleas. In one way or another, all of the reasons come down to the fact that these agencies can operate more efficiently and with less strain if the bulk of the offenders processed plead guilty. It is probable, as the quote from Justice Lummus implies, that the courts would come to a standstill if all defendants insisted on court trials, for at present the available manpower is insufficient to withstand the onslaught of a ninety-percent increase in trials. Furthermore, even if the personnel were available, trials are expensive, time-consuming, and the outcomes are rarely predictable. A guilty plea by the defendant assures that the case will be handled expeditiously. Little is gained even by the defendant by insisting on a trial when the likelihood is to incur a more severe penalty.

These practices and policies may be organizationally effective, but they create still another area of discrimination against the poor and the blacks. Since the guilty plea is obtained by a bargain between the defendant and the court, the benefit to the defendant will depend on the strength of his bargaining position.

The strength of his bargaining position, in turn, is a function of his ability to hire private counsel and of his knowledge of his legal rights and of law generally. Most middle- and upper-class persons arrested for crime may be as ignorant about the law as most lower-class persons, but they can pay for good legal counsel to inform them of their bargaining power. The professional thief is quite sophisticated about the legal system and can also afford legal counsel. It remains for the poor to receive the brunt of the disadvantageous possibilities of "bargain justice." Since the black persons who are processed in the courts tend to be poor, they will be the ones most likely to receive the short end of the "bargain."

The judge's role in Anglo-American law in sentencing allows for at least as great discretion as do the roles of the prosecutor and the police. In some respects, the judge's role is less encumbered by organizational restrictions than is the case with other agencies in the legal system. The fact remains, however, that in actual practice the judges' decisions are likely to be just as much determined by extra-legal factors as the decisions of other law-enforcement agencies. The demands for efficient and orderly performance of the court take priority and create a propensity on the part of the courts to dispose of cases in ways that ensure the continued smooth functioning of the system. The consequence of such a policy is to systematically select certain categories of offenders (specifically the poor and the black) for the most severe treatment. Thus, with all their presumed autonomy and independence from public control, judicial decisions, like decisions at every other level of the law-enforcement system, nevertheless remain a function of the organizational requirements of the legal system to a much greater extent than they are a function of the blueprint that supposedly guides those decisions.

21.5 SUMMARY

The effects of bureaucratization are rarely taken into account when laws are made or when law enforcement agencies are established. Neither are these effects given any consideration when the law is designed to have certain consequences, as when criminal sentences are supposed to serve the broader purposes of society. Yet, in fact, the tendency and necessity to bureaucratize is far and away the single most important variable in determining the actual day to day functioning of the legal system and its effect is clearly shown in the sentencing of offenders. Thus the large number of persons brought before municipal courts for minor transgressions of the law leads to an almost completely automatic sentence for certain types of offenders. Furthermore, even for more serious offenses the pressure to make the decision expeditiously (which is in large part a carry-over from the heavy burden created by the large number of minor offenders handled) leads to the judges relying heavily on the advice of "specialists"—in this case probation and parole officers who make pre-sentencing reports on offenders before the court for sentencing.

Under these circumstances, institutionalized patterns of discrimination against the poor are inevitable. They would no doubt be no less inevitable were the decisions solely in the hands of the judge (as it is ostensibly in the blueprint of the law); but were they solely in the hands of the judge the decisions would at least be more easily identifiable as reflecting the biases of a class. As things now stand, what with the trappings of "experts" and "objective personnel" who are presumably "interested only in the well-being of the offender and society" it is more difficult to discern the operation of bias and institutionalized discrimination against the poor because it is hidden behind a facade of bureaucracy. The judge can point to his "professional staff" as justification for his decisions and the "professional staff" can point to their position as an "expert" for protection against criticism.

It is only when the sum-total of the sentencing is added up that the real picture begins to emerge. Precisely how completely this process disadvantages the poor will be spelled out in the next chapter.

NOTES

1. Comment, "The influence of the defendent's plea on judicial determination of sentence," *Yale Law J.*, **66**, 1956, p. 204 at 218.

2. Caleb Foote, "Vagrancy type law and its administration," *U. Pa. Law. Rev.*, **104**, 1956, p. 605.

3. See Administrative Office of the United States Courts, *The Presentence Investigation Report*, Pub. No. 101 (1943); quoted in a footnote to *Williams v. New York*, 337 U.S. 241, 69 Sup. Ct. 1079, 93 L. Ed., 1337 (1949).

4. Robert M. Carter and Leslie T. Wilkins, "Some factors in sentencing policy," *J. Criminal Law, Criminology, and Police Science*, **58**, 1967, p. 503.

5. Advisory Council of Judges of the National Probation and Parole Association, *Guides for Sentencing*, Carnegie Press, New York, 1957, p. 46.

6. Sir Gerald Gardiner, "The purposes of criminal punishment," *Mod. Law Rev.*, **21**, 1958, p. 117 at 123.

7. Lloyd E. Ohlin and Frank J. Remington, "Sentencing structure: its effect upon systems for the administration of criminal justice," *Law and Contemporary Problems*, **23**, 1958, p. 495.

8. Jerome H. Skolnick, *Justice Without Trial*, Wiley, New York, 1966, p. 175.

9. Ohlin and Remington, *loc. cit.*

10. New York Penal Law, Section 2125.

11. New York Penal Law, Section 2010.

12. New York Penal Law, Section 407.

13. Livingston Hall, "Reduction of criminal sentences on appeal," *Columbia Law Rev.*, **37**, 1937, p. 521.

14. *U.S. v. Steinberg*, 62 F. 2d 77 (2nd Cir., 1932), at 78.

15. 246 Fed. 118 (4th Cir., 1917).

16. 182 F. 2d 416 (2nd Cir., 1950).

17. Leon Radzinowicz, *A History of English Criminal Law and Its Administration from 1750*, Vol. 1, Stevens, London, 1948, p. 5.

18. *Ibid.*, p. 10.

19. *Rex v. Palmer*, 2 Leach 692 (1795).

20. See Sir James F. Stephen, *A History of the Criminal Law of England*, Vol. 1, Macmillan, London, 1883, p. 471.

21. Radzinowicz, *op. cit.*, Vol. 1, pp. 110–111.

22. 8 Geo 3 c. 16.

23. Stephen, *op. cit.*, Vol. 1, p. 468.

24. *Ibid.*, pp. 471–472.

25. Radzinowicz, *op. cit.*, Vol. 1, p. 160.

26. See generally Stephen, *op. cit.*, Vol. 1, pp. 471–480.

27. *Ibid.*, p. 483.

28. Sir John Romilly, "Debates in the year 1810 upon Sir John Romilly's Bills for abolishing the punishment of death for stealing to the amount of forty shillings in a dwelling-house, for stealing to the amount of five shillings privately in a shop, and for stealing on navigable waters," cited in Radzinowicz, *op. cit.*, Vol. 1. p. 329.

29. *Ibid.*, pp. 370–371.

30. *Williams v. New York*, 337 U.S. 241, 69 S. Ct. 1079, 93 L. Ed. 1337 (1949).

31. *Supra*, p. 449.

32. Note, "Due process and legislative standards in sentencing," *U. Pa. Law Rev.*, **101**, 1952, pp. 257–258.

33. *Commonwealth v. Ritter*, 13 D. and C. 285 (Court of Oyer and Terminer, Philadelphia, 1930).

34. Livingstone Hall, "Reduction of criminal sentences on appeal," *Columbia Law Rev.*, **37**, 1937, pp. 521, 575. Reprinted by permission.

35. *Rex v. Shershewsky*, [1912] Times Law Reports 364.

36. 35 Criminal Appeal Reports (England, 1951), 164; [*Rex v. Ball* (No. 2)].

37. 35 Cr. App. Rep. 164 at 165.

38. 11 E.A.C.A. 114 (Uganda, 1944).

39. 9 E.A.C.A. 69 (Kenya, 1942).

40. 35 Cr. App. Rep. (1951), 164 at 165, 166.

41. *The Times*, October 3, 1964.

42. *The Times*, November, 6, 1962.

43. [1963] *Criminal Law Rev.*, 62.

44. [1964] *Criminal Law Rev.*, 68.

45. [1963] *Criminal Law Rev.*, 63.

46. [1961] All N.L.R. (Nigerian Law Reports) 782 (High Court, Lagos), 12.

47. [1963] N.R.N.L.R. (Northern Region Nigerian Law Reports) 54 (High Court, Jos, Northern Nigeria), 12.

48. Kenneth C. Davis, *Discretionary Justice: A Preliminary Inquiry*, Louisiana State University Press, Baton Rouge, 1969, pp. 133–141.

49. *Utah Code Ann.*, Section 77–35–12 (1953).

50. *Ibid.*, Section 77–35–13 (1953).

51. 334 U.S. 736, 68 S. Ct. 1252, 92 L. Ed. 1690 (1948).

52. 334 U.S. at 739.

53. 337 U.S. 241, 69 S. Ct. 1079, 93 L. Ed. 1337 (1949).

54. 337 U.S. at 249.

55. 337 U.S. at 246.

56. 337 U.S. at 250.

57. *Mempa v. Rhay*, 389 U.S. 129 (1967).

58. *Prive v. Zerbst*, 268 F. 72 (N.D. Ga., 1920); *Wilson v. Johnston*, 47 F. Supp. 275 (D. Cal., 1942); *Anderson v. Denver*, 265 F. 3 (8th Cir., 1920).

59. *Shockley v. U.S.*, 166 F. 2d 704 (9th Cir., 1948) cert. den. 334 U.S. 850, 92 L. Ed. 1173, 68 S. Ct. 1502.

60. *Calvaresi v. U.S.*, 216 F. 2d 891 (10th Cir., 1954), reversed on other grounds, 348 U.S. 961, 99 L. Ed. 749, 75 S. Ct. 522, 523.

61. 204 F. 2d 624 (3rd Cir., 1953).

62. 204 F. 2d at 628.

63. Edward Green, *Judicial Attitudes in Sentencing*, Macmillan, London, 1961, p. 6.

64. Caleb Foote, "Vagrancy type law and its administration," *U. of Pa. Law Rev.*, **104**, 1 1956, pp. 605–606. Reprinted by permission of the University of Pennsylvania Law Review.

65. Mary Owen Cameron, *The Booster and the Snitch: Department Store Shoplifting*, Free Press of Glencoe, New York, 1964, pp. 143–144.

66. Green, *op. cit.*, pp. 67–69.

67. Marvin E. Wolfgang, Arlene Kelly, and Hans C. Nolde, "Comparison of the executed and the commuted among admissions to death row," in Norman B. Johnson, Leonard D. Savitz, and Marvin E. Wolfgang (eds.), *The Sociology of Punishment and Correction*, Wiley, New York, 1962, pp. 63–69.

68. These statistics are taken from Frank E. Hartung, "Trends in the use of capital punishment," *Annals of the American Academy of Political and Social Science*, November 1952, and from *The National Prisoner Statistics Bulletin*, Bureau of Prisons, Washington, D.C.

69. Cited in Donald J. Newman, *Conviction: The Determination of Guilt or Innocence Without Trial*, Little, Brown, Boston, 1966, p. 62.

70. *Ibid.*, p. 3.

71. Comment, *supra* (n.1), pp. 206–207.

22

Poverty and the criminal process

The shape and character of the legal system in complex societies can be understood as deriving from the conflicts inherent in the structure of these societies which are stratified economically and politically. Generally, the legal system in its normative strictures and organizational operations will exhibit those norms and those practices that maintain and enhance the position of entrenched power-holders. Those broad principles underlying the legal order are ramified in and attenuated by the organizational aims of complex societies. The logical structure and its empirical implications, uncovered in our analysis of law, order, and power, may be set forth as a set of propositions. We begin with propositions about the relationship between a group's norms and the law:

Propositions
1 One's "web of life" or the conditions of one's life affect one's values and (internalized) norms.
2 Complex societies are composed of groups with widely different life conditions.
3 Therefore, complex societies are also composed of highly disparate and conflicting sets of norms.

4 The probability of a group's having *its* particular normative system embodied in law is *not* distributed equally among the social groups but, rather, is closely related to the group's political and economic position.

5 The higher a group's political or economic position, the greater is the probability that its views will be reflected in the laws.

According to these first five propositions, then, the law will differentially reflect the perspectives, values, definitions of reality, and morality of the middle and upper classes while being in opposition to the morality and values of the poor and lower classes. Given this twist in the content of the law, we are not surprised that the poor should be criminal more often than the nonpoor. The systematically induced bias in a society against the poor goes considerably farther than simply having values incorporated within the legal system which are antithetical to their ways of life. Since, in complex societies, the decision to enforce the laws against certain persons and not against others will be determined primarily by criteria derived from the bureaucratic nature of the law-enforcement agencies, we have the following propositions which explain what takes place within these agencies and the kinds of decisions they are likely to make:

1 The legal system is organized through bureaucratically structured agencies, some of which are primarily norm-creating agencies and others of which are primarily norm-enforcing agencies.

2 The formal role-expectation for each official position in the bureaucracy is defined by authoritatively decreed rules issuing from officials in other positions who themselves operate under position-defining norms giving them the power to issue such rules.

3 Rules, whether defining norm-creating positions or norm-applying positions, necessarily require discretion in the role-occupant for their application.

4 In addition, the rules are for a variety of reasons frequently vague, ambiguous, contradictory, or weakly or inadequately sanctioned.

5 Therefore, each level of the bureaucracy possesses considerable discretion as to the performance of its duties.

6 The decision to create rules by rule-creating officials or to enforce rules by rule-enforcing officials will be determined primarily by criteria derived from the bureaucratic nature of the legal system.

7 Rule-creation and rule-enforcement will take place when such creation or enforcement increases the rewards for the agencies and their officials, and they will not take place when they are conducive to organizational strain.

8 The creation of the rules which define the roles of law-enforcing agencies has been primarily the task of the appellate courts, for which the principal rewards are in the form of approval of other judges, lawyers, and higher-status middle-class persons generally.

9 The explicit value-set of judges, lawyers, and higher-status middle-class persons generally is that which is embodied in the aims of legal-rational legitimacy.

10 Therefore, the rules created by appellate courts will tend to conform to the requirements of legal-rational legitimacy and to the specific administrative requirements of the court organization.

11 The enforcement of laws against persons who possess little or no political power will generally be rewarding to the enforcement agencies of the legal system, while the enforcement of laws against persons who possess political power will be conducive to strains for those agencies.

12 In complex societies, political power is closely tied to social position.

13. Therefore, those laws which prohibit certain types of behavior popular among lower-class persons are more likely to be enforced, while laws restricting the behavior of middle- or upper-class persons are not likely to be enforced.

14 Where laws are so stated that people of all classes are equally likely to violate them, the lower the social position of an offender, the greater is the likelihood that sanctions will be imposed on him.

15 When sanctions are imposed, the most severe sanctions wil be imposed on persons in the lowest social class.

16 Legal-rational legitimacy requires that laws be stated in general terms equally applicable to all.

17 Therefore, the rules defining the roles of law-enforcement officials will require them to apply the law in an equitable manner.

18 Therefore, to the extent that the rules to be applied are potentially applicable to persons of different social classes, the role-performance of law-enforcement officials may be expected to differ from the role-expectation embodied in the norms defining their positions.

Taken as a unit, these propositions represent the basis of a theory of the legal process in complex societies. It is a theory derived essentially from the facts of the operation of criminal law—facts gathered by a large number of researchers into the criminal-law process at each level of the operation.

22.1 POVERTY AND THE LEGAL SYSTEM

The empirical data and the propositions based on them make it abundantly clear that the poor do not receive the same treatment at the hands of the agents of law-enforcement as the well-to-do or middle class. This differential treatment is systematic and complete. It includes the practice by the police and prosecuting attorneys of choosing to look for and impose punishments for offenses that are characteristically committed by the poor and ignoring those committed by the more affluent members of the community. Where offenses are equally likely to be committed by persons from different social classes (such as gambling), the police will look for these crimes in the lower-class neighborhoods rather than in middle- or upper-class neighborhoods. For example, in almost every American community, medical doctors, dentists, and practicing attorneys are the groups most actively engaged in placing bets with bookmakers. This is so not because of the inherently corrupt tendencies of people in these professions but rather because these people can hide substantial amounts of their income and thus avoid paying taxes on that income. They can then afford to gamble with this tax-free money and declare it as gains only when they substantially increase their wealth. They cannot simply spend the money they do not declare, since to do so would mean living at a much higher level than could be justified by their acknowledged income which makes good grounds for being prosecuted for income tax evasion. Hence, professional groups are the most important financial backers of many forms of gambling. Yet the police virtually never attempt to discover this practice and punish the professional people who are gambling, nor do they very often curtail the activities of those who take the bets (except, of course, where these operations are part of a criminal organization, which subject we shall take up shortly). By contrast, persons who bet on or sell policy numbers (a typically lower-class form of gambling) are often subject to arrest and prosecution. Similarly, middle- and upper-class suburbanites who play poker in their own homes are never sought out or prosecuted for gambling (though in most states there are statutes prohibiting this game). But lower-class persons who shoot dice in the alley or hallway of their apartment house (the apartment itself is of course too small to permit such activities) are constantly in jeopardy of legal intervention. To reduce the visibility of gambling, the devotees may be willing to pay someone a "cup" or the "pot" in order to use their apartment for a game. To do so, however, makes the entire group vulnerable, since this solution to the problem of finding space in which to gamble simultaneously increases the ability of the police and prosecutor to make the game appear as one run by "professional gamblers," thereby justifying arrest and prosecution. As we shall see, in most communities in the United States, there is a substantial amount of highly organized gambling activity which takes place with the complicity of the police and the prosecuting attorney's office. The purveyors of these enterprises are generally immune from prosecution. It is ironically the games between friends and acquaintances in lower-class areas which are likely to be chosen for prosecution; similar games among middle- and upper-class members of the community are ignored, as are games handled by truly professional gamblers.

That the selective enforcement by policing agencies is not merely a function of what is most pressingly needed by the society is clearly indicated by a comparison of civil rights law-enforcement and the enforcement of laws prohibiting the use of "dangerous drugs." On the one hand, although riots and general discontent are rampant in the urban areas were black ghettos are concentrated, the laws which prohibit discrimination in employment, unions, and housing, consumer fraud, housing violations, and other protections for the poor are effectively ignored at every level of the government, federal, state, and local. By contrast, despite the preponderance of scientific evidence demonstrating that the smoking of marijuana is a relatively harmless pastime (less harmful, most experts agree than drinking alcohol), laws prohibiting marijuana smoking are enforced vigorously. With respect to unfair employment, housing, and labor practices, enforcement would involve the enforcement agencies in conflicts with politically powerful groups. The federal government, for example, would be involved in serious conflict with the politically powerful trade unions if the section of the National Labor Relations Act prohibiting discrimination in unions were enforced. And if sanctions were inflicted for discrimination in employment, as it can be under Title VII of the Civil Rights Act of 1964, the federal and state governments would be at loggerheads with many of the nation's leading corporations. It is to avoid such clashes that only fourteen of some eight thousand complaints received by the Department of Justice between 1965 and 1968 complaining of discrimination in employment resulted in litigation.[1]

On the other hand, since marijuana smokers were, until quite recently, concentrated among the poor black and Chicano (Mexican-American) populations in the United States, these laws could be enforced at the will of the enforcement agencies and indeed they were. Recently, the spread of marijuana and other "drugs" to middle- and upper-class youths has increased the population of "criminals" substantially. It has also brought into public view some of the problems of selective enforcement which characterize America's legal process. It is possible that this increased visibility of police activities will bring about changes in policy and law. It is unlikely, however, that these changes will substantially alter the tendency of the legal system to select for enforcement laws dealing with acts of the poor.

Since 1941 there has been a constant stream of executive orders prohibiting discrimination in employment by any company holding government contracts. The latest order, Executive Order 11236 issued in 1965, is one of the most stringent. Despite the increased stringency of these executive orders, and despite the fact that most of the companies holding government contracts are covered by these orders, *there has never been a single contract with the government canceled nor sanctions applied because of job discrimination by the employer*,[2] though there are administrative board findings clearly showing discrimination in employment by companies holding government contracts.

By way of digression, this is an appropriate place to point out that it is because of the very great and real gap between "laws" and "enforcement" that the generally held ideal of a "fair" and "just" system of law can be maintained despite widespread tendencies subverting these goals. For few people would be so cynical as to doubt the sincerity of an executive order decrying discrimination in employment and providing for the cancelation of contracts with companies who engage in such practices. Yet the truth of the matter is that the order is totally meaningless; if the sanctions are never imposed and if the enforcement agencies do not seek out violators, it is apparent that the executive order does nothing— it is a rhetorical ritual, empty of content, whose principal significance is the acknowledgement of the need to placate dissentors. It succeeds indeed only in providing a false sense of the inherent justice of the system.

Perhaps the best way to grasp the all-encompassing nature of the differential treatment of the poor in the American legal system is through case studies. The intensive patrol by the police in slum areas presents a constant threat to everyone in the community, whether they are engaged in illegal activities or not.[3]

Case 1. Ralph worked the four-to-twelve shift in a factory. After work one night he decided to work on his car before going to sleep. Since he had no garage, the only place to work on the car was in the street. He was working on the engine, with the hood up when a policeman stopped and asked him what he was doing. He explained that he was fixing his car. The policeman asked to see his driver's license and registration card. Ralph showed these and the policeman left. Within five minutes another policeman had stopped and essentially the same scene took place. Five minutes after the second policeman left, a third patrol car turned the corner and asked Ralph what he was doing. According to the policeman and Ralph the conversation went like this:
Officer: Whatcha doing to the car, son?
Ralph (angrily): I'm stealin' the motherfucker.

Ralph was arrested and taken to the station. Later he was released after questioning by the lieutenant.

If a policeman suspects that someone had done something wrong, then the pattern of discriminatory treatment of the poor continues. The following case, adapted from the President's Crime Commission Report,[4] is illustrative of the kinds of problems encountered by the poor as they make their way from arrest through trial and conviction:

Case 2. Defendant A is spotted by a foot-patrol officer in the skid-row district of town, weaving along the street. When the officer approaches him, the man begins muttering incoherently and shrugs off the officer's inquiries. When the officer seizes his arm, A breaks the hold violently, curses the officer and the police. The patrolman puts in a call for a squad car, and the man is taken to the precinct station where he is booked on a double charge of drunkenness and disorderly conduct.

In the stationhouse
Defendant A's belt is removed to prevent any attempts at suicide, is put in the drunk tank to sober up.

His cellmate lies slumped and snoring on the cell's single steel bunk, sleeping off an all-day drunk, oblivious to the shouts ... There are at least two men in each 4 × 8 foot cell and three in some ... The stench of cheap alcohol, dried blood, urine and excrement covers the cell block. Except for the young man's shouts, it is quiet. Most of the prisoners are so drunk they gaze without seeing, unable to answer when spoken to. There are no lights in the cells, which form a square in the middle of the cell block. But the ring of naked light bulbs on the walls around the cell block throw the light into the cells, each of which is equipped with a steel bunk. There are no mattresses. "Mattresses wouldn't last the night," a policeman explains. "And with prisoners urinating all over them, they wouldn't be any good if they did last." The only sound in the cell block is the constant flowing of water through the toilets in each cell. The toilets do not have tops, which could be torn off and broken.

Every half hour or so a policeman checks to see if the inmates are "still warm."

After sobering up, a drunk or disorderly can usually leave the lockup in four or five hours if he is able to post the collateral ($10–$25). No matter how many times he has been arrested before, he will not have to appear in court if he chooses to forfeit the collateral. The drunk without money stays in jail until court opens the next morning. At 6 a.m., the police vans come to collect the residue in the precinct lockups and take them to the courthouse cell blocks to await a 10 a.m. arraignment.

Preliminary hearing and arraignment
Defendant A, charged with drunkenness and disorderly conduct, is brought into court from the bullpen in a shuffling line of dirty, beat, unshaven counterparts, many still reeking of alcohol. Each spends an average of 90 seconds before the judge, time for the clerk to intone the charge and for the judge to ask if he desires counsel and how he pleads. Rarely does a request for counsel or a "not guilty" break the monotony of muttered "guilty" pleas. Lawyers are not often assigned in police courts, and anyone who can afford his own counsel will already have been released from jail on bond—to prepare for trial at a later date or to negotiate with the city prosecutor to drop the charges.

Occasionally, an unrepresented defendant will ask for trial. If the arresting officer is present, he will be tried on the spot. There are no jury trials for drunkenness. The policeman will testify that the man was "staggering," "his breath smelled of some sort of alcholic beverage," his speech was "slurred," "his eyes were bloodshot and glassy." The man may protest that he had only a few drinks, but there are no witnesses to support his testimony, no scientific evidence to establish the level of alcohol in his blood at the time of arrest, no lawyers to cross-examine the officer. If the defendant pleads not guilty and hopes he can get counsel (his own or court-assigned), he may have his trial postponed a week or two. Meanwhile, he must make bond or return to jail.

Police-court sentencing is usually done immediately after a plea. A few courts with alcoholic rehabilitation court clinics may screen for likely candidates—

those not too far along on the alcoholism trail—in the detention pens. Counsel, when available, can ask for a presentence report, but delay in sentencing means jail or bail in the meantime. On a short-term offense it is seldom worth it. Other kinds of petty offenders—disorderlies, vagrants, street-ordinance violators— follow a similar route in court. Guilty pleas are the rule. Without counsel or witnesses, it is the defendant's word against that of the police. Even when counsel is present, defense efforts at impeachment founder on the scanty records kept by the police in such petty offenses. The only defense may be the defendant's word, which is suspect if he has a record, or hard-to-find "character witnesses" without records from his slum neighborhood.

Because the crime is more serious, the poor defendant accused of a felony fares even worse than one who is accused of a misdemeanor. Frequently the difference between a misdemeanor and a felony charge is the result of police work to a greater extent than it is a result of the defendant's criminal act. The following case from Chambliss' research is illustrative.

Case 3. Louie, a black militant active in organizing the black community in a middle-sized western city, had failed to pay two traffic tickets. One ticket was for running a stop sign (at three miles an hour); another was for driving without a tail light on his car. A warrant was issued for his arrest. The police pursued him into the night and confronted him at 11:00 p.m. with the warrant. He was approaching his car when the policeman commanded him to place his hands on the top of his car and allow them to search him. He did so, and as he took the stance with his legs spread apart, the policeman kicked his legs to make him spread them apart more widely. After searching him, the policeman handcuffed him and began pushing him across the street to the police car. The policeman also pushed him as he started into the car, causing Louie to hit his head against the top of the automobile.

A friend of Louie's, Dan, was in a nearby cafe when someone came in and told him Louie was being arrested. Dan confronted the officer and demanded to know what Louie was being arrested for. The policeman informed Dan that if he wanted to accompany them to the police station to see that Louie was not mistreated he could. Dan entered the car and went with Louie and the policeman to the station.

Dan and Louie argued vehemently at the police station and accused the police of being "white racists" and of arresting them because they were black. Louie was shoved down to the floor and taken by force into the elevator and to the jail. Dan began to leave the station but was informed that he, too, was under arrest for "obstructing arrest." Dan tried to leave and was forcefully restrained. The Police filed charges as follows:

Louie: charged with resisting arrest, public intoxication, and disorderly conduct (all misdemeanors).
Dan: charged with public intoxication, disorderly conduct, resisting arrest, and battery against a police officer.

The last charge, battery against a police officer, is a felony in the state and, as such, carried with it a possible prison sentence. The alleged battery came about when Dan "threw a pendulum which he was wearing around his neck at a police officer." The policeman claimed to have had his hand nicked by the pendulum.

Bail for Louie was set at $650. He was immediately released when friends posted bond, by paying a bail bondsman $65, which of course is never returned no matter what the result of the trial. Dan could not be bailed out until the hearing the next day, since a hearing is necessary to set the bail in felony cases. Since the arrest occurred on Friday, Dan had to spend the entire weekend in jail.

Friends contacted a lawyer. Dan and Louie insisted they were innocent. The lawyer agreed to talk to the district attorney. The lawyer they hired was with one of the best-known firms in the city. He arranged a bargain with the prosecuting attorney so that in exchange for a guilty plea to the disorderly conduct charges (and a possible six-months jail sentence or up to $1000 fine) the prosecution would drop the other charges. Louie and Dan said they wanted to plead not guilty. The lawyer then informed them that (a) if they pleaded guilty to the lesser offense, his fee would be $500, but (b) if they chose to plead not guilty and the case went to trial (which it probably would), his fee would be a minimum of $1500. He also told them that if they wished, they could ask for a court-appointed lawyer, and he acknowledged that court-appointed lawyers were sometimes excellent.

Ultimately, the men were able to raise $1500 (by a campaign for funds to defend themselves), and the case went to trial. Within two days of testimony the entire case was dismissed without ever going to the jury on the ground that the prosecution did not have sufficient evidence for bringing the case to court. At the hearing, the judge criticized the prosecution and pointed out the expense that the county had incurred. He failed to make note of the expense it had caused Louie and Dan. The two men who were accused of crimes which they did not commit and which were escalated by police because the latter's insensitivity and belligerence had elicited harsh words from Louie and Dan, were exonerated. But the whole episode cost them over two thousand dollars (the lawyer's fee turned out to be two thousand instead of fifteen hundred) and several nights in jail.

Case 4. The previous case contrasts sharply with that of Joe, who was arrested for disorderly conduct and malicious mischief against personal property. Joe was a black man who had been sharing an apartment with two white men. The three of them had an argument, and Joe broke some furniture in the apartment and cussed out his roommates. He moved from the apartment two days later, and one of the former roommates pressed charges. Joe was arrested. He spent the night in jail until he raised $125 to pay the bail bondsman (again, not refundable no matter what the outcome of the trial) so he could be released. The bondsman would *not* have been willing to provide bond except for the fact that Joe's employer signed the bond and put his home up for collateral. Joe asked for and was assigned a court-appointed lawyer. The lawyer encouraged Joe to plead guilty to whatever the prosecutor would offer. Joe refused. The lawyer requested that he be withdrawn from the case because he was "about to go on vacation." A new lawyer was appointed. Joe went to the new lawyer's office, and explained what had happened. He told the lawyer that he had witnesses that the property damages consisted of only a plate and that he had not assaulted anyone. The second lawyer suggested that he see still another lawyer, and the court appointed a third one. Each lawyer encouraged Joe to plead guilty. None of them acknowledged that he was being accused unjustly. Meanwhile, the man who had filed the original charge withdrew it and asked the prosecuting attorney's office to drop the charges.

The prosecuting attorney's office refused to do so and determined to pursue the case. After several weeks of postponement, indecision, and changing lawyers, during which no one would give Joe the satisfaction of telling him that he could perhaps win in a court fight, Joe pleaded guilty because, in his words, "I'm tired of all this fucking around, Chambliss." He was sentenced to three months in the county jail. As a consequence, he lost his job and had to drop out of a remedial reading program in which he was enrolled.

For the indigent, free representation by a lawyer is available in two ways: the court may appoint a lawyer chosen from a list supplied by the local bar association or, in states and communities with a public defender system, an indigent defendant may be assigned a public defender. In both instances, whether or not the defendant is indigent and therefore eligible for a court-appointed lawyer or a public defender is a question that must be decided by the judge. Standards of indigency are in no way prescribed and vary considerably from one judge to another:

Case 5. The defendant was charged with petty larceny. He had allegedly stolen a $19.95 sleeping bag from a Sears department store. He was brought to the courtroom handcuffed after spending a night in jail awaiting his preliminary hearing. The judge asked if he could afford a lawyer.
Def: No sir, I would like to have one appointed by the court.
Judge: It's up to me to decide whether or not you should have one appointed by the court. Do you work?
Def: Yes Sir.
Judge: What do you do?
Def: I make sandals.
Judge: How much do you earn making sandals?
Def: About $40 a month.
Judge: Can you live on $40 a month?
Def: (nods yes)
Judge: Do you own any personal property?
Def: No.
Judge: Any musical instruments?

Def: Yes, a sitar.

Judge: How much does a sitar cost?

Def: I paid $150 for it.

Judge: O.K., you can sell your sitar and hire your own attorney. Hearing is set for tomorrow at 11:00 a.m.

Def: How can I sell it and get a lawyer while I'm in jail?

Judge: You'll have to work that out for yourself.

But even when the indigent is assigned a free lawyer, as the case of Joe illustrates, the court-appointed lawyer will conscientiously pursue the best interests of his client only if he can put professional duty without reward of money or status ahead of other more lucrative employment. Even where the state provides public defenders, as was pointed out earlier, the tendency is for the public defender simply to become a pawn of the prosecuting attorney's office. In any event, it is a simple maxim that the best disposition of a poor defendant from the standpoint of the practicing attorney, public defender, prosecuting attorney, judge, police—indeed, everyone in the legal system—is to convince the defendant in one way or another that he should plead guilty to something and throw himself on the mercy of the court. Given the disadvantageous position of the impoverished when confronted with the legal system, it is not surprising that most defendants are coerced into doing just that. It is unlikely that many of them are met with the mercy they plead for.

NOTES

1. William F. Ryan, "Uncle Sam's betrayal," *The Progressive*, May 1968, pp. 25–28.

2. *Ibid.*, p. 25.

3. Field notes of William J. Chambliss.

4. President's Commission on Law Enforcement and Administration of Justice, *Task Force Report: The Police*, U.S. Government Printing Office, 1967.

23

The relationship between organized crime, professional theft, and the criminal process

Professional thieves and organized criminals enjoy an immunity from criminal prosecution second only to the immunity enjoyed by the very wealthy. This immunity appears at first glance to contradict the general principle that the law will be enforced most stringently against the poorest members of the community. This apparent contradiction evaporates when we realize, first, that the upper echelons of the organized-crime syndicate and the more successful professional thieves are in fact not poor (though they may have been poor at the beginning of their careers) and, second, although they live socially and economically outside the pale of "respectable" society, their activities are in fact convenient and rewarding for the law-enforcement agencies. For these reasons, the exceptional status of the organized criminal and professional thief is in reality simply a further illustration of the general principles that shape the criminal-law process.

Writing in the early 1900's, Lincoln Steffens observed that "the spirit of graft and of lawlessness is the American spirit."[1] He went on to describe the results of his inquiries:

in the very first study—St. Louis—the startling truth lay bare that corruption was not merely political; it was financial, commercial, social; the ramifications of boodle were so complex, various and far reaching, that our mind could hardly grasp them . . . St. Louis exemplified boodle; Minneapolis, police graft; Pittsburgh, a political and industrial machine; Philadelphia, general civic corruption . . .

In 1938, Frank Tannenbaum made a similar observation:

It is clear from the evidence at hand that a considerable measure of the crime in the community is made possible and perhaps inevitable by the peculiar connection that exists between the political organizations of our large cities and the criminal activities of various gangs that are permitted and even encouraged to operate.[2]

The Kefauver Commission summed up the results of its extensive investigation into organized crime in 1951 by observing:

1 There is a Nation-wide crime syndicate known as the Mafia, whose tentacles are found in many large cities. It has international ramifications which appear most clearly in connection with the narcotics traffic.

2 Its leader are usually found in control of the most lucrative rackets in their cities.

3 There are indications of centralized direction and control of these rackets, but leadership appears to be in a group rather than in a single individual.[3]

And in 1969, Donald R. Cressey, using data gathered by the Attorney General of the United States and local crime commissions, summed up the state of organized crime: .

In the United States, criminals have managed to organize a nation-wide illicit cartel and confederation. This organization is dedicated to amassing millions of dollars from usury and the illicit sale of lottery tickets, chances on the outcome of horse races and athletic events, and the sale or manipulation of sexual intercourse, narcotics, and liquor.[4]

The same general conclusion can be reached from the frequency with which major scandals break out in cities, linking organized criminals with major political and legal figures. Detroit, Chicago, Denver, Reading (Pennsylvania), Columbus (Ohio), Cleveland, Miami, New York, Boston, and a host of other cities have all been scandalized and cleaned up innumerable times. Yet organized crime persists and, in fact, thrives. Despite periodic law-enforcement forays, exposés, and reform movements prompted by journalists, sociologists, and politicians, organized crime has become an institution in the United States and many other parts of the world. How is this possible?

23.1 THE LAW AND PROFESSIONAL CRIMINALS: A STUDY IN SYMBIOSIS[5]

At first glance it seems that the professional criminal (be he a thief, gambler, prostitute, or hustler) could not be immune from punishment since he lacks an adequate base of political power. It therefore seems *unlikely* that a set of mutually advantageous relationships would emerge between law-enforcement agencies and professional criminals. In fact, our first impression is quite erroneous. Given the criteria by which law-enforcement agencies are judged and the conflicting pressures they are subjected to, it is virtually impossible for a law-enforcement system to operate effectively and efficiently without developing policies and practices which are mutually advantageous to the legal system *and* to professional criminals. This is of course the point made by Tannenbaum in the passage quoted above.

To understand more clearly this process of symbiosis, it will be well to consider, first, the peculiar relationship which develops between the professional thief and the legal system and, next, the relationship between other types of professional crime, especially gambling, drug distribution, and prostitution, which develops in urban centers.

The Professional Thief

Observers of crime in urbanized complex societies have often noted the considerable degree to which professional thieves enjoy immunity from the imposition of legal sanctions. A survey in Massachusetts conducted in 1933 of a group of eighty habitual offenders, many of whom presumably were professional thieves, disclosed some interesting facts. The eighty offenders had each been brought before the court between 9 and 103 times. Charges against them had been as follows: homicide 14; assault and battery 103; driving under the influence of alcohol 31; larceny 324; robbery 59; breaking and entering 154; larceny of auto 84; forging 12; receiving stolen goods 18; carrying concealed weapons 16; violations of narcotics laws 16; violations of liquor laws 71; and miscellaneous offenses 10. These charges represent a total of 912 cases involving this group of persistent offenders. The following table[6] shows the percentage of the final dispositions:

Dismissed	13% ($N = 118$)
No prosecution paper filed	3% ($N = 27$)
No bill	3% ($N = 29$)
Acquittal	12% ($N = 113$)
On file	14% ($N = 136$)
Suspended sentence	6% ($N = 51$)
Probation	14% ($N = 130$)
Prison sentence	25% ($N = 228$)
Fined	6% ($N = 54$)
No record and pending	3% ($N = 26$)

It is noteworthy that of these eighty offenders who accounted for 912 felonies, twenty were categorized officially as "public enemies." Despite the fact that these individuals were among the most serious violators of the law in Massachusetts at the time, only one-fourth of them received prison sentences.

These statistics are not peculiar. Indeed, they represent a fairly typical pattern throughout complex societies. How is this possible? The simple fact is that professional thieves are in a position to provide considerable benefit to agencies responsible for law-enforcement. And, more significantly, without cooperating with professional criminals, the agencies would not be able to function as efficiently as when they do cooperate.

A professional thief is in a position to perform a number of services for law-enforcement agencies. In return for these services, of course, the thief is rewarded by receiving only occasional sentences for criminal activities (if he receives any at all) and a host of other considerations which reduce the likelihood that he will be sent to prison.

To begin with, the professional thief can substantially aid law-enforcement agencies by promoting their appearance of being highly efficient in apprehending criminals. The law-enforcement agencies can scarcely control the number of crimes reported to them. And it is one of the facts of law-enforcement that it is exceedingly difficult in most instances to find the person who has committed a criminal offense. On the other hand, law-enforcement agencies are, to a large extent, judged by persons who control their resources, and indirectly by the public, on the number of crimes known to have been committed for which they make arrests. The professional thief is in an ideal position to help law-enforcement agencies maintain an appearance of efficiency and expertise in solving crimes, because he experiences no particular loss of status or of anything else by admitting that he had committed a large number of crimes. Thus, when confronted by a policeman or prosecutor with the proposition that they will "go easy" on him for a known offense if he agrees to admit having committed a large number of offenses that have not been solved by the police, the professional thief has everything to gain from such an agreement. Although this practice may undermine the whole thrust of the law, the fact remains that it is one which is organizationally sensible for law-enforcement agencies to engage in. The practice is called "clearing the books" and is used by police departments everywhere as a means of "solving" crimes.

Another service which the professional thief can perform for law-enforcement agencies is to provide important information. One type of information which law-enforcement agencies must frequently need is the name of the thief who committed a particular crime. While most victims of crime may not possess the power to disrupt the law-enforcement system, some few are in a position to do so. As a consequence, the law-enforcement agencies must be able to solve some crimes with greater efficiency than they do others. And if they have a working arrangement with some professional thieves in the community, then the recapturing of stolen goods in a particular crime is facilitated. The professional thieves are often able to provide the name of the person who committed the crime and his whereabouts much more rapidly than most law-enforcers can do by themselves. In this way also, then, the law-enforcement agencies can use professional thieves to help them maintain the image of an effective and efficient force. But, once again, the return for such favors is in one way or another a license for the professional thief to practice his trade.

Finally, and this is probably the most important means by which professional criminals maintain their legal immunity, there is the bribe. Professional thieves consistently claim that it is possible to "fix" almost any case in any city in the United States. Probably this is easier to do in some countries and more difficult to do in others than in the United States. Typically every community has a lawyer who is known to the law-enforcement agencies and the professional thieves as "the fix." His job is to take care of any charges brought against a professional thief. For this service the thief pays a high fee. In contemporary America the fee is frequently about $5000. The criminal lawyer who acts as a fix has extensive contacts with political leaders in the community and especially with judges and prosecuting attorneys. He is able to obtain a fix for a professional thief under some circumstances by paying money directly to the prosecuting attorney or a judge. If money is not the commodity which suffices to obtain a special favor needed, then the criminal attorney will develop other wedges to serve the purpose. This frequently involves him in making sizable contributions to political campaigns electing prosecuting attorneys or which will ensure the appointment of certain judges to the bench. At times the criminal attorney operates by obtaining evidence of criminal activities of some sort on the part of judges. For example, in one community studied, the criminal attorney gained favors from one of the judges by threatening to expose the judge's homosexuality if he did not comply with his demands.

More often than not, however, the relationship between the criminal attorney and the various officials in the legal system is a highly cooperative one which is mutually beneficial to everyone concerned. For the fact of the matter is that the judge and the prosecuting attorney who are willing to permit professional thieves to enjoy considerable immunity from criminal prosecution, are likely to be among the most successful people in the system. The general public and political figures are ordinarily ignorant of the immunity enjoyed by professional thieves, so that the system is enhanced by this symbiotic relationship between the thieves and the law-enforcers, without having this relationship in any way jeopardize the positions of the role incumbents or the organizations to which the latter belong. On the contrary, as we pointed out earlier, the entire organization maximizes its rewards and minimizes its strains by adopting just such a set of practices.

The Law and Organized Crime

Organized crime flourishes in the United States and is an intimate part of the political and economic structure of virtually every city and state. It has a similar stranglehold on many cities in other parts of the world. Whether organized crime represents one unified organization or a highly diversified group of organizations which operate in different areas of the country remains a subject of debate. Social scientists, until recently, tended to think that the existence of a "Mafia" or "Cosa Nostra" type of criminal organization dominating illegal activities throughout the country is a figment of fiction writers' imagination. Recently, however, Donald Cressey has systematically analyzed the data on organized crime obtained from the Attorney General's office and concluded that there is indeed such a nation-wide organization.

Since the data on the scope and character of organized crime in America come almost exclusively from informants and police wire-taps, they are sketchy and incomplete. Putting the pieces together, however, we find that the picture that emerges is best characterized as a confederation of groups which have organized criminal activities in various cities throughout the United States. The first successful steps at national organization took place in 1931, when a series of territorial disputes between rival local criminal organizations threatened to destroy the lucrative business of crime. A small group of representatives with interests in several cities met and agreed on the establishment of a decision-making hierarchy which divided up the then existing metropolitan areas of the country. Shortly after this meeting, assignments were made and the various groups moved into their territories and eliminated whatever competition existed. Significantly, many areas of the country were untouched by this organization. As a consequence, cities like Las Vegas (Nevada), Los Angeles, Seattle (Washington), and Portland (Oregon)—which were at the time simply "wastelands" of too little consequence to warrant the interests of the recently formed national organization—were left untouched. Local entrepreneurs were thus left to develop their own organizations to handle different types of criminal activities in these areas. Later, when organized crime attempted to move into these areas, it found through several murders that local syndicates had already been sufficiently entrenched with the police and other law-enforcement agencies that the territories could not be readily taken over.

From the standpoint of the sociology of legal systems, the most important aspect of the widespread presence of organized crime (whether organized locally or nationally) is that such organizations are impossible without the cooperation of the legal system. Malcolm X in his autobiography makes this point in reflecting on his past and his experiences with one of the "madams" in New York:

She would talk to me about the Dutch Schultz days—about deals that she had known, about graft paid to officials—rookie cops and shyster lawyers right on up into the top levels of police and politics. She knew from personal experience how crime existed only to the degree that the law cooperated with it. She showed me how, in the country's entire social, political and economic structure, the criminal, the law and the politicians were actually inseparable partners.[7]

At the very root where organized criminal syndicates emerge lies the legal structure itself. The laws prohibiting gambling, prostitution, drug use, and high interest rates on personal loans are laws about which there is a conspicuous lack of consensus. Whatever consensus may exist in the generalized notions proscribing rape, murder, aggravated assault, and theft—and we have suggested that that consensus ends where the actual laws begin—disappears abruptly when one turns to the laws controlling other types of activities. Furthermore, even among persons who agree that gambling, prostitution, and drug use are improper activities and should be controlled by law, there is considerable disagreement as to what the proper legal approach to them should be. (Should persons found guilty of committing such acts be imprisoned or counseled?) Finally and perhaps most important, there are large groups of people, some with considerable political power, who insist on their right to enjoy these pleasures without interference from law-enforcers. And, of course, there is an equally important group of persons who are willing to provide such illegal services if they can command a sufficient price to warrant taking the risk.

The law-enforcement system is thus placed squarely in the middle of two essentially conflicting demands. On the one hand, it is their job to "enforce the law," albeit with discretion; on the other hand, there is considerable disagreement as to whether or not certain particular activities should be declared criminal. The conflict is complicated by the fact that there are some persons of influence in the community who insist that all laws be rigorously enforced while other influential persons demand that some law *not* be enforced, at least not against *them*.

Faced with such a dilemma, the law-enforcers are likely to do what any well-managed organization would do under similar circumstances: follow the line of least resistance. They resolve the problem by establishing procedures which minimize organizational strains and provide the greatest promise of rewards for the organization and the individuals involved. Typically what this means is that the law-enforcers adopt a "tolerance policy" toward the vices and selectively enforce those laws only when it is to their advantage to do so. Since those demanding enforcement are generally middle-class persons who rarely go into the less prosperous sections of the city, by selective enforcement of the laws only in certain ecological locations, the enforcers can appease both those persons who demand the enforcement of the applicable laws and those who are politically powerful and who oppose enforcement at least against themselves.

Another advantage deriving from such a policy is that the legal system is in a position to exercise considerable control over potential sources of "real trouble." Violence which may accompany gambling can be controlled by having the cooperation of the gamblers. Since gambling and prostitution are profitable, there will be competition among persons who want to provide these services. This competition is prone to become violent, and if the legal system is not in control of those who are running the vices, competing groups may well go to war to obtain dominance in the rackets. If, however, the legal system cooperates with one group, then there may be a sufficient concentration of power to prevent these uprisings. Prostitution can be kept "clean" if the law-enforcers cooperate with the prostitutes; the law-enforcers can minimize the chance, for example, that a prostitute will steal money from a customer. In these and many other ways, then, the law-enforcement system maximizes its effectiveness by developing a symbiotic relationship with certain types of criminals.

How is this set of relationships perpetuated? For the individual policeman, it involves a gradual socialization from which few can escape save by giving up being a policeman altogether. A former Denver policeman tells "what makes a cop go wrong." Speaking of a rookie policeman who is serving his six-months probationary period before being commissioned as a police officer, he notes:

He knows he is being watched by all the older hands around him. He senses that an unfavorable report turned in by a senior man could blackball him. He watches closely what the others do. He's eager to be accepted.

He does what he can to show he has guts. He backs up his partner in any way he can. He accepts advice gracefully.

Then he gets little signs that he's making a good impression. It may happen like this: the older man stops at a bar, comes out with some packages of cigarettes. He does this several times: he explains that this is part of the job, getting cigarettes free from proprietors to re-sell and that as part of the rookie's training it is his turn to "make the butts."

So he goes into a Skid Row bar and stands uncomfortably at the end waiting for the bartender to acknowledge his presence and disdainfully toss him two packages of butts.

The feeling of pride slips away, and a hint of shame takes hold. But he tells himself this is unusual, that he will say nothing that will upset his probation standing.

In six months, after he gets his commission, he will be the upright officer he meant to be when he applied for the job, when he took his oath and when he left the Police Academy.

One thing leads to another for the rookies. After six months they have become conditioned to accept free meals, a few packs of cigarettes, turkeys at Thanksgiving and liquor at Christmas from the respectable people in their district.

The rule book forbids all this. But it isn't enforced. It's winked at, at all levels.

So the rookies say to themselves that this is okay, that all the men accept these things, that it is a far cry from stealing and they can still be good policemen. Besides, they are becoming accepted as "good guys" by their fellow officers.

This becomes more and more important as the young policeman begins to sense a hostility toward him in the community. This is fostered to a degree by some of the saltier old hands in the department.[8]

More generally, the involvement of the entire legal system in a symbiotic and mutually advantageous relationship with organized crime goes through a similar process. As we have seen, the law-enforcers will find that their job is best managed by cooperating with certain groups of organized criminals. It is, then, only a short step to cooperating with organized criminal syndicates to control the vices in the community, to accepting systematic payoffs and favors, both political and personal, from those who run the syndicates and the gambling houses. Ultimately what emerges is a tightly interwoven group of persons both within and without the officially recognized political leadership in the community, and one can no longer discern where the political system ends and the criminal syndicate begins.

This phenomenon has been consistently documented in America. One of the more recent studies which provides detailed information on the way the organized criminal syndicate becomes intertwined with the political system is provided by John Gardiner's study of a town to which he gives the pseudonym "Wincanton."[9]

Wincanton is a predominantly working-class community with something over 75,000 residents. The history of Wincanton politics shows a constant vacillation between the election of mayors and political figures who openly support gambling and prostitution and mayors who oppose them and attempt to "clean up the town." Gardiner concludes that "the people of Wincanton apparently want both easily accessible gambling and freedom from 'racket domination.'" Wincanton is apparently very much like other cities in complex societies.

The importance of gambling and prostitution to the city is revealed to some extent in the economics of gambling. (Keep in mind that Wincanton is a community of around 75,000 people. The following figures, then, represent the income from gambling in a relatively small city. In communities of a million or more people the income would be correspondingly higher.) Gardiner reports that bookies taking bets on horses earned several million dollars every year. A numbers game did an annual business in excess of one million three hundred thousand dollars a year. In this community of less than a hundred thousand people, there were over two hundred pinball machines which paid off like slot machines, and these machines each had a two-hundred-and-fifty-dollar federal gambling stamp attached—some indication of the amount of money taken in by the machines. A high-stakes dice game, which ran continuously in the town, attracted people from communities as far as a hundred miles away, and in one federal raid over twenty-five thousand dollars was found on the table. In addition, there was a still which produced over four million dollars worth of illegal alcohol each year operating within the city. Prostitution was rampant during the pro-vice mayors' reigns, and this activity no doubt added other monies to the take of corruption in the city.

Wincanton is also an interesting community not simply because it illustrates the basic pattern of corruption, but because the history of gambling organization and criminal syndicates in Wincanton parallels the history in other parts of the United States. The major figure in Wincanton's syndicate operations is a man whom Gardiner calls Irving Stern. Like most organized criminal groups, the one organized by Stern was the offspring of a bootlegging syndicate. Indeed it has happened in most American communities that the groups who formerly operated the speakeasies and provided the bootleg liquor during prohibition are the ones which have subsequently gone into organized gambling and prostitution and drug distribution. Interestingly, many of these groups were first formed in the early 1900's as strike breakers for large corporations attempting to undermine the collective-bargaining movements of the embryonic labor unions.

Irving Stern managed to create a gambling empire which kept the gambling and prostitution activities in Wincanton carefully controlled and which also systematically paid off political figures. The payoffs ranged all the way from a turkey or a bottle of liquor at Christmas and Thanksgiving for the partrolman on the beat, to payments of several thousand dollars a month to key political leaders.

Stern also paid a certain portion of the profits to out-of-state syndicates. The local opposition to the political groups in power frequently claimed that Irv Stern was simply the local agent of the "Cosa Nostra." Gardiner, however, suggests that Stern was the true boss of organized crime in Wincanton, though he did pay out-of-state syndicates fees for services. The out-of-state syndicates provided technical services for the operation of dice games and the still, and when needed, "enforcers" to help keep the gambling operation under control. Stern's ability, then, to control the gambling syndicate in the city and to eliminate outside competition was a function of his being able to control police activities in the city and his ability to call on outside syndicate help and advice.

The payoffs were of course the central feature of his relationship with the police and other political figures. Gardiner reports payoffs of twenty-four hundred dollars each week to the mayor, councilmen, district attorney, sheriff, state legislators, police chief, a captain in charge of detectives, and persons with the simple titles "county" or "state." The payoff was not the same for all these people. The mayor, when the gambling business was at its peak, received $750 a week, the chief of police $100 a week, and the captains and lieutenants on the police force somewhat smaller sums.

There were in addition other ways of paying off local officials and politicians: campaign contributions, holiday and birthday gifts, and many other kinds of favors.

The corruption became exceedingly widespread and involved virtually every phase of the decision-making process in the government. Even textbooks for the school were ordered and purchased according to payoffs made to the purchasing agent and other political officials. In short, over a period of years in this one community, the corruption which began with the organization of gambling and prostitution for the mutual benefit of a criminal syndicate and the law-enforcement agencies, gradually spread to include virtually every phase of the municipal government.

It must be acknowledged that the frequency with which reports similar to

Gardiner's are published whenever researches on municipal governments are conducted, suggests that such practices are extremely widespread in the United States; whether or not they are inextricably built into the structure of complex societies is still an open question. The fact of their being very prevalent is, however, no longer a matter for debate. It is one of the facts of law-enforcement in the United States, and one of the central facts that we must account for if we are to have an adequate theory of the law in action.

Since those who supply services such as gambling and prostitution are in a profit-making enterprise, they are generally in a position to see to it that among the many other advantages enjoyed by the law-enforcers for tolerating these activities is the added incentive of financial remuneration. From the perspective of the law-enforcers, since the entire enterprise must be surreptitious, and since it is clearly in the community's best interests to have the police control the vices in this way, accepting payments from gamblers and prostitutes is not really contrary to the best interests of law-enforcement.

Not all of the persons involved in the law-enforcement process will be seduced by the logic of this argument, but some will be and *some* is all that is necessary for such practices to reduce the effectiveness of the law-enforcement agencies in controlling crime. Once persons in positions of power accept the offer of the vice organizations to share in the profit, they become, of course, vulnerable. The fact that the "vice lords" are themselves vulnerable means that, though the law-enforcers can bargain with the crime syndicates, they must also now be receptive to the syndicate leaders' demands. Special favors that are beyond the pale of tolerated vice will have to be considered, if not always granted. Furthermore, the cooperative relationship must be kept from public view. Certain other illegal steps become necessary to ensure that disclosure does not take place.

Officials resort to different means to avoid public disclosure of widespread graft in law-enforcement agencies. One of the extralegal mechanisms which law-enforcement officials have been a party to in one community consisted of the following:[10]

A radio broadcaster agreed on the air to take "any and all phone calls" from people who knew anything about gambling and corruption in the city. With the apparent knowledge and complicity of the police, this broadcaster was shot at on his way home from work. He subsequently canceled his previous offer. A university professor who was investigating the relationship between the legal system and various types of professional criminals had his office and home telephones "bugged" and was tailed by a plain-clothes policeman. A man who had at one time been part of the vice operation in the city tried to publicize the existence of graft; he was shot at, his property was destroyed, and he was assaulted. His own efforts to bring charges were thwarted by the prosecutor's refusal to prosecute.

In recent years, however, the relatively "strong-arm" techniques have become less and less frequently used. The favored method of controlling the publicity likely to come from disclosure is to get information on prospective informants which makes them vulnerable. In the same city as before, this technique was used with great success in bringing a difficult sheriff into line. After this particular sheriff was elected, he refused to cooperate with the rackets. Since the wire services so crucial to the numbers and bookmaking operations were located in the county, this unyielding stance on the sheriff's part threatened to disrupt the entire vice business. The police, however, were able to get pictures of the sheriff in a motel room with a woman other than his wife. These pictures were then used to blackmail him with great success.

Since the legal system can often effectively conceal the presence of a symbiotic relationship between crime and legal order, it is fairly difficult to establish the extent to which this relationship exists in the American legal system. The fact, however, that fairly widespread scandals are exposed with alarming frequency in the large cities of the United States is reason to suspect that such a relationship is the rule rather than the exception. In recent years, for example, scandals have been exposed in Boston, Chicago, Denver, New York, Burlington (Vermont), Reading (Pennsylvania), and Detroit.[11] According to the President's Commission on Law Enforcement, large blocks of states in the United States are areas in which core groups of organized criminals reside and are active.[12]

Since only a handful of communities have been systematically studied in this connection, it can be argued that the number of communities involved in enforcement agencies and criminal syndicate symbiosis is relatively small. Such an argument seems untenable, however, in view of the consistency with which similar findings have been made wherever researchers, journalists, or independent police investigators have looked. The autobiography of Lincoln Steffens reports widespread corruption of the legal system by organized criminal syndicates at the turn of the twentieth century. Intermittently since that time, virtually every major city in the United States has experienced serious scandals unveiling the same phenomena.

The empirical evidence and the theoretical arguments produced here imply that an ongoing cooperative relationship between organized crime and the legal system is characteristic of virtually every community in the United States. Indeed, we would argue that only when a community has an unusually homogeneous class population (and thus one that does not have conflicting interests with regard to gambling, drug use, poor-risk loans, etc.) will there be an absence of a symbiotic relationship between crime and the legal system. Needless to say, homogeneous communities are rare in modern complex societies.

The consequences of an ongoing symbiotic relationship between crime and the legal system are far-ranging. Virtually every aspect of the legal process is affected by this relationship, and where it is fully developed the legal process is likely to exhibit all the worst characteristics attributed to law-enforcement agencies by critics. One legal scholar, Johannes Andenaes, states flatly: "Laxity and corruption in law enforcement in its turn is bound to reduce the general preventive effects of criminal law."[13]

One reason for this reduction of the general preventive effects of a legal system when it is corrupt is the lowering of personal and professional respect for the whole system created by the ongoing cooperation between the legal system and professional criminals. As James Wilson has observed:

the existence of large-scale corruption is a . . . source of demoralization for any policeman not part of the system and thus not sharing in the proceeds. Such corruption affects the entire department by bringing formal rules into contempt, providing a powerful induce-ment for participating in the system, and encouraging the officer to view the public as cynical and hypocritical.[14]

Where corruption is widespread, one generally finds a tendency for the police to be violent and for the prosecutor's office to request unusually stern punishment for relatively minor offenses. It is as though the law-enforcers feel that by over-zealous and harsh handling of other types of crime, they "make up" for the crimes they themselves are committing and those they are overlooking. In one of the cities studied the sheriff's department was relatively free from corruption and the police were thoroughly involved in a symbiotic relationship with vice. In general, the law-enforcement agents in the sheriff's department took pride in their work and viewed their job with respect. The police appeared to have little respect for their job or for their work. Observations of juvenile gangs' attitudes toward these two policing agencies disclosed that the juveniles generally looked on the officers in the sheriff's department as fair and on their authority as legitimate, but they regarded the police with complete disdain.

Thomas C. Schelling has presented an analysis of the "costs and losses" of organized crime from the perspective of an economist. He concludes that the costs to society of having black markets in vice must be weighed against the gains of having these things defined as crimes:

Essentially the question is whether the goal of somewhat reducing the consumption of narcotics, gambling, prostitution, abortion or anything else that is forced by law into the black market, is or is not outweighed by the costs to society of creating a criminal industry. In all probability, though not with certainty, consumption of the proscribed commodity or service is reduced. Evidently it is not anywhere near to being eliminated because the estimates of abortions runs to about a million a year, the turnover from gambling is estimated in the tens of billions of dollars per year, and dope addiction seems to be a serious problem. The costs to society of creating these black markets are several:

First, it gives the criminal the same kind of protection a tariff might give a domestic monopoly: it guarantees the absence of competition from people who are unwilling to be criminal, and guarantees an advantage to those whose skill is in evading the law.

Second, it provides a special incentive to corrupt the police, because the police not only may be susceptible to being bought off, but also can be used to eliminate competition.

Third, a large number of consumers who are probably not ordinary criminals—the conventioneers who visit houses of prostitution, the housewives who bet on horses, the women who seek abortions—are taught contempt, even enmity, for the law, being obliged to purchase particular commodities and services from criminals in an illegal transaction.

Fourth, dope addiction may so aggravate poverty for certain desperate people that they are induced to commit crimes or can be urged to commit crimes because the law arranges that the only (or main) source for what they desperately demand will be a criminal source.

Fifth, these big black markets may guarantee enough incentive and enough profit for organized crime so that the large-scale criminal organization comes into being and maintains itself. It may be—this is an important question for research—that without these important black markets crime would be substantially decentralized, lacking the kind of organization that makes it enterprising, safe, and able to corrupt public officials.[15]

As the preceding analysis of the relationship between professional crime and the legal system shows, the tacit assumption about the value of outlawing activities which are deemed undesirable or disruptive rarely takes into account the unintended consequences of such legislation. In the case in point, it seems clear that the costs of outlawing such things as high interest loans, abortions, gambling, prostitution, and narcotics is far greater than any benefit derived by society from maintaining such proscriptions. It may even be that, ultimately, such laws will totally undermine the democratic process, as they have in other countries with similar patterns of relationships between crime and the law.[16]

The Law and Petty Deviants

Gambling, prostitution, and professional theft are activities in which the mutual advantages to be had by law-enforcers and law-violators through the establishment of a "working relationship" are given their clearest illustration. The same arrangement yields similar mutual advantages in virtually any of the other illegal activities in this never-never land of law-enforcement morality.

Since no one obtains very great economic profit from homosexuality, there is not much economic exchange between the legal system and the homosexual community. What exchange there is, is generally limited to the hiring of off-duty policemen (at generous rates) by homosexual bars and clubs, where the policemen are expected to keep out "tourists," protect the anonymity of the bar, and if necessary, keep peace among the patrons.

A more important reward for the legal system is that cooperation keeps homosexuality "under control." As one police chief in a city studied expressed it, "This way we know where the perverts are and we can keep an eye on them. Otherwise we would constantly be bothered by their causing trouble in the wrong places."

Since many of the homosexuals in any community command respect by virtue of their social status in the community, processing such persons is always a potential source of trouble for the law-enforcers. By cooperating with them, the police can neutralize this source of potential trouble.

The legal system's handling of drug traffic poses an interesting contrast to some of the other vices. To begin with, traffic in drugs such as heroin, morphine, and cocaine shares with gambling and prostitution the characteristic of high economic reward. But unlike gambling and prostitution, community sentiment is much more likely to be univocally opposed to allowing persons to partake of this vice, especially where heroin or any of the opiates are concerned. Interestingly, it appears that law-enforcers generally attempt to enforce antidrug-use laws even in communities where there is a well-integrated and mutually dependent relationship between the legal system and purveyors of other forms of vice.[17] This fact is exceedingly important, since it suggests that profit alone is not a sufficient explanation for the mutual cooperation.

Marijuana use is in a different category. Here consensus is once again lacking, and profits may be high. From what data there are available it appears that law-enforcement agencies have generally been much more tolerant of and cooperative with the distributors and users of marijuana than with persons involved in the "hard-drug" traffic.

The use of LSD offers still another interesting contrast. In this case, community consensus is lacking, but in contrast to marijuana and opiates, there is very little profit to be had from its distribution because of the relative ease with which it can be produced. Although there has been some question about how the legal system would treat this new vice, the tendency seems to be *not* to tolerate it. Certainly the creation of a federal agency to control dangerous drugs following the wide-spread publicity concerning LSD suggests that this vice will be rather seriously dealt with.

There are other immoralities which have middle-class consensus and where the participants can offer few rewards to the legal system for nonenforcement. Where this is the case, the legal agencies are likely to enforce the law. The exemplification of this category of "immorality" is in the "down and outers" who inhabit the "skid rows" of our cities. These persons, who are frequently picked up as vagrants and sometimes as drunks, offer no reward to the legal system for nonenforcement. Since they do not have a real voice in the community, processing these offenders causes no trouble for the legal system; and there is something to be gained by processing them, for their presence bespeaks the diligence and watchfulness of the law. The fact that approximately fifty percent of the arrests every year are for offenses such as drunkenness, vagrancy, and "suspicion" suggests the extent to which these types of offenders furnish fodder to keep the bureaucracy operative.

Once all of the above detailed relationships between the legal system and the social classes, organized criminals, professional thieves and sexual deviants are fully developed, the organizations which administer the criminal law maximize the rewards they receive from their environment and minimize the strains which potentially plague bureaucracies. Much of the organizational effort of the legal system must go into efforts to keep the system functioning smoothly, once the necessary realationships have been worked out. Older policemen must socialize newer recruits into the system so that they will not disrupt the processes.[18] Judges will reprimand policemen from the bench for bringing cases to court that violate established procedures.[19] Prosecutors select cases and thereby communicate to the police what types of offenses to look for.

But errors occur even in the most efficiently organized systems. Not infrequently the legal system breaks down because someone fails to realize the potential source of trouble a suspect may be able to cause in the legal system.[20] For example, the recent arrest of Margot Fonteyne and Rudolph Nureyev for "disorderly conduct" while they were attending a party in the "hippie" section of San Francisco would probably not have taken place had the arresting officers realized whom they were arresting. Few policemen are ballet patrons, so the error was quite understandable.

Highly sophisticated techniques emerge in the law-enforcement agencies to cope with potential sources of disruption. Extensive "public relations" programs are instituted in order to "educate" the public about problems of law-enforcement and, hopefully, thereby to reduce public criticism of the law-enforcement agencies. Newspapers are neutralized in various ways in order to reduce the chances that reporters will uncover illegal or shoddy law-enforcement practices. The most effective means of obtaining support from the press is to offer ready access to valued information (that is, materials that make "good copy") to those reporters who report "sympathetically" on police activities and to exclude from this valued information any and all reporters who are critical of police activities. In some cases, the treatment is more direct. In one city studied by Chambliss, the editor of the newspaper was paid a monthly sum by the county prosecutor to see to it that no unfavorable news about the law-enforcement agencies was printed. This plan was apparently quite successful. In this particular community, the police and the prosecutor, as well as some members of the city council, were engaged in an extensive vice operation which was carried on with very little effort at concealment, a major reason being that the newspapers would not publish anything detrimental to the police and no one else had an effective mechanism available to bring the existing malpractices to public notice.

Where a symbiotic relationship exists between the legal system and criminal organizations, the potential for severe disruption of the ongoing process is omnipresent. Much of the criminal-law effort must therefore be devoted to protecting the system against outsiders learning about it. Since the only really reliable source of knowledge about the system must ultimately come from persons who are themselves involved, considerable protection is automatically afforded. However, new personnel may come in, especially where officials are elected, and the potential disruptive force is great indeed. A sheriff may be elected who refuses to cooperate with the organization and who thereby threatens the entire system. A reporter or a sociologist may discover what is taking place and threaten to make the information public. These potential threats are then dealt with by sanctioning bribery, collusion, threats, and even murder.[21]

23.2 CONCLUSION

It must be realized that many of the events and practices that shape the law are not intentional, but are instead the outgrowth of the relationships between the legal order and its social setting. The legal system, and certainly the law-enforcement officers, did not make the world in which public morality was systematically biased against the poor and favored the well-to-do. Given the problems of operating the law-enforcement system, it is no surprise to find that law-enforcement officials select for prosecution those persons whose processing not only cause no trouble for the organization, but also provides proof for the importance and quality of the legal order.

NOTES

1. Lincoln Steffens, *The Autobiography of Lincoln Steffens*, Harcourt, Brace, New York, 1931; see generally Part 3, pp. 357–361. Reprinted by permission of Harcourt Brace Jovanovich, Inc.

2. Frank Tannenbaum, *Crime and the Community*, Columbia University Press, New York, 1938, p. 128. Reprinted by permission.

3. Special Committee to Investigate Crime in Interstate Commerce (Kefauver Committee), *Third Interim Report*, U.S. Senate Report No. 307, 82nd Congress.

4. Donald R. Cressey, *Theft of the Nation*, Harper and Row, New York, 1969, p. 1. For a criticism of this view, see N. Morris and G. Hawkins, *The Honest Politician's Guide to Crime Control*, University of Chicago Press, 1970, pp. 202–235.

5. This discussion is based on a six-year study of the relationship between professional crime and the legal system in a large American city, conducted by William J. Chambliss.

6. Tannenbaum, *op. cit.*, p. 255. Used by permission.

7. *The Autobiography of Malcolm X*, Grove Press, New York, 1965, p. 117. Copyright © 1964 by Alex Haley and Malcolm X; Copyright © 1965 by Alex Haley and Betty Shabazz. Reprinted by permission.

8. Mort Stern, "What makes a policeman go wrong," *Sunday Denver Post*, October 8, 1961. Reprinted by permission of *The Denver Post*.

9. John A. Gardiner, "Wincanton: the politics of corruption," in William J. Chambliss, *Crime and the Legal Process*, McGraw-Hill, New York, 1969, pp. 103–135.

10. From Chambliss study cited in note 5.

11. The first four cities are mentioned in James Q. Wilson, "The police and their

problems: a theory," *Public Policy*, **22**, 1963. Scandals have appeared in other cities since Wilson's paper was published.

12. President's Commission on Law Enforcement and Administration of Justice, *The Challenge of Crime in a Free Society*, U.S. Government Printing Office, 1967, p. 7.

13. Johannes Andenaes, "The general preventive effects of punishment," *U. Pa. Law Rev.*, **114**, 1965–1966, p. 960.

14. James Q. Wilson, "The police and their problems: a theory," *Public Policy*, **2**, 1963, p. 189. Reprinted by permission.

15. Thomas C. Schelling, "Economic analysis and organized crime," in President's Commission on Law Enforcement and Administration of Justice, *Task Force Report: Organized Crime*, U.S. Government Printing Office, 1967, p. 125.

16. Cressey, *op. cit.*, Chapter 1.

17. This is the case in two communities studied by Chambliss and also in Wincanton.

18. Stein, *op. cit.*

19. Albert J. Reiss, Jr., and David J. Bordua, "Environment and organization: a perspective on the police," in David J. Bordua (ed.), *The Police*, Wiley, New York, 1967, pp. 25–26.

20. William J. Chambliss and John T. Liell, "The Legal process in the community setting: a study of local law enforcement," *Crime and Delinquency*, October 1966, pp. 310–317.

21. See Commission reports cited.

24
Conclusion

From the anthropological inquiries into primitive societies and the philosophical concerns with the law we have inherited a set of beliefs about legal systems that is best described as a myth. These beliefs take the form of "natural-law" (in various guises) perspectives in jurisprudence, of "value-consensus" perspectives in the social sciences, and "public-interest" assumptions in the culture at large. The popular view is that (1) the law represents the values of society; (2) if it does not represent the values of everyone, then it at least expresses the best common denominator of the society and operates through a value-neutral governmental structure, which is ultimately controlled by the choice of the people; and (3) in the long run the law serves the best interests of the society.

It is easy to maintain a myth like this provided that one does not look to see what in fact takes place in the day-to-day operations of the legal system. When everyday events that constitute the law in action are examined and brought together so as to represent the legal system as a dynamic, living institution, the mythical character of such claims becomes all too apparent. To suggest that the law represents the "value-consensus" in a pluralistic, stratified society is to assume that the only consensus that really matters is that of those whose views and interests are represented by the lawmakers. It is, as we have demonstrated,

patently absurd to argue that the law can ever represent everyone's views in stratified societies, since the patterns of life of the different strata differ so markedly that value-systems must differ correspondingly. Conflicting as well as competing value-systems cannot, by their very nature, coexist in a system of norms that strives to maintain some semblance of logical consistency.

It is logically possible, however, for the government, and the legal system as its principal norm-interpreter, to act as a value-neutral force working out reasoned solutions to conflict. But logic does not determine the shape of legal systems any more than it determines the shape of history. The reality of unequal power and control of resources, the selective process by which persons are moved from apprenticeship to decision-making, the criteria by which success is judged by those who have the power to make decisions—all these factors converge to influence the men who occupy the decision-making positions in the legal system and together they determine the output of the system. They make it inevitable that the legal system will *not* operate as a value-neutral arena in which conflicts are solved according to principles of justice and fairness. They create the conditions under which conflicts will be resolved in favor of those who control the resources of the system. If justice or fairness happen to be served, it is sheer coincidence.

The examination of the law in action also puts to rest the comfortable idea that the law represents the "public interest." One can of course define "public interest" as the maintenance of the existing system of power and privilege. In that case, it becomes a tautology that the law represents that interest. The law does, as we have argued and demonstrated, represent the interests of those in power. But if the interests of society are conceived more broadly (as they usually are, implicitly if not explicitly, by those who argue that the law serves the public interest), then they are not served by the law in practice. The interests of the disenfranchised in a stratified society are not served by a system in which adequate housing, medical care, and legal protection depend on being enfranchised.

In America it is frequently argued that to have "freedom" is to have a system which allows one group to make a profit over another. To maintain the existing legal system requires a choice. On this argument that choice is between maintaining a legal system that serves to support the existing economic system with its power structure and developing an equitable legal system accompanied by the loss of "personal freedom." But the old question comes back to plague us: Freedom for whom? Is the black man who provides such a ready source of cases for the welfare workers, the mental hospitals, and the prisons "free"? Are the slum dwellers who are arrested night after night for "loitering," "drunkenness," or being "suspicious" free? The freedom protected by the system of law is the freedom of those who can afford it. The law serves *their* interests, but they are not "society"; they are one element of society. They may in some complex societies even be a majority (though this is very rare), but the myth that the law serves the interests of "society" misrepresents the facts.

We have shown by example and study that complex, stratified societies are inevitably pluralistic. As such, the law will always represent the interests of one group as against the interests of others. We have argued that even the offenses on which there is a superficial consensus (such as murder, rape, theft) are not so unanimously viewed as wrongdoing if the surface of the abstract caricature is scratched.

In addition to shattering the myth that the law rests on value-consensus, the empirical study of the law in action also makes it abundantly clear that the State is hardly a value-neutral arena in which conflicts are worked out for the "good of everyone." Rather, these studies have shown that the upshot of the conflicting interests is such that law comes to represent the entrenched power groups.

The theory we have proposed as an alternative to a value-consensus model is heavily influenced by the conflict model of society. We think the evidence presented is the best possible defense for adopting this perspective. The basic notion derived from this model is that society is composed of groups that are in conflict with one another and that the law represents an institutionalized tool of those in power which functions to provide them with superior moral as well as coercive power in the conflict. As we have seen, however, this general proposition is not sufficient to account for all aspects of the legal order. We have supplemented this premise with a number of complementary propositions about the nature of the conflict in stratified societies and the relationship of the law to this conflict. We have also added to this perspective the critically important element of the bureaucratic character of the legal system—an element which in and of itself guarantees that the legal order will take on a shape and character at variance with what it might have been if the law reflected the "public interest."

Western man everywhere still bathes in the intellectual glow of the Enlightenment. He believes in a rational world, a society controlled and controllable by well-meaning human beings, making rational choices for the betterment of the human condition. Tensions, dysfunctions, violence, poverty, war can all be dissolved through rational effort of well-meaning men, tinkering with the social machinery to set the system aright.

It is a faith challenged by the daily headlines. War, riot, racial tensions, poverty, alienation—all bespeak problems so deep and profound as to cast doubts on the beliefs inherited from the Enlightenment. The inherent goodness and perfectability of man itself is called into question.

The myth is being challenged by facts. What Ought to be is confronted by what Is. The discrepancy between the ideal and the reality of modern life undercuts the ideal.

The realist perspective in law suggested a way of studying this discrepancy at the most sensitive point in the society, the law and the State. The realists' demand that we confront the law in the books with the law in action urges us to move out of the libraries, away from the reasoned opinions of appellate judges, to discover what happens "out there."

The empirical evidence of the law in action challenges the familiar normative map. Legislatures pass laws in response to interest-group pressures and the personal commitment of legislators, who are shaped and confined by the processes within which they operate. Appellate judges decide cases on the basis of unarticulated premises and hence miss the mark of rational decision-making, mainly because the norms of decision-making are dysfunctional to the actual agenda of decisions with which they are faced. The police, the prosecutors, the triers in courts, and the sentencing judges, to a greater degree than the appellate courts, are subjected to bureaucratic pressures which impel them to exercise the discretion which they possess under the norms defining their respective positions, in ways, sometimes illegal, conforming to the imperatives of those pressures.

Far from being mere slot-machines that feed on facts and rules, and grind out decisions in conformity to them, the entire legal process, so far as our examination shows, is shot with the exercise of discretion, sometimes in accordance with the law, sometimes in ways contrary to the law as nominally understood but made inevitable by the dysfunction of the norms to the decisions in question, and sometimes in clear violation of the law.

This discretion and the illegal behavior of some of those who man the bulwarks of power appear to be controlled, not by the public interest, obedience to norms, or rationality, but by naked self-interest, interest-group pressures, and irrationality.

How are we to explain or understand these dark forces that seem so impervious to rational control? How are we to control that which seems irrational except by sheer coercion? When those who must be controlled have a monopoly over means of violence?

The first sign of wisdom, we suggest, is to understand that there can be observed regularities in social behavior which are subject to study and analysis. The legacy of the Rational Man that we inherited from the Enlightenment assumes that man *en masse* is only the sum of the individuals who make up the crowd, and that individual man is rational and can be appealed to and swayed on rational grounds. The central teaching of modern social science is that this legacy is false. Social processes operate precisely because each individual tends to act as an individual. Multiplied thousands of times, his individual activity, however rational as a microphenomenon, frequently becomes irrational as a macrophenomenon. Man in society can and sometimes does act rationally. He can control his social environment. But he can do so only by recognizing that man in society acts along lines determined by the forces which structure his "field" and determine his activities in a way analogous to structuring of the "field" which determines the movement of inanimate objects.

Social science today has developed a number of "middle-level" propositions which express our present knowledge of these forces. If we are to try to control and tame the dark forces of irrationality that seem to defy the ideal of the Enlightenment, and until we have more accurate statements of how social forces operate, we must accept these propositions. Bureaucracies act so as to maximize rewards and minimize strains for the organizations and their members. The rich and the powerful have greater ability to maximize rewards and minimize strains for certain governmental organizations. Just as an engineer must fail who tries to design an aircraft without taking into account the laws of physics, so the lawyer must fail who tries to design a legal structure without taking into account the laws of social science. Freedom is the recognition of necessity; we are not free if we ignore the forces operative in the real world.

These forces explain why the institutions of law behave as they do. In a society racked by conflict, the conflicting elements make demands on the bureaucrats and officials who man the several positions in the hierarchy of the State. These demands on the whole are that the various officials act in ways that will favor those who make the demands and necessarily disfavor others in the society. Officials structured into a bureaucratic society will respond to the demands of the rich and the powerful, unless there are an ideology that forbids it, sanctions to inhibit it, and controls on the pervasive power of discretion. The State structure and its normative system, the law, thus become a system which is effectively a tool of power and privilege.

Given a society with conflicting interests, what variables can be changed so as to change the system and achieve the rational government of the Enlightment legend? In the short run, perhaps improvement depends on the control of discretion. There can be little doubt that the very broad discretion which now exists at every level of government can be reduced. The Ombudsman and declared policy guidelines, for example, offer some hope that police discretion can be controlled to some extent. In the long run, the ideology of officials may be changed to enable them to resist the forces which induce them to substitute unofficial goals and deviant behavior for official goals and conformity to the norms laid down for their guidance. The substitution of the realist mode of justification of judicial decisions for the formal style, for example, has tended to reduce the influence of evisceral judicial value sets in the judicial decision-making processes.

It may be doubted, however, whether a society divided sharply into haves and have-nots can ever completely achieve the ideal of neutrality of the legal process. In the first place, reforms must come through the very agencies of rule-making which already are subject to the interests of those who are economically and politically powerful. One may fairly question whether these men will ever reform themselves. In the second place, as we have seen, discretion of some sort is *inevitably* part of any rule-making and rule-applying system. No matter how specific the norms and sanctions are, there is still some room for choice. Given a conflict-ridden society, that choice is inevitably warped to some degree by the configurations of power in the society. Thirdly, since it is the web of life that shapes our consciousness, it is hard to believe that a conflict-ridden society can ever develop governing elites who are not imbued with the values of the very rich and powerful whose pressures warp the official goals of the legal institutions.

Justice in practice, not in theory, is dependent on the rule-making and rule-applying agencies. How these institutions exercise their discretion depends on who controls them. That is a political question. In short, justice and the working of the legal process is a political question. In the final analysis, control over the machinery of the State determines the output of the institutions of the legal process. Law and its institutions are the single most important force shaping the structure of society. Their output determines the nature of the economy, the openness of the society and the opportunity for mobility, the distribution of privilege and power, the very quality of life. Inevitably, in a stratified society where control over the legal process is finally lodged with the dominant group, the output of the legal institutions will tend to shape the society according to the interests of the dominant group.

The present condition, however, can be enormously improved, though it cannot be improved by pursuing law as a variant of library science. Law is a social science, a very general type of social science, to be sure, but nevertheless a form of social science. Behavior is its concern, not rules. The rules are merely a means of determining behavior. The rules cannot be formulated, the reforms planned, discretion narrowed, sanctions improved, recruitment and socialization of officers changed, or any of the manifold changes in the legal order made in order to ensure that the government represents all-of-us (so far as that is possible in a pluralistic society), unless we stop staring myopically at the law in the books, and mouthing mindlessly the shibboleths of value-consensus that are taught to school children. We must look at the law in action as well if we are to begin to make social fact conform to the myths of democracy.

NAME INDEX

NAME INDEX

SUBJECT and CASE INDEX

SUBJECT and CASE INDEX

Burglary, 196, 452
Bushell's Case, 434
Business, abuses of 177

Calculus of pleasure and pain, 197
Canons of judicial ethics, 121
Camana v. Municipal Court, 291
Capital punishment, 204, 453-454
"Captains of industry," 66
Case law, 8, 77, 83
Case method of instruction, 97, 144
Causality, 78
Cause of action, 76
Certainty in law, 436
Certiorari, 92
Chandler v. Fretag, 320
Change agent, 159
Chairman, Securities and Exchange Commission, 149
Chamberlain v. Milwaukee and Mississippi Railroad Co., 115
Charismatic legitimacy, 351
Chicago, 477
Chicago Jury Project, 438, 439, 443
Chicago Women's Court, 464
Chief Justice, 149
Child labor law, 177
Christian influence, 201
Civic order of national principles, 187
Civil actions for police misconduct, 375
Civil liberties, 91, 175-176
Civil rights, 91, 176
Civil Rights Act of 1964, 163, 477
Civil Rights Commission, 372
Civilian review boards, 218, 380-381
Civilized society, 140, 141
Class and group conflict, 444
Class biases, 175
Class position, 175
Classes, 140
Classical model, 143
Clear-case, 85-89, 107, 122, 123, 143, 151, 161, 187
Clear-case rules, 132, 133, 142, 144
  of recognition, 122
Clemency, 209
Coerced confessions, 305

Coercion, 53, 203, 303
Coercive powers, 77, 143
Cognoscible norms, 201, 353
Collins, v. Cloudy, 462
Colonial law, 43
Colonial society, 288
Command of sovereign, 131
Commerce, 67
Commercial and industrial classes, 47
Commercial law, 142
"Common conscience," 32
Common law, 3, 35, 38, 40, 83, 126, 131, 133, 139, 160, 194, 201, 202, 203, 222, 223, 225, 239, 241
Commonwealth v. Koczwana, 235
Commonwealth v. Morgan, 223
Commonwealth v. Pierce, 248
Commonwealth v. Ritter, 470
Communist Party, 94-5
Communists, 342, 443
Community tolerance, 67
Community-wide values, 140
Competing values, 143
Complaint, 76, 396
Complex technologies, 37
Comprehensive change, 159
Compromise, 28-34, 37
Confessions, 303, 304, 310, 314, 338, 419
Conflict, 17, 18, 29, 45, 50-51, 62, 162, 181, 194, 210
Conflict view of society, 56, 75, 140, 142, 157, 159
Conflicts, 3, 57, 261, 473, 477
Conformity, 148
Confrontation and countercharges to juveniles as well as adults, 314
Congress, 67, 72, 168
Connecticut sentencing review division, 237
Consanguinity, 72
Consciousness, 9
  of guilt, 202, 203
Consensus in norms, 18, 25
Conservation, 66
Conservative legal theory, 40-41
Conservative rulings, 174

Conspiracy, 71, 199, 223, 225, 227-229, 232

Constitution, 3, 78

Constitutional litigation, 167

Contingency fee, 103

Contract, 39, 42, 129, 165

Contract law, 164

Control of police discretion, 389-391

Conviction, 403, 438

Corruption, 67, 100, 476, 496

Cortez v. United States, 413

Cosa Nostra, 489

Cost of litigation, 102

Costliness of governmental processes, 52

Court decisions, influences of, 90

Court functions, 75

Courts, as rule-makers, 35, 40-42, 88, 106
 as applying customs, 40-42
 and role of reason, 146
 as sanctioning institutions, 373
 as taking sides, 143
 as value-neutral, 40-42

Creation of norms, 19, 34

Credibility of witnesses, 424

Crime-control model, 200, 272, 273, 298, 302, 307, 314, 341, 349, 358, 359, 410

Crime, defined, 70-73
 location of, 331
 in streets, 188

Crime rate, 331, 337

Crimes, of corporations, 339
 of status, 230, 231
 without victims, 230

Criminal actions for police misconduct, 374

Criminal procedure, 174, 301

Criminal sanction, 188

"Crisis" cases, 105

Criterion of relevance, 424

Cross-examination, 425, 426

Crowd and riot control, 282

Cumberland Plateau, 60

Custom and law, 22, 39

Darwinism, 19

Death sentences, 204, 454, 465, 466

Decision-makers, 112

Decisions and opinions, 118

Declaration of New Delhi, 44, 154

Defense counsel, 30, 40 408, 452

Definition of law, 5, 6, 136

Delinquency, 171, 335, 339, 411

Demeanor and arrest, 337, 338, 430

Democracy, 57

Democratic National Convention (Chicago, 1968), 282, 285, 372, 374

Demon, 203

Demonstrations, 390

Dennis v. United States, 247

Department of Health, Education, and Welfare, 163

Desegregation, 168

Deterrence, general, 197 199, 200, 204, 207, 209, 210, 455, 456
 special, 198, 199, 200, 201, 202, 203, 209, 210, 455, 456

"Developmental model," 157-158

Dewey's paradigm, 112

Discretion, 79, 81, 82, 84, 135, 210, 218, 219, 220, 221, 237, 239-245, 262, 265, 267, 268, 323, 325, 336, 374, 383, 384, 390, 391
 of appellate courts, 77
 in sentencing, 237

Discrimination, 105, 137, 168, 273, 467, 469, 477

"Disease of the mind," 87, 88, 161

Disorderly conduct, 292, 404, 449, 463, 479

Dispute-settlement, 28, 29, 34, 37, 54, 84, 165, 194, 257

Dispute-settlement function of the courts, 142

Dissent, frequency in appellate courts, 147

Divorce, 104

Domesday Book, 417

Dowling v. Inspector-General of Police, 457

Dragnet arrests, 295

Drinking, 195, 244, 292, 332, 339, 341, 449, 463, 479

Drugs, 68-69, 339-341, 490

Narcotics, 231, 244 (see also Drugs)
Nash v. United States, 241
National Advisory Commission on Civil Disorders, 352, 372, 392
National Association for the Advancement of Colored People, 91, 169, 380
National Commission on the Causes and Prevention of Violence, 282
National interest v. state's rights, 180
National Motor Vehicle Theft Act, 88, 222
Natural duties, 190
Natural law, 40, 46, 73, 178
Natural Gas Bill, 66
Natural law theories, 46, 47, 140, 143
Nature, of law, 174
    of man, 140
    of trial, 188
Necessity, 203
Negligent conduct, 202
Negotiated plea, 102, 404
Neoclassical theory, 208
Neo-Kantianism, 78
New Deal, 145, 177
New Haven project, 363
New York Penal Law, 222, 226
New York police department, 233
New York Times, 212, 247
Nigeria, 71, 134
Nigerian Code, 133, 205
Norm creation in simple societies, 37
Norman inquest, 417
Norman invasion, 194
Norms, defining judge's roles, 148
    and instincts, 22
    of judicial decision-making, 156
    and similarity of experiences, 25-26
Notification of charges, 314
Nuer, 71, 251-254
Nulla crimen sine lege, 134, 219, 421
Nulla poena sine lege, 221, 228, 243, 421, 454

Obayi, 204
Obligations, 7
Obscenity, 441
Officials, 8, 219

Ombudsmen, 381-383
Omission to act, 128
"One man, one vote," 95
Opinions, 121
"Ordinary" crimes, 189-210
Organic solidarity, 22, 31, 32, 37
Organizational interests, 100
Organized crime, 489-497
Organized criminals, 484
Original source, 78
Outputs of appellate courts, 156-185

Paradigm of social inquiry, 108
Pardon, 237
Parens patriae, in, 171
Patriarchal and industrial societies, 30
Peace demonstrations, 281
Peaceful social change, 177
Peace-keeping, 274
Penal Law, 187
Penal sanctions, 431
Penitentiary, 406
"Penumbra" case, 88
People v. Belcastro, 247
People v. Harris, 347
People v. Matlock, 313
People v. Miller, 226
People v. Picciotti, 413
People v. Portelli, 320
People v. Roberts, 87
People v. Schmidt, 182
People v. Utica Daw's Drug Company, 327
People v. Wakat, 313
Permissible rules of law, 105
Permissible scope of discretion, 219
Personal characteristics of judges, 95-97
Personal identity and goods and services, 32
Personal injury cases, 104
Peters v. New York, 292
Peterson v. United States, 452
Petty deviants, 497
Philip Muswi s/o Musola, 206
Physicians and drug laws, 68-69
Plaintiff, 76
Plea bargaining, 102, 405, 409, 410

Pleading, 224, 417 (see also Bargaining; Plea bargaining)
Pleasure-pain principle in law, 47
Plessey v. Ferguson, 137, 138
Pluralistic societies, 62, 143, 144
Police, 3, 53, 264, 265, 328
  and due process, 296
  historical development of, 35
  in slum areas, 478 (see also Ghettos; Black ghettos)
  and use of force, 276
Police administrator, 324
Police assaults, 374
Police brutality, 281, 307, 313
Police conduct, 300
Police controls, internal, 371
Police deviancy, general, 379
  control of, 371
  theory of, 358-366
Police discipline, internal, 379
Police discretion, 187, 189, 217, 218, 221, 223, 271
Police forces, 35
Police illegality, 370
Police mistreatment, 240
Police organizations, 391
Police riot, 282, 284
Police searches and seizures, 377
Police self-regulation, 371
Police socialization, 363
Police subculture, 365
Police violence, 274-286
Policing as organizational phenomenon, 328-330
Policing organizations, 339
Policeman's role, 359
Policeman's suspicion, 273, 448
Policeman's working personality, 359
Policy-choices, 143
Policy-makers, 51, 368
Political bargaining, 52
Political crimes, 230
Political incentives, 403
Political process, 52
Political science, 3
Political theory, 51
Polyarchy, 52

Poor, 3, 168, 218, 280, 298, 328, 359, 467
Pornography, 339, 441
Positive law, 194
Positive world of law, 137
Positivism, 46, 48, 78, 80
Potential criminals, 197
Poverty, 44, 104, 298
  and law, 90
  and police violence, 280-282
Powell v. Alabama, 320
Power, 3, 4, 33, 47, 52, 53, 58, 63, 64, 65, 66, 73, 79, 120, 167, 218, 221, 268, 350, 358, 473
  of arrest, 295
  and authority, 350
  of police, 223
  and privilege, 218
Power relations, 161
Pragmatic decision-making, 169, 178
Pragmatic method of problem-solving, 138, 145
Pragmatic philosophy, 137, 140
Pragmatic rule-making procedures, 144
Pragmatic tradition, 178
Pragmaticism, 145
Prayers in public schools, 169
Precedents, 123, 124, 133, 138, 139, 172, 175
Prejudice, 353
Presentence report, 449, 450, 468
President's Commission on Law Enforcement and Administration of Justice, 262, 269, 277, 296, 314, 318, 347, 392, 483
President's Commission on Crime in the District of Columbia, U.S., 269
President's Task Force on the Police, 373
Presumption, of guilt, 273
  of innocence, 272, 273, 426, 433
Pretrial conferences, 102
Pretrial interrogation, 300-302
Priestley v. Fowler, 126
Primary rules of law, 80, 81, 84, 86, 88, 120
Primitive societies, 20, 25
Primogeniture, 38

Revolution of 1688, 421
Revolutionary change, 159
Rex v. Atma Singh s/o Chanda Singh, 456
Rex v. Ball, 456
Rex v. Bourne, 153
Rex v. Edgal, 133
Rex v. Kyle, 457
Rex v. Mild and Reynolds, 457
Rex v. Nagong, 203
Rex v. Palmer, 470
Rex v. Petero Mukasa, 456
Rex v. Reeves, 456
Rex v. Schoenfield, 456
Rex v. Shershewsky, 470
Rex v. Walton, 456
Rex v. Wheat and Stocks, 212
Rights, 7
Right, to appeal, 76
    to bail, 423
    to counsel, 304-306, 314, 423
    to jury, 422
    to summon witnesses in defense, 423
Rights and obligations, 127
    of property, 440 (see Property rights)
Riots, 70, 328, 351, 372, 443
Robbery, 190, 225, 337
Robinson Patman Act, 242
Robinson v. California, 244, 248
Rogues, 195
Role differentiation, 31
Role expectation, 8, 11, 50, 80, 368
Role occupant, 10, 12, 31, 50, 368
Role performance, 8, 11, 12, 50, 368
Roles, differentiation of, 30, 31
Rule of law, 77, 79, 84, 85, 87, 107, 130,
    132, 134, 143, 145, 154, 187, 218,
    219, 224
    as distinguished from custom, 80-81
    as hypothetical judgment, 84
Rule of recognition, 143
Rule-enforcement, 28-34, 194
Rule-sanctioning agencies, 259
Rules, created by appellate courts, 156
    of evidence, 163
    of law, 8, 16, 44, 89, 144, 178
    of natural law, 139
    "of recognition," 85, 122, 132
    of seniority, 52

Ruling classes, 53, 67, 220, 419
Rural values, 60

Saboteurs, 150 (see also Steele, Marion
    F.)
Sacred and secular societies, 30
Sanction, 32
Sanctioning breaches of rules laid down
    for police, 374
Sanctioning institutions, 156
Sanctioning process, 9, 10
Sanctions, 10, 34, 142, 188, 194, 201,
    208, 210, 220, 368-370
Scandals, 65, 66, 495
Scientific inquiry, 108, 109
School desegregation, 91, 163, 169
Scruttons v. Midland Silicones, 153
Search, 83, 286
    and arrest, 292-296
    without warrant, 292
Search warrants, 288
Secondary rules, 81, 83, 84, 85, 99, 120,
    257
Securities and Exchange Act, 149, 190,
    231
Seditious intention, 232
Seditious libels, 232
Segregation, 137, 138, 142
Self-defense, 71, 204, 206
Self-fulfilling prophecy, 273, 331, 336
Self-incrimination, 179, 306-308, 314,
    423
Sentences, 237
    purposes of, 455
Sentencing, of convicted criminals, 76
    objectives of, 200
    and police, 451
Separate but equal, 137, 138
Serf, 39
Serious crime, 331-332
Seriousness of offense, 457
Service organizations, 266
Service to poor, 104
Sexual perversion, 223
Sherman Antitrust Act, 65, 199, 241
Shevlin-Carpenter, 245
Shoplifters, 339
Shot drill, 198

Sibron v. New York, 292
Sifting process of legal system, 262
Simple societies, 19
Simple technologies, 37
Sin, 191, 201
Sine ira et studio, 356
Sitakimatata s/o Kimwage, 213
Situational imperatives, 156
Sixth Amendment, 300
Skekanja, 214
Skid row, 293, 329, 345
Slattery's Spoilers, 294
Slums, 65, 70, 332 (see also Ghettos)
Small-claims court, 104
Small-group interactions, 156
Small-group sociological theory, 147-149
Smith Act, 232
Social action, 9
Social class, and institutions of law, 113
  and law enforcement, 476
Social conflict, 144
Social control, 80, 140, 189
Social engineering, 9, 11, 12, 50, 140,
  141
Social engineering function of law, 9
Social inquiry, 109, 110
Social issues, 144
"Social" leadership, 149
Social mobility, 42
Social order, 197, 200, 218
Social organization of police work, 328
Social security, 173
Social solidarity, 31, 32
Social system, 6
Social theory, 3
Social welfare legislation, 144
Social workers, 220
Socialization, 97, 175
  of judges, 97, 99, 156
  of lawyers, 174
  and recruitment processes for judiciary,
    127
Society of Good Neighbors v. Van An-
  twerp, 326
Sodomy, 457
Soliciting, 293
Solitary confinement, 198
Southern Pacific Co. v. Jensen, 153

Sovereignty, 46, 48, 78, 307
Soviet law, 129
Sparf v. United States, 436
Special interest groups (see Interest
  group)
Star Chamber, 221, 306, 307
State court judges, 148
State decisions, 94
State ex rel McKittrick, 413
State ex rel Pacific American Fisheries v.
  Darwin, 346
State ex rel Parker v. McKnaught, 346
State legislation, 168
State power, 8, 10, 39, 48, 83, 140, 143,
  144, 194
State structure, 258
  as source of law, 47
State v. Grenz, 240
State v. Lombardi, 346
Stateless societies, 28-36
  defined, 250-251
Status to contract, 42
Statute of Wills, 41
Statutes, core meaning of, 82
Statutory construction, 107
Statutory offenses, 189
Statutory penal law, 238
Steel Seizure case, 105
Stop and frisk, 290-299
Store detectives, 340
Stratification, 30, 33
Strict construction, 223
  of penal statutes, 222
Structural-functionalist model, 56, 157,
  158
Students and police, 282-285, 374
Subculture of police, 369
Substantive criminal law, general prin-
  ciples of, 186-216
Substantive irrationality, 129
Substantive laws, 52
Substantively rational law-making, 129
Summons, 76
Sunsum, 204
Superior courts, 76
Superstition, 204
Supreme Court, and developmental (or
  tension management) model, 172

discretion to select cases, 92
inability of, to create new organizations, 162
inability of, to determine potential consequences, 163
incapacity of, for planning, 162
informal leader of, 149
power of judicial review of, 167
revolution of, 145
Suspicion, 273, 340
Symbiotic relationship between crime and legal system, 495, 496, 499
Symbols, 83
"System model" (see Structural-functionalist model)

Tax cases, 168, 174, 176 (see also Income tax)
Taylor v. Goodwin, 88
Technology, 32
and society, 20
Terry v. Ohio, 291, 292, 318
Theft, 67, 70, 190, 196
by false pretense, 195
Theories of the middle range, 3
Theory, of justice, 136
of legal process, 475
Third degree, 313
Thomas v. Collins, 183
Throckmorton's Case, 419, 434
Tiller v. Atlantic Coast Line Railroad, 152
Title insurance, 165
Token sentences, 464
Tokoloshe, 203
Tool of social engineering, 13
Tort law, 165
Torture, 198, 307, 419
Townsend v. Burke, 458
Trade unions, 29, 477
Traditional and bureaucratic societies, 30
Traditional crimes, 231
Traditional felonies, 327
Traditional legitimacy, 351
Traditional offenses, 230
Traffic fines, 101
Traffic laws, 8

Traffic ticket, 325
Transvestitism, 293
Trespass, 219
Trial, as administrative process, 457
by battle, 417
by combat, 194
by jury, 175
by ordeal, 417
rationality of, 428-431
Trial court, 75, 76, 101, 396, 439
Trial judges, 402, 415, 452
Trial proceedings, 233, 304, 433
Tribal law, 206
Tribunals, 104
Trobriand Islands, 23
Trouble cases, 85-89, 95, 107, 122, 125, 130, 132, 135, 143, 144, 161, 174, 187
Trust law, 90
Twining v. New Jersey, 307, 308

Ultra vires, 219, 373
Uniform commercial codes, 148
Uniform crime reports, 347
United Nations, 57
United States Commission on Civil Rights, 372, 389 (see also Civil rights)
United States Supreme Court (see Supreme Court)
United States v. Balint, 245, 248
United States v. Caroline Products, 183
United States v. Chicago, 393
United States v. Darby, 149
United States v. National Dairy Products Corp., 242
United States v. Ponanno, 318
United States v. Sacher, 453
United States v. Wade, 286, 317, 319
Urban rioting, 58, 281, 284 (see also Riots)
Usury, 490
Utilitarianism, 47, 122, 131, 192, 202, 209

Vagrancy laws, 54, 233-234, 240-241, 244, 449, 463
Vagueness, 83, 123, 385

ABCDE7987654321